# Austrian Yearbook
on
# International Arbitration 2026

The Editors

**Christian Klausegger, Peter Klein, Florian Kremslehner, Alexander Petsche, Nikolaus Pitkowitz, Irene Welser, Gerold Zeiler**

The Authors

Matthew T. Adams, Antje Baumann, Katherine Bell, Lisa Berger, Dina Berkaliyeva, Vilius Bernatonis, James H. Boykin, Stavros Brekoulakis, Cavinder Bull, Rita de Carvalho, Ondrej Cech, Antonia Cermak-Kietaibl, Vod K.S. Chan, Chrystalla Christoforou, Barbara Concolino, Sofia Elena Cozac, Sára Darnót, Borna Dejanović, Egishe Dzhazoyan, Vivian Elvers, Sarah Yvonne Enzi, Catrice Gayer, Agis Georgiades, Amaryllis Germanidis, Duarte G. Henriques, Rishika Jain, Arush Khanna, Judith Knieper, Justin Friedrich Krahé, Niam Leinwather, Eric Leikin, Courtney Lotfi, Eveli Lume, Peter Machherndl, Tamara Manasijevic, Marlene Maurer, Maximilian Albert Mueller, Max Murtinger, Irina Nazarova, Pınar Noberi, Petra Pataki, Camilla Perera – de Wit, Markus Petsche, Nikolaus Pitkowitz, Jessica Puhr, Matej Pustay, Milica Savić, Helena Schnur, Albertas Šekštelo, Arman Shaikenov, Valikhan Shaikenov, Iain Sheridan, Ana Stanič, Ben Steinbrück, Wei Sun, Sofia Svinkovskaya, Johannes Tropper, Doğuhan Uygun, Florian Wagner, Anna Weinzierl, Irene Welser, Stephan Wilske, Mathias Wittinghofer, Roland Ziadé

C.H.BECK

ALLE KRAFT IST WILLE 1849

Wien 2026
MANZ'sche Verlags- und Universitätsbuchhandlung
Verlag C.H. Beck, München
Stämpfli Verlag, Bern

**To be cited as:**

Author [first and last name], *Title of Work*, in AUSTRIAN YEARBOOK ON INTERNATIONAL ARBITRATION 2026 [first page on which work appears, pincite] (Klausegger, Klein, Kremslehner, Petsche, Pitkowitz, Welser & Zeiler eds., 2026)

**Disclaimer**



FSC
www.fsc.org
MIX
Papier | Fördert gute Waldnutzung
FSC® C014138

ISBN 978-3-214-26622-6 (Manz)
ISBN 978-3-406-84834-6 (Beck)
ISBN 978-3-7272-2413-3 (Stämpfli)


Kohlmarkt 16, 1010 Vienna
Austria
Telephone: +43 1 531 61-0
E-Mail: verlag@manz.at
World Wide Web: www.manz.at

Data Conversion and Type Setting: EXAKTA GmbH, Wien, www.exakta.at
Printed by: FINIDR, s. r. o., Český Těšín

# Introduction

It is with great pleasure that we present the 20th anniversary edition of the *Austrian Yearbook on International Arbitration*. 2026 marks a special milestone: since the first publication in 2007 this Yearbook has become a trusted resource for arbitration practitioners, scholars, and students and established itself as a respected platform for discussing developments, challenges, and innovations in international arbitration. Over the past 20 years the Yearbook has steadily evolved into a work of broader relevance, shaped by the growing interconnectedness of the legal, political, and economic spheres in which Austria participates.

Authored by an exceptional group of experienced practitioners, this anniversary edition covers a wide range of highly relevant topics in the international landscape of arbitration. The valuable contributions, addressing global discussions and emerging challenges in arbitral practice, seek to assist readers in addressing and resolving issues in their daily work.

With the role of arbitration in resolving complex international disputes efficiently and fairly, it is of importance for arbitration itself to evolve with and adapt to the constant changes and shifts in the global landscape. This 20th edition's goal seeks to reflect on these transformations and provide a comprehensive selection of central developments and trends in arbitration worldwide.

We are especially pleased that this anniversary edition covers 39 contributions from authors around the globe giving most relevant insights in international developments and challenges. Among others the Yearbook contains forward looking keynote speeches by Cavinder Bull SC, Professor Stavros Brekoulakis and Roland Ziadé, articles addressing efficiency, diversity, technology and AI, procedural issues, enforcements and ISDS. Furthermore, the Yearbook covers specific regional developments, including those in Austria, the Balkans, China, Germany, Hungary and the United Kingdom.

We sincerely thank all authors, contributors, and supporters whose efforts made this anniversary edition possible. Your expertise and commitment continue to advance the discussion on international arbitration.

On the occasion of the 2026 anniversary edition, we are proud to also present an overview of all, over 300 authors, who have contributed to the Yearbook in the past 20 years (available under https://www.ayia.at/). In this regard, we are particularly thankful for the broad network developed in the past twenty years, facilitating the exchange of valuable perspectives between arbitration practitioners worldwide through their valuable contributions to the Yearbooks.

It is our hope that this edition will serve as a valuable resource for academics, practitioners, and all readers interested in understanding the dynamics shaping the world of arbitration now and in the years ahead.

*Vienna, January 2026*

*Nikolaus Pitkowitz*
On behalf of the Editors

# Contents

## Developments on the Austrian Market



## Chapter I
## The Arbitration Agreement and Arbitrability



## Chapter II
## The Arbitrator and the Arbitration Procedure

## Chapter III
## The Award and the Courts



## Chapter IV
## Investment Arbitration

# The Editors and Authors

Matthew T. Adams, Research Assistant at Gleiss Lutz in Germany
Barry Appleton, Managing Partner at Appleton & Associates International Lawyers and Professor at the New York Law School
Antje Baumann, Partner at BAUMANN Resolving Disputes in Germany
Katherine Bell, Partner at Schellenberg Wittmer in Switzerland
Lisa Berger, Senior Associate at Gorrissen Federspiel in Denmark
Dina Berkaliyeva, Partner at ADL Disputes in Kazakhstan
Vilius Bernatonis, Managing Partner and Chair of the Baltic Board at TEGOS in Lithuania
James H. Boykin, Partner at Hughes Hubbard & Reed in the US
Stavros Brekoulakis, the Michael and Laura Hwang Professor of International Arbitration at the National University of Singapore and Arbitrator at Three Verulam Buildings barristers in the UK
Cavinder Bull, Chief Executive Officer at Drew & Napier LLC in Singapore
Rita de Carvalho, Trainee Lawyer at Victoria Associates in Portugal
Ondrej Cech, Senior Associate and Head of Prague branch at ZEILER in Austria
Vod K.S. Chan, Barrister at RW Chambers in Hong Kong
Chrystalla Christoforou, Associate at Christos Georgiades & Associates in Cyprus
Barbara Concolino, Partner at BonelliErede in Italy
Sofia Elena Cozac, Counsel at Suciu Partners in Romania and VIAC Ambassador for Romania
Sára Darnót, Attorney-at-law at Lakatos, Köves & Partners in Hungary
Borna Dejanović, Counsel at Wolf Theiss in Croatia
Egishe Dzhazoyan, Partner at King & Spalding in the UK
Vivian Elvers, Associate/Rechtsanwältin at BAUMANN Resolving Disputes in Germany
Sarah Yvonne Enzi, Associate at CERHA HEMPEL in Austria
Catrice Gayer, Partner at Herbert Smith Freehills Kramer in Germany
Agis Georgiades, Partner and Head of International Disputes at Christos Georgiades & Associates LLC in Cyprus
Amaryllis Germanidis, Associate/Rechtsanwältin at BAUMANN Resolving Disputes in Germany
Duarte G. Henriques, Lawyer and Arbitrator at Victoria Associates in Portugal

Rishika Jain, Associate at Arendt & Medernach in Luxembourg and National Representative for Sweden at the International Bar Association
Arush Khanna, Partner at Numen Law Offices in India
Antonia Cermak-Kietaibl, Attorney-at-Law at Cermak Schwarz in Austria
Christian Klausegger, Partner at Binder Grösswang in Austria
Peter Klein, Partner at Petsch Frosch Klein Arturo Rechtsanwälte in Austria
Judith Knieper, Legal Officer at the Secretariat of the United Nations Commission on International Trade Law (UNCITRAL) in Austria
Justin Friedrich Krahé, Associate at SZA Schilling, Zutt & Anschütz in Germany
Florian Kremslehner, Partner at DORDA in Austria
Niam Leinwather, Secretary General of the Vienna International Arbitral Centre in Austria
Eric Leikin, Partner at Freshfields in Austria
Courtney Lotfi, Arbitrator, Counsel and Consultant at Courtney Lotfi ADR Consulting in Germany
Eveli Lume, Partner at Squire Patton Boggs in Germany
Peter Machherndl, Partner at Pitkowitz & Partners in Austria
Tamara Manasijevic, Attorney-at-law at ARP in Austria
Marlene Maurer, Associate at Pitkowitz & Partners in Austria
Maximilian Albert Mueller, Attorney at Law at Pitkowitz & Partners in Austria
Max Murtinger, Associate at KNOETZL in Austria
Irina Nazarova, Founding Partner at Engarde Attorneys at Law in Ukraine
Pınar Noberi, Associate at Paksoy in Turkey
Petra Pataki, Partner at Queritius in Hungary
Camilla Perera - de Wit, Arbitration and Mediation Specialist and immediate past Secretary General of the Netherlands Arbitration Institute
Alexander Petsche, Partner at Baker McKenzie in Austria
Markus Petsche, Professor at the Department of Legal Studies at Central European University in Austria
Nikolaus Pitkowitz, Founding Partner at Pitkowitz & Partners in Austria
Jessica Puhr, Legal Counsel at the Vienna International Arbitral Centre in Austria
Matej Pustay, Partner at Squire Patton Boggs in the Czech Republic and Slovak Republic and ICC YAAF representative for Europe & Central Asia
Milica Savić, Partner at Karanovic & Partners in Serbia
Helena Schnur, Associate at Gowling WLG in Germany
Albertas Šekštelo, Associate Professor at Vilnius University Law Faculty and Partner at MOTIEKA in Vilnius
Arman Shaikenov, Senior Counsel at ADL Disputes in Kazakhstan
Valikhan Shaikenov, Partner at ADL Disputes in Kazakhstan
Iain Sheridan, Barrister at Mountford Chambers in the UK
Ana Stanič, Founding Partner at E&A Law in the UK

Ben Steinbrück, Partner at SZA Schilling, Zutt & Anschütz in Germany and an honorary Professor at Trier University in Germany
Wei Sun, Managing Partner at Zhong Lun in China
Sofia Svinkovskaya, Principal Associate at Freshfields Austria
Johannes Tropper, Postdoctoral Researcher and Lecturer at the Department of European, International and Comparative Law at the University of Vienna in Austria
Doğuhan Uygun, Counsel at Paksoy in Turkey
Florian Wagner, Counsel at Gleiss Lutz in Germany
Anna Weinzierl, Associate at PARAGON Advocacy in Austria
Irene Welser, Senior Partner of CERHA HEMPEL and Head of the Contentious Business Department in Austria
Stephan Wilske, Partner at Gleiss Lutz in Germany
Mathias Wittinghofer, Partner and Head of Dispute Resolution Germany at Gowling WLG in Germany
Gerold Zeiler, Partner at ZEILER in Austria
Roland Ziadé, Partner and Global Co-Head of International Arbitration at Linklaters in France

# Developments on the Austrian Market

*Niam Leinwather/Jessica Puhr*

VIAC's Annual Report – 2025

Celebrating 50 Years of Excellence in Dispute Resolution

# VIAC's Annual Report – 2025
## Celebrating 50 Years of Excellence in Dispute Resolution

*Niamh Leinwather/Jessica Puhr*

## I. Introduction

2025 marked a significant milestone in the history of the Vienna International Arbitral Centre ("VIAC") as the institution celebrated its 50$^{th}$ anniversary. Over the past five decades, VIAC has continuously evolved: from rule adaptions over the expansion of services to embracing innovation. This past year, VIAC took a moment to reflect on its history, past achievements and challenges. Under the auspices of the Austrian Federal Economic Chamber and the guidance of founding figures and the VIAC Board, VIAC administered around 2,500 cases over the course of the past 50 years while at the same time maintaining the highest standards in case management.

On the case management front, VIAC launched its modernised Vienna Rules 2021 with new model arbitration and mediation clauses, the introduction of Annex 7, and an updated schedule of fees for mediation proceedings. VIAC also finalised and published its note on the use of artificial intelligence in arbitration proceedings. These efforts demonstrate VIAC's commitment to thought leadership in dispute resolution globally.

As part of its 50$^{th}$ anniversary, VIAC (co-)organised a series of events to commemorate this milestone. The VIAC Community Ambassador Network ("VIAC CAN") also continued to grow and is becoming a cornerstone of the institution's outreach efforts in the CEE and SEE regions. The initiative has facilitated invaluable connections and further reinforced VIAC's prominence in the region.

Institutional collaborations also took centre stage this year, with VIAC joining forces with a multitude of institutions. These initiatives reflect VIAC's enthusiasm and dedication to global thought exchange and collaboration.

On the team front, VIAC welcomed back two team members who returned from maternity leave and developed the position of managing counsel. The VIAC team now consists of the Secretary General and her deputy, a managing counsel, four case managers, two assistants and the VIAC CAN team. The newly established role as managing counsel demonstrates the institution's dedication to knowledge management and an overall excellent service.

This annual report takes a different approach this year as it reflects on the past, analyses the present and sets out VIAC's ideas about VIAC in the future.

## II. The Past: Reflecting on 50 Years of VIAC

### A. Reflecting on VIAC's Legacy and Evolution

In the late 1950s, the intensification of economic relations brought the recognition and enforcement of arbitral awards to the forefront of international discourse. In 1958, the founding father of VIAC, Werner Melis served as the Austrian delegate during the negotiations of the New York Convention on the Recognition and Enforcement of Arbitral Awards (New York Convention). Austria's ratification of the New York Convention in 1961 marked a pivotal moment in establishing Vienna as a recognised centre for alternative dispute resolution. Thereafter, an increasing number of parties from Central Eastern Europe and Southern Eastern Europe chose Austria as the place of arbitration for disputes due to its neutrality and location between East and West.

The Austrian Federal Economic Chamber (WKÖ) recognised this trend and saw the necessity for an international centre for arbitration and mediation. In 1974, the Vienna International Arbitral Centre was founded, and the institution began its work on 1 January 1975. VIAC registered its' first case on 21 March 1975 and the first final award was rendered two years later in 1977.

As the demands of the ever-changing dispute resolution world changed, VIAC adapted and steadily increased its offering. In 2013, VIAC added mediation to its portfolio providing its users with a broader range of conflict resolution mechanisms. In 2017, VIAC became the authority to also administer purely domestic cases.[1]) In 2021, VIAC also introduced stand-alone investment rules as the first European institution to do so. Since 2021, the Vienna Rules also allow VIAC to act as an administrative and appointing authority (Annex 4 and 5).

While being innovative on the offering front, VIAC tirelessly sought out expertise and the right people to improve its services. The VIAC Board has traditionally been comprised of numerous prominent arbitration practitioners, academics, and judges, the institution's decision-making body. In 2009, the VIAC International Advisory Board was inaugurated with a variety of well-known international arbitration experts. Almost a decade later, in 2019 the VIAC Domestic Advisory Board and the VIAC Mediation Advisory Board were established to focus on the development of the domestic arbitration and mediation market. VIAC's Advisory Boards provide invaluable input, function

[1]) Up until 2017, VIAC only administered international cases. Domestic cases were administered by the regional economic chambers.

as a sounding board, and assist the institution in developing and benchmarking its services.

At the same time, VIAC also sought cooperation with reliable partners on a global level. VIAC entered into its first Memorandum of Understanding with the Bulgarian Chamber of Commerce and Industry in 1982, and since then has made continuous efforts to establish and nurture new partnerships with organisations and institutions around the globe. As of 2025, VIAC has signed around 50 Cooperation Agreements and has proven to be a reliable partner on the global arbitration and mediation stage.

## B. 50 Years of Excellence in Case Management

Over the past fifty years, the world and VIAC have evolved, but VIAC's mission has remained consistent: offering excellency in dispute resolution. With excellency comes the need to uphold the highest standards, and in VIAC's case, this converted to numerous rule revisions. Since entering into force, the Vienna Rules have been amended eight times. The most significant changes were implemented in 2013, expanding the scope of the rules to important topics such as joinder and consolidation, multi-party proceedings, confirmation of the appointment of an arbitrator, and expedited proceedings.

In an effort to serve regional markets, VIAC, with the help of dedicated arbitration practitioners and translators had the Vienna Rules translated into numerous languages. The 2021 Vienna Rules have been translated into eleven – and counting – different languages.[2])

Another effort to bring the Vienna Rules closer to users was the publication of the VIAC Handbook in 2013. A second, revised version was published in 2018. The VIAC Handbook is designed for practitioners with each article of the rules reproduced in their entirety providing detailed comments and background information on each of the articles. The VIAC Handbook is a unique source for practitioners to guide them through each step of a VIAC arbitration proceeding.

The institution also did not stay idle in relation to its case management core. The institution has administered approximately 2,500 cases over the past 50 years. With an average duration of proceedings of 12 months and fast and reliable responses, VIAC is proud of the fruits of its efforts to increase efficiency in VIAC proceedings. While maintaining its standard of fast responses, VIAC further improved its internal procedures under the leadership if its Secretary Generals. Numerous improvements were implemented over the past five decades. One of the most significant improvements, was the implementation of

[2]) Translations of the Vienna Rules 2021 can be found on the VIAC website: https://www.viac.eu/en/arbitration-basics/arbitration-rules/ (last accessed on 23 October 2025).

the institution's award monitoring procedure and the expansion of its scrutiny light in 2023.[3])

### C. 50 Years of Excellence in Innovation

With technological advancements and the rise of digital technologies over the past few years, arbitral institutions had to radically adapt their daily work. VIAC has always been at the forefront of technology and introduced as one of the first arbitral institutions in Europe an electronic case management system. In 2021, VIAC introduced the VIAC Portal – an online case management platform hosted on HighQ, a cloud-based file sharing and collaboration software operated by Thomson Reuters. The VIAC Portal was developed to be used for all types of VIAC proceedings for communication among VIAC, the parties, and the arbitrators or other third-party neutrals.

## III. The Present: 50 Years of VIAC

### A. 2025 in Numbers

2025 has been a successful year for VIAC in many regards. The case numbers were no exception. VIAC observed an increase in case numbers once again while at the same time closing a record number of cases. Detailed statistics are available on the VIAC website and in the VIAC Annual Report.

### B. Advancements in Case Management: New Version of the Vienna Rules

A new version of the VIAC Rules of Arbitration and Mediation 2021 and the VIAC Rules of Investment Arbitration and Mediation 2021 entered into force on 1 January 2025. The rules apply to all proceedings that commenced after 31 December 2024.

Key changes of the Vienna Arbitration Rules included a new model arbitration clause[4]) for intra-corporate disputes providing corporations with a practical tool to include or update arbitration clauses in their articles of asso-

---

[3]) VIAC Arbitral Awards need to be rendered within three months of the last hearing concerning matters to be decided in an award or the filing of the last authorised submission concerning such matters (Art. 32 Vienna Rules). Arbitrators subject themselves to this time limit by completing and signing the VIAC Acceptance of Office form. VIAC closely monitors the Arbitral Tribunal's progress in the award drafting stage. Arbitrators are also provided with the VIAC Award Checklist and are required to submit their arbitral award in advance to allow for the informal review of the award.

[4]) The model arbitration clauses are available on the VIAC website: https://www.viac.eu/en/arbitration-basics/arbitration-clauses/ (last accessed on 20 October 2025).

ciation or partnership agreements, and the introduction of Annex 7 with specific supplementary rules for corporate disputes. This rule change was a response to jurisprudence from the Austrian Supreme Court (18 OCg 3/22y).

Key changes of the Vienna Mediation Rules also included the simplification of the model mediation clauses,[5]) and the introduction of a revised fee schedule for mediation proceedings. There are now two model clauses for mediation that also provide for numerous supplementary provisions. The registration fee is now a flat rate set at EUR 500 rather than a maximum amount of EUR 1,500, and the calculation of VIAC's administrative fees has been significantly revised. The administrative fees continue to be calculated on the basis of the amount in dispute (as outlined in Annex 3 of the Vienna Rules). However, the following maximum amounts have been introduced: EUR 2,000 for disputes up to EUR 500,000; EUR 5,000 for disputes between EUR 500,001 and EUR 5,000,000; and EUR 10,000 for disputes exceeding EUR 5,000,000.

| **Registration Fee** | |
|---|---|
| Flat rate | EUR 500 |
| **Administrative Fees** | |
| *Amount in dispute* | *Maximum Rate* |
| up to EUR 500,000 | EUR 2,000 |
| from EUR 500,001 to EUR 5,000,000 | EUR 5,000 |
| over EUR 5,000,001 | EUR 10,000 |

At the end of the mediation proceedings, the Secretary General has the discretion to set the administrative fees according to this scale, taking into account the specific circumstances of the case.

## C. Launch of Best Practices: VIAC Note on the Use of Artificial Intelligence in Arbitration Proceedings

To ensure that VIAC is fit for the future, the Legal Tech Think Tank (LTTT) met regularly throughout 2024 to consider potential risks the use of AI tools might pose in arbitration proceedings. A tangible outcome of these discussions was the publication of the VIAC Note on AI.[6])

[5]) The model mediation clauses are available on the VIAC website: https://www.viac.eu/en/mediation-basics/mediation-clauses/ (last accessed on 20 October 2025).

[6]) The VIAC Note on the Use of Artificial Intelligence in Arbitration proceedings in available on the VIAC website: https://www.viac.eu/wp-content/uploads/2025/04/VIAC-Note-on-AI-1.pdf (last accessed on 21 October 2025).

VIAC's Note on AI is non-binding and encourages arbitrators to use AI tools responsibly, in line with ethical standards and professional duties, while maintaining confidentiality and procedural fairness. VIAC has adopted a considered and balanced approach; rather than imposing rigid or prescriptive disclosure requirements on counsel or arbitrators, the Note entrusts parties and tribunals with the discretion to determine, on a case-by-case basis, how best to address the use of AI within the proceedings. Central to the Note's guidance is the promotion of early and open dialogue; parties and arbitrators are encouraged to discuss the potential use of AI tools at the outset of the arbitration, ideally during the case management conference. This conversation should encompass any disclosure obligations, and the anticipated impact of AI on procedural and substantive aspects of the case.

The Note also offers loose recommendations to arbitrators, such as supporting parties and relevant third parties in understanding and appropriately utilising AI tools where necessary and informing the parties of any intended use of AI tools by the arbitrator, if they see fit. In such cases, arbitrators may consider identifying the tool, explaining its intended purpose, and providing an opportunity for parties to respond. Ultimately, VIAC underscores that transparency in the use of AI is essential to preserving confidence in the arbitral process; the extent of this transparency is left in the hands of the arbitrators and parties.

This initiative was spearheaded by a working group consisting of the VIAC Secretary General Niamh Leinwather, VIAC CAN Coordinator Vladyslava Donchyk, and LTTT members Mihaela Apostol, Aija Lejniece, Sean McCarthy, Philipp Schwarz, and David Tebel.

## D. Meeting our Users: Launch of the VIAC Inhouse Counsel Breakfast

In March 2025, VIAC launched a breakfast series for inhouse counsel. This brand-new initiative is a quarterly get-together designed as a relaxed information and networking event. VIAC hosts an expert on a specific topic that is relevant to the everyday work of an inhouse counsel, while connecting arbitration law with other areas of law. The kick-off event was well attended and welcomed inhouse counsel from various sectors, moderated by VIAC Domestic Advisory Board members Ingeborg Edel and Christian Koller addressed practical questions of arbitration where VIAC as an institution used the opportunity to listen carefully to the needs of its' users. The second breakfast in May 2025 welcomed a growing number of inhouse counsels and focused on the topic of class actions expertly presented by VIAC Board Member, Prof. Paul Oberhammer while the breakfast in November tackled the ongoing challenge of sanctions, both in arbitration and more generally.

The initiative developed within the VIAC Domestic Advisory Board and is led by VIAC Secretary General, Niamh Leinwather and Legal Counsel, Jessica Puhr. Increased outreach activities and community engagement: 50 years of VIAC events

2025 was a milestone year for VIAC with its $50^{th}$ anniversary. VIAC rolled out a series of events dedicated to its Golden Jubilee over the course of the whole year. The year began with the Swiss Arbitration Summit taking place from 29 to 31 January 2025. On 29 January 2025, VIAC and Arb|Aut co-hosted "Take 1 of the Austrian Series: Taking a Closer Look at Modern Investment Arbitration" during the ASA – Swiss Arbitration Association 2025. Marking the start of VIAC's 50th anniversary celebrations, the event gathered leading practitioners to examine the evolving landscape of investment arbitration moderated by Claudia Annacker, VIAC Board Member. Speakers examined procedural innovations, including the balance between adversarial and inquisitorial approaches, recent ICSID rule changes, and transparency measures. The discussion also addressed substantive protections, damages and reflections on how arbitration can adapt to the complex realities of modern investor-State relations.

The year continued with the second VIAC CAN Congress on 28 February 2025. The VIAC CAN Congress plays a pivotal role in advancing the objectives of the VIAC Community Ambassador Network. By bringing together professionals from across the network, including VIAC Ambassadors, the event highlights recent developments in the market, explores future trends, and provides a dynamic platform for the exchange of ideas and networking. Aligning to this year's overall theme, the focus of the 2025 VIAC CAN Congress was VIAC's $50^{th}$ anniversary with the topic "Shaping the future of arbitration in CEE/SEE for the next 50 years". As in previous years, the event started with an exclusive programme for VIAC Ambassadors on 27 February 2025 and concluded with the prestigious Ball of Legal Professionals on 1 March 2025. A particular highlight of the VIAC CAN Congress was the exceptional keynote speech by Stavros Brekoulakis where he noted that "VIAC has evolved into this modern and vibrant arbitral institution that is more popular than ever. But it always kept this special character that distinguishes VIAC from any other institution in the world; in being this living historical symbol that international arbitration can be more than just resolving commercial disputes. That it can be a platform where people from very different backgrounds leave their parochialism, cultural assumptions and prejudices behind to find common ground. (...) international law and arbitration are at a crossroads today. In the next 50 years, VIAC's role should be not just to administer more arbitration cases; it should be to remind us all what international arbitration is all about."

The next event where VIAC celebrated its anniversary was at the Paris Arbitration Week from 7 to 11 April 2025. The main VIAC event hosted at the exclusive Cercle de l'Union Interalliée in collaboration with Arb|Aut under the theme "The Price of Justice: Rethinking Costs in Arbitration – Are arbitration costs out of control? Exploring allocation, discipline, and best practices". The panel brought together leading practitioners and arbitrators to explore the evolving landscape of cost decisions in arbitration. VIAC also introduced its "Practice Note for Decision on Costs in Arbitral Awards", a practice note aimed at promoting consistency in cost decisions.

As in previous years, VIAC also made a significant impact at the Vis Moot from 11 to 17 April 2025. VIAC's Vis Moot week started with an Arbitrator Moot Camp in collaboration with CIArb, a boot camp designed for this year's Vis Moot arbitrators to equip them with the insights, strategies, and practical know-how needed to navigate rounds effectively. VIAC's next event was the Mind and Motion: FAI – VIAC Wellbeing Morning, where participants were invited to join the two arbitral institutions for a morning yoga session. VIAC also co-organised an event under the auspices of the International Federation of Commercial Arbitration Institutions (IFCAI) of which VIAC's Secretary General is the Secretary General. The other institutions that participated included the Asian International Arbitration Centre (AIAC), the Cairo Regional Centre for International Commercial Arbitration (CRCICA), the German Arbitration Institute (DIS), and the SCC Arbitration Institute (SCC) who addressed the topic of "Pay me in full or you owe me one – Remunerating the Arbitrator, when, how, and how much?". During elevator pitches, the arbitral institutions outlined their institutions approaches to the renumeration of arbitrators. The last event VIAC organised during the Vis Moot week was an Oxford style debate on the topic of "Arbitr-AI-tion": Justice Meets the Algorithm which was spearheaded by VIAC's Legal Tech Think Tank (LTTT) and explored the pros and cons of AI in arbitration.

VIAC was also the proud co-organiser of the Vienna Arbitration Days which took place from 9 to10 May 2025. The Vienna Arbitration Days 2025 discussed "Orchestrating Efficiency in Arbitration – a symphony of modern solutions to the classic challenge" and offered dynamic discussions. VIAC hosted the session "Arbitral Institutions: Maintaining Harmony or Rethinking the Rhythm?" which sparked an insightful debate on the evolving role of arbitral institutions and included a live poll. The cherry on top of the session was the sneak preview of the VIAC Documentary.[7])

After a short summer break, VIAC continued its celebration at the Berlin Dispute Resolution Days from 8 to 11 September 2025. VIAC hosted the third edition of the Austrian Series titled "Challenges in M&A Disputes: W&I Insurance and Expert Determination" on 8 September 2025, co-hosted with Advantage Austria and Arb|Aut and organised by VIAC's Post M&A Expert Focus Group, which is spearheaded by VIAC's Board Member, Karl Pörnbacher.

---

[7]) The VIAC Documentary is available in three parts on VIAC's YouTube: Part I https://youtu.be/Ppr0RwwqH-k?si=OoDSGM_W4L8afLa5; Part II https://youtu.be/tX7o8pUCZSg?si=T5F0_wjtARJLfWQ5; Part III https://youtu.be/lf-L30FdJ9k?si=H84y0QjARet5aftx (all last accessed on 23 October 2025).

The event, held during the Berlin Dispute Resolution Days at the Austrian Embassy, brought together experts to explore the nuances of post-M&A dispute management and expert determination.

The grande finale of VIAC's celebrations was the "VIAC at 50" event together with the GAR Live Vienna on 2 and 3 October 2025. Under the theme "The Legacy and Future of Dispute Resolution in the Heart of Europe", VIAC welcomed a multitude of renowned speakers and almost 200 participants. It was an event of reflection, with nostalgia for the past and excitement for the future of the institution. Fitting this theme, the event was opened by the current VIAC President, Nikolaus Pitkowitz, and was rounded off by closing remarks from the incoming VIAC President, Franz Schwarz, whose presidency was announced at the VIAC at 50 event. The evening ended on the historic grounds of Palais Ferstel in Vienna, where participants enjoyed a Gala Dinner that was hosted together with GAR.

Under the auspices of the VIAC CAN initiative, VIAC organised a plethora of events in 2025. Each occasion addressed unique regional and professional needs. Exclusive, invitation-only sessions and online workshops complemented networking events. VIAC partnered with local law firms and institutions as well as with the foreign trade centres of the Austrian Federal Economic Chamber[8]) to host international conferences and roadshows in countries as far as India and China, first time appearances in Kazakhstan and Egypt as well as strong presences in Slovakia, Hungary, Montenegro, Türkiye, and Georgia to name but a few. 2025 was also a year of expansion for VIAC CAN, as VIAC announced a call for VIAC Ambassador applications in regions where VIAC does not yet have an Ambassador; this is a major milestone for the VIAC CAN project as it demonstrates that the initiative has become an established pillar of the institution and is growing in popularity and reach. Additionally, VIAC cooperated on two occasions with the Arbitration Association of Central and Eastern Europe (ArbCEE).

Overall, VIAC significantly enhanced its public presence and outreach in 2025, with a notable increase in activity on LinkedIn and other platforms.

## E. Improving Collaboration: New Cooperation Agreements

VIAC frequently signs cooperation agreements. In 2025, VIAC signed cooperation agreements with eight institutions, marking 2025 as a record year for collaboration.

[8]) The Austrian Federal Economic Chambers has over 700 experts in over 100 destinations across the globe. Find out more here: https://www.wko.at/aussenwirtschaft/about-us (last accessed on 23 October 2025).

On 11 January 2025, VIAC signed an Agreement of Cooperation with the Ukrainian Academy of Mediation (UAM), a public association established to promote the spread of mediation and other alternative dispute resolution methods in Ukraine. Given the current situation the signing ceremony took place online.

At the VIAC CAN Congress on 28 February 2025, VIAC signed an Agreement of Cooperation with the Scottish Arbitration Centre's CEO Andrew McKenzie, a non-profit company offering arbitration services as well as arbitral appointment services in ad hoc cases. As a first step in this cooperation, VIAC attended ArbFest in September 2025 contributing to a panel on ethics in arbitration.

On 17 March 2025, VIAC signed a Memorandum of Cooperation with the Beihai Asia International Arbitration Centre (BAIAC), the first international arbitration centre in Singapore established by a Chinese arbitration commission.

At the Vienna Arbitration Days (VAD) on 10 May 2025, VIAC signed a Memorandum of Understanding with Arbitral Women, a leading force for gender equality in alternative dispute resolution with the mission to elevate the presence and impact of women in ADR. VIAC has been a signatory of the ERA-Pledge (see also A. 2025 in numbers for VIAC's gender statistics) for many years and has been spearheading the organisation of the ArbitralWomen breakfast at the VAD for the past years, hence the signing of this cooperation was timely.

On 10 July 2025 during the IBA-VIAC CDRC Mediation & Negotiation Competition, VIAC signed an Agreement of Cooperation with the Finland Arbitration Institute (FAI), an autonomous arbitration body of the Finland Chamber of Commerce administering arbitrations and mediations. The FAI rules had been used as the rules for the Vis Moot competition, hence VIAC had already closely cooperated with the FAI during 2025, hence the signing of this agreement with the FAI's Chair Heidi Merikalla-Teir cemented the good relationship between the institutions.

During VIAC's India Roadshow on 13 September 2025, VIAC signed an Agreement of Cooperation with the Society of Indian Law Firms (SILF), the apex body of law firms in India. This landmark occasion was made possible by VIAC's Ambassador for India, Arush Khanna.

During VIAC's China Roadshow, the institution signed another Agreement of Cooperation. On 22 September 2025, VIAC Board Member Alexander Petsche signed an agreement with the Shenzhen Court of International Arbitration (SCIA), the first arbitration institution in the Guangdong-Hong Kong-Macao region. On the same day back in Vienna, VIAC Vice-President Patrizia Netal signed an agreement with the China Maritime Arbitration Centre (CMAC), a permanent international arbitration institution resolving admiralty, maritime, transport, logistics-related disputes and other commercial disputes.

Lastly, on 25 September 2025, VIAC's President Nikolaus Pitkowitz signed an Agreement of Cooperation with the Istanbul Chamber of Commerce Arbitration and Mediation Centre (ITOTAM), an arbitration and mediation centre set up by the Istanbul Chamber of Commerce.

VIAC is excited to enhance cooperation and promote best practices in international dispute resolution together with its new partners.

## F. VIAC Website

In March 2025 VIAC also launched its new website as part of the 50$^{th}$ anniversary celebration. The new website increased accessibility and provides VIAC's contents in a more user-friendly format. One of the highlights is VIAC's new interactive arbitrator and mediator search. Arbitration and mediation practitioners are invited to create a profile and present themselves on the VIAC website. The service is free of charge and allows practitioners to showcase their bio together with a profile photo. An interactive search function aids with the finding of suitable arbitrators and mediators. The arbitrators' profiles are non-binding and do not constitute as a recommendation by the institution. Parties and the VIAC Board are free to nominate and appoint arbitrators of their own choice.

## G. VIAC Handbook

In 2024 and 2025 VIAC worked on the Third Edition of the VIAC Handbook. The VIAC Handbook is written by leading arbitration and mediation experts, many actively involved in the institution and provides detailed commentary to each provision focusing on their practical application. The key updates include of the new edition of the VIAC Handbook include the following:

- expansion of VIAC's authority to administer investment proceedings;
- revision of the mediation rules;
- new and revised provisions regarding third-party funding, disclosure, use of digital technology, and costs;
- a new model arbitration clause for intra-corporate disputes; and
- special provisions for succession-related disputes.

The book also incorporates the Explanatory Notes prepared by the VIAC Secretariat, along with insights into the Secretariat's day-to-day practice. The Third Edition of the VIAC Handbook will be available soon.[9])

[9]) The VIAC Handbook will be available for purchase here: https://law-store.wolterskluwer.com/s/product/viac-handbook-rules-of-arbitration-and-mediation-3e/01t

## IV. The Future: Looking Ahead to the next 50 Years

Vienna, as a historic bridge between East and West, continues to serve as a key hub for international arbitration, fostering connections between diverse legal traditions and business cultures. In this ideal framework, VIAC remains dedicated to advancing international arbitration and mediation, and developing the highest standards in case management. Over the next few years and under the leadership of the incoming VIAC President, Franz Schwarz, and a new, even more diverse VIAC Board for 2026 to 2028,[10]) the institution will have a strong focus on the following three points: First and foremost, users first. The key is service excellence. Building on a strong foundation of its history of offering excellent service, the institution intends to excel in its user-oriented service offering. In particular, a focus will be on the full repertoire of VIAC's service, including mediations, investment proceedings and other services VIAC offers. Second, regional cooperation: VIAC has strong ties with the region, which VIAC intends to further strengthen. For VIAC this entails engaging and listening to the region's users, promoting regional practitioners, and – with the support of VIAC CAN – showcasing VIAC as a reliable partner for all ADR-needs. Third, global thought leadership: VIAC intends to stay on top of current trends and topics in international arbitration and mediation. As the premiere institution in the CEE and SEE, VIAC will enhance its contributions as a thought leader. Grateful for a fantastic year of celebrating VIAC at 50, VIAC with its' forward-looking perspective and the best people in its' Secretariat and Board, is poised to shape the evolving landscape of arbitration in Austria and the region – anchored in principles of efficiency, transparency, and innovation.

---

Pg00000Hd7kzIAB?srsltid=AfmBOoqt8e4IfMKhwJzrxX_MAk3OnEk8o0JXbjKYQCHmAfGwi5MFunhv (last accessed on 5 January 2026).

[10]) An overview of the current VIAC Board can be found on the VIAC website: https://www.viac.eu/en/about-viac/structure-at-a-glance/viac-board/ (last accessed on 2 January 2026).

# Chapter I

# The Arbitration Agreement and Arbitrability

*Helena Schnur/Mathias Wittinghofer*
German Federal Court Ruling of 9 January 2025 (I ZB 48/24) –
Free Rein to Opt Out of German General Terms and Conditions Law
via Arbitration Agreements?

*Ben Steinbrück/Justin Friedrich Krahé*
Arbitration without Agreements
Unilateral Arbitration Provisions under sec. 1066
of the German Code of Civil Procedure

# German Federal Court Ruling of 9 January 2025 (I ZB 48/24) – Free Rein to Opt Out of German General Terms and Conditions Law via Arbitration Agreements?

*Helena Schnur/Mathias Wittinghofer*

## I. Introduction

The following article examines the far-reaching implications of the decision of the German Federal Court (*Bundesgerichtshof*, BGH) of January 9, 2025[1]) for the possibility of opting out of the German law on standard terms and conditions in arbitration proceedings. In its ruling, the court has, for the first time, set out key guidelines for the application of Section 1051 of the German Code of Civil Procedure (*Zivilprozessordnung*, GCCP) in the context of Art. 28 of the UNCITRAL Model Law on International Commercial Arbitration (*"UNCITRAL Model Law"*) and specified the conditions under which such an opt-out can be legally valid in B2B-transactions.

The starting point for the underlying issue is Section 307 of the German Civil Code (*Bürgerliches Gesetzbuch*, GCC), which, under German law, also applies mandatorily in B2B transactions. The parties cannot simply "switch off" the review of general terms and conditions by state courts either by choice of law or by contract.

This principle entails that contracting parties cannot circumvent the review of general terms and conditions by state courts merely by choosing a different law or by agreeing on other contractual arrangements. A typical "escape" to foreign law is also limited by Art. 3 para 3 of the Rome I Regulation (Regulation (EC) No. 593/2008) in cases where the parties involved have a purely domestic connection. This provision ensures that mandatory provisions of German law remain applicable even if the parties have chosen a different law, but all other relevant elements of the case only have a connection to Germany at the time of the choice of law.

The following article will illustrate how Section 1051 GCCP in conjunction with Art. 28 of the UNCITRAL Model Law opens up a different decision-making corridor for arbitral tribunals, which the Federal Court has clarified with key guidelines (separability, *blue-pencil* test, *ordre public* control). At the

[1]) Federal Court, 9 January 2025, file no. I ZB 48/24, in NJW 896 (2025).

same time, the court affirmed the rights of arbitral tribunals to examine the choice of law on a case-by-case basis. Court review is shifted to the annulment/enforcement proceedings via Section 1059 para 2 sentence 2 b GCCP.

The use of arbitration agreements provides for an independent legal framework for parties to work with, albeit significantly influenced by Section 1051 GCCP and the corresponding Art. 28 of the UNCITRAL Model Law.

These provisions give the parties greater autonomy in determining the legal provisions applicable to the substantive contract. The Federal Court now confirmed this leeway in its landmark decision while at the same time attaching a clear *ordre public* reservation. Against this background, the central thesis of this article is as follows: Although it is legally possible to opt out of Sections 305-310 GCC in arbitration proceedings, this is by no means a *carte blanche* or (*"Freifahrtschein"* in German).

The following remarks will explain this thesis in detail on the basis of an analysis of the underlying case law and the associated dogmatic and practical implications.

## II. The Mandatory Framework of General Terms and Conditions Law in B2B Transactions

German law on standard terms and conditions, primarily regulated in Sections 305 *et seq.* GCC, aims to protect contractual partners from unilateral exploitation of drafting power when using pre-formulated contract terms. Although Sections 305 *et seq.* GCC are originally strongly focused on consumer protection, a large part of the provisions, in particular the content review under Section 307 GCC, also apply to transactions between businesses. According to Section 310 para 1 sentence 1 GCC, Sections 307 to 309 GCC apply to contracts between entrepreneurs only to a limited extent, with Section 307 GCC continuing to function as a central general clause.

This means that clauses in general terms and conditions that unreasonably disadvantage the user's contractual partner contrary to the principle of good faith are invalid. In B2B transactions, however, appropriateness is assessed pursuant to Section 310 para 1 sentence 2 GCC by *"taking into account the customs and practices applicable in commercial transactions"*. In its established case law,[2]) the German Federal Court has clarified that Section 307 GCC also functions as a key central general clause in terms of assessment between entrepreneurs, which can lead to a "consumer-like" content review of assessments, especially in cases of imbalance between the contracting parties or in atypical B2B constellations.

---

[2]) Federal Court, 19 January 1984, file no. VII ZR 220/82, in NJW 1350 (1984); 19 September 2007, file no. VIII ZR 141/06; 3 February 2021, file no. XII ZR 29/20.

This strict application of German law on standard terms and conditions is difficult to circumvent, even in cross-border cases. The limits of the choice of law are set by Art. 3 para 3 of the Rome I Regulation. This conflict-of-law rule states:

> *"If, at the time of the choice of law, all other elements of the situation are located in a country other than the one whose law has been chosen, the choice of law made by the parties shall not affect the application of those provisions of the law of that other country which cannot be derogated from by agreement."*

This means that in purely German domestic cases – *i.e.*, if all relevant connecting factors (*e.g.*, the parties' registered office, place of performance, location of property) are situated in Germany – mandatory German law, including Section 307 GCC, remains applicable even if the parties have chosen foreign law. The frequently mentioned "escape" to foreign law in order to circumvent German law on standard terms and conditions is thus effectively prevented by this provision. This leads to the interim conclusion that German law on standard terms and conditions cannot simply be "decoupled" contractually before state courts. A possible way out of this predicament, which gives the parties greater freedom of contract, is therefore only through arbitration.

## III. The Arbitration Bracket: Section 1051 GCCP and the Model Law

Compared to state jurisdiction, arbitration offers a broader framework for party autonomy, particularly with regard to determining the legal provisions to determine the substance of the dispute.

Section 1051 para 1 GCCP, which largely corresponds to Art. 28 para 1 of the UNCITRAL Model Law, provides that the arbitral tribunal must decide the dispute according *"to the legal provisions chosen by the parties"*. The wording of "*legal provisions designated by the parties*" (in German: *"mit den Rechtsvorschriften zu entscheiden, die von den Parteien als auf den Inhalt des Rechtsstreits anwendbar bezeichnet worden sind"*) in Section 1051 GCCP thus grants the parties the necessary leeway to determine the *"rules of law"* applicable to the merits of the dispute.

In addition, the arbitral tribunal may, pursuant to Section 1051 para 3 GCCP, decide *ex aequo et bono* or as *amiable compositeur* if the parties have expressly authorized it to do so. If such a choice of law is made, the arbitral tribunal must apply – and vice versa, exclude – the legal provisions chosen by the parties. In the absence of an agreement between the parties, the arbitral tribunal shall apply the law of the state with which the subject matter of the dispute is most closely connected.

The tribunal can come to a decision at its reasonable discretion, taking into account justice and fairness. The practical consequence of this option, which is left to the discretion of the parties, is of considerable significance: In arbitration proceedings, the parties can exclude the application of certain provisions, such as Sections 305–310 GCC, even if they have chosen German law. However, the effectiveness of such an exclusion depends largely on whether the arbitral tribunal accepts and implements such a choice of law.

Section 1051 thus serves as a substantive law opening clause that allows the parties to choose from positive *rules of law* and, if necessary, to make partial exclusions.[3]) In addition, there is discussion in the literature regarding the relationship between Section 1051 GCCP and Section 306a GCC, which regulates the legal consequences of the invalidity of general terms and conditions clauses.[4]) Nevertheless, the dominant opinion[5]) affirms the possibility of opting out of general terms and conditions control under Section 1051 GCCP, which paved the way for the court's decision.

In view of these discussions in the past, opting out of German law on general terms and conditions was associated with a substantial potential risk, if, in the absence of clear higher court rulings, a state court were to question the validity and consequences of such a choice of law clause and reject the opt-out in general.

With its decision, the Federal Court has now provided clearer guidelines for practice.

## IV. The Decision of the Federal Court of January 9, 2025 – I ZB 48/24

### A. Facts and Course of Proceedings

The decision marks a milestone for the review of general terms and conditions in arbitration proceedings. The decision was based on a case in which the parties had agreed on an arbitration clause recommended by the

---

[3]) *See Voit* in Musielak/Voit ZPO, Section 1051 ZPO at 2, *Münch* in MüKo ZPO, Section 1051 ZPO, at 1.

[4]) *See Kondring, Jörg*, § 1051 I ZPO und die Abwahl einfach zwingenden Rechts bei Binnensachverhalten, in ZIP 706, (2017); but *see Valdini, Daniel*, Gesetzesreform durch die Hintertür? Die Abwahl zwingenden Rechts durch Schiedsabreden bei Inlandssachverhalten ZIP 7, (2017).

[5]) *See Pfeiffer, Thomas*, Die Abwahl des deutschen AGB-Rechts in Inlandsfällen bei Vereinbarung eines Schiedsverfahrens, in NJW 1169 (2012) und NJW 866 (2025); *Leupertz, Stefan*, Die Vereinbarung deutschen Rechts unter Abwahl des AGB-Rechts in Schiedsverfahren, in RInPrax 2 (2025); *Wolff, Reinmar*, Empfiehlt sich eine Reform des deutschen Schiedsverfahrensrechts?, in SchiedsVZ 293 (2016) *Kondring, Jörg*, Flucht vor dem deutschen AGB-Recht bei Inlandsverträgen, in RIW 184 (2010).

German Institution of Arbitration (DIS). The designated place of arbitration was Berlin, and the language of the proceedings was German. A special feature of the clause setting was the choice of "German law" as the applicable law for the contract, combined with an express waiver of the application of Sections 305–310 GCC, *i.e.*, the German law governing the review of general terms and conditions. This waiver was the central point of dispute that required judicial clarification.

In a contract concluded under the German General Contract Conditions for the Execution of Construction Work ("*VOB/B*") between the parties on September 7, 2020, the applicant undertook to perform various works (including the ramming of prefabricated concrete foundations) for a carport solar power plant to be built in the Netherlands.

Clause 28.1 of the contract specified the applicable law:

> "*This contract and all contractual terms and conditions applicable to it are subject to German law, with the exception of the UN Convention on Contracts for the International Sale of Goods and the conflict of law rules of private international law.*"

Clause 28.3 of the contract contained an arbitration clause with the following wording:

> "*(i) All disputes arising out of or in connection with this contract or its validity shall be finally settled in accordance with the Rules of Arbitration of the German Institution of Arbitration (DIS), excluding recourse to ordinary legal proceedings.*
> *(ii) The arbitral tribunal shall consist of a single arbitrator.*
> *(iii) The place of arbitration shall be Berlin. The language of the proceedings shall be German. However, annexes to the written pleadings may also be submitted in English.*
> *(iv) The applicable law in this matter is governed by clause 28.1. The parties expressly agree to waive the application of Sections 305 to 310 of the German Civil Code (GCC).*"

In 2022, the claimant initiated arbitration proceedings and asserted claims for remuneration for work performed in the amount of approximately EUR 3.2 million against the respondent. The respondent contested the claims in its statement of defense and asserted counterclaims for defects, delay, and contractual penalties in the amount of up to EUR 1.35 million. An arbitration tribunal had not yet been constituted. The parties initially attempted unsuccessfully to settle their mutual claims through mediation proceedings.

The claimant argued that the contractual penalty claims invoked by the respondent, which was limited to 10% of the net order amount, was excessive and therefore invalid under the case law of the German Federal Court in the context of general terms and conditions. Due to the clause contained in

Section 28.3 (v), according to which the arbitral tribunal should not review the general terms and conditions, it saw the risk that the arbitral tribunal could apply the contractual penalty provision even though it violates the law on general terms and conditions. It therefore considered the arbitration clause to be invalid, even though they had initially started arbitration proceedings.

The claimant therefore filed an application with the Berlin Court of Appeal (*Kammergericht*) in October 2023 for a declaration of the inadmissibility of the arbitration proceedings pursuant to Section 1032 GCCP.

Section 1032 GCCP provides a procedural mechanism for parties to seek a judicial determination on the admissibility of arbitration proceedings before the arbitral tribunal is constituted. The provision has no equivalent in the UNCITRAL Model Law.[6]) It allows a party to apply to a state court for a declaration that arbitration is either admissible or inadmissible, typically in cases where there is doubt about the validity or scope of the arbitration agreement. A key feature of this procedure is its preliminary nature: The court's review is limited to the existence and validity of the arbitration agreement itself, without delving into the merits of the underlying dispute or the substantive validity of other contractual provisions. The aim is to provide legal certainty at an early stage, ensuring that parties do not invest time and resources in arbitration proceedings that may later be found inadmissible.[7]) Most importantly, the court's decision under Section 1032 is binding only with respect to the admissibility of arbitration, leaving all other issues, such as the interpretation of the contract or the application of specific legal provisions, to the arbitral tribunal. This mechanism thus balances judicial oversight with the principle of party autonomy in arbitration.

The Berlin Court of Appeal considered the application in its decision of June 24, 2024[8]) to be admissible but unfounded, stating in essence that the arbitration clause was valid even if German law on standard terms and conditions was excluded:

> *"However, the motion is unfounded. The arbitration clause in No. 28.3 (i) of the contract was validly agreed. The validity of the provision in No. 28.3 (v) waiving the application of Sections 305 to 310 of the German Civil Code (GCC) is not relevant to the decision. The provision is not part of the actual arbitration clause. In proceedings pursuant to Section 1032 (2) GCCP, the state court only decides on the validity of the arbitration agreement as sufficiently formulated in No. 28.3 (i) of the contract. Neither the examination of a procedural provision nor the choice of law by the parties is the subject of the state court's decision. Rather, the examination of the admissibility and merits of a possible arbitration claim is reserved for the*

[6]) *See Wolf, Christian/Eslami, Nassim* in BeckOK ZPO, Section 1032 ZPO at 1 (58th edition 2022).

[7]) *Id.* at 4.

[8]) Berlin Court of Appeal of June 24, 2024, file no. 12 SchH 6/23.

*arbitral tribunal. The validity of the arbitration clause would not be called into question even if the agreement in No. 28.3 (v) were invalid. An invalid procedural agreement would not render the arbitration agreement invalid."*

The applicant and claimant lodged an appeal against this decision with the Federal Court, which upheld and further elaborated on the legal opinions of the Berlin Court of Appeal.

## B. Key Statements of the Federal Court

In its decision, the Federal Court formulated several decisive guiding principles that significantly shape the legal landscape for the rejection of German law on standard terms and conditions in arbitration proceedings:

### 1. Separability of the Arbitration Agreement

One of the most important statements of the Federal Court pertains to the principle of separability of the arbitration agreement. According to this principle, the validity of an arbitration agreement is fundamentally independent of the validity of the main contract or other provisions that are part of the broader contractual arrangements, such as choice of law or procedural agreements. Even if other contractual clauses, including those providing for the opt-out of the law on standard terms and conditions, should be invalid, the arbitration clause generally remains unaffected and valid, provided that it does not itself suffer from a specific defect. This principle significantly strengthens the stability of arbitration agreements.

### 2. Blue-Pencil Test (Section 306 GCC) for Arbitration Clauses in General Terms and Conditions

In margin note 45 of its decision, the court clarified that the so-called *blue-pencil* test, which is provided for in Section 306 GCC for the invalidity of general terms and conditions clauses, also applies to general terms and conditions arbitration clauses. If part of a general terms and conditions clause contained in an arbitration agreement or a choice of law clause is invalid, the separable remainder of the clause – in particular the arbitration agreement itself – remains valid if the unlawful part can be "struck from the agreement" and a legally permissible part remains that makes sense on its own.

### 3. Individually Negotiated Clauses

In margin note 45 *et seq.*, the court also indicated that even if an arbitration clause containing a waiver of the right to apply general terms and conditions were to be regarded not as a general term and condition but as an individual agreement negotiated between the parties, it would remain valid, since the partial invalidity of the remaining agreements pursuant to Section 139 GCC would not affect the remaining agreements. In this context, severability clauses play a particularly important role, as they aim to ensure the validity of the remaining part of a contract in the event that individual provisions should be invalid. In such a case, the judicial interpretation of the contract would also tend to uphold the arbitration agreement as such.

### 4. Obiter Dictum on Public Policy (Section 1059 para 2 No. 2 letter b GCCP)

Of particular importance is the obiter dictum of the Federal Court on German *ordre public* principles contained in margin note 42 of the decision. The court emphasized that the primary examination of the choice of law – including the question of opting out of the law on standard terms and conditions – is the responsibility of the arbitral tribunal. State control of this decision only takes place "downstream" in the context of annulment or enforcement proceedings, in particular under Section 1059 para 2 No. 2 (b) GCCP. This provision is mostly congruent with Art. 34 para 2 UNCITRAL Model Law and Art. V New York Convention on the Recognition and Enforcement of Foreign Arbitral Awards ("New York Convention, NYC") and allows for the annulment of an arbitral award if its recognition or enforcement leads to a result that is manifestly incompatible with the essential principles of German *ordre public*. The court specifies here that intervention by the state's *ordre public* is only justified if the non-application of the law on standard terms and conditions leads *"to consequences that are simply unacceptable and fundamentally call into question essential self-determination or the rule of law"*. There is no provision allowing for a comprehensive substantive review of the arbitral award, but rather a review that is limited to extreme exceptional cases. The court reaffirmed therefore its stance on the prohibition of a *"révision au fond"* of state courts over arbitral awards.

## C. Implications of the Decision

The decision of the Federal Court must be carefully classified and must not be misunderstood. What the Federal Court *does not say* is that it gives blanket absolution for any opt-out of standard terms and conditions in arbitration agreements. Rather, it introduces a differentiated context and outcome review, which is carried out via the *ordre public* valve. The decision is not a blank check, but rather a nudge to careful drafting and application.

The practical message of the Federal Court to contractual practice and arbitration is clear: a choice of law clause that includes an opt-out of the law on standard terms and conditions does not automatically render the arbitration agreement null and void. The primary decision on the validity and scope of such an opt-out rests with the arbitral tribunal itself. The state judge only examines compatibility with fundamental legal principles in subsequent annulment or *exequatur* proceedings. This strengthens arbitration and its ability to respond to the specificities of international contractual relationships, while at the same time ensuring that international procedural law principles are ultimately safeguarded by state public policy.

## V. Consequences for Contract Drafting

The Federal Court's decision has direct and far-reaching consequences for contract drafting in the B2B sector, particularly with regard to the integration of arbitration clauses and the possibility of opting out of the right to review general terms and conditions. Careful drafting is essential in order to achieve the desired legal certainty and avoid subsequent challenges.

In order to ensure the effectiveness of opting out of standard terms and conditions in arbitration proceedings, certain principles of contract drafting should be observed:

### A. Formulate Clearly and Separately

The agreement on the choice of law and the opt-out of the right to review general terms and conditions should be set out in a separate, clearly distinct clause and structurally separated from the actual arbitration clause. This serves the purpose of *"blue-pencil test"*, *i.e.*, the possibility of separating invalid parts of the clause, without jeopardizing the entire agreement. A separate structure increases the chance that the arbitration agreement will remain valid even if the part opting out of the right to review standard terms and conditions is invalid. In particular, care should be taken to ensure that the wording is precise and unambiguous in order to minimize room for interpretation.

### B. Choose the Place of Arbitration and Institution Carefully

The choice of the place of arbitration and the arbitral institution is of strategic importance. Choosing renowned arbitral institutions can promote acceptance of the arbitration agreement and the choice of law due to their reputation and competence and can, by doing so, alleviate government concerns, as the court alludes to in margin note 48. The quality of the arbitrators and the arbitral institution chosen can reduce the likelihood that an arbitral award will later be set aside on the grounds of violation of *ordre public*.

## C. Documentation of Fairness

In order to comply with *ordre public* review, it is crucial to document the fairness and balance of the agreement. This includes the traceability of the parity of negotiation, the transparency of the clause, and the economic justification for deviating from the terms and conditions. Complete documentation of the contract negotiations, proving that the parties were aware of the implications of opting out of the standard terms and conditions and that this agreement was made in the context of a balanced business relationship, increases the validity of the agreements. This serves to ensure public policy resilience at a later date and can be of crucial importance in annulment or enforcement proceedings.

## D. Risk Management

Proactive risk management is essential to ensure the enforceability of the opt-out of the general terms and conditions and the validity of the arbitral award:

### 1. Annulment/Exequatur Risks

Potential annulment and *exequatur* risks should be anticipated as early as the contract drafting stage and during the arbitration proceedings. This includes developing a robust rationale that demonstrates the "viability" of opting out of the law of general terms and conditions in the context of the contractual relationship. Careful reasoning that highlights the commercial and legal background of the opt-out can be crucial in the event of a review.

### 2. Preservation of Evidence

It is very important to keep complete and timely records of considerations, negotiation processes, and industry-standard market practices. This creates a solid basis of evidence that can later be used to substantiate the legality of the opt-out from the general terms and conditions and to refute *ordre public* concerns. In particular, it should be documented to what extent the opt-out of the general terms and conditions was the result of a conscious and balanced decision by the parties.

# VI. Limits & Restrictions

The possibilities for opting out of the right to use standard terms and conditions in arbitration proceedings are not unlimited and are subject to strict restrictions in certain contexts and areas of law. It is crucial to clearly recognize these limits in order to avoid legal risks.

## A. Opting out of T&C in State Court Proceedings (Including Commercial Courts)

The option to opt out of the right to review general terms and conditions, as provided for in Section 1051 GCCP, applies exclusively in the context of arbitration. Such an opt-out is generally inadmissible before state courts, including the newly-formed specialized German commercial courts. In this case, the mandatory law on general terms and conditions in Sections 305 *et seq.* GCC applies in full, as explained above. The "way out" of opting out therefore only applies within the specific legal framework of arbitration proceedings. A lawsuit before a state court would lead to the full application of general terms and conditions control, even if there were a corresponding contractual agreement.

## B. Consideration of Persons and Areas of Protection

The increased party autonomy in the choice of law in arbitration proceedings is limited in special areas of protection. Opting out of the law on standard terms and conditions is excluded in the case of contracts with consumers or contractual relationships under labor law. In these areas, the protection needs of the contracting parties are so dominant that mandatory standard terms and conditions controls cannot be waived, even in arbitration proceedings. Even in purely B2B constellations, strict controls remain in place as a corrective measure to prevent extreme and obviously unfair outcomes. The state legal system ensures that fundamental principles of justice and the self-determination of the parties are upheld.

## C. International Enforceability

In the international enforcement of an arbitral award based on an opt-out clause, the provisions of the New York Convention must be observed. Here, too, *ordre public* reservations play a central role. Each recognizing state reserves the right to refuse to recognize or enforce an arbitral award if it violates its fundamental legal principles (Art. V para 2 (b) NYC). This means that careful drafting and justification of the opt-out clause in the general terms and conditions is important not only for the German legal system, but also for potential international enforcement.

## VII. Open Questions and Outlook

Although the Federal Court's decision has provided important clarity for the opt-out of the law on general terms and conditions in arbitration proceedings, there are still open questions and areas that require further clarification by case law and literature. These concern both dogmatic and practical aspects.

### A. Need for Clarification in the Legal Classification of Section 1051 GCCP

The exact legal nature of Section 1051 GCCP as a conflict-of-law rule or substantive legal authorization to choose "rules of law" and "legal provisions" remains the subject of discussion. An in-depth analysis of the relationship to national mandatory provisions, in particular § 306a GCC, which regulates the legal consequences of the invalidity of general terms and conditions in general, is desirable. Further academic contributions and future court decisions are needed here in order to clarify the demarcation and mutual effects of the norms even more precisely.

### B. Guidelines for *ordre public* Review

Although the Federal Court has emphasized the high threshold for intervention, it remains to be seen how lower courts and arbitration tribunals will develop these guidelines in practice. There is a need for ongoing judicial practice that underpins and fleshes out the criteria established by the Federal Court – in particular those contractual clauses with *"absolutely unacceptable consequences"* and *"lack of contractual self-determination"* for one party – with specific case constellations. Only in this way can a reliable casuistry emerge that offers clearer guidance to the parties and arbitral tribunals. This ruling will play a decisive role in this regard and has already advanced the discussion.

### C. Reform/Soft Law Perspectives

In view of the increased importance of opt-out clauses in arbitration proceedings, the question arises as to whether international arbitration institutions such as the DIS, VIAC or the ICC see a need for "soft law" regulations or specific guidance documents. Such guidelines could develop "best practice standards" for the drafting of opt-out clauses and provide reliable assistance to the parties, their advisors, and the arbitral tribunals. An outline of possible content could include recommendations on the documentation of negotiations, the transparency of clauses, and the justification of the economic necessity of opting out in order to strengthen resilience.

## VIII. Conclusion: Five Theses

In summary, five central theses can be derived from the analysis of the decision and the associated dogmatic discussion, which summarize the current legal situation and the practical implications for the opt-out of general terms and conditions law in arbitration proceedings:

**1. Opting out is possible, but with conditions**

The application of Section 1051 GCCP opens up a legal corridor for the parties in arbitration proceedings to opt out of the German law on the control of standard terms and conditions in Sections 305–310 GCC. However, this option is always conditional on the separability of the clauses, the transparency of the agreement, and fairness of results that comply with *ordre public*. A blanket opt-out without regard to these conditions is built on sand and can be set aside by a state court.

**2. Arbitral tribunal first, state second**

The examination of the validity and scope of a general terms and conditions opt-out clause is primarily the responsibility of the arbitral tribunal. A review on state court level only takes place ex post via the annulment or enforcement proceedings pursuant to Section 1059 para 2 No. 2 letter b GCCP. This strengthens the autonomy of arbitration, but at the same time ensures ultima ratio control by the state judiciary.

**3. Blue-pencil test as a protective shield**

A well-designed clause architecture that aims for clarity, separability, and precision acts as a protective shield. It ensures the validity of the arbitration agreement even if parts of the choice of law clause providing for the opt-out of general terms and conditions are deemed invalid. The blue pencil test allows the intended arbitration proceedings to be maintained.

**4. Observe public policy**

The *ordre public* review pursuant to Section 1059 para 2 No. 2 (b) GCCP remains strict but must be interpreted narrowly. Intervention by the state courts is only justified in cases of manifestly unacceptable results that are clearly incompatible with the fundamental principles of German law. There is no general review of the arbitral tribunal's considerations, but rather a review limited to exceptional cases.

### 5. Strengthening competitiveness

For long-term B2B contractual relationships, especially in an international context, the possibility of opting out of general terms and conditions in arbitration proceedings can strengthen the legal certainty and competitiveness of German companies – and German law as a whole. However, this requires a dogmatically sound and procedurally prudent implementation that complies with the guidelines established by the Federal Court. The Federal Court has thus sent an important signal to contractual practice.

# Arbitration without Agreements
## Unilateral Arbitration Provisions under sec. 1066 of the German Code of Civil Procedure

*Ben Steinbrück/Justin Friedrich Krahé**)

## I. Introduction

Arbitration is overwhelmingly seen as grounded in consent. The 1958 United Nations Convention on the Recognition and Enforcement of Foreign Arbitral Awards, the UNCITRAL Model Law on International Commercial Arbitration, the domestic law of many countries[1]) and the rules of various arbitration institutions[2]) presuppose an agreement to arbitrate.[3]) This agreement to arbitrate is simultaneously interpreted as a waiver of the parties' right to go to court.[4]) However, an understanding of arbitration as always requiring an agreement departs markedly from the overall doctrines of private law more generally. Private law is not limited to the reductive notion that the only relevant categories are obligations imposed by law and obligations willingly accepted under a contract. Instead, private law also typically allows certain situations where a party may unilaterally modify the legal situation regardless of the consent of others. Why not, then, allow the same for arbitration?

---

*) Prof. Dr. Ben Steinbrück, MJur (Oxford) is an attorney-at-law (*Rechtsanwalt*, Germany) and partner at SZA Schilling, Zutt & Anschütz in Mannheim, Germany, and an honorary professor at Trier University, Germany.

Dr. Justin Friedrich Krahé, LL.B. (UCL) ACIArb is dual-qualified as *Rechtsanwalt* (Germany) and solicitor (England & Wales) and an associate at SZA Schilling, Zutt & Anschütz in Frankfurt, Germany. The usual disclaimers apply.

[1]) *See e.g.* sec. 6 of the English Arbitration Act 1996; Art. 1442 of the French Code de Procédure Civile. To the extent ascertainable, the only countries with provisions similar to sec. 1066 ZPO appear to be Austria (sec. 581 (2) of the Austrian Code of Civil Procedure) and Switzerland (Art. 178 (4) of the Private International Law Statute and Art. 358 (2) of the Swiss Code of Civil Procedure).

[2]) *Cf. e.g.* Art. 4.3 (e), Art. 5.5 (c) ICC Rules 2021; Art. 1.1 (ii) LCIA Rules 2020; Art. 5.2 (vi) DIS Rules 2018.

[3]) Discussing whether this is always the case for the NYC *see Stacher/Röhl*, Arbitration Clauses in Articles of Associations of Companies Limited by Shares – Are They Arbitration Agreements in the Sense of the New York Convention?, ASA Bulletin 2024/4 (792).

[4]) *Born*, International Arbitration: Law and Practice (3rd ed., 2021) 2 *et seq.*; for a human-rights-based analysis *see* II.A. below.

In addition to the classic framework for contractual arbitration based on the UNCITRAL Model Law, for several centuries[5]) various German arbitral laws have also contained provisions by which powers to unilaterally modify the legal situation under substantive private law will correspond to a power to provide for arbitration. The comparatively humble sec. 1066 of the German Code of Civil Procedure (*Zivilprozessordnung,* "**ZPO**"), contained in a division of the ZPO entitled "Arbitral tribunals not established by agreement", provides simply that the provisions of German arbitral law apply *mutatis mutandis* to arbitral tribunals established, in a legally permissible manner, by last wills or other directions not based on an agreement.[6]) Where an arbitral tribunal is seated in Germany and the requirements imposed by sec. 1066 ZPO are met, a party to a dispute can insist on arbitration even if the other party has never agreed to arbitrate.[7])

This article provides an introduction to the concept of unilateral arbitration provisions under sec. 1066 ZPO. A first section (II.) explains the constitutional underpinnings of unilateral powers and provides an overview of areas of German private law in which such powers occur. A second section (III.) draws on German corporate law to provide a case study of unilateral arbitration provisions in action. Finally, a concluding section (IV.) summarises the practical impact of unilateral arbitration provisions under German law and this idea's potential for international transfer.

## II. Unilateral Powers under German Substantive Private Law

Sec. 1066 ZPO does not itself explicitly set out the situations in which German law allows for unilateral arbitration provisions, but instead simply expands unilateral powers under substantive private law by adding a procedural element. Where private law allows a person – whether as an individual or as a body corporate – to impose their will on others, that ability will also allow them to impose an arbitration provision which they or others can later rely on. An important distinction is that this does not mean that arbitration can be imposed against the will of *both* parties to a subsequent dispute; invoking the arbitration

[5]) *Schmidt,* Statutarische Schiedsklauseln zwischen prozessualer und verbandsrechtlicher Legitimation, JZ 1989 (1078).

[6]) Sec. 1066 ZPO reads, in the translation by the Federal Ministry of Justice and Consumer Protection, "The provisions of the present Book apply accordingly to the arbitral tribunals established, in a manner permissible under statute, by last wills or other directions not based on an agreement". The German original reads: *„Für Schiedsgerichte, die in gesetzlich statthafter Weise durch letztwillige oder andere nicht auf Vereinbarung beruhende Verfügungen angeordnet werden, gelten die Vorschriften dieses Buches entsprechend.“*

[7]) For a comprehensive analysis of sec. 1066 ZPO, *see Steinbrück* in beck-online. Grosskommentar ZPO (2025) § 1066 para 1 *et seq.*

provision remains a procedural defence and a return to the State courts is always open.

Sec. 1066 ZPO, at least in the interpretation followed by the legal mainstream, therefore requires as a precondition that a unilateral power to make directions exist as a matter of substantive law.[8]) Because these kinds of unilateral powers will have legal force irrespective of consent, they require justification under German fundamental rights law (*see* A.), typically by reference to other weighty private interests. In current German black-letter law, such powers are particularly widespread in probate law (*see* B.), the law of private foundations (*see* C.) and in corporate law (*see* D.). Where such unilateral powers are used to impose a unilateral arbitration provision, the result will be that German arbitration law will apply in a way modified to reflect the lack of agreement (*see* E.).

## A. Unilateral Powers in German Fundamental Rights Law

German constitutional law requires that all private law comply with the underlying minimum requirements of the Basic Law's fundamental rights.[9]) For contractual arrangements, this is usually not a significant issue. As long as the parties have entered into a contract of their own free will and there is no public interest in prohibiting such a contract, the parties' fundamental rights typically require the legal order to give their promises binding legal effect. The parties' consent, if given without vitiating factors such as duress, means that there is no interference with fundamental rights, and thus no need for justification.

Unilateral powers, conversely, require justification against the fundamental rights of the party who does not consent to be bound. Unilateral arbitration provisions in particular interfere with the basic position that anyone has a right to bring disputes over civil rights and obligations before the State courts, a right secured in German domestic constitutional law[10]) and at the European level in Art. 6 (1) ECHR (civil limb) as interpreted by the European Court of Human

[8]) This, at least, is the prevailing view, although it does conflate procedural and substantive questions in a problematic way. For criticism *see e.g. Geimer*, Nichtvertragliche Schiedsgerichte, in FS Schlosser 2005 (202).

[9]) For an English-language introduction *see e.g. Krahé*, European Journal of Comparative Law and Governance 2 (2015) 124, 127 *et seq.*; *see* Federal Constitutional Court, judgment of January 15, 1958 – 1 BvR 400/51, BVerfGE 7, 198.

[10]) Art. 2 (1) of the Basic Law in conjunction with the principle of the rule of law (Art. 20 (3) Basic Law); *see e.g.* Federal Constitutional Court, order of June 3, 2022 – 1 BvR 2103/16, NJW 2022 (2677 f.), English translation available at: https://www.bundesverfassungsgericht.de/SharedDocs/Entscheidungen/EN/2022/06/rk20220603_1bvr210316en.html, retrieved October 22, 2025.

Rights[11]) and under the Charter of Fundamental Rights.[12]) However, the right to bring disputes to the State courts is not absolute. It can be limited based on other interests, particularly in cases where a different form of dispute resolution does not lead to significant disadvantage to the rights-holders. While questions of limitation do not arise at all where a party has freely consented to a different form of dispute resolution, where arbitration is unilaterally imposed against the will of one of the parties, there is a limitation of that party's rights. This limitation will have to be justified under the traditional doctrines of human rights law.

Beyond public interests,[13]) unilateral powers and particularly restrictions on the right to go to court can be justified by reference to private interests recognised as particularly weighty. Private interests considered important enough that they can justify unilateral powers are *e.g.* the testator's freedom of testation[14]) and the constitutional provisions protecting individuals' collective action, particularly freedom of association for corporations.[15]) The right to act in conjunction with others and freely form corporations is a pillar of active civil society and an important counterweight to the role of the State.[16]) This general right to freedom of association comports a right for corporations to set legally binding rules for their members.[17]) From the point of view of the members, rules set by a corporation are not simply relative rights by one legal person against another. Instead, they are closer to the kind of objective law that the State sets, since they bind the members simply by virtue of their membership itself. This power to set binding rules for corporations' members can also justify prioritising the creation of separate dispute resolution mechanisms over the individual member's right to take a given dispute to court.[18])

Where the protection of these fundamental rights requires that the law grant a person or group of persons the power to unilaterally impose their will on others in certain circumstances, German private law also adds a unilateral power to provide that any dispute arising from such a unilateral disposition be

---

[11]) *See* European Court of Human Rights, *Golder v. The United Kingdom [GC]*, judgment of February 21, 1975 – App. no. 4451/70.

[12]) Art. 47 (1) EU Charter of Fundamental Rights.

[13]) On the relationship between private interests, public interests and balancing see *e.g. Krahé*, Legal Services and the European Convention on Human Rights (2025) 405 *et seq.*

[14]) Protected by the constitutional right of inheritance under Art. 14 (1) (1) Basic Law. Note that the Federal Constitutional Court also sees mandatory minimum shares as protected by constitutional law, explaining the limitations discussed below at text to note 23.

[15]) Protected under Art. 9 Basic Law.

[16]) *See e.g.* Federal Constitutional Court, order of December 18, 1974 – 1 BvR 430/65, 259/66, NJW 1975 (1266).

[17]) *See* Federal Constitutional Court, order of June 15, 1989 – 2 BvL 4/87, NJW 1990 (38).

[18]) *See Schwennicke* in STAUDINGER, BGB[Neubearbeitung 2023] (2025) § 25 para. 29 *et seq.*

heard not by a court, but by an arbitral tribunal. The considerations justifying the unilateral power, *e.g.* the right to form corporations or the right to make testamentary dispositions, outweigh the constitutionally protected right to go to court.

## B. Unilateral Arbitration Provisions in Probate Law

The only unilateral power referred to directly in sec. 1066 ZPO is the testator's power to make testamentary dispositions.[19]) Arbitration provisions in wills are a historically well-established area, as demonstrated not least – in a US context – by George Washington's last will and testament.[20]) Probate disputes can be particularly suitable for arbitration due to arbitration's confidential, flexible dispute resolution mechanisms, which can be particularly important in a family environment. Under sec. 1066 ZPO, the testator can exclude the State courts and refer questions such as the interpretation, validation and execution of wills or the ascertainment of beneficiaries to an arbitral tribunal.

However, probate law also shows some of the limitations of arbitration. Those matters which are assigned by law to the competence of a State probate court, such as matters relating to certificates of inheritance,[21]) cannot be relegated to arbitral tribunals, nor can the testator influence the forum for claims brought by parties claiming against the estate.[22]) Despite sec. 1066 ZPO's ostensibly generous power to refer matters to arbitral tribunals, in practice situations abound in which both an arbitral tribunal and a State court would have to deal with matters under a will. Therefore, testators often refrain from including an arbitration provision in their wills. This significantly limits sec. 1066 ZPO's practical importance.

Moreover, while sec. 1066 ZPO reflects the testator's freedom of testation, German law also contains certain provisions on forced heirship, awarding minimum shares to certain next-of-kin. These limitations on freedom of testation under substantive law will equally limit the testator's procedural ability to exclude the State courts and refer disputes with next-of-kin regarding their minimum shares to arbitration. Under the case law of the Federal Court of

---

[19]) *See* on German probate law *Gottwald/Schwab/Büttner*, Family & Succession Law in Germany (1st ed., 2001) 124 *et seq.*

[20]) https://founders.archives.gov/documents/Washington/06-04-02-0404-0001, retrieved September 18, 2025.

[21]) Celle Higher Regional Court, order of December 10, 2015 – 6 W 204/15, NJW-RR 2016 (332).

[22]) *Stallknecht*, Schiedsklauseln in Verfügungen von Todes wegen, RNotZ 2019 (439); Bavarian Supreme Court, order of June 1, 1956 – BReg. 1 Z 21/56, BayObLGZ 1956 (189); Federal Court of Justice, order of May 15, 2017 – IV ZB 25/16, NJW 2017 (2112).

Justice, arbitration over these compulsory minimum shares is therefore not possible against the will of the party seeking the minimum share.[23]) This severely limits the range of unilateral arbitration provisions possible under German probate law. In practice, unilateral arbitration provisions under wills are therefore seen as risky and, consequently, rarely used.[24])

## C. Unilateral Arbitration Provisions by Private-Law Foundations

A related area in which unilateral powers play a significant role, but which unlike probate law is not explicitly named in sec. 1066 ZPO, concerns private-law foundations under sec. 80 of the German Civil Code (*Bürgerliches Gesetzbuch*, "**BGB**"). Such arbitration provisions can be useful particularly where the founder wants to ensure that disputes are dealt with in a rapid and confidential manner. However, since the significant growth in private-law foundations as a means of managing wealth is a comparatively recent phenomenon in German law, there is little settled case law as yet.

On the basic principles of the law of private-law foundations, sec. 1066 ZPO will only apply to "true" foundations with separate legal personhood.[25]) In these cases, the founder, the foundation itself and the foundation's organs can all be bound to arbitrate, as well as any beneficiaries whose rights are related to the underlying endowment transaction.[26]) However, it will not generally be possible to bind the competent public authority supervising the foundation's activities.[27]) Third parties, including legal entities owned in whole or in part by the foundation, will also not be bound by a unilateral arbitration provision in the endowment transaction.

---

[23]) Federal Court of Justice, order of March 16, 2017 – I ZB 49/16, SchiedsVZ 2018 (40); criticising this *Pawlytta*, Erbrechtliches Schiedsgericht und Pflichtteilsrecht, ZEV 2003 (92 *et seq.*); *Geimer*, FS Schlosser 2005 (206 *et seq.*).

[24]) *See e.g. Raude* in Wetzel/Odersky/Götz, Erbengemeinschaft-HdB § 51 para. 4; *Zimmermann*, Sind vom Erblasser angeordnete Schiedsgerichte zweckmäßig?, ErbR 2021 (190).

[25]) *Stumpf*, Schiedsgerichtsbarkeit in Stiftungen, SchiedsVZ 2009 (267).

[26]) *See* the discussion in *Stumpf*, SchiedsVZ 2009 (267 *et seq.*); *Godron/Gollan* in Richter, StiftungsR-HdB (2nd ed., 2023) § 6 para. 384; *Roth* in Münchener Handbuch des Gesellschaftsrechts Band 7[6] (2020) § 96 para. 14; *Prantl/Bretscher/Gabriel-Oiwoh/Reich*, Privatstiftung und Schiedsrecht – Ausgewählte Problemfelder in Deutschland, Liechtenstein, Österreich und der Schweiz, SchiedsVZ 2023 (312).

[27]) *Stumpf*, SchiedsVZ 2009 (270); *Godron/Gollan* in Richter, StiftungsR-HdB (2nd ed., 2023) § 6 para. 384; *Prantl/Bretscher/Gabriel-Oiwoh/Reich*, SchiedsVZ 2023 (312).

## D. Unilateral Arbitration Provisions in Corporate Law

Moreover, there is a field of application for unilateral powers under German corporate law. Similarly to many other jurisdictions,[28]) German law by now[29]) sees a company's constitution as going beyond a simple contract and constituting a founding instrument for a separate legal entity. The accepted wisdom is that a company's constitution is therefore closer to statutory law than to any mere contract, since the company as a legal entity can bind even those members who vote against a certain provision and the members are bound as a result of their membership, not of any specific contractual arrangement. The courts have drawn on this analysis to class the company's ability to set binding rules in its constitution as akin to a power to make a "direction not based on an agreement". On that basis, the courts have applied sec. 1066 ZPO by analogy to arbitration provisions in the constitutions of commercial and non-commercial associations,[30]) limited liability companies (GmbH),[31]) stock corporations (AG),[32]) public partly limited partnerships (KGaA), cooperative societies (*Genossenschaften*) and European public limited-liability companies (SE).

While the application by analogy of sec. 1066 ZPO is universally accepted for corporations with separate legal personhood, whether sec. 1066 ZPO can also be applied to partnership agreements, which exist in various forms in German law,[33]) remains subject to debate. In a 1979 judgment, the Federal Court of Justice held that sec. 1066 ZPO did not apply to partnership agreements since at that stage partnerships were largely seen as contractual in nature and therefore fell under the general rules concerning arbitration agreements, in particular sec. 1029, 1031 ZPO.[34]) While the legal status of certain partnerships in German law has subsequently changed significantly, with subsequent legislative and jurisprudential shifts moving them closer to corporations, the Federal Court of Justice has not yet formally had occasion to revisit its case law. In practice, the

---

[28]) *See e.g.* in England sec. 33 Companies Act 2006.

[29]) *See e.g. Segna* in beck-online. GROSSKOMMENTAR BGB, January 1, 2025, § 25 para. 28–30.

[30]) Imperial Court of Justice, judgment of October 29, 1940 – VII 44/40, RGZ 165 (140).

[31]) Federal Court of Justice, judgment of October 15, 1962 – II ZR 188/61, NJW 1963 (203 *et seq.*); judgment of October 11, 1979 – III ZR 184/78, NJW 1980 (1049).

[32]) Federal Court of Justice, judgment of July 4, 1951 – II ZR 117/50, BeckRS 1951, 31203937; judgment of October 11, 1979 – III ZR 184/78, NJW 1980 (1049).

[33]) *E.g.* the partnership under sec. 705 *et seq.* BGB (*"Gesellschaft bürgerlichen Rechts"*, GbR), the commercial partnership under sec. 105 *et seq.* of the German Commercial Code (*Handelsgesetzbuch*, "HGB") (*"offene Handelsgesellschaft"*, oHG) or the partly limited partnership under sec. 161 *et seq.* HGB (*"Kommanditgesellschaft"*, KG).

[34]) Federal Court of Justice, judgment of October 11, 1979 – III ZR 184/78, NJW 1980 (1049 *et seq.*).

exclusion of partnerships significantly limits the ambit of sec. 1066 ZPO, since partnerships play a significant role in German corporate law. This exclusion is also inconsistent with the modern state of German corporate law, which otherwise applies many rules on corporations to partnerships as well.

For corporations, it can be particularly important to ensure a uniform mechanism of dispute resolution that uses classic arbitration advantages such as confidentiality and relative speed. Substantively, unilateral arbitration provisions can relate to any dispute arising from the membership itself as long as the matter is considered arbitrable under the general provisions of German arbitral law.[35]) This means that sec. 1066 ZPO can be used to require arbitration for fields of dispute such as voting rights, information rights, payment of membership duties and even the exclusion of members, all areas where there can be a legitimate interest in finally settling disputes without the involvement of the State courts. While German law also considers applications to set aside resolutions as arbitrable subject to certain procedural requirements,[36]) these procedural requirements generate significant complexity and have even led to the drafting of a further "Model Clause for Articles of Incorporation for Arbitrations Pursuant to the Supplementary Rules for Corporate Disputes" (known in German as the DIS-ERGeS) by the German Arbitration Institute.

While it is therefore possible to use sec. 1066 ZPO to refer corporate law disputes to arbitration, in certain situations there will be further restrictions arising from mandatory provisions of German corporate law. This is particularly relevant for stock corporations. Under the German Stock Corporation Act (*Aktiengesetz*, "**AktG**") the extent to which unilateral arbitration provisions will be permissible is not yet finally settled, since that law requires that at least certain disputes be decided by the State courts. This sits in tension with the modern position taken by the German legislator that arbitration is, in principle, equivalent to litigation as a means of dispute resolution.[37])

In terms of the concrete modalities of introducing unilateral arbitration provisions, matters are simplest where the unilateral arbitration provision is contained in the founding documents of the corporation itself. In that case, all of the founders must have agreed, and the provision can only have effect prospectively for disputes arising after its introduction. Similarly, no issue arises where a unilateral arbitration provision is introduced subsequently, but by a unanimous vote. In these situations, there is not only an interest by the corporation itself that is protected under sec. 1066 ZPO, but even an argument to be made that there is some form of agreement by the members. This construction is

[35]) *Cf.* on the issue of arbitrability sec. 1030 ZPO.

[36]) Federal Court of Justice, judgment of September 23, 2021 – I ZB 13/21, SchiedsVZ 2022 (86 *et seq.*); judgment of April 6, 2017 – I ZB 32/16, SchiedsVZ 2017 (197 *et seq.*); judgment of April 6, 2009 – II ZR 255/08, NJW 2009 (1962 *et seq.*); judgment of March 29, 1996 – II ZR 124/95, NJW 1996 (1753 *et seq.*).

[37]) *See* Draft bill of the Federal Government concerning the Act to Reform Arbitration Law, BT-Drucksache 13/5274, p. 1.

similar to that used to explain why members joining subsequently are bound by a unilateral arbitration provision: There is an argument that, since they must take the corporation as they find it, they have to some extent agreed to the arbitration provision.[38]) Nonetheless, this reasoning amounts to a legal fiction. A member who joins a corporation but protests against the arbitration provision will nonetheless be bound by it. This situation can be easily resolved without interpretative difficulties by recognising that the corporation's constitution binds its members because corporations are inherently able to bind their members, even against their will.

The complicated questions arise where a corporation subsequently adopts a unilateral arbitration provision by a majority vote, whether simple or qualified. For these cases, the consensus now appears to be that unilateral arbitration provisions can, in principle, be adopted by simple majority,[39]) at least where the corporation in question does not exhibit any special features such as *e.g.* membership being a requirement to exercise a specific profession.[40]) However, under the general principles of German corporate law, decisions made by majority decision can only have effect for the future.[41]) Where a dispute has already arisen, it will therefore not be possible to impose a unilateral arbitration provision against the vote of a party to that dispute. Any unilateral arbitration provision adopted by majority vote can have effect against dissenting voices only for the future.[42])

## E. German Arbitration Law to Apply *mutatis mutandis* in Unilateral Contexts

Where sec. 1066 ZPO's requirements are met, the provisions of German arbitral law will apply *mutatis mutandis*, with the non-contractual nature of such an arbitration reflected in a number of differences in the way that German

---

[38]) München Higher Regional Court, judgment of February 9, 1999 – 30 U 709/97, NZG 1999 (780).

[39]) München Higher Regional Court, judgment of February 9, 1999 – 30 U 709/97, NZG 1999 (780).

[40]) *See* below III.

[41]) *See* generally on limitations to majority decisions *Berger* in Münchener Handbuch des Gesellschaftsrechts Band 2 (6th ed., 2024) § 14 para. 40; on resolutions within sec. 244 AktG: Federal Court of Justice, judgment of December 15, 2003 – II ZR 194/01, NJW 2004 (1165); on amendments of the business year *Born* in beck-online. Grosskommentar GmbHG (2025) § 53 para. 343; Jena Higher Regional Court, order of July 21, 2021 – 2 W 244/21, FGPrax 2021 (266); on subsequent contri bution increases Federal Court of Justice, judgment of October 21, 2012 – II ZR 84/13, NJW 2015 (862).

[42]) *Anders* in Anders/Gehle, Zivilprozessordnung (83rd ed., 2025) § 1066 para. 16; *Wolf/Eslami* in BeckOK, Zivilprozessordnung (58th ed., 2022) § 1066 para. 7; *Voit* in Musielak/Voit, Zivilprozessordnung (22nd ed., 2025) § 1066 para. 8.

arbitration law is applied.[43]) Perhaps the most significant effect will be that the usual formalities that German arbitration law requires for a valid agreement to arbitrate under sec. 1031 ZPO will not apply. Instead, such formalities requirements are displaced by the requirements imposed under the substantive legal provisions referred to by sec. 1066 ZPO, since these constitute an equally effective means of securing legal certainty.[44]) Sec. 1066 ZPO and the corresponding formalities for the unilateral power thus take precedence over sec. 1031 ZPO. This is important because sec. 1031 ZPO can frequently be a pitfall for unwary drafters. Most notably, sec. 1031 (5) ZPO provides that the arbitration agreement must be contained in a separate document where one party is a consumer. This requirement can be easily missed because German law takes a comparatively wide interpretation of the term "consumer", requiring only that the person in question act for purposes that predominantly are outside their trade, business or profession, regardless of the extent to which they may understand the concept of arbitration and the significance of signing an arbitration agreement. Where sec. 1066 ZPO applies, there is no such restriction, and complying with the formalities of the unilateral power itself will suffice.

Beyond formalities, a further modification to the standard application of German arbitration law relates to the hierarchy of the rules on arbitration in sec. 1042 – 1050 ZPO. While typically the question would only be whether the parties have agreed to deviate from these rules in their arbitration agreement, either individually or in the form of a choice of institutional rules, or whether the default statutory rules apply, in cases involving a unilateral arbitration provision under sec. 1066 ZPO the tribunal will also have to inquire whether the statutory rules are displaced by directions in the unilateral arbitration provision. Arbitration in a corporate-law context, for example, often involves multiple parties, so it can make sense to specify a mechanism for the appointment of arbitrators in the arbitration provision (*e.g.* that the entire arbitral tribunal will be appointed by an arbitral institution or another independent third party). While any actual agreement between the parties to the arbitration will still reign supreme if it respects the general bounds of the right to be heard and the right to a fair trial, an arbitral tribunal will also have to look to the unilateral arbitration provision before resorting to institutional rules or the statutory rules for ad hoc arbitration.

More generally, the interpretation of German arbitration law in relation to unilateral arbitration provisions can also be used to ensure that the requirements of the right to be heard and the right to a fair trial are respected. The procedure followed by the arbitral tribunal must provide sufficient safeguards to

---

[43]) For an overview of the respective adjustments, *see Steinbrück* in beck-online. GROSSKOMMENTAR ZPO (2025) § 1066 para. 74 *et seq*.

[44]) Federal Court of Justice, judgment of October 11, 1979 – III ZR 184/78, NJW 1980 (1049); Federal Court of Justice, judgment of April 3, 2000 – II ZR 373/98, NJW 2000 (1713).

ensure that the limitation to the right to go to court[45]) is not unduly restrictive; for example, the Federal Court of Justice has held that it is not possible to order a unilateral arbitration provision where the arbitrator would effectively be adjudicating a matter in which they are personally involved, thereby violating the principal of impartiality.[46])

## III. Case Study: Unilateral Arbitration Provisions in German Corporate Law

How do unilateral arbitration provisions work in practice, then?

Consider the following situation:[47]) A non-commercial association dedicates itself, by its statutory objects, to the breeding of German Shepherds. This is protected by the general right to freedom of association.[48]) As part of these activities, it organises dog shows, assesses and accredits dogs and grants certification to dog breeders. In any organisation large enough, disputes will arise sooner or later. However, for such a specialist organisation, there is clearly an interest in ensuring that disputes are heard by persons who understand the world of competitive dog-breeding, as well as ensuring that disputes are resolved in a timely manner – dog years, after all, are shorter than human years.

The State judiciary cannot guarantee that it will be able to meet this need. Under German civil procedure, there is no way of ensuring that all of the judges hearing a case will have any experience of dog ownership or, even less likely, dog breeding. Arbitration, instead, allows the parties to a dispute to ensure that their dispute is heard and decided by a panel of arbitrators who can be selected to have exactly this expertise.

If arbitration is therefore clearly the dispute resolution mechanism of choice, a strict requirement that there always be an agreement to arbitrate will struggle to reach this result. It may be possible to interpret the association's constitution as some form of arbitration agreement, leaving aside formalities issues; it may also be possible to interpret subsequent members' decision to join as a form of consent to arbitration, although again this requires the formalities discussed above. However, neither of these approaches really captures the essence of why this dispute should go to arbitration. The possibility of imposing arbitration in these cases is a reflection of the freedom to form an association of dog breeders, which – like all other forms of freedom of association – enjoys constitutional protection in Germany under Art. 9 of the Basic Law.[49]) This

[45]) *See* II.A. above.

[46]) *See e.g.* Federal Court of Justice, order of November 8, 2018 – I ZB 21/18, NJW 2019 (857).

[47]) Modelled on Federal Court of Justice, judgment of April 3, 2000– II ZR 373/98, NJW 2000 (1713).

[48]) *See* II.A. above.

[49]) *See* II.A. above.

freedom of association also grants members the right to establish a set of rules for the association in the form of articles of association, binding all current and future members. Implied agreements to arbitrate protect a different interest than the one at stake: arbitration agreements derive from the individual's right to make legally binding commitments, freedom of contract, rather than from freedom of association.

Instead, practical and effective realisation of freedom of association requires that, for its members, the association can set rules even without requiring each member's consent in every case. In this sense, members who join an association accept that changes to the bylaws of that association will bind them in much the same way that they will be bound by changes to statutory law made by the State. Those binding rules set by the association can include insisting on arbitration in lieu of the State courts. Where freedom of association, which is constitutionally protected, outweighs the individual's interest in being able to bring disputes to the State courts, unilateral arbitration provisions will be permissible. Where the individual's interest in being able to bring disputes to the State courts outweighs the other members' interest in freedom of association – as, for example, where the individual's interest is reinforced by other constitutionally protected interests, such as occupational freedom under Art. 12 Basic Law –, the association will not be able to validly introduce a unilateral arbitration provision.

However, any limitation on the right to go to court must be a fair balance with countervailing interests. While there can be a general interest in ensuring that disputes within associations are heard by arbitration, the power to unilaterally order arbitration can also be misused to prejudice the position of parties to the dispute. In this respect, the original Federal Court of Justice judgment concerning the association for the breeding of German Shepherds contained several dimensions of added complexity. In the original case, the association had only added the unilateral arbitration provision after the dispute had already arisen. Moreover, the member concerned had voted against that motion. There were thus significant indications that the association was attempting to move a dispute that had already arisen into the association's preferred forum, particularly since the change to the constitution was only adopted eight days before the member filed his claim and thus at a point in time where pre-filing preparation would have been largely complete. The Federal Court of Justice therefore held that the unilateral arbitration provision was ineffective and that the member's claim in the State courts was admissible.

This decision sits well with the fundamental principle of German corporate law that, in general, majority decisions can only have effect in the future, not retroactively. Moreover, on the facts of the Federal Court of Justice's judgment, there were also significant human rights issues at stake. According to the courts' findings in that case, breeding German Shepherds was effectively impossible without membership in the association. On that basis, the Federal Court of Justice held that the member's continued membership could not reasonably be interpreted as entailing any kind of implied consent to the arbitration provision, since they could not have left the association without simultaneously losing the possibility to breed German Shepherds entirely. Given that the entire dispute concerned the imposition of a two-year membership suspension, leaving the association would have achieved the same result as losing the dispute.

While the Federal Court of Justice ultimately did not need to commit to a single line of reasoning, the approach chosen – arguing by reference to whether implied acceptance of an arbitration agreement is possible – is not necessarily the clearest way of addressing this issue. Inquiring into whether remaining in the association can be interpreted as tacitly accepting an arbitration agreement arguably misses the point of unilateral arbitration provisions. Sec. 1066 ZPO allows the imposition of arbitration as a means of dispute resolution precisely where there is no consent, if and only if there is a sufficient justification for arbitration and certain fair-trial safeguards are observed. Instead of blurring the boundaries between arbitration agreements and unilateral arbitration provisions, the general principle that changes to an association's constitution made by majority decision can only have effect for future situations would arguably have been sufficient justification on its own. At the level of human rights law, this result can be easily explained as the outcome of a balancing exercise between the association's and its members' interest in dispute resolution by arbitration only and the individual member's right to have access to the courts.

The advantages of recognising clearly that the justification for unilateral arbitration provisions is ultimately freedom of association become particularly clear if one takes the hypothetical example that the association, by a majority vote, decides that all future disputes shall be resolved only by arbitration, to the exclusion of the State courts. In this case, the decision by the majority and the unilateral arbitration provision would be valid and legally binding. As with any majority decision, it would then have been open to each member to decide whether they wish to continue enjoying the benefits of membership or whether, on the basis of the new rules of membership, they prefer to leave the association. Construing continued membership as a kind of implicit acceptance of the unilateral arbitration provision is misleading because the member may well explicitly object to the arbitration provision passed by majority vote, and yet still be bound. It is not that the member has waived their right to go to court by their continued membership. Instead, their right to go to court is outweighed by the interest in, in principle, giving effect to decisions reached by a majority vote within an association. Where, as in the case decided by the Federal Court of Justice, there are very serious disadvantages attached to leaving the association, these must be taken into account and weighed against the association's and the other members' interest in ordering arbitration. However, this is not a question of consent or lack of consent to the arbitration provision, but of the weight of the individual's protected interested in remaining a member of the association relative to the protected interests of the association and its other members in regulating the association's affairs by majority vote.

## IV. Conclusions

Agreement, therefore, is not the only possible justification for arbitration. If powers to act unilaterally recognised by substantive private law are taken seriously, there is arguably also a justification to allow the unilateral imposition of a specific dispute resolution mechanism, within, of course, the general boundaries of the right to be heard and to have a fair trial. This is particularly obvious for unilateral arbitration provisions in a corporate law context: There is a separate, legally recognised and protected interest in individuals being able to act collectively to further common goals. This freedom of association, which is reflected in the association's ability to make legally binding rules for its members, arguably also justifies the imposition of arbitration as a means of dispute resolution even without every member (actually or implicitly) agreeing to it. Put simply, collective action by humans will always give rise to disputes; the legally protected freedom to act collectively protects not only collective actions to further a specific object but can also mean that where the collective decides to resolve disputes in a certain way, that will bind individual members. German law implements this fundamental position at the level of its arbitration law by means of sec. 1066 ZPO, thus providing for a simpler means of binding parties to arbitration even against their will if general private law allows others to impose their will on such parties and the typical procedural safeguards for arbitration are respected. In light of Switzerland's recent adoption of a similar provision,[50]) it remains to be seen whether this development will find favour internationally.

[50]) *See* n 2 above.

# Chapter II

# The Arbitrator and the Arbitration Procedure

*Irene Welser/Sarah Yvonne Enzi*
"Last orders!" – But What About the Cut-Off-Date?

*Doğuhan Uygun/Pınar Noberi*
The Third-Party Dilemma in Arbitration:
Inclusion of Non-Signatories and Enforcement Challenges

*Eric Leikin/Sofia Svinkovskaya*
The State of Emergency Arbitration:
Between Promise and Performance

*Stephan Wilske/Matthew T. Adams*
Where the Streets Have No Name

When Arbitral Institutions Underestimate
the Seemingly Mundane Tasks

*Maximilian Albert Mueller*
Rising Cost of Performance: An Arbitral Perspective on Hardship and
Risk Allocation under Art 79 CISG

*Ana Stanič/Vod K.S. Chan*
The Tale of Two Cities:
The Impact of Sanctions on Arbitration in London and Hong Kong

*Albertas Šekštelo*
Clash of Titans or Contemporary Issues of *lis pendens* in the
EU Arbitration Law

*Barry Appleton*
Data, Sovereignty, and Arbitral Autonomy:
Confronting Extraterritorial Digital Regulations

*Irina Nazarova*
Deciding Minds in Justice's Looking-Glass: Human and AI
Where Intuition Meets Algorithm

*Katherine Bell/Catrice Gayer/Judith Knieper/Niamh Leinwather/ Petra Pataki/Camilla Perera-de Wit*
Diversity in Arbitration: Progress, Pushback & The Road Ahead

*Iain Sheridan*
Growth, the Rule of Law and Arbitration

*Stavros Brekoulakis*
VIAC 50th Anniversary:
"International Arbitration and the Rule of Law:
Between the Scylla of Politics and the Charybdis of Law"

*Roland Ziadé*
Mission Possible: Harnessing Power, Embracing Responsibility, and Seizing Opportunity in International Arbitration

*Wei Sun*
Recent Reforms and Emerging Trends in China's Arbitration Law and Practice

*Cavinder Bull SC*
Rediscovering the Simplicity of Arbitration

*Nikolaus Pitkowitz/Marlene Maurer and the 17 contributors*
The Vienna Proposition on Efficiency in Arbitration

# "Last orders!" – But What About the Cut-Off-Date?

*Irene Welser/Sarah Yvonne Enzi*

## I. From British Tradition to International Arbitration

"Last Orders!" is a long-standing and much-loved tradition in British pubs. The call for last orders is usually announced loudly by the bartender, sometimes even with a bell. This ritual does not only mark the final chance to buy a drink before closing time, but also carries a unique mix of practicality, courtesy and pub culture charm.

In international arbitration, things are less romantic. Still, there is something similar, namely the last chance to enter documents into the proceedings before the oral hearing takes place: the so called "cut-off-date". While each and every arbitrator has of course heard of the cut-off-date, a closer look reveals that the actual possibilities a cut-off-date offers after the regular submissions have been made are highly unclear. In fact, it is astonishing that while there is ample doctrine on the question whether, in exceptional cases, single documents may even be submitted after the cut-off-date has passed, the significance of the cut-off-date as such remains open. In particular, the question whether the cut-off-date is in fact a last hidden chance to file yet another submission not foreseen in the procedural timetable remains unanswered.

Does the cut-off-date therefore, just like the call for "last orders", offer yet another possibility to file an additional full submission accompanied by documents, or is it only a last resort to submit evidence that had not been available for use before or introduce new facts that could not have been pleaded in prior submissions? Funnily enough, this question remains totally unanswered in the arbitration literature.

## II. Sense and Limits of Cut-Off-Dates

Procedural efficiency and fairness are of the utmost importance in ensuring the timely and equitable resolution of arbitral disputes. In connection therewith, the so called "cut-off-date" plays a significant role. A cut-off-date, which is always timed before the hearing takes place, is designed to prevent ambushes on and unfair surprises for witnesses.

Cut-off-dates are therefore one of the procedural tools used to regulate the submission and exchange of evidence in arbitral proceedings. A cut-off-date marks a point in time after which new documentary and other evidence will not be admitted or only admitted subject to more stringent thresholds. Such a date is usually incorporated into procedural orders (POs) and procedural timetables. The primary purpose of including a cut-off-date is to prevent parties from submitting new evidence or facts at a late stage, thereby safeguarding both sides from unexpected developments and surprises during the hearing.

Despite the widespread use of cut-off-date clauses by tribunals around the world, their interpretation and application can differ significantly. These disparities often stem from contrasting understandings of the term itself or ambiguous definitions of the clause's scope. This gives rise to several key questions: What constitutes a cut-off-date in the first place? This is of particular importance if the cut-off-date is an additional date in the procedural timetable after the last round of submissions. How should a cut-off-date clause be construed when the applicable arbitration rules offer no explicit guidance? To what extent may parties continue to make submissions or introduce new evidence before, on and after the cut-off-date, and are they permitted to introduce new arguments beyond that point? Moreover, can a party submit a full additional brief by the cut-off-date to address arguments previously raised by the opposing side, particularly when the procedural timetable does not expressly provide for such filings? Such an opportunity would, in its effect, then result in an unequal number of submissions on the side of claimants and respondents. Finally, what procedural or substantive consequences arise when a submission falls outside the prescribed scope or procedural timeline? Can it simply be dismissed by the tribunal?

These are the issues considered in this contribution. The authors further show best practices for arbitrators, emphasizing the importance of carefully and clearly drafting the cut-off-date clauses and other provisions of the respective PO to prevent misunderstandings and potential conflicts.

## III. What Does a Cut-Off-Date Actually Cut-Off?

### A. Definition and General Concept of a Cut-Off-Date

In the context of any arbitration, the role of evidence is of paramount importance. No party can succeed without the presentation of credible and persuasive evidence to substantiate its claims or defences. This, however, does not imply that all the evidence is presented directly at the outset; rather, it is common for further evidence to be submitted as both parties develop their respective cases and the proceedings progress. Quite often, the point in time at which evidence is presented is of particular strategic importance and counsel might even withhold specific documents until the very last moment.

Nevertheless, it is necessary for the tribunal to ensure that neither party obstructs the proceedings by introducing new facts or evidence at an inconveniently late stage in the arbitration. This is particularly relevant in instances where the parties had ample opportunities to submit their respective evidence beforehand and were even obliged to do so by the concluding number of full submissions foreseen in the procedural timetable. Conversely, these actions may compromise the procedural efficiency of the arbitration. In order to circumvent such issues, and given that tribunals are generally expected to manage proceedings efficiently, they have a range of tools and procedures at their disposal. One such instrument is the implementation of a cut-off-date.[1])

First and foremost, a cut-off-date does of course not by itself constitute permission to file yet another submission. Rather, it is the date after which the introduction of new evidence into the proceedings will only be permitted under exceptional circumstances.

Thus, a cut-off-date does not stipulate that new substantive submissions and legal arguments may be filed at will until its expiry. The distinction is that, before the cut-off-date, a party may request leave of the arbitral tribunal to submit additional evidence without needing to demonstrate the existence of exceptional circumstances. Exceptional circumstances may, for instance, arise where the party concerned had no prior opportunity to present the relevant evidence earlier in the proceedings. By contrast, following the cut-off-date, the arbitral tribunal may insist on a higher standard and a party will be required, when seeking leave to submit new evidence, to also demonstrate that there are exceptional circumstances to permit its admission at such a late date. In other words: It is crystal clear that after the cut-off-date, only "fresh" evidence that was not accessible earlier or did not even exist before can be entered into the proceedings. But does this automatically mean that, until the cut-off-date, any evidence, as old as it may be, can still be successfully introduced?

In order to understand the purpose and function of the cut-off date, it is important to first look at the principal manner in which the submission of evidence and pleading in an arbitration is regulated; the procedural timetable (interpreted in accordance with the rules of procedure). The procedural timetable sets out the number of submissions the parties are to file, the date those submissions are due and (often) what those submissions should include.[2])

---

[1]) Lasse Lehtonen, Laura Parkkisenniemi, *Chapter 10: Submitting New Evidence after the Cut-Off Date: When Are Exceptional Circumstances Present?*, in Schöldström/Danielsson, Stockholm Arbitration Yearbook 2023, 161.

[2]) Kristoffer Löf, Aron Skogman, *et al.*, Chapter 9: *The Proceedings, in Magnusson/Ragnwaldh, et al., International Arbitration in Sweden: A Practitioner's Guide* (2nd ed. 2021), 243 [107]; Dorda/Sessler/Pfisterer, *C. Abschließende (post-hearing) Schriftsätze*, in Torggler/Schäfer/Wong/Mohs/Wed, Schiedsgerichtsbarkeit (3rd ed. 2024), 488 [1229 *et seq.*].

Any element not encompassed within the procedural timetable is, *per se*, not a solicited submission – as it has not been agreed between the parties and received approval from the arbitral tribunal in advance. The same principle applies to evidence and witness or expert statements. It is standard practice for the parties to include all supporting evidence and accompanying documentation that substantiate their claims and present their case within their respective written submissions that are explicitly and finally listed in the procedural timetable.[3])

Nevertheless, certain documents or pieces of evidence may only become relevant at a later stage or may not be available for submission earlier. In such cases, a party wishing to submit such new evidence outside the defined procedural timetable must request leave of the arbitral tribunal to submit such evidence *before* entering that evidence into the procedure.[4]) It is by requesting prior leave that the arbitral tribunal is put in a position to fulfil its role of ensuring the efficiency of the procedure and protect the parties' due process rights. Importantly, the tribunal will need to weigh the potential relevance of the evidence for which leave is sought against potential delays it may cause in the procedure and the opposing party's right to respond or comment on the newly submitted evidence. The cut-off-date is a regulatory measure that is intended to support arbitral tribunals in making this assessment.

As will be discussed in more detail below, the cut-off date is a date agreed between the parties and the tribunal as the latest date after which it may be assumed that a party being asked to respond to new evidence will suffer a higher degree of prejudice in having to do so. This hurdle must be understood in the context of the procedural timetable and the planning and scheduling the parties have undertaken to ensure they are properly positioned to present their respective cases. The admission of new evidence after the cut-off-date will generally (depending on the nature and breadth of evidence submitted) have some effect on the parties' preparation of their cases and may also necessitate a postponement of the already agreed hearing dates – a consequence most tribunals greatly prefer to avoid.

Understood in this context as an agreement between all the stakeholders involved in the arbitration, it is clear that the arbitral tribunal may consider this kind of prejudice, and the parties' agreement on its existence after the cut-off-date, in deciding whether the unsolicited submission of new evidence or pleading is permissible.

In practice, parties often submit their new evidence concurrently with making their request for leave to have the evidence admitted to the record of

[3]) Löf and Skogman, *supra* note 2, at 243 *et seq.*; Dorda/Sessler/Pfisterer, *supra* note 2, at 488.

[4]) Hahnkamper, *IX.Praxistipps für Schiedsrichter*, in Nueber, Handbuch Schiedsgerichtsbarkeit und ADR (1st ed. 2020), 980 [50].

the arbitration.[5]) This practice is to be discouraged and arbitral tribunals may wish to factor the breach of procedure in their assessment whether to grant leave to admit the evidence to the procedure or not. Ultimately, the circumstances of the case will be the determinative factor in whether any given request should be granted.

## B. The Time of Fixing a Cut-Off-Date

As previously established, the cut-off-date is generally defined as the "final" opportunity – or in other words: "last order" – for the parties to add new evidence or arguments to the file.

Historically, cut-off-dates were commonly used after the procedural timetable had already been fixed in arbitrations that were already pending and where it was evident that a party was regularly amending its claims or the grounds thereof. Furthermore, tribunals used cut-off-dates in instances where a party has persistently presented further evidence, resulting in complex and time-consuming proceedings or even the postponement of fixed hearing dates.[6])

*The dynamic has clearly shifted:* Nowadays, parties and tribunals typically agree on cut-off-dates when fixing the procedural timetable, thus shortly after the arbitrators receive the file, in most instances during or after the case management conference. Tribunals therefore frequently incorporate cut-off-dates into POs or procedural timetables, even when there is no apparent indication to anticipate that a party will submit additional claims, evidence or arguments.[7])

Regardless of the temporal context, it is imperative that arbitrators notify the respective parties prior to setting a cut-off-date. The purpose of this procedure is to ensure that there are no surprise decisions and that the parties are aware of the timeframe in which they are on the safe side to submit evidence. Consequently, they are able to arrange the presentation of their case in advance, which has a positive effect on both the efficiency and duration of the respective arbitral proceeding.[8])

---

[5]) *Id.*, at 980 [50].

[6]) Lehtonen and Parkkisenniemi, *supra* note 1, at 162.

[7]) Lehtonen and Parkkisenniemi, *supra* note 1, at 162.

[8]) Franz T. Schwarz, Christian W. Konrad, *Article 20: The Conduct of the Proceedings*, in Schwarz/Konrad, The Vienna Rules: A Commentary on International Arbitration in Austria (2009), 444 [20-072].

## C. The Scope of the Cut-Off-Date

Despite the fact that cut-off-dates are widely recognised and used, not many arbitration rules contain an explicit provision concerning the exact meaning thereof. Most of the rules tend to merely grant the tribunal the authority to conduct the proceedings in an efficient manner. This authority will include the implementation of cut-off-dates. In addition, the imposition of cut-off-dates is often the consequence of the applicable rules, stipulating that submissions shall be made and evidence shall be provided "within the time limits set by the tribunal".[9])

For instance, the Rules of Arbitration of the Danish Institute of Arbitration 2021 (DIA Rules) provide in Article 34 that all documents or other evidence must be submitted in accordance with the set time limits. A failure to comply with the set limits may cause the rejection of the respective submission unless the tribunal considers the failure justified, or if *special circumstances* exist.

Any preclusion of evidence or of any submission is, however, limited by the parties' right to be heard and their right to fair and equal treatment.[10])

Furthermore, the authority to implement cut-off-dates can also be inferred from the application of the IBA Rules on the Taking of Evidence as tribunals – or more specifically – the decisions of tribunals with respect to the taking of evidence are often guided or inspired by these rules.[11])

Article 3 of the IBA Rules on the Taking of Evidence provides: "*Within the time ordered by the Arbitral Tribunal, each Party shall submit to the Arbitral Tribunal and to the other Parties all Documents available to it on which it relies [...]*". Moreover, Article 9 establishes, that the Tribunal shall "*determine the admissibility, relevance, materiality and weight of evidence*".

The authority to set cut-off-dates is also derived from major arbitration frameworks: For example, the Vienna Rules 2021 stipulate in Article 28 (2) the following: "*Upon prior notice, the arbitral tribunal may inter alia consider pleadings, the submission of evidence, and requests for the taking of evidence to be admissible only up to a certain point in time of the proceedings.*"

Moreover, Article 22 (2) of the International Dispute Resolution Procedures (including Mediation and Arbitration Rules) 2021 (ICDR Rules) reads as follows "*The tribunal shall conduct the proceedings with a view to expediting the resolution of the dispute. The tribunal may, promptly after being constituted, conduct a procedural hearing with the parties for the purpose of organizing, scheduling, and agreeing to procedures, including the setting of deadlines for any submissions by the parties. [...]*"

---

[9]) Lehtonen and Parkkisenniemi, *supra* note 1, at 162.

[10]) Schwarz and Konrad, *supra* note 8, at 486 [20–183].

[11]) Lehtonen and Parkkisenniemi, *supra* note 1, at 163; Löf and Skogman, *supra* note 2, at 244 [109].

Furthermore, the International Chamber of Commerce (ICC) has published a Commission Report in 2021. These reports are developed by expert commissions with the aim of improving the efficiency, fairness and predictability of international commercial practices through commentary, practical tools and best practices. The ICC established the following as a *best practice* for arbitrators: "*In advance of any evidentiary hearing, consider setting a cut-off date after which no new documentary evidence will be admitted unless a compelling reason is shown.*"[12])

On the other hand, there are some arbitration rules that explicitly refer to a cut-off-date: For instance, the Arbitration Rules of the Finland Chamber of Commerce 2020 (FAI Rules) contain an explicit "cut-off-date" provision in Article 35. This Article stipulates that after the agreed upon date, no party will be allowed to present any new claims, arguments or documentary evidence on the merits of the dispute, nor invoke any new witnesses not previously nominated, unless the tribunal in "*exceptional circumstances decides otherwise*".

Furthermore, the Rules on the Efficient Conduct of Proceedings in International Arbitration ("Prague Rules") also contain an explicit provision in Article 3.3: "*The arbitral tribunal shall consider imposing a cut-off date for submission of evidence and not accepting any new evidence after that date, save for under exceptional circumstances.*"[13])

It is evident that, even in instances where explicit cut-off-date provisions are included in the rules, their scope may vary. For instance, the FAI Rules stipulate a rather extensive scope of application: The cut-off-date restriction covers new claims, arguments or documentary evidence on the merits of the dispute. In addition, it limits the introduction of new witnesses not previously nominated. On the other hand, the Prague Rules only refer to the submission of evidence. *Consequently, when drafting a cut-off-date clause, the Tribunal should be mindful of the wording of both the underlying rules, if any, and its own chosen terminologies.*[14])

This raises the question of how to proceed when the applicable rules do not contain any provisions regarding a cut-off-date clause. *The answer is straightforward*: It falls to the respective tribunal to establish the specific terms of such clauses, as it holds both the authority and the duty to determine the procedural framework governing the conduct and organization of the proceedings. In such instances, the tribunal is at liberty to decide whether and how to stipulate a cut-off-date provision and the other provisions of the PO to establish what may and may not be submitted. *In order to preserve the parties'*

[12]) The International Chamber of Commerce (ICC), *Controlling Time and Costs in Arbitration* 2021, 14 [73].

[13]) These rules were first introduced and developed by a Working Group of nearly 30 representatives of civil law countries in 2018. These rules are not mandatory but serve as a non-binding, soft-law supplement that parties and arbitral tribunals can agree to apply in international arbitration proceedings.

[14]) Lehtonen and Parkkisenniemi, *supra* note 1, at 164.

*right to a fair hearing, the tribunal should clearly define and stipulate this from the outset of the proceedings.*[15])

Established doctrine also reveals differing interpretations of the scope of a cut-off-date clause. Some authorities confine its application to the introduction of newly produced evidence; some extend it to the submission of previously undisclosed documents. Other interpretations adopt a broader view, extending the clause's scope to encompass the introduction of new factual as well as legal pleadings.[16]) In the majority of cases, however, the cut-off-date is set for the submission of "new" evidence, without further explaining whether the evidence existed before or not.[17])

In the absence of explicit provisions in the applicable arbitration rules, the determination of this matter rests within the discretion of the arbitral tribunal. As a result, the scope and effect of such clauses are defined by the arbitrators on a case-by-case basis. *Ultimately, the precise wording of the clause remains of paramount importance.*

## IV. A Cut-Off-Date After the Last Round of Submissions Does Not Constitute a Right to "a Very Last Submission"

All the above considerations show that it is, of course, best for the tribunal to *explicitly regulate* that the cut-off-date only serves for submitting documents that either did not exist when the last submission was due or could, despite reasonable efforts, not have been obtained or presented in this submission. If the procedural timetable fixes an equal number of submissions for both parties, "this is it". Setting an additional cut-off-date can therefore not be used – or abused – by either party to file yet another substantive submission including evidence that had been available well before that date.

[15]) *Id.*, at 164; A. Horvath, Meisinger, *Beweisverfahren*, in Czernich/Deixler-Hübner/Schauer, Handbuch Schiedsrecht (2018), 468 [13.43].

[16]) Dorda/Sessler/Pfisterer, *supra* note 2, at 488 [1230]; Gary Born, *Chapter 15: Procedures in International Arbitration (Updated March 2024)*, in Born, International Commercial Arbitration (3rd ed. 2024), [Y]; Eliane Fischer and Courtney Furner, *Chapter 48: Early Case Documents*, in Lotfi/Zielińska-Eisen, *et al.*, International Arbitration in Practice, 549.

[17]) Andrea Meier, Nadja Kull, *Chapter 17, Part II: Commentary on the ICC Rules, Appendix IV [Case management techniques]*, in Arroyo, Arbitration in Switzerland: The Practitioner's Guide (2nd ed. 2018), 2346 [11]; Irene Welser, Christian Klausegger, *Fast Track Arbitration: Just fast or something different?*, in Klausegger/Klein/Kremslehner/Petsche/Pitkowitz/Power/Welser/Zeiler, Austrian Arbitration Yearbook 2009, 266.

Such an understanding can also implicitly derive from a procedural timetable with a strictly specified number of rounds of written submissions.[18]) In the event that such a strict timetable with an exhaustive number of submissions (*e.g.*, Full Statement of Claim, Full Statement of Defence, Rejoinder, Rebutter, Re-Rejoinder and Re-Rebutter) exists, it is clear that no further submissions are allowed, even if an (additional) cut-off-date is fixed out of precaution. Such additional cut-off-date merely allows a party to draw conclusions from facts that did *not yet exist* when its last submission was due or to submit documents *that could not be filed before*. Adopting a good faith approach, this may include documents that already existed, but were not accessible to such party. By contrast, newly drafted written witness statements just to "rebut" the opponent's last submission to not fall under this exception.

When the tribunal, in cooperation with the parties, establishes the procedural timetable, it is perfectly clear that it will be one party – usually the respondent – to have the "last word". The stipulation of a cut-off-date is not an excuse to circumvent this rule and to file an extra "unsolicited" submission. Therefore, if the parties expressly agreed on a procedural calendar with a specified number of submissions, no additional submission may be filed by the cut-off-date.

Quite frequently, PO1 will contain wording more or less similar to the following:

> *"The number and sequence of pleadings was determined by the parties in the procedural calendar. However, the arbitral tribunal may at any time request the parties to submit further pleadings on specific issues which it considers essential for its decision."*.

Already such a provision makes it clear that, without substantive and unforeseen reasons, no party may "save" its final arguments or additional evidence that had been available before until the cut-off-date.

The cut-off-date is therefore not at all comparable with a call for "last orders" in a British Pub.

If the arbitral tribunal does not request the parties to submit any further pleadings after the last submission has been filed, no additional submissions are permissible as per the cut-off-date unless new facts arise or new documents become available.

Any party wishing to submit an additional written statement that is not provided for in the procedural calendar must therefore first submit a corresponding application. Written statements or submissions of substantial content that are submitted without prior permission from the arbitral tribunal

[18]) Dorda/Sessler/Pfisterer, *supra* note 2, at 488 [1229 *et seq.*]; Irene Welser, Susanne Wurzer, *Formality in International Commercial Arbitration – For Better or For Worse?*, in Klausegger/Klein/Kremslehner/Petsche/Pitkowitz/Power/Welser/Zeiler, Austrian Arbitration Yearbook 2008, 222 *et seq.*

are inadmissible, and the mere existence of an additional cut-off-date does not change this situation: they are to be rejected.

This is particularly clear if the PO1 expressly states that the parties must, in their respective filings, submit arguments in support of their positions and offer and include evidence to support them. Regularly, the factual and/or legal evidence, witness statements and/or expert opinions that a party intends to rely on must already be attached to these written submissions.

This automatically prohibits withholding certain documents until the very last minute for strategic reasons, even if a later cut-off-date is also foreseen in the procedural timetable.

Despite such a cut-off-date, it is inherent in any arbitration proceedings that the exchange of written submissions between the parties must come to an end at some point, whereby, for reasons of equal treatment, neither party may submit more written submissions than the other. Allowing one party to file yet another brief not provided for in the procedural timetable would violate the principle of equal treatment. Any other approach would result in an exchange of written submissions between the parties turning into a never-ending "ping-pong game".

Even if the cut-off-date is defined as "a date after which no party is permitted to submit new documents or request other evidence, unless the arbitral tribunal expressly permits this in individual cases", this does not automatically entitle any party to file yet another written submission *up to that date*. Quite to the contrary, if – as usual – the number of submissions is limited by number it follows that a further round of written submissions is not available and that the cut-off-date is intended for exceptional cases, such as those in which a party subsequently finds individual documents that it was previously unable to use.

In the above cut-off-date-definition containing the restriction to "new documents or other evidence", it is particularly clear that the cut-off date is not intended to allow parties to make submissions that they have previously failed to make, to submit documents that have long been known, and, in particular, to refute the arguments of the party that was entitled to submit the last written statement according to the agreed procedural calendar.

All this does not, of course, preclude the possibility that, in individual cases, a procedural order could take a different approach and grant the parties a "final, joint round of written submissions" at the time of the cut-off-date.

To sum up: If a cut-off-date is provided for in the procedural timetable, this is not a permission for another submission, raising arguments that could long have been raised before, rebutting arguments of the opposite party that had, according to the procedural timetable, had the last word or to even submit evidence that could have been submitted before. The cut-off-date merely serves as a possibility to bring latest developments to the tribunal's attention that could not have been addressed before, or to submit documents that were not accessible earlier. Never may a cut-off-date be used to file newly drafted written witness statements or expert reports serving solely to rebut the opponent's arguments or evidence.

This is further supported by the fact that, under most institutional arbitration rules, all parties to the arbitration proceedings must act in good faith; they shall use all means to ensure that the proceedings are conducted efficiently and avoid unnecessary costs and delays.

The cut-off-date cannot therefore not be interpreted as granting the parties autonomous discretion to submit documents at will or on a continuous basis until the cut-off-date elapses.

## V. Submissions Made On and After the Cut-Off Date: Legal and Practical Challenges

With regard to submissions made either before or after the stipulated deadline, two principal issues arise: the scope of application of the clause in question and the extent of the tribunal's discretion in addressing such submissions that fall outside the stipulated scope or are submitted belatedly.

Regarding the first matter, *i.e.*, the scope, the following points are noted: Arbitrators tend to interpret the cut-off-date clauses and thus the respective scope of these clauses strictly based on the wording. For instance, in *SCC case 2018/127*, a dispute arose concerning the scope of the respective cut-off-date clause. The clause in question in the respective PO read as follows:

> *"After the cut-off date mentioned in Section (1) of the Procedural Timetable, the parties are not permitted to submit any additional documentary evidence or legal texts. The Arbitral Tribunal will not accept any late submission unless the Arbitral Tribunal in exceptional circumstances decides otherwise upon a party's reasoned request showing sufficient cause for the delay."*

The arbitrators thus concluded that – seeing that the clause did not contain *oral* witness testimonies – new oral witness testimonies were admissible (even after the cut-off-date elapsed). This decision was justified on the basis that the clause in question was unambiguous and could not be subject to contradictory interpretation.[19]) This case shows how important it is to draft the relevant cut-off-date provision carefully and precisely. Unclear wording of the clause can lead to many conflicts and possible legal consequences, some of which are dealt with in Chapter VI.

With regard to the latter issue, specifically the arbitrators' handling of and discretion regarding belated submissions, the following should be noted: As previously stated, the cut-off-date does not constitute an invitation to

[19]) Lehtonen and Parkkisenniemi, *supra* note 1, at 164; SCC Case No. 2018/127, Final Award, 14 November 2019, paras 38, 161–170.

submit. Accordingly, irrespective of the timing – whether occurring before or after the cut-off-date – the submission remains one not previously consented to by the parties or the tribunal and, as such, is subject to the tribunal's prior authorization. The difference is that, after the designated date has passed, the burden of justification increases significantly for the parties, who are required to provide substantial justification for their submission. The tribunal will then have to determine the weight of the submitted materials, and whether this submission bears the risk of delaying the proceedings if accepted or whether it is only presented with the aim of surprising the other party. Furthermore, the Tribunal will have to consider whether there was a relevant reasoning for not making a prior submission.[20]) Ensuring the procedural efficiency is the tribunal's main priority. In order to achieve this, most POs grant the tribunals the authority to reject belated submissions, which do not follow from the agreed timetable or which are not specifically requested beforehand by the tribunals.[21])

It is evident that submissions made either before or after the designated cut-off-date may give rise to procedural disputes, particularly when the scope of the relevant clause lacks sufficient precision. As previously stated, submissions that are not submitted within the specified procedural timetable are generally regarded as unsolicited. In such instances, the tribunal retains the discretion to admit or reject these submissions.

From a legal standpoint, these circumstances test the balance between procedural fairness and the tribunal's duty to ensure efficiency and finality. From a practical perspective, they prompt consideration of how tribunals should address late or additional evidence without undermining the integrity of the arbitral process or causing undue prejudice to either party. The interplay of these factors underscores the necessity of defining clear procedural consequences for breaches of cut-off-dates and maintaining consistent and predictable standards for their enforcement.

## VI. Tribunal Discretion and Legal Consequences

As previously established, arbitral tribunals generally enjoy broad discretion in the conduct of arbitral proceedings. This discretion is recognized by many rules and conventions, such as the New York Convention. The tribunal may determine the arbitral procedure, including admissibility and relevance of evidence. This discretion is subject to the principles of fairness, equality and the right to be heard. In principle, the parties have procedural autonomy, meaning they can agree on rules to govern the arbitration, but failing such

[20]) Löf and Skogman, *supra* note 2, at 270 [212].

[21]) *Id.*, at 243 *et seq.*

agreement, the tribunal may conduct the proceedings as it sees appropriate. This is under the rationale of the applicable laws and rules.

POs intend to set specific procedural rules for the parties from the outset of the proceedings. This results in predictability and efficiency of the arbitration. The content of the POs depends on the level of detail both the parties and the tribunal consider necessary. Normally, the parties and the tribunal endeavour to resolve as many procedural matters as possible in the POs. The rationale behind this is to mitigate the risk of unforeseen and timely procedural issues arising.[22])

Disputes regarding the permissibility of certain submissions prior to and after the designated cut-off-date are sometimes used by the parties to invoke a violation of their right to fair treatment or their right to be heard. Arbitral Tribunals, however, should not be too timid *vis-à-vis* such complaints. *No "due process paranoia", please!*

Again, it needs to be stressed that the cut-off-date is the date, where the presentation of both parties is "cut-off", once *they had a reasonable chance to present their case.*[23]) Pleadings cannot go on forever.

Tribunals should therefore not be overly cautious while dealing with procedural decisions such as belated introduction of additional evidence. Only where a party has been totally denied the opportunity to be heard without a reasonable justification, this can be considered to be a ground for annulment of the award. This is, of course, not the case if a predefined cut-off-date is taken into account. In addition, both parties will of course have the right to react to the opposing party's submission during the oral hearing and therefore, the right to be heard is of course ensured.

Parties cannot be allowed to submit everything and at every single stage of the arbitration, until they are satisfied with presenting their case. *Therefore*, arbitral tribunals should not fear to formally reject belated submissions and evidence, as the rejection of late filings does not violate due process, if each party has had a reasonable opportunity to present its case before.[24])

Accordingly, the tribunal bears the duty to prevent the process from devolving into an unrestrained or continuous exchange of pleadings and documents.[25])

---

[22]) Fischer and Furner, *supra* note 16, at 536 [D].

[23]) Nikolaus Pitkowitz, *Chapter II: The Arbitrator and the Arbitration Procedure, The Vienna Predictability Propositions: Paving the Road to Predictability in International Arbitration*, in Klausegger/Klein, *et al.*, Austrian Yearbook on International Arbitration 2017, 135.

[24]) Rolf Trittmann, Ramona Schardt, *§2.05: The Proceedings Before the Arbitral Tribunal, Article 31: Closing of Proceedings*, in Flecke Giammarco/Boog, *et al.*, The DIS Arbitration Rules – An Article-by-Article Commentary (2020), 496 [14]; Schwarz and Konrad, *supra* note 8, at 445 *et seq.* [20-075 *et seq.*].

[25]) Trittmann and Schardt, *supra* note 24, at 496 [14]; Schwarz and Konrad, *supra* note 1, at 445.

## VII. "Best Practice" for Arbitrators

Tribunals should implement clauses which clearly define the scope of the cut-off-date. It is helpful if transparent guidelines are provided on what can and cannot be submitted.

*Therefore, draft with precision today to avoid deliberation regrets tomorrow.*

This principle also applies to the other provisions of the respective PO and to the procedural timetable. It is imperative to establish explicit criteria from the outset to determine acceptable submissions and those that are not.

*Drafting POs with foresight spares the tribunal from future friction.*

In addition, the cut-off-date in question, while making clear that it does not give room to make up for prior omissions, should be set within a reasonable margin to the last submissions of the parties as well as to the hearing. The cut-off-date clause should further, if necessary, allow the tribunal to grant the other party reasonable time to respond. This should happen without the possibility of delaying or jeopardizing the scheduled hearing.[26])

*Draft cut-off provisions to give room for response, not room for delay.*

While strict timelines are essential for POs, tribunals should retain the authority to permit reasonable accommodations when justified. This ensures that neither party is unfairly disadvantaged due to unforeseen circumstances. Any exception to the cut-off-date should be granted only upon showing substantial cause, and the other party must always be given adequate time to respond to new material.

*Therefore, maintain firm timelines, but let flexibility serve fairness, not convenience.*

Provisions should be drafted to prevent strategic or negligent behaviour. A party should not be able to use late submissions nor procedural requests as means to delay the proceedings or jeopardize the subsequent scheduled hearing.

*Procedural clarity is the best shield against strategic misuse and delay.*

The cut-off-date clause should clearly define what happens if a party submits materials after the cut-off-date or submissions, that fall outside of the stipulate scope of this clause. Consequences might include an exclusion of the submission, the denial of consideration or cost implications for the respective

[26]) Martin Agren, Niklas Astenius, *Chapter 3: Time and Cost in Arbitration*, in Magnusson/Ragnwaldh, *et al.*, International Arbitration in Sweden: A Practioner's Guide (2nd ed. 2021), 88 [105].

party. These measures encourage compliance and reinforce procedural discipline. However, flexibility should remain for the tribunal to accept late materials when refusal would compromise the fairness of the proceedings.

*Therefore, define consequences clearly – discipline thrives where uncertainty ends.*

To conclude: A well-drafted cut-off-date clause contributes significantly to clarity, predictability, and equality between the parties. It helps avoid negative surprises, promotes a timely management of the proceeding and supports the tribunal in conducting efficient and orderly hearings. When both parties understand the boundaries and potential impacts from the outset, the process becomes more transparent and less predisposed to contention.

And, at long last:

*Don't let due process paranoia get hold of you!*

# The Third-Party Dilemma in Arbitration: Inclusion of Non-Signatories and Enforcement Challenges

*Doğuhan Uygun/Pınar Noberi*

## I. Introduction

Arbitration's defining characteristic is its contractual nature. Consent expressed through an arbitration agreement constitutes both the source and the limit of an arbitral tribunal's jurisdiction.[1]) Yet, the increasing complexity of global commerce, with its networks of subcontractors, financiers, guarantors, and corporate groups, often frustrates this ideal of bilateralism. Unlike litigation, where jurisdiction may be asserted on territorial or statutory grounds, arbitration participation typically turns on the existence of an arbitration agreement; mere economic interest in a dispute does not confer standing.[2]) Many commercial actors that are intimately involved in a project never sign the arbitration clause that subsequently governs disputes. This structural mismatch between contractual consent and economic reality produces the third-party dilemma: Should a non-signatory who stands at the heart of a transaction be brought within the arbitral process, and if so, on what legal basis?

Courts and arbitral tribunals have responded with a range of doctrines that seek to reconcile arbitration's consensual foundations with commercial efficiency. These include assignment and succession (the arbitration clause follows the contract), third-party beneficiary rights, agency and apparent authority, estoppel and abuse of rights, and the much-debated group of companies doctrine, alongside exceptional remedies such as piercing the corporate veil.[3])

---

[1]) *Gary B. Born, International Commercial Arbitration,* Third Edition (Kluwer Law International 2021), Chapter 10, 1401–1402.

[2]) *Stavros Brekoulakis, Chapter 24: The Various Forms of 'Consent' in International Arbitration,* in Stefan M. Kröll, Andrea Kay Bjorklund, et al. (eds), Cambridge Compendium of International Commercial and Investment Arbitration (Cambridge University Press, 2023), 697–698.

[3]) *Bernard Hanotiau, Non-signatories, Groups of Companies and Groups of Contracts in Selected Asian Countries: A Case Law Analysis* (Journal of International Arbitration, December 2015), 571–620.

This article explores how and when those doctrines are applied, and the legitimacy and enforcement challenges that follow. It further examines how major jurisdictions draw the line between autonomy and practicality.

## II. Conceptual Foundations

Arbitration's legitimacy rests on the idea that private parties may, through contract, remove their disputes from state courts and submit them to an arbitral forum.[4]) This notion of autonomy, however, has never been absolute. In modern commercial practice, the web of participants surrounding a transaction often extends beyond the signatories of the arbitration clause. The conceptual challenge is therefore to define whose consent matters and how far it may be inferred.

### A. The Classical View: Consent as a Constitutive Requirement

In classical doctrine, arbitration is a creature of contract; the arbitration agreement is both the source and the limit of jurisdiction. According to this view, jurisdiction cannot exist without the parties' meeting of minds.

United Nations Convention on the Recognition and Enforcement of Foreign Arbitral Awards (New York, 10 June 1958) (New York Convention), Article II, codifies this orthodoxy by requiring that an arbitration agreement be "in writing" and "signed by the parties".[5]) UNCITRAL Model Law on International Commercial Arbitration (1985, as amended 2006) (UNCITRAL Model Law), Article 7, mirrors this requirement.[6]) The rationale is twofold: first, to ensure that the waiver of access to courts is voluntary and unequivocal; and second, to furnish an objective record for enforcement under the New York Convention.

Turkish law takes a similar stance. International Arbitration Law No. 4686 (*Milletlerarası Tahkim Kanunu* – IAL) and Code of Civil Procedure No. 6100 (*Hukuk Muhakemeleri Kanunu* – CCP) Article 412 explicitly require a written arbitration agreement signed or otherwise evidenced in writing. The Turkish Court of Appeal (*Yargıtay*) has repeatedly characterized arbitration as an exceptional jurisdiction that may not be extended by analogy.[7])

---

[4]) *Brekoulakis, Chapter 24, supra,* at 699.

[5]) New York Convention, Art II.

[6]) UNCITRAL Model Law, Art 7.

[7]) *The Turkish Court of Appeal (Yargıtay) General Assembly of the Civil Chambers, E. 2023/103 K. 2023/1185, 29.11.2023.*

## B. The Evolution Toward Implied and Functional Consent

Despite the contractual ideal, arbitral reality soon exposed its limitations. International trade and complex projects seldom involve neatly bilateral relationships. Participants such as subcontractors, guarantors, or parent companies often perform essential obligations or derive substantial benefits without ever signing the contract. Refusing to include them in arbitral proceedings could fracture the dispute into multiple forums and frustrate efficiency which is the very rationale of arbitration. In response, tribunals and courts began to interpret consent more broadly, giving rise to implied and later functional notions of consent.

### 1. Implied Consent

An entity may become a party to a contract, including an arbitration agreement, impliedly (by conduct or non-explicit declarations) as well as by express agreement or formal execution. Ordinary principles of contract law apply to issues of implied consent regarding arbitration agreements. The fundamental question is whether the parties' intention was that a particular entity be a party to the arbitration agreement.[8])

This theory assumes that the fact that a party has had direct and decisive participation in the negotiation, execution or termination of the contract, can be considered a good indication that it has consented to be part of the arbitration agreement. This implied consent to the arbitration agreement, on the part of those who have not signed it, is deduced from their participation in the main legal act; and from their effective relationship (at the time the arbitration agreement is signed) with the company that has signed said agreement.[9])

Tribunals have inferred consent from a party's participation in negotiations, submission of claims in the arbitration, or reliance on the contract's terms. The principle draws on the objective theory of contract, which measures intent by outward manifestations rather than subjective will.

### 2. Functional Consent

Functional consent goes further: it permits inclusion when denial of arbitration would contradict good faith or constitute an abuse of rights. The idea emerged from Swiss jurisprudence, particularly under Article 2 of the

[8]) *Born, supra,* at 1520 1530.

[9]) *Carlos Alberto Matheus López, Global Analysis of the Extension of the Arbitration Agreement to Non-signatories, and Proposed Model Norm and Guideline for Standard Use*, Chapter 5 in Ben Beaumont, Alexis Foucard, et al. (eds), International Arbitration: Quo Vadis? (Juris Publishing, December 2022), 83.

Swiss Civil Code[10]) (*Schweizerisches Zivilgesetzbuch* – SCC) and Article 178(2) Swiss Private International Law[11]) (*Bundesgesetz über das Internationale Privatrecht* – Swiss PILA) and has since influenced French and ICC practice. In this view, consent can be "constructed" where conduct makes exclusion inequitable.

The practice of the Swiss Federal Tribunal regarding extension of an arbitral clause may be summarized as follows: *A non-signatory party is obliged to arbitrate where the statements and behaviour of such party must in good faith be interpreted so as to meaning that such party considered itself bound by the main contract as a whole or at least by its arbitral clause.*[12])

This has been described as "consent theory plus": tribunals first look for genuine or implied consent; if absent, they assess whether a party's behavior makes refusal abusive.[13]) *In Switzerland, the issue of non-signatory parties to an arbitration agreement is dealt with based on general principles of contract law, with the Supreme Court developing a two-step method for interpreting contracts including arbitration agreements governed by Swiss law: (i) establishing "true and common intent" of the parties, and (ii) if that fails, applying objective interpretation based on the principle of confidence.*[14])

Swiss courts have adopted this dual method. In the *Butec* case, the Federal Tribunal upheld jurisdiction against a company that had actively participated in contract execution and correspondence, reasoning that denying consent would violate good faith.[15])

In cases where involvement of non-signatories to arbitral proceedings is present, the concept of dispute is crucial in establishing the arbitral tribunals' jurisdiction. Tribunals may take on jurisdiction in cases where a non-signatory interferes with the contractual relationship of its performance. Even though this investigation is fact-specific and case-specific by nature, its factual character does not make the test arbitrary or unpredictable. Comparative case law from various jurisdictions provides consistent guidance on the minimal requirements of such evaluation, to ensure predictability and coherence in the application of such test.[16])

---

[10]) SCC, Art. 2.

[11]) Swiss PILA, Art. 178(2).

[12]) *Michael Mráz, Extension of An Arbitration Agreement to Non-Signatories: Some Reflections on Swiss Judicial Practice*, Annals of Faculty of Law in Belgrade, Issue 3 (2009), 58.

[13]) *Nathalie Voser, The Swiss Perspective on Parties in Arbitration: 'Traditional Approach With a Twist regarding Abuse of Rights' or 'Consent Theory Plus'*, Chapter 9, in Stavros Brekoulakis, Julian David Mathew Lew, et al. (eds), The Evolution and Future of International Arbitration, International Arbitration Law Library, Volume 37 (Kluwer Law International, 2016), 161–182.

[14]) *Ibid.* at 165–166.

[15]) *Swiss Federal Tribunal, ATF 129 III 727 (Butec), 16 October 2003.*

[16]) *Stavros Brekoulakis, Rethinking Consent in International Commercial Arbitration: A General Theory for Non-signatories* (Journal of International Dispute Settlement, December 2017), 630.

Yet, beneath the rhetoric of consent lies a more complex reality. Many inclusion theories are ultimately equity-based or rely on constructive consent to the main contract rather than true consent to arbitrate. Some systems even accept mere awareness of the arbitration clause as sufficient, which invites critique that the consensual foundation is being eroded in favor of functional or policy-driven outcomes.[17])

# III. Doctrinal Bases for Inclusion of Non-Signatories

The inclusion of non-signatories in arbitration challenges the very principle that arbitration is a matter of consent. Yet, arbitral and judicial practice have developed a spectrum of doctrines that stretch consent beyond formal signature, reflecting commercial realities whilst trying to preserve legitimacy. These doctrines can be grouped into three broad families: consent-based, conduct-based, and equity-based theories.

## A. Consent-Based Theories

### 1. Assignment and Transfer of Rights

When a contract is transferred, the key question is whether the arbitration clause travels to bind the assignee or not. The prevailing rule across most jurisdictions is one of automatic transfer: general consent to take the contract brings the arbitration clause with it, enabling assignees to compel or be compelled to arbitrate. Indeed, in most jurisdictions, it is presumed that assignment of the underlying contract entails the assignment of the associated arbitration agreement.[18])

Closely related is assumption, where a third party adopts contractual duties by conduct or express declaration. Arbitral tribunals have repeatedly found that an entity that performs the core obligations of a contract – such as issuing invoices, accepting payments, or managing the project – thereby assumes the arbitration clause unless it clearly objects.[19])

### 2. Third-Party Beneficiaries

A similar rationale underlies third-party beneficiary cases. Non-parties to a contract may, in certain circumstances, claim the benefits of that contract as third party beneficiaries. In such circumstances, the third party may either be

17) Brekoulakis, *Chapter 24, supra,* at 698.

18) *Born, supra,* at 1579.

19) *Born, supra,* at 1574.

able to invoke or may be bound by an arbitration clause contained in the contract. It is generally accepted that if a third party is bound by the same obligations stipulated by a party to a contract and this contract contains an arbitration clause or, in relation to it, an arbitration agreement exists, such a third party is also bound by the arbitration clause, or arbitration agreement, even if it did not sign it.[20])

A party claiming rights under a contract cannot reject its procedural terms; *qui sentit commodum sentire debet et onus*. The principle of reciprocity ensures equilibrium between advantage and responsibility.

## B. Conduct-Based Theories:

### 1. Agency and Apparent Authority

The most established of these theories is agency. According to the agency theory, a non-signatory will be bound by an arbitration agreement, when an agent executes a contract on behalf of its principal. It is well-settled, under all developed legal systems, that one party (an "agent" or similar representative) may in certain circumstances, legally bind another party (a "principal") by its acts.[21])

Apparent/ostensible authority is closely related to agency as a basis for binding non-signatories. Also referred to as "principle of appearance" or "*mandat apparent*" in some jurisdictions. Under this theory, a party may be bound by another entity's unauthorized acts if the putative principal created the appearance of authorization through words or conduct, leading a counter-party to reasonably believe authorization existed.[22])

To extend jurisdiction to a non-signatory party on the basis of apparent or ostensible authority, a tribunal must first be satisfied that the apparent principal has induced, by false representations, the claimant to believe that the apparent agent had the authority to enter into an arbitration clause; second, that the claimant actually relied on the misrepresentations of the apparent principal, and that such reliance was reasonable and in good faith in the circumstances.[23])

A leading ICC award illustrates this approach: applying Swiss law as the law of the seat, the tribunal held that a state could not rely on internal irregularities in the agent's authority to defeat jurisdiction when the counterparty reasonably relied on the agent's ostensible power. The tribunal reasoned that

---

[20]) *Born, supra,* at 1569.
[21]) *Born, supra,* at 1531.
[22]) *Born, supra,* at 1538.
[23]) *Born, supra,* at 1537.

allowing the state to invoke domestic formalities would contradict good faith and the principle of legitimate expectations in international commerce.[24])

## 2. The Group of Companies Doctrine

Beyond agency lies the more ambitious group of companies doctrine. Under this principle, non-signatories of a contract may be deemed parties to the associated arbitration clause based on factors often roughly comparable to those relevant to alter ego analysis. Where a company is part of a corporate group, is subject to the control of (or controls) a corporate affiliate that has executed a contract and is involved in the negotiation or performance of that contract, then that company may in some circumstances invoke or be subjected to an arbitration clause contained in that contract, notwithstanding the fact that it has not executed the contract itself.[25])

The doctrine has its arbitration pedigree in extending clauses within corporate groups based on common intention or implied consent. One of the landmark group of companies decisions is in *ICC Case No. 4131 Dow Chemical*, between Dow Chemical Company, together with various of its subsidiaries, and Isover Saint Gobain.[26]) The tribunal stated in its decision that: "*Irrespective of the distinct juridical identity of each of its members, a group of companies constitutes one and the same economic reality (une réalité économique unique) of which the arbitral tribunal should take account when it rules on its own jurisdiction.*"[27])

The decision rested not on legal unity but on economic reality and implied will. Since then, French courts and numerous arbitral tribunals have applied similar reasoning, often citing the need to reflect "the true commercial matrix" of a transaction. The doctrine's application, however, begins from the baseline that separate corporate personality remains the rule. Tribunals look for common intention or implied consent to bind non-signatories, rather than automatically disregarding corporate form.[28])

In practice, tribunals examine a range of indicators: close group structure and control, shared resources and branding, active involvement in negotiation, performance, or termination of the contract, and confusing representations suggesting one economic identity. Factors such as gross undercapitalization, common management, intermingled finances, absence of corporate formalities,

---

24) *Bernard Hanotiau, Chapter 1: Who Are the Parties to the Contract(s) or to the Arbitration Clause(s) Contained Therein? The Theories Applied by Courts and Arbitral Tribunals*, in Bernard Hanotiau, Complex Arbitrations: Multi-party, Multi-contract, Multi-issue – A comparative Study (Second Edition) International Arbitration Law Library, Volume 14, 2020, 16.

25) *Born, supra*, at 1559.

26) *Born, supra*, at 1559.

27) *Born, supra*, at 1560.

28) *Born, supra*, at 1547.

in terms of behavior and documentation, and coordinated conduct in contract execution all point toward a finding of implied consent.[29])

## C. Good Faith Based Theories

### 1. Equitable Estoppel

Estoppel, rooted in common law, is a well-recognized legal doctrine which can be invoked to preclude parties from denying that they are a party to arbitration (or other) agreements. In these jurisdictions, "estoppel" is defined in various ways, but generally means that a party is barred by considerations of good faith and equity from acting inconsistently with its own statements or conduct.[30])

As several US courts have held, if a non-signatory party seeks to exercise substantive rights under a contract which contains an arbitration clause, then this party has to be bound by the arbitration clause, too. As the courts have pointed out: "To allow [a plaintiff] to claim the benefit of the contract and simultaneously avoid its burdens would both disregard equity and contravene the purposes underlying enactment of the Arbitration Act."[31])

Estoppel found renewed force in *GE Energy Power Conversion France v Outokumpu Stainless USA (US Sup Ct, 2020)*, where the Court held that the New York Convention does not exclude domestic doctrines such as equitable estoppel. The ruling signalled that international enforcement need not rest solely on formal consent.[32])

### 2. Abuse of Rights

In civil-law systems, the functional equivalents to the estoppel are good faith and abuse of rights. Under Article 2 of Turkish Civil Code No. 2004 (*Türk Medeni Kanunu*), a right exercised contrary to its purpose constitutes abuse.[33])

---

[29]) Brekoulakis, *Chapter 24, supra,* at 713; *Born, supra,* at 1550.

[30]) *Born, supra,* at 1585.

[31]) *Stavros Brekoulakis, Chapter 8: Parties in International Arbitration: Consent v. Commercial Reality,* in Stavros Brekoulakis, Julian D.M. Lew, et al. (eds), The Evolution and Future of International Arbitration, International Arbitration Law Library, Volume 37, 130.

[32]) *GE Energy Power Conversion France SAS v Outokumpu Stainless USA LLC, 590 U.S. (2020).*

[33]) *Hatice Özdemir Kocasakal, Tahkim Anlaşmasının Dürüstlük Kuralı Çerçevesinde Üçüncü Kişilere Teşmili* (Extension of Arbitration Agreement to Third Parties within the Framework of the Principle of Good Faith), in Tahkim Anlaşması (Arbitration Agreement) (On İki Levha Publishing, 2020), 47.

Swiss jurisprudence has long invoked this principle to include non-signatories who actively benefited from a contract yet later denied arbitration.[34]

### 3. Piercing the Corporate Veil

The most extreme equitable tool is piercing the corporate veil. Authorities from all jurisdictions hold that a party who has not assented to a contract containing an arbitration clause may nonetheless be bound if that party is an "alter ego" of an entity that did execute or was otherwise a party to the agreement. This is a significant but exceptional departure from "*the fundamental principle ... [that] 'each company in a group of companies (a relatively modern concept) is a separate legal entity possessed of separate legal rights and liabilities*'".[35]

Veil-piercing criteria typically include complete domination and control, undercapitalization, disregard of corporate formalities, commingling of assets, and fraud or abuse of the corporate form. Tribunals occasionally pierce the veil to assert jurisdiction over a controlling parent where the subsidiary was a mere instrumentality used inequitably, though the remedy remains exceptional and fact-intensive.[36]

The remedy is exceptional: it aims not to enlarge consent but to prevent its abuse. As it is emphasized in the doctrine, veil-piercing is a "jurisdictional last resort", permissible only when necessary to prevent injustice.[37]

## IV. Comparative Approaches

### A. France

French jurisprudence views arbitration as autonomous from national contract law. In *Korsnas Marma v. Durand-Auzias*, the Court of Appeal of Paris noted that an arbitration clause in an international contract has autonomous validity and effectiveness, calling for extension to parties directly involved in contract performance and disputes, provided their activities raise the presumption that they were aware of the existence and scope of the arbitration clause, irrespective of whether they signed the contract.[38]

The *Cour de Cassation* has held that an arbitration clause binds all parties "*directly involved in the performance of the contract*".[39] Cases such as *Dow Chemical* demonstrate France's preference for inferred intent over written

[34] *Swiss Federal Tribunal, ATF 129 III 727, 735 (Butec).*
[35] *Born, supra,* at 1640.
[36] *Born, supra,* at 1645–1650.
[37] *Born, supra,* at 1650.
[38] *Hanotiau, Non-signatories, supra,* at 590.
[39] *Hanotiau, Non-signatories, supra,* at 591.

formality. The result is broad inclusion, justified by participation and international commercial practice.

## B. England

In contrast, English law adheres to strict contractual principles. Arbitration clauses bind only those who have expressly agreed to them. English courts are sceptical of the group-of-companies doctrine and maintain high clarity standards for intention to arbitrate.[40)]

*In Dallah Real Estate and Tourism Holding Co v Government of Pakistan, UK Supreme Court, Judgment of 3 November 2010, UKSC 46, Dallah Real Estate and Tourism Holding Co.* entered into a Memorandum of Understanding with the Government of Pakistan under which it agreed to purchase land and provide accommodation to pilgrims from Pakistan in Mecca. The Pakistan Government created a trust and subsequently Dallah entered into a formal agreement with the trust containing an arbitration clause. When disputes arose, Dallah invoked arbitration against the Pakistan Government before a French arbitral tribunal, with the Pakistan Government arguing that it was not party to the arbitration agreement since it had not signed the agreement.[41)]

The UK Supreme Court, whilst acknowledging the principle of kompetenz-kompetenz, *i.e.* that the tribunal can decide on its own jurisdiction, observed that Courts were not bound by the Tribunal's reasoning and findings. It held that when a party resists enforcement under Article V(1)(a) of New York Convention, the Court must "Revisit the tribunal's decision on jurisdiction". The Court refused enforcement of the Paris-seated ICC award, holding that Pakistan had never agreed to arbitrate.

## C. Switzerland

Swiss law strikes a balance. Under Article 178 Swiss PILA, an arbitration agreement is valid if it meets the requirements of any one of (i) the chosen law, (ii) the law governing the main contract, or (iii) Swiss law.[42)]

Swiss Federal Tribunal employs a two-step analysis: it first seeks actual common intent, then interprets according to the principle of confidence (*Vertrauensprinzip*) – how reasonable parties would have understood the clause in good faith.[43)]

---

40) *M.P. Bharucha, Sneha Jaisingh, and Shreya Gupta, The Extension of Arbitration Agreements to Non-Signatories – A Global Perspective, Indian Journal of Arbitration Law* (February 2016), 47–48.

41) *Ibid.* at 49.

42) Swiss PILA, Art. 178.

43) Voser, *supra*, at 165–166.

Academics characterize this as "consent theory plus": tribunals look for consent but may infer it when denial would amount to an abuse of rights.[44]) The *Butec* decision confirmed that the written-form requirement applies only to signatories, not to later-joined non-signatories whose inclusion rests on conduct.[45])

Furthermore, in the *Turkish Contractor* case, the Swiss Federal Tribunal held that a non-signatory Turkish contractor was bound by an arbitration clause where it had actively participated in contract performance and its conduct objectively manifested acceptance of the contractual framework, including the arbitration clause.[46])

Similarly, in the *Company Sale Guarantee* case, the Tribunal extended jurisdiction to non-signatory companies within a construction consortium that had jointly negotiated and performed the contract, reasoning that their integrated participation created a legitimate expectation of arbitral commitment.[47])

### D. United States

United States has developed robust estoppel and intertwined claims doctrines. U.S. courts have demonstrated greater willingness than many other authorities to apply alter ego analysis to subject non-signatories to arbitration agreements.[48])

Courts compel arbitration where a non-signatory seeks benefits under a contract containing an arbitration clause, or where claims are so closely related to the contract that arbitration is necessary to avoid inconsistent outcomes.[49])

## V. Enforcement Under the New York Convention

The inclusion of non-signatories finds its ultimate test not before arbitral tribunals, but before enforcement courts applying the New York Convention.

---

44) Voser, *supra,* at 175.
45) Mráz, 56; *Swiss Federal Tribunal, ATF 129 III 727 (Butec).*
46) *Swiss Federal Tribunal, 4P.126/2001 of 18 December 2001.*
47) *Swiss Federal Tribunal, 4P.48/2005 of 20 September 2005.*
48) *Born, supra,* at 1549.
49) *Hanotiau, Chapter 1, supra,* at 55.

## A. Article V(1)(a): Validity of the Arbitration Agreement

Article V(1)(a) of the New York Convention authorizes refusal of enforcement where "*the parties to the agreement … were under some incapacity, or the said agreement is not valid under the law to which the parties have subjected it*". The clause presupposes a clear notion of "the parties to the agreement". Yet, when arbitral tribunals rely on conduct-based or equity-based theories to include non-signatories, enforcement courts must determine whether such inclusion violates the New York Convention's requirement of a valid arbitration agreement.

The *Dallah Real Estate* and *Tourism Holding Co v Government of Pakistan* saga epitomizes this problem. The ICC tribunal in Paris extended the arbitration clause to Pakistan based on its participation in the project's negotiations. The Paris Court of Appeal upheld enforcement, emphasizing the "common intention" evidenced by conduct. However, the UK Supreme Court refused recognition under Article V(1)(a), finding that Pakistan had never consented in the manner required by English law.[50)]

Soon after the English Court's decision, the Paris Court of Appeal rejected the Government of Pakistan's application for annulment under Article 1502(1) of the French Code of Civil Procedure (*Code de procédure civile* – French CCP). The Paris Court of Appeal also applied French Law, *i.e.* looking into the parties' intentions and the decision in *Dalico*, but, unlike the UK Supreme Court, the Paris Court of Appeal had no difficulty in holding that the Government of Pakistan was intended to be a party to the arbitration agreement.[51)]

The two decisions, rendered on the same facts, show that "validity" under Article V(1)(a) depends less on treaty interpretation than on national conceptions of consent.

In contrast, the Swiss Federal Tribunal has tended to uphold awards where consent was functionally inferred under Article 178(2) Swiss PILA, reasoning that the Convention does not prohibit the application of good-faith principles.[52)] Similarly, the U.S. Supreme Court held that the Convention permits enforcement based on domestic doctrines such as equitable estoppel, thus confirming that functional consent can coexist with the Convention's validity requirement.[53)]

The emerging trend is to interpret Article V(1)(a) flexibly, allowing domestic doctrines – assignment, estoppel, good faith – to operate so long as

---

50) *Bharucha, Jaisingh, and Gupta, supra,* at 49–50.

51) *Bharucha, Jaisingh, and Gupta, supra,* at 50.

52) *Voser, supra,* at 175–178.

53) *GE Energy Power Conversion France SAS v Outokumpu Stainless USA LLC, 590 U.S. (2020).*

they reflect a rational connection between the party's conduct and the arbitration clause. What enforcement courts increasingly require is foreseeability: whether the non-signatory could reasonably have anticipated being bound.[54])

## B. Article V(2)(b): Public Policy and Due Process

The Convention also allows refusal where enforcement would violate the public policy of the enforcing state.[55]) Non-signatory enforcement challenges often invoke public policy under the guise of due process: that compelling a true non-consenting party to arbitrate offends fundamental fairness.

Courts would consider public policy *ex officio*, however, such claims are generally raised by the resisting party and not evaluated by the court itself. The standard applicable in annulment proceedings is the *lex fori* public policy, while recognition and enforcement courts would tend to apply the less stringent standard of international public policy. In any event, reliance on public policy manifests as a last resort when other arguments fail, and such arguments rarely succeed in invalidating non-signatory awards. In countries like France, where extension of arbitration agreements is accepted on essentially economic grounds, a public policy challenge against such awards would most likely be futile.[56])

In this regard, some courts treat inclusion without signature as a breach of due process. In *Westmoreland v Sadoux*, the U.S. Court of Appeals refused to enforce an award against a corporate officer, holding that binding him without clear consent, "Frustrates the ability of persons to settle their affairs against a predictable backdrop of legal rules-the cardinal prerequisite to all dispute resolution".[57])

# VI. The Turkish Perspective

Turkish arbitration law reflects a tension between contractual formalism and functional consent. Whilst Turkish courts and doctrine remain anchored in the principle that arbitration is founded on express and written consent, an evolving line of jurisprudence – strongly influenced by good faith – has

[54]) *Brekoulakis, Rethinking Consent, supra,* at 635.

[55]) Article V(2)(b) of the New York Convention.

[56]) *Vladimir Pavic, 'Non-Signatories' and the Long Arm of Arbitral Jurisdiction,* in P. Hay, L. Vekas, Y. Elkana, N. Dimitrijevic (eds), Resolving International Conflicts – Liber Amicorum Tibor Varady (CEU Press 2009), 227–228

[57]) *Westmoreland v Sadoux, 299 F.3d 462 (5th Cir. 2002).*

opened the door for the inclusion of non-signatories in limited but significant circumstances.[58)]

## A. The Starting Point: Formal Consent and the Relativity of Contracts

The Turkish legal system, consistent with its civil-law heritage, has long adhered to the principle of relativity of contracts. As a rule, a contract produces rights and obligations only between the parties who have signed it. This principle extends naturally to arbitration clauses: under Article 4(1) of the IAL and Article 412 of the CCP, the arbitration agreement must be in writing and signed by the parties.[59)]

The Turkish Court of Appeal has frequently reaffirmed this orthodoxy, emphasizing that arbitration is an exceptional jurisdiction requiring a clear waiver of access to state courts.[60)]

## B. The Emergence of Functional Consent: Good Faith as a Corrective Principle

Against this background, modern Turkish doctrine and arbitral reasoning have progressively embraced functional consent grounded in good faith and the prohibition of contradictory conduct. Article 2 of the Turkish Civil Code provides that every person must act in good faith in the exercise of rights, and that any abuse of rights is not protected by law.

This principle serves as a doctrinal bridge between strict formalism and commercial fairness. Where a non-signatory has participated in the negotiation, performance, or termination of a contract containing an arbitration clause,

---

58) *Kocasakal, supra,* at 35; *Mehmet Murat İnceoğlu, Cemile Demir Gökyayla, Tahkim Anlaşmasının Yetkisiz Temsilci Tarafından Yapıldığına İlişkin İddiaların Dürüstlük Kuralı Çerçevesinde Değerlendirilmesi* (Evaluation of Allegations Concerning the Conclusion of the Arbitration Agreement by an Unauthorized Representative Within the Framework of the Principle of Good Faith), PPIL 40(1) (2020), 404.

59) *Simel Sarıalioğlu, Tahkim Sözleşmesi Hazırlarken Dikkate Alınması Gerekenler* (Considerations While Drafting the Arbitration Agreement), in Tahkim Anlaşması (Arbitration Agreement), Vol 1, (On İki Levha Publishing, 2020), 129; *Süleyman Yasir Zorlu, Tahkim Anlaşmasının Yazılı Olma Şartı* (The Written Form Requirement for the Arbitration Agreement), in Tahkim Anlaşması (Arbitration Agreement), Vol 1 (On İki Levha Publishing, 2020), 105.

60) *The Turkish Court of Appeal (Yargıtay) General Assembly of the Civil Chambers, E. 2023/103 K. 2023/1185, 29.11.2023.*

and where its conduct has led the other party to reasonably believe that it accepts arbitration, good faith may justify inclusion.[61])

Turkish scholars – including Pekcanıtez, Özdemir Kocasakal, Demirkol, and Yeşilova[62]) – have emphasized that this approach does not undermine the written form requirement, because the written clause remains in place; what is extended is its subjective reach, not its formal validity. In this sense, Turkish law mirrors the Swiss "consent theory plus" and the French concept of common intention, but with a narrower, equity-based rationale rooted in Turkish Civil Code Article 2.

## C. The Prohibition of Contradictory Conduct (*Venire Contra Factum Proprium*)

A particularly powerful tool in Turkish law is the doctrine of *venire contra factum proprium*, a subset of the good-faith principle. It prevents a party from acting inconsistently with its prior behavior when such inconsistency harms another's legitimate expectations.[63]) In the arbitration context, a non-signatory who has benefited from or relied upon a contract containing an arbitration clause cannot later deny the clause's applicability.

## D. Conceptual Position: Turkish Law Between Formalism and Equity

In sum, Turkish law stands between the poles of formal consent and equitable inclusion. Whilst it remains formally conservative, its courts and scholars – most prominently Pekcanıtez – have developed a nuanced doctrine that permits the extension of arbitration agreements in the presence of active participation, continuity of legal or economic identity, or contradictory conduct, all under the umbrella of good faith. The guiding thread is not a transposition of foreign doctrines like the group of companies, but a native synthesis rooted in Turkish Civil Code Article 2, ensuring that arbitration remains both consensual and just.

By grounding inclusion in good faith and legitimate expectation, Turkish law mirrors the Swiss functional model whilst maintaining fidelity to its codified civil-law structure. In doing so, it provides a distinctive contribution to comparative arbitration theory: a model where formal consent and moral fairness coexist in pragmatic equilibrium.

---

61) *İnceoğlu, Gökyayla, supra,* at 410.

62) *Kocasakal, supra,* at 29; *Berk Demirkol, Tahkim Anlaşmasının Üçüncü Kişilere Teşmili* (Extension of Arbitration Agreement to Third Parties), in Tahkim Anlaşması (Arbitration Agreement), Vol 1 (On İki Levha Publishing, 2020), 307.

63) *Kocasakal, supra,* at 33.

## VII. Conclusion

The inclusion of non-signatories in arbitration lies at the intersection of consent and commercial necessity.

Contractual doctrines (assignment, agency, succession) maintain conceptual purity; equitable doctrines (estoppel, abuse of rights) safeguard fairness. The group of companies theory pushes further, accepted in France, rejected in England, and treated with nuanced restraint in Switzerland and Türkiye.

Predictability under the New York Convention demands a common denominator: foreseeability. A non-signatory should be bound only if, through its conduct, it could reasonably foresee being treated as a party to the arbitration agreement. That standard preserves both efficiency and legitimacy.

A general trend is emerging in favor of extending arbitration agreements to non-signatories, with the only bar being that the parties must have intended it to be so and that an arbitration agreement was concluded by the parties either expressly or impliedly.

In advocacy and practice, the recommended approach is to emphasize genuine common intention or clear benefits-and-burdens logic where possible, and to be candid about jurisdictional variance to mitigate enforcement risk.

Türkiye's jurisprudence demonstrates that a system can remain faithful to formal consent yet evolve through good faith to meet modern commerce's complexity. As arbitration grows more multi-party, maintaining this equilibrium will be crucial to its credibility and enforceability worldwide.

The future of arbitration depends not on abandoning consent but on refining it – transforming it from a static formality into a dynamic expectation grounded in conduct, equity, and legitimate commercial expectations. Only through such evolution can arbitration remain both consensual in principle and effective in practice.

# The State of Emergency Arbitration: Between Promise and Performance

*Eric Leikin/Sofia Svinkovskaya*

## I. Introduction

One of the key advantages of arbitration is offering parties a measure of control, with disputes decided by independent and qualified decision makers chosen by the parties themselves. Yet this key strength reveals a procedural vulnerability at the very start of the arbitral process – specifically, before the constitution of the arbitral tribunal, when arbitration effectively stands still for weeks or even months. During that time, valuable assets can be dissipated, evidence destroyed or lost, contractual obligations altered, leaving one party exposed and disadvantaged and the arbitration at risk of being rendered meaningless.

Historically, the only available remedy during this critical gap before the tribunal's constitution was recourse to national courts for interim relief. Such a solution, however, appears to be fundamentally at odds with the very decision to arbitrate and begs the question: why should parties, having deliberately chosen arbitration to escape the publicity and procedural formality of state court litigation, be forced to return to that same system simply to obtain urgent protection? The development of emergency arbitration can be seen as a direct response to this dilemma, and its fundamental appeal is the continuity it provides by allowing parties to seek urgent relief from an independent arbitrator within the same institutional framework as the main dispute, ensuring procedural coherence and preserving the confidentiality that parties expect from arbitration.

Over the past decade, emergency arbitration has developed from a novel concept into a standard fixture within the rules of most major arbitral institutions. Yet, empirical data suggests that the mechanism is used relatively sparingly. Moreover, the enforceability of emergency arbitrator decisions continues to differ across jurisdictions, with courts divided on whether such decisions possess the same status as final awards under the New York Convention. To address these shortcomings, in recent years several arbitral institutions and key arbitral jurisdictions have undertaken efforts to refine and adapt the framework for emergency arbitration, aiming to enhance its effectiveness and enforceability.

This article examines how emergency arbitration operates within the broader effort to make arbitration more efficient and responsive. It outlines how the mechanism functions in practice, examines recent institutional and judicial developments, and analyses what empirical evidence reveals about its usage and performance. In doing so, it explores whether emergency arbitration represents a true innovation and to what extent its initial promise has translated into actual utility for parties.

## II. The Genesis and Function of Emergency Arbitration

Historically, the need to seek urgent relief exposed a core vulnerability in the arbitral process – without an impaneled arbitral tribunal, parties seeking urgent relief had little choice but to turn to national courts.[1]) While this recourse can be effective, particularly in jurisdictions with a reputation for speed and efficiency,[2]) it is not a universally reliable solution. In many jurisdictions, court proceedings are notoriously slow, and the potential for multiple levels of appeal often means that urgent relief may not be granted in time.

More fundamentally, this forced reliance on domestic courts directly undermines the core advantages of arbitration, re-exposing parties to a system they may have sought to avoid due to concerns over impartiality, efficiency, and the lack of specialized commercial expertise among judges.[3]) Moreover, the public nature of court proceedings further compromises the confidentiality that parties sought to preserve, whereas procedural formalities do not leave any room for flexibility required in complex cross-border disputes. The territorial constraints of the domestic court system would also sometimes require a party to initiate an inefficient and expensive exercise of seeking interim relief in multiple parallel legal proceedings across different jurisdictions.[4])

---

[1]) Amir Ghaffari & Emmylou Walters, *The Emergency Arbitrator: The Dawn of a New Age?* 30(1) Arb. Int'l 155 (2014); Patricia Shaughnessy, *The Emergency Arbitrator* in Shaughnesy/Tung, *The Powers and Duties of an Arbitrator: Liber Amicorum Pierre A. Karrer* 340 (2017); Hermann J Knott & Martin Winkler, *The Arbitrator and the Arbitration Procedure, Emergency Arbitration Securing Advantages at an Early Stage* in Klausegger/Klein/Kremslehner/Petsche/Pitkowitz/Welser/Zeiler (eds.), Austrian Yearbook on International Arbitration 2022, 171–172.

[2]) Ghaffari & Walters, *Emergency Arbitrator* 155.

[3]) Gary B Born, *International Commercial Arbitration* § 17.01 (3rd ed. 2021, updated 2023); Ghaffari & Walters, *Emergency Arbitrator* 155; Knott & Winkler, *Emergency Arbitration* 171. *See* Shaughnessy, *The Emergency Arbitrator* 340.

[4]) *See* Cameron Sim, *Emergency Arbitration Meets the Courts* in Schöldström/Danielsson, Stockholm Arbitration Yearbook 2023, 97 (2023).

Collectively, these limitations expose a structural gap: lack of an internal, coherent mechanism capable of delivering urgent relief before the constitution of the tribunal within the arbitration realm.[5]) As an innovation conceived by arbitral institutions to provide urgent protection entirely within the arbitral framework, the emergency arbitrator mechanism was intended to address this procedural deficiency.[6])

## A. Origins and Institutional Adoption

A precursor to modern emergency arbitration emerged in 1990 with the International Chamber of Commerce's ("ICC") introduction of the "Pre-Arbitral Referee Procedure" to address urgent issues that arise during contracts – particularly long-term ones – when waiting for a final court or arbitral decision is impractical.[7]) This framework allowed parties in time-sensitive contractual disputes to obtain temporary orders from a designated "Referee", empowered to grant urgent protective or restorative measures, require payments, enforce contractual duties, and preserve evidence.[8]) These orders were strictly provisional and did not interfere with the authority of the tribunal or court deciding the case's merits.[9])

The Pre-Arbitral Referee Procedure enjoyed very limited use: only 14 cases were brought under its rules over a 24-year period.[10]) This may be attributed to two design elements of the mechanism: first, unlike contemporary "opt-out" systems, the Pre-Arbitral Referee Procedure required parties to "opt-in" through explicit written agreement, as Pre-Arbitral Referee Procedure was not part of the ICC Arbitration Rules.[11]) Second, the characterization of the decision-maker as a "Referee" rather than an arbitrator suggested a purely contractual rather than arbitral authority and thereby undermined confidence in the process.[12]) Nevertheless, despite being rarely used, the Pre-Arbitral Referee Procedure was a seminal development that paved the way for the evolution of contemporary emergency arbitration frameworks.

---

[5]) *See* Ghaffari & Walters, *Emergency Arbitrator* 155; Born, *International Commercial Arbitration*, § 17.02[A][5][d]; Guilherme Piccardi, *17. Emergency arbitration: historical context, current landscape, and practical issues* in Carlos González-Bueno (ed.), 40 under 40 International Arbitration 259–260 (2024).

[6]) ICC Commission on Arbitration and ADR, Report on Emergency Arbitrator Proceedings, at p. 3 (2019); Andrea Carlevaris & José Ricardo Feris, *Running in the ICC Emergency Arbitrator Rules: The First Ten Cases* 25(1) ICC Int'l Court of Arb. Bull. 3, 22 (2014); Sim, *supra*, at 96–99.

[7]) ICC Pre-Arbitral Referee Rules (1990/2012).

[8]) ICC Pre-Arbitral Referee Rules (1990/2012), p. 2.

[9]) ICC Pre-Arbitral Referee Rules (1990/2012), Introduction and Art. 2(4).

[10]) Carlevaris & Feris, *supra*, at p. 2.

[11]) ICC Pre-Arbitral Referee Rules (1990/2012), p. 1.

[12]) Carlevaris & Feris, *supra*, at p. 2.

The institutionalization of emergency arbitration began to take shape in 2006 with the *International Centre for Dispute Resolution ("ICDR"),* which pioneered an opt-out EA mechanism in its rules.[13]) Gradually, other major institutions followed suit and incorporated similar mechanisms into their rules by mid-2010s.[14]) Despite its now-established presence, applications for emergency arbitration remain relatively infrequent – a point addressed in more detail below – but the very availability of the mechanism enhances the autonomy and effectiveness of the arbitral process, reducing the need to resort to domestic courts.

This broad institutional embrace of emergency arbitration, however, has not been universal. Among leading arbitral institutions, the Vienna International Arbitral Centre ("VIAC") remains one of the few that has not adopted emergency arbitration provisions. The Vienna Rules contain no mechanism for an emergency arbitrator, a deliberate choice the institution attributes to concerns of enforceability, cost-effectiveness and institutional practicality, given the uncertain legal status of emergency arbitrator decisions and the effective availability of interim relief from Austrian courts.[15]) Like VIAC, the German Arbitration Institute ("DIS") also does not have an emergency arbitrator mechanism; instead, DIS Rules empower arbitral tribunal to grant interim relief while explicitly preserving the traditional role of national courts as a parallel forum available to parties at any time.[16])

---

[13]) ICDR Rules (2006), Art. 37.

[14]) The Stockholm Chamber of Commerce ("**SCC**") introduced an emergency arbitrator procedure in its 2010 Rules; *see* SCC Rules (2010), App. II. In the same year, the Singapore International Arbitration Centre ("**SIAC**") adopted comparable provisions; *see* SIAC Rules (2010), Sch. 1. The Swiss Arbitration Centre followed in 2012; *see* Swiss Rules (2012), Art. 43. ICC also incorporated provisions in its 2012 Rules; *see* ICC Rules (2012), Art. 29 and App. V. The Hong Kong International Arbitration Centre ("**HKIAC**") added its provisions in 2013; *see* HKIAC Rules (2013), Art. 23 and Sch. 4. Finally, the London Court of International Arbitration ("**LCIA**") incorporated its provisions in 2014; *see* LCIA Rules (2014), Art. 9B.

[15]) VIAC, *VIAC Arbitration – Vienna Rules 2021: A Step-by-Step Guide*, at p. 44, https://www.viac.eu/wp-content/uploads/2025/01/VIAC-arbitration-Vienna-Rules-2021-a-step-by-step-guide.pdf (last visited Oct. 17, 2025). *See also*, Mishcon de Reya, *A Q&A with the Secretary General of the Vienna International Arbitral Centre*, at pp. 2–3, https://www.viac.eu/wp-content/uploads/2025/01/A-QA-with-the-Secretary-General-of-the-Vienna-International-Arbitral-Centre.pdf (last visited Oct. 17, 2025). Austrian commentators have noted this caution is well-founded, as the legal status of an emergency arbitrator and the enforceability of their orders under Austrian law remains disputed. *See, e.g.*, Lisa Beisteiner, *The Award and the Courts, To Be or Not to Be an Arbitrator – On the Nature of Emergency Arbitration* in Klausegger/Klein/Kremslehner/Petsche/Pitkowitz/Welser/Zeiler, Austrian Yearbook on International Arbitration 2022, 289, 292, 329.

[16]) DIS Rules (2018), Arts. 25.1, 25.3; *see also*, Bernard Bell, *Arbitration or Court Proceedings in Emergencies – Tipping the Scale from a German Perspective*, Kluwer Arbitration Blog (Feb. 8, 2021), https://legalblogs.wolterskluwer.com/arbitration-blog/

## B. The Lifecycle of Emergency Arbitration

In modern arbitration practice, the framework for emergency arbitration is characterized by two distinct yet complementary pillars: procedurally, the rules of most major institutions share a common architecture focused on efficiency progressing from application to a decision in a matter of weeks. Substantively, practice appears to be guided by a transnational standard for relief derived from the international arbitral practice. Recent institutional reforms have refined this mechanism even further, streamlining procedures to deliver faster and more effective relief.

### 1. Commencing and Conducting an Emergency Arbitration

Most major institutional rules allow an application for emergency arbitration to be filed before, concurrently with, or after the submission of the request for arbitration (or notice of arbitration, collectively "RfA"), provided it precedes the constitution of the main arbitral tribunal.[17])

The jurisdiction of the emergency arbitrator is generally not exclusive. Modern arbitration framework provides for concurrent jurisdiction, allowing both arbitral tribunals and national courts to grant provisional relief unless the parties agree otherwise.[18]) This is mirrored in the majority of institutional rules, which preserve a party's right to seek urgent interim relief from a competent judicial authority: The LCIA Rules, for example, state that the emergency arbitrator procedure *"shall not be treated as an alternative to or substitute for"* the right to apply to a court, while the ICC Rules provide that such an application *"shall not be deemed to be an infringement or a waiver of the arbitration agreement"*.[19])

---

arbitration-or-court-proceedings-in-emergencies-tipping-the-scale-from-a-german-perspective/.

[17]) *See, e.g.,* ICC Rules (2021), Art. 29(1); SIAC Rules (2025), Sch. 1, para. 2; HKIAC Rules (2024), Sch. 4, para. 1; SCC Rules (2023), App. II, Art. 1(1); Swiss Rules (2021), Art. 43(1).

[18]) For a comprehensive discussion of this principle, *see, e.g.,* Born, *supra,* at § 17.02[E]; Philippe Cavalieros & Janet Kim, *Emergency Arbitrators Versus the Courts: From Concurrent Jurisdiction to Practical Considerations,* in Maxi Scherer (ed), Journal of Int'l Arb., p. 283 (2018); Sim, *Emergency Arbitration Meets the Courts* 99.

[19]) *See* LCIA Rules (2020), Art. 9.13; ICC Rules (2021), Art. 29(7). Similar provisions exist in other major institutional rules. *See, e.g.,* HKIAC Rules (2024), Sch. 4, para. 20 ("The Emergency Arbitrator Procedure is not intended to prevent any party from seeking urgent interim or conservatory measures from a competent authority at any time."); SIAC Rules (2025), Rule 45.2 ("A request for interim or conservatory relief made by a party to a judicial authority is not incompatible with these Rules and shall not be considered a breach or waiver of the arbitration agreement."); SCC Rules (2023), Art. 37(5) ("A request for interim measures made by a party to a judicial authority is not incompatible with the arbitration agreement or with the Arbitration Rules."); Swiss Rules (2021), Art. 29(5) ("A request for interim measures addressed by any party to a

In practice, however, the approach of national courts to the concurrent jurisdiction to grant emergency relief has been cautious, as courts appear to be reluctant to intervene when an emergency arbitrator mechanism is available. In *Gerald Metals v Timis* case, the English High Court declined to intervene after the LCIA refused to appoint an emergency arbitrator, holding that it could only act where the arbitral process was *"inadequate, or where the practical ability is lacking to exercise those powers"*.[20]) It emphasized that the LCIA's refusal to appoint an emergency arbitrator did not demonstrate such inadequacy, stating that *"the only inference"* to be drawn from LCIA's rejection was that the institution had considered the matter and *"was not persuaded that the application was so urgent that it needed to be decided before the arbitral tribunal is constituted"*.[21]) Similarly, in *Ashwani Minda v U-shin* case, the Delhi High Court rejected an attempt to seek emergency relief before national court after a failed emergency arbitrator application. The Court held that the applicants had *"invoked the mechanism of the Emergency Arbitrator and invited a detailed and reasoned order"*, and thus it was *"not open for the Applicants to take a second bite at the cherry"*.[22]) The Court also noted that the petition was *"really in the nature of an appeal pointing out flaws and infirmities in the order of the Emergency Arbitrator"* and concluded that the applicants had *"consciously chosen to tread on a path and cannot turn around only because they were unsuccessful"*.[23]) This practice demonstrates that courts are increasingly deferential to arbitration and will intervene only when emergency arbitration is not available to provide an effective remedy.

To ensure that the emergency proceedings are properly anchored to the subsequent arbitration proceedings, the rules typically impose strict deadlines for filing the request for arbitration. For instance, the RfA must be filed within 10 days under the ICC and Swiss Rules[24]) and within 7 days under the HKIAC and SIAC Rules.[25]) The SCC Rules tie the deadline for commencing main arbitration to the issuance of the decision of emergency arbitrator ("EA Decision"), providing that it ceases to be binding if arbitration is not formally commenced *"within 30 days from the date of the emergency decision"*.[26]) In

judicial authority shall not be deemed to be incompatible with the Arbitration Agreement, or to constitute a waiver of that agreement.").

[20]) *Gerald Metals S.A v. Timis & Ors*, EWHC 2327 (CH), para. 8 (Eng.).

[21]) *Gerald Metals S.A v. Timis & Ors*, EWHC 2327 (CH), para. 9 (Eng.).

[22]) *Ashwani Minda & Anr. v. U-Shin Ltd & Anr.*, OMP (I) (COMM.) 90/2020 (Delhi High Ct. 2020), para. 55 (India).

[23]) *Ashwani Minda & Anr. v. U-Shin Ltd & Anr.*, OMP (I) (COMM.) 90/2020 (Delhi High Ct. 2020), para. 56 (India).

[24]) *See* ICC Rules (2021), App. V, Art. 1(6); Swiss Rules (2021), Art. 43(3).

[25]) *See* HKIAC Rules (2024), Sch. 4, para. 21; SIAC Rules (2025), Sch. 1, para. 6.

[26]) SCC Rules (2023), App. II, Art. 9(4)(iii).

contrast, the LCIA mandates that an EA application must be filed *"together with a copy of the Request* [for arbitration] *or a copy of the Response"*.[27])

Together with the application, the requesting party must pay a fixed deposit to cover both the administrative fees of the institution as well as the fees and expenses of the emergency arbitrator.[28]) While the upfront cost is initially borne by the applicant, the rules generally provide for its apportionment in the EA Decision, subject to final review and allocation by the arbitral tribunal in the main arbitration.[29])

Following the submission of an application, the administering institution typically undertakes a screening process and may exercise its discretion to reject it for a manifest lack of jurisdiction or if the emergency provisions are otherwise inapplicable.[30]) If application is accepted, the emergency arbitrator is appointed expeditiously, generally within 24 to 72 hours.[31]) Upon appointment, the emergency arbitrator is subject to the same duties of impartiality and independence as a tribunal member and may be challenged, albeit under significantly condensed timelines.[32])

The emergency arbitrator generally has broad discretion as to the structure and conduct of the proceedings and can tailor the process to the urgency of the matter, including by deciding the application on a documents-only basis.[33]) In practice, emergency arbitration is a compressed "mini-arbitration" with its own set of submissions and, often, a hearing. Such a process requires significant

[27]) LCIA Rules (2020), Art. 9.5.

[28]) The emergency arbitration fees vary across institutions. *See, e.g.*, SCC Rules (2023), App. II, Art. 10(2) (EUR 20,000); SIAC Rules (2025), Sch. 1, para. 4 and Sch. of Fees (S$ 35,000); Swiss Rules (2021), App. B, sec. 1.5 (CHF 25,000); HKIAC Rules (2024), Sch. 4, para. 5 and Sch. of Costs (2024) (HKD 250,000); ICC Rules (2021), App. V, Art. 7(1) (US$ 40,000); LCIA Rules (2020), Art. 9.5 and Sch. of Costs (2023) (£ 35,000).

[29]) *See, e.g.*, SCC Rules (2023), App. II, Art. 10(5); HKIAC Rules (2024), Sch. 4, para. 16; SIAC Rules (2025), Sch. 1, para. 24; LCIA Rules (2020), Art. 9.10; Swiss Rules (2021), Art. 43(9).

[30]) *See, e.g.*, SCC Rules (2023), App. II, Art. 4(2); Swiss Rules (2021), Art. 43(2); ICC Rules (2021), App. V, Art. 1(5); LCIA Rules (2020), Art. 9.6; HKIAC Rules (2024), Sch. 4, para. 4; SIAC Rules (2025), Sch. 1, para. 7.

[31]) *See, e.g.*, HKIAC Rules (2024), Sch. 4, para. 4 (within 24 hours); SCC Rules (2023), App. II, Art. 4(1) (within 24 hours); SIAC Rules (2025), Sch. 1, para. 7 (within 24 hours); ICC Rules (2021), App. V, Art. 2(1) (within two days); LCIA Rules (2020), Art. 9.6 (within three days). Swiss Rules (2021), Art. 43(2), in turn, require an appointment "as soon as possible".

[32]) *See, e.g.*, SCC Rules (2023), App. II, Art. 4(3) (24-hour deadline); SIAC Rules (2025), Sch. 1, para. 9 (24-hour deadline); ICC Rules (2021), App. V, Art. 3(1) (three-day deadline); HKIAC Rules (2024), Sch. 4, para. 7 (three day deadline); Swiss Rules (2021), Art. 43(4) (three-day deadline).

[33]) *See, e.g.*, ICC Rules (2021), App. V, Art. 5(2); LCIA Rules (2020), Art. 9.7; HKIAC Rules (2024), Sch. 4, para. 10; SIAC Rules (2025), Sch. 1, para. 13; SCC Rules (2023), App. II, Art. 7; Swiss Rules (2021), Art. 43(6).

availability from the arbitrator and imposes a dual burden on the applicant, who must concurrently manage the emergency proceeding and prepare its case for the filing of the RfA in the main arbitration.

The decision of emergency arbitration must be issued within a prescribed period, typically ranging from 5 to 15 days, although this deadline may be extended by the administering institution where the rules allow.[34]) The form of the EA Decision – another key variable – also differs across institutions. The ICC Rules, for example, mandate the issuance of an "order", a choice that circumvents the ICC Court's formal award scrutiny process.[35]) In contrast, other leading institutions (such as LCIA, SIAC, ICDR and HKIAC) explicitly empower the emergency arbitrator to render an "award",[36]) while the SCC uses the distinct term "emergency decision".[37])

Irrespective of its formal designation as an "order", "award", or "decision", the rules generally provide that the EA Decision is binding on the parties upon its issuance.[38]) Its authority, however, is provisional in nature, which is reflected by the ultimate authority of the arbitral tribunal in the main arbitration to confirm, modify, or vacate the emergency arbitrator's decision.[39]) While it reflects the auxiliary function of emergency arbitration to serve as an interim remedy in urgent circumstances that does not usurp the final authority of the main arbitral tribunal, the lack of finality continues to raise concerns about the enforceability of EA Decisions, regardless of what label they carry.[40])

---

[34]) *See, e.g.,* SCC Rules (2023), App. II, Art. 8(1) (five days; extendable by the Board); HKIAC Rules (2024), Sch. 4, para. 12 (14 days; extendable by HKIAC); LCIA Rules (2020), Art. 9.8 (14 days; extendable by the LCIA Court); SIAC Rules (2025), Sch. 1, para. 17 (14 days; extendable by the Registrar); ICC Rules (2021), App. V, Art. 6(4) (15 days; extendable by the President); Swiss Rules (2021), Art. 43(7) (15 days; extendable by the Court).

[35]) ICC Rules of Arbitration (2021), App. V, Art. 6(1).

[36]) *See* LCIA Rules (2020), Art. 9.8 ("order or award"); SIAC Rules (2025), Sch. 1, para. 17 ("order or award"); HKIAC Rules (2024), Sch. 4, para. 12 ("decision, order or award"); ICDR Rules (2021), Art. 7(4) ("order or award"). *See also*, Swiss Rules (2021), Arts. 43(8) and 29(2). Article 43(8) provides that an emergency arbitrator's decision has "the same effects as a decision pursuant to Article 29." Article 29(2) in turn states: "Interim measures may be granted in the form of an interim award."

[37]) SCC Arbitration Rules (2023), App. II, Art. 8(1).

[38]) *See, e.g.,* SIAC Rules (2025), Sch. 1, para. 23; SCC Rules (2023), App. II, Arts. 9(1), 9(3); HKIAC Rules (2024), Sch. 4, para. 17; ICC Rules (2021), Art. 29(2); LCIA Rules (2020), Arts. 9.9 and 26.8; Swiss Rules (2021), Art. 16(1).

[39]) *See, e.g.,* ICC Rules (2021), Art. 29(3); SIAC Rules (2025), Sch. 1, para. 21; LCIA Rules (2020), Art. 9.11; HKIAC Rules (2024), Sch. 4, para. 18(a); SCC Rules (2023), App. II, Art. 9(5); Swiss Rules (2021), Art. 43(8).

[40]) *See, e.g.,* Born, *supra*, at §17.03[A]; Cavalieros & Kim, *Emergency Arbitrators Versus the Courts: From Concurrent Jurisdiction to Practical Considerations*, p. 287 (2018).

## 2. The Scope of Emergency Relief

Through emergency arbitration, parties can request a wide array of remedies, which are functionally equivalent to the interim measures that may be ordered by an arbitral tribunal in the main arbitration. While the scope is generally wide, the relief is limited to the parties in the arbitration, and must not overstep mandatory provisions of applicable national laws or the specific terms of the parties' arbitration agreement.

The most commonly requested form of relief concerns preserving the current state of affairs,[41]) such as contractual or legal relationships, as well as relevant factual circumstances, until the primary underlying dispute is resolved in the main arbitration.[42]) The underlying purpose of this category of emergency orders is to avert changes that could cause serious harm to the other party during the course of the proceedings,[43]) or undermine the enforceability of a future award.[44]) Some institutional rules, such as those of HKIAC, now explicitly codify this power, allowing an emergency arbitrator to order a party to *"maintain or restore the status quo pending determination of the dispute"*.[45])

In practice, the requested measures within this category often include requests to prevent the disruption of agreements, such as restraining the termination of contracts, the disclosure of trade secrets or breach of a non-competition clause.[46]) In a recently reported case, an emergency arbitrator ordered an ex-Meta employee to refrain from promoting and distributing a memoir that allegedly contained confidential company information.[47]) Other examples include requests to i) enjoin the enforcement of bank guarantees or letters of credit,[48]) ii) halt pursuit of parallel litigation,[49]) iii) preserve assets and property, like requesting placement of funds into escrow account, or seeking orders to prevent a party from transferring equity interests or disposing

---

[41]) ICC Report on Emergency Arbitrator Proceedings indicates that 51 out of the first 80 ICC EA Applications concerned preserving the status quo. *See* p. 40.

[42]) *See, e.g.*, Born, *supra*, at § 17.02[G][a]; Cavalieros & Kim, *supra*, at 275.

[43]) *See, e.g.*, Born, *supra*, at § 17.01.

[44]) Born, *supra*, at § 17.02[G][4][a]; *see* Markus Wirth, *Interim or Preventive Measures in Support of International Arbitration in Switzerland*, ASA Bull., p. 33 (2000).

[45]) HKIAC Rules (2024), Art. 23.3(a). This power is extended to the emergency arbitrator by Sch. 4, para. 11, which applies Art. 23 to emergency arbitrator proceedings.

[46]) *See, e.g.*, Born, *supra*, at § 17.02[G][4][a]. *See also*, SCC Arbitration Institute, SCC Practice Note on Emergency Arbitrator Decisions 2019–2022, at pp. 10–11 (2023).

[47]) *Meta Platforms, Inc. v. Wynn-Williams*, ICDR Emergency Proceeding (2024).

[48]) *See, e.g.*, SCC Arbitration Institute, SCC Practice Note on Emergency Arbitrator Decisions 2017–2018, p. 3 (2020); ICC Report on Emergency Arbitrator Proceedings, para. 179.

[49]) *See* Born, *supra*, at § 17.02[G][j]; ICC Report on Emergency Arbitrator Proceedings, para. 179. SCC case law also includes requests for orders Both the ICC and SCC reports confirm that parties have sought anti-suit injunctions. *See* ICC Report on Emergency Arbitrator Proceedings, para. 179; SCC Practice Note on Emergency Arbitrator Decisions 2019–2022, p. 6.

of company assets,[50]) and iv) protect the physical subject matter of the dispute by means of inspection or its placement into appropriate custody.[51])

A party can also request emergency arbitrator to issue an order for specific performance, compelling the respondent to perform a specific act, for example, to maintain existing supply arrangements or provide access to information.[52]) In one SCC arbitration, the emergency arbitrator had ordered the respondent to continue the performance of its contractual obligations relating to sales orders placed by the claimant.[53]) In this case, the emergency arbitrator recognized the *"very special"* relationship between the parties in a niche market for specialized equipment, and held that the respondent's non-compliance would irreparably hurt the claimant's reputation with intermediaries and customers.[54])

However, a fundamental limitation on an emergency arbitrator's authority is the duty to refrain from prejudging the merits of the underlying dispute.[55]) Requests for specific performance can create a particular tension with this principle, as granting the relief may require a preliminary assessment of the very contractual obligations at the heart of the core dispute. The recent case of *Beyond Gravity v. Ensign-Bickford Aerospace & Defense* is a good example of that: here, the ICC emergency arbitrator refused to grant a preliminary injunction that would have ordered Ensign-Bickford to continue supplying certain equipment at agreed-upon prices.[56]) In his reasoning, while finding the application inadmissible primarily for lack of urgency, the emergency arbitrator held that he could not decide whether Ensign-Bickford was obliged to provide

50) *See* Carlevaris & Feris, *supra*, at p. 33. The ICC Report on Emergency Arbitrator Proceedings found that requests to preserve assets were common, specifically noting applications for the *"preservation of assets or property"* and the *"transfer of money into an escrow account (in seven cases)". See,* p. 29, 39; SCC Practice Note on Emergency Arbitrator Decisions 2017–2018, p. 5. In the investment arbitration context, *see, e.g., Liormand Holdings Ltd. v. Republic of Armenia*, SCC Emergency Arbitration No. 2019/143, Decision on Interim Measures (Apr. 2, 2020) (ordering a state to refrain from enforcing laws aimed at expropriating the claimant's energy company).

51) *See* Born, *supra note* 1, at §17.02[G][4][g]. An SCC case involved a request to "prevent the respondent from delivering the product to the third-party buyer." *See*, SCC Practice Note on Emergency Arbitrator Decisions 2019–2022, at p. 9.

52) *See, e.g.*, Born, *supra note* 1, § 17.02[G][4][c]; *See* ICC Report on Emergency Arbitrator Proceedings, para. 179 (2019).

53) Case 6 in SCC Practice Note on Emergency Arbitrator Decisions 2019–2022, pp. 13–14.

54) *Id.* at 13.

55) *See, e.g.*, ICC Commission on Arbitration and ADR, Report on Emergency Arbitrator Proceedings, para. 163 ("When deciding applications for emergency relief, the EA should avoid prejudging or predetermining the dispute itself.").

56) *Beyond Gravity Sweden AB v. Ensign-Bickford Aerospace & Defense Co.*, ICC Case No. 29155/HBH (EA), Emergency Arbitrator's Order (Feb. 7, 2025).

the equipment, as this was precisely the *"issue for the arbitral tribunal* [to] *decide on the merits of the dispute".*[57])

Other practical examples of requested relief are predominantly financial in nature, such as orders for security for claims, requiring preservation of assets or providing a guarantee to ensure that a final award will not be rendered meaningless,[58]) or requests for security for costs, aimed at providing financial assurance for the opposing party's legal costs.[59]) Parties have also pursued interim payment orders, which mandate the payment of largely uncontested sums; however, such relief can be seen as a form of a partial award on the merits and is therefore granted with caution.[60])

The emergency arbitration practice demonstrates that the scope of available emergency relief is fairly broad. However, granting such measures is contingent upon the applicant's ability to satisfy the substantive criteria that govern the issuance of emergency relief, which represent a demanding threshold for any party seeking urgent protection.

## 3. The Substantive Test for Emergency Relief

The substantive standard for emergency relief starts with the requirement of urgency: an applicant must first and foremost demonstrate that the requested measure cannot await the constitution of an arbitral tribunal.[61]) In addition to being an admissibility requirement, some emergency arbitrators may treat urgency as part of the substantive test on the merits.[62]) Within the ICC practice, the Report of the ICC Commission on Arbitration and ADR on Emergency Arbitrator Proceedings ("ICC EA Report") notes that the distinction has strategic implications, as a dismissal on admissibility grounds alone in this case allows the applicant to re-argue the urgency aspect with the request for interim measures before the constituted tribunal.[63])

---

[57]) *Beyond Gravity Sweden AB v. Ensign-Bickford Aerospace & Defense Co.*, ICC Case No. 29155/HBH (EA), Emergency Arbitrator's Order (Feb. 7, 2025), para. 52.

[58]) *See, e.g.*, Born, *supra*, at § 17.02[G][4][d]. The UNCITRAL Model Law, for instance, codifies the power to order measures that *"provide a means of preserving assets out of which a subsequent award may be satisfied".* UNCITRAL Model Law on International Commercial Arbitration, Art. 17(2)(c) (2006).

[59]) *See, e.g.*, LCIA Rules (2020), Art. 25(2). *See* Born, *supra*, at §17.02[G][4][e]. *See, e.g.*, SCC Practice Note on Emergency Arbitrator Decisions 2019–2022, p. 7.

[60]) The ICC Report on Emergency Arbitrator Proceedings identifies "interim payment" as a distinct category of requested relief, noting its occurrence in 8 of the first 80 cases. *See* p. 29, 39. Born notes that this type of relief *"differ materially from other types of provisional relief in that [it] resolve[s] ... the merits of the parties' dispute." See* Born, *supra*, at § 17.02[G][i].

[61]) *See, e.g.*, ICC Rules (2021), Art. 29(1); HKIAC Rules (2024), Sch. 4, para. 2(d).

[62]) ICC Report on Emergency Arbitrator Proceedings, para. 83.

[63]) *Id.* at 85.

Beyond the urgency requirement, the institutional rules are generally silent on both the specific substantive test for emergency relief and the law that governs it. While the lack of explicit guidance raises a question whether the law of the seat (*lex arbitri*) or the law governing the contract (*lex causae*) should be decisive in that regard,[64]) the prevailing approach in practice resorts to a transnational standard derived from international arbitral practice.[65]) This international test is generally understood to comprise several elements requiring the applicant to demonstrate both a credible claim and a genuine need for urgent protection:[66]) i) a *prima facie* case on the merits;[67]) ii) a risk of harm not adequately reparable by a subsequent award of damages;[68]) and iii) the balance of equities requiring the emergency arbitrator to weigh the harm

[64]) Beisteiner, *supra*, at p. 297, paras. A–B.

[65]) *See* Born, *supra*, at § 17.02[G][2]. This approach is supported *see, e.g.*, ICC Report on Emergency Arbitrator Proceedings, para. 89; Carlevaris & Feris, *Running in the ICC Emergency Arbitrator Rules: The First Ten Cases* 19–20.

[66]) *See, e.g.*, Knott & Winkler, *supra*, p. 164.

[67]) Gabrielle Kaufmann-Kohler & Antonio Rigozzi, *International Arbitration: Law and Practice in Switzerland* para 6.120 (3rd ed. 2015). ("[A]rbitral tribunals are reluctant to venture an assessment of the merits at an often early stage of the proceedings when the record is still scarce; they are concerned about prejudging and giving the impression that they have lost their objectivity. As a result, they soften the traditional requirement and tend to be satisfied with a showing that the claim is not manifestly without merit"); Born, *supra*, at § 17.02[G][3][b][iv]. *Sergei Paushok, et al. v. The Government of Mongolia* (UNCITRAL), Order on Interim Measures, para. 54 (Sept. 2, 2008) (stating the tribunal need only decide that the claims are *"not, on their face, frivolous"*).

[68]) ICC Report on Emergency Arbitrator Proceedings, para. 157; The SCC Practice Note on Emergency Arbitrator Decisions 2019–2022, p. 2. In practice, the requirement of "irreparable harm" is often understood to require a threat of substantial or serious injury, not harm that is literally impossible to compensate with money. This practical interpretation is reflected in the UNCITRAL Model Law, which phrases the standard as "harm not adequately reparable by an award of damages". *See* UNCITRAL Model Law on International Commercial Arbitration, Art. 17A(1)(a) (2006). Authoritative commentary confirms that tribunals generally require a showing of "grave, substantial, or serious injury". *See* Born, *supra*, at § 17.02[G][b][i]. This is also supported by institutional reports. *See, e.g.*, ICC Report on Emergency Arbitrator Proceedings, para. 157 (confirming that in practice, the requirement has "often been interpreted to require a showing of serious or grave harm, even if compensable by money"). Commentary on the LCIA Rules connects this concept to urgency, noting that the "'common denominator of this requirement is that the circumstances of the case (i.e., the risk of harm) are such that the measure cannot await the final resolution of the dispute'". *See* Maxi Scherer, *Chapter 10: Expedited Formation of the Arbitral Tribunal, Emergency Arbitrator and Expedited Replacement of Arbitrators*, in Scherer/Richman/Gerbay, *Arbitrating under the 2020 LCIA Rules: A User's Guide*, para. 75 (2021).

to the applicant if relief is denied against the harm to the respondent if it is granted.[69])

Institutional reports and commentary demonstrate that this international standard has found consistent application in practice. The ICC EA Report observed that in the majority of the first 80 ICC EA cases, emergency arbitrators adopted the international test approach rather than relying on any particular domestic legal standards.[70]) The SCC Practice Notes reflect the same framework, acknowledging that *"a set of criteria have been formed, commonly accepted as prerequisites for granting interim relief"*.[71]) The commentary on the LCIA Rules explains that emergency arbitrators should *"take into account the standards and laws applicable in the context of the arbitration"*, thereby affording them the discretion to apply the same international standard.[72])

Crucially, the ICC EA Report clarifies that these elements are not applied as a rigid, cumulative checklist. Instead, emergency arbitrators tend to weigh the relevant criteria based on the specific circumstances of the case, affording themselves significant discretion.[73]) HKIAC Rules, for example, already reflect that, requiring the EA to consider factors such as whether *"harm not adequately reparable by an award of damages is likely to result"* and whether there is *"a reasonable possibility that the requesting party will succeed on the merits"*.[74])

## 4. Enforcement of Emergency Arbitrator Decisions

The enforceability of EA decisions remains one of the more controversial and unsettled issues in international arbitration. The issue turns on the inherent tension between the provisional character of an emergency arbitrator's decision and the finality required for enforcement under the New York Convention.[75]) Given that emergency orders or awards are generally subject to review by the main arbitral tribunal, it is contended by some commentators, and has been concluded by the courts of some countries,[76]) that emergency

[69]) Born, *supra*, at § 17.02[G][b][i].

[70]) ICC Report on Emergency Arbitrator Proceedings, para. 138.

[71]) SCC Practice Note on Emergency Arbitrator Decisions 2017–2018, p. 12.

[72]) Scherer, *supra*, at para. 75.

[73]) ICC Report on Emergency Arbitrator Proceedings, para. 33 ("*EAs tend to assess which elements are relevant in light of the particular circumstances of the case, and similarly which weight is to be afforded to each of them*").

[74]) HKIAC Rules (2024), Art. 23.4.

[75]) *See, e.g.,* ICC Report on Emergency Arbitrator Proceedings, para. 182 (noting that enforceability concerns have "*given rise to numerous debates*"); Nigel Blackaby, Constantine Partasides, et al., *11. Recognition and Enforcement of Arbitral Awards* in *Redfern and Hunter on International Arbitration*, para. 11.103 (7th ed. 2023) (observing that the finality of emergency awards leads to "*vastly different decisions across jurisdictions*"); Born, *supra*, at § 17.03[A]; Cavalieros & Kim, *supra*, at 287.

[76]) *See* Blackaby, *supra*, para. 11.103. Courts in Australia, Russia, and Chile, for example, have refused to enforce interim awards on the grounds that they are not final

arbitrator decisions do not satisfy the "final and binding" criterion of Article V(1)(e) of the NYC, which allows national courts to refuse enforcement of an award that *"has not yet become [...] binding on the parties"*.[77]) This hurdle persists regardless of the decision's formal designation as an "award" or an "order", as its provisional nature – namely, its being subject to review by the main arbitral tribunal – is seen as incompatible with the finality required for enforcement.[78])

A contrary view within the scholarship, however, regards emergency arbitrator decisions as capable of enforcement, on the basis that they are "final" in relation to the specific issue of interim relief they determine, and that denying enforcement would risk rendering the emergency arbitration mechanism futile.[79])

Notably, this pro-enforcement view has been adopted in recent case law in certain important jurisdictions. In *Yahoo! v. Microsoft Corp.*, the US District Court for the Southern District of New York upheld an emergency arbitrator award that required Yahoo to continue migrating its search capabilities to Microsoft's Bing platform.[80]) Similarly, the US District Court for the Southern District of Florida confirmed the enforceability of an EA order in *Vital Pharmaceuticals v. PepsiCo*,[81]) which had ordered the specific performance of a distribution agreement.[82])

---

and binding. *See Resort Condominiums Int'l Inc. v. Bolwell*, XX Y.B. Comm. Arb. 628 (Queensland Sup. Ct. 1993) (Austl.); *Living Consulting Group AB v. OOO Sokotel*, XXXVI Y.B. Com. Arb. 317 (Russian S. Arbitrazh Ct. 2011) (Russ.); *Western Technology Services International Inc. v. Cauchos Industriales SA*, No. 5468-2009 (Chilean S. Ct. 2010).

[77]) New York Convention on the Recognition and Enforcement of Foreign Arbitral Awards, Art. V(1)(e) (Jun. 10, 1958). *See* also, *e.g.*, Born, *supra*, at §17.03[A] (discussing authorities who hold that provisional measures are not "*final*"); Cavalieros & Kim, *supra*, at 291–292; ICC Report on Emergency Arbitrator Proceedings, paras. 38, 192.

[78]) *See ICC Report*, paras. 192–194.

[79]) Born, *supra*, at §17.03[A]. The ICC Report on Emergency Arbitrator Proceedings also acknowledges this school of thought, citing "prominent authors" who "consider that an arbitral award providing for interim relief may be enforced under the New York Convention". *See*, at fn. 156 (2019).

[80]) *Yahoo! v. Microsoft Corp*, No. 13cv7237, Opinion & Order (S.D.N.Y 2013).

[81]) *Vital Pharmaceuticals, Inc. v. Pepsico, Inc.*, No. 20cv62415, Order (S.D. Fla. 2020).

[82]) *Id.* at pp. 1–3, 11. In *Al Raha v PKL Services* case, the US District Court for the Northern District of Georgia refused to enforce an interim emergency award which prevented termination of a sub-contract between the parties pending constitution of the full arbitral tribunal. In its reasoning, the court concluded that it lacked subject-matter jurisdiction because the interim emergency award was not *"a final arbitral award, because it did not finally and definitely dispose of any independent claim"*, *see Al Raha Group for Technical Services v. PKL Services Inc.*, 2019 WL 4267765, (N.D. Ga. 2019).

In India, in its landmark *Amazon.com v. Future Retail* decision, the Supreme Court affirmed the enforceability of an interim award issued in a domestic SIAC emergency arbitration, holding that it was enforceable as an interim order under Section 17 of the Indian Arbitration Act.[83]) However, the legal status for enforcing decisions in foreign-seated emergency arbitrations in India remains uncertain, and parties in such cases often must still apply directly to national courts for identical relief under Section 9 of the Indian Arbitration Act.[84])

In an effort to address these enforcement challenges, a number of key arbitral jurisdictions have amended their arbitration laws by enacting specific legislative reforms. In 2012, Singapore amended Section 2(1) of the Singapore International Arbitration Act 1994 (**IAA**) to extend the definition of "arbitral tribunal" to emergency arbitrators.[85]) However, because this amendment did not expressly apply to Part 3 of the IAA, which governs the enforcement of foreign awards, whether a decision from a foreign-seated emergency arbitrator would be enforceable in Singapore remained an open question.[86]) The ambiguity was resolved in 2022, when the Singapore High Court confirmed the enforceability of foreign EA awards under Section 29 of the IAA in its ruling in the *CVG v. CVH* case.[87]) Here, an ICDR emergency arbitrator in a Pennsylvania-seated arbitration had issued an "emergency interim award" preserving the status quo of a franchise agreement.[88]) When the enforcement reached the Singapore High Court, it confirmed that EA orders, both domestic and foreign, were enforceable under the IAA, explaining that "*the interpretation that the term 'arbitral award' in s 27(1) of the IAA includes awards by emergency arbitrators was clearly consistent with the legislative purpose of the statute*".[89])

Hong Kong has also implemented legislative changes to ensure the enforceability of emergency arbitrator decisions. In 2013, its Arbitration Ordinance (Cap. 609) introduced a new Part 3A, which expressly addresses the

---

[83]) *See Amazon.com NV Investment Holdings LLC v. Future Retail Ltd.*, Judgment of the Supreme Court of India, at 6 (Feb. 1, 2022). *See* Rahul Jain, *Enforceability of Emergency Arbitration Awards in India*, Daily Jus (May 6, 2025), https://dailyjus.com/world/2025/05/enforceability-of-emergency-arbitration-awards-in-india.

[84]) Vijayendra Pratap Singh, Abhijnan Jha & Arnab Ray, *India*, in The Asia-Pacific Arbitration Review 2022, GAR, p. 8 (2022).

[85]) *See* International Arbitration (Amendment) Bill 2012, cl. 2(a) (Sing.).

[86]) *See* Yasaschandra Devarakonda, *When Not to Enforce: Status of Enforcing Foreign Emergency Awards in Singapore*, Kluwer Arbitration Blog (Dec. 6, 2022), https://legalblogs.wolterskluwer.com/arbitration-blog/when-not-to-enforce-status-of-enforcing-foreign-emergency-awards-in-singapore/; *CVG v. CVH* [2022] SGHC 249, paras. 26, 30 (Sing.).

[87]) *CVG v. CVH* [2022] SGHC 249.

[88]) *Id.* at paras. 4, 17.

[89]) *Id.* at para. 34.

enforcement of emergency relief.[90]) Section 22B provides that any emergency relief granted by an emergency arbitrator – whether issued inside or outside Hong Kong under the relevant arbitration rules – may be enforced in the same manner as a court order or direction.[91]) This provision applies in arbitrations seated in Hong Kong or elsewhere, so long as the emergency relief was granted under the applicable rules and the court's leave is obtained. Notwithstanding this pro-enforcement stance, the Hong Kong courts have underscored that the enforcement remains subject to mandatory statutory limits. Example of that is *HY v. GD* case, in which the Hong Kong Court of First Instance set aside an emergency arbitrator's order on the ground that no valid arbitration agreement existed.[92])

Most recently, the English Arbitration Act 2025 followed suit in modernizing the existing legislative framework by introducing a new Section 41A, which expressly recognizes emergency arbitrators.[93]) Under this provision, where (a) the parties have agreed to arbitral rules that provide for the appointment of an emergency arbitrator, and (b) an emergency arbitrator has in fact been appointed pursuant to those rules, the emergency arbitrator may issue a peremptory order if a party fails to comply with any prior order or direction issued by him/her.[94]) Such peremptory orders are in turn directly enforceable by courts, ensuring that emergency measures granted under institutional rules before constitution of the main tribunal are actionable.[95]) This reform removes previous uncertainty about the enforceability of emergency arbitrator decisions in the UK and brings it into line with other jurisdictions that provide clear legislative support for emergency relief.

While the recent pro-enforcement legislative reforms and case law are a positive development, the global landscape for enforcing emergency arbitrator decisions remains fragmented and unsettled. The absence of a harmonized approach, together with the limited availability of case law in many jurisdictions, results in legal uncertainty regarding the fate of emergency arbitrator decisions, especially within the context of the New York Convention.[96]) However,

---

[90]) Arbitration Ordinance (Cap. 609), Part 3A (H.K.). *See also*, Cavalieros & Kim, *supra*, at 288.

[91]) Arbitration Ordinance (Cap. 609), Part 3A, Sec. 22B (H.K.).

[92]) *HY v. GD* [2021] HKCFI 3900.

[93]) Arbitration Act 2025, C. 4, Sec. 8(2) (E&W). *See also*, Eleanor Scogings, *The English Arbitration Act 2025: What Does This Mean for LCIA Arbitration?*, Kluwer Arbitration Blog (Mar. 18, 2025), https://legalblogs.wolterskluwer.com/arbitration-blog/the-english-arbitration-act-2025-what-does-this-mean-for-lcia-arbitration/.

[94]) Arbitration Act 2025, C. 4, Sec. 8(2) (E&W) (inserting s. 41A into the Arbitration Act 1996).

[95]) *See* Arbitration Act 2025, c. 4, s. 8(4)(a) (E&W).

[96]) *See, e.g.*, Cavalieros & Kim, *supra*, at 291–292 (concluding that the enforceability of EA orders in most jurisdictions is unsettled); ICC Report on Emergency Arbitrator Proceedings, para. 185 (noting the "wide range of interpretations" across national legal systems).

it is crucial not to overstate the impact of these formal enforcement challenges on the actual practice. Institutional reports and commentary consistently observe that voluntary compliance with emergency arbitrator decisions is rather the norm, not the exception.[97]) The ICC Report, for example, found that compliance issues arose in only a small fraction of its early cases.[98]) This high rate of compliance is often attributed to the practical reality that few parties are willing to openly defy a binding order and risk losing the confidence or goodwill of the main arbitral tribunal before the merits of their case have even been heard.

## III. Recent Institutional Developments: Preliminary Protective Orders and an *Ex Parte* Relief

Emergency arbitration was designed to address the procedural limbo that exists before a full arbitral tribunal is constituted. However, a further procedural gap can be found within the emergency arbitration process itself: the standard requirement to notify the responding party of the EA application creates a window of opportunity for it to take preemptive action, such as dissipating assets, and render any subsequent emergency relief futile. To mitigate this risk, some leading institutions have introduced additional mechanisms for preliminary orders that can be issued on an accelerated, and in some cases even *ex parte* basis.

One of the first institutions to address this issue was SIAC. The 2016 SIAC Rules expressly granted emergency arbitrators the authority to "*order or award any interim relief that he deems necessary, including preliminary orders that may be made pending any hearing, telephone or video conference or written submissions by the parties*" prior to issuing their order or award.[99]) In 2024, HKIAC followed suit by expanding the powers of emergency arbitrators under the HKIAC Rules, allowing them to "*make any preliminary or interim order the emergency arbitrator deems necessary before making the Emergency Decision*".[100]) Although these revisions did not provide for an *ex parte* option that would allow the responding party not to be notified of the request, they gave the concerned party an option to seek temporary preservation of the status quo for the duration of the emergency arbitration proceedings.

[97]) *See* ICC Report on Emergency Arbitrator Proceedings, para. 183; Born, *supra*, at § 17.03 (noting a "*strong historical tendency towards voluntary compliance with arbitral awards and orders*").

[98]) *See* ICC Report on Emergency Arbitrator Proceedings, para. 210; *see* also Blackaby, *supra*, para. 7.35 (explaining that arbitrators have persuasive power as parties do not wish to "*defy instructions given to them by those whom they wished to convince of the justice of their claims*").

[99]) SIAC Rules (2016), Sch.1, para. 8.

[100]) HKIAC Rules (2024), Sch. 4, para. 10.

The availability of a true *ex parte* relief within the emergency arbitration has been a highly controversial topic, due to inherent tension between the need for urgent action and the principles of due process.[101]) On the one hand, emergency relief is designed to provide a prompt safeguard to prevent the irreversible harm, and in some situations, providing advance notice would simply allow the responding party to take the very action the applicant is trying to prevent, rendering the process futile.[102]) On the other hand, granting relief without prior notice – even on a provisional basis – can undermine the respondent's right to be heard, creating a risk of unfairness and biased decisions.[103])

This dilemma is typically resolved in favor of due process, as the rules of most major institutions effectively preclude *ex parte* relief through mandatory notice provisions. Under Article 1(5) of Appendix V to the ICC Rules, the ICC Secretariat must send the application and its supporting documents to the responding party if the President of the ICC Court determines that EA provisions apply under Articles 29(5) and 29(6) ICC Rules, which implies that *ex parte* proceedings are not allowed.[104]) However, the ICC EA Report considered that an emergency arbitrator could, in theory, issue a short provisional order to preserve the status quo after notifying the respondent but before receiving their full response, a step that occurred in at least one early case in the ICC practice.[105]) At the same time, the ICC EA Report noted significant opposition to this practice, noting that an *ex parte* measures *"cannot be reconciled with the respondent's right to be heard, particularly where the ICC Rules do not expressly authorise the EA to grant such temporary measures"*.[106]) Similarly, other major institutions effectively preclude such relief through their notification requirements.[107])

---

[101]) *See, e.g.*, Born, *supra*, at § 17.02[G][10] (describing the *"substantial controversy"* surrounding *ex parte* relief and its tension with the right to be heard).

[102]) *See, e.g.*, UNCITRAL Model Law on International Commercial Arbitration (2006), Art. 17B(2) (permitting an *ex parte* preliminary order where *"prior disclosure* [...] *risks frustrating the purpose of the measure"*).

[103]) *See* ICC Report on Emergency Arbitrator Proceedings, para. 114 (noting critics argue that such measures "cannot be reconciled with the respondent's right to be heard"; *see also* Rania Alnaber, *Emergency Arbitration: Mere Innovation or Vast Improvement*, 35 Arb. Int'l 441, 447 (2019) (arguing that *ex parte* relief may not be enforceable under the New York Convention due to the denial of the right to be heard).

[104]) ICC Report on Emergency Arbitrator Proceedings, para. 24.

[105]) *Id.* at 24, 113.

[106]) *Id.* at 114.

[107]) *See, e.g.*, SCC Rules (2023), App. II, Art. 3 ("As soon as an application for the appointment of an emergency arbitrator has been received, the Secretariat shall send the application to the other party."); HKIAC Rules (2024), Sch. 4, para. 2(j) (requiring the applicant to provide a "confirmation that copies of the Application [...] have been or are being communicated simultaneously to all other parties to the arbitration");

By contrast, some institutions have adopted a different approach by introducing special procedures permitting ex parte relief in exceptional cases. The earlier outlier was Article 43 Swiss Rules, which allows the tribunal, in *"exceptional circumstances"*, to issue a preliminary order before the request is communicated to the responding party, so long as it is promptly notified and *"immediately granted an opportunity to be heard"*.[108])

Building directly on its earlier emergency arbitration framework, the newest 2025 edition of the SIAC Rules expanded the authority of emergency arbitrators even further by introducing a novel "Protective Preliminary Order" mechanism ("PPO"). Applicable on an opt-out basis,[109]) PPO allows a party to obtain an *ex parte* emergency relief.[110]) It provides an applicant with an effective tool designed to alleviate the risk that a respondent, upon receiving notice of the application, might take immediate steps to frustrate the purpose of the requested measures.

The procedure is exceptionally swift: once the PPO application is accepted by the President of the SIAC Court of Arbitration, the emergency arbitrator will be appointed within 24 hours. The decision has to be issued within 24 hours of the appointment,[111]) which is then transmitted to all parties by the SIAC Secretariat.[112]) The applicant is in turn required to provide all parties with the case papers, the PPO, and all related communications within 12 hours of its transmission,[113]) otherwise the issued PPO will expire within three days.[114]) The affected party must be provided with an opportunity to present its case *"at the earliest practicable time"* and the emergency arbitration must decide *"promptly"* on any objection to the PPO.[115]) Just as with the 'regular' emergency relief, the main arbitral tribunal has the authority to reconsider any decision made by the emergency arbitrator, including the PPO.[116]) In any event, PPO automatically expires 14 days after its issuance, although the emergency

SIAC Rules (2025), Sch. 1, para. 3 (requiring the application to include a "statement certifying that all parties have been provided with a copy of the Application").

[108]) Article 29(3) of the Swiss Rules applies to emergency arbitration by virtue of Article 43(8), which provides that an emergency arbitrator's decision has the "same effects as a decision pursuant to Article 29", *see* Swiss Rules (2021), Arts. 29(3), 43(8). *See also*, Christoph Müller & Sabrina Pearson, *Waving the Green Flag to Emergency Arbitration under the Swiss Rules: the Sauber Saga*, ASA Bull. 815–816 (2015).

[109]) The PPO mechanism applies by default but can be excluded by agreement. *See* SIAC Rules (2025), Sch. 1, para. 25 ("Unless otherwise agreed by the parties [...]").

[110]) SIAC Rules (2025), Sch.1, para. 25.

[111]) SIAC Rules (2025), Sch.1, paras. 26–27.

[112]) SIAC Rules (2025), Sch.1, para. 28.

[113]) SIAC Rules (2025), Sch.1, para. 29.

[114]) SIAC Rules (2025), Sch.1, para. 30.

[115]) SIAC Rules (2025), Sch.1, para. 31–32.

[116]) SIAC Rules (2025), Sch.1, para. 21.

arbitrator may subsequently adopt, modify, or replace it with another order or award for emergency interim relief after hearing all involved parties.[117])

SIAC's PPO mechanism is one of the most ambitious procedural innovations in recent institutional rulemaking, as it directly confronts the tension between due process and the need for effective, preemptive relief. Its practical application and reception will therefore be closely observed to see if it sets a precedent for other institutions that have historically favored a more prohibitive stance on *ex parte* orders. It remains to be seen whether SIAC's forward-looking approach will inspire a broader institutional trend to introduce more innovative procedural tools that address the commercial realities and practical needs of high-stakes disputes.

## IV. Emergency Arbitration in Practice: Empirical Trends Across Selected Institutions (2019–2024)

The data drawn from institutional statistical reports between 2019 and 2024 indicates that emergency arbitration, while an important procedural innovation, remains a specialized and relatively infrequently used mechanism. Across the five leading arbitral institutions examined – the ICC, LCIA, SIAC, HKIAC, and SCC – applications for emergency arbitration constitute only a minor fraction of the overall caseload. During the considered six-year period, these institutions collectively administered 12,876 arbitrations, of which 336 involved applications for emergency measures, representing just 2.61 % of all cases.

| Institution | Total Registered Cases | Filed EA Applications | EA as % of Total Cases |
|---|---|---|---|
| ICC[118]) | 5,016 | 163 | 3.25 % |
| LCIA[119]) | 2,013 | 27 | 1.34 % |
| HKIAC[120]) | 1,248[121]) | 27 | 2.16 % |
| SIAC[122]) | 3,524[123]) | 89 | 2.53 % |

[117]) SIAC Rules (2025), Sch.1, para. 33.

[118]) Data for the ICC are based on the ICC Dispute Resolution Statistics (2019–2024).

[119]) Data for the LCIA are based on the LCIA Annual Casework Reports (2019–2024).

[120]) Data for the HKIAC are based on the HKIAC Annual Reports (2019–2024).

[121]) This figure includes cases administered by HKIAC under the HKIAC Administered Arbitration Rules and the UNCITRAL Arbitration Rules.

[122]) Data for the SIAC are based on the SIAC Annual Reports (2019–2024).

[123]) This figure includes arbitration cases administered by SIAC.

| Institution | Total Registered Cases | Filed EA Applications | EA as % of Total Cases |
|---|---|---|---|
| SCC[124]) | 1,075 | 30 | 2.79 % |
| **Total** | **12,876** | **336** | **2.61 %** |

At the ICC, such applications accounted for between 2.05 % and 5.18 % of annual filings, with a weighted average of approximately 3.25 % over the 2019–2024 period.[125]) The LCIA recorded even lower proportions, ranging from 0.29 % to 2.48 % per year and averaging at about 1.34 % across the same timeframe.[126]) By comparison, the SCC and SIAC reported moderate but still limited use of the mechanism, with averages of approximately 2.79 % and 2.53 %, respectively.[127]) At the HKIAC, EA applications comprised approximately 2.16 % of registered arbitrations between 2019–2024.[128])

These statistics make clear that emergency arbitration has not become a routine feature of international arbitration practice. Its relatively sparing use reflects both the exceptional nature of the circumstances that may justify such proceedings and the demanding criteria that govern them, particularly urgency and irreparable harm. In this sense, emergency arbitration functions not as a routine procedural step, but as an extraordinary mechanism reserved for disputes requiring immediate and compelling interim protection, where other avenues of protection are either unavailable or inadequate.

---

[124]) Data for the SCC is based on the SCC Annual Reports (2019–2024) and the SCC Practice Note on Emergency Arbitrator Decisions (2019–2022).

[125]) The annual share of emergency arbitration (EA) applications was calculated as the number of EA requests divided by total cases filed under the ICC Rules for each year: 2019 (23/851; 2.70 %), 2020 (32/929; 3.44 %), 2021 (27/840; 3.21 %), 2022 (36/695; 5.18 %), 2023 (28/870; 3.22 %), and 2024 (17/831; 2.05 %). The weighted average, computed as total EA applications (163) divided by total cases filed (5,016), equals approximately 3.25 %.

[126]) The percentage of EA applications per year was determined by dividing the number of EA requests by total LCIA arbitrations filed: 2019 (1/346; 0.29 %), 2020 (5/407; 1.23 %), 2021 (8/322; 2.48 %), 2022 (3/293; 1.02 %), 2023 (6/327; 1.83 %), and 2024 (4/318; 1.26 %). The weighted average for the period, calculated as 27 EA applications out of 2,013 arbitrations, is 1.34 %.

[127]) For the SCC, EA applications represented 8/175 (4.57 %), 5/213 (2.35 %), 7/165 (4.24 %), 2/143 (1.40 %), 4/175 (2.29 %), and 4/204 (1.96 %) of total cases, yielding a weighted average of 2.79 %. For SIAC, the corresponding figures were 10/454 (2.20 %), 20/1,063 (1.88 %), 15/446 (3.36 %), 12/336 (3.57 %), 11/640 (1.72 %), and 21/585 (3.59 %), producing a weighted average of 2.53 %.

[128]) The number of EA applications ranged from none in 2019 to a maximum of 14 in 2020, representing 0/173 (0 %), 14/203 (6.90 %), 4/183 (2.19 %), 1/256 (0.39 %), 3/184 (1.63 %), and 5/249 (2.01 %) respectively. The weighted average, calculated across the six-year period (27 applications out of 1,248 total cases), equals 2.16 %.

Data published by institutions such as the ICC and SCC reveal that emergency arbitrators grant relief in approximately forty percent of cases, confirming that the mechanism, while effective in some instances, remains far from a guaranteed avenue of interim protection.

At the ICC, the aggregate success rate for 2020–2024[129]) (counting both fully and partially granted applications) stands at approximately 39.2 %,[130]) only marginally higher than the 33.3 % success rate recorded for the first 80 cases decided under the ICC Emergency Arbitrator Rules between 2012–2018.[131]) This relative stability indicates that parties' and counsel' growing familiarity with the mechanism has not significantly increased the likelihood of obtaining emergency relief.

The SCC's aggregate success rate is similar:[132]) approximately 43 % of all applications result in measures being granted.[133]) In the 14 SCC cases decided between 2014–2019, the tribunals denied EA applications on the basis of i) lack of urgency;[134]) ii) lack of irreparable/serious harm;[135]) iii) failure by the claimant to establish a reasonable possibility of success on the merits;[136]) iv) failure by the claimant to establish that damages would not be a sufficient remedy;[137]) and v) proportionality.[138])

[129]) No outcome data were published in the ICC Dispute Resolution Statistics for 2019. Accordingly, the aggregate success rate of approximately 39 % is based on the 2020–2024 period only.

[130]) Annual success rates were as follows (the first number representing successful and partially granted applications, and the second the total number of decided applications): 2020 (11/27; 40.74 %), 2021 (10/25, 40 %), 2022 (13/34, 38.24 %), 2023 (12/27, 44.44 %) and 2024 (5/17, 29.41 %). The weighted average for 51 successful outcomes out of 130 decided applications equals approximately 39.2 %.

[131]) ICC Report on Emergency Arbitrator Proceedings, pp. 5–9 (2019), covering the first 80 applications filed up to 30 April 2018 (of which 69 resulted in orders and 23 were granted in full or partially).

[132]) The SCC's annual statistics include both commercial and investment treaty arbitrations, including cases filed under bilateral investment treaties and, in some years, the Energy Charter Treaty. While emergency arbitrator proceedings are overwhelmingly commercial, certain years (notably 2020) recorded EA applications within investment treaty disputes. The aggregate figures therefore reflect the combined total of commercial and investment-related cases.

[133]) Annual success rates were as follows (the first number representing successful and partially granted applications, and the second the total number of decided applications): 2019 (6/7; 85.71 %), 2020 (1/5; 20 %), 2021 (3/6; 50 %), 2022 (0/2; 0 %), 2023 (2/4; 50 %), and 2024 (0/4; 0 %). The weighted average for 12 successful outcomes out of 28 decided applications equals approximately 42.86 %

[134]) *Ibid.* at Cases 8, 9, 10, 11 and 13.

[135]) *Ibid.* at Cases 8, 10, 11, 12, 13 and 14.

[136]) *Ibid.* at Cases 11, 13 and 14.

[137]) *Ibid.* at Case 14.

[138]) *Ibid.*

Unfortunately, other major institutions do not publish data on the substantive outcome of emergency arbitrator proceedings. The LCIA reports only reflect the number of applications for the appointment of an emergency arbitrator and how many of those applications were granted or rejected by the LCIA Court.[139]) SIAC and HKIAC statistics confirm the number of emergency applications filed each year, without specifying the outcome of the applications, which precludes assessment of their success rates.[140]) Nonetheless, the consistently low incidence of such applications supports the broader conclusion that emergency arbitration remains a narrowly confined and exceptional procedural mechanism, invoked only in limited circumstances where urgent interim relief is truly indispensable.

Taken together, the available data suggest that the threshold for emergency relief remains high, with urgent relief being granted only where applicants establish both genuine urgency and a credible risk of grave or irreparable harm.[141]) For practitioners, the data underscore that emergency arbitration should be approached strategically, not reflexively. Its effectiveness depends less on its procedural availability than on the applicant's ability to meet demanding substantive standards. This necessitates a thorough and realistic pre-application assessment, including a candid evaluation of evidentiary strength, the specific institutional requirements, and the potential costs and benefits relative to other available remedies. The data therefore caution against viewing emergency arbitration as a purely tactical instrument, instead affirming its greatest utility in truly exigent circumstances where delay would irrevocably undermine the fundamental objective of the arbitration. Ultimately, emergency arbitration serves as a critical safeguard within the international arbitration system, designed to preserve the integrity and ultimate enforceability

[139]) Under Article 9.6 of the 2020 LCIA Rules, parties may apply for the appointment of an Emergency Arbitrator with the LCIA Court, which then must decide on the application *"as soon as possible in the circumstances"*, based on whether the requirement of *"emergency"* is met, *see* Scherer, *supra*, at 168. The authors understand that the term "granted" application means the LCIA Court agreed to appoint an emergency arbitrator and allow the EA proceeding to move forward; it does not indicate whether the emergency arbitrator ultimately granted the requested relief. The annual rates for LCIA Court's acceptance of EA application were as follows (the first number representing the number of applications that were granted, and the second the total number of filed applications): 2019 (1/1; 100 %), 2020 (3/5; 60.00 %), 2021 (3/8; 37.50 %), 2022 (0/3; 0 %), 2023 (1/6; 16.67 %), and 2024 (1/4; 25.00 %). The weighted average of 9 granted applications out of 27 submitted applications equals approximately 33.33 %.

[140]) Neither SIAC nor HKIAC publishes data distinguishing between applications granted, partially granted, or denied. Their reports indicate only the number of EA applications filed and, in some cases, whether an order or award was issued.

[141]) The criteria for granting interim measures, as reflected in institutional summaries and practice notes (e.g., SCC Practice Note on Emergency Arbitrator Decisions 2019–2022; ICC Dispute Resolution Statistics, 2023–2024), consistently require a showing of urgency, risk of irreparable harm, and prima facie jurisdiction.

of future arbitral awards, rather than to function as a routine preliminary step in dispute resolution.

## V. Conclusion

Emergency arbitration has quickly spread from a procedural innovation into an integral feature of the international dispute resolution landscape. As the empirical evidence makes clear, it has not however been invoked as a routine procedural step, but rather remains an exceptional mechanism exercised only in especially urgent circumstances. Although some uncertainty remains regarding the enforcement of emergency arbitrator decisions under the New York Convention, its practical utility is largely sustained by a high rate of voluntary compliance, as parties are generally unwilling to risk the strategic disadvantage of defying a preliminary order. It thus seems safe to say that emergency arbitration is here to stay – and as legislative reforms and pro-enforcement judicial interpretations across jurisdictions continue to establish clearer and more reliable pathways for enforcement, the strategic significance of this specialized remedy is likely to increase further.

# Where the Streets Have No Name

## When Arbitral Institutions Underestimate the Seemingly Mundane Tasks

*Stephan Wilske/Matthew T. Adams**)

> *"You think I'll mess it up, mess it up,*
> *mess it up all for you."*[1])

## I. Introduction

For decades now, international arbitration has been growing more prominent and the disputes it handles have become more complex. Proceedings can run for years on end and feature dozens of different parties, counsel, arbitrators, and institutional staff.[2]) Yet, as these disputes only continue to increase in procedural complexity, scale, and value, there are also more potential points of failure in the process. These procedures deal with rather mundane tasks, which nevertheless can be of significance and sometimes require special knowledge and experience. Indeed, one of the main reasons why parties turn to institutional arbitration rather than *ad hoc* proceedings is to secure the services of experienced professionals to carry out these procedures, often paying handsomely for the administration of the dispute. So what, then, happens when the arbitral institution fails to live up to its side of the agreement?

---

*) Stephan Wilske Partner, Gleiss Lutz, Stuttgart (Germany); FCIArb; admitted to the New York and German bar as well as to the U.S. Supreme Court; Maîtrise en droit (Université d'Aix-Marseille III, France); LL.M. (The University of Chicago; Casper Platt Award); Dr. iur (Tübingen); lecturer at the University of Heidelberg and Honorary Professor at the University of Jena; visiting Professor at the National Taiwan University, College of Law (Spring 2010). The author can be reached at stephan.wilske@gleisslutz.com.

Matthew T. Adams, Attorney-at-law admitted to the North Carolina Bar; J.D., University of North Carolina School of Law. He currently works on Stephan Wilske's Dispute Resolution team at Gleiss Lutz, as well as serving on the editorial teams for the *Transatlantic Law Journal* and the *ICSID Rules and Regulations Commentary* 2nd Edition 2026 (forthcoming).

1) The Rolling Stones, *Mess It Up*, Hackney Diamonds (2023).

2) For more on this, *see* Wilske/Adams, *Between Scylla and Charybdis: Copy-and-Paste Method as Another Peril of the 'Time-Efficient' Arbitrator*, Liber Americorum for Paolo Michele Patocchi, 2026 (forthcoming).

For any other institution, a breach of an agreement has a quick remedy in contract law, yet arbitral institutions are often able to avoid the ultimate liability for their mistakes. While some jurisdictions like the United States base this lack of accountability for arbitral institutions on judicial theories of absolute or qualified immunity,[3]) this is in no way a settled position. Rather, many may rightfully point to these arbitral institutions being sophisticated market players, and that the agreements made between them and the parties to the arbitration demand accountability for the institutions, just as attorneys or doctors may be liable for malpractice when they fail to live up to their promised standard.[4]) This is not to say that arbitral institutions are immune to being sued, however. There have been several cases, even in the last few years, where arbitral institutions have been pulled into court to defend themselves.[5]) So far, at least, these cases have been successfully defended by the arbitral institutions.

Imagine a scenario where an arbitral institution, tasked with transmitting a request for arbitration to a major, well-known office building, fails to do so, and then simply turns to the party and says its courier cannot find the building and thus they cannot transmit the request? Is this failure simply now the responsibility of the party, despite the fees paid to the institution to carry this task out and the fact that a quick plausibility check (or Google research) would have shown that the courier service is either blatantly ignorant, incompetent, unwilling,[6]) or unable to do its job? If there is a deadline missed or additional interest imposed because of this delay, must the party simply bear this conse-

---

[3]) For a critique of the American doctrine of absolute judicial immunity in arbitration and the emerging trend of administrative exceptions, *see* Jenny Brown, *Expansion of Arbitral Immunity: Is Absolute Immunity a Foregone Conclusion*, 10 J. Disp. Resol. 1 (2009).

[4]) For more on the theories of how arbitral institutions can and should be liable, *see* Barbara Alicja Warwas, *The Liability of Arbitral Institutions: Legitimacy Challenges and Functional Responses*, (T.M.C. Asser Press, The Hague 2017).

[5]) *See, e.g., Uber Tech., Inc. v American Arbitration Assn., Inc.*, Case No. 2021-03782, Slip Op 02503 (14 April 2022, N.Y. App. Ct.), *Société Kraydon Ltd v. Chambre de commerce internationale de Paris*, Court of Cassation of France, First Civil Law Chamber, Arrêt n° 194 F-D, Pourvoi n° J 21-16.238 (22 March 2023), *Oil investor sues ICSID over annulment case*, Glob. Arb. Rev. (03 June 2013), https://globalarbitration review.com/article/oil-investor-sues-icsid-over-annulment-case.

[6]) An unfortunate phenomenon exists whereby couriers will, rather than deliver their packages, simply dump them all in a remote location: a common-enough practice to earn the moniker "*forest deliveries*". *See, e.g.*, Marlene Lenthang, *'Stressed' Amazon driver abandons 80 packages in Mass. woods during holiday shipping rush*, NBC News (24 December 2024) https://www.nbcnews.com/news/us-news/stressed-amazon-driver-abandons-80-packages-mass-woods-holiday-shippin-rcna185343, Marc Levy, *With 30 packages dumped in the wrong lobby, resident tried harder to correct it than Amazon*, Cambridge Day (11 November 2021) https://www.cambridgeday.com/2021/11/11/with-30-packages-dumped-in-the-wrong-lobby-resident-tried-harder-to-correct-it-than-amazon/, Kate Hawkinson, *A FedEx driver running late on his routes ditched dozens of parcels in woods, Florida cops say*, The Independent (23 Dec. 2024) https://www.inde

quence? In light of the lack of a comprehensive framework or understanding of arbitral institutional liability, these authors wish to highlight some examples in recent cases of seemingly routine responsibilities carried out by institutions which, if not properly performed by the arbitral institution, could lead to unexpected consequences for the parties. Arbitral institutions should not underestimate the potential ramifications of these mistakes, no matter how minor.

## II. What Happens when the Arbitral Institution Fails?

There has been no shortage of both academic and public attention focused on the question of arbitrator liability, *i.e.*, whether an arbitrator may be personally liable for actions taken in the course of their role as an adjudicator. What is seemingly less discussed, however, is the question of who becomes responsible when it is the arbitral institution itself that messes up. If the institution, which is paid money to administer the proceedings, fails in upholding its standards, would it be a basis for a breach of contract? If a properly filed request for arbitration fails to be transmitted to the opposing party in time to begin the accounting of interest, is that a risk that the claimant must bear? Or would the institution be liable for the damages which would have been won?

Perhaps the greatest problem with some of the potential avenues for arbitral institutional liability lies in their seemingly mundane nature. It is often not the most exciting aspect of a dispute when the parties are dealing with things like service of process, transmission of documents, or forwarding payments, yet each of these routine tasks holds great power over the proceedings. It is precisely this underestimated potential for consequences that makes these small steps in arbitration so critical, especially for an arbitral institution hoping to avoid being pulled into court.

### A. Failure to Locate a Well-known Respondent

As referenced in our introduction, these authors had a particularly frustrating experience when claimants in a case, after paying over EUR 65,000 in arbitral administrative fees, submitted a request for arbitration against a well-known and publicly listed blue-chip company, anticipating no issues in transmitting the request to such a recognized company. Not only had claimants provided the arbitral institution with the address that corresponded with all

pendent.co.uk/news/world/americas/crime/fedex-package-dumping-florida-arrest-b2669253.html.

publicly available information and documentation for the company, but this company itself was easily findable from a simple Google Maps search. This is not to mention the fact that the company is based in a large building with its company name and logo clearly visible from the outside. Nor had this company even moved offices in the past several decades. Rather than needing a specialized and experienced courier, even the most novice pizza delivery driver would be able to easily find this building.

Yet, to the authors' surprise, the arbitral institution reached out to the claimants to inform them that delivery "*was not possible at this address*" and requested another address. Harkening back to the words of the band U2, for the arbitral institution and their courier, it was as if the streets had no names, not even conducting a basic check to see if the address or the company actually existed where hundreds of sources pointed them out to be. It took local counsel directly setting out GPS coordinates, creating a map, and providing detailed instructions for the arbitral institution to attempt a second delivery. Ultimately, this well-known company was found right where claimants had pointed it out to be, but with the omission of the arbitral institution to carry out even a basic plausibility check as to the company's location, it delayed the proceedings, which involved hundreds of millions of Euros in dispute, by over a month. With this amount of money at stake, a considerable amount of interest may have already accrued in this period. Nor was the arbitral institution the one who rectified this mistake; rather, they simply returned to the claimant and asked them how to proceed, only attempting a second delivery after the claimant themselves had to spell out step-by-step how to find the front desk of this public company. One wonders how much of the EUR 65,000 in administrative fees went to transmitting this request for relief.

## B. The Case of the Disappearing Office Building

In another case involving the same arbitral institution, the explanations given for the failures proved to be paradoxically impossible. Even while the respondent in this case was playing "*hard to get*" and making proceedings difficult, claimants had already managed to successfully transmit the request for arbitration to the respondent. However, the next time documents needed to be sent, the arbitral institution claimed they could not be served. When pressed for details, the institution indicated that its courier had said the offices were closed. Yet, implausibly, the next day that courier claimed that delivery was impossible as the respondent's contact information was invalid. If the address was invalid, how was there an office to be closed as claimed in the courier's first excuse? How was the initial submission of the request for arbitration successful? When pressed for an acceptable explanation, the arbitral institution simply returned saying that its inquiry to the courier as to the failed deliveries "*has not led to any clear results*" and asked the claimant how to proceed. Both the previous cases suggest that arbitral institutions must be careful with whom it selects for third-party services, and arbitrators and attorneys should be aware that, often, when these third parties fail, the question inevitably gets returned to the parties rather than the institutions dealing with it.

But should it not be the task of an arbitral institution to ask its chosen service provider why service of process was initially possible, then was claimed impossible because the office was closed before pointing to the *Fata Morgana* of the disappearing office building as a follow-up excuse? Even more blatantly, imagine there is a courier who adheres to the conspiracy theory that Bielefeld, Germany, does not actually exist.[7]) If an arbitral institution must deliver a request for arbitration to this town, would it be acceptable for it to simply accept its courier's claim that delivery to such a non-existent town is impossible? At the very least, the arbitral institution should check to make sure the proffered explanation is at least plausible, as these institutions cannot escape liability simply by outsourcing their duties to third parties. Rather, no matter what law is applicable, the arbitral institution retains some responsibility to both select a proper and well-suited third-party service provider, as well as make sure they are doing an appropriate job.

## C. Taking Time to Transmit Documents

In another case involving these authors, a different, yet very well-known, arbitral institution engaged in perhaps even more blatant errors, highlighting an instance where, unlike the previous example, there is no third-party courier service that could be blamed. In this case, the author was serving as the responding party to the request for arbitration and noticed that the document had been initially received by the arbitral institution six weeks prior. Curious as to the delay in the transmission, it was confirmed that the arbitral institution had already received the payment advances when they received the request for arbitration. This author inquired why the institution had sat on this document despite having their payment. Incredulously, the arbitral institution sloppily retorted that, given their prominence and scale, they had simply been too busy

[7]) There is a satirical conspiracy in Germany which claims the town of Bielefeld does not actually exist. https://en.wikipedia.org/wiki/Bielefeld_conspiracy. While a google search may suggest this town does, in fact, exist, even former chancellor Angela Merkel has her doubts. *Auch Merkel zweifelt an Existenz Bielefelds (Merkel also doubts Bielefeld's existence)*, Welt (27 November 2012) https://www.welt.de/newsticker/news3/article111575893/Extra-Auch-Merkel-zweifelt-an-Existenz-Bielefelds.html. These theories are not limited to Bielefeld but are featured around the globe, such as doubts to the existences of Wyoming, USA, or Australia. Jake Goodrick, *Growing online theory says Wyoming doesn't exist*, AP News (22 Nov. 2020) https://apnews.com/article/wyoming-coronavirus-pandemic-gillette-d7d2bbf5e2040b4e1e5498c8131bc376; James Ball, *Australia doesn't exist! And other bizarre geographic conspiracies that won't go away*, The Guardian (25 April 2018) https://www.theguardian.com/technology/shortcuts/2018/apr/15/australia-doesnt-exist-and-other-bizarre-geographic-conspiracies-that-wont-go-away.

and had more important work to prioritize. Though it should not matter, it is not as if this dispute was small and insignificant, rather it contested an amount between EUR 10 and 15 million.

In a field that is almost entirely reliant on the choices of parties to select their institution and arbitrators, a reputation is one of the most critical tools of anyone involved in international arbitration. This is what makes the risk of mistake so powerful, as an arbitral institution that develops a reputation as unreliable, slow, or prone to mistake will quickly find itself less frequently recommended by lawyers or chosen in contractual provisions. And when an arbitral institution – despite holding themselves out as an attractive destination for business and taking fees in the five-digit range for their services – simply explains a mistakes as being "*too busy with more important matters*," it leaves a bad taste in the mouths of the parties and leaves them questioning the priorities of the institution: are they focused on quantity or quality?

## D. Late Payments and Reimbursements

A more common and perhaps frequently seen ground for complaints highlights the double standard that surrounds much of the discussion around institutional liability and obligations. It is all too typical, as is one of these authors' own personal experience, for the arbitrator's fees or repayments of cost advances to take up to four to six weeks following the final award and administrative decisions on costs to be paid out, despite lacking any reason for the delay. These payments can entail huge amounts of money that were once planned and accounted for by the arbitrators and parties, but which are now being held in limbo without so much as an explanation. And this is not to mention the impact that late payments can have on parties, as the sums involved in these cases can mean that there are substantial cash balances waiting to be paid rather than being used by the parties to pay their attorneys, to fund experts, or even keep their lights on in the office. Thus, failing to return or forward payments to the parties or the arbitrators promptly is not merely harmless lethargy, but something that can have seriously harmful consequences in the right (or wrong) circumstances.

Even when there may be justifiable explanations for a delayed payment, there should be, at a minimum, communication of the status of the payments or activity of the arbitral institution. These authors are aware of one case in which payments were delayed by five months, and while the parties were sitting and wondering where their payments could be, the arbitral institution was checking to make sure payments were not forbidden by sanction regimes. Just as it is a common professional courtesy to inform a client or colleague if you are running late in traffic, arbitral institutions should not be able to operate in secrecy and non-transparency, especially when it is concerning the distribution of payments after a disposition. This may also prove to be in the best interest of the institutions, as they can avoid constant inquiries as to the status of payments if they would just communicate openly with the parties. As a double standard, there is no punishment for late payment by the arbitral institution, yet a failure by a party to pay on time could mean the wholesale dismissal of their case. As it stands, arbitral institutions have "*rules for thee, but not for me.*"

## E. The Burden of Knowledge

An even more contentious question revolves around the obligations of an arbitral institution to share knowledge which it has, but which one party lacks. Consider a situation where there is a local arbitral institution, one local party, and the other party is from a far-remote foreign country. The local party appoints its arbitrator, who the arbitral institution knows has been appointed by this same local party in dozens of preceding cases with the very same institution, yet that arbitrator fails to disclose that information to the foreign party. Would the arbitral institution have a duty to inform the foreign party of these repeated appointments, given that the foreign party may have no way to uncover this to object to the appointment? While this may not represent the current views of the German Arbitration Institute (*Deutsche Institution für Schiedsgerichtsbarkeit*, DIS) anymore, former president Klaus-Peter Berger claimed in an academic publication that the DIS, if it has such knowledge unknown to the party and undisclosed by the arbitrator, will "*in principle, not contact the nominee and bring these circumstances to his attention, even if the Secretariat considered these circumstances relevant.*"[8] Even if the parties are not informed and thus do not object, he says the Secretariat will "*respect the autonomy of the parties and the fact that it remains the nominee's decision as to what he wants to disclose.*"[9] To these authors, this seems an untenable position, and greatly impedes on the equality of arms between the parties. While the arbitrator certainly has the duty to disclose relevant facts about a close relationship with one of the parties, this will not shield the institution from the risk of having the award challenged if this information does eventually come to light.

One may even imagine a much more blatant scenario to illustrate the position that arbitral institutions may find themselves in. Imagine, if you will, a situation where there is a conference organized by an arbitral institution with a subsequent dinner. Then, the secretary general or the president of the arbitral institution went into a side room after dessert and found a prominent local arbitrator and the lead counsel for a party to an ongoing dispute in a, shall we say, compromising position? Would the arbitral institution then have a duty to

---

8) *Berger* in Böckstiegel, Kroll, and Nacimiento (eds.), Arbitration in Germany, The Model Law in Practice 2nd ed. 2015, Section 16 para 9.

9) *Id.*

disclose its awareness of this relationship, even if it's a well-known "*secret*" for the local parties? Going even further, what should the arbitral institution do when this friendly encounter turns into an ongoing relationship, even with children, but is still undisclosed – assuming that this situation is well-known to the institution but not to the foreign party and their lawyers? According to Berger, the answer may be no, but it is these authors' view that it is in the best interests of the parties, arbitrators, and the institution itself if they were to take a more proactive approach to disclosing this one-sided information. Otherwise, certain institutions may quickly find themselves with a reputation for disfavoring foreign parties – not the best position for a provider of international arbitrations.

## III. Conclusion

While the exact mechanisms of and confines for arbitral institutional liability would better be the subject of a separate paper, these authors wanted to highlight some recent frustrating experiences and raise questions as to the extent of the arbitral institutions' attention to these details. It must be a priority of arbitral institutions to focus on accurately performing their "*bread and butter*" work, such as transmitting documents or forwarding timely payments, so as to generate a consistent reputation for good work, not just a lot of work. Like the institution that held on to documents for weeks due to being "*too busy*," many institutions have been focused too much on soliciting business from around the world – sending representatives and employees to conferences and galas – and not as much on making sure the functions which it provides are properly administered.

It may be that some arbitral institutions are simply doing too much: concerned more with the volume of cases and not with the quality of the services rendered. Just as a doctor may have to decline new patients due to a full schedule, perhaps arbitral institutions must become more comfortable with declining non-case-related activities when their resources are spread too thin. Otherwise, we may get situations as detailed above, where the transmission of a multi-million-dollar request for arbitration is deferred to an overworked and under-qualified employee who cannot be bothered to make sure their courier even attempted to google an address. For the arbitral institutions that fail to shore up their administration of these seemingly mundane tasks, we leave them with the eternal wisdom of our most favorite contemporaneous philosophers, the *Glimmer Twins*:

*"Don't get angry with me ... If we go separate ways."*[10])

[10]) Mick Jagger and Keith Richards (with Andrew Watt), *Angry*, The Rolling Stones, Hackney Diamonds (2023).

# Rising Cost of Performance: An Arbitral Perspective on Hardship and Risk Allocation under Art 79 CISG

*Maximilian Albert Mueller*

## I. Introduction

Businesses increasingly face price volatility driven by factors, such as disruptions in global shipping or shortages of certain goods or raw materials. In extreme cases, changes of market conditions can significantly raise the cost of performance, making it difficult for obligors to meet contractual obligations. In this context, the United Nations Convention on Contracts for the International Sale of Goods 1980 (CISG) entails some significant peculiarities with regard to performance failures in cross-border supply contracts.

Unlike many other legal regimes and uniform contract laws, the CISG does not explicitly regulate or define hardship or force majeure.[1]) Instead, Art 79 provides for an exemption from liability for damages caused by the failure to perform contractual obligations. This provision can be understood as reconciling the concepts of both force majeure and hardship, providing a single mechanism to deal with factual impossibility as well as economic onerousness, while maintaining a stringent standard of proof. In essence, an obligor may invoke Art 79 if the impediment causing its non-performance was (i) beyond its control, (ii) unforeseeable and (iii) unavoidable. Assessing these criteria can be rather contentious, in particular when rising performance costs constitute the relevant impediment. The below analysis will examine the intricacies of Art 79 in this context, with a particular focus on arbitration practice.

## II. Application of Art 79 CISG

Traditionally, Art 79 has been understood as reflecting the **force majeure** principle, focusing on impediments beyond the obligor's control that render

---

[1]) For example, Art 6.2.2 Principles of International Commercial Contracts (hardship) and Art 6.1.1 Principles of European Contract Law (change of circumstances); Art 89 Common European Sales Law.

performance unfeasible.[2]) However, it is widely accepted that **economic unreasonableness or unaffordability** of performance may also entitle an obligor to invoke Art 79.[3]) This provision therefore extends beyond factual impediments (impossibility) to also encompass cases of economic **hardship** where performance has become excessively onerous for the obligor (while still technically possible).

Both the seller and the buyer may rely on the exemption under Art 79 for the non-performance of any obligation arising from their contractual relationship.[4]) However, Art 79 only applies (superseding domestic law provisions) if the parties have not deviated from it by agreement (Art 6). This is often the case as many international supply contracts include limitations of liability, force majeure or hardship clauses.[5])

In the absence of such provisions, a non-performing obligor may rely on Art 79 if the impediment causing its non-performance was (i) beyond its control, (ii) unforeseeable and (iii) unavoidable.[6]) The obligor bears the burden of proof for the presence of these requirements.[7]) The following sections examine each element in turn.

---

[2]) See *Brunner*, Force Majeure and Hardship under General Contract Principles: Exemption for Non-performance in International Arbitration, International Arbitration Law Library, p. 103 *et seqq.*

[3]) See CISG Advisory Council Opinion No. 7 (2007), para 3.1 and Comments 26–39; *Schlechtriem/Schwenzer*, Commentary on the UN Convention on the International Sale of Goods (CISG), Art 79 mn 31; *Brunner*, Force Majeure and Hardship under General Contract Principles: Exemption for Non-performance in International Arbitration, International Arbitration Law Library, p. 213 with further references.

[4]) For the seller, this might be the case if its production, procurement or delivery costs increase exorbitantly rendering the performance of its own delivery obligations excessively onerous. It is also possible that the seller's performance becomes indirectly more onerous if the value of the counter-performance – namely, the purchase price – declines due to depreciation of the currency. For the buyer, a significant fall in value of the goods purchased from the seller may give rise to Art 79.

[5]) The effectiveness of such provisions (*e.g.*, unequal terms or bargaining positions), falls outside the regulatory scope of the CISG and is subject to domestic legal systems.

[6]) In addition to these requirements, Art 79(4) CISG requires a party to give notice (in any form) of an impediment and its effects on the ability to perform its obligations within reasonable time. The failure to give such notice does not deprive the party of the right to claim the exemption from liability under Art 79 CISG. However, there is a risk that the party is held liable for any damages suffered by the other party, which could have been avoided if it had given timely notice.

[7]) See Art 79(1) CISG.

## A. Impediment Beyond Control

First, it must be determined whether the obligor has assumed the risk for the impediment it is invoking under Art 79. The requirement that the impediment lies "beyond the control" of the obligor, thus ultimately requires examining the (explicit or implicit) **allocation of risks between the parties.** This is primarily based on the underlying supply contract, the parties' past practices and relevant international usages.[8]) For example, the selection of a specific Incoterms rule in the contract can place specific risks (such as regarding shipping costs or tariffs) on one of the parties.

As a general rule, financial difficulties are attributed to each party's own sphere of responsibility.[9]) The procurement risk typically lies with the seller.[10]) However, the application of Art 79 is not categorically excluded in this context, but rather the standards applied to the assessment of the invoked impediment are higher.[11]) Also, when (substantial) financial difficulties with the contractual performance exclusively result from external and uncontrollable events (*e.g.*, global shortages in a necessary raw material), tribunals may consider the impediment to be beyond the control of any party.[12]) Increases in the cost of performance due to typical force majeure events (such as natural disasters, governmental interventions, piracy, pandemics) can qualify in this category.[13])

In case the performance impediment invoked by the seller stems from its own **external supplier**[14]) (who is unable to bear the increased cost of performance of its own delivery obligation), it is generally considered as part of the seller's procurement risk in (arbitral) case law.[15]) However, tribunals may qualify such impediment to be beyond the seller's sphere of responsibility

---

[8]) See *Schlechtriem/Schwenzer*, Commentary on the UN Convention on the International Sale of Goods (CISG), Art 79 mn 12; *Brunner*, Commentary on the UN Sales Law (CISG), Article 79, para 6.

[9]) See *Schlechtriem/Schwenzer*, Commentary on the UN Convention on the International Sale of Goods (CISG), Art 79 mn 26 with further references.

[10]) For example: Higher Regional Court of Hamburg, 28 February 1997, CISG-online 261; Swiss Federal Court of 12 June 2006, 4C.92/2006.

[11]) See *Salger* in *Witz/Salger/Lorenz*, International Einheitliches Kaufrecht Art. 79 mn 7.

[12]) See *Huber*, Münchener Kommentar (2008), Art 79 para 12.

[13]) See *Brunner*, Commentary on the UN Sales Law (CISG), Article 79, para 20.

[14]) External (sub)suppliers generally do not fall within the definition of "third person whom [the non-performing party] has engaged to perform the whole or a part of the contract" under Art 79(2) CISG. As a result, the stricter exemption standards of Art 79(2) CISG, pursuant to which the non-performing party must establish that the conditions for exemption are met not only for itself but also for the third-party supplier, do not apply in this context.

[15]) See for example: Arbitration Court of the International Chamber of Commerce, 1995 (Arbitral award No. 8128); Tribunal of the Hamburg Chamber of Commerce, 21 March 1996, NJW 1996, 3229-323 = CLOUT case No. 166; Tribunal of the International Commercial Arbitration at the Russian Federation Chamber of Commerce,

(control) if the external supplier holds a monopoly, either because it actually holds a monopoly in a particular market or because contractual arrangements designate it as the seller's sole source.[16])

## B. Unforeseeability

As second requirement, the impediment to performance must have been unforeseeable in the sense that it could not be expected to be taken into account by the obligor at the time of the conclusion of the contract. The key question in this context is what a "reasonable" contracting party in the same position could have anticipated – regardless of whether the impediment existed at the time of contract formation or arose later.[17]) The *Steel Rope* case[18]) illustrates this approach: The seller had invoked economic disruptions in Bulgaria, including currency devaluation, after a governmental collapse. However, because the parties had entered into the supply contract at a time when Bulgaria's severe economic instability was already in full force and presumed to be widely known, the arbitral tribunal rejected the application of Art 79.

Arbitral and judicial practice generally treat market fluctuations as foreseeable and part of the risk of commercial activities that each party has to bear.[19]) Yet exceptions remain possible where an increase of the cost of performance occurs with unprecedented magnitude or speed. This might especially be the case for short-term supply contracts. Conversely, parties entering into long-term delivery obligations are generally expected to exercise greater care to address potential price fluctuations, for instance through value protection clauses.

Some scholars[20]) as well as the CISG Advisory Council[21]) propose assessing the foreseeability requirement by examining historical price movements

16 March 1995, case no. 155/94 = CLOUT case No. 140; Higher Regional Court of Hamburg, 28 February 1997, CLOUT case No. 277.

[16]) See *Salger* in *Witz/Salger/Lorenz*, International Einheitliches Kaufrecht Art. 79 mn 8.

[17]) See *Salger* in *Witz/Salger/Lorenz*, International Einheitliches Kaufrecht Art. 79 mn 4; CISG Advisory Council Opinion No. 20, Comment 6.4.

[18]) Arbitration Court at the Bulgarian Chamber of Commerce and Industry, 12 February 1998 (CISG-online 436).

[19]) For example: RB Hasselt, 2 May 1995, CISG-online 371; ICC Ct Arb, 6281/1989, CISG-online 8; ICC Award, 26 Aug 1989, No 6281, CISG-online 8; Audiencia Provincial de Valladolid, Sección 1a, no. 69/2015, 6. 4. 2015, CISG-online No. 2619; RB Tongeren, 25 January 2005, CISG-online 1106; Cass civ 1ère, 30 June 2004, CISG-online 870; CA Colmar, 12 June 2001, CISG-online 694; Int Ct Russian CCI, 16 March 1995, CISG-online 526; Tribunale di Monza, 14 Jan 1993, CISG-online 540.

[20]) *Ishida*, CISG Art 79 at 367, 68; *Schwenzer/Muñoz*, Duty to Re-negotiate and Contract Adaptation in Case of Hardship, IHR 2020, 150 mn 19.

[21]) See CISG Advisory Council Opinion No. 20, Comment 4.6.

over a reasonable past time period. This approach reflects the expectation that (reasonable) market participants would monitor and evaluate pricing trends. With the growing availability of AI-based predictive pricing and risk analytics, what is considered foreseeable under Art 79 may evolve. As technologies enable (sophisticated) market participants to anticipate price volatility with increasing precision, arbitral tribunals might raise their expectations regarding a party's duty to foresee and manage supply cost fluctuations.

## C. Unavoidability

The final requirement of Art 79 – unavoidability of the impediment – is typically the most controversial. An impediment is considered "unavoidable" when the obligor cannot reasonably be expected to avoid or overcome it or its consequences. This requirement obliges the obligor to take all reasonable steps in its power to fulfill its obligations and counteract any difficulties as soon as it is aware of them, even if doing so entails considerable additional costs or results in a loss on the overall transaction.[22]) This approach is reflected in various arbitral awards.[23]) As an example, in the "Canned Oranges" case, the arbitral tribunal rejected the application of Art 79 since the seller was expected to overcome the invoked impediment (a flood that had severely reduced the oranges harvest in a particular province) by sourcing the oranges from another province, which was found to be a commercially reasonable substitute.[24])

However, drawing the line between reasonable and unreasonable measures remains difficult and **highly context-dependent**. As a general rule, an obligor may be exempted from liability under Art 79 when the expenditures associated with performance are grossly disproportionate to the value of the contract, resulting in a financial burden exceeding what a "reasonable person" would be expected to assume at the time of contract formation. In a comparative law study, a 100–125 % increase in the cost of the performance was suggested as a point of reference under general contract principles.[25])

As far as can be seen, publicly available arbitral awards addressing Art 79 in the context of economic hardship are limited and offer little guidance on the

---

[22]) See *Fischer*, Praxishandbuch UN-Kaufrecht Chapter VII.5.1(a); *Schlechtriem/Schwenzer*, Commentary on the UN Convention on the International Sale of Goods (CISG), Art 79 mn 14 *et seq*; Higher Regional Court of Hamburg, 28 February 1997, No. 167, CISG-online 261.

[23]) International Centre for Dispute Resolution of the American Arbitration Association, 23 October 2007 (Macromex Srl. v. Globex International Inc.); CIETAC, 30 November 1997 ("Canned Oranges" case), CISG-online No. 1412.

[24]) Ibid.

[25]) See *Brunner*, Force Majeure and Hardship under General Contract Principles: Exemption for Non-Performance in International Arbitration, International Arbitration Law Library, p. 426 *et seqq*.

precise "limit of sacrifice" an obligor must bear before it can rely on Art 79. In the absence of extensive arbitral case law, domestic state court decisions interpreting Art 79 also serve as valuable references for the uniform application of the CISG.[26]) From both arbitral and judicial practice, it emerges that an increase in the cost of performance of **less than 100 % generally does not suffice** to reach the obligor's "limit of sacrifice". Such an increase is typically not regarded as fundamentally or drastically altering the contractual equilibrium so as to justify the application of Art 79.[27])

A variety of factors of the individual case may influence the assessment. For example, the fact that the financial ruin of the obligor was imminent has been acknowledged in certain cases to lower the threshold of hardship.[28]) Also, tight revenue margins in a specific business sector may be argued to lower the threshold. On the other hand, if the obligor has hedged against market changes (*e.g.*, with insurance policies), the threshold can typically be considered higher.

The assessment of "unavoidability" typically needs to be **considered in conjunction with the other requirements of Art 79**. For example, any part of the cost increase that is attributable to the obligor's sphere of responsibility (i.e., not "beyond the control" of the obligor) must be deducted for the assessment of the "limit of sacrifice". Furthermore, the threshold for hardship can be lower in (domestic) procurement markets where price fluctuations are not to be expected to the same degree as in more speculative (international) markets that involve foreign currencies (thus, relating to the "unforeseeability" requirement).[29]) For instance, a German court has held that a seller had not reached its "limit of sacrifice" even after its supply prices had skyrocketed by 300 % because the respective market had been subject to a foreseeable volatility of prices.[30])

In essence, the yardstick used to measure the efforts of the non-performing party is (i) what can reasonably be expected from that party, (ii) what is

---

[26]) See Art 7 CISG; Austrian Supreme Court, legal proposition RIS-Justiz RS0008820.

[27]) See for example: Cour d'appel de Colmar 12 June 2001, CISG-online No. 694 (50 % price increase insufficient); Cour de cassation 30 June 2004, CISG-online No. 870 (50 % price increase insufficient); Tribunale Civile di Monza, 29 March 1993, CISG-online 102 (30 % price increase insufficient); CIETAC, 2 May 1996, CISG-online 1067; Int Ct Bulgarian CCI, 12 February 1998, CISG-online 436; Cour de cassation, 17 February 2015, CISG-online No. 2598 (price increases of 118 %, causing a 58 % drop in profits, insufficient). Deviating: Hof van Cassatie van Belgie, 19 June 2009, CISG-online No. 1963 (70 % price increase was considered sufficient for the application of Art 79; however, this decision has been widely criticized for its low standard of value alteration).

[28]) See *Brunner*, Force Majeure and Hardship under General Contract Principles: Exemption for Non-Performance in International Arbitration, International Arbitration Law Library, p. 435 *et seqq.*

[29]) See also CISG Advisory Council Opinion No. 20, Comment 7.

[30]) Higher Regional Court of Hamburg, 28 February 1997, No 167, CISG-online 261.

customary, or (iii) what similar individuals would have done in a similar situation. While applying an abstract guideline to determine the "limit of sacrifice" may represent a practical need, Art 79 rather requires a **comprehensive case-specific assessment** that takes all relevant circumstances into account. The available case law suggests that there is a general reluctance to apply economic hardship in the context of Art 79 as a **rather high "limit of sacrifice" is generally required**. Consequently, it was also noted in the UNCITRAL Digest of CISG Case Law 2016 that Art 79 had been invoked by parties with some frequency, but with limited success (e.g., sellers were successful with it in five cases, but denied in 27 cases).[31])

## III. Legal Effects and Alternative Remedies

Within the scope of application of the CISG, Art 79 sets the boundaries of the obligor's performance obligation in an exhaustive manner and does not leave any room for other potentially applicable domestic law remedies relating to hardship (such as "Wegfall der Geschäftsgrundlage", "clausula rebus sic stantibus", or frustration of contract).[32]) However, the application of Art 79 does not preclude other remedies available to the parties under the CISG, such as contract termination or reduction of the purchase price.[33])

Art 79 sets out an **exemption from liability for damages** (arising under Art 74–77) in connection with the failure to perform contractual obligations for as long as the impediment is present.[34]) Whether contractual penalties or liquidated damages are also covered by Art 79 remains controversial, though the majority opinion seems to favor such an approach when the underlying contract offers no clear guidance.[35]) Beyond the strict wording of Art 79, which does not expressly discharge an obligor from its (primary) obligation to perform, it is widely accepted that **claims for performance** – whether the

---

[31]) See UNCITRAL Digest of CISG Case Law 2016, p. 375 mn 7; p. 376 mn 15.

[32]) See CISG Advisory Council Opinion No. 7 (2007), Comments 34–35; *Brunner*, Force Majeure and Hardship under General Contract Principles: Exemption for Non-performance in International Arbitration, International Arbitration Law Library, p. 218 with further references; *Laimer*, Internationale Warenlieferungsverträge in der COVID-19-(Wirtschafts-)Krise, JBl 2020, 553; Landgericht Aachen, 14 May 1993, CLOUT case No. 47; Tribunale Civile di Monza, 14 January 1993, CLOUT case No. 54.

[33]) See Art 79(5).

[34]) Therefore, if the impediment is no longer present and the seller subsequently delivers, the buyer is not entitled to claim damages for any delay. In cases where the seller is temporarily prevented from delivering, yet ultimately fails to perform, the additional damages for the buyer caused by the ultimate non-performance need to be compensated.

[35]) See *Schlechtriem/Schwenzer*, Commentary on the UN Convention on the International Sale of Goods (CISG), Art 79 mn 52 with further references.

original delivery obligation or claims for substitute or replacement delivery – are also excluded for the duration of the impediment.[36])

Some scholars argue that the legal effects of Art 79 should not be applied in a rigid manner as the drafting history of Art 79 as well as the general characteristics of economic hardship rather call for the use of more flexible approaches to resolve fundamental value alterations. It is rather suggested that the obligor shall have a right to request the renegotiation of the contract or that an adaption of the contract by the arbitral tribunal or court be possible.[37])

The availability of these remedies, in particular a duty to renegotiate contractual terms, is argued by some based on the general rule to interpret the CISG in good faith (Art 7) – with the aim of restoring the balance of the performances.[38]) This approach is also supported by an earlier decision of the Belgian *Cour de Cassation*, where it assumed a right to request the renegotiation of a contract follows from the inherent equilibrium of contractual performances.[39]) Others argue a duty to renegotiate based on Art 9(2), which considers the parties to have impliedly made applicable to their contract any usages of international trade.[40]) As an important usage of international trade, Art 6.2.3 UNIDROIT Principles of International Commercial Contracts stipulate that "*in case of hardship the disadvantaged party is entitled to request renegotiations*". Despite these arguments, the predominant opinion rejects the existence of a duty to renegotiate under the CISG.[41])

[36]) See *Salger* in *Witz/Salger/Lorenz*, International Einheitliches Kaufrecht Art. 79 mn 12; CISG Advisory Council Opinion No. 7.

[37]) See CISG Advisory Council Opinion No. 7, Comments 29–30 and 40; *Brunner*, Force Majeure and Hardship under General Contract Principles: Exemption for Non-Performance in International Arbitration, International Arbitration Law Library, p. 216–227, 400, with further references.

[38]) See, for example, *Laimer*, Internationale Warenlieferungsverträge in der COVID-19-(Wirtschafts-)Krise, JBl 2020, 553 (560); CISG Advisory Council Opinion No. 7, Comment para 40.

[39]) Hof van Cassatie, 19 June 2009, CISG-online 1963 – However, this decision has been widely criticized for the application of the UNIDROIT rules to fill in a gap in the CISG that – according to the predominant opinion – does not exist (see *Eckardt/Magnus/Piltz*, Art. 79 CISG in der internationalen Rechtsprechung, IHR 2020, 140, para 22 with further references).

[40]) *Schlechtriem/Schwenzer*, Commentary on the UN Convention on the International Sale of Goods (CISG), Art 79, para 31, para 55, with further references.

[41]) See CISG Advisory Council Opinion No. 20, Comment 11; *Eckardt/Magnus/Piltz*, Art. 79 CISG in der internationalen Rechtsprechung, IHR 2020, 140, para 22, with reference to *Honnold/Flechtner*, mn 432.2; *Kröll/Mistelis/Perales Viscasillas/Atamer*, Art. 79 mn 84; *Schlechtriem/Schroeter*, Internationales UN-Kaufrecht mn 682; dissenting opinions: *Brunner* in *Brunner/Gottlieb*, Commentary on the UN Sales Law (CISG) Art. 79 mn 33; *MünchKomm/BGB/P. Huber*, Art. 79 CISG mn 21.

## IV. Conclusion

The general notion under the CISG is that parties are expected to do everything reasonably possible to fulfill their contractual obligations, even if doing so entails significant added costs or financial loss on the overall transaction (*pacta sunt servanda*). In the context of rising cost of performance due to changed market conditions, Art 79 can provide an exemption from liability for obligors in exceptional circumstances of economic unreasonableness or unaffordability of performance. In essence, this requires that (i) the non-performing obligor has not (explicitly or implicitly) assumed the risk for the change in market conditions, (ii) the change was unforeseeable at the time of contract formation and (iii) the efforts associated with the contract performance exceed what can reasonably be expected from the obligor.

While this approach is not inherently problematic, the rather restrictive (arbitral) case law on the application of Art 79 may raise doubts as to whether the current use and interpretation of this provision adequately reflect the commercial realities of post Covid-19 trade that is marked by increased global uncertainty and supply-chain volatility. Conversely, one might argue that the highly individual and fact-specific nature of the Art 79 assessment allows this provision to function effectively across time and commercial contexts. In any case, however, since there is no general point of reference to pinpoint when rising cost of performance can qualify as a sufficient impediment to the contractual performance, parties relying on Art 79 must often do so with considerable legal uncertainty. This underscores the importance of thoughtful contract drafting. Parties should consider proactively addressing risk allocation and the related legal consequences through force majeure, indexation, value-protection, or delivery-against-supply clauses to ensure a predictable balance of rights and obligations when circumstances change.

# The Tale of Two Cities: The Impact of Sanctions on Arbitration in London and Hong Kong

*Ana Stanič/Vod K.S. Chan**)

## I. Introduction

The 2022 invasion of Ukraine by Russia prompted an expansion of unilateral sanctions against Russian entities, particularly from by the European Union. In response, Russia introduced counter-legislation enabling sanctioned entities to turn to domestic courts to challenge the enforcement of those sanctions or to seek alternative pathways for redress. The sanctions, aimed at exerting political and economic pressure, and the counter-responses thereto are not only affecting sanctioned states but also critical hubs for international arbitration world-wide. This situation presents complex challenges for courts especially in leading arbitration hubs like London and Hong Kong ("**HK**") including concerning the enforceability of arbitration agreements.

What follows is the tale of the challenges faced by the courts in these two cities as a result of EU sanctions prohibiting (i) Linde and Renaissance from complying with the terms of the EPC Contracts they had entered into with RusChemAlliance ("**RCA**") to construct the gas processing plant in Russia[1]) and (ii) UniCreditBank GmBH ("**UniCredit**") from paying out pursuant to the performance bonds[2]) and the attempts by Russia to shield RCA from such

---

*) Mr Chan would like to thank Letty Lam for her assistance.

[1]) Article 3(b) of Regulation (EU) No 833/2014 concerning restrictive measures in view of Russia's actions destabilizing the situation in Ukraine as amended by Council Regulation (EU) 2022/576 of 8 April 2022 ("**Regulation**") provides that it "shall be prohibited to sell, supply, transfer, or export, directly or indirectly, goods and technology suited for use in oil refining and liquefaction of natural gas, as listed in Annex X, whether or not originating in the Union, to any natural or legal person, entity or body in Russia or for use in Russia. Text of the consolidated Regulation as it is in force today is available at https://eur-lex.europa.eu/legal-content/EN/TXT/HTML/?uri=CELEX:02014R0833-20250720#tit_1.

[2]) Article 3(b)(2)(b) states that it is prohibited to provide financing or financial assistance related to the goods and technology referred to in paragraph 1 for any sale, supply, transfer or export of those goods and technology, or for the provision of related technical assistance, brokering services or other services, directly or indirectly to any person, entity or body in Russia or for use in Russia. In addition, Article 11 (1)(b) provides that "[n]o claims in connection with any contract or transaction the performance

sanctions. The tale of another city, that of Moscow, will not be told expect as it impacted on the proceedings in London and Hong Kong.

## II. Background

In 2021 RCA entered into an Engineering Procurement and Construction ("**EPC**") contracts with Linde and Renaissance to construct liquefied natural gas (LNG) and gas processing plant facilities in Russia (the "**EPC Contracts**"). Under the EPC Contracts, RCA was obliged to pay the contractors approximately EUR 10 billion. The contractors were entitled to advance payment of EUR 2 billion, which RCA made. UniCredit issued seven on-demand performance bonds (the "**Bonds**") in favor of the RCA to a total value of approximately EUR 420 million, four of which were to guarantee the performance of the EPC Contracts and three of which were to secure repayment of the advance payment. Both the EPC Contracts and the Bonds were governed by English law. Both agreements provided for arbitration as a mechanism for resolving disputes, the former provided for arbitration seated in Hong Kong under the arbitration rules of the HK International Arbitration Centre ("**HKIAC**") and the latter in Paris under the arbitration rules of the International Chamber of Commerce ("**ICC**").

On 8 April 2022 the EU extended the sanctions regime to "the sale, supply, transfer, or export, directly or indirectly, of goods and technology suited for use … in the liquefaction of natural gas" pursuant to Article 3(b) of the Regulation. Shortly thereafter Linde wrote to the RCA advising that it was no longer able to perform the EPC Contracts and was also not able to return the advance payment. RCA terminated the EPC Contracts and also demanded payment under the Bonds issued by UniCredit. UniCredit, invoking Article 11 of the Regulation, asserted that it was prohibited from making any payment under the Bonds.

Relying on Article 248.1 of the Russian Arbitration Procedural Code ("**APC**"), RCA commenced proceedings against (i) Linde seeking repayment of the advance payment and (ii) UniCredit to recover the EUR 448 million under the Bonds in St Petersburgh court in March 2023 and August 2023 respectively. Article 248.1 had been adopted by the Russian Parliament on 8 June 2020 in order to "*protect the rights of natural and legal persons in connection with*

of which has been affected, directly or indirectly, in whole or in part, by the measures imposed under this Regulation, including claims for indemnity or any other claim of this type, such as a claim for compensation or a claim under a guarantee, notably a claim for extension or payment of a bond, guarantee or indemnity, particularly a financial guarantee or financial indemnity, of whatever form, shall be satisfied, if they are made by" any "Russian person, entity or body".

*restrictive measures introduced by foreign states or unions*".[3]) In particular, it grants Russian Arbitrazh Courts exclusive jurisdiction in respect of disputes arising from foreign sanctions and overriding contractually agreed arbitration if such sanctions *"obstruct such party's access to justice"* rendering arbitration no longer feasible.[4]) Article 248.2 also empowers these courts to issue anti-suit injunctions prohibiting the initiation or continuation of proceedings in foreign courts or international arbitration and to impose fines for breach thereof.

## III. The Tale of Hong Kong

In response to the proceedings brought in Russia, Linde initiated on 4 March 2023 arbitration before HKIAC, and obtained on 17 March 2023 an *ex parte* interim anti-suit injunction ("**ASI**") from the HK Court of First Instance ("**HKCFI**") seeking to restrain RCA from continuing the case before the court in St Petersburgh.

On 31 March 2023, RCA applied by summons to discharge the ASI on the following grounds: (i) that the Russian courts had exclusive jurisdiction over the dispute pursuant to Article 248.1; (ii) that the arbitration agreement was invalid as a result of the operation of such mandatory rule; and (iii) that as a result of EU sanctions HK would be biased against RCA as a Russian entity as HK has a close connection to the UK which is unfriendly towards Russia and in similar way denies RCA's access to justice.

In *Linde GMBH v. Ruschemalliance LLC* [2023] HKCFI 2409[5]) Mimmie Chan J rejected RCA's application to discharge the ASI for the following reasons. First, she affirmed the basic principle that HK is ready to grant an injunction to restrain proceedings brought in breach of an agreement to arbitrate [relying on *Donohue v Armco Inc* [2002] CLC 440; *Angelic Grace* [1995] 1 Lloyd's Rep 87], unless RCA can show that there is a strong reason to the contrary. She further noted that when considering whether to grant an ASI there is no need for parties to prove that arbitration in HK is the more convenient forum as the court is not comparing *forum conveniens* but deciding whether or not to enforce the agreement to arbitrate. Given that the parties had agreed to arbitration in HK, she concluded that Russian law lacked jurisdiction over the matter. She rejected the expert evidence that as a matter of Russian law the dispute between the parties under the EPC Contracts gives rise to matters of public law, rather than private law. Noting that a question

---

[3]) *See* Federal Law N 171-FZ, http://publication.pravo.gov.ru/Document/View/0001202006080017?index=1. English translation https://www.acerislaw.com/wp-content/uploads/2020/07/Anti-Russian-Sanctions-Law-English.pdf.

[4]) Article 248.1(4).

[5]) *Linde GMBH v. Ruschemalliance LLC* [2023] HKCFI 2409, https://legalref.judiciary.hk/lrs/common/search/search_result_detail_frame.jsp?DIS=155389&QS=%2B&TP=JU.

of foreign law is a question of fact she noted that "on the plain reading of Article 248.1, the exclusive jurisdiction of the Russian Court may not apply if there is an agreement between the parties to submit their dispute to international arbitration".[6]) Second, in response of RCA's claims that granting the ASI was neither just nor convenient given (i) the exclusive jurisdiction of Russian courts, and (ii) the invalidity of the arbitration agreement under Russian law, which renders any arbitral award unenforceable in Russia, she noted that the claim that Russian courts had exclusive jurisdiction is unfounded. Based on the evidence presented, she found that Article 248.1(4) applied only if foreign sanctions create obstacles to justice for a party in the dispute. The judge found RCA's arguments to be "*grossly exaggerated, if not totally based on false premises*" as (i) EU sanctions have no legal effect in HK and (ii) RCA clearly had access to lawyers in HK which represented it from the time of the initial *ex parte* application for the ASI until the case before her and (iii) its choice of arbitrator, the former Chief Justice of HK, Geoffrey Ma, was confirmed by the HKIAC. Accordingly, she concluded that there was no indication that RCA faced any difficulties in relation to its dealings with the HKIAC as a result of the sanctions nor before courts in HK. Third, that there was no "strong" reason to discontinue the ASI, noting existing case law that if an arbitration agreement is valid and enforceable under the law chosen by the parties (in this case, HK law), the mere fact that a foreign court might assert jurisdiction under its own law should not, as a general rule, prevent courts in HK to grant an ASI. She found that the present case there was no "strong reasons" for suing in a non-contractual forum as the effect of EU sanctions was foreseeable at the time of contracting and arbitration in HK, as stipulated in the EPC Contracts, would provide a fair trial to RCA. Fourth, that Article 284.1 was inapplicable to the present case, and that there was, in fact, a valid arbitration agreement covering the dispute between the parties. Accordingly, Mimmie Chan J issued an enforcement order requiring RCA to take all necessary steps to seek a stay of and take no further steps in the Russian courts.

In August 2025, RCA lodged an application before Anthony Chan J in HKCFI to discontinue and set aside the ASI order made by Mimmie Chan J on the ground that RCA was not able to comply with it. In ***RusChemAlliance LLC v Linde GMBH [2025] HKCF I3720***[7]) the learned judge rejected the application for the following reasons: (i) that this was not a case where RCA was unable to comply with the ASI order, but of compliance disadvantaging it; and (ii) that compliance with a court order is strict.

[6]) *Ibid.*, paragraph 45.

[7]) https://legalref.judiciary.hk/lrs/common/search/search_result_detail_frame.jsp?DIS=171513&QS=%26%2340%3B%7BRusChemAlliance%C2%A0%7D+%25parties%26%2341%3B&ID=AAATwKAAAAADpbz A1&TP=JU.

The above rulings were confirmed in ***Bank A v Bank B*** [2024] HKCFI 2529.[8]) In particular, in that case HKCFI affirmed that sanctions *per se* do not impede access to justice and granted an ASI together with an anti-enforcement injunction in favor of a German bank against a Russian bank, that was subjected to EU sanction.

Both cases illustrate the growing complexity at the intersection of EU sanctions and jurisdictional challenges in international arbitration. In both cases, HKCFI took a decisive stand by upholding an ASI restraining court proceedings initiated in Russia. The HK Court's rulings exemplify how the judiciary in HK is willing to protect the rights of parties who choose arbitration as their preferred mechanism of dispute resolution, affirming the sanctity of arbitration agreements in the face of conflicting legal actions.

## IV. The Tale of London

With a hearing before the Russian Arbitrazh Court scheduled against it for 27 September 2023, UniCredit obtained from the English High Court an interim ASI to restrain them on an *ex parte* basis on 22 August 2023. It had applied to the English High Court to do so even though the seat of arbitration was in Paris.

Since RCA is not domiciled in England or Wales and has no presence there, the ability of the English court to grant an ASI depended on whether service could be effected on RCA out of the jurisdiction. This required three tests to be satisfied: (i) that there is a serious issue to be tried, (ii) that there is a good arguable case that the claim falls within one of the relevant gateways in Practice Direction 6B, and in particular, that the contract was governed by English Law (the "**Contract Gateway Test**"); and (iii) that England is the proper place in which to bring the claim (the "**Appropriate Forum Test**"). The first point was not disputed as between the parties.

The hearing with regard to the final relief was held on 22 September 2023 at which in an *extempore* judgement Sir Nigel Teare held that English courts did not have jurisdiction over RCA on the following two grounds.[9]) First, that the starting point under Enka v Chubb [2020] UKSC 38,[10]) in which the UK Supreme Court found that in the absence of a choice of law governing the arbitration agreement the parties' choice of English law as the governing law of the main contract generally governs the arbitration agreement, is negated by

[8]) *Bank A v Bank B* [2024] HKCFI 2529, https://legalref.judiciary.hk/lrs/common/search/search_result_detail_frame.jsp?DIS=163107&QS=%2B&TP=JU.

[9]) *Unicredit Bank GmbH v RusChemAlliance LLC* [2024] UKSC 30. https://www.supremecourt.uk/cases/judgments/uksc-2024-0015.

[10]) *Enka Insaat Ve Sanayi AS v OOO Insurance Company Chubb* [2020] UKSC 38, ("**Enka**"), https://www.bailii.org/uk/cases/UKSC/2020/38.html.

the non-statutory principle of French law (as the *lex arbitri*) whereby the existence and effectiveness of an arbitration agreement is determined in accordance with parties' common intention, which since the parties had chosen Paris as the seat of arbitration, was to be taken to be French law. Accordingly, the judge found that UniCredit did not satisfy the Contract Gateway Test as the arbitration agreement was governed by French law. Second, Sir Nigel Teare found that the ICC arbitration was the appropriate forum for UniCredit to seek damages for breach of the arbitration agreement. He, thus, found that the Appropriate Forum Test was also not satisfied albeit acknowledging that an ASI could not be obtained from a French court and an award of damages may be difficult to enforce.

As UniCredit appealed the decision, the interim ASI stayed in place. The Arbitrazh Court in St Petersburgh suspended proceedings pending the appeal to the Court of Appeal and subsequently the appeal to the Supreme Court. Both the Court of Appeal[11]) and the Supreme Court held that the English court had jurisdiction and that both tests were satisfied. In particular, in ***UniCredit Bank GmbH v RusChemAlliance LLC [2024] UKSC 30***[12]) the Supreme Court in an unanimous decision held that English law governed the arbitration agreement confirming its ruling in Enka noting that the fact that the courts of France as the seat of arbitration may take the view that French law is the governing law was not a good reason to depart from Enka. With reference to the Appropriate Court Test the court clarified, as had the HK court, that the case before it did not concern the issue of whether England is *forum conveniens* but whether or not England was the proper place to enforce the parties' agreement to arbitrate. Noting that "*where the contractually agreed forum is arbitration, the policy of securing compliance with the parties' contractual bargain is further reinforced by the strong international policy of giving effect to agreements to arbitrate disputes. The main pillar on which international arbitration rests is the 1958 Convention on the Recognition and Enforcement of Foreign Arbitral Awards, known as the New York Convention, which now has more than 170 state parties and has been implemented through national legislation in almost all contracting states*".[13]) It then went on to find that RCA had not sought to argue that Article 248.1 was a mandatory principle of foreign law (*lois de police*) which overrode English law by rendering the arbitration agreement null and void. It, therefore, held that (i) the power to grant injunctive relief does not derive from or require supervisory jurisdiction and is able to be exercised by courts other than the courts of the seat and in any event, on the evidence before it French courts would not have jurisdiction over RCA and

[11]) *Unicredit Bank GmbH v RusChemAlliance LLC* [2024] EWCA Civ 64, https://www.bailii.org/ew/cases/EWCA/Civ/2024/64.html.

[12]) *Unicredit,* [2024] UKSC 30, https://www.bailii.org/cgi-bin/format.cgi?doc=/uk/cases/UKSC/2024/30.html&query=(2024)+AND+(UKSC)+AND+(30).

[13]) *Ibid.*, at [68].

(ii) England was the proper place to seek an ASI due to the arbitral tribunal having no coercive power and the undisputed evidence that as a matter of French law French courts have no power to enforce an arbitral order prohibiting the continuation of court proceedings in Russia.

In a further twist, revealing the complexities sanctions and measures introduced to counter-sanctions have introduced in arbitration, UniCredit applied to the English Court of Appeal to revoke the anti-suit injunction in February 2025. It did so after RCA obtained a ruling from the St Petersburg court (i) prohibiting UniCredit from initiating arbitrations or court proceedings against RSA except in the Russian courts in respect of the Bonds; (ii) prohibiting UniCredit from continuing any proceedings or enforcing any judgments against RCA, except in Russian courts; (iii) obliging UniCredit to take all measures within its control to cancel the effect of the ASI by the UK Supreme Court within two weeks of its decision; and (iv) ordering UniCredit to pay RCA €250 million should it fail to comply with its decision. Weighing, on the one hand, that pursing contempt of court proceedings in England would have little practical effect since RCA had no assets outside of Russia and its officers did not travel outside Russia and on the other hand the fact that it still had significant assets in Russia, UniCredit told the Supreme Court that it wished to have the ASI lifted and would proceed to have the dispute resolved before the court in St Petersburg. The Supreme Court obliged by finding that (i) UniCredit could not be considered as having been coerced in making this request and (ii) there were no public policy reasons which would militate against refusing the application since "UniCredit is a commercial party acting in its own interest and is entitled to tell the court that it no longer needs or wants the anti-suit injunction".[14]) The Court clarified that Article 11 (c) of the Regulation which was inserted in December 2024 prohibits EU Member States giving effect to any order made by the Russia Court pursuant to Article 248 of the APC did not have legal effect in UK and that no equivalent measures were adopted in the UK.

Although the Supreme Court's decision granting ASI was welcomed by many in the international arbitration community as pro-arbitration, others noted that it was at odds with the approach taken in other leading arbitration hubs. In most jurisdictions around the world (including in HK) the default rule in absence of express parties' choice is that the law governing the arbitration agreement is the law of the seat. As part of the modernization of the English Arbitration Act and on the recommendation of the Law Commission, which found that the principles in Enka to be "complex and unpredictable"[15]) Section 6A(1)(b) of the English Arbitration Act 2025 provides that the law

---

[14]) *Ibid.*, at [43].

[15]) Law Commission, *Review of the Arbitration Act 1996: Final report and Bill* (Law Com No 413), published on 5 September 2023, paragraph 12.20, https://webarchive.nationalarchives.gov.uk/ukgwa/20250109103833mp_/https://cloud-platform-e218f50a

applicable to an arbitration agreement is the absence of an express agreement is the law of the seat of arbitration. The English Arbitration Act entered into force on 1 August 2025. Accordingly, going forward the English court will not be in a position to grant ASI in support of arbitrations in other jurisdictions as it did in the case of UniCredit.

As at the time of writing this article, the dispute under the Bonds is being heard by the St Petersburgh Court and the dispute under the EPC Contracts in HK.

## V. Conclusion

The tale of the two cities illustrates the growing complexity at the intersection of EU sanctions and jurisdictional challenges in international arbitration. The use of sanctions as a way to exert political and economic pressure is not new. However, the sanctions introduced against Russia after its invasion of Ukraine by the EU, in particular, have been much more extensive both in depth, sectors of the economy covered as well as breadth, for example sanctioning access to the SWIFT financial system. Secondary sanctions have also been adopted in recent sanctions packages by the EU sanctioning third parties including from China and India for doing business with Russian companies. In fact, in today's interconnected economy, no company is immune to the disruptions caused by the imposition of sanctions. In response to the broad-based sanctions introduced against Russian individuals and entities, Russia, as well as other countries subject to sanctions, have increased efforts to assert jurisdiction over disputes involving sanctioned parties by according jurisdiction to local courts.

The courts in jurisdictions outside the EU have found themselves in the cross-fire of these measures. The tale of the two cities illustrates how the courts in HK and UK have dealt with the challenges of sanctions as concerns the enforcement of arbitration agreements. It is clear from the HK and UK decisions that unilateral sanctions imposed by EU are not binding on their courts. The HK decision also makes clear that the introduction of sanctions does not *per se* automatically invalidate an arbitration agreement. The readiness of both courts to issue ASI to uphold arbitration agreements is also important in promoting trust in arbitration as a reliable mechanism for resolving cross border disputes.

Looking ahead, as the legal landscape continues to evolve, the principles established in these cases are likely to shape future arbitration practice. They reinforce the notion that parties should be able to rely on their chosen dispute resolution mechanisms, even in the face of external legal and political chal-

4812967ba1215eaecede923f.s3.amazonaws.com/uploads/sites/30/2023/09/Arbitration-final-report-with-cover.pdf.

lenges. Preserving arbitration as an effective avenue for resolving international disputes contributes meaningfully to a resilient international and depoliticized legal framework that supports global trade and investment in an increasingly complex geopolitical environment. It contributes also to keeping and fostering peace.

# Clash of Titans or Contemporary Issues of *lis pendens* in the EU Arbitration Law

*Albertas Šekštelo**)

## I. Introduction

"Zeus understood clearly that war was inevitable. Kronos would not rest as long as his children lived, and Zeus was just as determined to dethrone his father. He heard louder than ever the sound he had heard within him since infancy: a softly insistent whisper from Moros telling him that it was his destiny to rule".[1])

Moros's prophecy that Kronos would be overthrown by his children so possessed him that he devoured all his children born to his wife Gaia. But he was deceived and had to face his last son, Zeus, in the bloody, violent, and destructive conflict known as Titanomachy – the clash of Titans. Zeus defeated the Titans, just as his father Kronos had done before him. This led to the Third Order of divine beings.

Interestingly, "[t]he origins of international arbitration are sometimes traced, if uncertainly, to ancient mythology"[2]) as well. Deities aside, ancient Greeks often resorted to international arbitration to resolve disputes between city-states.[3])

Throughout history we have seen many views towards arbitration. Gaillard distinguished three representational paradigms: "[t]he first relegates international arbitration to a component of a single national legal order. The second anchors international arbitration in a plurality of national legal orders. The third representation [...] recognizes an autonomous character to international arbitration".[4]) And the form of representation impacts the understanding of such concepts, as *e. g.*, *lis pendens*. Just as there was a clash of Titans, we now witness a clash of representations, where, on the one hand, the CJEU sticks to the old concept of the single European legal order and squeezes arbitration into

---

*) Associate professor at Vilnius University Law Faculty and partner at MOTIEKA Law firm.

[1]) Stephen Fry, *Mythos*. Penguin Books 43 (2018).

[2]) Gary B. Born, *International Commercial Arbitration*. Wolters Kluwer 7 (2nd ed. 2014).

[3]) *Id.* at 8.

[4]) Emmanuel Gaillard, *Legal Theory of International Arbitration*. Martinus Nijhoff Publishers 15 (2010).

it. On the other hand, arbitration stands for an independent legal order and faces severe consequences not only by itself but also by the courts that support this concept.

This publication demonstrates that the CJEU adheres to Gaillard's first representational paradigm that "assimilates the arbitrator to a national judge" rather than recognizing arbitration's autonomous character.[5]) To prove this thesis, we examine three pivotal clashes between the CJEU and arbitration: first, the West Tankers and Steamship Owners cases, which established the framework for EU interference with arbitration; and second, the Royal Football Club Seraing case, which further eroded arbitration's autonomy. The reader may then judge whether the CJEU acts as Kronos – devouring arbitration's independence – or as Zeus – establishing a new, more integrated legal order.

## II. 1st Clash – Two Ships Shatter Arbitration in the EU

In August 2000, the Front Comor, a vessel owned by West Tankers and chartered by Erg Petroli SpA, collided in Syracuse (Italy) with a jetty owned by Erg and caused damage, with the charterparty governed by English law and containing a clause providing for arbitration in London.

Two years later, in November 2002, the oil tanker Prestige sank off the coast of Spain, causing significant environmental damage to the Spanish and French coastlines, and a criminal investigation was subsequently initiated in Spain at the end of 2002 against, amongst others, the master of that vessel.

These two unrelated vessels caused considerable damage not only to the aggrieved parties but also to arbitration within the EU. Both cases led to the Court of Justice of the EU ("**CJEU**"). The first is known as "*West Tankers*",[6]) the second as "*Steamship Owners*".[7])

### A. *West Tankers'* Impact on Arbitration in the EU

In the *West Tankers* case, Erg claimed compensation from its insurers Allianz and Generali up to the limit of its insurance cover and commenced arbitration proceedings in London against West Tankers for the excess with West Tankers denying liability for the damage caused by the collision.

In turn, having paid Erg compensation under the insurance policies for the loss it had suffered, Allianz and Generali brought proceedings against West

---

[5]) *Id.* at 15.

[6]) CJEU Judgment in the case C-185/07 *Allianz SpA and Generali Assicurazioni Generali SpA v West Tankers Inc.* ECLI:EU:C:2009:69.

[7]) CJEU Judgment in the case C-700/20 *London Steam-Ship Owners' Mutual Insurance Association Limited v Kingdom of Spain.* ECLI:EU:C:2022:488.

Tankers before the Tribunale di Siracusa (Italy) to recover the sums they had paid to Erg. The action was based on their statutory right of subrogation to Erg's claims, and West Tankers raised an objection of lack of jurisdiction based on the existence of the arbitration agreement.

In parallel, West Tankers brought proceedings before the High Court of Justice of England and Wales seeking a declaration that the dispute between itself and Allianz and Generali was to be settled by arbitration pursuant to the arbitration agreement, and also seeking an anti-suit injunction restraining Allianz and Generali from pursuing any proceedings other than arbitration and requiring them to discontinue the proceedings commenced before the Tribunale di Siracusa.

The High Court of Justice upheld West Tankers' claims and granted the anti-suit injunction sought against Allianz and Generali, who then appealed against that judgment to the House of Lords, arguing that the grant of such an injunction is contrary to Brussels I Regulation. The House of Lords referred to the CJEU. The House of Lords referred to the judgments in *Gasser*[8]) and *Turner*[9]) cases, which decided in substance that an injunction restraining a party from commencing or continuing proceedings in a court of a Member State cannot be compatible with the system established by Brussels I Regulation. However, the House of Lords considered that this principle could not be extended to arbitration, which is completely excluded from the scope of Brussels I Regulation.

However, the CJEU held that "the objection of lack of jurisdiction raised by West Tankers before the Tribunale di Siracusa on the basis of the existence of an arbitration agreement, including the question of the validity of that agreement, comes within the scope of [Brussels I Regulation] and that it is therefore exclusively for that court to rule on that objection and on its own jurisdiction, pursuant to Articles 1(2)(d) and 5(3) of that regulation".[10]) The judgment established that whilst arbitration is excluded from the scope of the Brussels I Regulation, anti-suit injunctions issued by courts of one Member State to prevent proceedings in another Member State are incompatible with the Regulation, even when granted in support of arbitration agreements. The Court emphasized the principles of mutual trust between Member State courts and the right of each court to determine its own jurisdiction, including preliminary issues concerning the validity and applicability of arbitration agreements. In other words, comity was the key factor limiting the intra-EU application of anti-suit injunctions.

[8]) CJEU Judgement in the case C-116/02 *Erich Gasser GmbH v MISAT Srl.* ECLI:EU:C:2003:657.

[9]) CJEU Judgement in the case C-159/02 *Gregory Paul Turner v Felix Fareed Ismail Grovit, Harada Ltd and Changepoint SA.* ECLI:EU:C:2004:228.

[10]) CJEU Judgment in the case C-700/20 *London Steam-Ship Owners' Mutual Insurance Association Limited v Kingdom of Spain.* ECLI:EU:C:2022:488, para. 27.

This represented the first clash between EU civil procedure law as embodied in the then-Brussels I Regulation and arbitration. *West Tankers* resulted in the prohibition of arbitration-related anti-suit injunctions granted by courts. But it did not touch upon the *lis pendens*, as there was no parallel arbitration then. However, in the later *Gazprom* case, the CJEU left the anti-suit injunctions granted by the arbitral tribunal outside the scope of Brussels I Regulation but warned the courts that any potential limitation of the courts' power should be assessed under the procedural law of the *lex fori* Member State and the New York Convention.[11]) Interestingly, the New York Convention does not expressly address the *lis pendens* issue.[12]) Member State courts could, at the stage of challenge or recognition and enforcement of the award in question, in principle, argue that such an anti-suit injunction award is against the public policy under Article V(2)(b) of the New York Convention.[13])

## B. *Steamship Owners'* Impact on Arbitration in the EU

In the *Steamship Owners* case,[14]) the dispute arose after the oil tanker sank off the coast of Spain, causing considerable environmental damage to the Spanish and French coastlines.

Various legal entities, including the Spanish State, brought damage claims against the ship's master, owners, and insurer. Rather than participating in these proceedings, the insurer commenced UK arbitration based on its insurance agreement's arbitration clause, seeking declarations that the Spanish State was bound by arbitration and that the insurer bore no liability. The arbitral tribunal granted these claims. The insurer then obtained UK court leave to enforce the award. Despite not participating in arbitration, the Spanish State opposed enforcement but was unsuccessful. Subsequently, Spanish courts rendered judgment against the insurer, and the Spanish State secured recognition and enforcement of this judgment from the UK High Court. The insurer appealed, arguing the judgment conflicted with the arbitral award. The High Court referred to the CJEU and asked whether Article 34(3) of Brussels I Regulation must be interpreted as meaning that a judgment entered by a court

[11]) CJEU Judgment in the case C-536/13 *"Gazprom" OAO v Lietuvos Respublika*. ECLI:EU:C:2015:316, para. 42.

[12]) Gary B. Born, *International Commercial Arbitration*. Wolters Kluwer 3796 (2nd ed. 2014).

[13]) In fact, in the *Gazprom* case, the Lithuanian Court of Appeals (Lietuvos apeliacinis teismas) refused to recognize the award precisely because of public policy; however, the Supreme Court of Lithuania quashed its ruling when the latter received the CJEU's Judgment.

[14]) CJEU Judgment in the case C-700/20 *London Steam-Ship Owners' Mutual Insurance Association Limited v Kingdom of Spain*. ECLI:EU:C:2022:488.

of a Member State in the terms of an arbitral award may constitute a 'judgment', within the meaning of that provision, which prevents the recognition, in that Member State, of a judgment given by a court in another Member State if those two judgments are irreconcilable.[15])

The CJEU held that exclusion of Article 1(2)(d) of the Brussels I Regulation covers arbitration, including proceedings brought before national courts.[16]) Likewise, recital 12 of Brussels I bis Regulation now emphasizes that the Regulation does not apply to any action or judgment concerning the recognition or enforcement of an arbitral award.[17]) The logical conclusion would be that "a judgment entered in the terms of an arbitral award is caught by the arbitration and that it cannot, therefore, enjoy mutual recognition between the Member States and circulate within the EU judicial area".[18])

However, the CJEU emphasized that the notion of „judgment" is rather broad and thus should encompass any judgment, including one related to the recognition or enforcement of an arbitral award.[19]) Mutual trust in the administration of justice in the EU does not extend to decisions made by arbitral tribunals or to judicial decisions entered in their terms.[20]) The CJEU noted that the court's judgment cannot be recognized as irreconcilable with the award, only if the latter does not infringe the right to an effective remedy guaranteed in Article 47 of the Charter of Fundamental Rights of the EU and enables the objective of mutual trust in the administration of justice within the EU.[21])

The CJEU went even further and stated that "[i]n the present case, it should be noted that the content of the arbitral award at issue in the main proceedings could not have been the subject of a judicial decision falling within the scope of [Brussels I Regulation] without infringing two fundamental rules of that regulation concerning, first, the relative effect of an arbitration clause included in an insurance contract and, secondly, *lis pendens*".[22]) In other words, the CJEU examined the merits of the award in question and stated that the court would not have granted such a decision, *inter alia*, because of the *lis pendens*. But why?

When the arbitral proceedings commenced, the case that involved the same cause of action had already been pending before the Spanish courts.[23]) This was against Article 27 of the Brussels I Regulation, as the court first seized should have established its jurisdiction first.[24]) The CJEU then "punished" the

---

[15]) *Ibid.* at 41.
[16]) *Ibid.* at 44.
[17]) *Ibid.* at 46.
[18]) *Ibid.* at 47.
[19]) *Ibid.* at 49, 53.
[20]) *Ibid.* at 57.
[21]) *Ibid.* at 58.
[22]) *Ibid.* at 59.
[23]) *Ibid.* at 64–68.
[24]) *Ibid.* at 69.

award by stating that objections of the Brussels I Regulation should not be circumvented, including the *lis pendens* rule, and, consequently, by stating that judgment entered by a court of a Member State in the terms of an arbitral award does not constitute a 'judgment', within the meaning of that provision, where a judicial decision resulting in an outcome equivalent to the outcome of that award could not have been adopted by a court of that Member State without infringing the provisions and the fundamental objectives of that regulation, in particular as regards the relative effect of an arbitration clause included in an insurance contract and the rules on *lis pendens* contained in Article 27 of that regulation, and that, in that situation, the judgment in question cannot prevent, in that Member State, the recognition of a judgment given by a court in another Member State.[25])

Moreover, the CJEU emphasized that „the recognition or enforcement of a judgment from another Member State cannot be refused as being contrary to public policy on the ground that it would disregard the force of *res judicata* acquired by the judgment entered in the terms of an arbitral award".[26])

The clash between EU policy and arbitration was even more apparent and striking in *Steamship Owners*. In *West Tankers*, there was no evident issue of *lis pendens*, but in *Steamship Owners*, it indeed was.

These two cases established a troubling precedent: the CJEU's willingness to apply EU procedural rules to arbitration despite arbitration's formal exclusion from the Brussels I bis Regulation's scope. The Court's reasoning reveals a fundamental misunderstanding of arbitration's nature as an autonomous dispute resolution mechanism, treating it instead as merely another form of national court proceeding subject to EU coordination rules.

## C. 1st Clash – Analysis of the Impact

### 1. *Lis pendens* vs. Competence-Competence

The first issue is that the CJEU considered arbitration as operating in the same realm as national courts. As demonstrated above, in the *Steamship Owners* case, the CJEU stated that the courts in the given situation would not have granted a similar decision because of the *lis pendens*.

First of all, in the previous case, the CJEU decided that a violation of the *lis pendens* rule in the event of parallel court proceedings in matrimonial matters does not amount to violation of public policy.[27]) However, suddenly, in

[25]) *Ibid.* at 71–73.

[26]) *Ibid.* at 80.

[27]) CJEU Judgment in the case C-386/17 *Stefano Liberato v Luminita Luisa Grigorescu*. ECLI:EU:C:2019:24; Vesna Lazic, Peter Mankowski, *The Brussels I-bis Regulation. Interpretation and Implementation.* Edward Elgar Publishing 49 (2023).

the *Steamship Owners* case *lis pendens* became relevant in the event of arbitration.

Second, it is correctly pointed out that "[m]ost puzzling is how the 'relative effect of an arbitration clause' can be considered one of the fundamental objectives of the Regulation considering that arbitration is excluded altogether from its scope".[28])

Third and foremost, many authors deny the existence of any question of *lis pendens* in the context of arbitration (between an arbitral tribunal and a State court) "based on the notion that a contractual undertaking to arbitrate is sufficient, in and of itself, to preclude the concurrent exercise of jurisdiction by public authorities, thus rendering moot the problem of *lis pendens*".[29]) In other words, the arbitral tribunal has inherent power to decide on its own jurisdiction by virtue of the competence-competence doctrine. Such a power is expressly granted by all progressive States that implemented the UNCITRAL Model Law on International Commercial Arbitration and the main arbitration rules. This means that the arbitral tribunal has the priority to decide on jurisdiction. Therefore, the *lis pendens* rule is inapplicable in such a situation.

However, the CJEU ignored this concept, although Articles 25 and 31(1) of the Brussels Ibis Regulation have the same exception of *lis pendens* in terms of the prorogation of jurisdiction: where a court of a Member State on which an agreement as referred to in Article 25 confers exclusive jurisdiction is seized, any court of another Member State shall stay the proceedings until the court seized based on the agreement declares that it has no jurisdiction under the agreement.[30])

[28]) *Ead.* at 49.

[29]) Filip J.M. De Ly and Audley William Sheppard, *ILA Final Report on Lis Pendens and Arbitration Seventy-second International Law Association Conference on International Commercial Arbitration* in William W. Park (ed), Arbitration International, pp. 3–34; Gary B. Born, *International Commercial Arbitration*. Wolters Kluwer 3794 (2014); Emmanuel Gaillard, *Legal Theory of International Arbitration*. Martinus Nijhoff Publishers 87 (2010); Geisinger & Lévy, *Lis Alibi Pendens in International Commercial Arbitration, in ICC, Complex Arbitrations* 53 (2003).

[30]) Recital (22) of the Brussels I bis Regulation is more than clear in this regard: „in order to enhance the effectiveness of exclusive choice-of-court agreements and to avoid abusive litigation tactics, it is necessary to provide for an exception to the general lis pendens rule in order to deal satisfactorily with a particular situation in which concurrent proceedings may arise. This is the situation where a court not designated in an exclusive choice-of-court agreement has been seised of proceedings and the designated court is seised subsequently of proceedings involving the same cause of action and between the same parties. In such a case, the court first seised should be required to stay its proceedings as soon as the designated court has been seised and until such time as the latter court declares that it has no jurisdiction under the exclusive choice-of-court agreement. This is to ensure that, in such a situation, the designated court has priority to decide on the validity of the agreement and on the extent to which the agreement applies to the dispute pending before it. The designated

Thus, viewed through the lens of a choice-of-court agreement, the issue that emerged in the *Steamship Owners* case would not have been relevant. The second court (in England) would have had an exclusive right to deal with its competence, and the first court seized (in Spain) would have stayed the proceedings until the first seized court deals with its jurisdiction and merits. In turn, such an English court's decision would not have raised any issues regarding the *lis pendens*. Thus, the CJEU made an apparent mistake in not treating arbitration as having exclusive jurisdiction.

However, the CJEU deprived arbitration of its inherent exclusive rights to deal with the competence and thus threatened the mere existence of the competence-competence doctrine.

## 2. Attack on *res judicata*

In the *Steamship Owners* case, the referring court asked the third question whether Article 34(1) of Brussels I Regulation must be interpreted as meaning that, in the event that Article 34(3) of that Regulation does not apply to a judgment entered in the terms of an arbitral award, the recognition or enforcement of a judgment from another Member State may be refused as being contrary to public policy on the ground that it would disregard the force of *res judicata* acquired by the judgment entered in the terms of an arbitral award. The CJEU stated that the recognition or enforcement of a judgment from another Member State cannot be refused as being contrary to public policy on the ground that it would disregard the force of *res judicata* acquired by the judgment entered in the terms of an arbitral award.

The CJEU held that „the arbitral proceedings which gave rise to the award confirmed by that judgment were completed in breach of the rules on *lis pendens* laid down in Article 27 of that regulation and the relative effect of an arbitration clause included in the insurance contract in question".[31]) As stated above, the CJEU not only disregarded the competence-competence doctrine recognized in all Member States but also, *ipso facto*, deprived the arbitral award of the *res judicata* effect by disregarding the force of *res judicata* acquired by the judgment entered in the terms of the arbitral award. Such deprivation was confirmed three years later.

The implications of this approach extend far beyond the specific facts of these cases. By denying *res judicata* effect to arbitral awards that allegedly violate EU procedural rules, the CJEU has created a mechanism whereby any arbitral award touching on EU law issues becomes vulnerable to collateral

court should be able to proceed irrespective of whether the non-designated court has already decided on the stay of proceedings".

[31]) CJEU Judgment in the case C-700/20 *London Steam-Ship Owners' Mutual Insurance Association Limited v Kingdom of Spain*. ECLI:EU:C:2022:488, para. 75.

attack in Member State courts. This fundamentally undermines the finality that makes arbitration an attractive dispute resolution mechanism.

## III. 2nd Clash – CJEU again Scores the Goal! 2:0

The Grand Chamber of the CJEU again shook the arbitration community on August 1, 2025 in the *Royal Football Club Seraing* case.[32])

The main dispute concerned the FIFA Regulations on the Status and Transfer of Players, the essence of which was to establish restrictions on transferring players from one club belonging to different associations to another. FIFA established prohibitions on third-party ownership of footballers, whereby private investors acquire economic rights to footballers to profit from future transfer fees. FIFA, having established violations of the regulations, prohibited transfers for two years and imposed a fine of approximately EUR 138,000 (CHF 150,000) on Seraing for two contracts it concluded with the Maltese investment fund Doyen Sports regarding the transfer of economic rights to three players.

Seraing club appealed this FIFA decision to the FIFA Appeals Committee, which rejected the appeal.

Seraing then lodged an appeal with the Court of Arbitration for Sport and, inter alia, argued that the contested FIFA Appeals Committee decision violated the European Union's freedom of movement of workers, services, and capital, as well as Swiss competition rules. The Court of Arbitration for Sport dismissed the appeal. When this arbitration award was appealed to the Swiss Federal Supreme Court (*Tribunal fédéral*), the latter dismissed the appeal, even though Seraing based its appeal on the grounds that the arbitration award was incompatible with "substantive public policy" because it prohibited the freedom of movement of workers, capital, and services, as well as competition rules.

A dispute concerning the FIFA regulations also took place in Belgium, in which Seraing club intervened, requesting the Belgian court to declare void the relevant provision of the FIFA regulations, which later gave rise to the dispute in arbitration. The court of first instance found that it lacked jurisdiction, and when the dispute reached the Brussels Court of Appeal (*Cour d'appel de Bruxelles*), the latter, after the Court of Arbitration for Sport decision discussed above, dismissed Seraing's appeal. When Seraing lodged an appeal on points of law with the Belgian Court of Cassation (*Cour de cassation*), the latter referred a request for a preliminary ruling to the CJEU. The Belgian Court of Cassation raised the following questions: (1) whether it is prohibited to apply the principle of *res judicata* to an arbitration award if the review of such award's compliance with European Union law was not carried out by a court of an EU

[32]) CJEU Judgment in the case C-600/23 *Royal Football Club Seraing SA v. Fédération internationale de football association (FIFA) et al.* ECLI:EU:C:2025:617.

Member State that cannot refer a preliminary question to the CJEU; (2) whether it is prohibited to grant such an arbitration award evidential force?

Through the lens of the effective judicial protection enshrined in Article 47 of the Fundamental Rights of the European Union, the CJEU stated that the courts must be able "to carry out an effective judicial review of the acts, measures or behavior alleged, in the context of a given dispute, to have infringed the rights or freedoms which EU law confers on individuals. That requirement means, in principle, that those courts or tribunals must have the power to consider all the issues of fact and of law that are relevant for resolving that case".[33]) And such remedies "must enable the competent national court or tribunal to request the Court of Justice to give a preliminary ruling on any question concerning the interpretation of EU law or the validity of an act of EU law".[34]) In other words, the preliminary ruling procedure constitutes an essential component of the system established by the Treaties to enable national courts or tribunals to ensure effective judicial protection of the rights which individuals derive from EU law.[35])

Therefore, at least awards in the mandatory arbitrations "must be amenable to judicial review such as to guarantee the effective judicial protection to which the individuals concerned are entitled".[36]) Consequently, the courts of the Member States' scope of review of the arbitral award must be extended "as to whether such awards are consistent with the principles and provisions which form part of EU public policy and which are relevant to the dispute concerned".[37]) The CJEU concluded that it is prohibited to give an arbitral award a res judicata effect and probative value unless the national court checks its consistency with EU public policy.

The Royal Football Club Seraing decision represents the culmination of the CJEU's systematic approach to subordinating arbitration to EU law. Unlike the earlier cases, which focused on procedural coordination between Member State courts, this decision directly attacks the substantive finality of arbitral awards by requiring extensive judicial review for compliance with EU public policy. This transforms arbitration from a final dispute resolution mechanism into a preliminary step subject to comprehensive court oversight.

---

[33]) CJEU Judgment in the case C-600/23 *Royal Football Club Seraing SA v. Fédération internationale de football association (FIFA) et al.* ECLI:EU:C:2025:617, para. 75; *see also* CJEU Judgement in the joined cases C-245/19 and C-246/19 *État luxembourgeois.* ECLI:EU:C:2020:795, para. 66.

[34]) *Ibid.* at para. 77.

[35]) *Ibid.* at para. 77.

[36]) CJEU Judgment in the case C-600/23 *Royal Football Club Seraing SA v. Fédération internationale de football association (FIFA) et al.* ECLI:EU:C:2025:617, para. 83.

[37]) *Ibid.* at paras. 85 and 101. *See also* CJEU Judgments in the case C-126/97 *Eco Swiss* ECLI:EU:C:1999:269, para. 37; and the case C-124/21 P *International Skating Union* v *Commission*, ECLI:EU:C:2023:1012, para. 193.

# IV. Conclusion

The trilogy of cases examined – *West Tankers*, *Steamship Owners*, and *Royal Football Club Seraing* – reveals a systematic erosion of arbitration's autonomy within the European Union. Like the mythological clash of Titans, these decisions represent a fundamental struggle between competing legal orders: the unified European judicial system and the autonomous realm of international arbitration.

The CJEU's approach consistently reflects Gaillard's first representational paradigm, treating arbitration as merely a component of national legal orders rather than recognizing its autonomous character. This perspective has led to several problematic outcomes: the prohibition of *anti-suit injunctions* in support of arbitration agreements, the application of *lis pendens* rules that ignore the competence-competence doctrine and exclusive nature of the arbitration competence, the denial of *res judicata* effects to arbitral awards, and the requirement for extensive judicial review of awards to ensure compliance with EU public policy.

These developments pose significant challenges for international arbitration within the EU. The CJEU's disregard for fundamental arbitration principles such as competence-competence and the finality of awards undermines the very foundations upon which modern arbitration is built. The requirement that national courts conduct extensive reviews of arbitral awards for compliance with EU public policy effectively transforms arbitration from a final dispute resolution mechanism into a preliminary step in a broader judicial process.

The implications extend beyond procedural concerns to fundamental questions about the relationship between EU law and international arbitration. While the CJEU's emphasis on effective judicial protection and the preliminary ruling procedure serves important constitutional functions within the EU legal order, the wholesale subordination of arbitration to these principles threatens to make arbitration an unattractive option for resolving disputes involving EU law issues.

Moving forward, the EU legal system must develop a more nuanced approach that recognizes arbitration's legitimate autonomy while preserving essential EU legal principles. This requires several concrete reforms: first, clarifying that the competence-competence doctrine grants arbitral tribunals priority in determining their own jurisdiction, even in parallel proceedings with Member State courts; second, establishing clear and narrow criteria for when EU public policy justifies intervention in arbitral proceedings; third, limiting judicial review of arbitral awards to genuine public policy violations rather than routine compliance checks; and fourth, developing procedural mechanisms that allow arbitral tribunals to seek preliminary rulings from the CJEU when EU law interpretation is central to their decisions.

The mythological parallel proves apt: like Zeus's victory over the Titans, the CJEU's decisions represent a fundamental reordering of the dispute resolution landscape in Europe. However, unlike the mythological resolution that established a lasting divine order, the current approach creates ongoing instability and uncertainty. The CJEU has positioned itself as the supreme arbiter of all dispute resolution within the EU, but this supremacy comes at the cost of arbitration's effectiveness and predictability. Whether this represents necessary evolution or destructive overreach will ultimately be determined by the practical consequences for international commerce and dispute resolution within the European Union. The challenge now lies in finding a sustainable balance that preserves both the integrity of EU law and the autonomy that makes arbitration a valuable alternative to litigation.

# Data, Sovereignty, and Arbitral Autonomy: Confronting Extraterritorial Digital Regulations

*Barry Appleton**)

## I. Introduction

International arbitration has long styled itself as the neutral guardian of party autonomy and contractual certainty. Yet in the digital age, governance power projected through code, digital standards, and cloud infrastructure is reshaping the landscape of international arbitration. No longer confined to questions of party intent and contractual performance, arbitral tribunals now face disputes where extraterritorial regulation of artificial intelligence, data flows, and platform infrastructure silently predetermines contractual validity and enforcement. This article argues that international arbitration is becoming the crucible in which the legitimacy of extraterritorial digital regulation will be tested.

Whether via the European Union's "Brussels Effect" of digital regulation,[1]) the United States' assertion of jurisdiction through the CLOUD Act,[2]) or China's mandatory algorithm registration,[3]) private bargains and arbitral clauses no longer operate in isolation.

This article anticipates a broader inquiry into what may be termed a *lex data* – a framework of digital procedural law that governs the collection, processing, and transfer of arbitral data across jurisdictions.[4]) While the present discussion stops short of developing that theory, it identifies the structural tension between arbitral autonomy and the extraterritorial reach of mandatory digital regimes.

---

*) This contribution has already been published.

[1]) Anu Bradford, The Brussels Effect: How the European Union Rules the World (2020); Shoshana Zuboff, The Age of Surveillance Capitalism (2019).

[2]) *Clarifying Lawful Overseas Use of Data* (CLOUD) Act, Pub. L. No. 115–141, div. V, 132 Stat. 1214 (2018).

[3]) Provisions on the Administration of Algorithm Recommendation Services (promulgated by Cyberspace Admin). China, Jan. 2022.

[4]) This article forms part of a broader research project on digital procedural law in arbitration. A companion work, *Lex Data: Reconceptualizing the Law of the Digital Seat in International Arbitration*, develops the theoretical framework previewed here.

Arbitration's tried-and-true heavy reliance on the law of the seat may also be insufficient to address these new issues. Tribunals now confront disputes in which compliance with an award may require breaching a sovereign's digital laws.[5] International arbitration, therefore, occupies a constitutional role in international law, balancing state sovereignty, private autonomy, and the governance of data.

This article employs doctrinal analysis of data protection law combined with normative argumentation about arbitral legitimacy, supported by comparative examination of enforcement regimes across three jurisdictions. Overall, this article argues that international arbitration is becoming the crucible in which the legitimacy of extraterritorial digital regulation will be tested. This dual challenge of autonomy under siege and arbitration as a potential handmaiden of hegemony reframes arbitration as a constitutional arena in international law. To ignore the algorithmic empire is to risk arbitral complicity in its expansion.

## II. Digital Sovereignty and Extraterritorial Regulation

"Digital sovereignty" refers to governance by code: the projection of regulatory authority through technical standards, infrastructure, and interoperability rules, rather than territorial control.[6] Digital sovereignty represents a new form of jurisdictional claim – rooted not in geography but in informational control. States now regulate access, storage, and transmission of data as expressions of sovereign authority. Arbitrators, who once treated data merely as evidence, must now recognize it as a vector of sovereignty itself. It builds on Anu Bradford's "Brussels Effect", extending into infrastructure lock-in,[7] and echoes Shoshana Zuboff's concept of "surveillance capitalism", but emphasizes governance rather than mere extraction.[8] The phenomenon echoes earlier extraterritorial claims in *Hartford Fire Insurance Co. v. California*[9] and *Al-Skeini v. UK*,[10] but differs in its seamless embedding of compliance into global commerce.

Legal scholarship increasingly recognizes that digital law functions as a form of constitutional ordering. The algorithmic age poses a structural challenge to arbitral autonomy, while scholars such as Veeder and Paulsson

---

[5] Convention on the Recognition and Enforcement of Foreign Arbitral Awards art. V(2)(b), June 10, 1958, 330 U.N.T.S. 3 [hereinafter New York Convention], Art. V(2)(b).

[6] Bradford, The Brussels Effect, *supra* note 1.

[7] Bradford, The Brussels Effect, *supra* note 1.

[8] Zuboff, The Age of Surveillance Capitalism, *supra* note 1.

[9] *Hartford Fire Insurance Co. v. California*, 509 U.S. 764 (1993).

[10] *Al-Skeini v. United Kingdom*, 53 Eur. H.R. Rep. 18 (2011).

stress that arbitration cannot be a haven from overriding mandatory norms.[11]) Recent blogs on Kluwer Arbitration, EJIL:Talk!, and IAPP also highlight GDPR's reach into arbitral proceedings, noting the risks of annulment or non-enforcement when tribunals disregard EU data law.[12])

For arbitration, the implication is stark: party autonomy may prove illusory where embedded standards silently dictate obligations. Arbitrators must now confront disputes in which regulatory lock-in, rather than contractual consent, structures the outcome.

Algorithmic empire describes governance-by-code: the projection of regulatory authority through technical standards, infrastructure, and interoperability rules rather than territorial control.[13]) It builds on Anu Bradford's "Brussels Effect" while extending into infrastructure lock-in, and contrasts with digital colonialism by emphasizing governance rather than mere extraction.[14]) For arbitration, the implication is stark: party autonomy may prove illusory where embedded standards silently dictate obligations.

## III. Mandatory Local Law in Arbitration: VAT, Privilege, and Privacy

### A. VAT as Overriding Mandatory Norm

Tribunals have long acknowledged the need to apply local fiscal obligations, such as VAT, in calculating costs and awards.[15]) This prevents awards from undermining sovereign fiscal policy. The logic applies equally to digital regulation: GDPR and AI laws represent sovereign prerogatives to protect citizens, just as tax regimes protect fiscal sovereignty.

---

[11]) Gary B. Born, International Commercial Arbitration 3062-63 (3d ed. 2021); Jan Paulsson, The Idea of Arbitration (2013). V.V. Veeder, *Is There a Crisis in International Arbitration?*, 11 Arb. Int'l 1 (1995).

[12]) *See, e.g.*, Maxi Scherer, *The Invisible Arm of the GDPR in International Treaty Arbitration: Can't We Make It Go Away?*, Kluwer Arb. Blog (Aug. 29, 2019); https://legalblogs.wolterskluwer.com/arbitration-blog/the-invisible-arm-of-gdpr-in-international-treaty-arbitration-cant-we-make-it-go-away/; Christopher Kuner, *International Data Transfers and Data Protection*, 25 Eur. Bus. L. Rev. 1 (2014).

[13]) Bradford, The Brussels Effect, *supra* note 1.

[14]) Barry Appleton, *Algorithmic Empire and Arbitral Autonomy: The Challenge of Extraterritorial Digital Regulation* (2025); forthcoming publication in the International Lawyer (Vol 59, No. 2-2026). Paulsson, The Idea of Arbitration, *supra* note 11.

[15]) Born, International Commercial Arbitration, *supra* note 11, at 3062-63 (3d ed. 2021).

## B. Legal Privilege as Mandatory Norm

Tribunals respect attorney–client privilege as a cornerstone of procedural fairness, even across divergent legal systems.[16] The protection of confidentiality transcends party agreement and ensures trust in the arbitral process. Data protection plays a parallel role in the algorithmic age, safeguarding the informational integrity of proceedings.

## C. Privacy and GDPR as *Lois de Police*

The European Union's General Data Protection Regulation (GDPR) establishes binding obligations on controllers and processors of personal data, with extraterritorial effect.[17] It reflects not only statutory design, but a constitutional right enshrined in Article 8 of the EU Charter. Privacy must therefore be understood as an overriding mandatory norm in arbitration, no less than anti-corruption laws or competition statutes.

Leading commentary in the *Journal of International Arbitration* and the *Arbitration International* journal has underscored GDPR's unique status, noting that even where arbitral seats fall outside Europe, EU-based arbitrators, counsel, or secretariats trigger obligations.[18] The ICCA-IBA Joint Task Force has reinforced this view, warning that ignoring data protection undermines enforceability.[19]

This author submits that arbitral legitimacy in the digital age will depend on the recognition of dual procedural sovereignty: one territorial, one informational. The growing interaction between arbitral procedure and data protection suggests the emergence of a dual procedural structure: the territorial *lex arbitri* that defines juridical supervision, and a concurrent layer of digital obligation – what some commentators have begun to describe as a *lex data*. While the latter will be explored in depth elsewhere, its presence is already visible in the mandatory character of regimes such as the GDPR and the CLOUD Act.

---

16) Catherine A. Rogers, *Arbitrator Ethics: The Intersection of Codes and Law*, 7 PEPP. DISP. RESOL. L.J. 115, 132 (2007).

17) Regulation (EU) 2016/679 of the European Parliament and of the Council of 27 April 2016 on the Protection of Natural Persons with Regard to the Processing of Personal Data and on the Free Movement of Such Data (General Data Protection Regulation), 2016 O.J. (L 119) 1 [hereinafter GDPR].

18) Markus Petsche, *Privacy in International Arbitration*, 38 J. Int'l Arb. 303 (2021).

19) ICCA-IBA Joint Task Force on Data Protection in International Arbitration, *Roadmap to Data Protection in International Arbitration*, ICCA Reports No. 7 (2022).

## D. GDPR: EDPB Guidance, Joint/Co-Controller Allocation, and Practical Obligations for Arbitral Proceedings

The GDPR applies to arbitral proceedings whenever one or more controllers or processors are established in the Union, processing takes place in the Union, or processing relates to offering goods or services to data subjects in the Union (*see* GDPR Arts. 3, 4, 26). The European Data Protection Board (EDPB) guidance on the distinction between controllers and processors, on joint controllership, and on transfers of personal data is directly relevant to tribunals, arbitrators, institutions, and service providers involved in arbitration. Tribunals should adopt the EDPB's practical approach when determining roles and allocating responsibilities,

There are foundational EDPB principles of immediate relevance to arbitration:

**Functional analysis of roles (controller vs processor)**

The EDPB emphasizes a facts-and-circumstances test to determine who decides on the purposes and means of processing. Where tribunal members, institutional secretariats, or thirdparty service providers (cloud hosts, transcription/translation services, edisclosure platforms) have decisionmaking authority about the purposes/means of processing personal data, they may be controllers or joint controllers.[20])

- Joint controllership and transparency (Art. 26): Where two or more entities jointly determine the purposes and means, they must transparently allocate responsibility for compliance (including handling data subject rights) and publish that arrangement. The EDPB treats the surface requirement of a written arrangement as the minimum; allocation must be substantive and enforceable by data subjects.
- Processor obligations (Art. 28): Where entities process on the controller's documented instructions (*e.g.*, PCA secretariat, cloud provider), the controller must have a written contract that meets Art. 28 minimum terms; processors must implement appropriate technical and organizational measures (Art. 32).
- DPIA and prior consultation (Arts. 35–36): Large-scale or highrisk processing (profiling, special categories, systematic disclosure of personal data in public awards, automated decisionmaking using AI tools) may

[20]) European Data Protection Board, *Guidelines 07/2020 on the Concepts of Controller and Processor in the GDPR*, Version 2.0 (July 7, 2021). Also *see* GDPR Arts. 4(7), 4(8), 26.

trigger the requirement to carry out a DPIA and, where risks cannot be mitigated, prior consultation with the competent supervisory authority.

- International transfers (Arts. 44–49): Transfers to third countries require an adequacy decision, appropriate safeguards (*e.g.*, SCCs), and supplementary measures in light of the EDPB's recommendations (postSchrems II). The EDPB's transfer guidance requires casebycase transfer impact assessments.
- Security and breach notification (Arts. 32–34): Controllers/processors must implement stateoftheart security; breaches affecting data subjects' rights must be notified to supervisory authorities within 72 hours and to data subjects where there is a high risk.

## E. The Practical implications for arbitration

At the outset, the tribunal should identify all entities involved in data processing (tribunal members, institutional secretariat staff, transcription/translation vendors, cloud providers, edisclosure platforms, experts) and classify them as controllers, joint controllers or processors using an evidentiary, functionbased test.

If joint controllership exists, the parties and affected data subjects (witnesses, experts, counsel staff) must receive or have access to a clear Article 26 arrangement setting out respective responsibilities for data subject rights, legal bases, security, transfers and contact points.

### 1. DPIA trigger review

The tribunal should consider whether a DPIA is required under Art. 35 (*e.g.*, systematic processing of large categories of sensitive data or use of automated decision tools). If required, a DPIA must be completed before the relevant processing begins and the supervisory authority consulted where residual high risks remain (Art. 36).

Where data will be stored, accessed, or processed in nonEEA jurisdictions, a transfer impact assessment consistent with EDPB recommendations must be prepared and documented; where appropriate, SCCs and supplementary measures must be put in place (Arts. 44–46).

### 2. Contracts and DPAs:

All processor relationships must be governed by a written Data Processing Agreement that satisfies the requirements of Art. 28. Where joint controllership exists, the written joint controller arrangement required by Art. 26 must be signed and published or otherwise made available to data subjects.

# IV. The Tennant Energy Tribunal and Its Flawed Reasoning

## A. Introduction: Data Privacy Questions Before the Tribunal

The issue of data protection first came squarely before an arbitral tribunal in *Tennant Energy, LLC v. Canada*, a NAFTA treaty claim administered under the 1976 UNCITRAL Arbitration Rules and seated in Toronto.[21] The procedural issue regarding data privacy was a technical procedural issue – mostly unrelated to the cut and thrust of the arbitration about the fairness of Ontario's Feed-in-Tariff program administration.

The investor, Tennant, argued that the tribunal and its participants were subject to obligations under the European Union's General Data Protection Regulation (GDPR), due to the participation of a United Kingdom-domiciled arbitrator and the involvement of the Permanent Court of Arbitration (PCA) secretariat staff located in The Hague.[22] Canada opposed the application of GDPR on the basis that the applicable procedural and substantive law was not EU law, and neither of the parties was from the EU.[23]

These procedural submissions raised a novel but unavoidable question: whether international investment arbitration can ignore overriding mandatory data protection laws when clear connecting factors link the proceedings to jurisdictions with strong privacy protections.

There is no provision on data privacy in the UNCITRAL Arbitration Rules that governed this NAFTA arbitration. The NAFTA provided no specific

---

[21]) *Tennant Energy, LLC v. Government of Canada*, PCA Case No. 2018-54 NAFTA, (UNCITRAL Rules). The author acted as lead counsel for the investor in the *Tennant Energy v. Canada* arbitration and argued in favor of a procedural order to take into account the role of a UK arbitrator who admitted to being covered by the GDPR in his data privacy notice, and PCA staff and facilities supporting the arbitration falling outside of the terms of the Headquarters Agreement. The author represented the claimant in *Tennant Energy v. Canada*. The views expressed are solely those of the author.

[22]) *Tennant Energy*. Questions and Investor's Response to Tribunal GDPR Questions and Data Privacy Questions (June 4, 2019) (addressing applicability of the GDPR to NAFTA Chapter 11 arbitration) paras 8.–9. In the UK arbitrator's own data privacy notice, he confirmed that the GDPR covered him and that he was both a data 'processor' and a 'controller' (referenced in para 9).

[23]) Tennant Respondent's Response to Claimant's Submission on the European Union General Data Protection Regulation (June 11, 2019) paras 2–3. Canada conceded that the GDPR might apply to individual participants or arbitrators, but that the provisions would be inapplicable to Canada because it was a sovereign state not subject to the GDPR (*see* paras 3–5).

guidance either. There is little guidance available from treaties and procedural rules to assist Tribunals in identifying applicable local data protection law.[24])

The GDPR applies to arbitration.[25]) Within the UK, arbitration activities are covered under the UK Data Protection Act 2018 and the GDPR.[26])

## B. The Tribunal's Position

The tribunal declined to apply GDPR. It reasoned that since neither the European Union nor its Member States were parties to NAFTA, and the arbitration was seated in Canada, EU data protection law had no application.[27])

On June 19, 2019, the Tribunal issued a brief direction. The provision on data privacy was one paragraph long:

> On the potential application of the General Data Protection Regulation 2016/679 ("GDPR") to this arbitration, having carefully considered Parties' submissions on this issue, the Tribunal finds that an arbitration under NAFTA Chapter 11, a treaty to which neither the European Union nor its Member States are party, does not, presumptively, come within the material scope of the GDPR. Accordingly, the Confidentiality Order makes no reference to the GDPR. This is without prejudice to the importance of ensuring a high level of data protection, and language to this effect has been added into the Confidentiality Order.[28])

In deciding that the GDPR did not apply to this arbitration, the Tennant Tribunal relied upon GDPR Article 2.2(a) material scope, which provides: '[t]his Regulation does not apply to the processing of personal data: (a) in the course of an activity which falls outside the scope of Union law.[29]) But the Tribunal did not address the issue of the UK Arbitrator's personal obligations, nor the obligations of the secretariat at the Permanent Court of Arbitration (PCA), which were also covered by GDPR obligations in their own right and with respect to where the data was stored. As a matter of EU law, GDPR obligations arise whenever between an arbitrator based under GDPR scope, or

---

[24]) There are data protection international treaties such as the Council of Europe Convention No 108 on Data Protection, [Convention for the protection of individuals with regard to automatic processing of personal data] (ETS No. 108, 28.01.1981), the OECD Guidelines Governing the Protection of Privacy and Trans-border Flows of Personal Data, or the APEC Cross-Border Privacy Rules and the Privacy Framework.

[25]) GDPR Recitals 20 and 91, *supra* note 12.

[26]) Data Protection Act 2018, c. 12 (U.K.); Data Protection, Privacy and Electronic Communications (Amendments etc.) (EU Exit) Regulations 2019, S.I. 2019 No. 419 (U.K.) [hereinafter UK GDPR].

[27]) *Tennant Energy, LLC v. Government of Canada*, Tribunal Decision on GDPR Submissions (June 19, 2019).

[28]) *Ibidem.*

[29]) GDPR, *supra* note 12 at Article 2.2.

the PCA engages in a "data transfer" which would occur as a matter of course within the Tribunal and with the parties.[30])

The Tennant Tribunal did not address the issues under the law of the seat under Canadian law. At the time of *Tennant Energy*, Canada had a comprehensive privacy statute in place: the **Personal Information Protection and Electronic Documents Act** (PIPEDA).[31]) PIPEDA, enacted in 2000 and updated regularly, imposes binding obligations on private organizations that collect, use, or disclose personal information in the course of commercial activities.[32]) While PIPEDA applied primarily to commercial enterprises, it encompassed many of the same categories of personal data – such as identification numbers, employment records, and financial information – that routinely circulate in arbitral proceedings. Its existence demonstrates that Canada itself did not treat data protection as optional or peripheral, but rather as a central aspect of lawful information handling. Thus, even under domestic law, a Canadian-seated tribunal faced potential obligations to ensure that personal data processed in the arbitration was adequately safeguarded.

The tribunal did not meaningfully engage with the submissions regarding the GDPR obligations of the UK-based arbitrator or the PCA's European secretariat staff. In essence, the Tribunal wished the problem away. However, the responsibility to ensure that the Tribunal acts lawfully does not fall upon the parties to the arbitration. That obligation is for the Tribunal to discharge.[33])

## C. Why GDPR and PIPEDA Should Have Applied

This reasoning was flawed for several reasons. First, the GDPR expressly extends its territorial scope beyond the EU, applying to the processing of personal data by controllers or processors established in the European Union, regardless of whether the processing itself occurs within the EU.[34]) Thus, the participation of a UK-domiciled arbitrator, who publicly declared himself subject to GDPR in his arbitrator profile, created a direct connection to EU law.[35]) Similarly, PCA staff in Europe were engaged in case management functions – including the handling of pleadings, correspondence, and records –

[30]) *Tennant Energy*. Investor's Response, *supra* note 22 at para 30.

[31]) Personal Information Protection and Electronic Documents Act, S.C. 2000, c. 5 (Can.) [hereinafter PIPEDA]. Office of the Privacy Commissioner of Canada, *A Guide for Businesses on the Personal Information Protection and Electronic Documents Act (PIPEDA)* (2023 update).

[32]) Id. PIPEDA, *supra* note 30, § 4(1) (defining scope of application).

[33]) Paulsson, The Idea of Arbitration, *supra* note 11, at 90–95 (arguing that the tribunal's legitimacy depends on adherence to public law principles, not merely party agreement).

[34]) GDPR, *supra* note 12, art. 3(1)–(2).

[35]) Jie Jeanne Huang & Dan Xie, *Data Protection Law in Investment Arbitration: Applicable or Not?*, 37 Arb. Int'l 167, 176 (2021).

placing them squarely within the scope of GDPR, absent specific institutional immunities.[36])

In any event, having one member of a tribunal subject to data protection means that there are co-data controllers among the tribunal members. This imposes an obligation for the covered arbitrator arising from the activities of the other arbitrators or the covered institution. As a practical matter, these obligations need to be addressed, not ignored.

The tribunal's reasoning was misguided for several reasons. GDPR is not limited to disputes between EU parties. Article 3 GDPR establishes extra-territorial reach whenever the processing of personal data takes place within the EU, or involves controllers or processors based in the EU. Thus, the participation of a European arbitrator and secretariat, along with EU-based data servers, created obligations under GDPR, regardless of whether the disputing parties themselves were subject to European jurisdiction.[37])

International arbitration regularly implicates sensitive personal and corporate data, including birthdates, national identification numbers, passport details of witnesses, financial account records, internal emails, and privileged communications. Cybersecurity obligations further extend to preventing unauthorized access, ransomware attacks, and inadvertent disclosure.[38]) Indeed the Permanent Court of Arbitration itself was the subject of a high profile data breach in 2015.[39]) GDPR compliance is not merely formalistic; it is essential to safeguarding the integrity of proceedings and the privacy rights of individuals involved when EU nationals are involved.

Furthermore, GDPR covers categories of data processing that are ubiquitous in arbitration: transmission of documents via institutional platforms, case management by secretariats, storage of awards in digital repositories, and even transcription and translation services that process personal identifiers. A tribunal ignoring GDPR risks exposing participants to liability, undermining both party's confidence and the enforceability of awards.

Second, the tribunal overlooked PIPEDA, which was in force at the seat of arbitration. As Huang and Xie note, the applicability of local data protection laws can be determined by several connecting factors, including the domicile of arbitrators, the seat and place of hearings, the location of data processing, and the place of enforcement of awards.[40]) By ignoring both GDPR and PIPEDA, the tribunal failed to recognize that data protection functions, like taxation and privilege, operate as overriding mandatory norms in arbitration.

---

[36]) *Eid.* at 183–85.

[37]) GDPR, *supra* note 12, art 3.

[38]) Catherine A. Rogers & Maxi Scherer, *Cybersecurity in Arbitration*, 41 Arb. Int'l 1 (2022).

[39]) Permanent Court of Arbitration, *Statement on PCA Website Cyberattack During Philippines v. China Proceedings* (July 2015), https://pca-cpa.org/en/news/statement-on-pca-website-cyberattack-during-philippines-v-china-arbitration/.

[40]) Ibid. at 172–73.

## D. Broader Implications for Arbitral Autonomy

The *Tennant Energy* award highlights the risk of tribunals establishing a self-contained legal order that is immune to the reach of mandatory public law. GDPR and PIPEDA obligations attached to arbitral participants not by treaty but by function: arbitrators, counsel, and secretariats necessarily process personal data. Declaring data protection norms inapplicable therefore exposes participants to regulatory liability and places the enforceability of awards at risk. Under Article V(2)(b) of the New York Convention, courts may refuse recognition of an award rendered in violation of mandatory EU data protection law as contrary to European public policy.[41]) Awards tainted by disregard of mandatory laws risk annulment or refusal of enforcement under Article V(2)(b) of the New York Convention. Nevertheless, enforcement courts have shown varying degrees of willingness to refuse recognition based on public policy grounds, with some jurisdictions applying a more restrictive interpretation of what constitutes violations of public policy.

Additionally, arbitrators, counsel, and secretariat staff may face personal liability for breaches of the GDPR or equivalent privacy regimes. This may create conflicts between the arbitration parties and the arbitrators, who may seek indemnity for such personal liability from the parties. Finally, unbalanced decisions invite inconsistent practice, weakening arbitration's appeal as a harmonized system of dispute resolution.

The tribunal's refusal to engage meaningfully with GDPR demonstrates arbitration's vulnerability to being cast as hostile to fundamental rights. The proper approach would have been to adopt GDPR-compliant protocols, striking a balance between transparency and privacy while ensuring that neither arbitrators nor institutions contravened binding EU law. Commentators in *Kluwer Arbitration Blog* and *Transnational Dispute Management* argue that the Tennant tribunal's approach risks alienating European arbitrators and undermining public confidence in arbitration.[42])

To safeguard legitimacy, arbitral tribunals must integrate data protection regimes into their procedural frameworks. Just as tribunals have long respected VAT obligations and privilege protections, they must recognize GDPR and national data protection statutes as *lois de police* applicable to the arbitral process itself. Failing to do so undermines arbitral credibility, subjects' participants to liability, and risks annulment or non-enforcement of awards.

---

41) New York Convention. *supra* note 5, art. V(2)(b).

42) Maxi Scherer, *Data Protection in Arbitration*, KLUWER ARB. BLOG (2020); Kuner, *International Data Transfers, supra* note 12.

# V. Extraterritorial Digital Regulation: EU, U.S., and China

## A. The EU: Rights-Based Digital Constitutionalism

The EU AI Act (2024) applies extraterritorially to high-risk systems impacting EU markets. It mirrors GDPR in design and reach. Arbitrators cannot disregard such measures, as they constitute overriding mandatory norms.[43]) Academic commentary frames the AI Act as a constitutional statute of the Union, thereby reinforcing its status as public policy.[44])

## B. The United States: CLOUD Act and AI Action Plan

The U.S. CLOUD Act (2018) requires American providers to comply with subpoenas, regardless of the data's location.[45]) The 2025 AI Action Plan further integrates AI into national security frameworks. For arbitrators, this means U.S.-based digital infrastructure imports non-derogable compliance obligations.

## C. China: Algorithm Registration as Ideological Governance

China's 2022 Provisions on Algorithm Recommendation Services mandate registration and ideological conformity.[46]) Awards inconsistent with these rules risk non-enforcement under Article V(2)(b) of the New York Convention. Scholars in *Chinese Journal of Comparative Law* stress that China's approach reflects a sovereignty-driven model, fundamentally at odds with EU rights-based constitutionalism.[47])

---

[43]) Regulation (EU) 2024/1689 of the European Parliament and of the Council of 12 July 2024 Laying Down Harmonised Rules on Artificial Intelligence (Artificial Intelligence Act), 2024 O.J. (L 211) 1 [hereinafter EU AI Act].

[44]) Sartor, *Constitutionalizing AI Regulation in Europe*, 61 COMMON MKT. L. REV. 1121 (2024).

[45]) CLOUD Act, *supra* note 2.

[46]) Provisions on the Administration of Algorithm Recommendation Services, *supra* note 3.

[47]) Han Zhu, *Algorithmic Regulation with Chinese Characteristics*, 9 CHINESE J. COMP. L. 445 (2023).

### D. The Geopolitical Squeeze

Arbitration increasingly sits at the intersection of these competing models: EU rights-based law, U.S. corporate-infrastructure jurisdiction, and Chinese sovereign control. Algorithmic empire is not theoretical; it is the daily terrain of arbitral legitimacy.

## VI. Treaty Regimes and Digital Standards

### A. EU Treaties and Austria's Context

While Austria is not party to CPTPP or USMCA, it is firmly within the EU legal order. EU treaties, notably the Treaty on the Functioning of the European Union (TFEU) anchor the Union's competence in digital markets, data protection (Art. 16), and trade (Art. 207).[48]) For Austria-seated arbitrations, EU law has constitutional status, and tribunals cannot disregard EU mandatory rules without jeopardizing enforceability.

### B. UNCITRAL Model Laws

UNCITRAL has developed frameworks such as the Model Law on Electronic Commerce (1996) and the Model Law on Electronic Signatures (2001).[49]) These instruments, adopted widely, establish recognition of digital transactions and standards for electronic evidence – providing useful interpretive tools for arbitrators confronting AI and algorithmic disputes. The 2017 UNCITRAL Model Law on Electronic Transferable Records further affirms the international legal architecture underpinning digital commerce.[50])

### C. WTO E-Commerce Negotiations

WTO talks on e-commerce aim to transplant CPTPP/USMCA-style provisions into global rules, threatening to constrain digital sovereignty.[51])

---

[48]) Treaty on the Functioning of the European Union, May 9, 2008, 2008 O.J. (C 115) 47, arts. 16, 207 [hereinafter TFEU].

[49]) U.N. Commission on International Trade Law, Model Law on Electronic Commerce with Guide to Enactment, U.N. Doc. A/51/162 (1996). UNCITRAL Model Law on Electronic Signatures (2001). U.N. Doc. A/56/17 Annex I (2001).

[50]) UNCITRAL Model Law on Electronic Transferable Records (2017). U.N. Doc. A/72/17 Annex II (2017).

[51]) WTO, Joint Statement on Electronic Commerce, WT/L/1056 (January 25, 2019).

Tribunals interpreting such commitments may determine whether AI regulation is a legitimate objective or disguised restriction.

### D. CPTPP and USMCA

The CPTPP and USMCA enshrine digital trade commitments prohibiting source code disclosure and data localization mandates, subject to public policy exceptions.[52]) Arbitrators must balance investor expectations against sovereign claims.

## VII. Toward a Coherent Arbitral Framework

The Tennant case and the spread of digital regulation underscore the need for structured arbitral responses:

1. **Procedural Orders.** Arbitrators must issue GDPR-compliant protocols: data minimization, encryption, transfer agreements.[53])

2. **Transparency.** Tribunals should disclose how data is processed to ensure compliance.[54])

3. **Harmonization.** Institutions should develop standard protocols, similar to the ICCA–IBA Roadmap on Data Protection.[55])

4. **Public Policy Recognition.** Privacy, like anti-corruption, must be recognized as part of transnational *ordre public.*[56])

## VIII. Comparative Enforcement Perspectives

### A. European Union

EU courts have consistently treated GDPR as a constitutional norm. Following *Schrems II*, data transfers outside the EU without adequate safeguards are prohibited.[57]) If an arbitral award disregards GDPR or AI Act obligations, EU courts may refuse enforcement under Article V(2)(b) of the New York

---

[52]) CPTPP, signed March 8, 2018, in force December 30, 2018, ch 14; USMCA, signed November 30, 2018, ch 19.

[53]) ICCA-IBA Roadmap, *supra* note 19, at 13–15.

[54]) ICCA-IBA Roadmap, *supra* note 19, at 13–15.

[55]) ICCA-IBA Roadmap, *supra* note 19, at 13–15.

[56]) ICCA-IBA Roadmap, *supra* note 19, at 13–15.

[57]) Case C-311/18, *Data Protection Commissioner v. Facebook Ireland Ltd.* (Schrems II), ECLI:EU:C:2020:559 (July 16, 2020).

Convention on public policy grounds.[58] Commentators such as Christopher Kuner and Giovanni Sartor argue that EU courts will interpret privacy obligations expansively to safeguard fundamental rights.[59]

## B. United States

U.S. courts traditionally adopt a narrow reading of the New York Convention's public policy exception.[60] While they may enforce awards even where foreign privacy rules were disregarded, U.S. statutes such as the CLOUD Act impose mandatory obligations on U.S.-based parties and cloud providers.[61] As Susan Franck notes, U.S. courts rarely overturn awards on public policy grounds, but the growing intersection with national security and digital governance could expand scrutiny in future.[62]

## C. China

Chinese courts treat data sovereignty as a core national security matter. Under the PRC's Data Security Law (2021) and the 2022 Algorithm Provisions, awards inconsistent with state-mandated data localization or algorithmic conformity may be refused enforcement as contrary to public order.[63] As Han Zhu emphasizes, Chinese enforcement practice reflects a statist conception of sovereignty, prioritizing ideological alignment over transnational arbitral norms.[64]

## D. Implications for Arbitrators

This comparative analysis underscores the enforcement risk arbitrators face when ignoring digital regulation. EU courts may strike down awards for failing to apply GDPR; Chinese courts may do so for failing to respect data sovereignty; U.S. courts may be more lenient but constrained by CLOUD Act

58) New York Convention, *supra* note 5, art. V(2)(b).

59) Christopher Kuner, *Reality and Illusion in EU Data Transfer Regulation*, 18 Ger. L.J. 881 (2017); Sartor, *Constitutionalizing, supra* Note 44.

60) *Parsons & Whittemore Overseas Co. v. Societe Generale de L'Industrie du Papier* (RAKTA), 508 F.2d 969, 974 (2d Cir. 1974).

61) CLOUD Act, *supra* note 2.

62) Susan D. Franck, *The Legitimacy Crisis in Investment Treaty Arbitration: Privatizing Public International Law Through Inconsistent Decisions*, 73 Fordham L. Rev. 1521 (2005).

63) Data Security Law of the People's Republic of China (promulgated June 2021).

64) Han Zhu, *Algorithmic Regulation, supra* note 47.

obligations. Arbitrators sitting in international disputes must craft procedural orders that balance these regimes or risk fragmentation of enforceability.

In practical terms, the enforceability of digital-era awards depends on a tribunal's ability to navigate overlapping data regimes. Future procedural orders must therefore incorporate a dual analysis – of the seat and of the data.

## IX. GDPR-Compliant Procedural Order

To provide guidance to tribunals, the following model order illustrates GDPR-compliant practices that can be adapted:

**Model Procedural Order on Data Protection and Cybersecurity**

1. **Scope and Purpose.** This order governs the collection, processing, storage, and transfer of personal data in these arbitral proceedings, ensuring compliance with GDPR and equivalent data protection frameworks.
2. **Data Minimization.** Parties and the tribunal shall collect and process only data strictly necessary for the conduct of these proceedings.
3. **Secure Transmission.** All electronic communications shall be encrypted, and secure file transfer systems shall be used for submission of evidence and pleadings.
4. **Data Storage.** Case files shall be stored on servers located in jurisdictions that ensure adequate protection under GDPR. Cloud services must incorporate EU Standard Contractual Clauses or equivalent safeguards.
5. **Access Control.** Access to personal data shall be restricted to authorized individuals directly involved in the arbitration (tribunal members, secretariat staff, counsel, and experts).
6. **Data Subject Rights.** Parties shall respect rights of access, rectification, and erasure of personal data consistent with GDPR requirements, subject to the integrity of the arbitral record.
7. **Retention and Deletion.** Personal data shall be retained only for the duration necessary to conduct the arbitration and enforce any award. Upon conclusion, parties and the tribunal shall ensure secure deletion of unnecessary data.
8. **Cybersecurity Protocols.** The tribunal adopts baseline cybersecurity measures in line with ICCA–IBA Cybersecurity Guidelines, including incident response planning and regular risk assessments.
9. **Conflicts with Other Laws.** In the event of conflict between GDPR and other applicable mandatory regimes (*e.g.*, U.S. CLOUD Act, PRC Data Security Law), the tribunal shall confer with the parties to adopt solutions minimizing violation risk while ensuring due process.

This model order demonstrates how tribunals can operationalize GDPR compliance while balancing competing extraterritorial obligations.

## X. Arbitral Autonomy Under Pressure and the Need for Pluralism

Party autonomy is constrained by mandatory rules, as in *World Duty Free v. Kenya*.[65]) Algorithmic regulation introduces a new category of non-derogable law. Awards enforcing contracts reliant on U.S. cloud providers, EU markets, or Chinese platforms risk entrenching foreign rules ("regulatory lock-in").[66]) Unless institutions adapt – through technical experts, algorithmic disclosure, or guidance akin to the IBA Rules on Evidence – arbitration may become an instrument of empire rather than a guardian of balance.[67])

Pluralism demands respect for technological non-alignment, treating it as a legitimate policy objective under treaty exceptions.[68]) Soft law instruments (UNIDROIT Principles, OECD AI Principles) provide harmonizing guidance.[69]) Ultimately, arbitrators must frame algorithmic governance as a matter of transnational public policy, akin to anti-corruption or environmental law, to preserve legitimacy.[70])

## XI. Conclusion: Arbitration in the Algorithmic Age

International arbitration now sits at the hinge of sovereignty and technology. Algorithmic empire challenges both party choice and tribunal neutrality by embedding extraterritorial standards into digital commerce. Arbitration must respond. It must treat algorithmic governance as part of transnational public policy, incorporate the UNCITRAL frameworks, and respect the EU's constitutional obligations. Only by doing so can arbitration preserve its legitimacy as a forum for balancing law, sovereignty, and technological transformation.

---

[65]) *World Duty Free Company Limited v. Republic of Kenya*, ICSID Case No. ARB/00/7, Award (October 4, 2006).

[66]) *Microsoft Corp. v. United States*, 829 F.3d 197 (2d Cir. 2016), cert. granted, 138 S. Ct. 356 (2017), vacated as moot, 138 S. Ct. 1186 (2018).

[67]) ICC, *Note to Parties and Arbitral Tribunals on the Conduct of Arbitration* (2021).

[68]) Appleton, *Algorithmic Empire, supra* note 14, at 33–37.

[69]) OECD, *OECD Principles on Artificial Intelligence* (2019); UNIDROIT, *Principles of International Commercial Contracts* (2016).

[70]) *Philip Morris Brands Sàrl, Philip Morris Products S.A. and Abal Hermanos S.A. v. Oriental Republic of Uruguay*, ICSID Case No. ARB/10/7, Award (July 8, 2016).

Peripheral questions in arbitration can be complicated. But arbitrators must resist the fight or flight instinct. We cannot escape technology or the law. Arbitration Tribunals must resist the urge to be horse-and-buggy leaders on the AI Autobahn. Otherwise, arbitration will become outdated, slow, and potentially hazardous to others. It will have an undesirable effect of being avoided by users, who expect arbitrators to have the competency and fluency to address the economic realities of the times.

Suppose arbitration is to remain a legitimate form of global adjudication. In that case, it must evolve a digital constitutionalism of its own – grounded in procedural fairness, respect for human rights in data processing, and transparency in algorithmic governance. The conceptual scaffolding for this evolution – what this author elsewhere calls the *lex data* – will define the procedural legitimacy of the twenty-first century

The *Tennant* tribunal's reaction is a cautionary tale. The tribunal's decision not to apply data privacy law raises significant questions about how arbitral proceedings should address mandatory regulatory requirements in the digital age. It presented a challenge to the rule of law and a troubling erosion of the privacy rights of those whose data was involved in the consideration of the claim. This reasoning is difficult to reconcile with GDPR's extraterritorial scope when data processing occurs within EU jurisdiction. In addition, this decision, claiming that a general-purpose data law could not apply ab initio, was strategically shortsighted.

In a world where digital regulation defines sovereignty, arbitral tribunals must acknowledge that tribunal autonomy has limits, just as party autonomy does. Arbitration must evolve into a guardian of this intangible digital evolution, or risk irrelevance as states and courts reclaim authority. The pathway forward demands recognizing privacy, algorithmic accountability, and digital sovereignty as core elements of arbitral legitimacy.

The next step in this inquiry is to define how these overlapping digital obligations might coalesce into a coherent procedural framework – one that parallels the *lex arbitri* but operates through data itself. Such a framework, once articulated, could determine the future legitimacy of arbitration in the algorithmic era.

# Deciding Minds in Justice's Looking-Glass: Human and AI
## Where Intuition Meets Algorithm

*Irina Nazarova*

## I. Introduction

The role of artificial intelligence (AI) in the administration of justice has become a pressing issue in the legal world. Current debates focus on the absence of AI's "jurisdiction", potential for bias, the extent and the ethical limits of AI's use, the risks of errors undermining justice and the absence of any clear liability for AI-driven decision. The core question, however, remains: Can AI truly assume the role of human judgment in the administration of justice?

Soft-law guidance on the use of AI by arbitrators is still in development, but some of the leading arbitral institutions have already strongly asserted that the delegation of the decision-making process to AI is impermissible.

To illustrate, the Chartered Institute of Arbitrators (CIArb) in its *Guideline to the Use of AI in Arbitration* explicitly prohibits delegating an arbitrator's personal decision-making mandate to an AI tool. CIArb notes that arbitrators remain fully responsible for every aspect of an award, regardless of any assistance received from AI tools during the decision-making process; arbitrators should not delegate to AI tasks such as legal analysis, research, interpretation of facts and law where such use could influence procedural or substantive determinations. CIArb further emphasizes that arbitrators must independently verify the accuracy of AI-generated information, conduct their own research and maintain critical oversight to prevent undue influence.[1])

The Vienna International Arbitral Centre (VIAC) strongly recommends that arbitrators retain full control over the decision-making process and refrain from transferring any part of this responsibility to AI.[2])

---

[1]) Chartered Institute of Arbitrators (CIArb), *Guideline on the Use of AI in Arbitration*, Section 8, at 16 (September 2025), available at https://www.ciarb.org/media/bpndtcgu/guideline-on-the-use-of-ai-in-arbitration_updated-sept-2025.pdf (all websites last accessed on November 6, 2025).

[2]) Vienna International Arbitral Centre (VIAC), *Note on the Use of Artificial Intelligence in Arbitral Proceedings* (April 2025), available at https://www.viac.eu/wp-content/uploads/2025/04/VIAC-Note-on-AI-1.pdf.

The Silicon Valley Arbitration & Mediation Center (SVAMC), in its *Guidelines on the Use of Artificial Intelligence in International Arbitration*, likewise emphasizes that personal responsibility for rendering decisions rests solely with the arbitrator and the decision-making must remain entirely human-driven. The SVAMC Guidelines note that arbitrators must review any output produced by AI tools and verify that it accurately reflects their own independent reasoning. The arbitrators are liable for the use of AI.[3])

This article, however, explores only one aspect – how human and AI decision-making differ when viewed through the lens of morality and emotion, and how reasoning and empathy together influence justice.

## II. Emotion and the Moral Mind

AI has become an inseparable part of modern reality, both as a promise and a paradox. AI offers a tempting vision: the elevation of human work, delivering significant improvements in quality in seconds and restoring balance through saving time, efforts and costs. On the other hand, the abundance of information that AI provides may deepen the human burden: The more data AI generates, the greater is the responsibility on humans to identify the truth. Recent survey data, however, indicate that "the respondents predict that arbitrators will increasingly rely on AI (52 %) and that new roles to work with AI will emerge (40 %)".[4]) Whether this new technological reality will ultimately ease or intensify human endeavor remains a rhetorical question. What is certain is that the greatest task is to preserve oneself – to remain conscious and responsible for one's own decisions, conclusions and words. This calls for a deeper consideration of human nature as a driving force in the administration of justice.

The phenomenon of human nature remains a mystery despite countless attempts to describe the structure of personality. The more we know, the less certain we become. Nevertheless, the attempts to understand human nature are of fundamental importance to justice.

Numerous psychological scholars have sought to explain the motivation of human behavior, from the pursuit of pleasure to the pursuit of meaning. To illustrate: Sigmund Freud viewed personality as comprising the *Id* (a reservoir of instincts that motivates the pursuit of pleasure) the *Superego* (a reservoir of

---

[3]) Silicon Valley Arbitration & Mediation Center (SVAMC), *Guidelines on the Use of Artificial Intelligence in International Arbitration*, Guideline 6, at 19–20 (2024), available at https://svamc.org/wp-content/uploads/SVAMC-AI-Guidelines-First-Edition.pdf.

[4]) White & Case LLP, *2025 International Arbitration Survey: Arbitration and AI*, at 1, available at https://www.whitecase.com/insight-our-thinking/2025-international-arbitration-survey-arbitration-and-ai.

the moral, social standards and the highest ideals) and the *Ego* (the mediator between the Id and the external world).[5]

Alfred Adler argued that personality is driven by the striving for superiority.[6]

Abraham Maslow emphasized the hierarchy of needs in motivation, culminating in self-actualization (the highest need to realize one's personal meaning).[7]

Finally, Viktor Frankl proposed that the "will-to-meaning" – the desire to find meaning in life – is a person's primary driving force.[8]

Despite their different perspectives the author suggests that these theories share a common recognition: A person's motives are often unconscious, hardly accessible, and ultimately lie beyond one's own full understanding. When people attempt to explain their own motives, they frequently engage in *post hoc* rationalization, offering logical explanations for decisions that may, in fact, be driven by unconscious processes. People tend to believe that such rationalizations are true, while their genuine motives often only become apparent through psychotherapeutic work, and even then clarity is not guaranteed.

This interplay between conscious and unconscious processes demonstrates the complexity of moral reasoning and human nature. Psychologist Richard Lazarus saw emotion as a personal evaluation of meaning that connects thinking and feeling.[9]

Likewise, Robert Plutchik viewed emotions as adaptive responses essential for survival, each triggered by significant life events.[10]

The author notes that emotion serves as a channel through which information about personal relevance and meaning is received.

From another point of view, cognitive theory suggests that our thoughts and beliefs can shape our feelings and actions. Aaron Beck observed that when people change negative patterns of thought, they often feel better and behave differently as a result.[11]

---

[5]) Sigmund Freud, *The Ego and the Id* (1923) (introducing the id–ego–superego structure of the mind).

[6]) Alfred Adler, *Understanding Human Nature* (1927) (describing the drive for superiority as a fundamental motive).

[7]) Abraham H. Maslow, *A Theory of Human Motivation*, 50 Psychol. Rev. 370 (1943) (introducing the hierarchy of needs culminating in self-actualization).

[8]) Viktor E. Frankl, *The Will to Meaning: Foundations and Applications of Logotherapy* 1–4 (Meridian ed. 1988).

[9]) Richard S. Lazarus, *Emotion and Adaptation* (1991) (characterizing emotions as personal appraisals of meaning).

[10]) Robert Plutchik, *The Nature of Emotions*, 89 Am. Sci. (2001) (explaining basic emotions as evolutionary adaptations to life events).

[11]) Judith S. Beck & Sarah Fleming, *A Brief History of Aaron T. Beck, MD, and Cognitive Behavior Therapy*, Clin. Psychol. Eur. 3 (2021).

A simple illustration is the difference between telling oneself, *"I have a financial problem"* and *"I have a financial task"*. These two phrases mean almost the same thing, but they carry different emotional weight, the first can cause anxiety, while the second can lead to motivation.

It follows that there is a constant interplay between emotion and thought in human. Different emotions evoke different thoughts, and different thoughts, in turn, generate different emotions. Emotional and cognitive processes are therefore inseparable and continuously interacting components of human nature including decision-making.

*Moral psychology* explores how emotions shape moral judgment. Research in this field suggests that moral decision-making follows a very interesting sequence: emotion → intuition → reasoning → action. In other words emotions generate moral signals, intuition turns them into judgments, and reasoning provides later justifications.[12])

Moral judgments arise mainly from intuition, while reasoning serves to explain or defend these intuitive reactions. Moral emotions also extend beyond the self, shaping how people treat others and form social bonds. Morality, as Jonathan Haidt observes, uplifts and unites people by connecting them to something greater than themselves – each other.[13])

## III. Empathy and Justice

Empathy is the ability to feel and understand another person's emotions without losing one's own boundaries. Through the integration of emotion and cognition, empathy is both a feeling and a form of understanding. It must be emphasized that empathy encompasses both emotional and cognitive levels. It creates emotional resonance that allows people not only to recognize someone's suffering but also to feel it and to respond with care. In other words, empathy is about putting yourself in others' shoes. Neuroscience shows that it activates the same brain areas as when we feel our own emotions. So, the author might say that moral understanding is rooted into our biology.

While empathy lies at the core of moral understanding, its absence reveals much about how morality functions. Some individuals show a greatly reduced emotional response to others' suffering, a trait often associated with dysfunction of the *amygdala*. Individuals known as psychopaths, for example, may fully understand moral rules on a cognitive level but lack the emotional engagement

[12]) Jonathan Haidt, *The Emotional Dog and Its Rational Tail: A Social Intuitionist Approach to Moral Judgment*, 108 Psychol. Rev. 814 (2001) (proposing that moral judgments arise from quick intuitions, with reasoning serving as post hoc rationalization).

[13]) Jonathan Haidt, *The Moral Emotions,* Oxford Press (2003), abstract available at https://pages.stern.nyu.edu/~jhaidt/articles/alternate_versions/haidt.2003.the-moral-emotions.pub025-as-html.html.

that gives those rules a moral weight. Blair's "Violence Inhibition Mechanism" (VIM) model of psychopathy explains that emotional reactions to others' suffering trigger an aversive response that normally inhibits aggression. According to Blair, psychopathy is defined as a lack of empathy, psychopaths understand moral rules yet fail to act in accordance with them.[14)]

In other words, psychopaths understand morality intellectually but not emotionally. This highlights the crucial role of emotions in empathy and application of the moral principles. Because of this link with emotions, the author concludes that empathy itself cannot simply be taught, although it can be cultivated and improved through experience and training.

Legal scholars have explored the concept of judicial empathy from various perspectives. Professor of Law Thomas B. Colby argues that judicial empathy does not weaken neutrality but rather reinforces it. He explains that empathic judges do not allow emotions to distort legal balance; instead, they use empathy to understand the facts more deeply and apply the law with greater accuracy. As he concludes, *"empathy is not an obstacle to judicial neutrality; it is its requirement"*.[15)]

In line with this view, Professor Susan A. Bandes, one of the founders of the *Law and Emotion* movement, notes that empathy in judging is not about taking sides but about understanding what is at stake for all participants. As she observes *"a judge may – and I would argue should – feel empathy for all the litigants before her. It is her job to try to understand what is at stake for the parties. Once she has done so, she must make a legal determination about which side prevails"*.[16)]

While empathy, when exercised by judges or arbitrators, enriches judicial reasoning, it must be balanced by emotional awareness, which requires training. Professor Lisa Feldman Barrett emphasizes that judges should develop the ability to experience emotions with high *granularity*, noting that such awareness allows them to explore their feelings wisely and use them constructively in the process of justice. In her words, "Without empathy, anger can foster the type of retributive punishment that risks undermining the very notion of justice as the foundation of the legal system".[17)]

Therefore, moral dimension of empathy naturally extends into law, where legal decisions must balance moral values, human behavior, rational legal

---

14) R. J. R. Blair, *Applying a Cognitive Neuroscience Perspective to the Disorder of Psychopathy*, 17 Dev. & Psychopathol (2005).

15) Thomas B. Colby, *In Defense of Judicial Empathy*, 96 Minn. L. Rev. 1944, 2015 (2012) ("Empathy is not an obstacle to judicial neutrality; it is a requirement of judicial neutrality.").

16) Susan A. Bandes, *Compassion and the Rule of Law*, 13 Int'l J. Law in Context 184, 185 (2017).

17) Lisa Feldman Barrett, *How Emotions Are Made: The Secret Life of the Brain* 247–48 (2017) ("Without empathy, anger can foster the type of retributive punishment that risks undermining the very notion of justice as the foundation of the legal system.").

reasoning and correct application of law. Empathy appears to be essential for translating moral knowledge into moral judgment and should be seen as a safeguard of justice. As a unique source of understanding, it enables judges and arbitrators to render legally sound and morally fair decisions. To balance impartiality with empathy, decision-makers must remain aware of their own emotions and thoughts. This self-awareness can help to uphold the principle of *"empathy in, bias out"*. It can be trained which is especially recommended for judges and arbitrators. Last but not least, the goal is not to suppress empathy, but to use it wisely in the service of humanity and justice.

## IV. The Boundaries of Justice: Human and AI Minds

While empathy anchors human judgment, AI operates through fundamentally different mechanisms. Human reasoning integrates emotion, intuition, rational thought and ethical reflection, while AI relies on data processing, probability, and logic-based optimization.

Experts in law and technology warn that although AI can assist courts by processing information and detecting patterns, it must remain a tool rather than a replacement for human judgment. Algorithms, while often perceived as neutral, mirror the biases and assumptions embedded in their training data and may thus reproduce or even amplify existing inequalities. This underscores the enduring necessity of human empathy and moral awareness in ensuring fairness, qualities no algorithm can replicate.[18)]

Attempts to prompt GPT-4 to reason like human judges proved revealing. Even when instructed to consider sympathy or predict how a jury might decide, it remained strictly formalist, acknowledging emotions only to dismiss them as legally irrelevant. The findings show both the potential and the limits of AI in judicial reasoning. It cannot weigh moral or social context, although it can apply rules consistently. Thus, AI may assist judges, but only humans can interpret meaning exercise equitable discretion, and ensure that justice – as a moral concept – is served.[19)]

Researchers have also observed that algorithmic errors differ fundamentally from human ones. While human mistakes are typically isolated and context-specific, algorithmic flaws tend to replicate across all cases processed by the same model, thereby amplifying their systemic effect. In this way, a single

---

[18)] Paul W. Grimm, Cary Coglianese & Maura R. Grossman, *AI in the Courts: How Worried Should We Be?*, 107 Judicature (2024), available at https://judicature.duke.edu/articles/ai-in-the-courts-how-worried-should-we-be/.

[19)] Eric A. Posner & Shivam Saran, *The Role of AI in Judicial Decision-Making*, CLS Blue Sky Blog, Columbia Law School (February 19, 2025), available at https://clsbluesky.law.columbia.edu/2025/02/19/the-role-of-ai-in-judicial-decision-making/.

defect in an algorithm can evolve into a structural distortion of justice. This underscores, from another perspective, the utmost importance of the errors made by AI when it is delegated the task of rendering arbitration decisions or judgments.

## V. Conclusion

In today's world, the use of AI is inevitable as it becomes an inseparable part of everyday life. AI can either enhance or diminish the quality of human work; it can reduce effort or increase it, improve results or worsen them. Everything depends on the human using AI.

The soft law that advises against delegating an arbitrator's duties to AI plays an essential role in safeguarding the human essence of justice. Equally important, however, is understanding why justice can only be exercised by humans. This awareness can help to preserve justice as a purely human moral, philosophical and legal concept.

Human decisions in the realm of justice are inseparable from their emotion and empathy. Empathy rooted in the emotional level allows judges and arbitrators to see situations through others' eyes, to understand the motives behind actions, and to balance legal reasoning with moral awareness. AI, by contrast, operates only through logic, data, and probability. It can assist in analyzing information, detecting patterns, and improving efficiency, but while it may process millions of facts, AI cannot feel; it may calculate, but it cannot comprehend human pain, compassion, or fairness.

Justice, however, is not a mechanical act; it is a profoundly human concept grounded in moral and emotional reflection. A person who understands moral rules intellectually but lacks emotional sensitivity is capable of grave moral errors. Decisions made without empathy may not only fail to achieve fairness but may even lead to tragedy. The parallel of justice without empathy to a psychopathic application of rules illustrates this danger: knowledge of moral norms alone does not ensure moral conduct.

It is empathy, moral intuition, and emotional awareness that give true weight and meaning to moral norms, qualities embodied exclusively in human nature. Therefore, the most suitable model for integrating AI into the legal process is the "human-in-the-loop" approach, where AI functions as a technical instrument while humans retain full responsibility for decision-making. Justice cannot be delegated to AI, just as it cannot be entrusted to those incapable of empathy. It requires a healthy human heart, for only the human heart can give morality its depth and weight.

# Diversity in Arbitration: Progress, Pushback & The Road Ahead

*Katherine Bell/Catrice Gayer/Judith Knieper/Niamh Leinwather/ Petra Pataki/Camilla Perera-de Wit*

VIAC has long been a strong advocate for diversity, including through its endorsement of the Equal Representation in Arbitration Pledge.[1]) VIAC is not only a signatory to the Equal Representation in Arbitration Pledge but also acts on this commitment in arbitrator appointments and other institutional activities. For instance, VIAC's statistics in 2024 showed that the VIAC Board appointed 64 % of women to arbitral tribunals, thus, achieving gender parity in its' institutional appointments.[2]) UNCITRAL shares this commitment. For example, the UNCITRAL Mediation Rules (notably Article 3(5)) call on institutions to consider both gender balance and geographical diversity when selecting mediators. Similarly, UNCITRAL's Working Group III on ISDS reform has explicitly addressed the lack of diversity among decision-makers, taking a broad and inclusive approach that reflects both gender balance and geographical diversity. These considerations are already visible in instruments such as the UNCITRAL Guidelines on Investment Mediation, and the Working Group continues to explore concrete solutions.

Both VIAC (represented by its' Secretary General, Niamh Leinwather) and UNCITRAL (represented by Judith Knieper, Legal Officer) were therefore pleased to co-organise the ArbitralWomen breakfast event during the 2025 Vienna Arbitration Days[3]) – a welcome space to connect, reflect, and push progress forward. The panel featured Catrice Gayer, Partner at Herbert Smith Freehills Kramer, Petra Pataki, Counsel, Queritius, and Camilla Perera-de Wit, Independent Arbitrator, with moderation by Katherine Bell (Partner at Schellenberg Wittmer and Vice-President of ArbitralWomen), and touched upon the following topics: (i) Diversity Fatigue and Developments in International Arbitration, (ii) The Value of Diversity in International Arbitration, (iii) Efficiency of Diverse Tribunals, (iv) Appointment of female arbitrators, and last but not least the question on (v) How to Achieve More Diversity?

---

[1]) https://www.arbitrationpledge.com/ [last accessed on October 31, 2025].

[2]) https://www.viac.eu/wp-content/uploads/2025/01/2024-Statistics-for-Web-2.pdf [last accessed on October 31, 2025].

[3]) https://www.viennaarbitrationdays.at/ [last accessed on October 31, 2025].

## I. Diversity Fatigue and Developments in International Arbitration

With the diversity agenda increasingly questioned in the current political climate, the panel began by highlighting that the international arbitration community is not insulated from these broader developments. When analyzing the global diversity discussion, the panel noted the very different starting points across regions. For example, at some arbitral institutions in Central and Eastern Europe, only about 10 % of arbitrators on rosters are women, highlighting the uneven uptake and implementation of global diversity initiatives. Without local engagement and buy-in, international efforts may struggle to achieve meaningful and lasting impact.

The panel also highlighted the risk of diversity fatigue[4]) – especially in contexts where diversity measures are seen as externally imposed or politicized. This can lead to tokenism[5]) or box-checking rather than genuine progress. From a psychological perspective, diversity fatigue can stem from perceived overexposure, lack of visible progress, or defensive reactions when inclusion efforts challenge entrenched hierarchies or comfort zones.[6])

Participants emphasized the importance of taking these developments seriously. Law firms, in particular, are increasingly targeted in the public debate, and the current climate risks emboldening voices that previously would have remained on the margins. As one speaker noted, 'the door is wide open' for society to backslide, with people now feeling encouraged to voice views that were previously seen as inappropriate.

Ultimately, the panel agreed that it is the responsibility of the arbitration community to keep these discussions alive – just as was being done at this panel. Only through continuous dialogue, commitment, and collective responsibility can progress toward greater diversity in arbitration continue and withstand the challenges ahead.

---

[4]) Gassam, J. (2019, June 18). *Is America tired of talking about diversity and inclusion? Forbes.* https://www.forbes.com [last accessed on October 31, 2025] and Chartier, D. (2019, March 20). *Pushing through "diversity fatigue". Law Week Colorado.* https://www.lawweekcolorado.com [last accessed on October 31, 2025].

[5]) Singh, S. J. (2021, August 31). *Boards need real diversity, not tokenism. Harvard Business Review.* https://hbr.org/2021/08/boards-need-real-diversity-not-tokenism [last accessed on October 31, 2025].

[6]) Trabue, C. (2019, September 25). *5 ways to fight diversity fatigue in the legal profession. The Talent Whisperer,* Carrington Legal. https://www.carringtonlegal.com, [last accessed on October 31, 2025].

## II. The Value of Diversity in International Arbitration

The panel returned to a fundamental question: why is diversity, particularly gender diversity, important in international arbitration? Speakers emphasized that decision-making improves when it draws on a range of perspectives, including professional diversity (such as law firms, academia, in-house counsel, and the judiciary), geographical and cultural diversity, which allows for a better understanding of varying legal and commercial contexts, and generational diversity, where younger practitioners bring fresh insights, availability, and motivation.

Cognitive diversity was highlighted as a key factor in improving problem-solving and the overall quality of decisions. The discussion noted the importance of addressing entrenched and self-reinforcing selection practices and informal networks that tend to exclude underrepresented groups. A broader range of perspectives can lead to stronger group performance and more robust deliberations, while also reducing the risk of groupthink and confirmation bias -particularly relevant in complex disputes. One study cited in support of these claims was McKinsey's 2021 report *"Female Empowerment Unlocks Value"*, which found that companies with the highest gender diversity in executive teams achieved 26 percent higher profitability.[7]) Law firms with higher racial and ethnic diversity among attorneys consistently report significantly higher partner compensation, up to $260,000 more per partner, due to "diversity dividend".[8]) This financial advantage is also likely linked to the cognitive benefits diverse teams offer, including improved problem-solving, better decision-making, and stronger workplace cultures

The panel further explored how diversity contributes to the quality and credibility of arbitration. Appointing the best-suited arbitrator involves more than traditional credentials; it includes relevant language skills, legal training, and awareness of the context. Diversity not only strengthens perceptions of fairness but also enhances the practical effectiveness of proceedings. For example, when parties see arbitrators or mediators who share cultural or linguistic backgrounds, this can foster trust and mutual understanding.

It was stressed that the aim is not to appoint individuals solely on the basis of gender, but to ensure that qualified candidates from a broader, more inclusive pool are considered. This includes newer voices and younger arbitrators, who may have more time, capacity, and drive to contribute meaningfully to the process.

---

[7]) McKinsey & Company, "Win Win: How empowering women can benefit Central and Eastern Europe" (2021).

[8]) Nath, Y., & Parker, E. (2021, June 27). *Nothing not to like: Diversity and law firm profitability* (238). Legal Evolution. https://www.legalevolution.org/2021/06/nothing-not-to-like-diversity-and-law-firm-profitability-238/, [last accessed on October 31, 2025].

Finally, the panel highlighted the need to cultivate a sustainable pipeline of new talent. As senior arbitrators gradually retire, encouraging the development of a vibrant and diverse pool is essential to ensure that the arbitration system continues to evolve and meet the needs of its users.

## III. Efficiency of Diverse Tribunals

The panel then turned to the theme of this year's Vienna Arbitration Days: efficiency in arbitration. Are diverse tribunals or diverse counsel teams inherently more efficient? Or could the opposite be true?

Speakers agreed that efficiency is a mindset, much like being 'international'. Selecting the best fit for a team often means including a mix of experienced professionals and younger colleagues, who are typically eager to prove their preparedness and efficiency. Efficiency is a shared responsibility, among arbitral institutions, tribunals, counsel, party representatives, and experts, and it depends not only on speed but on effective processes.

Diversity was viewed as an asset in this regard. While repeat appointments can sometimes streamline collaboration, they may also reduce checks and balances and involve arbitrators with overloaded schedules. Including newer voices often adds capacity and technological fluency.

The panel also questioned whether speed should be the primary measure of efficiency. Diverse teams may deliberate longer, but they are more likely to avoid groupthink and identify blind spots early, leading to more robust and resilient decisions. While such teams might require more discussion upfront, they are better equipped to handle cross-cultural nuances and avoid inefficiencies later – such as miscommunication, perceived bias, or enforcement issues.

Ultimately, the panel concluded that efficiency is not simply about doing things quickly; it is about doing the right things and doing them well. From that perspective, diversity is not an obstacle to efficiency, but rather an essential component of it.

## IV. Appointment of Female Arbitrators

The panel addressed the recurring challenge of appointing female arbitrators. While recent statistics show progress (roughly one-third of all appointments under leading rules are women[9])) this progress is largely driven by arbitral institutions. However, most statistics do not disaggregate by amount

[9]) ICC: 30 %, LCIA: 33 % in 2023 [https://www.lcia.org/News/lcia-news-annual-report-on-2023-lcia-court-and-african-users-c.aspx], VIAC: 37 % in 2024 [https://www.viac.eu/wp-content/uploads/2025/01/2024-Statistics-for-Web-2.pdf] [both last accessed on October 31, 2025].

in dispute. VIAC's data shows a clear trend: the higher the amount, the lower the share of women appointed – highlighting the need for continued efforts.[10])

While institutional progress is at least encouraging, the real gap lies in appointments by parties and co-arbitrators, where female representation remains low. The reasons are complex and interconnected. Parties and co-arbitrators tend to favor familiar names, often senior, male arbitrators with established reputation. Female and younger arbitrators are less likely to make it onto shortlists, particularly in high-value cases. The 'safe choice' reflex still dominates, driven by familiarity bias, 'club culture', and perceived assumptions about authority.

Anecdotes highlighted this dynamic: in one case, a (male) party chose a male arbitrator over a qualified woman because he believed he would be less intimidated by a difficult witness. It was also mentioned that where the list procedure under Article 8 of the UNCITRAL Arbitration Rules is used, female candidates are often the first to be struck off. A further illustration: when ChatGPT was asked to suggest arbitrator candidates for a complex international construction arbitration, it generated ten names – with only male candidates. Female candidates were suggested only when specifically prompted – reflecting the visibility gap even in algorithmic outputs.

Structural issues were also raised: women remain underrepresented in older professional networks and among top repeat users. Some male colleagues are more confident in selling their experience, while women are more hesitant to put themselves forward unless they meet all criteria – what one speaker called 'imposter syndrome'. There was also a call for senior lawyers to be mindful of how opportunities are distributed: male associates frequently ask to be staffed on high-profile cases, while female colleagues are more likely to wait for assignments and be reluctant to speak up. Equal opportunity must begin in the workplace, and female associates should be encouraged – and empowered – to proactively seek out challenging assignments.

The panel highlighted that diversity in counsel teams has increased and noted a positive trend towards counsel teams expected to reflect the diversity of the in-house legal teams they represent. The more diverse the in-house team the more they expect to see this mirrored in the external counsel team and ultimately in the arbitration tribunal. It is indeed becoming more common for clients to openly address this imbalance during pitches. For example, one speaker recounted arriving at a client headquarters to deliver a pitch and, in the hallway, encountered the team from a competing law firm – consisting of only senior male lawyers of the same nationality. As the in-house legal team was visibly diverse, both in terms of gender and geographical background, the more diverse external team made a better impression, and later indeed won the pitch.

---

[10]) https://www.viac.eu/wp-content/uploads/2025/01/2023-Statistics-for-Web-5.pdf [last accessed on October 31, 2025].

Ultimately, more progress is needed, especially in building confidence among parties and peers in the capabilities of women arbitrators, across all levels and types of disputes, and also in ensuring that women are encouraged and empowered to seize opportunities when they arise.

## V. How to get to More Diversity?

The panel agreed that one key is early exposure: young women lawyers must be brought to hearings, involved in strategic decisions, and given small advocacy opportunities from the outset — even during internships or traineeships. Women need to be visible, and visibility starts early.

Another essential factor is mentorship. Close, proactive support can make a substantial difference in identifying and fostering strengths and actively supporting women in their progression. This includes both structural changes – like flexible work models – and cultural ones, such as normalizing women in leadership roles and challenging ingrained assumptions about "who looks like an advocate".

Indeed, the panel agreed that:

- Visibility is unevenly distributed. Women are still less frequently offered lead speaking roles in hearings or client meetings. Yet advocacy is a visibility game. Firms must ensure that the women can shine and convince their clients, if need be.
- Mentors becoming sponsors is important to note here. A sponsor takes a more active role in advocating on behalf of a female talent with senior leadership as well as the arbitration community. This remains much needed.
- Assertiveness vs. likability. Women who advocate often face a double standard – confidence may be misread as aggression. All stakeholders in the arbitration process must be made aware of this still existing (unconscious) bias, so the perception can be changed.
- The practical demands of arbitration remain rigid. Late nights, extensive travel, and high-pressure deadlines often conflict with caregiving responsibilities. While COVID-19 introduced more flexible working models (including remote work), much more needs to be done to retain women at key career stages.
- Client expectations can be a hurdle. There are still (explicit or implicit) preferences for 'battle-tested' male advocates. Firms must educate clients and advocate internally for diverse teams.

Following the panel discussion, VIAC and ArbitralWomen[11]) officially signed a Memorandum of Understanding (MoU) to promote diversity, inclusion, and collaboration in international arbitration. The MoU was signed by Niamh Leinwather, Secretary General of VIAC, and Katherine Bell, Vice President of ArbitralWomen. Also in attendance was the Secretary of ArbitralWomen, Nata Ghibradze, whose presence further underscored the importance of this new partnership. This agreement marks a meaningful step in strengthening ties between the two organizations and advancing shared goals in the arbitration community.

[11]) https://arbitralwomen.org/ [last accessed on October 31, 2025].

# Growth, the Rule of Law and Arbitration

*Iain Sheridan**)

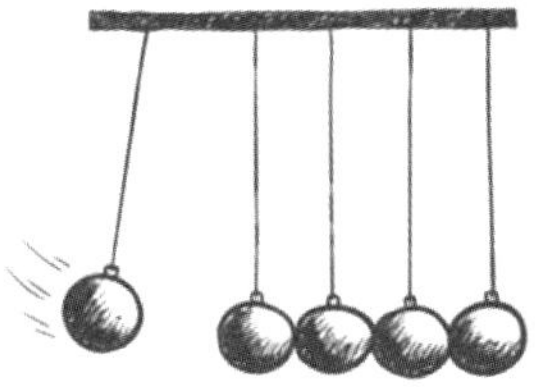

## I. Introduction

The genesis of this article arises from the reality that economic growth in Europe has slowed compared with past periods of consistent prosperity. The so-called *Draghi Report* highlighted an alarming innovation gap across the continent. Not only is labour productivity slowing compared with the US, but Europe is also entering the first period in which GDP growth will not be supported by sustained net growth of the labour force. By 2040, the EU's workforce is projected to shrink by close to two million workers each year, while the ratio of working to retired people is expected to fall from around 3:1 to 2:1. In sum, by 2040 growth in Europe will stall.[1])

The *Draghi Report* also spelt out the complexity for the EU with its approaches to competition law and historical aversion to state aid. The report observed that the "lack of innovation in Europe is sometimes blamed on competition enforcement. Although stronger competition will in theory generally both lower prices and foster innovation, there are cases where it can be harmful to innovation [...] in some cases the Commission has come under attack

---

*) The views expressed in this article are those of the author and do not reflect the official opinion of the Bar of England and Wales, the Bar of Ireland, or any arbitral institution.

[1]) EC (2025), *The future of European competitiveness – Part A – A competitive strategy for Europe*, Chapter 2, Closing the Innovation Gap, at 23. UK contributions to the *Draghi Report* included the *London School of Economics*, *Rolls Royce* and *Vodafone*. From the author's viewpoint, conspicuous for its absence was any Asian contributors that could have illustrated how they assess opportunities for European growth. What do *Samsung*, *TSMC* and *Xiaomi* think?

for not allowing mergers that would create companies of sufficient scale to invest to compete with Chinese and American superstar companies".[2])

Across Europe, sustained growth requires stimulation at varying business scales and sectors.[3]) Further, the solution to each scale is quite different and often conflicting. There are many established star performers at the gargantuan multinational level, such as Switzerland's *ABB*, the Netherlands' *ASML*, and Germany's *Infineon*. But cutting-edge smaller firms, such as the UK's *DeepMind*, France's *Mistral*, and Germany's *Black Forest Labs* are at earlier stages of growth experiencing markedly different competitive dynamics. Europe as a business region needs to encourage and fuel its entrepreneurialism. Sometimes that will involve competition enforcement. Sometimes that will involve strategically targeted state aid.

## II. Growth

Imagine modern capitalism as Newton's cradle. By which is meant picture free market activity as a set of five motionless steel balls suspended by wires. When one ball is raised and released its kinetic energy passes to the second ball, then onto the third ball, the fourth ball, and the fifth ball. Consequently, that fifth ball rises into the air, then returns significant energy back through to the first ball. Innovation, the vital component of modern capitalism, is that first ball. In turn, that first ball rises then returns energy to the second ball, and so forth. The energy passing from each successive ball is economic growth. *Click ... click ... click ...*

The greatest contributor to highlighting the critical role innovation-led growth plays in capitalist economies is *Joseph Schumpeter*, an Austrian-born economist and doctoral alumnus of *Vienna Law Faculty*. His concept of 'creative destruction' captures the evolutionary nature of free markets where established ways of doing things are replaced by new ones.[4]) New entrants to existing markets tend to succeed when introducing significant improvements.

To elaborate, *Schumpeter* encapsulated creative destruction in this way: "But in capitalist reality ... the competition from the new commodity, the new technology, the new source of supply, the new type of organization (the largest-scale unit of control for instance), competition which commands a decisive cost or quality advantage and which strikes not at the margins of the profits

[2]) EC (2025), *The future of European competitiveness – Part B – A competitive strategy for Europe*, Section 2 Horizonal policies, at 298.

[3]) To be differentiated with sustainable growth. *See* Mitsi, M. and Lim, B. (2025), *Environmental, Social and Governance Disputes – Litigation and Arbitration* (Wolters Kluwer); and *Austrian Yearbook of International Arbitration* (2024), *Greener Arbitration: How to Achieve More Sustainable Practices in International Arbitration*, at section H.

[4]) Schumpeter, J. (1950), *Capitalism, socialism and democracy* (Harper & Brothers).

and the outputs of the existing firms but at their foundations and their very lives."[5])

In essence, creative destruction is the most dynamic form of innovation. Examples of creative destruction include motor cars overtaking horse-drawn carts, personal computers breaking the dominance of mainframes, and the supplanting of *Nokia* traditional mobile phones by App-driven *Android* and iOS smart phones.

Turning back to the image of Newton's cradle, the first steel ball is creative destruction – innovation. Everything else in modern capitalism, arbitration, bureaucracy, court litigation, industrial policies, law and tax, are other steel balls. *Click ... click ... click ...* These are steel balls that play a positive contribution helping growth to continue. Alternatively, like gravity they play a negative role by dragging momentum down to a slower pace or a recessionary stop.

## III. The Rule of Law

The rule of law needs to be consistently applied in any jurisdiction to maintain its positive influence on growth. But how can such a set of values be consistently measured if at all? How does its application vary across EU member states, Norway, Iceland, Liechtenstein, and the UK?

On first reflection there might not be a consensus across all of Europe on what is meant by the rule of law. Further, it cannot be ignored that the concept of the rule of law has its critics. For instance, consider *Judith Shklar*. The first woman to be given tenure in Harvard's Government Department, she argued that the expression has lost its meaningfulness because of abuse and over-use, commenting, "it may well have become just another one of those self-congratulatory rhetorical devices that grace the public utterances of Anglo-American politicians. No intellectual effort need therefore be wasted on this bit of ruling-class chatter".[6])

*Shklar's* was observing our world in the latter part of the 20th century. Yet in some ways her view resonates more so now given the frequent rhetorical noises of social media that distract rational minds from the evidence-based signals communicated by the quality press and leading science-based journals.

From a judicial stance, Lord *Bingham's* famous Cambridge University lecture on the rule of law is widely accepted as a rounded characterisation of a multifarious concept.[7]) Lord *Bingham's* lecture revolved around eight areas.

[5]) Mason, E. (1951), *Schumpeter on Monopoly and the Large Firm*, The Review of Economics and Statistics, Vol 33, No.2, at 139 (MIT Press).

[6]) Shklar, J. (1987), *"Political Theory and The Rule of Law" in Hutchinson and Monahan (eds), The Rule of Law: Ideal or Ideology* (*Carswell*) at 1.

[7]) Bingham, T. (2006), *The Rule of Law*, lecture delivered on 16 November 2006, *see* transcript at 29. Available at https://www.cpl.law.cam.ac.uk/sir-david-williams-

These eight elements are widely accepted among senior judiciary around the world. Naturally, among other universally applied principles, the eight principles include, among other things, accessibility for each citizen to know the legal rules applicable to a given case, the right to a fair hearing, respect for human rights, and civil redress at reasonable cost, predictability, and finality without undue delay.

## A. Obligations under International Law

Figure 1 captures three vital aspect of the rule of law that singularly and in combination influence growth. First, that each nation-state must comply with their obligations under international law.[8])

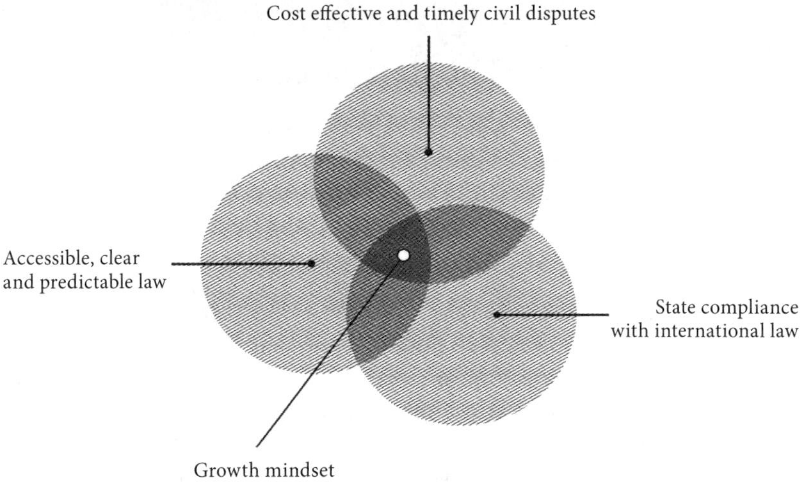


Figure 1 – Growth Mindset

This is predominantly derived by compliance with treaties. Put another way, every jurisdiction must comply with international customs, rules, norms, principles, and procedures. Three global examples are postal, shipping and telecommunications services.

Lord *Bingham's* seminal lecture on the rule of law concluded in this way. "The state for its part accepts that it may not do, at home or abroad, all that it has the power to do but only that which laws binding upon it authorise it to do."

---

lectures/rt-hon-lord-bingham-cornhill-kg-rule-law. These eight concepts are greatly expanded in his later book: Bingham, T. (2010), The Rule of Law (*Penguin*).

[8]) *Ibid.*, at 29.

Compliance with international law fundamentally requires applying the Vienna Convention on the Law of Treaties (VCLT) which has often played a crucial role in solving a recurring range of arbitration issues. A recent example is the published French-language decision in Switzerland. The Swiss Supreme Court held it was not bound by the CJEU decision in *Republic of Moldova v Komstroy LLC*.[9]) The Swiss judges concluded there were no grounds to consider under public international law that EU law should prevail over the Energy Charter Treaty (ECT).[10])

The brief background facts to this case were that Spain challenged an arbitration award made by a Swiss tribunal in favour of EDF under the ECT. Among other grounds, Spain asserted that there was a conflict between Article 26 of the ECT and EU law. The Swiss Supreme Court focused on the fact that the ECJ's reasoning in *Komstroy* omitted to apply the rules of treaty interpretation. The Swiss judiciary analysed that there was a requirement to apply Article 41 VCLT which allows for changes by two or more parties to a multilateral treaty if certain conditions are fulfilled. The Article 41 conditions are (a) that the possibility of such a change is provided for by the treaty, or (b) the change in question is not prohibited by the treaty.

Article 16 ECT states that where two or more parties who have entered a prior international agreement or enter a subsequent international agreement, whose terms concern the subject matter of the ECT, nothing in the ECT can act to nullify the relevance of the terms of the other international agreement. Further, Article 26 ECT provides that each party to a dispute gives its unconditional consent to submit a dispute to international arbitration. In sum, the Swiss judges concluded there was no conflict between Article 26 of the ECT and EU law.

## B. Civil Disputes Managed Cost Effectively and Expeditiously

Second, Lord *Bingham* argued that rule of law requires resolving civil disputes without prohibitive costs and delay. This includes the option of arbitration as what he classifies as an "additional" means of dispute resolution. This does not mean it is peripheral to court civil disputes in the context of commerce. The learned judge also made a significant comment about arbitration. He made clear that in his view arbitration and other means of dispute

[9]) *Republic of Moldova v Komstroy LLC*, Case C-741/19. The central tenet of the *Komstroy* ruling was that ad hoc arbitral proceedings derived from rights set out in bilateral investment treaties are incompatible with EU law.

[10]) Swiss Supreme Court (2024) *Case 4A_244/2023*.

resolution, "have a supremely important contribution to make to the rule of law".[11])

Therefore, we can say that one of the best judicial minds who possessed an unwavering dedication to fairness values the role of arbitration. Equally, the judges of the CJEU must value more the contribution of arbitration to influencing economic growth. As Europe increasingly builds its own technology infrastructure, including semiconductor fabrication plants, bilateral and multilateral investment treaties play a pivotal role in securing the billions of euros needed for many economies.[12])

Additionally, when judges are tasked with cases that they are less familiar with their sense of professionalism causes them to simply delay dealing with that particular type of case. In these instances when arbitrary tribunals are very experienced and dealing with cross border issues, there is an argument for judges to delegate cases to arbitration. An example is where a sector that has ongoing geopolitical tensions and presents elevated risk levels risk exacerbated by continuous media attention that is likely to damage international relations. In these instances, there is every sense for appropriate cases to be delegated to experienced, vetted arbitral tribunals.

### C. Accessible, Clear and Predictable Law

Third, Lord *Bingham* propounded that the rule of law must be accessible, clear and predictable. That seems uncontroversial for most European jurisdictions, albeit to varying degrees. Given commercial law is complex making the support of legal experts is essential, the judiciary have responsibilities to also communicate that reality.

In recent years decisions by the Court of Justice of the European Union (CJEU) have held that bilateral investment treaties (BITs) between EU member states are incompatible with EU Law. From one view, the CJEU's *Achmea* decision neglected the importance of growth to the EU. To date, if growth is not part of the CJEU mindset. Yet investment treaty arbitration, whether under ICSID or other rules, plays a vital role in long-term international business confidence to make foreign direct investment (FDI) decisions.

## IV. Arbitration

Arbitration is the preference of many corporations that have the freedom to make long term strategic global investments. Arbitration also allows cross-

[11]) Bingham, T. (2006), *The Rule of Law*, lecture delivered on 16 November 2006, *see* transcript at 20. Available at https://www.cpl.law.cam.ac.uk/sir-david-williams-lectures/rt-hon-lord-bingham-cornhill-kg-rule-law.

[12]) Sheridan, I. (2025), *Semiconductors – Law, Strategy and Tax*, Edward Elgar Publishing, at 5.4 to 5.5.2.

border disputes to be dealt with fairly without clogging up national courts. Cost, quality and speed are all addressed.[13]) Growth requires certainty of outcome as well. Every company invests *x* to achieve *y* profits, accepting existing and unknown risks. If courts and arbitral tribunals move from reasonable certainty to uncertainty, growth will slow down.

What future solutions could prevent the EU from commercial self-harm? A potential remedy would be to apply the judicial approach adopted in Ireland when a law is judged to be in incompatible with the Irish constitution. When faced with such scenarios, the Irish Supreme Court makes what is referred to as a '*suspended declaration of invalidity*'. The practical consequences are that the offending law is not judged invalid for a period of six months – long enough for the legislature to alter the law. This way there is not a flooding of the courts of claims surrounding the offending law. Additionally, a dialogue can start between the judiciary and the legislature to find the best workable solutions.[14])

If the suspected declaration of invalidity approach was applied by the CJEU to EU law, it would enable a growth-oriented change to be made to Article 267 of the Treaty on the Functioning of the EU (TFEU) which does not classify or include an arbitral tribunal as a court or tribunal "of a Member State" within the meaning of Article 267 TFEU concerning references for a preliminary ruling, and therefore has no power to make a reference to the Court for a preliminary ruling. Alternatively, each Member State's domestic law could be changed to make arbitral tribunals an exception to Article 267 TFEU.

## A. The Treaty on the European Union

Additionally, the EC seems to take a selective approach to applying the Treaty on the European Union ("TEU") in the context of state aid. For instance, the EC challenged the UK for, among other things, failing to apply Article 4(3) of the TEU that sets out the duty to apply the principle of sincere cooperation

[13]) Sheridan, I. (2016), Journal of International Arbitration, *Qualitative Analytical Models for Arbitration* (Wolters Kluwer).

[14]) The Irish Supreme Court has acknowledged that the suspended declaration of invalidity is an established concept in other jurisdictions. In *Heneghan v Minster for Housing, Planning and Local Government, Government of Ireland, Attorney General and Ireland* ([2023] IESC 18), Chief Justice O'Donnell makes clear that this jurisprudence has developed in detail from the Canadian Supreme Court. In *Reference Re Manitoba Language Rights, [1985] 1 S.C.R. 721* the Canadian Supreme Court highlighted that the primary logic of a suspended declaration is that without more, making a law invalid immediately would undermine the rule of law. Further, in the same Irish Supreme Court judgment O'Donnell CJ pointed out that the German Constitutional Court applies a similar approach.

to "facilitate the achievement of the Union's tasks".[15]) The duty of sincere co-operation contained in Article 4(3) TEU was described in *Deutsche Lufthansa AG v Flughafen Frankfurt-Hahn GmbH (Ryanair Ltd intervening)* (Case C-284/12) [2014] 2 CMLR 20, para 41, that "national courts must take all the necessary measures, whether general or specific, to ensure fulfilment of the  bligations under European Union law and refrain from those which may jeopardise the attainment of the objectives of the Treaty, as follows from Article 4(3) TEU. Therefore, national courts must in particular, refrain from taking decisions which conflict with a decision of the Commission [...]".

This approach by the EC ignores Article 4(2) that states "The Union [...] shall respect their essential State functions, including ensuring the territorial integrity of the State [...] In particular, national security remains the sole responsibility of each Member State." Events in Europe throughout and after the Covid-19 pandemic highlighted the need for regional supply chains.

An example might be when a sector that has ongoing geopolitical tensions. In these instances, there is every sense for appropriate cases to be delegated to experienced, vetted arbitral tribunals. Supply chains currently undergoing geopolitical tensions include, among others, EV batteries, rare earth elements, solar panels, semiconductors and steel. Indeed, there is no coincidence that most of the sectors covering these goods form chapters in the *Draghi* Report.

## B. Arbitration and Transparency

To maintain respect for the rule of law in each jurisdiction there needs to be not only the choice of arbitration as a dispute resolution mechanism, but also appropriate levels of transparency. By which is meant, there are instances where it is important for multiple diverse stakeholders to have access to information on how companies operate. However, arbitrations generally concern business disputes with the key advantage of confidentiality. Yet increasingly in the context of climate change and global technology supply chains,[16]) geopolitics play a significant role in challenging the form and substance of corporate activity. That cannot be achieved without some published data.[17])

The happy medium, in many but not all cases, in such scenarios is for (a) no publicity on the names of the businesses involved, and (b) the publication

[15]) *European Commission v United Kingdom of Great Britain and Northern Ireland* (2024), Case C-516/22.

[16]) Sheridan, I. (2025), *Semiconductors – Law, Strategy and Tax* (*Edward Elgar Publishing*).

[17]) Readers may have noticed that the penultimate year's VIAC Yearbook included an article proposing the standardised reporting of statistics as a key benefit of meaningful data. *See Austrian Yearbook of International Arbitration* (2024), *The Vienna Propositions for Streamlining Arbitral Proceedings: Keeping Pace with New Developments and User Expectations*, at 149.

of the arbitral seat, the choice of arbitral rules, and the outcome. In this way there would be data available on outcomes relevant to other interest groups. Simultaneously businesses would continue to have confidence in specific jurisdictions because they see that there is predictability in dispute management. VIAC for more than 10 years has made transparency a priority. At the end of 2023 VIAC published 25 anonymised summaries of VIAC arbitral awards in a special edition of the ITA Arbitration Report.[18])

If a balance is not maintained, any CJEU decision making, EU regulations, and EC policies may influence businesses to be reluctant to agree arbitration in EU seats. This would include commercial disputes between public limited or private companies or other business entities such as private equity firms.

## V. Conclusions

The main arguments in this article can be crystalised into the following four points:

1. The rule of law requires predictability at both domestic and international levels.
2. The rule of law demands the consistent application of international treaties.
3. Growth is influenced by the consistent application of international treaties.
4. Arbitration facilitates growth.

Given growth is an existential priority, how can senior judges as elite professionals influence political leaders to appreciate the importance of the rule of law? During a 2025 event in Dublin organized by the Bar of Ireland and the Law Society of Ireland, three chief judges from England & Wales, Ireland, and Northern Ireland, made up a panel on a seminar focused on the rule of law. They were Sir *Geoffrey Vos*, the second most senior judge in England & Wales, Mr Justice *Donal O'Donnell*, Chief Justice of Ireland, and Lady Chief Justice *Siobhan Keegan* of Northern Ireland. Collectively, they have over 100 years of judicial experience. Further, the combined GDP of England & Wales, Ireland, and Northern Ireland is comparable to that of France.

My specific question posed to this eminent trio was given many political leaders struggle to be interested in the rule of law as an influential factor in economic growth, should the concept be communicated to them as a source of

[18]) Other arbitral institutions apply transparency principles, albeit in different ways. For instance, LCIA has been a thought leader in publishing challenge decisions. *See* www.lcia.org/News/lcia-releases-additional-challenge-decisions-online.aspx In investment treaty arbitration, ICSID publishes not only challenge decisions, but also awards and procedural orders.

'soft power'? To briefly remind readers, soft power is a concept from international relations, developed by Professor *Joseph Nye* of Harvard University. Soft power forms part of foreign policy, whereby non-coercive aspects of a country attract other actors into that jurisdiction. The opposite is 'hard power', such as how many bullets, fighter planes and tanks are available to a country. The rule of law can be characterised as a non-coercive source of attraction any jurisdiction can offer – soft power.[19])

The individual responses of the three judges had two contrasting aspects. First, there was a consensus that external to a jurisdiction the rule of law is a form of soft power. Second, the rule of law cannot be expressed in soft power language because the judiciary in any jurisdiction are a third pillar of a civilised society – the Executive, the Legislature, and the Judiciary. Therefore, in their collective view, judges within each jurisdiction have a duty to consistently communicate that the rule of law applies to all citizens. While arbitrators and commercial lawyers can make contributions to the rule of law by promoting it as a form of soft power, judges cannot do so because they would be delivering mixed messages to all the citizens they serve. Judges are both guardians of human rights and business.

In the Swiss Supreme Court decision discussed earlier in this article, the judges remarked that for several years EU institutions have been waging a *"crusade"* against international arbitration. From a foreign direct investment viewpoint, such a mindset cannot be conducive to economic growth.[20]) When new firms seek to grow they will achieve a sustainable mass in business environments where their free-flowing creativity is maximised by the predictable interaction of the rule of law and arbitration. European court decisions that weaken arbitration and the rule of law weaken growth. EU law becomes, to return to the Newton's cradle analogy, a force of gravity slowing down European business activity in a fiercely competitive global marketplace.

---

[19]) The concept of soft power was created by the leading foreign policy professor Joseph Nye of Harvard University. The author had two encounters with him at Oxford, which left a deep impression that soft power is a key catalyst for economic growth. Sadly, Joe Nye passed away in 2025. His last book is a rich source of soft power examples from around the world. *See* Nye, J. (2024), *A Life in the American Century* (Polity Press).

[20]) *Ibid.* Case 4A_244/2023 at 7.6.5: *"Depuis plusieurs années, les organes de l'UE mènent, en effet, une croisade contre de tels arbitrages internationaux."*

# VIAC 50th Anniversary: "International Arbitration and the Rule of Law: Between the Scylla of Politics and the Charybdis of Law"

*Stavros Brekoulakis**)[1]

28 February 2025

1. Distinguished guests, Ladies and gentlemen. I would like to start by thanking VIAC for the honor to invite me to speak at its Golden Jubilee Anniversary. I have a tremendous respect for VIAC because it has a long and remarkable history and contribution to international arbitration which goes far beyond its caseload. At the time it was conceived, in the middle of the cold war, VIAC was possibly the only arbitration institution together with the Stockholm Chamber of Commerce that was trusted by both the east and the west. It became thus the prime example as to how international commerce and international arbitration can function as a bridge that brings people closer.

2. Since then, VIAC has evolved into this modern and vibrant arbitral institution that is more popular than ever. But it always kept this special character that distinguishes VIAC from any other institution in the world; in being this living historical symbol that international arbitration can be more than just resolving commercial disputes. That it can be a platform where people from very different backgrounds leave their parochialism, cultural assumptions and prejudices behind to find common ground. As I will come to explain shortly, international law and arbitration are at a crossroads today. In the next 50 years, VIAC's role should be not just to administer more arbitration cases; it should be to remind us all what international arbitration is all about.

3. But it is not just about VIAC that I am pleased to be here today. It is also Vienna. For those of you who know me, will also know that this city is

*) Professor Stavros Brekoulakis is the Michael and Laura Hwang Chair in International Arbitration, NUS Law. This contribution features his keynote for the VIAC CAN Congress on February 28, 2025.

near and dear to me – I have great friends here and beautiful memories. I am also fond of Vienna because it is one of the few places who still keep alive this wonderful legal tradition where practice and academia still work together. The majority of the legal practitioners in Vienna have either completed a Doctoral thesis or they have an active interest in academic scholarship and publications. You do not find this unified approach to law in many other places in the world, and certainly not in the Anglo-Saxon tradition where legal practitioners tend to reside in a very different world from that of academics.

4. I said a minute ago that it is an honor to be here with you this morning. But it is also a daunting task to speak to you about international law and politics in today's complex world. But I thought that there is no better occasion to address these broad and big questions that trouble us today than the occasion of the 50th Anniversary of VIAC whose history, as I mentioned, transcends international law and politics all these years. I hope you will bear with me as I now turn to this task in the next 45–50 minutes.

5. Should a private international tribunal of three individuals decide whether the decision of a foreign government on matters concerning its economy, public health, and environment are lawful or unlawful under international law? Should important decisions of public policy and governance be subject to a rules-based system of independent justice?

6. As I will come to explain shortly, the answer that most of us would have given to these questions forty years ago might be different from the answers that we might give today. While previously most people would answer these questions with a resounding yes, today a critical mass is likely to say that governmental decisions on public policy are essentially political questions and should be left to the discretion of governments; not international law and tribunals. This is the first thing that I will argue today: that the space for international law is currently narrowing down.

7. The second thing that I will address is the question of "what's changed" and we now consider that international law should occupy a narrower space. As I will argue, after a constant growth in the first sixty years after the WWII, international law reached a point of saturation; of excess. And at this point, the broader political context started to shift from liberalism to sovereignty. This shift has had profound implications for the scope and role of international law. And I will spend some time to speak about those implications.

8. I pause here to say that the proposition that international law may change because the political context changes is a counter-intuitive, perhaps even controversial, proposition speaking in Vienna within a short distance from the place where Kelsen taught for many years. Indeed, since Kelsen's legal revolution, international lawyers are hardwired to think that the law is firmly separated from religion and politics. That the law is a self-contained system that reflects lasting notions of fairness and justice that transcend the ephemeral whims of politics. But of course, this is not true. The relationship between the law and politics is one of continuous struggle. Take any conceptual analogy you want to illustrate the point: think of it as a zero-sum game; a roller-coaster; a pendulum.

9. The analogy I have chosen for today's lecture is slightly more dramatic: it is that of two mythical creatures: Scylla and Charybdis, these immortal and irresistible sea monsters from Greek mythology. And I choose this analogy first to honor my Greek heritage; and second because as I will come to explain to, international arbitration's struggle between law and politics is a struggle between two equally ferocious monsters. As the myth has it, Scylla and Charybdis were located on opposite sides of the Strait of Messina between Sicily and Calabria. And they were located close enough to each other that they posed an inescapable threat to passing sailors; avoiding Scylla meant passing too close to Charybdis and vice versa. And it is this analogy that I find ideal to describe how, today, international arbitration needs to be very careful and always navigate between the hazards of excessive law and excessive politics.

10. The third thing I will do today is to provide a normative assessment of this shift from international law to politics. As I will argue here, we are now at a sorry state of affairs which is unsatisfactory by any account.

11. And the final thing I will do is to propose a possible way forward and out of this sorry state of affairs.

12. So, this is an overview of the four things I propose to do today: while in the first two I will mainly describe/explain, in the last two I will set out my main contribution and ideas to the current debates.

13. But before I start to explain the rise and decline of international law I need to briefly define the main concepts that I will use to set out my theses.

14. First comes international law: I am using international law in its liberal conception; that is a system of rules-based global governance that seeks

to limit sovereignty and to keep states' power in check. To do that, international law provides that the conduct of states is subject to review by an independent system of justice, which can take the form of international courts and tribunals, including international investment tribunals (which is the focus of my Lecture).

15. Right opposite to this idea of international law is the idea of politics. The idea of politics I will use today is drawn from Schmitt's foundational work on *The Concept of the Political.* In summary, Carl Schmitt argued that the political concerns of the state are above the rule of law. For Schmitt, the ultimate source of power in any constitutional order is the power of the executive; not the judiciary. It is the sovereign executive that must have the ability to decide how to protect the essential interests of the people, especially in times of crisis (what Schmitt called, the state's power to decide *the exception*). And the decisions that the executive will take in those circumstances should not be subject to any form of judicial review. Let me say up front that Schmitt's association with the Nazi regime was of course heinous. But some of the questions that Schmitt has posed are difficult for anyone who is committed to defend the rule of law. If we are serious about international law and the rule of law, we are intellectually obliged to provide an answer to these questions.

16. Having set up my two main conceptual blocks, I now turn to the first point I want to argue today: the rise and decline of international law; and correspondingly the decline and rise of politics.

17. After the horrors of the WWII, international lawyers considered that more international law was the answer to make our world a better place. And they embarked in a relentless project of setting up more international legal institutions and drafting more international legal rules. The lofty aim here was that more international law would foster global peace, economic cooperation, and human rights. The number of international treaties and international institutions that were produced in the first forty years after WWII was more than the number of international treaties and institutions that had been produced since the inception of international law by Hugo Grotius. In this period, a wide range of international treaties were signed: from the Geneva Conventions on war crimes to the GATT agreement on tariffs and trade, the Bretton Woods Agreements on international economic law, and of course a number of treaties on human rights and the environment.

18. In the field of investment law and property rights that I am concerned with today, the expansion of international law took the form of a large network of international trade and investment treaties. These inter-

national trade and investment treaties had two immediate and two broader implications for the power of states.

19. The first immediate implication was that, by entering into those treaties, states were agreeing to protect property rights of foreign individuals and corporations. Specifically, states were agreeing to do three things: first, that they could not expropriate private property without compensation and due process; second, that they had to treat private property and investment in a fair and equitable manner; and third, that they could not discriminate against foreign owners of property rights. With the passage of time more states were entering into more international treaties agreeing to protect property rights of almost every national in the world. Treaty-making became a frantic project: from the first modern Investment Treaty in the late 50s between Germany and Pakistan and until today more than 3,000 investment treaties have been signed.

20. The second immediate implication was that, not only did these treaties provide that states had to protect foreign property rights; they also provided, for the first time, that individuals or corporations could bring a direct claim against a state every time a state breached its obligations. Never before had individuals direct and actionable rights against states in such a far-reaching manner. This is important because it gave rise to the idea of international investment tribunals. If individuals and corporations had rights against states, they also had to be able to adjudicate these rights somewhere. And this somewhere could not be the courts of the state itself; because, evidently, national courts were not trusted to fairly adjudicate a claim against their own state. We had to create a system of international justice that would sit outside the reach of states. And, in the minds of the liberal international lawyers of the last century, another international treaty was the answer to whatever the world's problem was. And *a presto*, they drafted the Washington Convention in 1965 that created a system of independent justice which took the form of ad hoc international tribunals that had the power to review states' actions and hold them accountable for any violation of property rights.

21. This all sounds common place today. But they were most certainly not 60 years ago; back then, states had very thin obligations to protect property rights in accordance with minimum only standards of protection under customary international law. Importantly, even when states were breaching their bare minimum obligations, individuals and corporations had no recourse against the states. If property rights of a foreign investor were violated, the investor had to rely on their home country to intervene on their behalf and engage in either diplo-

matic negotiations with, or use its force against, the state that violated property rights. Back then, international law was thin, patchy and state-centered. It was the liberal project of treaty-making and institutional building of last century that effected the dramatic shift in international law from state-centered power to individual rights and state accountability.

22. This brings me to the two profound implications that the liberal project of international law had for states and sovereignty:

23. First, it turned national to international. Before WWII, states were mainly constrained by their domestic constitutions only and their conduct was reviewed by domestic courts (constitutional or administrative). But, as the Weimar experience showed, the idea that the executive could be constrained by its own national law and national courts was fanciful. The executive could always trigger the emergency clause that we find in all constitutions to suspend national law and national courts. International lawyers had learned their lesson: national constraints were hopeless; we had to set up a form of international constitution and international judicial review so that states could no longer practice their escape art and remove their constitutional straight-jacket at will. Turning national to international was key to limit state power and keep the executive in check.

24. Second, the liberal project turned politics to law. From that time on, questions of policy were framed as legal questions that should be answered by reference not to political expedience but legal rules and legal tests. Thus (and I am drawing here on real cases who are well-known to this audience):

25. Whether Uruguay could pass anti-tobacco legislation that included placing graphic health warnings onto cigarette packaging was no longer a question of whether the state's regulation to implement anti-tobacco policy was expedient. It became a question of whether the state's regulation had violated trademark rights of the tobacco companies (*Philip Morris v Uruguay*).

26. Whether Ecuador could decide to terminate the exploration of fossil fuels in Amazon was no longer a question of whether the state's decision to protect its environment and control its natural recourses was an expedient policy. It became a question of whether the state's decision met the legal test of the fair and equitable standard under international treaties (*Occidental v Ecuador*).

27. Whether Argentina could take emergency economic measures, such as to abandon the peso's fixed exchange rate with US dollar, was no longer a question of whether these measures seeking to address the state's unprecedented financial crisis were expedient; it became a question of whether the state's measures breached the legal test for expropriation and fair and equitable standard (*CMS vs Argentina*).

28. Finally, whether Germany could decide to close down a nuclear plant was no longer a question of whether the state's decision to abolish its policy for *nuclear energy* was expedient; it became a question of whether closing down the nuclear plant met the legal test of rationality under the fair and equitable standard (*Vattenfall v Germany II*).

29. Importantly, the answer to these legal questions were to be given by three individuals acting as arbitrators; the state had no saying in that. In answering these questions, international tribunals sometimes found that the state's decisions were compliant with international law; and sometimes they found that they were not. But this is beside the point. What matters was that by turning national to international, and politics to law, the system of national sovereignty that was at play since the Westphalian truce of 1648 had now been displaced in favor of a system of international legal order.

30. At the time, there was a genuine sense of moral gratification among liberal international lawyers that the global constitution and independent justice that they had put together would govern international affairs in a principled and dignified, if not always peaceful, manner. At last, the Rule of Law was accomplished, it was thought.

31. In the next fifty years, law would thrive over politics. These were the years of law's empire (to steal from Dworkin). Schmitt's conception of the political was defeated both on the ground and in the field of ideas.

32. But there was a problem with the triumph of international law over politics. In fact, there were three problems. The first was a problem of scale. Because a system of global adjudication was now available, crafty international lawyers soon realized that they could frame almost any political question in legal terms and send them for adjudication to international tribunals. While initially the questions that were referred to international tribunals were relatively straight-forward questions of expropriation, increasingly more international law was laid at the feet of international arbitrators. There came a point where arbitrators were asked to decide on fundamental questions of public policy, including how states should respond to pandemics, or to financial and climate

change crises. In some cases, arbitrators were asked to decide whether the measures that some European states took to satisfy the conditions for their accession to the European Union were lawful or not. These are matters of profound economic and geopolitical importance. And the more matters were referred to arbitrators, the more matters arbitrators would take. By way of example of that scale: in 70s, there were only about 5 registered cases against states; by 2010 this number had risen to more than 400. Today there are more than 1,300 known cases challenging a wide number of executive decisions taken by states. There were fifty claims filed only against Argentina to challenge the measures Argentina took in response to its financial crisis in the 90s. More recently there have been more than 40 claims against Spain for decisions it took in respect of its renewable energy policies.

33. Many have accused arbitrators of accepting these cases mainly because of the handsome financial reward that comes with them. I cannot deny that monetary considerations may have been part of this. But I think it is too simplistic to argue that international arbitrators have been motivated mainly, or indeed exclusively, by profit. The majority of arbitrators, *we*, are international lawyers who are genuinely excited by complex questions of international law and, *we*, want to be part of the settlement of big matters dealing with the hard questions. In many respects, this is a healthy and lofty ambition.

34. The second problem was judicial activism on the part of arbitrators. Not only more political questions were referred to arbitrators dressed up as questions of international law; but also (and importantly), arbitrators started to push the boundaries of international investment law to dramatically develop the standards of protection for private property and, at the same time, increase the scope of liability for states. International arbitrators were allowed to do so because the system of investment adjudication was set up with wide discretion in the form of broadly formulated legal standards (such as that of fair and equitable treatment) but with none of the typical balances that keep decision-making discretion in check. There was no doctrine of judicial precedent and no appellate body to guide the jurisprudence of international tribunals. And while, in many cases states were winning, in many other cases states were losing for having taken decisions which, states thought, were ordinary executive decisions that were traditionally within their political discretion. States were genuinely perplexed that the traditionally minimum protection of property rights had evolved through a series of arbitration decisions to occupy increasingly more political space.

35. The third was a problem of attitude: I mentioned a few moments above that I do not consider that arbitrators accepted more cases and pushed the limits of international law merely for monetary reasons. Greed was not our cardinal sin; pride was. As we were dealing with more and bigger questions of international law, international lawyers and arbitrators gradually developed a sense of intellectual vanity that *we* were the global arbiters of the word's affairs. Not only we have the legal authority to deal with any question no matter how big it is; but we have the indisputable moral prerogative to decide when a state is right or wrong. Most international arbitrators, we, were born at the time when the shift from sovereignty to global governance had either started or was underway. In that sense most of us are liberal lawyers by outlook; not in the US sense of the word; but in the sense of classic liberalism which understands international law as a tool that can correct the injustices of the world. Many international arbitrators genuinely thought that it is our mandate to use international law to do so. Again, whatever the reasons behind it, this attitude of entitlement was perceived by many as *hubris*.

36. All these three problems together (scale of international law, judicial activism, and attitude) started to give rise to questions from the public, the media and of course from states:
- How can three individuals decide important questions of public policy? How can they award damages of hundreds of millions against a state?
- Who are these people? Where do they draw their power from?
- Who elected them to be the arbiters of the world?

37. Initially, the answer of international lawyers to these questions was that international arbitration tribunals were formed in accordance with rules of international treaties which states had signed. This may well be, but it is not a reassuring answer to the minds of the public and politicians. The fundamental issue here was not the process of appointment of arbitrators (although it was admittedly an important issue too); the fundamental question from the public was that we elected a government to deal with these questions; not three foreign legal technocrats.

38. And questions bring about pushbacks and reactions. In this case, we had two kinds of reactions:

39. The first was a project to *reform* international investment law and arbitration and their excesses. Some reforms are seeking to address the way that arbitrators are appointed and the way they decide. The idea here is to replace arbitrators with tenured judges to eliminate arbitral activism.

A tenured system of justice, together with an appellate body and a form of judicial precedent may lead to consistent and predictable jurisprudence.

40. There are many other proposed reforms that I do not need to repeat here. What I need to say however is that all these proposed reforms essentially aim to preserve the status quo. They are all underpinned by the idea that states' decisions of policy should, as a matter of principle, be subject to international law and a system of independent justice. The reforms aim to improve this system.

41. I personally consider that some of these ideas, although not all, are reasonable. But for better or worse, we have now come to a point that none of the proposed reforms can placate the criticism. They are considered to be too little, too late. A critical mass of states does not want to correct the excesses of the system; they want to change the *paradigm*; to reinstate the primacy of the political; to grant national sovereignty the power to decide the question of exception again.

42. It is against this background that, in the last 10 years, law has started to retreat. Politics are winning again both on the ground and in the field of ideas.

43. On the ground, in a series of decisions, the European Court of Justice has declared that investment arbitration is a system of independent justice that sits outside the EU, and -as such- it is not acceptable. The decisions of the ECJ in *Komstroy*, *Achmea* and *PL Holdings* are well-known decisions to this audience and I do not intend to discuss them in any detail. I would only say that the fundamental point that the ECJ makes in all these decisions is that the question of how an EU state can deal with questions of policy is a question that falls outside the purview of international law and tribunals.

44. In compliance with these decisions, a number of European state courts are now striking down arbitral awards on the grounds that questions of investment law referred to tribunals were matters of "*public policy*" and, as such, these questions were [and I quote] "non-arbitrable". Courts do not simply strike down awards because a tribunal made an error or violated due process. Courts say these matters are now matters of public policy and fall altogether outside the scope of international arbitration.

45. A year ago, the EU member states collectively decided to withdraw from Energy Charter Treaty (ECT). The main objection of the EU states was that this international treaty (the same treaty that the EU states had

originally negotiated and signed in the 90s) was now curtailing the political discretion of EU to set its own policies on the environment. And what was the solution of the EU the constraints of the ECT? To withdraw from this treaty with immediate effect and to reassert their political authority to take policy decisions unconstrained by international treaties and tribunals.

46. A number of bona fide international lawyers pointed out the obvious: a state cannot simply withdraw from a treaty with immediate effect. The ECT (as many international treaties do) have a clause also known as survival or sunset clause. As you know, a survival clause says that if a state decides to withdraw from the treaty, the treaty still binds the state for the next 20 years. The logic here is that you cannot just pull the plug suddenly. And it makes good sense: states must give sufficient notice to investors that have acquired rights and protection under the treaty to gradually adjust to the prospect that the treaty will no longer protect these rights in the future. And what was the solution of the EU commission and EU states to this fundamental problem of international law? To declare survival clauses and international law away: in June last year, the EU and 26 out of the 27 EU States, signed a formal Declaration to declare that the Treaty survival clause has no effect on them and, thus, with immediate effect, no further claims can be brought against EU states under the Treaty. The EU states declared that not only future claims against states are now impossible; all pending arbitrations against states are also retroactively terminated. If you ask any third-year law student, they will immediately tell you that this is plainly against the rules of international law and the Vienna Convention on the Law of Treaties. The answer would of course be correct; but entirely beside the point. The point being that matters are now firmly back into the hands of sovereignty.

47. Now the most alert of you must have noticed that I said a moment ago that the Declaration to withdraw from the ECT with immediate effect was taken by 26 out of 27 EU members. The odd one out here was Hungary which disagreed with the majority's decision on the ground (by now banal) that such a declaration would infringe international law. What was the EU Commission's reaction to Hungary's opposition? It initiated proceedings against Hungary and threatened it with a fine for undermining the EU position.

48. EU states are not just withdrawing from international law and independent justice. They also refuse to abide by awards that have been issued years ago. In the last ten years, Spain has lost more than 20 arbitrations for violation of investment treaties; the outstanding amount of

damages that Spain has to pay from these awards is more than 1.5 billion US $. Spain staunchly refuses to pay any of these awards on the grounds of (you guessed it) sovereign immunity, a defense which is effectively Schmitt's idea of exception dressed up as international law.

49. The EU Commission has directed Romania not to pay up, an award that was issued by a competent international tribunal before Romania joined the EU, on the ground that payment of the award would breach EU law on state aid. To point out the obvious here: an executive body orders a state to entirely disregard the decision of international independent justice taken on the basis of international law.

50. But it is not just EU states. The Global South is witnessing a number of withdrawals from international investment treaties. Their new policy is to agree that disagreements over investment disputes will be decided not on the basis of a system of independent justice; but on a firmly state-to-state basis.

51. I pause here to say that the expansion of politics over the law is obvious not only in the field of investment law and arbitration. It the broader direction of travel right now with sovereign governments retreating at will from a rules-based international order. Just look at the imposition of tariffs, the paralysis the Appellate Body of the WTO, the withdrawal from international organizations as well as international treaties on environmental law.

52. We are experiencing the full return of politics over international law. States are not just moving the goalposts here; they are moving the entire pitch from the Peace Palace in the Hague to 1600 Pennsylvania Avenue in Washington DC and number 200 of Rue de la Loi in Brussels where the EU Commission resides.

53. In the field of ideas, Francis Fukuyama's famous declaration about the ultimate victory of a liberal legal order is now, at best, perceived as naïve or, at worse, widely ridiculed. In the aftermath of the pandemic's experience and realization that sovereign decisions must be taken on a decisive basis, Schmitt's theories on sovereignty and the state of exception are quickly catching up with intellectual discourse and have significant impact on debates about constitutional theory and international law. Schmitt is now hailed by many commentators as "a household name in the academic world whose work is more popular than ever". And other commentators have built on Schmitt's ideas to mountain a full-scale critique against liberal law and international legal order.

54. The specter of Carl Schmitt and politics are now haunting international legal order again. How many decades can the dish of revenge stay cold before finally served?

55. Now I recognize that, for a keynote speech, I am offering a rather bleak account of current affairs; I sense that you all look forward to hearing the words "in conclusion" and to rushing to lunch where I hope that some wine will be served. But stick with me for a few minutes more – it will get better.

56. Having explained how the politics have now encroached on the law, I will now turn normative and seek to give an account of what ought, in my view, happen from here. Let me preface what I am going to say with this: the forthcoming observations are broad-brush propositions. I admit that they account for no comprehensive theory. But I do believe that they are getting at something potentially important that warrants further exploration in the years to come.

57. The starting point is that the state of unabashed international liberal order is unsustainable. And by unsustainable I don't just mean difficult to survive in the current political climate. I also, and mainly, mean normatively wrong. The idea that we can depoliticize disputes on broad policy questions by simply casting them in the legal discourse about rights is entirely fanciful. Political contestation always catches up with the law. And when political contestation eventually captures the law, the law collapses. This is exactly what happened in the field of investment law and arbitration; for some decades liberal lawyers thought that they had managed to insulate property rights from politics, but as I described above, politics have now caught up with the law and have effectively nullified it. So here is proposition number one: Litigation cannot substitute for political reasoning.

58. Equally, though, a world that is guided by a Schmittian conception of the political is a dangerous world that paves the way to totalitarianism. I do not need to remind this audience what followed Schmitt's theories in Germany in the late 30s. Even if we stripped down the inflated doctrine of the Rule of Law to its bare minimum, the idea that states must be accountable to a system of independent justice ought to be the lodestar for any form of political structure worth living in. So here is proposition number two: states' conduct *must* be assessed against certain standards; and if state's conduct is assessed and found wanting, states must be liable for that.

59. In other words, we must recognize the necessity of the political and the importance of the law and find a principled way to mediate between these two. To do that, we need to identify the space where the political and the law intersect. And that space, I say, is the concept of the public interest.

60. All disputes that give rise to these hard cases in investment law have the question of the public interest at their heart. And here is the big issue in my view: the current law of investment has no legal doctrine to properly account and protect the public interest. The closest functional equivalent is the doctrine of FET which we find in all investment treaties. But the abstract formulation of this standard as well as the evolution of arbitral jurisprudence make this standard problematic. It might sound paradoxical, but lawyers cannot deal with abstract conceptions of fairness and equity. Being all positivists, we best deal with narrow legal rules and specific legal tests. It is only natural therefore that when lawyers were asked to apply the abstract standard of fair and equitable treatment, we analytically dissected this standard to a set of rules and requirements. And as a result, we ended up with a deconstructed standard that simply draws the line of demarcation between law and politics too generously in favor of the former and leaves little room for political discretion.

61. Equally, the doctrines of necessity and police powers are so restrictively formulated that do not allow states to meaningfully exercise political discretion; for example, most tribunals have rejected Argentina's defense of necessity to justify the emergency economic measures it took to address the severe financial crisis it faced in the 90s.

62. On the other hand, retreating to the Minimum Standard of Treatment under customary international law would not be an appropriate alternative either: this standard which is effectively the lowest common denominator of state conduct is too thin to offer meaningful protection to investors.

63. I would therefore submit that we need to develop a new theory of the public interest. It should be a modern and coherent theory that properly accounts for, and protects, the public interest. And use this new theory to develop appropriate standards to assess state conduct in investment arbitration. Importantly, I would submit that this theory cannot be the work of lawyers only. Important interdisciplinary work in international law in the last thirty years has taught us that law alone does not have the intellectual tools to construct a theory to transcend the fields of law and politics.

64. Law cannot pull itself up by its bootstraps here.

65. The concept of the public interest is interdisciplinary by nature. To understand this concept, we need contributions from different disciplines, including law, political science, economics, sociology, public policy and environmental studies. While the law can address the narrow question of legality of state conduct, political science can address the question of what kind of collective good should elected governments pursue. Equally, economics can assist us to understand whether certain policies aim to maximize social welfare whereas the discipline of public policy can address questions about the effectiveness and fairness of governmental actions.

66. A proper assessment of the public interest involves a wide range of considerations, that cannot be addressed only by law. Investment law is running out of road here. But this does not mean that we should replace law with politics. Rather, we should collaborate *with* politics, as well as other disciplines. In other words, we need to roll up our sleeves to work across disciplines and develop a principled and coherent theory of the public interest for the purposes of assessing questions of international investment law.

67. And once we come up with such an interdisciplinary standard for the protection of the public interest, we need to also agree on a forum that should adjudicate this standard. And here, for better or worse, *international arbitration is* not perceived as an appropriate form of justice to adjudicate this question. This is not because international arbitration is currently under severe criticism. I have argued elsewhere that a large part of this criticism is unfair. Arbitration largely works at the majority of investment disputes; it is the few hard cases that have brought about arbitration's demise.

68. The main reason that international arbitration is not appropriate to adjudicate hard cases that involve the public interest is exactly because, as I explained, the concept of the public interest transcends disciplines; we thus need broader resources and expertise that equally transcend disciplines to properly assess the public interest. In other words, we need a system of justice that breaks down the barriers of law. There is no reason that the task of administering justice should be a matter of law only. This is especially the case in disputes that involve complex assessments, broader considerations and potentially far-reaching political, social and economic implications.

69. I pause here to say that a great colleague of ours and a prominent arbitrator has argued that we need to insert politics back into the process. I certainly agree with the premise; but I consider that we should approach this differently. The way it has been suggested that we should insert politics back into the process is by making the process more inquisitorial to allow tribunals to call interested social groups to give evidence in the arbitration. In that way, it is argued, arbitrators can decide with a better understanding of the political context. However, this approach effectively doubles down on the law. While it allows social groups to provide *evidence* in the arbitration process, the final decision will still rest with arbitrators who will have to decide on the basis of the same legal standards and tests. It is not the process that is the issue here; in fact, counsel and witnesses in arbitrations do give the broader stories to tribunals about how the public interest has been affected by investors (and vice versa about how states' conduct has wrecked businesses and sometimes personal lives). But arbitrators rarely take those stories into account when we decide; not because we are a group of insensitive, impervious individuals. But because the legal tests, in their current formulation, do not allow for this sort of wider considerations to be taken into account. In fact, lawyers and arbitrators are not trained or equipped to make assessments outside the law. Even if the process was more inquisitorial, the outcome would be the same every time that lawyers are asked to decide broad policy matters on the basis of narrow legal tests.

70. I thus I submit that instead of legal panels of adjudication in the form of international arbitration, we need panels or standing committees that incorporate expertise and insights from other disciplines and have wide fact-finding powers and resources to support their decision-making task. In all cases, we should place this system of justice outside the reach of the states. Complete independence from states would be important to ensure neutrality.

71. This would not be the first time that such an interdisciplinary approach to justice existed. By way of example only, several competition authorities and tribunals, such as the European Commission department for enforcement of competition rules or the US Federal Trade Commission, the UK Competition Appeal Tribunal include economists in their decision-making panels.

72. The Unified Patent Court that decides disputes on European patents is comprised of distinct pools of 'legally qualified' and 'technically qualified' judges sitting in panels of three or five recognizing thus that legal expertise does not suffice to determine complex questions of patent law.

73. In all these examples, an interdisciplinary approach to adjudication and delivery of justice has both improved accuracy of the outcome and enhanced the legitimacy of the process.

74. In conclusion, if we are serious about addressing the inadequacies of the current system of justice for international investment disputes, we should be willing to let go of the legal grip, develop a new interdisciplinary standard of assessing public interest disputes, and include non-legal expertise in the *decision making* process.

Happy 50th Anniversary; long live VIAC.

*Stavros Brekoulakis*

# Mission Possible: Harnessing Power, Embracing Responsibility, and Seizing Opportunity in International Arbitration

*Roland Ziadé**)

## I. Introduction

International arbitration is not just a tool for resolving complex disputes – it is a dynamic system built and shaped by the energy and insights of all its participants. Whether you are a client seeking a just and efficient resolution of a dispute, a lawyer advocating for your client's interest, an arbitrator seeking to decide wisely and ensure due process, an expert imparting specialist knowledge, or a counsel at an arbitral institution administering the procedure, everyone has a key role to play.

The theme of this article – *Heroes of Arbitration: Great Power, Great Responsibility, Great Opportunity* – aptly captures our unique shared endeavour. The term "hero" is sometimes over-used and of course is not to be confused with the fictional "superhero" figures who populate movies and other parts of popular culture these days. As actors in the domain of international arbitration, we are nevertheless collectively entrusted with significant power – power to resolve commercial disagreements or investor-state disputes, to uphold and apply the rule of law across borders, and to safeguard parties' interests in conflictual circumstances and, in particular, in uncertain and volatile times. With this power comes obvious responsibility: the need to maintain and even increase credibility, fairness, efficiency and trust in arbitration as a means of dispute resolution.

And today, faced with evolving industries, rapidly advancing technology, and a changing global landscape, we face challenges, but also great new opportunities to achieve more together. The intent of this article is to reflect on the evolution of international arbitration over the past decade and to consider the

---

*) Roland Ziadé is the Global Co-Head of International Arbitration at Linklaters and a member of the Paris, New York, and Beirut Bars. This article is the written version of the keynote speech delivered by the author at Vilnius Arbitration Day 2025 on 12 September 2025. The author would like to thank Andrew Plump and Lédéa Sawadogo-Lewis for their assistance with the preparation of this publication.

several challenges currently confronting arbitration, before concluding with a forward-looking perspective on some of the opportunities ahead of us.

It is hoped that readers will come away both inspired and better equipped to advance excellence in arbitration: in other words, ready to play their role as, and amongst, arbitration heroes.

## II. Achievements and Lessons from the Past Decade

### A. Ongoing Popularity and Growth

Let us begin with a look at international arbitration's continued popularity and growth over the past decade. It seems quite unquestionable overall.

Sixteen more states adhered to the New York Convention in the last decade, bringing the total to 172 states,[1]) a notable increase from the 156 contracting states that had ratified it as of 2015,[2]) evidence that a key element of arbitration's power – its global enforceability – remains robust.

In the same period, 32 more jurisdictions have adopted legislation based on the UNCITRAL Model Law, bringing that total to more than 90 states.[3])

Caseload statistics from the leading international arbitration institutions confirm that arbitration has remained a popular option over the last decade. For example, the ICC registered 841 new cases in 2024;[4]) it had registered 801 new arbitration cases in 2015.[5]) Similarly, the LCIA registered 362 new cases in 2024;[6]) it had registered 332 new cases (an "all time high" at the time) in 2015.[7]) Although these numbers indicate that their caseloads have not grown exponentially, they also demonstrate that parties have continued to resort to

[1]) Albert Jan van den Berg, *Contracting States*, New York Convention (7 November 2025, 10:45 AM), https://www.newyorkconvention.org/contracting-states/contracting-states.

[2]) United Nations, *United Nations Commission on International Trade Law Yearbook* XLVI:2015 (2018).

[3]) United Nations, *United Nations Commission on International Trade Law*, Status: UNCITRAL Model Law on International Commercial Arbitration (1985), with amendments as adopted in 2006 (7 November 2025, 10:50 AM), https://uncitral.un.org/en/texts/arbitration/modellaw/commercial_arbitration/status.

[4]) International Chamber of Commerce Dispute Resolution Services, *ICC Dispute Resolution 2024 Statistics* (7 November 2025, 10:50 AM), https://iccwbo.org/wp-content/uploads/sites/3/2025/06/2024-Statistics_ICC_Dispute-Resolution.pdf.

[5]) International Chamber of Commerce, *ICC Dispute Resolution Bulletin* (2016, Issue 1).

[6]) London Court of International Arbitration, *2024 Annual Casework Report* (7 November 2025, 10:53 AM), https://www.lcia.org//LCIA/reports.aspx.

[7]) London Court of International Arbitration, *Registrar's Report 2015* (7 November 2025, 10:53 AM), https://www.lcia.org//LCIA/reports.aspx.

international arbitration on a steady basis, even as the market has become more competitive and diverse.

The most explosive growth in caseloads and amounts in dispute, of course, has occurred in parts of the world other than traditional arbitration hubs in Europe and North America. In Asia, for example, SIAC and HKIAC caseload values each doubled in the past decade. The latest HKIAC statistics report a record US$ 13.6 billion in dispute across all arbitrations in 2024,[8]) compared with US$ 6.2 billion a decade ago,[9]) for example, and SIAC reports US$ 11.86 billion of total sums in dispute in 2024,[10]) compared to US$ 4.36 billion in 2015.[11])

Arbitration centers in Africa and in the Middle East are also experiencing significant growth, with the Cairo Regional Centre for International Commercial Arbitration (CRCICA), for example, reporting 76 new cases filed in 2024,[12]) for a total of US$ 238,902,561 of total sums in dispute, as opposed to US$ 10,296,930 in 2020.[13])

Matter value has also increased significantly. At the ICC in 2024, for example, the average amount in dispute in new cases soared to US$ 130 million, and the aggregated value of the entire caseload was an unprecedented US$ 354 billion.[14]) This is an almost US$ 70 billion increase in aggregated matter value over the last decade from USD$ 286 billion in 2015,[15]) reflecting the ever-expanding role of arbitration worldwide in the resolution of cross-border disputes.

---

[8]) Hong Kong International Arbitration Center, *2024 Statistics* (7 November 2025, 10:51 AM), https://www.hkiac.org/news/hkiac-releases-statistics-2024.

[9]) Hong Kong International Arbitration Center, *Annual Report: 2015 Reflections* (7 November 2025, 10:53 AM), https://www.hkiac.org/sites/default/files/annual_report/2015_Annual_Report_Final.pdf.

[10]) Singapore International Arbitration Centre, Annual Report 2024 (7 November 2025, 10:55 AM), https://siac.org.sg/wp-content/uploads/2024/08/SIAC_AR2024_FA-spread-Online.pdf.

[11]) Singapore International Arbitration Centre, Annual Report 2015 (7 November 2025, 10:58 AM), https://siac.org.sg/wp-content/uploads/2022/06/SIAC_Annual_Report_2015.pdf; https://www.globalarbitrationnews.com/2016/08/25/global-arbitration-cases-still-rise-arbitral-institutions-caseload-statistics-2015/#1066216-v1-GAN_Statistics_in_2015.docx.

[12]) Cairo Regional Centre for International Commercial Arbitration, 2024 Annual Caseload Report (7 November 2025, 11:00 AM), https://crcica.org/arbitration/annual-caseload-reports/.

[13]) Cairo Regional Centre for International Commercial Arbitration, 2020 Annual Caseload Report (7 November 2025, 11:01 AM), https://crcica.org/arbitration/annual-caseload-reports/.

[14]) International Chamber of Commerce Dispute Resolution Services, *ICC Dispute Resolution 2024 Statistics* (7 November 2025, 11:04 AM), https://iccwbo.org/wp-content/uploads/sites/3/2025/06/2024-Statistics_ICC_Dispute-Resolution.pdf.

[15]) International Chamber of Commerce, *ICC Dispute Resolution Bulletin* (2016, Issue 1).

The ever-increasing expansion of arbitration is of course not just reflected in statistics and amounts in dispute. We have seen a sustained and ever-growing interest in the field of arbitration among law students and young lawyers. The diversity, quality, and number of participants in the Vis Moot Competition and the expansion of and creation of new masters programs in international arbitration in key arbitration centers around the world are also representative of this undeniable trend.

## B. Adaptability and Flexibility

A few words about the adaptability and flexibility of arbitration: Heroism is often marked by how one confronts changes – sometimes by choice, often by necessity.

Over the past ten years, international arbitration has displayed resilience and ingenuity in the face of global uncertainty. Whether adapting proceedings amid global shutdowns linked to the COVID-19 pandemic, or maintaining the continuity of arbitration proceedings even when courts have been closed or on limited sessions, for these and other reasons, arbitration proved capable of transforming crisis into opportunity.

Similarly, arbitral institutions have been responding to user demand for procedural flexibility and efficiency. A number of leading institutional rules now provide for emergency arbitration, allowing a party to seek urgent interim relief before an arbitrator as opposed to a court, a concept virtually unknown 20 years ago. It has now become a rather standard feature of arbitration. The ICC has for instance reported receiving more than 250 applications for emergency arbitrations between 2012 and 2024,[16] while the SIAC reports 173 emergency arbitrations since 2010.[17]

Some institutional rules, such as those of the ICC, now provide for expedited arbitration of smaller value claims, with streamlined procedures and tighter overall deadlines.

The increasing availability of summary disposition procedures, enabling the determination of clearly unmeritorious claims at an early stage in the proceedings, also shows arbitration adapting to the evolving needs of users.

---

[16]) International Chamber of Commerce Dispute Resolution Services, *ICC Dispute Resolution 2024 Statistics* (7 November 2025, 11:10 AM), https://iccwbo.org/wp-content/uploads/sites/3/2025/06/2024-Statistics_ICC_Dispute-Resolution.pdf.

[17]) Singapore International Arbitration Centre, Annual Report 2024 (7 November 2025, 11:15 AM), https://siac.org.sg/wp-content/uploads/2024/08/SIAC_AR2024_FA-spread-Online.pdf.

## C. Technology

Technology is another area where arbitration shows its adaptability. Given party-driven procedural flexibility and the nimbleness of the actors in international arbitration, we in the arbitration community are frequently early adopters of new technology.

The adoption of and use of online and hybrid arbitral hearings was a sea change forced for a time by the COVID-19 pandemic but otherwise embraced by the arbitral community for their time and cost savings where appropriate. Arbitration counsel and experts have also been early and enthusiastic adopters of improved visual display technology; tools used notably in construction or industrial disputes and in others involving technical and expert testimony.

A number of major arbitral institutions now also offer electronic filing platforms, and while electronic legal research may have been less relevant to international commercial arbitration in many places than to national court litigation, advances in artificial intelligence and the development of more robust search engines, with more expansive data bases, have seen greater use of such technology in commercial arbitration.

Further discussion of artificial intelligence will follow, particularly regarding the significant challenges that accompany the opportunities it presents. There is little doubt, however, that arbitration practitioners will find ways to take advantage of these developments.

## D. Diversity and Inclusion

A look at the past decade would not be complete without mentioning diversity and inclusion. The international arbitration community has recognized for some time the importance of diversity to the legitimacy of arbitration.

The Equal Representation in Arbitration Pledge, which was launched in 2015, now boasts over 5,000 signatories,[18]) including numerous major law firms, reflecting the broader arbitration community's desire to continue diversifying its arbitrator pool. Encouragingly, nearly half of the arbitrators appointed by the LCIA last year were women, with an increase in the diversity of nationalities amongst arbitrator appointees.[19]) Also in 2024, women com-

[18]) Equal Representation in Arbitration, *Signatories* (7 November 2025, 11:30 AM), https://www.arbitrationpledge.com/signatories

[19]) London Court of International Arbitration, *2024 Annual Casework Report* (7 November 2025, 11:33 AM), https://www.lcia.org//LCIA/reports.aspx.

prised 43 % of sole arbitrator appointments made by the ICC.[20]) This is a significant evolution compared to ten years ago.[21])

Arbitration's expanding global footprint beyond "traditional" seats such as Paris, London, Geneva and Stockholm clustered in Europe, has seen the emergence of seats in, among others, Singapore and Hong Kong in Asia, the UAE in the Middle East, and Brazil and Mexico in the Americas, on some recent lists of most selected seats.[22])

These collective efforts show that the quest for diversity and representation in arbitration is not the work of a single champion, but of many everyday heroes pushing for positive change.

## E. Evolving Legal Frameworks

Arbitration heroes not only require individual resolve, but also a supportive legal environment. Legislative reforms continue to support arbitration's growth and evolution. In the UK, for example, the Arbitration Act 2025 that has very recently entered into force has (i) introduced clearer rules on the law governing an arbitration agreement and the power of arbitrators to summarily dismiss claims or defenses, (ii) has expressly recognized emergency arbitration under applicable institutional rules, and (iii) has enhanced the powers of UK courts as to third parties to an arbitration.

At the date of writing, Singapore, China, and India are all currently reviewing their arbitration frameworks, whilst France is considering further refinements to its arbitration laws, including possibly consolidating all of its arbitration laws and regulations into a single Arbitration Code.

Several emerging arbitration hubs are also adjusting their arbitration laws to align with best practice.

---

[20]) International Chamber of Commerce Dispute Resolution Services, *ICC Dispute Resolution 2024 Statistics* (7 November 2025, 11:34 AM), https://iccwbo.org/wp-content/uploads/sites/3/2025/06/2024-Statistics_ICC_Dispute-Resolution.pdf.

[21]) International Chamber of Commerce, *ICC Dispute Resolution Bulletin* (2016, Issue 1).

[22]) International Chamber of Commerce Dispute Resolution Services, *ICC Dispute Resolution 2024 Statistics* (7 November 2025, 11:35 AM), https://iccwbo.org/wp-content/uploads/sites/3/2025/06/2024-Statistics_ICC_Dispute-Resolution.pdf; Hong Kong International Arbitration Center, *2024 Statistics* (7 November 2025, 11:41 AM), https://www.hkiac.org/news/hkiac-releases-statistics-2024; Dubai International Arbitration Center, *Annual Report 2023* (7 November 2025, 11:51 AM), https://www.diac.com/wp-content/uploads/2024/11/DIAC-Annual-Report-2023.pdf.

## F. Arbitration as a Merchant of Peace

Beyond the advances and milestones covered so far, and particularly relevant in today's global landscape, international arbitration has continued to serve a more profound societal role: that of a merchant of peace.

From the Jay Treaty of 1794, by which Great Britain and the US undertook to resolve certain unsettled issues of the Anglo-American Peace of 1783 which terminated the American War of Independence, to more recently in disputes involving claims linked to the Russia-Ukraine war, arbitration has provided a neutral platform for dispute resolution. In doing so, arbitration arguably not only upholds the rule of law, but also actively contributes to international stability and economic development.

The Iran–US Claims Tribunal is a prime example of how international arbitration can serve as a "merchant of peace". Established in 1981 following the Iran hostage crisis, the Tribunal provided a neutral and effective forum for resolving over 4,700 claims between Iranian and US nationals, as well as government-to-government disputes.[23])

Its success in fairly and peacefully settling complex and politically fraught claims has made it, for many, a model for using arbitration to maintain stability and attempt to foster reconciliation between states, or at least between their nationals, even amidst profound diplomatic tensions.

International arbitration has also been used effectively for years for border disputes between States and for resource utilization disputes, including for example water use or undersea exploration rights. An example of a maritime boundary dispute was the Ghana/Côte d'Ivoire (Ivory Coast) case before the International Tribunal for the Law of the Sea (ITLOS), concerning their maritime boundary in the Atlantic Ocean.[24]) Both nations eventually accepted the Tribunal's 2017 decision while committing to peaceful cooperation.

Recent years have also witnessed arbitration's involvement in disputes concerning renewables and those arising from resource nationalism – disputes which can have genuine repercussions for communities and economies. For example, further to the numerous claims brought by investors against Spain under the Energy Charter Treaty (ECT) following the reduction of feed-in tariffs for renewable energy projects starting in 2012, arbitration provided a structured process for resolving these claims and helped channel tensions through legal mechanisms rather than political or economic retaliation.

---

[23]) Iran – United States Claims Tribunal, *Background* (7 November 2025, 11:51 AM), https://iusct.com/.

[24]) *Dispute concerning delimitation of the maritime boundary between Ghana and Côte d'Ivoire in the Atlantic Ocean (Ghana/Côte d'Ivoire), Judgment,* Reports of judgments, advisory opinions and orders, List of cases No. 23 (International Tribunal for the Law of the Sea, 2017).

Therefore, even as we mark its growth, it is worth reaffirming that arbitration's enduring value also lies in its ongoing role as an enabler of dialogue, cooperation, and even peace across borders.

## III. Responsibility Amidst Complexity and Challenges

As every hero knows, power also comes with responsibility. Indeed, the legitimacy and sustainability of international arbitration rests on, among other things, how we respond to the challenges it is now facing.

### A. Procedural Complexity and Costs

Arbitration faces mounting criticism for excessive complexity and cost – the latter sometimes rivalling (or even exceeding) that of national court litigation, depending on the applicable jurisdiction. The latest ICC and LCIA statistics show that cases concluded by way of final awards over recent periods of years have averaged around two years in duration.[25]) As for ICSID, a study found that for the period June 2017 to May 2020, the mean length of proceedings was five and a half years,[26]) which seems too long by any standard.

Of course, a significant proportion of filed arbitration cases are settled or otherwise resolved prior to a final award, but these average durations for obtaining a final award are nevertheless concerning. Although the most recent version of the ICSID rules[27]) has tried to address this, notably by providing rather strict time limits on the issuance of an award, no doubt progress remains to be made.

---

[25]) The latest ICC statistics report that the average arbitration duration was 26 months, and the median duration 22 months: International Chamber of Commerce Dispute Resolution Services, *ICC Dispute Resolution 2024 Statistics* (7 November 2025, 12:00 PM), https://iccwbo.org/wp-content/uploads/sites/3/2025/06/2024-Statistics_ICC_Dispute-Resolution.pdf. The median LCIA arbitration, covering all cases which reached a final award between 1 January 2017 and 12 May 2024, lasted a total of 20 months: https://www.lcia.org/News/lcia-releases-updated-costs-and-duration-analysis-2024.aspx.

[26]) Matthew Hodgson, Yarik Kryvoi, Daniel Hrcka, *2021 Empirical Study: Costs, Damages and Duration in Investor-State Arbitration*, British Institute of International and Comparative Law and Allen & Overy (7 November 2025, 12:05 PM), https://www.biicl.org/documents/136_isds-costs-damages-duration_june_2021.pdf.

[27]) International Centre for Settlement of Investment Disputes, *ICSID Arbitration Rules* (2022), *see, in particular,* Rule 58.

## B. Sanctions

The proliferation of sanctions in recent years has also made arbitration more complicated, creating significant challenges around party representation, payment of arbitral institutions and arbitrators, and enforcement of awards, particularly when individuals or entities involved are subject to international restrictions. Countermeasures, retaliations, and anti-suit injunctions of some national courts are obviously also an issue. Navigating these sanctions regimes and their ramifications requires additional due diligence and specialized legal knowledge and expertise, may delay proceedings, and can expose parties, counsel, arbitrators and arbitral institutions to substantial compliance risks.

## C. 'Over Lawyering' and Judicialization of Proceedings

So-called "over lawyering" has also become a growing concern.

The seemingly ever-increasing length and complexity of written arbitration memorials and submissions – amounting to hundreds or sometimes even thousands of pages of materials – is pointed to by many as a clear indicator of a 'judicialization' of arbitration proceedings. 22 % of respondents of the latest QMUL arbitration survey found that 'counsel over-lawyering', *e.g.*, over-detailed or long submissions, had the most negative impact on the efficiency of arbitration proceedings.[28)]

Parties often choose arbitration in order to benefit from the time and resources that prominent international arbitrators can devote to a case as compared to the time and resources available to many national court judges. However, the burden such voluminous submissions can place on arbitrators and on the schedule of a case is increasingly threatening the efficiency and efficacy of an arbitration.

In addition, the number and variety of interim applications – such as requests for interim measures, early determinations, security for costs, or even concerning document production disputes – has risen significantly over the years. These can contribute to modern day arbitration being challenged to live up to arbitration's promise of a faster, more flexible and less formal dispute resolution process. These also risk undermining some of the advantages that draw users to arbitration in the first place.

Adapting, tailoring and customizing processes to accommodate parties' interests to comprehensively present their cases, their desire for flexibility but

---

[28)] Queen Mary University of London and White & Case, *2025 International Arbitration Survey, The path forward: Realities and opportunities in arbitration* (7 November 2025, 12 :05 PM), https://www.qmul.ac.uk/arbitration/media/arbitration/docs/White-Case-QMUL-2025-International-Arbitration-Survey-report.pdf.

also foreseeability, as well as efficiency, and their paramount interest in just, well-reasoned and enforceable awards, is a delicate balancing act.

## D. Guerilla Tactics

Another related demanding test for practitioners is the rise of tactics aimed at disrupting the arbitration process, so-called "guerrilla tactics", the unexpected and at times creative strategies to influence, disrupt or even derail proceedings.

These can vary widely: from late document submissions and surprise new arguments at the hearing, to repeated challenges of arbitrators, to attempts at intimidating witnesses or arbitrators, to deliberate and untimely efforts to stall or delay the process.

The increasing use of these tactics and other factors have led some to call for more clear and binding guidance for international arbitration counsel and arbitrators on permissible and ethical behavior. In this sense, arbitration may stand at a crossroads between more self-regulation and preserving its defining hallmarks of flexibility, but also between self-regulation and otherwise being regulated (and possibly over regulated) from the outside. The two draft laws of the Ministry of Justice of the State of Qatar currently available for public consultation regarding the regulation of arbitration centers and the granting of licenses, and the licensing of arbitrators themselves are typical and extreme examples.[29]) What to do and how to do it in this area is undoubtedly one of the challenges faced by today's arbitration heroes.

## E. Competition from International Commercial Courts

As another challenge, the international commercial courts in certain legal systems are trying to position themselves as alternatives to international arbitration. Such specialized courts have been established as chambers of the Paris Commercial Court and Paris Court of Appeal, and are also present in, for example, Qatar, Bahrain, Singapore, and the Netherlands. These courts generally offer certain features traditionally associated with arbitration, such as the option to conduct proceedings in English and in some instances to more readily accommodate the use of foreign law.

[29]) Qatar Ministry of Justice, Draft Decree of the Minister of Justice No. () of 2025 on the conditions and rules for registration of arbitrators in the registry, their deletion and the determination of fees (7 November 2025, 12 :15 PM), ريزو رارق عورشم موسرلا ديدحتو مهبطشو لجسلاب نيمكحملا ديق دعاوقو طورشب 2025 ةنس ( ) مقر لدعلا | Sharek.

It remains to be seen whether such courts, which are after all mostly staffed by court judges and which operate pursuant to an established set of court rules and procedures, will become truly viable and effective competitors (and alternative) to international arbitration.

However, the mere fact that they have been established and promoted by these jurisdictions is an indication of some perception that arbitration may not be fully fulfilling its promises and may at least to some extent be vulnerable to such competition.

## F. Investment Arbitration Backlash

Investment arbitration backlash is another issue facing arbitration. The proponents of ISDS emphasize that it has afforded cross-border investors legal recourse and promoted regulatory stability.

However, its critics contend that permitting private investors to challenge state policy reforms – even when such reforms are aimed at legitimate public interests like public health, environment, fiscal responsibility or climate adaptation – could restrict democratic policymaking and undermine state sovereignty. This backlash has had a direct impact: according to a recent UNCTAD report, the total number of international investment agreement terminations reached almost 600 in 2023, with about 70 per cent of these terminations occurring over the last decade.[30)]

The perception, fair or not, that investor-state arbitration prioritizes foreign investor interests above those of domestic communities or broader societal goals, particularly when governments are required further to adverse awards to use public funds to pay compensation, as well as concerns over appointments of arbitrators and consistency of decisions, have also intensified criticisms as to the fairness and legitimacy of the system. This has sparked calls for reform and, in some cases, led countries to reconsider or withdraw from bilateral or multilateral treaties like the Energy Charter Treaty.

Balancing these competing considerations, while responding to the growing backlash, will be a continuing task for the arbitration community over the coming months and years.

---

[30)] United Nations Conference on Trade and Development, *International investment agreements trends: the increasing dichotomy between new and old treaties*, IIA Issues Note, October 2024.

## G. Threats to Intra-EU Commercial Arbitration and the Recent ECJ Decision

Concerns have also been expressed in recent years about whether the anti-ISDS backlash might end up impacting (and in any way contaminating) commercial arbitration.

Commercial arbitration, like investor-state arbitration, and arguably even more so than the latter, ultimately relies upon national court enforcement of awards in situations where the condemned party fails to voluntarily comply with an award. The latest Queen Mary/White & Case International Arbitration Survey reported, however, that only around 40 per cent of practitioners surveyed found that award debtors complied voluntarily with arbitral awards when the award debtors were non-ICSID, private parties.[31]) In this sense, were the notion of such State judicial support for private arbitral decision-making to be more generally eroded, consistent enforcement of commercial arbitration awards could possibly also suffer.

More immediately and concretely, a case involving decisions of the Court of Arbitration for Sport which resulted in a judgment by the European Court of Justice in August 2025 has garnered attention.

The ECJ ruled in the Seraing case[32]) that if mandatory sports arbitration is to be implemented within the EU, it is necessary to ensure that it is compatible with the judicial architecture of the EU and that it is consistent with EU public policy.

The decision emphasized that arbitral awards – particularly those arising from mechanisms unilaterally imposed, such as in the sports sector – should always be subject to effective judicial review by national courts to ensure compliance with EU public policy and fundamental rights, including the ability to seek interim relief and full review of EU law issues.

There had been fears that the ECJ might go farther, especially after the ECJ's Judge Advocate had issued an opinion in January 2025 questioning whether the New York Convention should apply at all to "mandatory arbitration" such as CAS arbitration and suggesting that the public policy exception to enforcement under the New York Convention might in any event serve as a

[31]) Queen Mary University of London and White & Case, *2025 International Arbitration Survey, The path forward: Realities and opportunities in arbitration* (7 November 2025, 12 :05 PM), https://www.qmul.ac.uk/arbitration/media/arbitration/docs/White-Case-QMUL-2025-International-Arbitration-Survey-report.pdf.

[32]) *Judgment of the Court (Grand Chamber) of 1 August 2025 (request for a preliminary ruling from the Cour de cassation – Belgium) – Royal Football Club Seraing SA v Fédération internationale de football association (FIFA), Union des associations européennes de football (UEFA), Union royale belge des sociétés de football association ASBL (URBSFA),* Case C-600/23 (European Court of Justice, 1 August 2025).

"gateway" to full review of CAS arbitration awards in respect of applicable EU law.[33])

Commentary following issuance of the ECJ's decision has revealed differing interpretations, including as to any potential implications for arbitration more generally. While there is much to be said for the prevailing view that the decision does not extend to "consensual" commercial arbitration, it is also true that it cannot be ruled out that the ECJ's expansive view of the public policy exception under the New York Convention as articulated in Seraing could potentially have a domino effect and significant implications for commercial arbitration.

## H. Technology, Data Protection, and Cybersecurity

As to technology, data protection, and cybersecurity, these are also issues requiring careful and clear-eyed handling. While the arbitration community's embrace of new technology has generally had positive effects, there is no denying that it comes with risks.

The already known and widely discussed risks have included exposure to cyberattacks, data breaches, confidentiality concerns and compliance issues. Model cybersecurity protocols have been developed, and arbitrators, counsel, and parties have cooperated in adopting them and making them work. But the arbitration community will no doubt need to maintain vigilance in this area, just as do all businesses and individuals, for that matter, in today's electronically connected world.

The newer development, of course, is the exponential growth and disruptive effect in just the past couple of years of readily accessible Artificial Intelligence tools.

We have not yet heard many horror stories in arbitration like those in some common law court litigation where lawyers have submitted legal briefs with some case citations that were simple fabrications or "hallucinations" of Chat GPT or other AI tools. However, we have already seen at least one instance reported where a party's counsel made a submission in an international arbitration with case citations that did not exist.[34])

Another important question is whether and, if so, under what circumstances and in what manner arbitrators might take advantage of AI in the performance of their duties. For example, were AI-powered tools to be used by arbitrators to analyze evidence or applicable contractual or legal principles or

---

[33]) *Opinion of Advocate General Capeta*, in the case of *Royal Football Club Seraing SA v Fédération internationale de football association (FIFA), Union des associations européennes de football (UEFA), Union royale belge des sociétés de football association ASBL (URBSFA)*, Case C-600/23 (European Court of Justice, 16 January 2025).

[34]) Tom Jones, *Niger challenges French academic in uranium case* (Global Arbitration Review, 9 September 2025).

for the drafting of their award, there could be a host of issues around that, not the least being the possible erosion or even loss of the fundamentally human dimension of arbitral analysis and judgment.[35]) This could raise issues as to, among others, transparency, consent, fairness, confidentiality, and even validity of the award.[36]) At least one arbitral award has been reported to have been challenged on grounds that the arbitrator was believed to have relied extensively on artificial intelligence to draft it.[37])

Additionally, the disparate access to and availability of technological resources for the users of international arbitration might in the future result in arguments about lack of equality of arms, if parties with more limited access to such technology tools consider that they are being at a significant disadvantage during proceedings.

The arbitral community is quite alive to these concerns, and some protocols and guidelines have already been issued, with more on the way. However, this is such a fast-moving area that our community will need to remain very alert in order to stay ahead of the curve and to maintain a proper and healthy balance between taking advantage of technology that may streamline (or even revolutionize) aspects of the work and increase efficiency while at the same time protecting fundamental due process and all of the core interests at stake in an arbitration.

Another concern and challenge is, naturally, the impact of artificial intelligence on the training and professional development of junior lawyers. As AI systems and tools not only further automate document review, where they have indeed been assisting for some years now, but potentially play ever larger roles in research and drafting of written submissions and oral presentations, and even in preparation of witness and expert examinations and cross-examinations, there will likely be fewer opportunities for early-career lawyers to gain some of the essential first-hand experience to develop core analytical and advocacy skills.

## I. New emerging world order

Finally, in discussing challenges, we cannot ignore that arbitration's popularity and ability to serve as an effective dispute resolution mechanism was notably strengthened during the decades in which the world was moving to a more globalized and inter-connected economy.

---

[35]) A. O. Onyefulu, *Artificial Intelligence in International Arbitration: A Step Too Far?*, in Stavros Brekoulakis (ed), Arbitration: The International Journal of Arbitration, Mediation and Dispute Management, pp. 56–77, February 2024.

[36]) *Id.*

[37]) Tom Jones, *Arbitrator accused of relying on AI* (Global Arbitration Review, 15 May 2025).

Now, however, the tide of economic nationalism is shifting the ground. We have not yet seen all the impacts of governments putting domestic priorities and regulatory powers front and center, and of States increasingly wielding higher tariffs and resource nationalism, no less seen how they may affect international arbitration.

In the short term, one can imagine such developments resulting in more claims and disputes that could potentially be brought to arbitration. However, the nature of these trends is such that the international cooperation and trust that underpins the international conventions and treaties on which the global ecosystem of international arbitration is so dependent might itself be questioned or even potentially jeopardized.

While it is to be hoped that this does not occur, the international arbitration community will likely wish to remain vigilant in safeguarding this fundamental principle.

## IV. Looking Forward: Perspectives and Opportunities

As just discussed, the journey of international arbitration is not without its current challenges. These will test the arbitration community's resolve and adaptability. However, it is often through overcoming adversity that individuals achieve some of their greatest opportunities. A few examples of these are set out briefly below.

### A. Harnessing Technology Responsibly

It is going to take careful thought, good judgment, and widespread co-ordination and cooperation for international arbitration to define best practices for the manner in which the newest technology, especially Artificial Intelligence, is used.

At the same time, used properly and wisely under those conditions, Artificial Intelligence and related digital tools have the potential to help achieve greater efficiency in the work of counsel and arbitrators, which may help control the costs and duration of arbitration.

### B. Expanding and Adapting to New Sectors

The use of arbitration is likely to continue to expand, with the potential for growth in new sectors. Recent examples include disputes concerning renewable energy, digital assets, outer space, and the business of sports.

Even though the current administration in the U.S. has announced different priorities, the global push elsewhere towards renewable energy involves often complex projects with new technologies. For example, large-scale infrastructure upgrades in less developed regions and emerging markets likewise involve large and complex projects, often in challenging environments, and frequently involve project owners, contractors and subcontractors from different countries and regions. Arbitration has long served as a preferred means of settling construction disputes, and there is still much potential for growth here.

In the technology sector, with the rapid expansion of digital infrastructure, cloud computing, and cross-border data flows, for example, commercial disagreements are increasingly likely to arise over data protection, platform governance, technology licensing, and intellectual property rights, to name a few. International arbitration, with its adaptability and ability to encompass technical expertise, is well-suited to provide efficient dispute resolution that addresses the fast-changing realities of the digital economy.

We also know that financial institutions have traditionally been cautious about using arbitration. However, recent statistics from arbitral institutions show that financial institutions seem to be increasingly opting for arbitration to resolve some of their disputes.[38]) These might notably arise from complex financial products, syndicated loans, and cross-border investments.

Further, as part of the economic nationalism mentioned earlier among the challenges for arbitration, resource nationalism also offers the opportunity for international arbitration to serve as an efficient means of addressing the disputes which will inevitably arise from states taking action to increase control over their natural resources. As an example, over the period February to July 2025, ICSID had registered not less than six disputes filed against African States involving resource nationalism.

As regards sports, arbitration before the Court of Arbitration for Sport has long played a vital role for resolution of disputes in respect of the Olympic Games and other major international sports competitions and events. The business side of sports has perhaps garnered less attention, but the international reach and commercial value of major sporting events, media rights deals, and sponsorship agreements have been reaching unprecedented levels. This also can open greater opportunities for commercial arbitration.

---

[38]) *ICC Dispute Resolution 2024 Statistics* (7 November 2025, 14:30 PM), https://iccwbo.org/wp-content/uploads/sites/3/2025/06/2024-Statistics_ICC_Dispute-Resolution.pdf.

### C. Resilience and Responsiveness as Opportunity

As touched upon at the beginning of this article, the COVID-19 pandemic served as both a stress test and, in many ways, a "great leveller" for the field of dispute resolution. Among its most significant effects was the clear demonstration of arbitration's resilience and adaptability in the face of external crisis. These and other swift adaptations showcase arbitration's unique capacity to maintain momentum even when other fora had difficulty doing so, a clear advantage and creator of opportunity in today's fast-changing world.

## V. Conclusion

Returning to the theme of international arbitration's power, responsibility, and opportunity: the last decade has shown that when the arbitration community acts with imagination and integrity, it can extend both its reach and its legitimacy. The challenges ahead are therefore not roadblocks, but invitations to – why not – further heroic action.

So, what will it take to become an arbitration hero of the future? With complexity also comes a demand for new skills: digital literacy, project management, cultural sensitivity, and crisis management. Arbitration heroes of the future must therefore not only be legal experts, but also strategists, technologists, managers, and leaders of inclusive teams. The future holds many opportunities for arbitration practitioners to innovate, adapt, and respond to tomorrow's challenges. This is, indeed, a Mission Possible.

As we shape the future of arbitration together, may we use our collective power wisely, shoulder our responsibilities with pride, and seize every new opportunity to further build and shape a fair, efficient, and global international arbitration system for the generations to come.

# Recent Reforms and Emerging Trends in China's Arbitration Law and Practice

*Wei Sun*

2025 marks a pivotal year for arbitration reform in China. In this year, China enacted the newly revised Arbitration Law, representing the third official amendment since its initial promulgation in 1994. The year also serves as a crucial window for the recovery and further development of the national arbitration sector following the waning impact of COVID-19 and coincides with an era of rapid expansion in artificial intelligence.

Under the combined forces of globalization, internationalization, and the broader societal trend toward digital and intelligent transformation, Chinese arbitration has shown increasing alignment with international standards and the demands of the intelligent age. Nevertheless, it continues to face a range of challenges in both theory and practice as reforms deepen.

This article begins with an overview of the 2025 revision of China's Arbitration Law and, together with an examination of evolving institutional rules, explores the current state and future trajectory of arbitration development in China.

## I. Changes in China's Arbitration Legal System and Arbitration Rules

### A. Key Revisions of the Arbitration Law (2025)

In the 1990s, alongside China's economic reform and opening up, the *Arbitration Law of the People's Republic of China* was promulgated in 1994 and came into effect on September 1, 1995. The Law was subsequently amended twice, in 2009 and 2017, and has now been in force for over three decades.

Over this thirty-year period, China's arbitration system has expanded dramatically. By the end of August 2025, a total of 285 arbitration commissions had been established across the country, collectively handling more than five million cases involving disputes valued at over nine trillion RMB. Parties to these arbitrations have come from over one hundred countries and regions, and the subject matters have spanned diverse fields including finance, e-commerce, construction, maritime affairs, and intellectual property. Arbitration has thus played a vital role in facilitating China's economic growth and international engagement.

Yet, despite this progress, the existing legal framework has revealed shortcomings in terms of openness, innovation, and the regulation of arbitral institutions and personnel. Against this backdrop, China undertook a third and comprehensive revision of the *Arbitration Law* in 2025. The latest amendments center on three main dimensions:

- Enhancing the regime for foreign-related arbitration;
- Aligning domestic arbitration practices with internationally accepted standards; and
- Improving the institutional and professional framework governing arbitral institutions and arbitrators.

## 1. Enhancement of the Foreign-Related Arbitration System

The 2025 revision of the *Arbitration Law* significantly expands the scope of "foreign-related arbitration"[1]) in China. It introduces a new, open-ended clause – "and other foreign-related disputes" – to the previously closed list of categories limited to economic, trade, transport, and maritime matters. This revision allows a wider range of cross-border disputes to fall within the ambit of "foreign-related arbitration".

The Law also introduces explicit provisions on the seat of arbitration and, for the first time, formally recognizes the option of *ad hoc* arbitration for certain types of disputes.[2]) At the same time, the Law expressly encourages

[1]) China adopts a dual-track arbitration system, under which *domestic arbitration* and *foreign-related arbitration* are subject to different procedural regimes. *Foreign-related arbitration* applies to disputes involving a foreign element and reflects China's effort to align its practice with international standards.

[2]) Article 82 of the *Arbitration Law 2025* stipulates:

"Where a foreign-related maritime dispute, or a foreign-related dispute between enterprises established and registered within a State Council–approved pilot free trade zone or the Hainan Free Trade Port, arises and the parties have reached a written agreement to arbitrate, the parties may choose to submit the dispute to an arbitral commission for arbitration.

Alternatively, they may agree to conduct arbitration within the territory of the People's Republic of China, with the seat of arbitration in China, and have the arbitral tribunal composed of individuals meeting the qualifications prescribed by this Law, to conduct the proceedings in accordance with the arbitration rules agreed upon by the parties.

The arbitral tribunal shall, within three working days after its constitution, file with the Arbitration Association the names of the parties, the agreed place of arbitration, the composition of the arbitral tribunal, and the arbitration rules to be applied."

arbitral institutions to strengthen international cooperation and exchange, and to further liberalize the arbitration sector to foreign participation.

China's open and accommodating stance toward international arbitration has deep institutional roots. As early as April 8, 2015, the State Council issued the *Plan for Further Deepening the Reform and Opening-Up of the China (Shanghai) Pilot Free Trade Zone*, which called for supporting "internationally renowned commercial dispute resolution institutions" in establishing a presence in China, enhancing the internationalization of commercial arbitration, and building an Asia-Pacific hub for dispute resolution.

Most recently, on April 22, 2025, the Shanghai Bureau of Justice amended the *Administrative Measures for Overseas Arbitration Institutions Establishing a Business Presence in Shanghai*, setting out clear application procedures and imposing a duty on the Bureau to process such applications promptly. Prominent international arbitration institutions – including HKIAC, ICC, and SIAC – have since established representative offices in Shanghai, Beijing, and other major cities, underscoring China's continued integration into the global arbitration landscape.

## 2. Integration with Internationally Accepted Practices

The newly revised *Arbitration Law 2025* also advances innovation in arbitral practice by aligning more closely with internationally accepted standards.

To safeguard the integrity of arbitration, the Law introduces explicit provisions against sham or collusive arbitration. Where an arbitral tribunal determines that a party has fabricated essential facts to initiate arbitration, or that the parties have maliciously colluded to harm state interests, public interests, or the lawful rights of others, the tribunal is required to dismiss the claim.

The Law further refines the appointment procedures for arbitrators. It clarifies that the chairperson of an arbitral institution must appoint the sole or presiding arbitrator strictly in accordance with the procedures set forth in the institution's arbitration rules.

To facilitate greater accessibility, lower costs, and better adaptation to technological advancement, the Law introduces a formal regime for online arbitration, expressly providing that online arbitral proceedings have the same legal validity as those conducted in person.

## 3. Institutional Reform and Independence of Arbitral Bodies in China

Since the promulgation of the 1994 *Arbitration Law*, both academia and practice have debated the institutional nature of China's arbitral bodies. Under the *Notice on the Plan for Re-establishing Arbitration Institutions* issued in 1995, the government initially guided the formation of arbitration commissions by reference to regulations applicable to public institutions. Consequently, most arbitral institutions nationwide were classified as public institutions, with their assets incorporated into the unified administrative system for state-owned assets.

The 2025 *Arbitration Law* resolves this ambiguity by expressly defining arbitral institutions as public welfare non-profit legal persons, subject to the governance regime for non-profit entities under the *Civil Code*. This transition, however, raises complex legal and practical issues: How should previously state-owned assets be transferred, converted, or supervised? Can retained property be donated or transferred without compensation to the new legal person in accordance with statutory procedures? Should the use, disposal, and proceeds of such property be subject to special restrictions? And which authorities – judicial administrative bodies, finance departments, audit offices, or registration authorities – should exercise supervisory power, or should a joint oversight mechanism be established? These questions highlight a legal and regulatory vacuum that remains to be filled.

Moreover, while the principle of institutional independence is essential for fostering a healthy, market-oriented arbitration ecosystem, the legacy of administrative involvement continues to cast a shadow. In practice, certain judicial administrative departments still exert considerable influence over institutional reforms. In some instances, government officials concurrently hold senior positions within arbitral institutions, or civil servants are encouraged to transfer into such roles. In certain regions, major institutional decisions – such as senior appointments, project approvals, and the allocation of significant funds – continue to require administrative authorization.

## B. Recent Revision Trends in Chinese Arbitral Institutions Rules

In recent years, to adapt to new trends in the development of international commercial arbitration and the growing demands of parties for efficient, flexible, and transparent dispute resolution mechanisms, China's major arbitral institutions have successively refined or systematically revised their arbitration rules. The common trends reflected in these revisions are summarized below.

### 1. Improving Arbitration Efficiency and Procedural Flexibility

In complex commercial transactions, it is not uncommon for parties, based on various commercial considerations, to split parts of the same transaction or a series of transactions into different contracts. Considering this practical situation and the needs of parties, Chinese arbitral institutions have introduced or improved the "arbitration application under multiple contracts" and the consolidation of arbitration systems. For example, China International Economic and Trade Arbitration Commission (CIETAC) Arbitration Rules 2024 improved the systems for arbitration applications under multiple contracts and consolidation of arbitration, moderately relaxing their conditions for application.

Meanwhile, driven by the demand for efficient dispute resolution, some arbitral institutions have actively optimized expediated procedures in revisions of the rules. Raising the applicable monetary threshold has been a key measure, aiming to allow more cases to proceed quickly via simplified procedures, thereby enhancing overall arbitration efficiency. For example, Shenzhen Court of International Arbitration (SCIA) raised the applicable monetary threshold for its fast-track procedure from 3 million RMB to 10 million RMB in its arbitration rules 2024. The China Maritime Arbitration Commission Arbitration Rules (2021) also adjusted the upper limit from 2 million RMB to 5 million RMB. These revisions reflect the institutions' proactive response to the trends of an accelerating market pace and differentiating case complexity, making arbitration procedures better aligned with commercial practice.

## 2. Aligning with International Rules and Strengthening Institutional Innovation

The internationalization of Chinese arbitration rules is manifested in the introduction and localized adaptation of several internationally accepted mechanisms. Representative mechanisms include:

- Emergency Arbitrator Mechanism: Since 2015, arbitration institutions including CIETAC, Beijing Arbitration Commission (BAC), Shanghai Arbitration Commission (SHAC), SCIA, have successively incorporated the emergency arbitrator mechanism into their rules.
- Early Dismissal Mechanism: Drawing on the experience of international institutions such as ICSID and ICC, both the CIETAC 2025 and SHAC 2025 rules provide that when an arbitration claim manifestly lacks basis or falls outside the scope of jurisdiction, the arbitral tribunal may dismiss the case at an early stage. This mechanism helps filter out abusive proceedings and enhances overall arbitration efficiency.
- Interim Award Mechanism: Interim awards allow the arbitral tribunal to rule on key disputed issues before the final award, thereby accelerating the case's progress. Both the CIETAC 2024 and SHAC 2022 editions have reinstated or established this mechanism, providing institutional support for the phased handling of complex disputes.

### 3. Strengthening Procedural Fairness and Transparency

Recent rule revisions also reflect the arbitral institutions' higher standards for good faith and fairness. In arbitration practice, there exists bad faith conduct by parties, such as maliciously changing counsel, appointing new counsel who has grounds for challenge in relation to an arbitrator or intentionally delaying the proceedings, all of which seriously affect the arbitral process and its fairness. Institutions like Shanghai International Arbitration Centre (SHIAC) and SHAC have introduced targeted restrictions on such conduct in their rules.

Article 34(7) of the SHAC Rules 2025 stipulates:

*"A party who, after becoming aware of the constitution of the arbitral tribunal, appoints authorised representatives whose appointment gives rise to grounds for the challenge of any arbitrator, shall be deemed to have waived its right to challenge the arbitrator on those grounds; the right of the other party to challenge the arbitrator shall not, however, be affected. The arbitral tribunal shall also have the power to refuse the authorised representatives to participate in the arbitral proceedings."*

### 4. Optimizing Fee Structures and Arbitrator Incentive Mechanisms

To reduce parties' dispute resolution costs and enhance the transparency of arbitration costs, several institutions have optimized their mechanisms for arbitration costs and arbitrators' remuneration.

BAC, CIETAC, and SCIA have in recent years all set a cap on arbitration fees and implemented refund and discount mechanisms in specific circumstances. Furthermore, some institutions have introduced an hourly billing mechanism for arbitrators' remuneration, allowing parties and arbitrators to negotiate and determine the rates, with a cap set to prevent excessive expenses. This flexible fee structure aligns with international practice and enhances the competitiveness of Chinese arbitral institutions in the global arbitration market.

## II. Efficiency Improvements and Technological Application Innovations in Chinese Arbitration Practice

Currently, Chinese arbitration practice is achieving systematic improvements in efficiency and modernization through procedural innovations and technological applications. At the procedural level, mechanisms such as lists of issues and preliminary hearings have effectively enhanced hearing efficiency.

At the technological level, online arbitration platforms and artificial intelligence tools are driving the digital transformation of the arbitration process. Concurrently, courts are strengthening coordination with arbitral proceedings through mechanisms like online preservation measures, forming a pattern of collaborative support.

## A. Procedural Efficiency

In recent years, arbitration practice in China has adopted several effective measures to enhance procedural efficiency and incorporate innovative procedural techniques.

One such measure is the use of issue lists. In international arbitration, parties often become aware of the arbitral tribunal's principal concerns only at the hearing stage, which may result in extensive written submissions and multiple rounds of exchange. By contrast, in China – particularly in complex cases such as construction disputes – the arbitral tribunal may issue a list of key issues midway through the proceedings. This approach enables the parties to focus their subsequent submissions and streamlines the overall presentation of arguments.

Another notable practice is the preliminary hearing. While international arbitration typically involves a single hearing after all written submissions have been exchanged, it is not uncommon in complex Chinese cases to hold two or even three hearings. During the first hearing, the tribunal listens to the parties' core arguments and raises clarifying questions. The parties then prepare supplementary submissions and evidence for the second hearing, with the goal of resolving the central issues efficiently in the subsequent session.

This procedural approach reflects China's practical context: given that the quality of legal representation across the country remains uneven, the international model of "submissions first, hearing later" may not always be efficient. The preliminary hearing mechanism allows tribunals to provide early procedural guidance, thereby improving efficiency, reducing costs, and ensuring more focused adjudication.

## B. Technology Application

The integration of electronic platforms and AI into arbitration practice has become a powerful driver of procedural efficiency and cost reduction.

### 1. Online Arbitration

As noted earlier, the *2025 Arbitration Law* explicitly affirms that online arbitration carries the same legal validity as traditional in-person proceedings. Even prior to this legislative clarification, several Chinese arbitral institutions had already taken steps to institutionalize online arbitration and electronic service mechanisms.

BAC took an early lead in 2022 by codifying the use of electronic service and online hearings, thereby laying a solid institutional foundation for digital arbitration procedures. Article 71 of the BAC Arbitration Rules (2022) provides that arbitral documents, notices, and other materials may be served "in person, by mail, courier, facsimile, email, or other electronic means", and that the BAC or arbitral tribunal "has the right to decide the appropriate mode of service in light of the circumstances of the case". Furthermore, Article 25 of the same Rules expressly recognizes online hearings as a valid mode of proceeding and grants the arbitral tribunal discretion to determine the hearing format based on the specific case context.

Similarly, the 2022 amendment of the SCIA Arbitration Rules, building upon its 2019 edition, advanced the default use of technology in arbitration. It replaced the prior "party-choice" approach with a presumptive rule authorizing the arbitral tribunal or arbitration court – unless the parties agree otherwise – to adopt electronic service and remote hearings by default (Articles 6, 23, and 67 of the SCIA Rules). The subsequent 2025 revision further reinforced this framework, reducing the potential for tactical delays arising from objections to online hearings and mitigating the risk of enforcement challenges based on alleged procedural defects in electronic or remote proceedings.

## 2. Virtual Platform

With the global advance of digitalization, leading international arbitral institutions have increasingly encouraged parties to submit documents electronically through secure online case management systems.

Following this global trend, a number of Chinese arbitral institutions have invested heavily in the development of intelligent arbitration platforms, encouraging parties, counsel, and arbitrators to manage cases digitally. These platforms typically include functions such as document uploading, online storage, categorized file management, and real-time access, enabling all participants to retrieve and exchange materials efficiently. Moreover, they support end-to-end online proceedings – from case filing and evidence submission to hearings, deliberations, and the rendering of awards – thereby creating a unified digital workflow for arbitration.

A notable example is the SHIAC, which, concurrent with the release of its 2024 amended arbitration rules, launched the SHIAC Digital Intelligence Platform (E-Platform). Article 20(1) of the SHIAC Arbitration Rules (2024) provides that, unless otherwise agreed by the parties or decided by the tribunal, "arbitration documents and evidence submitted under these Rules may, if the parties so prefer, be submitted in electronic form through the E-Platform". This provision establishes electronic submission as the default method, allowing parties to directly upload documents and evidence online. In addition, arbitrators use these secure systems for deliberation and internal communication.

Looking ahead, the nationwide integration and interconnection of such digital platforms may require unified technical standards and institutional coordination, potentially under the guidance of the Supreme People's Court or a national arbitration association

### 3. AI-Assisted Drafting

With the rapid advancement of AI-generated content technologies, the routine components of an arbitral award – such as the confirmation of the parties' identities and the procedural history – can now be automatically produced. This automation allows arbitrators to dedicate more time and attention to the substantive reasoning and analytical portions of the award.

For example, SHIAC has equipped its Digital Intelligence Platform with AI functions capable of automatically generating the procedural sections of arbitral awards. This feature significantly reduces the drafting workload of arbitrators and enhances the overall efficiency and timeliness of award rendering.

## C. Coordination between Arbitral Tribunals and Courts

The relationship between tribunals and courts plays a crucial role in shaping the conduct and evolution of arbitration in China. In recent years, China has adopted a distinctly collaborative and supportive approach toward this relationship.

The *2025 Arbitration Law* strengthens the finality of arbitral awards by shortening the time limit for filing an application to set aside an award – from six months to three months after receipt of the award. In addition, the new Law explicitly requires People's Courts to "handle arbitration-related preservation matters in a timely manner".

A notable illustration of this enhanced coordination is the introduction of online preservation mechanisms. For instance, SHIAC has established a digital interface with court systems that enables the online submission, inquiry, payment, and transfer of property preservation applications through the arbitration preservation filing portal of China's national litigation service network. This digital innovation streamlines preservation procedures, simplifies judicial interaction, and improves procedural efficiency for parties and institutions alike.

## III. Conclusion

China's arbitration system is entering a new stage of structural maturity and international integration. The 2025 revision of the *Arbitration Law* marks not only a legislative milestone but also a redefinition of the institutional foundations of Chinese arbitration – clarifying the legal nature of arbitral bodies, strengthening their independence, and modernizing procedural norms. These reforms signify China's determination to build a rule-based, transparent, and internationally credible arbitration framework.

At the same time, practice is evolving in parallel with law. The refinement of institutional rules, the adoption of online arbitration, and the deepening coordination between arbitral tribunals and courts collectively demonstrate China's pragmatic approach to reform – combining technological innovation with procedural sophistication.

Looking ahead, the continued success of China's arbitration modernization will depend on how effectively legislative intent is implemented in practice and how consistently arbitral institutions uphold fairness, efficiency, and transparency. As China's arbitration community deepens its engagement with global norms and embraces technological advancement, it is well-positioned to emerge as a pivotal jurisdiction in shaping the future architecture of international dispute resolution.

# Rediscovering the Simplicity of Arbitration

*Cavinder Bull SC**)

## I. Introduction

It is a pleasure and privilege to deliver the keynote address at the 2025 Vienna Arbitration Days.

Sincere thanks are due to the organising committee for the invitation to address such a distinguished and diverse audience. It is an honour to contribute to the discussions and to engage with the impressive lineup of speakers and panels that have been organised for the event. Warmest congratulations are also extended to VIAC on occasion of its 50th anniversary.

It is appropriate when such milestones are celebrated that we take the opportunity for reflection. We gather as colleagues in the arbitration community, and we believe in the efficacy of the arbitral process, a force for good in resolving disputes. However, we also know that there is much room for improvement.

Arbitration was once heralded as the simpler and more efficient alternative to traditional litigation. As Alan Redfern once said, arbitration was originally conceived of as *"a system of justice, born of merchants, which allies law and trade usage"*.[1]) So, arbitration was meant to be an effective and business-like method of resolving commercial disputes. It was supposed to be a simple, straightforward means of resolving a dispute before a commercially-minded decision maker, who may or may not be a lawyer. In contrast to litigation, arbitration promised a streamlined process that would be less formalistic, quicker, and less expensive.

This almost romantic paradigm of a simpler, more commercial, quicker and cheaper way of resolving disputes, contrasts sadly with what arbitration often looks like today. The arbitral process of today has become marred by unnecessary complexity – with proceedings becoming longer, more expensive, and increasingly bogged down by needless procedural hurdles. Many of us would agree that counsel and arbitrators spend far too much time involved in arguments over how to get the dispute resolved, rather than actually resolving

---

[*]) Sincere thanks are due to the efforts of Tan Yuan Kheng and Charlotte Tang from Drew & Napier in the preparation of this paper.

[1]) *Alan Redfern*, Stemming the Tide of Judicialisation in International Arbitration (2008) 2 World Arbitration & Mediation Review 21 (**"Stemming the Tide"**) at 22.

the dispute. This has led to growing criticism and discontent over the many inefficiencies and often eye-wateringly high costs in getting a dispute arbitrated.

One of the major problems facing arbitration today is the judicialisation of arbitration. This has occurred because over the years, arbitrators and counsel who are accustomed to litigation before the national courts have brought to arbitration the processes and practices of litigation with which they are familiar and comfortable,[2]) so much so that Thomas Stipanowich called arbitration "the new litigation".[3]) As more and more litigation practices get ported over to arbitration, counsel and arbitrators come to expect cookie-cutter models of arbitration resembling court processes, without putting any real thought into how the procedure may be tailored to the needs of the dispute in question. The end result is that instead of being a true alternative to litigation, arbitration today has essentially become litigation by a different name, with all the complexity and rigidity that litigation entails. The severity of the judicialisation of arbitration has not gone unnoticed. Speaking at the 2018 ICCA Congress in Sydney, former Chief Justice James Allsop observed that *"arbitration has developed the same process-driven costs that accompany poorly managed litigation"*, which he described as a *"cancer"* in the body of both.[4])

The original idea was very simple. Arbitrators would be appointed, and they would then have the flexibility to design a bespoke procedure to deal with the dispute at hand. If document production was not needed, they would dispense with that. If cross-examination of a class of witnesses was unnecessary considering the documentary record, then there was no need for those witnesses to appear in person. Unfortunately, we've lost sight of that as more and more focus has been given to designing an arbitral process that can take care of any and every type of case. It is difficult to say whether this is a symptom of the over-judicialisation of arbitration or whether it is its cause. It is probably a little of both.

It is true that the disputes being heard in arbitration have, over the decades, increased in complexity. Commerce has become more sophisticated and advancements in technology affect almost every industry. Lawyers and arbitrators have to grapple with many technical issues that surpass our experience and expertise. However, the growing complexity of disputes does not mean that arbitral procedure should become more complex. Just because the substance of what arbitrators have to decide has become more complex, it does not mean that the way in which arbitrators conduct proceedings should become

[2]) *Alan Redfern,* Stemming the Tide at 25, 28.

[3]) Thomas Stipanowich, Arbitration: The 'New Litigation' (2010) University of Illinois Law Review 1 at 8–9.

[4]) *Former Chief Justice James Allsop,* ICCA Congress 2018, Sydney, opening keynote address, Commercial and Investor-State Arbitration: The importance of recognising their differences (April 16, 2018), accessed on October 31, 2025 at <https://www.fedcourt.gov.au/digital-law-library/judges-speeches/speeches-former-judges/chief-justice-allsop/allsop-cj-20180416> (**"Allsop"**) at 38–39.

more complicated. Far too often, complex disputes are handled in unnecessarily complex ways, only deepening the inefficiencies that already plague the arbitral process. We seem to have forgotten how powerful the simplicity of arbitration can be.

The foundation for international arbitration's success is the commercial world's confidence in it as a powerful tool to resolve disputes and therefore to keep the wheels of international commerce turning. That confidence was originally won by a system that was simpler, more commercial, faster and cheaper than litigation in court. However, if we continue to forget the simplicity of arbitration, if we continue to inject unnecessary complexity into arbitral processes and if we continue to engage in over-judicialisation, then arbitration will provide no efficiencies over litigation, and we will lose our way. As former Chief Justice Allsop previously forewarned, *"if arbitration cannot exist as an efficient and cost-effective means of dispute resolution, then it will simply not find favour with commercial parties"*.[5])

In the 2021 edition of the White & Case Queen Mary University of London survey, 59 % of the participants stated that their preferred approach for dispute resolution was not arbitration alone, but rather a combination of arbitration and other alternatives such as mediation.[6]) In other words, arbitration was not enough for more than half of the participants in that survey. Only 31 % chose arbitration as a standalone method.[7]) This was down from 56 % who chose arbitration as a standalone method in the 2015 survey.[8]) When interviewed, participants in 2021 stated that they were increasingly resorting to other methods of dispute resolution *"in the hope that a swifter and more cost-efficient resolution could be found before resorting to arbitration"*.[9]) This is tragic. From a beginning where arbitration was portrayed as a simpler, less formal and more efficient way to resolve commercial disputes, it is now being characterised as the slower and less efficient mode of dispute resolution from which one seeks change.

This keynote contribution includes the thesis that we can help make arbitration become more efficient, even in today's complex world, if we rediscover the simplicity of arbitration. We need to go back to our roots and re-learn why arbitration was introduced; why it was, in the beginning, seen as

---

[5]) *Former Chief Justice James Allsop*, Allsop at 39.

[6]) Queen Mary University of London and White & Case, 2021 International Arbitration Survey: Adapting Arbitration to a Changing World, accessed on October 31, 2025 at <https://www.qmul.ac.uk/arbitration/research/2021-international-arbitration-survey/> (**"2021 QMUL Survey"**) at 5.

[7]) 2021 QMUL Survey at 5.

[8]) Queen Mary University of London and White & Case, 2015 International Arbitration Survey: Improvements and Innovations in International Arbitration, accessed on October 31, 2025 at <https://www.qmul.ac.uk/arbitration/research/2015/> at 5.

[9]) 2021 QMUL Survey at 6.

such a streamlined process which could quickly resolve commercial disputes in a straightforward manner. If we root out unnecessary complexities and rediscover the power behind the simplicity of arbitration, we will see efficiency flourish again in our international arbitration community.

## II. Rediscovering the Simplicity of Arbitration

What does rediscovering the simplicity of arbitration mean, exactly? This will be explained in practical terms, with reference to the life cycle of an arbitration.

### A. Memorials

Let's begin with memorials.

Memorials used to be concise documents which explained the party's position. They were of modest length so that they could communicate well, bearing in mind that arbitrators were not necessarily lawyers but included "commercial people". This is no longer the case. As unfortunate as it is, it has become commonplace to see memorials taking the form of much less disciplined documents, written in rampantly free-flowing prose, spanning hundreds of pages, with piles and piles of footnotes at the bottom of each page. Memorials, mammoth in scale, and churned out by an army of associates, have now become par for the course in almost all arbitrations that we see today. They are position papers, the walls of the city which the opponent is challenged to assault. Much less thought is given to communicating simply and clearly, than to ensuring that every angle is covered off regardless of materiality.

In a fascinating article, Professor Jörg Risse described the burgeoning length of memorials in the following manner.[10]) Consider an arbitration in which 10,000 pages of memorials are filed. Assuming the arbitrator takes six minutes on average to read a page, and therefore reads ten pages an hour, reading the 10,000 pages of memorials would require 1,000 working hours – equivalent to over *six months* of concentrated reading for a full-time lawyer. And that is just to read the memorials *once* through, without taking into account the time he or she would need to refresh their memory of what had been read weeks or months earlier.

Professor Risse recognises that 10,000 pages of memorials is an extreme illustration, though he gives the example of some complex windfarm project

---

[10]) *Jörg Risse*, An Inconvenient Truth: The Complexity Problem and Limits to Justice (2019) Arbitration International 291 (**"An Inconvenient Truth"**) at 292–294, cited in Chief Justice Sundaresh Menon, The Complexification of Disputes in the Digital Age, 9 November 2021.

arbitrations.[11]) Having said that, Professor Risse was not even including the witness statements, documentary exhibits and legal authorities that accompany memorials and which we all behave as if the arbitrators must read in full. It is not uncommon for documentary exhibits to run into a thousand pages. Legal authorities will also often contribute another 1000 pages. Add those to the page count for witness statements and the text of the memorials, it is no stretch of the imagination for each of four main memorials to reach 2,500 pages in total. In one case, involving a disputed amount of less than US$10 million, the claimant filed about 4,500 pages of papers in an uncontested arbitration. Professor Risse's example of ten thousand pages of memorials is no exaggeration.

In any case, the point Professor Risse makes rises above the illustration he uses. Are we being realistic in expecting arbitrators to read prolix written materials, to remember what is read and to be able to apply all the materials in their decision-making?

This is the sad reality of unnecessary complexity and attendant inefficiency that bedevils the arbitral process today. Many of us here would admit to having previously used Artificial Intelligence ("**AI**"), or even a junior associate, to highlight key points and summarise memorials received from parties or from opposing counsel. The need for such summaries confirms the existence of the problem it addresses, namely, that memorials today are far too long for any human to reasonably read and digest. Much of this may be attributed to what Jan Paulsson has described as "*endless over-lawyering*",[12]) where counsel prepare memorials with the intention of leaving all options open as opposed to narrowing the case to specific points in issue.

What can we do to rediscover the simplicity of arbitration, particularly in terms of memorials? One simple way would be to keep memorials within reasonable limits through the imposition of page limits. This is not a new idea. It is noteworthy that default page limits play a prominent role in the Ad Hoc Rules implemented by Derains & Gharavi for their standing ad-hoc arbitration tribunal launched earlier this year. In recognition of the fact that the arbitral process has become besieged with inefficiencies and unnecessary complexities, the Ad Hoc Rules have imposed default page limits not only for pleadings, but also for witness statements and expert reports.[13])

---

[11]) *Jörg Risse*, An Inconvenient Truth at 292, 294.

[12]) *Jack Ballantyne*, Paulsson warns of 'over-lawyering', *Global Arbitration Review*, 3 June 2024, accessed on October 31, 2025 at <https://globalarbitrationreview.com/article/paulsson-warns-of-over-lawyering> (**"Paulsson"**).

[13]) Article 22 of the Derains & Gharavi Ad Hoc Rules of Arbitration in force as of January 31, 2025 states that "*Unless otherwise agreed by the parties or directed by the Arbitral Tribunal, the Statement of Claim and Statement of Defense (and counterclaim(s) if applicable) shall not exceed 100 pages, and any Reply and Rejoinder shall not exceed 50 pages*". Article 24 states that "*Unless otherwise agreed by the parties or directed by the Arbitral Tribunal, [witness statements and expert reports] shall be limited to 20 and 40 pages, respectively for the first round, and to 10 and 20 pages for the second round*".

Is this too simplistic a solution or too blunt a tool to be accorded serious consideration? Arguably not. The power and wisdom of default page limits should not be underestimated. With such limits, counsel and parties will be forced to evaluate their case and pick their best arguments from an early stage of the proceedings, instead of adopting the usual kitchen-sink approach. While tribunals always have the discretion to grant an increase in page limits, the existence of defaults would set a baseline norm for parties. Such baselines would, over time, allow experienced arbitrators and arbitral institutions (if their users allow) to actively reset what the norm should be for the length of memorials. Not so that arbitrators can be lazy, but so that parties and lawyers can reclaim the opportunity for advocacy that memorials used to present, and so that arbitrators can be better assisted by counsel in understanding the case.

It's quite a simple point really: concise memorials communicate better. Succinct memorials are more persuasive. This is supposed to be a simple process where commercially-minded arbitrators are presented with a case in writing which they can understand and then apply their wisdom and experience to solving. There should be no prizes for building the haystack within which the needle is found.

It is recognised that everything is relative. There are arbitrations where there are so many issues that a 50-page memorial may not be sufficient. A one-size-fits-all approach is certainly not advocated. However, the prevailing norms for length of memorials have gone beyond the pale and something must be done to achieve a reset.

If norms are established for 'big', 'medium' and 'small' arbitrations, we will still need arbitrators to have the steel to enforce these norms. Arbitrators must, of course, have the flexibility to design the procedure appropriate for each case. It is precisely the abdication of this duty that has resulted in the burgeoning length of memorials. However, if we are to achieve a reset, we first have to give arbitrators a new norm to work from, and then we will need arbitrators to seriously apply their minds at the first procedural meeting to whether and to what extent deviation from page limit norms should be permitted.

At the GAR-LCIA roundtable held last year, the common sentiment amongst participants was that tribunals play a crucial role in imposing page limits, as there are no real incentives for counsel or parties to police themselves.[14] In particular, it was remarked that from counsel's point of view, it is always easier to draft more than to draft less. Mark Twain's famous quote was also recited: *"I didn't have time to write a short letter, so I wrote a long one instead"*.[15] Even if counsel may not wish to be verbose, they are sometimes

[14] Report of the GAR-LCIA Roundtable (October 2024), accessed on October 31, 2025 at <https://www.lcia.org/News/gar-lcia-roundtable-recommendations.aspx> (**"GAR-LCIA Roundtable Report"**) at 12, 17 19–20, 33.

[15] GAR-LCIA Roundtable Report at 27.

forced to by clients who think that more pages mean better quality. From the parties' point of view, no in-house counsel wants to restrict their lawyers to a certain page count as they rely on external counsel to know what is acceptable and effective.[16)]

While the views shared at the roundtable are largely agreed with, it may be worth highlighting that perhaps there is one important point that has not been sufficiently emphasised. If we really think about this, there *are* incentives for counsel to strive for brevity. The role of each party and each counsel is to effectively communicate their case. We would do it better being succinct. Disputes lawyers love to win, so why don't we see that the prolix, rambling memorial takes us further away from victory, not closer? We would be so much more effective if we would bravely seek to deliver the well-drafted and focussed memorial rather than the verbose and lengthy tome. As Jan Paulsson put it, it is "*wonderful to answer a 300-page brief with a 30-page answer*".[17)]

So, whether from the arbitrator's perspective or counsel's, page-limited memorials would be more efficient and effective. In the 2021 Queen Mary survey cited earlier, 61 % of arbitration users expressed that they would be most willing to do without unlimited length of written submissions, if that would make their arbitrations cheaper or quicker.[18)]

Focussed and page-limited memorials are the first step to rediscovering the simplicity of arbitration. Setting default page limits to achieve a reset of our norms can be simple and powerful. This will go a long way in clarifying the issues in dispute and also, simplify the document disclosure process. This leads to the next point.

## B. Document Disclosure

Document production has become overly costly and time-consuming in recent years, often with very little perceived benefit or effect on the outcome of the case. In a 2023 survey conducted by FTI Consulting and the ACICA,[19)] participants shared that more so than expert evidence and witness evidence, they were likely to spend greater than 20 % of the value in dispute for the preparation of documentary evidence.[20)] This is worrying, especially when one

---

[16)] GAR-LCIA Roundtable Report at 10, 19–20.

[17)] *Jack Ballantyne*, Paulsson.

[18)] QMUL 2021 Survey at 13.

[19)] Australian Centre for International Commercial Arbitration.

[20)] FTI Consulting and the Australian Centre for International Commercial Arbitration, 2023 Evidence in International Arbitration Report, accessed on October 31, 2025 at <https://acica.org.au/evidence-in-international-arbitration-report/#:~:text=The%202023%20Evidence%20in%20International%20Arbitration%20Report%20indicates%20that%20expert,representation%20and%20other%20key%20trends> (**"2023 Evidence in International Arbitration Report"**) at 30.

considers the oft-occurring mismatch between the volume of material presented to the tribunal, and the volume of material that actually motivates the tribunal's determinations.[21])

Let's begin with the Redfern Schedule. The Redfern Schedule was designed in the year 2000, as a tool for addressing disputed requests for the production of documents. In that case, counsel for the parties, three major oil companies, had spent several months in correspondence and discussions about their respective requests for document production, with the picture changing constantly as some requests were met, others were withdrawn, and others still were added to each party's lists. Finally, when the parties' counsel had done all they could to reach agreement, the tribunal was given an agreed bundle of emails and memoranda and asked to rule on the remaining disputed requests. This meant that the tribunal would have had to examine the ebb and flow of the parties' communications to find out what precisely were the requests on which it was expected to make a ruling. This was somewhat unrealistic but also completely inefficient.[22])

Accordingly, it was proposed that each requesting party should draw up a schedule showing in the first column what documents it wanted to seek production of, and in the second column, why these documents were relevant and material to the case. This schedule would then be sent to the opposing party who would then state, in the third column, its objections to production of the documents requested. The schedule would then be forwarded to the tribunal for its decision on the disputed requests.[23]) In this manner, the Redfern Schedule was conceived as a useful tool to make the document production exercise efficient.

This was the simplicity of arbitration on display. There was a complicated set of communications that the arbitrators were asked to review, and the arbitrators came up with a simple solution. Let's formulate a table which would *succinctly* set out requests and responses to document production.

It can be assumed that the tribunal which conceived the Redfern Schedule back in 2000 would be distressed by what has become of Redfern Schedules today. Instead of the narrow columns naturally forcing lawyers to be concise, counsel have insisted on being verbose and their entries in the narrow columns run for pages. This is perhaps why the Stern Schedule – which really is just a Redfern Schedule turned on its side – was created. But the problem was not the format of the Redfern Schedule or that the columns were narrow. That format was supposed to incentivise brevity.

---

[21]) 2023 Evidence in International Arbitration Report at 38.

[22]) *Nigel Blackaby*, *Constantine Partasides* and *Alan Redfern*, Redfern and Hunter on International Arbitration (OUP, 7th Edition, Feb 2023) (**"Redfern and Hunter"**) at 6.100–6.102.

[23]) *Nigel Blackaby*, *Constantine Partasides* and *Alan Redfern*, Redfern and Hunter at 6.100–6.102.

Aside from issues with Redfern Schedules, document production is frequently criticised as a major cost of arbitration. It is often a time-consuming process which takes up a significant bulk of the procedural calendar. This has been further aggravated in recent times with the proliferation of electronic document production. Yet, in spite of this lengthy and expensive process, the benefits of document production are not always immediately apparent. A smoking gun is seldom found. In view of this, why is it that parties and counsel still get caught up in protracted rounds of document production today?

One reason is that counsel have a natural desire to be thorough, to leave no stone unturned. This results in numerous requests, many of them overly broad. Another reason is that some parties engage in guerilla tactics and procedural abuse, seeking to delay proceedings by making hundreds of requests. This is often justified by a misguided attempt to say that above all, parties want to win; as if this validates guerilla tactics or justifies waste of time and costs even if there is a positive result.

As for the arbitrators who find themselves presented with numerous document production requests, being diligent people, they inevitably feel that they have to go through each one substantively, resulting in great inefficiencies. What is to be done, then?

There is a need for a fundamental shift in the attitude towards document production. A renewed focus on rediscovering the simplicity of arbitration and on rediscovering how arbitration was supposed to function is encouraged. Document production used to be far more restrained. Influenced by European procedural norms, the starting point was that parties were expected to prove their case or defence with the documents they had. Certainly, they would have to decide whether to start arbitration proceedings or defend arbitration proceedings on that basis, not on the basis of what documents they might hope to find during document production. The inclusion of document production in arbitration proceedings generally was a good thing. However, the putative commercial person would not have thought arbitration was an avenue to ransack the other side's files to find material to build a case.

There are a few things we can do. First, we need to re-educate ourselves as arbitration practitioners. We need to realise that it is just a waste of time and costs for us to engage in extensive document production exercises. We also need to realise that we are much more likely to have the tribunal's full attention if we have a small number of requests, each of which are narrowly focused. Simplifying our approach to requesting document production will make us more effective. We need to be brave enough to learn this and to teach this to the next generation of arbitration counsel.

Secondly, we should welcome limitations on document production. Whilst a blunt tool, arbitrators should consider limiting the number of document production requests. If the arbitrators know the case and hear counsel briefly on how many document production requests are needed, a fair number can be stipulated for both parties to abide by. Thirdly, tribunals should consider putting page limits on Redfern Schedules. If we put page limits on written submissions, why would we not do the same for Redfern Schedules which are essentially a submission on document production. Fourthly, tribunals could consider being more stringent about the amount of time that they will allow in the procedural calendar for the document production phase.

While arguments against each of these suggestions can immediately be identified, serious efforts to improve the efficiency of arbitration, will enable experienced arbitrators to use deploy of these measures in the right circumstances to limit the excesses of document production.

## C. Written Opening Submissions

Next, let us consider the written opening statement submitted just before the evidential hearing. Sometimes this is in the form of a written submission. Other times, it is in the form of a powerpoint presentation that the arbitrators are taken through orally at the start of the hearing.

Far too often, such written openings are a wasted opportunity. Instead of being used as a piece of written advocacy that draws the tribunal's attention to the key points in one's case, written openings are frequently prepared without much thought and end up being a cut-and-paste of vast chunks of memorials over which the tribunal has already laboured. While this is wholly inefficient, it is regrettably still the prevalent practice today. Tribunals have time and again been disappointed by opening submissions that are all too often just a re-run of the arguments in the memorials, with no focus on the key issues.

Instead, written openings should be pitched at the level of an exchange between highly informed persons. It should be a discourse between people who have already spent hours studying the papers. The opening should not start with "once upon a time". Instead, it should be the final chapter, the climax of a novel. Necessarily, it would be direct and to the point, and waste no time repeating what has already been said in the memorials.

The antithesis to an impactful opening submission is the lazy powerpoint. A rambling presentation that tries to capture every single point in the memorials without highlighting the main points on which the case will turn.

We would be rediscovering appropriate simplicity in arbitration procedure if we used oral and written openings to highlight key points and to articulate the main thrust of a case or defence. Achieving this is easy with page limits on written openings and parties being given a shorter amount of time for oral openings. That is much more like the simple and straightforward model that arbitration was supposed to be.

## D. Post-hearing Briefs

There is an interesting article by Campbell Walker and Gilbert Walker titled, *"International Arbitration: Return to Eden?"* There, the authors say that the practice of filing post-hearing briefs came about in the mid-1990s.[24]) However, it was likely not envisaged that post-hearing briefs were originally intended to run into hundreds of pages like they often do today, followed by lengthy reply briefs.

Often, these post hearing briefs restate a party's entire case, repeating what was in the memorials. That should not be the case. Post-hearing briefs should be limited to addressing the evidence that has been seen for the first time at the hearing, how it supports a party's case or how, despite first impressions, it does not damage a party's case. Perhaps parties doubt that arbitrators have read their lengthy memorials from before the hearing and that is why they insist on restating their entire case in the post-hearing briefs. However, if we keep memorials short and arbitrators demonstrate at the hearing through intelligent questions that they are fully across the materials in the memorials, parties can be more confident in limiting their post-hearing briefs to addressing the evidence of witnesses who testified at the hearing and the questions that the tribunal posed. That would be much more efficient and would accord with keeping the arbitral process simple and straightforward.

It has been suggested that tribunals should not allow or require post-hearing briefs except where it is truly necessary to pull one's case together. As one author put it, *"just because one side asks for post-hearing briefs, that does not mean that the arbitrators should permit them. Arbitrators frequently do so in order to be fair and to give parties every opportunity to present their case. However, by then, the parties will already have had substantial opportunities to present their case, and they are not entitled to one more shot"*.[25])

If post-hearing briefs are allowed, they should be page-limited, and their scope clearly defined by the tribunal. Ideally, that scope would be only to address the oral evidence and specific questions that the tribunal have. A growing number of tribunals do this, often to good effect.

## E. Utilising Tools to Help Achieve Efficiency

We have now walked through the key stages of the arbitral process. Some thoughts have been shared about how we can help ourselves rediscover the simplicity of arbitration and reject unnecessary complexity within the main architecture of an arbitration. These steps will not only make the arbitration

[24]) *Campbell T. Walker* and *Gilbert Walker*, International Arbitration: Return to Eden? (2008) New Zealand Law Journal 301 (**"Walker"**) at 302.

[25]) *David W. Rivkin*, Towards a New Paradigm in International Arbitration: The Town Elder Model Revisited (OUP 2008, Volume 24, Issue 3) at 384–385.

more efficient, they will also allow parties to be more effective in presenting their cases. Before concluding, a few words will be said about two vital tools that will help us be more efficient throughout the arbitral process. The first is active case management and the second is the use of technology.

*First,* on case management, various things that arbitrators need to do to make proceedings more efficient have throughout been addressed, some more difficult than others. Arbitrators will have to have some steel in them to make these directions and that really is the key to effective case management. Indeed, the discretion of an arbitral tribunal has been described as a *"one of the foundational elements of the international arbitral process"*.[26]) The principle that an arbitral tribunal may conduct the arbitration in such manner as it considers appropriate is a trite one. It is not only enshrined in the UNCITRAL Model Law but is also a mainstay in every institution's arbitration rules.

This is the epitome of the simplicity of arbitration. Arbitration was supposed to be a simple process where the rules essentially helped parties to commence arbitration and select their panel. Then, the arbitrators would design a straightforward process for the case. This quintessentially requires active case management guided by an early and accurate understanding of the case.

Arbitrators will also need to eschew the litigation mentality of exercising discretion only where necessary and instead take the reins in managing the arbitral process.[27]) Initial pleadings like Requests or Notices of Arbitration, and the Answers, need to be studied. There needs to be a real discussion about the issues at the first procedural meeting. Arbitrators may need to help parties to frame the issues and to indicate early to the parties which issues deserve more attention. Only then will the Procedural Calendar and Procedural Order No. 1 be a truly effective output of active case management.

With that said, effective case management should not be bandied around as the magic antidote to all of arbitration's ills. In fact, it is possible for case management to be counter-productive and for it to introduce unnecessary complexity and inefficiency in arbitral proceedings. For example, active case management may result in a proliferation of protocols to address a host of issues such as the overall framework of the proceedings, confidentiality, document disclosure (including e-discovery), and the hearing. The proliferation of such protocols would open up further avenues for parties to get caught up in satellite disputes. It would be a pity if these protocols, which are meant to aid parties in resolving the substantive dispute, end up luring parties into needless

---

[26]) *Gary B. Born*, International Commercial Arbitration (Kluwer Law International, 3rd Edition, 2021) at §15.03.

[27]) *Alexander Baykitch* and *Edmund Bao*, A Return to Innate Arbitration Culture: Implications from a Cost and Efficiency Perspective (OUP, 2019, Volume 35, Issue 1) at 66.

disputes about *how* to arbitrate and detract from the task of actually resolving the dispute.

Proposing active case management as a way to promote efficiency in arbitration also presumes that tribunals are able to make the right decisions on case management. Where an arbitrator, learned in the law but inexperienced in procedural matters, makes all the wrong case management decisions, this could be a catastrophe for the arbitral process. For instance, an arbitrator caught up with due process paranoia may end up acceding to every request by the parties however unreasonable, so as to avoid being the subject of natural justice complaints. Such an arbitrator would also be completely ineffectual in curbing abuses of the arbitral process.

Last but not least, a word will be said about technology. Arbitration has a track record of being at the forefront of adopting technology. And we should continue to uphold this ethos. We take it as a given today that arbitral hearings would have hearing room technologies such as real-time transcripts and videoconferencing, but we should not forget that many of these tools gained traction in arbitration before local courts adopted them.

This leads to the topic of Artificial Intelligence (AI). There has been a steady uptick in the use of AI in arbitration; arguably more so than in local courts. Many of us would be familiar with how AI is already supporting lawyers in performing traditional tasks. It is becoming an invaluable tool in areas such as legal research, drafting and preparing summaries. In fact, lawyers are increasingly relying on a variety of platforms to perform legal tasks that were once time-consuming and resource intensive.

Take, for example, the area of document review. AI platforms have revolutionised the process of document production through the use of predictive coding, particularly in identifying documents responsive to a document request or tribunal order. Instead of the traditional method where a lawyer would have to manually review each and every document in the case, a lawyer need only review a sample set of documents on the platform and mark them as "relevant" or "not relevant". Using machine-learning algorithms, the platform then identifies patterns in the marked documents and applies them to the wider set of documents, thereby reducing the number of documents that need to be reviewed manually. Using AI in this manner would obviously increase efficiency in arbitration.

Of course, the use of AI could quickly result in unnecessary complexities and inefficiencies if not properly managed. It can be a source of much satellite dispute. Guidance is needed and some arbitral institutions[28]) are already publishing guidelines on the use of AI in arbitrations.

We need as a community to harness this powerful tool for efficiency by coming up with guidance on crucial issues such as (a) whether the use of

---

[28]) For example, the Stockholm Chamber of Commerce (SCC) Arbitration Institute and the Silicon Valley Arbitration & Mediation Center.

predictive coding must be disclosed to or agreed with the opposing party; (b) whether the user of predictive coding is subject to any obligation to ensure its reliability, and the consequences for failing to do so; and (c) whether the user of predictive coding must disclose how many documents were reviewed manually for purposes of machine-learning, and the accuracy level of the platform used. Without such guidance, it will not be long before parties get caught up in protracted satellite disputes over the algorithms and methodology used in predictive coding. It would be a tragedy if what could be a significant tool to promote simplicity in arbitration, instead brings unnecessary complexity to the process.

## III. Concluding remarks

Arbitration was initially conceived as a cheaper, quicker means of resolving commercial disputes. It was marked by speed, affordability, simplicity and practicality. It also promised to offer flexibility and efficiency that local courts lacked. Unfortunately, arbitration has strayed from its simple origins. As one commentator put it: *"Having started life as a sleek but risky sports-car, international arbitration has come to resemble a cumbersome charabanc"*.[29]

We need to rediscover the simplicity of arbitration. We need a generation of brave and decisive arbitrators who will impose page and time limits, and weed out unnecessary complexity from arbitral procedures. We need a generation of enlightened arbitration counsel who will know that less is more, that short memorials persuade better than the rambling thesis and that focusing on the tribunal's questions in post-hearing briefs is more effective than repeating their entire case yet again. We need, all of us, arbitrators and counsel, to rediscover the simplicity of arbitration.

[29]) *Campbell T. Walker* and *Gilbert Walker*, Walker at 303.

# The Vienna Proposition on Efficiency in Arbitration

*Nikolaus Pitkowitz/Marlene Maurer and the 17 contributors*[1])

## I. Introduction

In 2025, Austria's leading arbitration conference, the Vienna Arbitration Days ("**VAD**"), was held under the theme *"ORCHESTRATING EFFICIENCY IN ARBITRATION – A SYMPHONY OF MODERN SOLUTIONS TO THE CLASSIC CHALLENGE"*. Since its inception in 2008, the conference has earned a reputation for presenting distinguished speakers addressing topical issues and giving insights into contemporary challenges and future directions in international arbitration as well as dispute resolution more generally. It is the conference's tradition to foster meaningful and high-level discussions among practitioners, academics, and industry experts.

As usual, the two-day conference explored the latest developments and emerging trends in dispute resolution, but this time with a particular focus on achieving the fast, fair, cost-efficient and final resolution of complex disputes through arbitration.

In this regard, the **Arbitration World Café** session is a central feature of the VAD. Introduced as a new concept by Nikolaus Pitkowitz in 2016 and run by him since then, the Arbitration World Café has evolved as a cornerstone of the conference. The World Café session is an interactive format, designed to mirror the vibrant atmosphere of a traditional Viennese coffee house. The participants – consisting of a wide range of professionals from diverse professional backgrounds, varying levels of experience, and different legal specializations – are invited to actively engage in focused discussions. These discussions are structured through certain themed tables with respectively two moderators carefully selected by the organizers, who lead two rounds of discussions, encouraging a lively and in-depth debate among the attendees.

In 2025, the World Café session included nine themed tables, each dedicated to a topic aligned with the overarching theme of the 2025 VAD. The participants of the VAD selected their respective tables based on their interest.

---

[1]) *Vilius Bernatonis, Lisa Berger, James Boykin, Antonia Cermak-Kietaibl, Ondrej Cech, Barbara Concolino, Borna Dejanović, Egishe Dzhazoyan, Catrice Gayer, Courtney Lotfi, Peter Machherndl, Tamara Manasijevic, Maximilian Murtinger, Petra Pataki, Camilla Perera – de Wit, Florian Wagner, Anna Weinzierl.*

As with the last years, these small and dynamic group conversations have resulted in the following valuable contributions.

- Toolkit of Innovative Procedural Instruments: Keys to Greater Efficiency in Arbitration?
- Early Disposition of Issues: Overcoming the Risk of Premature Decisions and Bias Perception
- Practical Strategies for Balancing Speed, Cost, and Quality in the Iron Triangle
- How Can Mediation Serve as a Catalyst for More Efficient Dispute Resolution?
- AI in Arbitration: Efficiency Booster or Ethical Minefield?
- The (Lacking) Role of Arbitrators in Driving Efficiency
- The (Lacking) Role of Institutions in Driving Efficiency
- The (Lacking) Role of Parties (and Counsel) in Driving Efficiency
- Wish List and Impulses from Young Arbitration Voices and for Greater Efficiency in ADR Proceedings

**Part II** of this chapter provides a comprehensive overview of the key findings and insights gained from these nine World Café discussions, summarized as the "Vienna Propositions".

**Part III** presents detailed reports prepared by the World Café moderators, showcasing the diverse perspectives and valuable contributions of the participants. These reports are shared with the explicit consent of all participants and reflect the collective ideas and insights generated during the sessions.

We sincerely thank the moderators for their thorough preparation before the session, for leading the discussions, and for their dedication in finalizing the discussion reports afterwards. Our heartfelt appreciation also goes to all VAD 2025 participants, whose engagement and expertise ensured the success of the World Café.

## II. Proposition for Driving Efficiency in Arbitration

Based on the lively discussions held during the 2025 World Café sessions, the moderators and participants collaboratively developed the following key propositions

### A. Propositions for Procedural Efficiency

**Tighten deadlines and procedural calendar:** Several World Café tables examined whether the current procedural rules would suffice for modern challenges. The discussions emphasized the possibility to enhance efficiency by setting deadlines and incorporate procedural timetables without compromising legitimacy. In order to achieve a tailored and proactive case management tribunals have to be forthright with their schedule as well as their capacities and the extensions of deadlines shall (only) be possible under certain circumstances.

**Promote page limits:** Another measure several World Café tables discussed is the limitation of the number of written submissions and/or their pages. While some participants generally approved this measure, others – being more hesitantly – referred to the dangers of a trade-off between quality and efficiency. The shared consensus is that efficiency must not come at the expense of accurate representation of the client's case.

**Focus of early disposition:** One World Café table explored early dismissals and summary judgments as an opportunity to save time and costs. By dismissing claims that have no plausible chance of success prior to engaging in the substance and evidentiary assessment, proceedings may concentrate their effort on issues that truly warrant determination. This rather severe consequence is balanced by the high threshold for early dismissal. Accordingly, early disposal should be available only in clear-cut cases and must be accompanied by comprehensive reasoning, while summary judgment should be granted only when the result advocated by the moving party is legally unavoidable.

**Mediation as hybrid-mechanisms:** One World Café table addressed how mediation can improve the efficiency of resolving disputes. Participants did recognize mediation as a growing and evolving approach in corporate disputes, though it has not yet unleashed its full potential. With concerns regarding enforceability or confidentiality and parties being unwilling to engage in meaningful settlement discussions, mediation seems to be behind in some aspects. Therefore, the round table proposed a hybrid-mechanism combining arbitration with mediation in order to unite procedural flexibility, enforceability and finality.

## B. Propositions for Technological Toolkits

While most World Café tables considered technology as a major efficiency booster, views diverged on its impact. Some supposed it widens resource gaps for smaller teams lacking technical support, others felt it levels the field.

Overall, virtual hearings were praised for cutting travel and speeding scheduling, and arbitrators found digital platforms ideal for preliminary or procedural matters.

While virtual tools work well for logistics, restraint was expressed for complex evidentiary hearings, which still benefit from in-person conduct.

One World Café focused primarily on the opportunities and challenges of AI as the booster for efficiency. With several practical applications like formatting submissions, organizing documents or billing reviews already in use, the group discussed more experimental or speculative applications as well. The discussion, however, also indicated severe concerns regarding documentary reliability and authenticity issues. In light of the numerous existing use cases, participants concurred that proactive regulation of AI use is necessary.

## C. Propositions regarding the Composition of Tribunals and Future Generations

**Promoting arbitration already at university-level:** Two World Café tables expressed the need to prepare the next generation for arbitration practice. Participants emphasized the values of the combination of academia and practice, which many law schools take too little advantage of. Moot competitions, early internships and alternative dispute resolution-focused clinics would enhance visibility and accessibility while giving young minds the opportunity to gain hands-on experience. There the next generation may also be trained to consider efficiency as a professional asset instead of a procedural risk.

**Promote diversity in the tribunal:** Other World Café tables explored the opportunities presented by different tribunal compositions. For more straightforward disputes, a single arbitrator may be sufficient, whereas more complex matters tend to benefit from three-member tribunals. In this context, the tension between availability and eminence was discussed: a highly reputable – and therefore frequently engaged – arbitrator may ultimately be less desirable than a more efficient but slightly less experienced one. Likewise, greater diversity within tribunals can enhance both fairness and efficiency.

## D. Propositions for Financial Incentives for Efficiency

Several World Café tables addressed the lack of (financial) incentives for procedural efficiency.

Participants noted, on one hand, that a prevailing culture of overcaution requires measures that actively reward efficient conduct. On the other hand, the current billing structures for lawyers were seen as reinforcing inefficiency.

One suggestion was to treat cost-information requirements related to document production as a separate line item, with the possibility that – where the procedure is abused or ultimately unsuccessful – the associated costs would not be recoverable.

While end-stage sanctions also exist, participants observed that measures applied only at the conclusion of proceedings may have limited influence on parties' procedural behavior throughout the process.

# III. World Café Reports

## A. Toolkit of Innovative Procedural Instruments: Keys to Greater Efficiency in Arbitration?

*Barbara Concolino*[2])

### 1. Introduction

The 2025 Vienna Arbitration Days were dedicated to the evergreen topic of efficiency in arbitration. While some suggested that there is too much discussion about efficiency and questioned whether efficiency is considered a priority by the parties, this old topic is (again or still) under the spotlight. Arbitral proceedings are often overly complex, lengthy, and expensive, frequently disproportionately to the actual complexity of the case. There is much discussion about who is to blame for this inefficiency. While identifying the cause of the inefficiency might be relatively straightforward, determining the key to efficiency in international arbitration presents a greater challenge. This question inevitably leads to others: are new procedural instruments required to boost efficiency? Are we making good use of the existing instruments? To answer these questions, moderators and participants discussed both traditional and innovative techniques, ranging from page limitations and sanctions for inefficiency to lists of issues and the use of AI. The discussion highlighted the pros and cons of these various techniques and instruments, and their potential impact on boosting efficiency. Ultimately, a broad consensus emerged: the key to efficiency lies in adopting a more tailored approach to each case, recognizing that there is no 'one-size-fits-all' solution. We need to adapt both existing and new instruments to the needs of the case and the parties. This can only be achieved with an early, open, and ongoing dialogue between the parties and the arbitrator(s).

---

[2]) Participants included: *Shane Daly* (co-moderator), *Anna Förstel-Cherng, Daniela Karollus-Bruner, Nico Köppel, Justin Krahé, Nikolaus Pitkowitz, Peter W. Steindl, Thaïs Stemmelin, Artúr Tamási, Stephan Wilcke* and *Lea Zieger.*

## 2. Innovative and Less Innovative Procedural Instruments

The participants and the moderator discussed various procedural instruments to understand what impact, if any, they could have in boosting efficiency in arbitral proceedings.

### a) Page (and Other) Limitations

Participants agreed that parties often file written submissions that are disproportionately long compared to the complexity and value of the case. Lawyers often believe that each argument, no matter how peripheral to the issues in dispute, should be addressed and no affirmation from the counterparty should go unanswered. This often means that, instead of having shorter reply submissions that only focus on disputed matters, the second round of submissions is even longer than the first one. This, of course, negatively impacts costs and efficiency.

While imposing page limitations is widely accepted for certain submissions, such as post-hearing briefs or skeleton arguments, significant skepticism persists regarding their application to other submissions. This is understandable.

Parties are reluctant to agree on page limitations before they have laid down their cases with the Statement of Claim and Statement of Defence. After this first exchange of submissions, parties would be better placed to assess and determine an acceptable page limitation for their reply submissions. However, this rarely happens. The reasons are many: if there is a document production phase – whose real necessity is rarely questioned – parties will, most of the time, not be willing to agree on a page limitation before the document production phase is closed; procedural timetables rarely include a second case management conference to assess the status of the proceedings and, even when they do, page limitations for the second exchange of submissions are seldom included in the case management conference agenda; and, perhaps the main reason, lawyers dislike page limitations and do not like to commit to them before they have a clear and full picture of the case. This is why, when it comes to post-hearing briefs, page limitations are generally accepted.

While there was general agreement that page limitations can be a useful instrument, participants largely agreed that they are not a primary solution for boosting efficiency in international arbitration.

Participants also discussed limiting the number of document requests that parties can submit during the document production phase. Many arbitral proceedings involve parties and legal systems that are not used to American-style discovery. The document production phase framed in the IBA Guidelines on Taking Evidence in International Arbitration envisions the document production phase as an option, not a rule. Yet, at least in the last decade, the document production phase is included in virtually all timetables of arbitral proceedings without questioning its actual need.

There was wide consensus that a document production phase is not always needed and that parties often abuse this phase with requests that are unreasonable in terms of number and scope. Arbitrators' approaches to these requests vary significantly. One participant reported a case in which the tribunal, in its decision on the parties' document production requests, noted that while it believed that the parties had requested documents well beyond what should be permissible in document production, it accepted most of the requests because the parties had adopted a similar 'broad approach'. This, of course, led to an undesirable outcome in terms of costs and efficiency with no real benefit for either party.

Yet, lawyers are often reluctant to agree to a limitation on the number of document production requests that they can submit at the time of the first case management conference. The reason is the same one discussed above: parties are yet to file their first submissions and they (especially respondents) may not have a full and clear picture of how the case will evolve.

After the first round of submissions, however, parties could, and should, be in a position to know if they need a document production phase and what kind of documents they may need. Parties and arbitrators should actively engage in this discussion at the first case management conference and, if parties are not ready to commit at that stage, in a second case management conference.

Arbitrators should take an active role in this discussion and, at least in the author's opinion, should sanction parties' failures to comply with the agreed course of action.

The need for a second management conference and the desirability of arbitrators sanctioning parties' procedural misconduct have been the subject of lengthy discussions and are addressed below.

### b) Hard Deadlines

Once upon a time, there were deadlines for submissions that the parties would adhere to. Now, more often than not, parties submit one request for extension after another and, at the end of the proceedings, the original timetable is a distant memory. While this may not immediately be perceived as the main cause of inefficiency, the impact is often underestimated. The postponement of deadlines often leads to lengthier submissions, with a cascade effect on the subsequent submissions. Moreover, this sometimes leads to the postponement of the hearing, which means that the parties will have to wait longer for the award. Perhaps this may be welcomed by some respondents, but our ultimate goal, as arbitration practitioners, should be for arbitration to be the fast and efficient means of dispute resolution that we have studied in books.

Participants expressed different views on this issue. Some emphasized that, after all, arbitration is an instrument in the hands of the parties and, especially when parties agree on postponement of deadlines, arbitrators should not interfere with the parties' will. Yet, often, parties do not agree, especially on lengthy extensions of time and, even when they do, this often reflects the lawyers' desire more than the clients'.

In the author's view, the rules of the game agreed upon at the beginning of the case, including the procedural timetable, should be respected, and arbitrators should take an active role in making sure that they are. Deviations from the agreed rules should, of course, be possible, but they should be the exception, not the rule. Any request to deviate from these rules should be motivated, and the requesting party should explain the reasons why compliance with the agreed rules is no longer possible. This should not be a mere formality, and parties should not assume that any request will be granted.

### c) Sanctions for Inefficiency

Should arbitrators sanction inefficiency? How and when should arbitrators sanction inefficiency? Is this going to have an impact on the overall efficiency of the proceedings? Participants discussed all these questions and expressed various views.

There was general agreement that arbitrators have the power to award costs and enjoy some discretion in the allocation of costs. Not everyone agreed, however, that using that discretion to sanction parties' inefficiency is an effective instrument in boosting efficiency.

Some participants noted that if the decision on costs comes at the end of the proceedings, it is unlikely to have any impact on the parties' procedural behavior. For this reason, some suggested that it is crucial for arbitrators to use this instrument in the course of the proceedings. If, for instance, one of the parties files plainly groundless motions or an excessive number of meritless document production requests, arbitrators should not reserve the decision on costs for the final award. Arbitrators should use their discretion and allocate the costs of unnecessary procedural activities to the party that caused them. This would, hopefully, discourage parties from adopting inefficient and disruptive behavior as the arbitration proceeds.

### d) Early List of (Disputed/Undisputed) Issues

Dozens of pages in written submissions and expert reports are often devoted to issues that are undisputed. Often parties feel the need to give a complete account of all matters connected to the dispute, no matter how peripheral they are to the disputed issues between the parties.

Some participants suggested that having a list of disputed and undisputed issues early in the case could help streamline the proceedings, assisting both parties in focusing on the real matters in dispute. While, in principle, this could be a useful exercise, skepticism remains as to whether and when this could be done in practice. Parties to a case are unlikely to be able or willing to agree on a list of agreed/disagreed issues before they have both set out their cases in the first round of written submissions. At that point, agreeing on a list of agreed/disagreed issues before filing their second round of submissions is likely to require time and effort that the parties may not be willing to invest.

In reality, a list of agreed/disagreed issues is, most of the time, something that parties feel is an imposition from the arbitrators requiring it before the hearing. In these cases, rather than being an instrument to boost efficiency, they end up contributing to an increase in costs and inefficiency.

According to the author, it is possible to turn lists of agreed/disagreed issues into an instrument for boosting efficiency only if the approach to this instrument is changed. One option could be to consider the list of agreed/disagreed issues as a living instrument. During the first case management conference, parties could agree on a preliminary list that could then be updated in the course of the proceedings and especially after the first round of submissions. Alternatively, parties could agree during the first case management conference that a list of agreed/disagreed issues will be drawn up after the first round of submissions to assist both parties in streamlining their second round of submissions. Being aware of this requirement early on may assist parties in identifying disputed issues sooner and will perhaps change the way parties view lists of issues, from foe to friend.

### e) Case Management Conferences and Procedural Order No. 1

Case management conferences and Procedural Order No. 1 ("PO1") have been widely cited as potentially the most useful instruments to boost efficiency. However, all participants agreed that parties and tribunals need to radically change their approach to case management conferences and procedural orders no. 1.

Currently, parties often receive a draft PO1 before the case management conference. In virtually all cases, this is a standardized PO1 that includes rules regarding documents and witness evidence, written submissions, document production, and the hearing. Parties are usually invited to comment, but their comments rarely question whether the PO1 is correctly tailored to the needs of the case. Participants generally agreed that this is not the best way to approach the PO1 and the first case management conference.

Some participants suggested that the PO1 should be drafted during, or perhaps right after, the case management conference. Before then, arbitrators should ask the parties what they envision for their case: Is it necessary to have two rounds of written submissions? Is this a case in which witness or expert evidence will be needed? Is a document production phase necessary? Would the parties accept setting a page limit for their submissions? Should parties and arbitrators reassess the answers to these questions (or some of them) in a second case management conference after the first round of written submissions?

All these questions are rarely asked. Most of the time, arbitrators assume that the answer to all the above questions is "yes, of course" (except for the question on page limitation) and most of the time parties assume that the arbitrators' assumptions cannot be questioned.

In many cases, the answer arbitrators will receive is likely to be "yes, of course", but this does not mean these questions should not be asked. Arbitration cases are not always massive disputes worth billions of euros involving very complex technical and legal matters. There is a wide range of disputes, but somehow along the way, arbitration practitioners decided that no matter how small or large, complex or simple, highly technical or purely legal their case is, there is only one way to approach it: with a standardized procedure set forth in PO1.

Participants agreed that this reality is highly undesirable and should be changed. There was a strong call for a first case management conference in which the applicable procedure and rules are discussed and agreed between the arbitrators and the parties to make sure that they meet the case's requirements and the parties' expectations. This should be then recorded in a customized PO1.

Many participants also suggested that the procedural timetable should always include a second management conference after the first round of written submissions. This meeting should not be a mere formality but should be used by the parties and the arbitrators to discuss the status of the case and the way forward. Many of the important issues discussed above can and should be addressed in this second case management conference: is a document production phase needed? Can page limitations for the next round of submissions be agreed? What are the issues actually in dispute, and can the agreed-upon issues be left aside?

A second case management conference is rarely held. Even when the original timetable provides for one, it often happens that it is ultimately cancelled with the agreement of the parties because "there is nothing to discuss". This is a lost opportunity.

#### f) The Use of Artificial Intelligence

The use of artificial intelligence as an instrument to boost efficiency in international arbitration was the most divisive topic for the participants. Views ranged from an absolute ban on the use of artificial intelligence (especially by arbitrators) to complete openness, subject to the understanding that everything should be reviewed and vetted by whoever makes use of AI.

The reality is that artificial intelligence is already part of arbitral proceedings. Parties began using it years ago for document review and will continue to use it more and more, including for legal research and drafting. And yes, arbitrators use it too. In the author's view, artificial intelligence should be considered a tool like any other technological tool. Lawyers and arbitrators remain responsible for each word they write and for any decision they make. There should be no outcry over an arbitrator using AI to summarize the parties' positions in a final award, provided that the arbitrator has indeed read the parties' submissions, reviewed the AI's draft, and adopts it as her or his own.

### 3. Conclusion

The participants in the discussion provided a variety of inputs and shared a range of experiences and best practices. While it is not possible to include all of them in these pages, what emerged from the discussion is that, even among different views and opinions, there is a lot of common ground. Arbitration practitioners do feel the need for more efficient and cost-effective arbitral proceedings. They also agree that there is no magic tool for that. The key to efficiency lies in adopting a more tailored approach to each case through an early, open discussion between the arbitrators and the parties. Arbitrators and parties should abandon the old standardized PO1 and should instead discuss the case's needs and the parties' expectations to ensure that the rules of the game and the procedural instruments adopted are best suited for the case.

## B. Early Disposition of Issues: Overcoming the Risk of Premature Decisions and Bias Perception

*Egishe Dzhazoyan/Lisa Berger*[3])

### 1. Introduction

Early disposition mechanisms have become a recurring topic in procedural reform debates in international arbitration in the last decade. Since 2006, a growing number of arbitral institutions have adopted provisions enabling tribunals to dismiss claims, defenses, or discrete issues that are manifestly without legal merit or otherwise manifestly outside the tribunal's jurisdiction. The newly enacted English Arbitration Act 2025 now also confers broad powers to arbitrators to make awards on a summary basis on issues that have no real prospect of success. In contrast, the practice of early disposition of claims and issues has a long tradition in court litigation in common law jurisdictions through motions to dismiss or motions for summary judgment, also referred to judgment as a matter of law.

The developments within the institutional and statutory frameworks governing international arbitrations are considered *one* response to widespread concern and sometimes criticism international arbitration has been facing in

[3]) The authors thank all participants of the Vienna Arbitration Days 2025 World Café Session on Early Disposition of Issues for their valuable insights and contributions to a thought-provoking discussion.

recent years – that it is no longer delivering on its promise of efficiency. While inefficient proceedings can have many root causes – dragging along clearly hopeless claims or issues throughout the entire course of an arbitration and into the final award is undoubtedly one of them. In response, early disposition mechanisms are intended to narrow down the claims or issues in disputes at a relatively early stage in the proceedings with a view to saving time, cost and allowing increased focus on the relevant issues.

However, despite these (potential) upsides, the widespread use of early disposition mechanisms in court litigation in many jurisdictions, and their express inclusion in major arbitration rules, their practical application in international arbitration is still rather limited. Indeed, all of the participants of the roundtable discussion dedicated to early disposition of issues during the Vienna Arbitration Days 2025 World Café Session reported never or extremely rarely having encountered arbitral tribunals applying such early disposition mechanisms.

The participants at the table included a diverse group of practitioners in private practice and at arbitral institutions as well as academics from a variety of civil and common law jurisdictions. Together, the group discussed the promises and limitations of early disposition mechanisms, what challenges need to be overcome for these tools to achieve more widespread application in practice and whether this is at all desirable.

After establishing a common understanding of what the group considered early disposition of issues (2.), and the basis for arbitral tribunal's power to apply such mechanisms (3.), the participants discussed which risks or obstacles they saw in applying early disposition as a procedural tool in practices and which measures could help alleviate these issues (4.). There was overall consensus among participants that, given the exceptional character of these early disposition mechanisms, their limited application in practice does not in itself call for correction and the objective should be to achieve reliable, targeted use rather than more widespread use (5.).

## 2. Delineation of Early Disposition Mechanisms

For the purpose of the Roundtable discussion, it was important to gain a joint understanding of what is – in this context – meant by early disposition or early determination of issues and claims as there is no precise, let alone uniform definition of the concept.[4]) It was therefore considered helpful to take departure from a negative definition of what the group did *not* consider early disposition mechanisms in this context – bifurcation and expedited proceedings, and to approach what hallmarks early disposition mechanisms entail by reference to

---

[4]) Gary B. Born & Kenneth Beale, *Party Autonomy and Default Rules: Reframing the Debate over Summary Disposition in International Arbitration*, 21 ICC BULL. 19, 23 (2010).

the common law concepts of early dismissal and summary judgment before determining the potential scope of these procedural tools in international arbitration.

### a) Bifurcation and Expedited Proceedings

The concept of determining issues or claims sequentially or based on a compressed procedure is not at all foreign to international arbitration and well known as bifurcation and expedited proceedings. These mechanisms, though equally aimed at increasing procedural efficiency, are different from early disposition mechanisms.

Expedited proceedings are designed to streamline the arbitration process in cases of lower complexity or value, or where the parties have agreed to prioritize speed (and usually lower costs) over extensive proceedings and usually entail shorter time limits, limited written submissions and limited use of time and cost intense procedural steps such as document production or the use of fact and expert witnesses. Expedited proceedings apply to the entire dispute and are intended to deliver a final award disposing of the entire dispute within a relatively short period of time. Early disposition on the other hand generally entails that the arbitral tribunal determines (only) a distinct issue or question on the basis of an abbreviated procedure, often after a limited exchange of written submissions and without a complete presentation of evidence, either on a written basis or after a limited oral argument in contrast to a full evidentiary hearing.

Bifurcation refers to the procedural division of an arbitration into separate phases, most commonly addressing in order either (i) jurisdiction and liability or (ii) liability and quantum. Where questions arise as to the arbitral tribunal's competence to hear all or part of the claims, the proceedings may be bifurcated to allow an initial determination on jurisdiction. Alternatively, the parties or the tribunal may decide to address liability first and defer the assessment of damages to a subsequent phase. In practice, the tribunal will typically render a decision on liability before inviting submissions on quantum. In contrast to early disposition mechanisms, each phase of the bifurcated proceedings commonly entails a full exchange of written submissions and evidence including an evidentiary hearing related to the questions at issue in the relevant phase. Prior to the more widespread codification of options for early determination in arbitral rules, bifurcation has been described as the *"acceptable face of early disposition"*.[5])

---

[5]) Judith Gill, *Applications for the Early Disposition of Claims in Arbitration Proceedings*, in Albert Jan van den Berg (ed), 50 YEARS OF THE NEW YORK CONVENTION. ICCA INTERNATIONAL ARBITRATION CONFERENCE 513, 513 (2009).

### b) Early Dismissal and Summary Judgment

The most common reference points for explaining early disposition mechanism in international arbitration are two procedural mechanisms with firm roots in common law jurisdictions, namely early dismissal and summary judgment.

Early dismissal, as the name suggests, usually occurs very early in the proceedings, usually before the parties start exchanging evidence prior to discovery. A motion to dismiss is one of the first procedural tools available to a defendant to challenge the legal sufficiency of a plaintiff's complaint before filing a substantive answer, for example pursuant to the Federal Rules of Civil Procedure 12(b), in the US. Common grounds for such motions include lack of (personal or subject matter) jurisdiction, res judicata, improper venue, statute of limitations or failure of the complaint to state a claim on which relief can be granted. This motion tests whether, assuming all factual allegations in the complaint are true, the law recognizes a plausible right to the requested relief. While motions to dismiss are almost a standard first line of defence in US litigation – a fact which in itself might offset their potentially positive effect on efficiency if viewed across proceedings – the underlying idea is to efficiently dispose of claims that have no or no plausible chance of success as a matter of law before engaging in the substance and evidentiary assessment of the dispute.

In contrast, motions for summary judgment are usually filed later in the proceedings, usually after discovery when the parties have exchanged evidence but before trial. In the US, the motion is governed by the Fed. R. Civ. P. 56 and entitles the moving party to summary judgment on all or part of the claims if it can show "that there is no genuine dispute as to any material fact and the movant is entitled to judgment as a matter of law". If successful, the motion leads to a judgment with prejudice regarding the concerned claim(s) and the case ends before trial (assuming no claims remain).

Considering these two established avenues for early disposition, it seems that the motion to dismiss is overall more suitable for analogous application in international arbitration, as it is aimed at disposing of claims that could not possibly be met with success at the outset, and thus prima facie seems to at least have the potential of increasing efficiency albeit at the "cost" of one party's claim not even reaching the phase of substantive written submissions and evidence on the merits. This harsh result is offset by the high threshold for early dismissal. Summary judgment on the other hand requires the judge or arbitrator to have considered the evidence and be convinced that – even viewing the non-moving party's evidence in the most favorable light – the outcome as argued by the moving party would be legally inevitable. That such summary decision requires the development and assessment of evidence suggests that the costs and time saved are more limited compared to a motion to dismiss.[6]) However, depending on what preparing and conducting an evidentiary hearing would entail in terms of inconvenience, time and costs, this option might still be attractive in certain cases. This is where the upside of the lack of a clear definition of early disposition mechanisms in international arbitration comes into play: In international arbitration, arbitral tribunals are predominantly (though not without exceptions) considered to have broad power to dispose of issues early in a manner that promotes efficiency within the outer limits of the parties' rights of due process, without being bound by the strict requirements and processes of the established common law mechanisms. While this great freedom has been framed as an upside in this report, the participants of the roundtable discussion by-and-large considered the lack of more detailed procedures and rules for early determination of issues as one of the main reasons for its limited use in practice.

### c) Early disposition in international arbitration

Compared to its common law counterparts described in the preceding section, early disposition presents a relatively recent procedural innovation in international arbitration which conceptually borrows from the motion to dismiss and summary judgment. Despite the absence of a universally accepted definition and different regulation in detail (see below), early disposition in international arbitration (and for the purpose of the roundtable discussion) includes and refers to mechanisms that allow an arbitral tribunal to resolve discrete issues, claims or defenses at an early stage of the arbitral proceedings, typically after no more than a limited exchange of written submissions and in any event without conducting a full evidentiary hearing on the relevant issue or claim. The ultimate determination might be based solely on written submissions or include an oral hearing, and the scope could be limited to arguments or include the taking of evidence. Commentary and arbitration rules generally do not limit early disposition to any particular form the procedure needs to take, or character of the decision whether in an order or an award, and different terms such as early disposition, summary disposition and early determination are all frequently used for (presumably) the same concept. The distinctive feature of all early disposition mechanisms is therefore not what they offer but what they lack – namely a full hearing on the merits. Importantly, and contrary to what the name *summary* disposition might suggest, the purpose of these procedural tools is not to dedicate less attention or a lower level of scrutiny to the determination of the issues subject to early disposition, but to identify discrete issues or claims, the success of which does not depend the assessment of the evidence in the case, or which can be

---

[6]) Caline Mouawad & Elizabeth Silbert, *A Case for Dispositive Motions in International Commercial Arbitration*, 2:1 BCDR INTERNATIONAL ARBITRATION REVIEW 77, 92 (2015).

determined based on limited, clearly delineated evidence.[7]) Also common to all instances of early disposition is that they are not only an end in themselves – to resolve the issue subject to early disposition, but also a means to an end – to promote efficiency and to reduce the time and costs of arbitration proceedings.[8])

The following section will examine what rules and standards currently do exist to empower arbitrators to make use of early disposition mechanisms.

## 3. Institutional Evolution and Comparative Standards

Until 2006, no major set of arbitration rules contained an express regulation of early disposition mechanisms. The International Center for the Settlement of Investment Disputes (ICSID) was the first major institute to adopt an early disposition procedure in its arbitration rules in 2006 and would remain the only one for the next ten years, after which several major arbitral institutions[9]) followed suit. In 2016, the Singapore International Arbitration Center (SIAC) introduced Rule 29 titled "Early Dismissal of Claims and Defences". In 2017, the Arbitration Institute of the Stockholm Chamber of Commerce (SCC) added a new "Summary procedure" in Article 39 of its arbitration rules. In 2018, the Hong Kong International Arbitration Centre (HKIAC) added inter alia an "Early Determination Procedure" in Article 43. Similarly, the London Court of International Arbitration (LCIA) has included early disposition provisions in its arbitration rules since October 2020. While neither the 2017 nor the 2021 Rules of Arbitration of the International Chamber of Commerce (ICC) contain an express provision codifying the possibility of early determination or summary procedure, the ICC in 2021 issued a "Note to the parties and arbitral tribunals on the conduct of the arbitration under the ICC Rules of Arbitration" in which it provided guidance how Article 22 can be relied on for this purpose. The note explained that "[a]*ny party may apply to the arbitral tribunal for the expeditious determination of one of more claims or defences, on grounds that such claims or defences are manifestly devoid or merit or fall manifestly outside the arbitral tribunal's jurisdiction*".[10]) Also in 2021, the International Centre for Dispute Resolution (ICDR) amended its rules and included early disposition procedures in rule 23. Most recently, the English Arbitration Act was reformed and now also empowers arbitrators, upon an

[7]) David L. Wallach, *The Emergence of Early Disposition Procedures in International Arbitration*, in William W. Park (ed), 37:4 ARBITRATION INTERNATIONAL, 835, 836 f (2021).

[8]) *Id.*

[9]) *Id*, at 838.

[10]) International Chamber of Commerce, *Note to the parties and arbitral tribunals on the conduct of the arbitration under the ICC Rules of Arbitration*, paragraphs 109 ff (1 January 2021).

application of a party, to summarily dismiss a claim or a particular issue arising in a claim or a defense that has no real prospect of success.

### a) Rule Frameworks

The starting point for discussion was a comparative overview of early disposition provisions in major institutional rules. The ICSID Arbitration Rules 2022 permit objections that a claim is manifestly without legal merit if raised within 30 days of the tribunal's constitution (Rule 41(5)). Similarly, the SIAC Rules 2025 allow early dismissal of claims or defenses "manifestly without legal merit" or "manifestly outside the jurisdiction" within the early days of the arbitration. The LCIA Rules 2020 similarly empower tribunals to render an early determination of claims that are manifestly without merit, inadmissible, or manifestly outside jurisdiction.

The standards, while similar in wording, vary in breadth. Some focus purely on legal merit (ICSID), others extend to factual unsustainability (SCC, HKIAC). The English Arbitration Act 2025, recently enacted, now provides arbitrators with express authority to render awards on issues having no real prospect of success (Section 39A(1)), "*with a view to expediting the proceedings on the claim or issue*" (Section 39A(2)). Before making an award on a summary basis, the tribunal "*must afford the parties a reasonable opportunity to make representations to the tribunal*" (Section 39A(3)). Participants noted that this legislative endorsement may encourage other jurisdictions or institutions to follow suit.

### b) Two-Step Processes and Safeguards

Some modern rules employ a two-step process. First, the tribunal determines whether an application for early disposition should proceed at all; only then, if leave is granted, does the tribunal decide on the merits. This model – prominently used by SIAC – was seen as a procedural filter that may deter tactical or unfounded applications while maintaining fairness. It also offers arbitrators an opportunity to invite focused submissions and schedule limited oral argument, thereby balancing efficiency with the parties' right to be heard.

While institutional rules rarely address cost shifting explicitly, tribunals may under general principles allocate costs to the unsuccessful party when an early disposition motion is evidently unfounded. Participants agreed that cost consequences, if predictable, could serve as both deterrent and incentive, but that arbitral discretion should remain paramount to preserve flexibility.

### Absence of Express Provisions

With the increased adoption of express provisions governing the application of early disposition mechanisms in the rules of major arbitral institutions, the group discussed what effect this would have on arbitration rules which do *not* contain such express provisions. Prominent examples of arbitration rules which do not contain express early disposition mechanisms include the UNCITRAL Rules as well as the arbitration rules of the *Deutsche Institution fuer Schiedsgerichtbarkeit* (DIS) and the 2021 Vienna Rules of the Vienna International Arbitration Center (VIAC).

It was discussed whether early determination of issues is and has always been part of the broad powers and, in fact, the duty of the arbitral tribunal under most sets of arbitration rules to conduct the arbitration in an efficient and expeditious manner, as it considers appropriate with a view to any party agreements and duly considering the parties' due process guarantees. The majority of participants leaned towards considering that arbitral tribunals did have the requisite power to dispose of issues early under certain circumstances even without express provisions to that effect.[11]) However, by the same token, the majority of participants expressed that they would have concerns in regard to the enforceability of the award if early disposition procedures were undertaken without such possibility having been discussed and aligned among the parties and the arbitral tribunal from the outset of the arbitration, for example in procedural order number 1, and/or if the facts in the given case did not *clearly* point to a manifestly frivolous or hopeless claim.

Everybody agreed that it is neither in the interest of international arbitration nor its users if a framework of dispute resolution that advertises efficiency was incapable of swiftly disposing of obviously bogus claims. In addition to a claimant's right of access to justice, all participants recognized a corresponding right of the respondent to be free from arbitration that lacks merit, and protection from having to defend against clearly hopeless claims. The need to balance these interests warrants the existence of procedural filters such as motions to dismiss, summary judgment or more broadly early disposition mechanisms. Where a claim is manifestly without legal or factual basis, compelling a respondent to arbitrate through a full evidentiary proceeding undermines efficiency and procedural fairness.

## 4. Countering the Risks of Early Disposition Mechanisms

The anecdotal evidence exchanged around the table suggested two things: (i) most practitioners had experienced what they labelled as "clearly hopeless" claims by a (counter) party in an arbitration or court proceeding. (ii) Nobody – or, erring on the side of caution: hardly anybody – had experienced that such claims were "thrown out" early by an arbitral tribunal. How is this possible when more and more arbitration rules expressly allow for early disposition and most agreed that the arbitral tribunal probably has the power

[11]) For a brief discussion on the different opinions on this point, see Wallach, *supra*, at 840.

to dispose of claims early even without express codification through the arbitration rules? The participants agreed that concerns about pre-judgment and bias perception remain central to the reluctance to employ early disposition.

The following sections describe what the participants considered to be (necessary) roadblocks to the application of early disposition, and how these challenges could be overcome (and if they should be).

### a) Threshold of Manifest Unmeritorious Claims

The discussion revealed a shared perception that the manifestly without merit standard, which informs many sets of arbitration rules, is high and so vaguely defined that it will be difficult to confidently apply it in practice. Considering the head start of ICSID in the adoption of early disposition rules compared to all other arbitral institutions, it is not surprising that ICSID awards until today shape the body of precedent of what is considered manifest absence of (legal) merit. The relevant case law essentially describes a vague standard with further terms that are no more clear: whether a claim is manifestly without legal merit should be clear and obvious.[12]) In contrast, ICSID precedent confirms that early disposition *"is not intended to resolve novel, difficult or disputed legal issues, but instead only to apply undisputed or genuinely indisputable rules of law to uncontested facts"*.[13]) Yet at the same time, ICSID case law accepts that *"this exercise may not always be simple"*,[14]) and *"may thus be complicated, but it should never be difficult"*.[15])

The participants discussed that the undoubtedly high threshold which limits early disposition to very clear-cut cases is needed to offset the finality of such decisions in an arbitration context. By contrast, court decisions applying similar mechanisms are usually appealable. While this does not change the fact that decisions disposing of claims should be correct, the existence of a second chance was considered by the participants to be conducive to an increased use of such mechanisms.

One practitioner remarked that the goal is not to conduct mini-trials under the guise of early disposition, but to filter claims that clearly fail as a matter of law, thus making a very high threshold necessary. Others remarked that three sets of lawyers will hardly ever agree that a critical question is "clear and obvious" when one party stands to lose – at least a claim – as a result.

---

[12]) *Trans-Global Petroleum, Inc. v. The Hashemite Kingdom of Jordan,* ICSID Case No. ARB/07/25, Decision on the Respondent's Objection under Rule 41(5) of the ICSID Arbitration Rules. para. 90 (12 May 2008).

[13]) *PNG Sustainable Dev. Program Ltd. v. Indep. State of Papua N.G.*, ICSID Case No. ARB/13/33, Decision on the Respondent's Objections under Rule 41(5) of the ICSID Arbitration Rules, para. 89 (28 October 2014); cf. also *Mainstream Renewable Power Ltd. & Others v. Fed. Republic of Ger.*, ICSID Case No. ARB/21/26, Decision on the Respondent's Application under Arbitration Rule 41(5), para. 61 (30 June 2022).

[14]) *Trans-Global v. Jordan,* para. 90.

[15]) *Ibid.*

Accordingly, it was discussed that the standard may – more than being high – also be too opaque to be operational, especially for counsel and arbitrators who are not used to early disposition as a matter of their legal background and training.

With the threshold being what it is and should be, the participants overall speculated that over time, the body of precedent of early dispositions will grow and – provided the relevant decisions can be accessed by a wider public – the nuances of the threshold will become clearer, which in turn may entail more confidence in applying early disposition mechanisms by parties and arbitral tribunals alike.

### b) Unjustified Stigma and Lack of Experience

The experience of the majority of the participants suggests that there appears to be a marked cultural difference between arbitrators when it comes to their willingness to pro-actively address a potential (partial) resolution of the dispute before the award stage. While arbitrators from certain common law systems have been perceived as comparatively comfortable with classic early disposition tools, in particular German arbitrators have been experienced to be very open to offering various avenues of narrowing down – if not settling – disputes before the award stage. Short of that, one participant suggested that employing *"Rechtsgespräch"*-style early dialogues with the parties to clarify legal issues *without* formal determination might yield the same result as more harsh early determination mechanisms, but on a more consensus-driven basis.

Not just the legal tradition but also the professional background of arbitrators was seen as determinative of their level of comfort dealing with early determination. By way of example, most participants considered experienced state court judges to be more eager to engage in such discussions. However, there appears to still be a (perceived) great overall reluctance of arbitrators to even expressly prompt the parties to *consider* the option of early disposition. It was suggested that arbitrators fear that addressing such option in an environment where this is not standard practice at the outset of most arbitrations might suggest that the arbitrator considers there might be grounds for early disposition in the particular case, which in turn might create a perception of bias or pre-judgment of the case in the parties.

The group discussed that, while these concerns may not be fully rational, arbitral institutions could be instrumental in "de-stigmatizing" early disposition mechanisms, for example by providing more detailed guidance on specific points that should be discussed at the preparatory meeting and how potential processes could look like. This would open the door for arbitrators to raise such options for party consideration as a matter of course, without fear of being perceived as biased or pre-judgmental, and it would perhaps increase their confidence in structuring the proceedings and actually handling any such requests. This could contribute to leveling the playing field when it comes to arbitrators' legal background and professional experience mentioned above.

### c) Alignment of Expectations and Procedural Transparency

Participants agreed that for early disposition mechanisms to be received well in practice, it is imperative to consider the consensual nature of arbitration. The group discussed that the express inclusion of such mechanisms in institutional rules provides a first anchor point for party agreement that early disposition might be an option if parties opt to conduct their arbitration under such rules.

While the existence of specific early disposition clauses – considering their relative novelty and sparing application in practice – may not be specifically known to parties when they opt for a particular set of rules, the preparatory meeting provides another natural opportunity for arbitral tribunals to discuss this potential avenue with the parties at a very early stage of the arbitration.

Participants debated the optimal procedural moment for early disposition. While ICSID requires applications within 30 days of the constitution of the arbitral tribunal, commercial arbitrations often allow greater flexibility. If the goal is to promote an increased willingness to consider and apply early disposition in practice, it is essential that the relevant applications are not tied to too short deadlines early on. The rules of most arbitral institutions are more lenient than the ICSID Rules when it comes to cut-off dates for applications for early disposition, thus mirroring this sentiment. Overall, some participants favored permitting applications after the Terms of Reference but before document production, striking a balance between informed decision-making and time savings. Others proposed that tribunals themselves could invite party submissions on potentially dispositive issues identified during early case assessment. While party consent remains advisable, such proactive engagement can enhance procedural economy without undermining neutrality.

Sequencing requests for early determination in two phases – leave to apply, and if granted, merits of the application, as done in the SIAC rules was considered helpful to increase predictability of the process and parties' confidence in the ultimate outcome, as they would get two clearly delineated opportunities to be heard on the application, thus avoiding a blindsiding effect, and would ultimately receive (if the motion should proceed) two reasoned decisions explaining the outcome. Of course, it was also mentioned that adding another step in the process might require an efficient and confident tribunal. Overly cautious tribunals may prolong early determination proceedings unnecessarily, defeating the efficiency goal.

### d) Costs as a Steering Tool

From a party perspective, early disposition serves not only as a procedural shortcut but as a strategic lever. Experienced counsel may use it to narrow issues, signal case confidence, or induce settlement discussions. However, participants cautioned that less sophisticated parties or inexperienced counsel might perceive such applications as aggressive or even unethical, potentially escalating costs instead of reducing them. Participants suggested that effective applications should target discrete legal issues, clearly identify the governing standard, and frame the request as a contribution to procedural economy rather than a tactical ambush.

Participants suggested that the threat of potential cost consequences or even orders to provide security for costs may provide a filter for meritless tactical applications. Participants also discussed the relationship between early disposition and interim or preliminary cost orders. By allocating costs progressively, tribunals can subtly encourage parties to focus on the most material disputes. While such practices require cautious implementation, they reflect the increasing managerial role of modern arbitral tribunals.

However, in line with the previous sections, participants agreed that whether costs work as efficient steering tools (within the scope of what they can possibly achieve) will often again hinge on the experience of the arbitral tribunal, their confidence in pro-actively structuring the proceedings and their willingness to align expectations with parties early on.

## 5. Conclusion – Balancing Efficiency and Fairness

The discussion at the Vienna Arbitration Days 2025 World Café Session confirmed that early disposition remains rarely utilized, not due to lack of legal authority but due to cultural caution and limited experience within the arbitral community. At a systemic level, participants emphasized the need for data transparency. Institutions rarely publish statistics on early disposition, leading to a persistent perception that the mechanism is risky. Collecting anonymized case examples, publishing procedural models, and offering educational outreach could normalize use and build jurisprudential consistency. In parallel, institutions might consider integrating soft-law guidance – such as indicative timeframes or cost principles – to reduce hesitation among arbitrators unfamiliar with the concept.

Participants agreed that efficiency and fairness are not competing imperatives but mutually reinforcing objectives when guided by procedural clarity and transparent reasoning.

Three insights emerged as common ground: (1) Confidence and clarity: tribunals should not fear allegations of bias when acting within a defined procedural framework; (2) Design and discipline: institutions should continue refining rule texts and guidance to ensure predictable, fair thresholds; and

(3) Transparency and communication: reasoned orders and proactive case management can reconcile efficiency with due process.

Ultimately, early disposition represents both an opportunity and a responsibility: when used prudently, it strengthens rather than compromises the legitimacy of international arbitration. The group saw a potential to improve the targeted use of early disposition mechanisms, while confirming that it's exceptional character in the context of the inherent finality of arbitration provides a logical barrier to broad adoption.

## C. Balancing the Iron Triangle: Practical Strategies for Aligning Speed, Cost and Quality in International Arbitration

*Petra Pataki/Borna Dejanović*

### 1. Introduction: The Iron Triangle

International arbitration has long been hailed as the faster and more cost-effective alternative to litigation. As procedural layers have multiplied and the financial and reputational stakes have risen, users remain focused on ensuring that the process continues to deliver on its original promise. The concept of the "Iron Triangle" provides a useful framework for articulating this challenge: speed, cost, and quality exist in constant motion, and strengthening one element may result in strain on the others.[16])

During the World Café session at the Vienna Arbitration Days 2025, our table brought together a diverse group of participants: in-house counsel from various industries, experienced arbitrators, counsel from both international and regional law firms, as well as representatives of arbitral institutions. The mix ensured that the conversation reflected not only different procedural traditions but also distinct incentives and pressures that shape how each stakeholder perceives efficiency in practice.

The discussion that unfolded at our table revealed both convergence and contrast in how participants approach the balance between time, cost, and quality. The sections that follow distil those insights: first, by examining how the components of the Iron Triangle are understood by different actors

[16]) The "Iron Triangle" in international arbitration is frequently employed as an analytical model and framework for analyses and discussions among scholars and practitioners (*see*, *e.g.*, Prof. William W. Park, *Arbitrators and Accuracy*, 1(1) J. Int'l Disp. Settlement 25 (2010), Dr Joerg Risse, *Ten Drastic Proposals for Saving Time and Costs in Arbitral Proceedings*, 29(3) Arb. Int'l 453 (2013), Jennifer Kirby, *Efficiency in International Arbitration: Whose Duty Is It?*, 32(6) J. Int. Arb. 689, Hafez R Virjee, *A Circle For A Triangle – Geometry In Aid Of Efficiency In International Arbitration*, (2021) Delos Dispute Resolution).

[Chapter 2]; second, by exploring strategies and innovations that have proved effective in practice [Chapter 3] third, by considering the respective roles and responsibilities of key stakeholders [Chapter 4]; and finally, by reflecting on what these perspectives may suggest for arbitration's ongoing effort to reconcile efficiency with legitimacy [Chapter 5].

## 2. Understanding the Components of the Triangle

Before turning to concrete strategies, we examined how the three dimensions of the Iron Triangle are defined in practice. While "speed", "cost", and "quality" appear intuitive, the discussions revealed a nuanced understanding, with differing defining elements by users. Moreover, the participants demonstrated differing views on ranking the three pillars under the Iron Triangle, as well as regarding which constituent aspect is most compromised in practice.

### a) Speed

For in-house counsel, speed was often described as the most visible measure of value. Corporate users, particularly from industries with fast changing and complex commercial relationships, spoke of the practical cost of delay: stalled projects, suspended cash flow and uncertainty on financial reporting, especially during on-going projects. One participant suggested that *"delayed decision may lead to a contractual relationship destroyed"*.

Arbitrators, in contrast, warned against equating speed with efficiency. Several experienced arbitrators observed that genuine time efficiency arises not from compressed deadlines, but from disciplined management and clear communication. They noted that party cooperation at the outset (especially during procedural scheduling) prevents the later friction that generally creates real delay.

Practitioners from civil law traditions expressed greater comfort with firm timetables and limited discovery, while common law participants tended to equate procedural flexibility with fairness.

### b) Cost

High cost of proceedings is seen as a major concern for stakeholders in international arbitration.

The discussion on cost seemed tied to the notion of transparency. In-house participants voiced concern at the unpredictability of legal and expert fees, which they described as *"the black box of arbitration"*. They advocated for budget discipline and early case assessment as the most valuable precursors.

Counsel, on the other hand, cautioned that cost cannot be isolated from strategy. *"Efficiency is not always cheap"*, one practitioner remarked. Cutting submissions or expert input too aggressively may produce a false economy if it compromises the persuasiveness or enforceability of the result.

Arbitrators offered yet another angle: they noted that parties often over-invest in procedural moves and unnecessary advocacy, while under-investing in early settlement or narrowing of issues. The tribunal's ability to nudge parties toward proportionate expenditure, particularly through early case conferences, was seen as an underused tool.

### c) Quality

The participants demonstrated a differing understanding of the notion of quality, in terms of the fairness of the process and the outcome. While the correctness of the award and the procedural fairness appeared non-controversial, related aspects such as party satisfaction and enforceability implications appear to play an important role in defining the quality segment.

While lengthy reasoned awards might hypothetically imply quality of the arbitration, some participants argued that this might appear problematic if taking too long, especially in relation to overlapping business relationships and considering the inherent issues in the enforcement stage, which oftentimes becomes impossible. Accordingly, some participants voiced their preference that quality might also amount to a faster and cheaper result allowing the parties to move forward, rather than having an elaborate award after a lengthy and costly arbitration.

Despite the arguably diverging viewpoints, the participants ultimately agreed that cutting time and cost should not compromise the fact-finding integrity and the fairness of the outcome.

## 3. Strategies to Efficiency: Lessons from Practice

Having clarified the competing priorities that shape perceptions of efficiency, the conversation opened to practical experiences. Participants exchanged examples of strategies and procedural innovations that have helped them rebalance the Iron Triangle in real cases. These ranged from institutional steps to individual techniques applied by tribunals, counsel, and parties.

### a) Tribunal Composition and Arbitrator Selection

Participants agreed that the composition of the tribunal remains one of the earliest and most consequential choices affecting both cost and timing. Corporate representatives showed a growing willingness to appoint sole arbitrators for mid-value or technically straightforward disputes, provided that institutional safeguards for review exist. In contrast, counsel handling complex, fact-heavy matters noted the benefits of three-member tribunals for the diversity of perspective and deliberative rigour they provide.

The group also examined the familiar question of availability versus eminence. Well-known arbitrators seem to experience scheduling difficulties, with the use of tribunal secretaries being on the rise. Participants were divided on this trend. Several in-house counsel questioned whether the premium on reputation always translates into quality, asking candidly whether they would trade a famous name for a faster award. Arbitrators themselves acknowledged that timeliness should become a visible part of professional reputation. Institutional representatives observed that some arbitral institutions now collect and publish data on average time to award, signalling that efficiency may soon be valued as highly as prestige.

The discussion turned to diversity, which several participants described as improving, but not at desired levels. Gender balance among arbitrators has improved in the past decade but remains uneven across institutions and case types. Counsels noted that clients are sometimes less likely to appoint female practitioners and are generally more drawn to tried and tested names, who are usually male. Some participants from Central and Eastern Europe observed that practitioners from their region remain underrepresented in prominent appointments, while jurisdictions such as Switzerland or France continue to dominate international rosters.

### b) Tailored Case Management

Across the discussions, there was near-unanimous agreement that proactive case management remains the single most effective way to balance time, cost, and quality. Tribunals that truly seek to tailor procedure to the dispute, rather than defaulting to standards, tend to achieve proportionate processes and greater party satisfaction.

Practitioners shared examples of effective techniques: limiting document production to categories that are both relevant and material; imposing page limits and restricting the number of written submissions; and insisting on detailed procedural timetables that are rigorously enforced. Consolidation and joinder were cited as tools that, when used judiciously, prevent duplication and inconsistent findings.

Arbitrators described how chess-clock hearings, which allocate equal blocks of time to each side, help focus advocacy and reduce interruptions. The consensus was that firmness, coupled with early consultation, is the key to efficiency. Tribunals earn authority not by asserting control but by exercising it predictably and transparently.

### c) Expedited and Fast-Track Procedures

Participants reported that fast-track rules are now being considered in a broader range of cases, not only small-value disputes, but resorting to such procedures is not automatic or without hesitation. Participants recognised the trade-offs inherent in such mechanisms. Shorter time frames and limited submissions can be highly effective for disputes that turn mainly on documents, but they may be unsuitable for matters requiring extensive evidence or complex legal analysis.

Some participants from emerging arbitration markets noted a cultural reluctance toward abbreviated procedures, which are sometimes perceived as limiting advocacy. Yet users with experience in well-run expedited cases observed that, when expectations are clear, a faster process can maintain both fairness and quality. The collective view was that expedited procedures should remain optional and guided by case complexity rather than by monetary thresholds.

### d) Early Dismissal and Procedural Efficiency

Several arbitrators shared that they have become more comfortable disposing of manifestly unmeritorious claims or defences at an early stage. Far from undermining due process, this practice was seen as reinforcing it by keeping proceedings focused on issues that truly warrant determination.

Counsel reactions were mixed. Some valued the predictability and savings in cost, while others warned that premature dismissal may erode confidence if used too readily. The prevailing sentiment was pragmatic. Early disposal is valuable when applied only to clear-cut cases and accompanied by detailed reasoning. Participants agreed that institutions can encourage judicious use of summary powers by providing model guidance and confirming that such decisions, when reasoned, do not breach due process.

### e) Technology and Virtual Hearings

Technology was singled out as a major driver of efficiency, though participants also observed some drawbacks. In-house counsel praised virtual hearings for eliminating travel costs and accelerating scheduling. Arbitrators found digital platforms particularly effective for preliminary meetings and short procedural hearings. Counsels noted that searchable electronic bundles changed the way they work.

However, several counsel warned that online hearings can accentuate disparities in advocacy resources, as smaller teams may lack dedicated technical support. Others countered that virtual formats have in fact levelled the playing field, allowing regional counsel to appear in major cases without the burden of travel. Arbitrators agreed that while virtual tools are invaluable for logistics, complex evidentiary hearings still benefit from physical presence. The shared conclusion was that technology should be used with purpose, not by default.

Discussions on AI reflected both enthusiasm and restraint. Younger practitioners reported using AI tools for document review, translation and transcription, significantly accelerating preparation. Arbitrators and institutional representatives, while recognising these efficiencies, highlighted the need for confidentiality safeguards and human oversight.

There was broad agreement that AI can contribute to the management and handling of a case but cannot replace human judgment and oversight. Tasks involving factual synthesis, credibility assessment or legal reasoning must remain in the hands of counsel and tribunals. As one participant put it, *"AI may quicken the pace, but it must never dictate the process"*.

#### f) Culture and Attitude of Stakeholders

Participants agreed that inefficiency in arbitration rarely stems from defective rules; it is often a by-product of excessive caution. Arbitrators fear challenges against awards, counsel fear client criticism, and institutions fear user dissatisfaction. The result is a culture of over-caution.

Participants called for a collective realignment of incentives that rewards proportionality instead of verbosity and decisiveness instead of deference, respectively. Several institutions have already begun experimenting with tangible incentives for efficient conduct. Some link tribunal fees to performance, offering higher remuneration when awards are rendered within agreed timelines and applying reductions in cases of unjustified delay. Others use post-case feedback or time-tracking mechanisms to promote accountability and transparency.

Education and mentoring were also highlighted as essential levers for long-term change. The next generation of practitioners and arbitrators must be trained to view efficiency as a marker of professional excellence rather than a procedural risk.

### 4. Stakeholders in the Triangle: Shared Responsibilities

The discussion revealed how differently each group perceives its own role in maintaining balance. Parties and clients recognised that they often contribute to inefficiency through over-lawyering or risk aversion, with an inherent tension between claimants and respondents. Many accepted that genuine change must begin with realistic expectations at the contract stage, by choosing the appropriate institution, the right tribunal size and clear procedural clauses.

Counsel reflected candidly on their dual role as advocates and custodians of efficiency. Some admitted that adversarial reflexes still drive unnecessary procedural disputes, especially where *"guerilla tactics"* are employed. Others highlighted that cooperation between opposing counsel on procedural logistics can dramatically reduce time and cost without compromising advocacy.

Arbitrators acknowledged that efficiency ultimately depends also on their willingness and capability to manage the process actively. In particular, efficient conduct of arbitration often depends on the tribunal's internal dynamics and arbitrator cooperation, with the diligent management of their own workload. Several observed that transparency about reasoning, explaining why certain requests are denied, builds party confidence even when rulings are firm.

Institutions were widely credited as catalysts for change. Representatives shared experiences with rule amendments introducing expedited tracks, time limits for awards, as well as rewards for efficiency and consequences for delay. Participants agreed that institutions are uniquely positioned to embed efficiency as a norm rather than an exception.

Beyond procedural technique, several participants reflected on diversity as a factor that influences both quality and perception of fairness. Participants noted that gender diversity among arbitrators has improved in the past decade but remains uneven across institutions and case types. Geographical representation drew sharper criticism with preferred jurisdictions and "arbitration friendly" regimes.

The discussion agreed that diverse tribunals tend to bring complementary approaches to case management, leading to more adaptable procedures and enhanced party trust. Institutional representatives confirmed that user demand for diversity is increasingly shaping appointment practices.

## 5. Conclusions

The World Café concluded with an acknowledgment that the Iron Triangle is not a zero-sum model. While perfect balance may be theoretical, conscious calibration should always be exercised. Efficiency, in the collective view of participants, is not synonymous with speed or austerity. It is about proportionality: allocating procedural attention in line with what truly matters to the dispute.

This requires confidence and trust. Tribunals must trust that firm procedural decisions will not be punished on enforcement, under the often seen "*due process paranoia*" dilemma. Counsel must resist the instinct to litigate every procedural detail. Clients must internalise that "faster" and "cheaper" are not sufficient results in themselves, but only pathways to a credible result.

As one senior arbitrator observed during the closing discussion, arbitration need not be faster or cheaper than litigation, but it must be worth the time and cost it demands. The Iron Triangle remains a fitting metaphor for the arbitral process: its strength lies not in rigid perfection along any single side, but in equilibrium across all three. Viewed not as a constraint but as a compass, the Iron Triangle can continue to guide the evolution of arbitration toward a practice that is both principled and practical.

# D. How Can Mediation Serve as a Catalyst for More Efficient Dispute Resolution? – Unlocking Value Through Mediation in Commercial Disputes.

*Camilla Perera – de Wit/Anna Weinzierl*

## 1. Introduction

In recent years, the use of mediation as a dispute resolution mechanism has garnered popularity. Yet the level of uptake can differ significantly per jurisdiction, depending on the legal culture and the legal framework. At a national level, mediation can get addressed through a variety of legislative or procedural approaches.

In Austria, for example, in the context of commercial disputes, mediation is slowly gaining increased popularity in recent years. In 2004, Austria enacted its first mediation law, exclusively addressing mediation in civil law matters (Civil Law Mediation Act). This codification of mediation law also served as a model for the development of mediation legislation in other EU member states.[17]) Austrian state court judges are however not obligated to require parties to mediate but must merely encourage settlement discussions between the parties during the first hearing.[18]) Additionally, in Vienna, some courts are currently testing the use of so-called "*judicial settlement proceedings*" ("*gerichtliche Einigungsverfahren*"), offering parties the possibility to interrupt any ongoing litigation proceedings to engage in mediation proceedings with separate judges acting as mediators.

In the Netherlands, as another example, the Directive 2008/52/EC, focused on cross-border civil and commercial mediation, was implemented into the Dutch Code of Civil Procedure and the Dutch Civil Code in 2012. Despite several efforts, this implementation did not lead to further specific legislation with respect to mediation. Dutch courts may propose mediation as a means of resolving disputes, however it is typically not mandated. Although mediation is not the standard approach in corporate disputes, it is a current evolving landscape due to companies seeking greater efficiency and reduced legal costs in resolving their disputes. Moreover, in a recent judgment, the Dutch Supreme Court clarified that mediation clauses can be binding and/or enforceable if the mediation clause stipulates that parties are required to attempt mediation prior to proceedings.[19]) This judgement has strengthened

---

[17]) Günther J. Horvath, Katherine Khan, et al., *Chapter 10: Michael Moser's Journey in Mediation: The 'Triple-A' Approach*, in Neil Kaplan, Michael Pryles, et al. (eds.), International Arbitration: When East Meets West –Liber Amicorum Michael Moser (2020) 121.

[18]) *See* Section 258 Austrian Code of Civil Procedure.

[19]) Supreme Court, 12 July 2024, ECLI:NL:HR:2024:1078.

the position of mediation in the Netherlands.[20]) Moreover, in 2024 a research study, conducted in cooperation with Platform Business Mediation, concluded that both lawyers and companies in the Netherlands have gained more experience with business mediation in recent years, mainly in the areas of labor disputes, shareholder disputes, and commercial conflicts between companies. From this study, it appeared that familiarity breeds affection; once a party has experienced mediation it is more open to using mediation again.[21])

Roundtable participants from the United Arab Emirates explained on this note that mediation is still in its early stages of development in the UAE, largely because the state courts are working highly efficiently. Similarly, Austria traditionally has a tendency for litigation or arbitration proceedings, partly due to the comparatively highly efficient state court system.[22]) The discussion highlighted a connection between court efficiency and the growing popularity of mediation, driven by a shared objective of achieving more efficient dispute resolution.

On a related note, and having recognized the possible advantages of mediation as a complementary mechanism next to arbitration, arbitral institutions are increasingly expanding their offerings to include mediation services by providing model clauses to its users, either as stand-alone mediation clauses or as part of multi-tiered dispute resolution clauses, as well as support with respect to the appointment of qualified mediators and guidance through dedicated mediation rules.[23])

These initial observations led us to the very core of the roundtable discussion and the *Gretchenfrage:* How can mediation be used to serve as a catalyst for more efficient dispute resolution? The authors were happy to welcome participants from different regions around the world – amongst others from Croatia, UAE, Greece, Poland, Hungary, Ukraine, the Netherlands, Germany and Austria – providing valuable insights which have been compiled in this article.

[20]) Peter Kamminga & Bart Fleuren, *Chapter 12: Corporate Mediation: The Dutch Approach to Mediation vs. Anglo-American Practices and the Enforceability of Mediation Clauses*, in Carla Klaassen, Gerard J. Meijer, et al. (eds), Arbitration in the Netherlands, in Particular NAI Arbitration, Serie Onderneming en Recht (Volume 158, 2025), 310.

[21]) *See* https://platformbusinessmediation.nl/wp-content/uploads/2024/04/PBM-Onderzoeksrapport-4-2024.pdf, p. 75/ (accessed on 23 September 2025).

[22]) Horvath, Khan, et al., *Michael Moser's Journey in Mediation*, *supra*, at 120.

[23]) *See, e.g.,* https://www.viac.eu/en/mediation-basics/mediation-rules/; https://www.hkiac.org/mediation; https://iccwbo.org/dispute-resolution/dispute-resolution-services/adr/mediation/mediation-rules/; https://nai.nl/nai-mediation-rules/ (all accessed on 23 September 2025).

## 2. Unleashing the Potential of Mediation in Complex Commercial Disputes

### a) Why Use Mediation?

The roundtable participants shared their experiences with the use of mediation in resolving disputes, focusing on the advantages and pitfalls they have encountered in mediation proceedings. We will share the identified benefits and drawbacks in this section.

One of the main benefits of mediation proceedings shared by the participants is its efficient nature, being generally faster and less costly than arbitration. At the same time, mediation allows for the preservation of business relationships while adversarial means of dispute resolution – potentially costly and protracted – frequently result in irreparable breakdowns between parties.

Furthermore, the participants highlighted the flexible and informal nature of mediation, noting that this structure not only fosters open dialogue but also creates a more conducive environment for uncovering underlying interests, concerns, and issues that may remain hidden in more formalistic and adversarial processes such as arbitration and litigation. On a related note, many of the participants shared that mediation often helps in disputes with heightened emotions as it provides a structured yet supportive space for dialogue – even in situations where previous negotiations have failed to establish common ground.

Despite its benefits, mediation also presents several drawbacks. One limitation that was referred to quickly was the status of the enforceability of settlement agreements. By contrast, global enforceability of arbitral awards is regarded as one of the most important advantages in international arbitration and a key reason why parties choose arbitration for their cross-border disputes.[24]) Currently, and especially for international disputes, mediation does not offer the same advantages as only a limited number of countries have currently ratified the Singapore Convention on Mediation (2019).[25]) With the Singapore Convention on Mediation being more recent, it is still viewed as being in its early stages.

Another identified drawback was the impact of – and experience with – poorly drafted multi-tiered dispute resolution clauses. Such clauses can be used to challenge the admissibility of the arbitration or the jurisdiction of the tribunal, based on claims that a prior procedural step was not properly fulfilled. On this note, participants also highlighted that poorly drafted mediation clauses can similarly negatively affect the entire dispute resolution process.

---

[24]) *See* 1958 – Convention on the Recognition and Enforcement of Foreign Arbitral Awards ("The New York Convention").

[25]) *See* United Nations Convention on International Settlement Agreements Resulting from Mediation ("Singapore Convention on Mediation").

Participants also found that mediation – in contrast to the previously identified advantage of creating space to talk – may proof inefficient if a dispute has already evolved too far with parties being unwilling to engage in meaningful settlement discussions. In such cases, mediation proceedings are likely to delay the final resolution of the dispute.

Concerns were similarly expressed regarding the confidentiality of the documents and information shared during mediation proceedings, specifically in case the mediation remains unsuccessful, and the parties move on to arbitration or litigation. Finally, some participants pointed out that the choice of counsel can also negatively impact the success of the mediation procedure, as some counsels are not able or not willing to look beyond the legal matter at hand and engage in the process of finding a solution through mediation.

Related to some of these drawbacks and what makes a mediation process (un)successful, the authors also want to highlight the importance of a skilled mediator. More specifically, in complex commercial disputes there seems to be a growing call for proactive mediators who actively guide the discussions and think along as regards possible solutions.[26]) In the United States, for example, the evaluative style of mediating disputes is the most common approach in corporate disputes, with the mediator often having sound legal expertise and insight into likely court outcomes. In the Netherlands, there is an increased preference of the evaluative style (as opposed to merely facilitating), particularly in complex multi-party, multi-issue and cross border disputes, as this reflects better the need for timely resolutions and legal certainty.[27]) Appointing the right mediator for the dispute at hand can make a difference in how the parties experience the overall process.

### b) Which Disputes Benefit from Mediation?

In principle, mediation is suitable for the resolution of almost any kind of dispute across various sectors, including family, commercial, governmental, financial, employment matters and more.[28]) During the course of the discussions, some participants, however, expressed that certain kinds of disputes may benefit more from the possible advantages of mediation proceedings than others.

[26]) *See* https://platformbusinessmediation.nl/wp-content/uploads/2024/04/PBM-Onderzoeksrapport-4-2024.pdf, p. 77. (accessed on 23 September 2025).

[27]) Peter Kamminga & Bart Fleuren, *Chapter 12: Corporate Mediation: The Dutch Approach to Mediation vs. Anglo-American Practices and the Enforceability of Mediation Clauses*, in Carla Klaassen, Gerard J. Meijer, et al. (eds), Arbitration in the Netherlands, in Particular NAI Arbitration, Serie Onderneming en Recht (Volume 158, 2025), 292.

[28]) Carrie Menkel-Meadow, *Chapter 3: The Future of Mediation Worldwide: Legal and Cultural Variations in the Uptake of or Resistance to Mediation*, in Ian Macduff (ed.), Essays on Mediation: Dealing with Disputes in the 21st Century, Global Trends in Dispute Resolution (Volume 6, 2016) 29.

Apart from the traditional field of family law, where mediation has long been an established means of dispute resolution, the participants generally found that disputes which mainly concern factual issues may be well suited for being resolved through mediation proceedings. Furthermore, disputes involving parties engaged in longstanding and ongoing business relationships or disputes concerning ongoing projects are often well-suited for mediation. These kinds of disputes generally benefit from holistic solutions which take into account that the parties typically value not only the resolution of the immediate dispute but also preserve their broader commercial relationship. Mediation offers the flexibility to craft holistic solutions that address both legal and relational dimensions of the conflict.

Additionally, some participants pointed out that claims seeking specific performance as opposed to monetary damages may benefit from the flexibility of mediation proceedings, allowing for practical, tailored, and forward-looking outcomes.

### c) Mediation and Arbitration: A Perfect Match?

Having established at the roundtable that mediation may present benefits in terms of flexibility and preserving business relationships but at the same time holds certain disadvantages, for example with respect to the enforcement stage, the discussion turned to the question of whether the use of hybrid mechanisms can promote increased efficiency in the resolution of disputes.[29)]

Hybrid mechanisms are dispute resolution processes combining two or more means of dispute resolution, such as mediation and arbitration. Practice has shown that these hybrid mechanisms can take a variety of forms. Commonly used hybrid mechanisms include "Med-Arb", "Arb-Med" or "Arb-Med-Arb".[30)]

"Med-Arb" commonly refers to a two-step dispute resolution process which may be used in two different scenarios. First, parties will try to resolve their disputes in mediation proceedings. In case the parties are unable to resolve (all) disputes in mediation, they will initiate arbitration proceedings. If the parties are able to resolve their disputes in mediation, they may still turn to arbitration to finalize their settlement agreement in the form of an enforceable arbitral award, enhancing enforcement in those cases. This model is typically seen as attractive by users because it combines the flexibility of mediation with the finality and enforceability of arbitration.

---

29) For a more detailed exploration of multi-tiered dispute resolution clauses/escalation clauses, *see* Klaus Peter Berger, *Law and Practice of Escalation Clauses, supra*; Michael Pryles, *Multi-Tiered Dispute Resolution Clauses, supra*.

30) *See* Hiroyuki Tezuka, *Chapter 23: Rise of Hybrid Arbitration/Mediation in the Era of the Singapore Mediation Convention*, in Neil Kaplan, Michael Pryles, et al. (eds.), International Arbitration: When East Meets West – Liber Amicorum Michael Moser (2020), 279.

"Arb-Med" commonly refers to a dispute resolution process that starts with arbitration proceedings, followed by mediation (if desired) during the ongoing arbitration to save time and costs. This hybrid mechanism may also be used to prevent the expiration of any statute of limitations.[31]) As another alternative, parties may also include clauses in their contracts providing that mediation proceedings take place at a specific point in the arbitration proceedings, *e.g.*, after the parties' first round of substantive submissions or following document production.

Finally, "Arb-Med-Arb" combines the two preceding hybrid models. Parties will first initiate arbitration proceedings, followed by a separate mediation process. If the parties fail to reach a settlement, they will continue the already initiated arbitral proceedings. Should the parties find a settlement, however, they have the option to finalize their agreement in the form of an enforceable arbitral award.

The International Dispute Resolution Survey 2024 performed by the Singapore International Dispute Resolution Academy ("SIDRA") confirms that parties choose hybrid dispute resolution mechanisms over standalone mediation for reasons of procedural flexibility, enforceability and finality. Similarly, if parties choose hybrid mechanisms over standalone arbitration, they do so – amongst other things – for reasons of efficiency, confidentiality, procedural flexibility and the preservation of business relationships.[32])

Invited to share their experiences or perceptions of hybrid dispute resolution mechanisms, the participants of the roundtable shared wide range views on whether hybrid mechanisms, specifically multi-tiered dispute resolution clauses, contribute to efficient dispute resolution.

On the one hand, some participants – including the authors – reported positive experiences in the use of hybrid dispute resolution models. Several participants specifically shared experiences of commercial disputes that were effectively resolved through contractual multi-tiered dispute resolution clauses incorporating a mandatory mediation phase. Notably, in some cases, parties were able to reach an agreement during mediation, despite having previously engaged in extensive but unsuccessful negotiations. This highlights the added value mediation can bring even when prior direct discussions have failed to produce results.

On the other hand, some participants expressed skepticism regarding multi-tiered dispute resolution clauses, particularly in scenarios where one party is unwilling to engage in good-faith settlement discussions or has no genuine interest in reaching an amicable resolution. It was noted that, in such cases, mandatory mediation requirements may be exploited by the un-

---

[31]) *Id.* at 280.

[32]) *SIDRA International Dispute Resolution Survey: 2024 Final Report*, available at: https://sidra.smu.edu.sg/sites/sidra.smu.edu.sg/files/survey-2024/SIDRA_Final_Report_2024.pdf (accessed on 9 September 2025).

cooperative party as a tactical tool to delay proceedings. This strategic misuse can obstruct progress and undermine the effectiveness of the dispute resolution process, ultimately wasting time and delaying access to arbitration.

However, as also pointed out during the discussion, part of the skepticism can be addressed through the proper drafting of the multi-tiered dispute resolution clause.[33]) We will address this point in the next section.

### d) A Short Guide for Drafting Multi-Tiered Dispute Resolution Clauses

Correct drafting of a multi-tiered dispute resolution clause is crucial for an effective and efficient dispute resolution process.[34]) Poorly conducted mediations – *e.g.*, due to poorly drafted clauses – can backfire, leading to longer and more costly procedures. Mediation clauses which include broad and unclear language or, for instance, give the parties little time to successfully attempt mediation, can provide the gateway for dilatory tactics and unnecessary, burdensome and futile procedures without results. The following points should be carefully considered when drafting a multi-tiered dispute resolution clause.

First, it is essential to use clear and unambiguous wording to establish that mediation is to be understood as a mandatory pre-trial step. Such clear wording may include phrases such as that the parties "shall" or "must" attempt mediation before moving to arbitration/litigation.

Secondly, any multi-tiered dispute resolution clause should clearly establish how far the parties' obligation to mediate goes. Specifically, parties should establish which steps they need to take before initiating arbitration or litigation proceedings. As an example, the clause may require parties to appoint a mediator, to attend a first substantive meeting under the participation of the mediator, or to conclude a mediation agreement before initiating arbitration/litigation.

It would be similarly desirable to establish a fixed period of time for the conduct of the mediation proceedings before parties are allowed to initiate arbitration/litigation proceedings.[35])

---

[33]) *See* Michael Pryles, *Multi-Tiered Dispute Resolution Clauses*, in Albert Jan van den Berg (ed.), ICCA Congress Series No. 10: International Arbitration and National Courts: The Never Ending Story (Volume 10, 2000) 25.

[34]) For a further exploration on the construction of multi-tiered dispute resolution clauses, *see* Michael Pryles, *Multi-Tiered Dispute Resolution Clauses*, *supra*, at 72 *et seqq*.

[35]) *See also*, Peter Kamminga & Bart Fleuren, *Chapter 12: Corporate Mediation: The Dutch Approach to Mediation vs. Anglo-American Practices and the Enforceability of Mediation Clauses*, in Carla Klaassen, Gerard J. Meijer, et al. (eds.), Arbitration in the Netherlands, in Particular NAI Arbi-tration, Serie Onderneming en Recht (Volume 158, 2025), 319.

Parties are generally well-advised to draft their multi-tiered dispute resolution clauses or mediation clauses in accordance with model clauses provided by established arbitration or mediation institutions. The Vienna International Arbitral Centre for example provides the following clause for supplementary arbitral proceedings:

> *"The parties agree to first refer any disputes or claims under this agreement to mediation. Only if it has not been resolved by mediation within [insert a time limit (e.g. 90 days up to a maximum of six months)] from commencing the proceedings as defined in the Vienna Mediation Rules, this dispute or claim may be initiated or continued in court, arbitral, or other proceedings with the exception of proceedings to obtain provisional or protective measures."*[36])

## 3. Conclusion

The participants of the roundtable discussion, while having had different experiences on whether mediation can boost efficiency in the resolution of commercial disputes, agreed that the effectiveness and efficiency of mediation hinges on three key factors: (i) the parties' willingness to reach an amicable solution, (ii) the specific construction of the dispute resolution clause itself, and (iii) the mediator's profile and style.

Furthermore, the participants generally expressed the desire for more information and education on mediation to promote the use of mediation, particularly to enhance its broader acceptance and uptake at the client level.[37]) Encouragingly, various arbitral institutions are already taking the lead by offering mediation rules, guidelines, protocols, and model clauses, thereby integrating mediation and hybrid mechanisms into their dispute resolution frameworks. The authors welcome and support these developments as important steps toward more efficient and flexible dispute resolution.

---

[36]) *VIAC Model Clause 1: Mediation Agreement for Integration into a Contract*, available at: https://www.viac.eu/en/mediation-basics/mediation-clauses/model-clause-1-mediation-agreement-to-be-inserted-into-a-contract/ (accessed on 9 September 2025).

[37]) For a detailed exploration of arbitrator-facilitated settlement, *see* Gabrielle Kaufmann-Kohler, *When Arbitrators Facilitate Settlement: Towards a Transnational Standard*, in William W. Park (ed.), Arbitration International (2009) 187–205.

# E. AI in Arbitration: Efficiency Booster or Ethical Minefield?

*Peter Machherndl/James Boykin*

## 1. Introduction

Artificial Intelligence (AI) has rapidly transitioned from a futuristic concept into an everyday reality of legal practice. AI tools now appear in law firms, arbitral institutions, and even client-side legal departments. It has become an everyday staple of modern legal practice, as it is not unusual for lawyers to use AI to prepare first drafts of submissions, tribunals to rely on machine translation for key documents, and parties to analyze entire case files using RAG[38])-enhanced large language models (LLMs).

This shift brings undeniable benefits. AI promises faster document production, improved accuracy, and cost efficiency. At the same time, the embrace of AI raises new and serious questions. Can tribunals still rely on the integrity of evidence when deepfakes blur the line between authentic and synthetic? Do clients have greater freedom to use AI than lawyers, given the professional and ethical duties that bind (outside) counsel? And should arbitral institutions step in to regulate how AI can be used in proceedings, or is self-regulation by parties and tribunals sufficient?

These and related questions were the subject of this World Café session. The format encouraged participants to share practical experiences and speculate about future scenarios.

## 2. Defining Artificial Intelligence

The session opened with the task to establish a definition of "artificial intelligence". While AI is generally used as a broad catch-all phrase, participants emphasized the need for precision. Reference may be made to existing definitions such as Art 3(1) Regulation (EU) 2024/1689 (AI Act)[39]) or in the OECD Explanatory Memorandum.[40]) In broad terms, AI can be understood as

---

[38]) Retrieval-augmented generation (RAG) enables large language models (LLMs) to consider new information, such as private documents of the user or updated information not yet integrated into the LLM. Cf https://en.wikipedia.org/wiki/Retrieval-augmented_generation for a more detailed description.

[39]) 'AI system' means a machine-based system that is designed to operate with varying levels of autonomy and that may exhibit adaptiveness after deployment, and that, for explicit or implicit objectives, infers, from the input it receives, how to generate outputs such as predictions, content, recommendations, or decisions that can influence physical or virtual environments.

[40]) OECD, *Explanatory Memorandum on the Updated OECD Definition of an AI System*, OECD Artificial Intelligence Papers No. 8, at 4 (2024), https://doi.org/10.1787/623da898-en ("An AI system is a machine-based system that, for explicit or implicit

an algorithmic system capable of identifying patterns, making predictions, and adapting through iterative learning. But within this umbrella definition, important distinctions must be drawn.

Most participants shared that they already use AI in their professional practice. DeepL is a fundamental pillar for fast translations of documents and correspondence. GPT[41]) Models such as ChatGPT and Harvey are being used to brainstorm arguments, summarize large volumes of text, or provide initial research on various legal and non-legal topics. Document management systems increasingly rely on AI to sort, tag, and retrieve material.

Yet there is a clear difference between automation – such as software that checks citations or applies formatting rules – and large language models (LLMs) that produce reasoning-like outputs. The former will always generate the same output if given the same input, and the system is fully transparent, while the latter generates its outputs through complex algorithms that even developers cannot explain (the so-called "Black Box Problem"[42]). When institutions or tribunals draft rules on AI, they must decide whether their scope covers only advanced generative models or also traditional automation.

The participants agreed that precision in terminology is necessary not only for purpose of debate but also for everyday legal practice. Without a common understanding of what is considered "AI", it will be impossible to develop consistent procedural rules.

## 3. Opportunities and Challenges: Where Can AI Make a Difference?

### a) Opportunities

The conversation quickly turned to the many opportunities that AI presents for arbitration. Several practical applications are already in use.

#### aa) Drafting and Formatting Submissions

AI tools can prepare skeleton drafts of pleadings or standard sections of submissions. By automating tasks such as formatting and citation checking, they free up valuable time for lawyers to focus on strategy.

objectives, infers, from the input it receives, how to generate outputs such as predictions, content, recommendations, or decisions that can influence physical or virtual environments. Different AI systems vary in their levels of autonomy and adaptiveness after deployment.").

41) A generative pre-trained transformer (GPT) is the technical basis for most of the current established generative AI systems, such as ChatGPT, Gemini, Claude, etc. Cf https://en.wikipedia.org/wiki/Generative_pre-trained_transformer for for a more detailed description.

42) Cf https://www.ibm.com/think/topics/black-box-ai for a detailed analysis of the issue.

### ab) Document Organization

Certain AI-driven systems can color-code documents or separate submissions into thematic sections. This allows teams to visually track arguments across issues, improving clarity in large cases with sprawling records.

### ac) Billing Review

Clients are increasingly using AI to audit legal bills. These systems identify duplicate entries, inconsistencies, or possible double billing. This not only helps clients control costs but also puts pressure on law firms to ensure billing practices are transparent and defensible.

### b) Concepts

Beyond current practice, the group discussed more experimental or speculative applications:

### ba) Tribunal AI for Procedural History

Arbitrations generate large volumes of procedural correspondence and orders. AI could extract key events, dates, and procedural steps to automatically generate a structured history of the proceedings. This would save tribunals time when drafting awards and reduce inconsistencies in describing the procedural background. More advanced versions could even produce interactive timelines, allowing readers to click on entries to access the underlying documents.

### bb) AI as a Mock Arbitrator

Before hearings, parties could submit arguments to an AI trained on case law and arbitral awards. The AI would generate indicative assessments of potential outcomes, highlighting weak arguments or overlooked precedents. This would not replace arbitrators but could serve as a tool for stress-testing submissions and refining strategy. Participants emphasized, however, that results must be treated with caution: an AI cannot capture the nuances of witness demeanor, tribunal dynamics, or equitable considerations.

### bc) Real-time AI Questioning Experts

A more futuristic idea involved using AI to listen to expert testimony during hearings and generate clarifying questions in real time. Such a system might function as a "tribunal appointed AI expert", ensuring that complex technical evidence is fully understood. While appealing in theory, this raised concerns about fairness: should parties be subject to questioning by a system they cannot cross-examine? Still, the idea illustrated how far participants were willing to stretch the imagination when considering AI's role.

## 4. Arbitrator Selection

AI could analyze databases of prior appointments, awards, and professional profiles to help parties identify suitable arbitrators. By highlighting decision-making patterns, industry expertise, or potential conflicts, AI could make the selection process more transparent. While this could disrupt the reliance on personal or informal networks, it also raised questions about privacy and the risk of over-relying on statistical patterns.

### a) Risks

The enthusiasm for these opportunities was tempered by serious caution. Participants repeatedly pointed out that AI systems remain prone to hallucinations: outputs that appear convincing but are factually (or legally) incorrect. Lawyers shared experiences of fabricated case citations, flawed legal reasoning, and oversimplified summaries.

The Black Box Problem compounded these risks. With advanced AI systems, neither users nor developers can fully explain how outputs are generated. This lack of transparency poses a major challenge when tribunals must assess reliability. If counsel present AI-generated analysis, how can tribunals verify its accuracy without effectively redoing the entire task?

Participants agreed on one principle: AI can support but not replace human judgment. Lawyers must learn to craft precise prompts, carefully review AI outputs, and perform rigorous proofreading – "AI can write your first draft, but only you can make it fit for submission".

## 5. Evidence in the Age of AI – Deepfakes and Documentary Reliability

### a) Authenticity Issues

Perhaps the most heated part of the discussion concerned evidence. Arbitration has traditionally applied a relatively low threshold for admissibility, relying on Article 9 of the IBA Rules to balance relevance against prejudice. Yet in an era of deepfakes and synthetic evidence, this presumption may no longer be sustainable.

Participants considered whether the burden of proof should shift. Should the party presenting AI-generated evidence be required to prove its authenticity? Or should authenticity be presumed until the opposing party raises serious doubts? Both options carry risks: the first could stifle legitimate use of AI, while the second could allow fabricated material to slip through.

Several practical safeguards were discussed:

First, there was strong support for mandatory disclosure whenever AI is used to generate or translate a document. This would not automatically discredit the document, but it would give tribunals and opposing parties the necessary context to assess reliability.

Second, participants highlighted the value of requiring original electronic files rather than PDF printouts. Original files preserve metadata such as creation dates, editing history, and digital signatures. This information can be crucial in verifying authenticity, whereas static PDFs strip away such indicators.

Third, some participants proposed certification systems for AI-generated evidence. Similar to notarization, an independent body could confirm that a document was generated by a specific AI tool at a specific time and has not been altered since.

Technical safeguards were also considered. Cryptographic hashes such as MD5[43]) values can provide a digital fingerprint of a file. Any alteration would produce a different hash, making tampering detectable. Blockchain-based time stamps offer another way to demonstrate that a file has remained unchanged since its creation.

Communication security was another focus. Parties could use encrypted communication protocols such as S/MIME[44]) when exchanging evidence to reduce the risk of interception or manipulation in transit. In cases of doubt, tribunals could appoint independent forensic experts to verify authenticity, ensuring that questions of technical integrity are addressed by specialists rather than left to speculation.

Interestingly, AI itself could become part of the solution. Just as AI can generate convincing deepfakes, it can also detect them. Tools that identify manipulated images, videos, or documents are already being developed. Some participants suggested that future systems might include automatic watermarks for AI-generated content, making it easier to distinguish synthetic from authentic evidence.

### b) Institutional Rules

Institutional frameworks are beginning to emerge. **VIAC** has already published initial guidelines on the use of AI in proceedings,[45]) while some judges in common law jurisdictions have issued practice notes requiring

---

[43]) The MD5 message-digest algorithm is a broadly used hash function, used for verifying data integrity. Cf https://de.wikipedia.org/wiki/Message-Digest_Algorithm_5.

[44]) S/MIME (Secure/Multipurpose Internet Mail Extensions) is a standard protocol for securely signing (and optionally also encrypting) e-mails (and its attachments). Cf https://en.wikipedia.org/wiki/S/MIME.

[45]) VIAC, *Note on the Use of Artificial Intelligence in Arbitration Proceedings* (April 2025), https://www.viac.eu/wp-content/uploads/2025/04/VIAC-Note-on-AI-1.pdf.

disclosure when AI is used in submissions.[46]) Participants suggested that **Procedural Order No. 1** (PO1) could include clauses regulating AI, such as requiring parties to disclose the use of machine translation or prohibiting reliance on undisclosed AI-generated analysis.

The group also debated how tribunals should **weigh AI-assisted evidence.** Should it be treated with less weight than traditional evidence, or assessed on a case-by-case basis? Should parties be allowed to agree on the AI tools to be used, for example by designating a single translation platform? These questions remain open, but there was agreement that institutions and tribunals cannot ignore them for much longer.

## 6. Broader Issues and Experiences

The session ended with a broader exchange of experiences and reflections.

Copyright and intellectual property were recurring concerns. AI systems trained on massive datasets may inadvertently reproduce protected works. This creates uncertainty about whether AI-generated content – whether text, images, or music – infringes third-party rights. In arbitration, where parties may use AI to generate demonstrative exhibits, this risk could have tangible consequences.

The asymmetry between clients and lawyers was another theme. Clients often face fewer regulatory constraints than counsel. They can experiment freely with AI without worrying about professional ethics rules or confidentiality obligations. This imbalance could shift expectations: clients may expect lawyers to deliver work faster and cheaper with AI, while lawyers are constrained in how they can use it.

Participants also highlighted the promise of retrieval-augmented generation (RAG).[47]) By linking LLMs directly to case-specific documents, outputs become more reliable and less prone to hallucination. RAG systems can provide grounded responses while keeping sensitive data within secure repositories – an important foundation for compliant use of AI in confidential settings.

Data protection was a constant concern. Compliance with GDPR and the risks of cross-border data transfers must be considered whenever cloud-based AI platforms are used. Sensitive case material may be exposed to jurisdictions with weaker privacy protections if not carefully managed.[48])

---

[46]) Supreme Court of New South Wales, Practice Note SC Gen 23 – Use of Generative Artificial Intelligence (Gen AI) (21 November 21, 2024), https://supremecourt.nsw.gov.au/documents/Practice-and-Procedure/Practice-Notes/general/current/PN_Generative_AI_21112024.pdf.

[47]) See *supra* fn 38.

[48]) European Data Protection Board, *Opinion 28/2024 on Certain Data Protection Aspects Related to the Processing of Personal Data in the Context of AI Models (Dec. 18,*

Questions of transparency and disclosure also surfaced. Should lawyers inform clients whenever AI tools are used in drafting or analysis? Some argued that disclosure builds trust and ensures clients understand what they are paying for. Others warned that over-disclosure might overwhelm clients with technical details and create confusion about the role of AI.

Finally, **confidentiality** was recognized as a cornerstone of arbitration that must not be undermined. Feeding sensitive case documents into third-party AI systems could breach confidentiality unless strong safeguards are in place. This issue will likely become more pressing as parties adopt AI tools more widely.

### 7. Conclusion

The World Café discussion revealed the dual nature of AI in arbitration. On the one hand, AI offers powerful tools for efficiency, consistency, and cost reduction. On the other hand, it introduces serious risks to evidence integrity, professional ethics, and procedural fairness.

Participants agreed on a few core principles. First, AI can support but not replace human legal judgment. Second, transparency and disclosure are essential to maintaining trust. Third, institutions and tribunals must take proactive steps to regulate AI use, whether through procedural orders, institutional rules, or practical safeguards.

The conversation also highlighted the need for ongoing education. Lawyers, arbitrators, and institutions must develop the skills to work with AI responsibly – crafting precise prompts, verifying outputs, and understanding technical safeguards.

AI may change how we practice arbitration, but it will not change the essence of arbitration itself. Ultimately, disputes are resolved not by algorithms, but by human judgment.

## F. The (Lacking) Role of Arbitrators in Driving Efficiency

*Courtney Lotfi/Vilius Bernatonis*

### 1. Introduction

Arbitration is often lauded for its relative speed compared to other forms of dispute resolution – but speed does not always equal efficiency. Truly efficient proceedings depend on seamless coordination among parties, counsel, arbitrators, institutions, and other key players.

*2024),* https://www.edpb.europa.eu/our-work-tools/our-documents/opinion-board-art-64/opinion-282024-certain-data-protection-aspects_en.

This World Café session examined how arbitrators can – and at times must – shape the efficiency of the process: when they *may*, *should*, or *must* act, and when they are expected to or must refrain from doing so. At the heart of this discussion lies a recurring tension: whether the parties actually *want* the tribunal to intervene or if they would prefer to retain control, even if it compromises efficiency.

The discussion moderators (Lotfi and Bernatonis) led a candid, interactive discussion grounded in real-life hypotheticals. Participants were encouraged to share their perspectives and experiences as discussions explored how arbitrators can effectively balance procedural fairness with the demands of an efficient process.

The article that follows documents some of the discussions which were held over two separate sessions in roughly chronological order on 10 May 2025 in Vienna with Mohamed Amara, Mark Campbell, David Coyne, Gabor Damjanovic, Sara Darnot, Nadja Jaisli-Kull, Stephan Klebes, Lilia Kolochenko, Stefan Kroll, Anton Maurer, Maximilian Menz, Vilija Parvan, Yurgita Petkute, Ileana Smeureanu, Artur Tamaji, and Philipp Wagner.

## 2. A Starting Point and Universal Agreement Amongst Participants

### a) The Tools Available to Tribunals

Tribunals possess tools with which to foster efficiency in arbitration. These tools are inherently and expressly conveyed when the tribunal is constituted and the file transmitted to them. For example, the 2025 VIAC Rules of Arbitration and Mediation (the "***Vienna Rules***") expressly and inherently grant the tribunal the power to control efficiency at every stage of the proceedings. These powers are enshrined in, *inter alia*, the following:

- Article 27 (Applicable Law, Amiable Compositeur), which requires the tribunal to apply the applicable law or rules of law which it considers appropriate if the parties have not done so.[49])
- Article 28 (Conduct of the Arbitration), which requires the tribunal to conduct the arbitration "in accordance with the Vienna Rules and the agreement of the parties *in an efficient and cost-effective manner, but otherwise at its own discretion*".[50]) It also grants the tribunal to power to set time limits and cutoffs by accepting pleadings, evidence, and

49) Vienna Rules, Art. 27(2).

50) Vienna Rules, Art. 28(1) (emphasis added).

requests for the taking of evidence up to a certain point in the proceedings;[51]) and facilitate the parties' endeavors to reach settlement.[52])

- Article 29 (Establishing the Facts of the Case), which grants the tribunal wide discretion in establishing the facts of the case including collecting evidence, questioning parties and witnesses, and requesting the parties submit evidence.[53]) It may do so even if a party fails to participate (*i.e.*, failure of a party to participate may not stall or derail proceedings).[54])
- Article 30 (Oral Hearing), which, absent party agreement to the contrary, requires that tribunal determine whether an oral hearing shall be held or whether the proceedings shall be conducted solely in writing.[55]) The date of any hearing is decided by the chair of the tribunal or sole arbitrator.[56])
- Article 32 (Closure of the Proceedings and Time for Rendering the Award), which requires the tribunal to declare the proceedings closed with respect to matters to be decided in the award as soon as it is "convinced that the parties have had sufficient opportunity to make submissions and to offer evidence".[57]) Absent a reasoned request by the tribunal on extensions, awards must be rendered within three months of the last hearing or the filing of the last authorized submission (whichever is later).[58])
- Article 33 (Interim and Conservatory Measures/Security for Costs), grants the tribunal broad powers in granting interim and conservatory measures and security for costs as soon as the file has been transmitted to it.[59]) Further, the tribunal is granted the power to suspend (in whole or part) or terminate the proceedings.[60])
- Article 34 (Means of Termination of the Proceedings), which permits the tribunal to terminate the proceedings by award or order, the latter of which includes the possibility to terminate if it becomes impossible to pursue the arbitration.[61])

---

[51]) Vienna Rules, Art. 28(2).
[52]) Vienna Rules, Art. 28(3).
[53]) Vienna Rules, Art. 29(1).
[54]) Vienna Rules, Art. 29(2).
[55]) Vienna Rules, Art. 30(1). Oral hearings are required if requested by any party.
[56]) Vienna Rules, Art. 30(2).
[57]) Vienna Rules, Art. 32(1).
[58]) Vienna Rules, Art. 32(2).
[59]) Vienna Rules, Art. 33.
[60]) Vienna Rules, Art. 33(7).
[61]) Vienna Rules, Art. 34(2.3-.4).

- Article 38 (Decisions on Costs), which requires the tribunal to determine who shall bear the costs of the proceedings (in whole or part), and allows the tribunal to take into consideration "[t]he *conduct of any or all parties as well as their representatives*..., and in particular their contribution to the conduct of efficient and cost-effective proceedings".[62]) Tribunals may make costs decisions at any stage of the proceedings.[63])

Soft law tools such as the 2020 IBA Rules on the Taking of Evidence in International Arbitration (the "***IBA Rules***") similarly convey powers of efficiency to tribunals.[64]) For example,

- Article 2 (Consultation on Evidentiary Issues) requires the tribunal consult the parties "at the earliest appropriate time" with a view of agreeing on an efficient, economical, and fair process on the taking of evidence.[65]) This may extend to scope, timing, and manner and apply to witness statements and expert reports, oral testimony, and the production of documents, etc.[66]) Furthermore, the tribunal is encouraged to identify issues it regards as relevant to the case and material to its outcome and/or for which a preliminary determination may be appropriate.[67])
- Article 3 (Documents) permits the tribunal to determine the time for which documents upon which a party relies shall be submitted,[68]) and to determine issues related to the requests for production of documents including manner, timing and scope of requests, objections and responses thereto, and production.[69]) It may also take a more active role in the taking of evidence by requesting a party produce documents, request a party use its best efforts to take or itself take any step appropriate to obtain documents from third parties.[70])
- Article 6 (Tribunal-Appointed Experts) permits tribunals to appoint one or more experts to report to it on specific issues.[71])

---

[62]) Vienna Rules, Art. 38(2) (cross-reference omitted, emphasis added).

[63]) Vienna Rules, Art. 38(3).

[64]) The stated purpose of the IBA Rules is "to provide an efficient, economical, and fair process for the taking of international arbitrations". IBA Rules, Art. 1.

[65]) IBA Rules, Art. 2(1).

[66]) IBA Rules, Art. 2(2).

[67]) IBA Rules, Art. 2(3).

[68]) IBA Rules, Art. 3(1).

[69]) IBA Rules, Art. 3(2) *et seq.*

[70]) IBA Rules, Art. 3(10).

[71]) IBA Rules, Art. 6.

- Article 7 (Inspection) permits tribunals to inspect/require the inspection of a site, property, machinery or any other goods, samples, systems, processes or documents it deems appropriate.[72]
- Article 8 (Evidentiary Hearing) grants the tribunal broad discretion on the conduct of the hearing, including whether it will be in-person or remote.[73]
- Article 9 (Admissibility and Assessment of Evidence) grants the tribunal broad discretion in determining the admissibility, relevance, materiality and weight of evidence, and permits adverse inferences.[74]

These powers enable tribunals to shape and control arbitration proceedings and make determinations necessarily enable the tribunal to foster efficiency. They cannot, however, be used at the expense of due process,[75] which may inevitably leave any award open to challenge and possible set-aside.[76]

### b) Universal Agreement Amongst Participants

It was clear that participants of the World Café largely favored tribunals using the tools available to them to foster and maintain efficiency in proceedings. It was universally agreed that this should take place at each stage of the proceedings, beginning immediately from constitution through final party submissions and the timely rendering of the award.

The lone exception was – again, universally – when the parties jointly seek to implement processes and procedures that are inefficient. Examples include lengthy document production phases which, while beneficial in some instances, may not result in a "smoking gun" in most instances. To dissuade from lengthy document production requests (and procedures in general) one experienced arbitrator shared that he routinely requests parties submit costs information at the end of the proceedings with costs associated with document production as a separate line-item. This enables the tribunal to separately consider costs associated with document production irrespective of success on the merits and, in instances where the procedure was abused/not fruitful, no costs for that separate line-item will be awarded.

In this connection, some participants noted the role of the counsel, especially in procedural matters. It was suggested that the tribunal should take

---

[72]) IBA Rules, Art. 7.

[73]) IBA Rules, Art. 8.

[74]) IBA Rules, Art. 9.

[75]) Doug Jones, The Remedial Armoury of an Arbitral Tribunal: The Extent to Which Tribunals Can Look Beyond the Parties' Submissions, 78 Arbitration, Issue 2, p. 102, 115 (2012).

[76]) *E.g.*, Courtney Lotfi, Practical Insights on Setting Aside and Enforcement of Awards (Kluwer Arbitration 2025), available at https://www.kluwerarbitration.com/practical-content/setting-aside-and-enforcement-of-awards.

a proactive role and assess any proposed procedural agreements among the parties' counsel, potentially testing how much the agreement between counsel is in line with the process efficiency requirements.

### 3. Constitution of the Tribunal

Whether the tribunal has any role in fostering efficiency in arbitration at the time it is constituted was debated. It was agreed that nominees should be forthright with their schedules so that parties are aware of any major time restrictions or limitations on the part of potential tribunal members (*e.g.*, a heavy case load or an inability to participate in a hearing during a specified time).

Tribunal members may be in a position to determine the parties' approach to the arbitration even before accepting a nomination. The example of parties submitting voluminous request for arbitrations and answers that were more akin to statements of claim and defense was discussed. (See below on how to potentially deal with this)

### 4. Case Management Conference, Procedural Calendar and Procedural Order No. 1

The case management conference or early meeting (the "***CMC***") is likely the first time where tribunals can influence the conduct of the proceedings; it is the time at which documents such as the procedural calendar and the first procedural order ("***Procedural Order No. 1***" or "***PO1***") are discussed and possibility finalized. Arguably, the CMC may be the best opportunity for the tribunal to set ground rules and openly discuss process efficiency related risks with the parties. Many participants were amenable to tribunals expressly referencing efficiency at this juncture.

It was recommended that the tribunal arrive prepared, with an understanding of the parties' submissions to date so that it could most effectively participate in this meeting.

One discussion revolved around tribunals circulating the draft PO1 before the CMC. This has many benefits, including the parties' abilities to review and confer with each other on points contained therein before the first meeting with the tribunal at CMC. In doing so, the parties can focus on points of disagreement – thereby streamlining the meeting.

One experienced arbitrator shared that he routinely excludes a phase for document production from his proposed PO1 if it wouldn't be usual when taking into account the type of case, and the parties and their counsel's expectations. This same arbitrator also shared that he requests at the case management conference that the parties record time spent on document production separately so that it can be considered when apportioning costs and states that this will be considered irrespective of success on the merits. The express purpose of this request is to encourage the parties to submit legitimate requests (*i.e.*, no fishing expeditions) in a time- and cost-effective manner.

Another viewpoint was for the tribunal to suggest the parties confer on the PO1 – without providing them a draft – thereby forcing them to collaborate on what is best for their case/desired by the parties.

One more viewpoint was a suggestion that in the context of the CMC the arbitrators could discuss the reasonableness of costs of representation. For instance, suggesting that, while the cost submissions will be assessed in due course, the tribunal will consider procedural efficiency in this regard. Some suggested going even as far as stating that, as a matter of principle, the representation costs should not exceed a certain proportion of the amount in dispute.

Finally, timing of the proceedings and the establishment of the procedural calendar was discussed. It was agreed that, wherever possible, this document should be drawn up with an eye to the nature and circumstances of dispute and availability. For example, it would be inappropriate to have relatively short time periods between written submissions when the merits hearing could not be scheduled for a comparatively long period due to party, counsel, or arbitrator availability (*i.e.*, the seemingly efficiency in producing written submission would be lost during the long break before the hearing).

## 5. Document Production

Document production is a topic of much discussion in international arbitration circles and the World Café was no different, where unnecessary complication, drawn-out processes and high costs were considered negatives associated with the process. On the other hand, the ability of parties to obtain documents not otherwise in their possession that were both relevant to their case and material to its outcome was seen as a clear benefit.

To ensure efficiency and discourage abuse, participants suggested tribunals apply standards such as those of the IBA Rules (relevance and materiality) and impose limits on the number of requests that can be made. One arbitrator and counsel also suggested the use of the traditional Redfern Schedule in a vertical format as opposed to the now prevalent horizontal format. When others lamented this made for tough advocacy given then arrow vertical columns, the response was "that's exactly the point!" – *i.e.*, the parties should be concise in their requests, justifications and objections and not use the Redfern Schedule as another means to advocate their case.

## 6. Written Submissions

Tribunals frequently influence the (in)efficiency of proceedings by detailing the number and timing of written submissions. It is not uncommon for straightforward cases to have five rounds of written submissions: (i) request-answer, (ii) statement of claim-defense, (iii) reply-rejoinder, (iv) post-hearing briefs, and (v) submissions on costs. This number can grow exponentially if the proceedings contain counter and/or cross-claims, are bifurcated, if post-hearing briefs and/or submissions on costs include replies, and if there are applications for interim or conservatory measures or security for costs.

Participants engaged in animated discussions on how to ensure the parties have the right to present their claims and defenses in full while still maintaining a modicum of procedural efficiency. Ideas included:

- Limiting the number and length of submissions,
- Requiring exhibits be focused, limited in length, and with the expectation that all submissions will be read by the tribunal, and
- Requesting the parties focus on certain areas identified by the tribunal (*e.g.*, where information is lacking)

While many accepted these suggestions, others raised concerns of tribunals infringing on party autonomy or their right to present their case, and appearances of pre-judging the dispute or bias.

When confronted with the hypothetical of parties submitting voluminous briefs and evidence with their request for arbitration, one experienced arbitrator questioned whether the tribunal could (should) not consider these documents as the statements of claim and defense and adapt the procedural calendar as such. Others thought this may face resistance from the parties and, it was agreed, that party autonomy would likely prevail (*e.g.*, a "normal" number of submissions over a truncated number if jointly sought by the parties).

One participant, a quantum expert, shared a recent experience with respect to written expert reports that streamlined the experts' involvement in the case. In that arbitration, the tribunal requested the same questions be posed to both party-appointed experts and that they be given the same data to review and upon which they would base their opinions. By reducing the risk that the expert reports would not address precisely the same points or analyze the same data, the tribunal was given two substantially similar reports in terms of structure and content, with the points of agreement and disagreement being clear. The reports could not have been described as *i.e.* the risk of "ships passing in the night".

## 7. The Hearing

Most rules provide that an oral hearing on the merits will take place if requested by any party. In the participants' experience, oral hearings are more common in international arbitration than a tribunal deciding the case on the written submissions alone. This is true despite the fact that few participants experienced a case where the case was won on oral advocacy. Rather, it was the contrary – cases were undermined and even lost at hearings.

All participants saw value in holding pre-hearing conferences to discuss the timing and procedure to be followed at the hearing. Efficiency elements to consider are:

- Whether the parties should present opening statements and, if so, whether those statements should be limited to the key issues in dispute (*i.e.*, omitting a recitation of the pleadings and case theory in favor of the main points of contention),
- Whether all witnesses and experts should be heard as witnesses,
- Whether there will be a direct examination or only cross,
- Issues of time allocation – *e.g.*, whether there will be limitations on the length of witness testimony, whether time allocation is to be determined by the number of witnesses presented or by issue.

Expert witness conferencing or "hot tubbing" was considered a valuable addition to hearings by most participants provided it is run effectively. Most agreed that the tribunal should be prepared to lead the questioning of the experts during this process. Providing experts with questions in advance or requiring the experts to meet and confer in advance was also seen as a means of promoting efficiency. Another suggestion was to introduce additional stages prior to "hot-tubbing", including asking experts appointed by both parties to analyze the same fixed set of facts, as well as performing a separate cross examination of experts (without the presence of the opposing party nominated expert) before moving to the "hot tubbing".

## 8. Rendering the Award

Many institutional rules require tribunals to render the award within a given time. The Vienna Rules, for example, require awards to be rendered within three months of the last hearing or the last authorized written submission (whichever is later) unless an extension is granted. Efficient tribunals may seek to direct the parties to provide clear and concise written submissions – including post-hearing briefs – to help their drafting process. They may also direct the parties' attention to certain issues which require further clarification.

## 9. Concluding Remarks

Tribunals possess a range of procedural tools designed to foster efficiency in arbitration, such as early case management conferences, streamlined procedures, limitations on document production, and bifurcation of proceedings. These tools aim to reduce time and cost, prevent unnecessary delays, and ensure that the arbitration process remains fair, focused, and effective.

However, the principle of party autonomy, a cornerstone of arbitration, can significantly influence whether and to what extent these tools are employed. Party autonomy grants the disputing parties substantial control over procedural matters, including the ability to agree on the rules governing the arbitration, the selection of arbitrators, timelines, and the scope of evidence. This means that even where a tribunal identifies an opportunity to improve efficiency, its ability to act may be curtailed by the parties' prior agreements or their resistance to procedural innovations.

Tensions may arise as a result between the tribunal's duty to manage the process efficiently and the parties' right to shape the procedure as they see fit. While arbitral rules increasingly empower tribunals to take proactive steps to ensure procedural efficiency (*e.g.*, expedited proceedings, early disposition), the extent to which these powers are exercised often depends on the tribunal's interpretation of its mandate and the parties' willingness to accept or encourage such measures.

Ultimately, efficiency in arbitration requires a careful balance: respecting party autonomy while also using procedural tools to avoid unnecessary delay or cost. Tribunals must navigate this balance thoughtfully, often by engaging in early dialogue with the parties to align expectations and secure consent for efficiency-enhancing measures.

## G. The (Lacking) Role of Institutions in Driving Efficiency

*Catrice Gayer/Maximilian Murtinger*

### 1. Introduction

Efficiency remains a cornerstone of international arbitration's appeal. However, the system faces mounting pressure to meet the evolving expectations of parties navigating an increasingly complex geo-political landscape. While procedural flexibility is a core advantage of arbitration, users continue to express concerns about procedural delays and rising costs.

Recent statistics indicate that the average duration of arbitration proceedings from Request for Arbitration to the Final Award ranges from 12 and 27 months[77]) depending on the administering arbitral institution. While many argue that the parties themselves are primarily responsible for costs and delays, the question persists: are arbitral institutions doing enough to foster expeditious and cost-effective proceedings, or is there scope – and need – for them to assume a more proactive role?

[77]) https://iccwbo.org/news-publications/news/icc-dispute-resolution-statistics-2024/; https://www.lcia.org/News/lcia-releases-updated-costs-and-duration-analysis-2024.aspx; https://www.hkiac.org/about-us/statistics; https://siac.org.sg/siac-year-in-review-2024.

The 2025 Vienna Arbitration Days World Café brought together practitioners (counsel, inhouse counsel and arbitrators) and representatives of arbitral institutions to examine these issues and discuss potential solutions.

## 2. Summary of the Discussions

### a) Defining Efficiency in Arbitration

The participants first explored how users – counsel, clients, institutions and arbitrators – define and interpret "efficiency" in arbitration. The discussion revealed that efficiency is a multi-dimensional concept, encompassing not only time and cost, but also procedural fairness, the quality of the award, and its enforceability. Delegates agreed that measuring efficiency solely by the duration of the proceedings is overly simplistic. A holistic approach is essential: efforts to expedite proceedings and reduce costs must not come at the expense of award quality or enforceability.

The conversation underscored the inherent tension between these often competing objectives. Many contributors noted that institutional arbitration is frequently chosen precisely to help manage this balance. Representatives of arbitral institutions acknowledged this role, emphasizing that while they strive to promote efficiency and design rules to support it, they must also ensure that procedural safeguards – such as the right to be heard and the equal and fair treatment of parties – are not compromised. These principles are fundamental to the legitimacy of arbitral awards and the integrity of the process.

### b) Institutional Capacity to Drive Efficiency

The second topic addressed was whether arbitral institutions can meaningfully drive efficiency, or whether the responsibility lies primarily with arbitrators, counsel and parties.

Participants agreed that institutions play an important role, but emphasised that there is no one-size-fits-all solution. Some delegates advocated for a more proactive institutional approach, while others cautioned that this could undermine procedural flexibility and party autonomy. Representatives of institutions noted that a more interventionist role would require increased staffing and, consequently, higher administrative costs to be borne by the parties.

Among the various approaches discussed, delegates highlighted the effectiveness of institutions adjusting arbitrators' fees to incentivise efficient conduct and discourage delay, with particular reference to the ICC's practice. This mechanism was widely regarded as a practical and impactful tool for promoting efficiency in arbitral proceedings.

### c) Tribunal Constitution and Composition Issues

The third topic considered was whether institutions should have greater authority over the constitution of the tribunal, such as appointing a sole arbitrator for straightforward cases even though the parties have agreed to a three-member tribunal.

Delegates firmly rejected this proposal, emphasizing the primacy of party agreement in arbitration. Nevertheless, in light of the costs and potential delays associated with three-member tribunals, it was suggested that institutions could take a more proactive role in reminding parties of the option to appoint a sole arbitrator, even where the arbitration agreement provides otherwise.

The discussion also addressed the selection of arbitrators. Delegates observed that delays are often caused by overburdened arbitrators and suggested that institutions should adopt a more rigorous approach to verifying arbitrator availability before appointments are confirmed. As part of this, institutions should consider implementing even stricter disclosure requirements regarding arbitrator caseloads and availability.

### d) Institutional Guidelines and Best Practices

The fourth topic addressed was the practical utility of institutional guidelines, reports, and notes on efficiency, such as the ICC Report on Techniques for Controlling Time and Costs in Arbitration, the VIAC Explanatory Notes, the LCIA Guidance Note for Parties and Arbitrators and CIArb Professional Practice Guidelines, among others.

Feedback was mixed. Some delegates found these resources valuable, especially for less experienced counsel and arbitrators, as they offer practical strategies for streamlining proceedings and managing costs. It was suggested that institutions might explore ways to enhance both the accessibility and the practical relevance of these materials. However, others questioned their practical impact, observing that many practitioners do not consult these materials in practice. There was also concern expressed that some arbitrators may use such guidelines to justify procedural decisions without adequately considering the specific circumstances and expectations of the parties in a case.

### e) Award Scrutiny and Quality Control Mechanisms

The fifth topic concerned the scrutiny of awards, such as the ICC's review process. The discussion centred on whether such scrutiny genuinely enhances the quality and enforceability of awards, or whether it introduces unnecessary delay.

Some delegates argued that institutional review is valuable because it helps to prevent obvious errors and strengthen the enforceability of awards, thereby safeguarding and enhancing the institution's reputation. Others questioned whether the benefits of scrutiny justify the additional time and cost involved. It was noted that scrutiny processes often concentrate on correcting minor typographical errors and formatting issues. Many participants agreed that while minor corrections are less significant, substantive quality control aimed at improving enforceability is crucial. Where scrutiny processes focus on substantive review rather than mere formalities, most agreed that the investment of time and cost is justified.

### f) Institutions and Sanctions

The discussion then turned to how arbitral institutions are adapting to contemporary geopolitical challenges, particularly those arising from sanctions-related issues affecting arbitration proceedings. Delegates highlighted the difficulties associated with non-participating parties and sanctioned entities.

A primary concern is the payment of arbitrator and institutional fees. Delegates agreed that arbitral institutions should establish clear policies for handling cases involving sanctioned parties and assist in identifying suitable banks to facilitate payment. At the same time, institutions must ensure strict compliance with applicable sanctions and maintain full transparency throughout the process.

Another challenge is appointing suitable arbitrators in cases involving sanctioned entities. Institutions need to ensure that appointed arbitrators have relevant experience and are from jurisdictions that minimise the risk of challenge.

While delegates generally found existing institutional procedures helpful in addressing these issues, they noted that delays in tribunal constitution due to difficulties in finding suitable, non-conflicted arbitrators remain a concern.

### g) Fast-Track and Expedited procedures

The final topic addressed were the benefits and drawbacks of fast-track and expedited procedures. Many arbitral institutions have incorporated such provisions into their rules, typically using either opt-in mechanisms or monetary thresholds to determine their application.

Delegates noted that, while these procedures can be valuable, there is no universal solution. Many expressed a preference for opt-in over opt-out approaches, and cautioned that case complexity, not just the amount in dispute, should determine suitability. Attendees agreed that, when appropriately applied, expedited processes can significantly enhance speed and cost-efficiency without compromising the legitimacy of the proceedings. However, they also recognised that achieving this balance is delicate, and both arbitrators and institutions are justified in approaching such measures with caution.

Drawing on their experience, most delegates agreed that the use of fast-track and expedited procedures has improved overall efficiency in arbitration. Notably, certain measures, such as limited document production, single rounds of pleadings and preliminary merits assessments, are increasingly being adopted even outside formal fast-track frameworks.

## 3. Conclusion

The Vienna Arbitration Days discussions highlighted both the potential and the limitations of institutional efforts to enhance efficiency in arbitration. While institutions play a significant role by establishing frameworks, offering procedural tools, and promoting best practices, they cannot address efficiency challenges in isolation.

Key findings suggest that institution should continue to prioritise high-quality case management, invest in administrative technology, refine robust expedited procedures, and develop effective mechanisms for managing multi-party disputes. These initiatives can provide a strong foundation for more efficient proceedings.

At the same time, the arbitration landscape is shaped by evolving geopolitical realities, including sanctions compliance and increasingly complex multi-jurisdictional disputes. Institutions must remain agile and innovative to address these external pressures, ensuring that their rules and practices remain fit for purpose in a changing environment.

Crucially, the discussions made clear that the responsibility for efficiency does not rest with institutions alone. Arbitrators, counsel, and parties must actively support and engage with institutional initiatives. Arbitrators must embrace efficient case management practices, and parties and counsel must cooperate in good faith, avoiding tactics that cause unnecessary delay or escalate costs.

Importantly, the pursuit of efficiency must never come at the expense of procedural fairness or award quality. The legitimacy of arbitration depends on upholding its core principles while seeking improvements in cost and time efficiency.

Ultimately, it is the collective commitment of the entire arbitration community that will determine whether the promise of efficient, fair, and effective dispute resolution is realised.

# H. The (Lacking) Role of Parties (and Counsel) in Driving Efficiency

*Tamara Manasijevic/Florian Wagner*[78])

## 1. Introduction

What would Vienna be without its coffee houses?

Coffee houses are undoubtedly one of Vienna's lifelines. They are tourist magnets and cultural monuments, simply an institution.

Anyone who has ever had a coffee in a Viennese café would not immediately think that efficiency is the order of the day. Compared to the thirty-second espresso in a Milanese bar, drinking coffee in Vienna is more of a celebration. From finding a suitable seat and selecting from the many coffee specialties to savoring the impeccable service and settling the bill, the entire ritual can easily take 30 minutes.

But does that really mean that drinking coffee in Vienna is less efficient than in Milan? Is efficiency not much more than just speed? Is it not also about the coffee drinker going home satisfied and happy at the end of the day? That the whole experience was harmonious and the guest wants to come back? As always, it is a question of perspective. While some prefer a quick and undifferentiated solution, others prefer a well-thought-out and varied selection and are happy to endure a longer wait for it.

The situation regarding efficiency in arbitration proceedings is very similar. In addition to the mere duration of the proceedings, numerous other factors such as costs, practical benefits and, last but not least, the overall experience also play a role. The importance of each of these factors is largely determined by the parties and their counsel. Table 4 therefore discussed the role that parties and their lawyers (can) play in improving efficiency in arbitration proceedings. In particular, the discussion focused on what exactly efficiency means from the perspective of the parties and counsel, how efficiency and due process relate to each other, and what measures should be taken to improve overall efficiency.

## 2. What are Efficient Arbitral Proceedings from the Parties' Perspective?

The participants in the discussion quickly agreed that the question of efficiency must first be assessed by comparing it with alternatives.

---

[78]) Discussion participants (among others): Varvara Artinkh, Balazs Fazakas, Manuela Grosu, Lukas Hellmayr, Soren Henriksen, Lilia Klochenko, Mojca Logar, Anton Maurer, Agnes Oppitz, Camelia Seghedi, Malte Stübinger, and Sarolta Szabo.

The numerous in-house lawyers participating in the discussion emphasized in particular that, when considering efficiency, arbitration proceedings must always stand up to comparison with state court proceedings. The costs of arbitration proceedings, which are generally (significantly) higher, could, particularly in complex cases, be offset by the often more stringent conduct of proceedings by arbitral tribunals and their greater competence in certain matters. However, one difficulty is that it is necessary to assess which route to take – arbitration or state court proceedings – (long) before the dispute arises.

Both the participating external and in-house counsel agreed that a particularly fast procedure is often not desirable. Rather, it is important for all internal and external stakeholders to feel that the arbitral tribunal has reached a fair and balanced solution. This is especially important in arbitration proceedings because there is no second instance in which the decision can be reviewed.

The in-house counsel present also pointed out that compliance with deadlines and schedules is an essential feature of efficiency. Even a delay of just a few days consumes significant resources. Often, the arbitrators and counsel involved are not aware of the effort involved in preparing all internal stakeholders and coordinating schedules.

## 3. Efficiency as a Shared Responsibility

At the beginning of the discussion, some participants saw the responsibility for efficient arbitration proceedings as lying primarily with the arbitrators. As the discussion progressed, the prevailing opinion was that efficiency can only be achieved jointly. The in-house lawyers in particular emphasized that they regard arbitration proceedings as a service that they purchase. They therefore expressed the expectation that it should be possible to remind an arbitral tribunal of its procedural duties. The external lawyers present stated that they often exercise restraint in this regard and expressed concern that inquiries to the tribunal could be perceived as presumptuous and might jeopardize their client's position. By the end of the lively discussion that followed on this point, it was agreed that these fears should not stop parties from making inquiries to the arbitral tribunal or subtly reminding the tribunal of its duties when appropriate.

The discussion then turned to whether it is also the responsibility of lawyers to encourage their clients to conduct proceedings efficiently. Although there is often one party that may have an interest in delaying proceedings and conducting them inefficiently, most of the lawyers present were of the opinion that these client interests can only be considered to a certain extent in arbitration proceedings. Moreover, they are superseded by the overriding interests and obligations of the lawyers for reasons of professional ethics. Most participants agreed that by submitting to arbitration, the parties have assumed the obligation to be (significantly) more disciplined than they might be in – non-agreed – state court proceedings.

## 4. Due Process vs. Efficiency

The table participants identified the relationship between due process and efficiency as a delicate balance in arbitral proceedings.

*On the one hand*, they observed that pursuing greater procedural economy could undermine the quality of the process and the correctness of the outcome. Efficiency measures that restrict how parties present their case (such as the imposition of page limits or tight procedural deadlines) can, if applied without sensitivity to the parties' or arbitrators' experience and the complexity of the dispute, prevent relevant information from reaching the tribunal. Parties will not prioritize speed or cost if they believe that doing so could compromise the rigor of the tribunal's analysis and the correct outcome.[79]) This attitude reflects the logic of the "iron triangle" theory, according to which: (i) a good arbitration cannot be both fast and cheap; (ii) a fast arbitration that is good will be expensive; and (iii) a cheap arbitration that is good will be slow.[80])

Indeed, the efficiency of proceedings must be pursued in parallel with the competing goals[81]) of safeguarding due process and ensuring that the arbitral award is not only enforceable but also substantively correct.[82]) At the same time, as Jennifer Kirby aptly framed it, *"[t]o the extent people spend time and*

---

[79]) *See* Rouven Bodenheimer, *The Tribunal Visualized Approach: Improving Proceedings by Visualized Case Introduction*, in Scherer, JOURNAL OF INTERNATIONAL ARBITRATION (2024, Issue 4), 469.

[80]) Jennifer Kirby, *Efficiency in International Arbitration: Whose Duty Is It?*, in Gerbay, JOURNAL OF INTERNATIONAL ARBITRATION (2015, Issue 6) 690–691; Tim Robbins, *The Efficiency Apex: Rethinking the Approach to Procedure in International Commercial Arbitration*, INDIAN JOURNAL OF ARBITRATION LAW (2023, Issue 2) 48, 49.

[81]) William W. Park, *Arbitration and Fine Dining: Two Faces of Efficiency*, in No. 17-25 Boston University School of Law, Public Law Research Paper (2017) 1, draws an analogy between arbitration and fine dining, highlighting that the balance of several competing goals can make the experience better or worse: "*Aiming to provide fine dining, a restaurant chef will pay attention to several goals, not all of which marry well one with another. Guests must not wait too long for their meal. Yet a good dish often takes time to prepare. The wine list should offer quality and choice, but without being pretentious or overpriced. Shortcomings in any one area could turn dinner into disappointment. Few points will be scored if tasty cuisine arrives two hours late, even assuming the customer has not departed in the interim. Prompt service will rarely save bad food. The evening would be ruined by a chef who had become preoccupied with any single aspect of fine dining, to the exclusion of the others.*"

[82]) Robbins, *supra*, proposes a procedural framework for the implementation of what he terms as the "Efficiency Apex", where the arbitral tribunal has sufficient information to render a correct and enforceable award without unnecessary procedural steps.

*money on things that don't go towards producing awards that are correct and enforceable, many parties would probably agree that such time and expenses could be saved without reducing quality".*[83])

*On the other hand*, the participants noted that, where parties wish to press for procedural choices that protract proceedings, such as late submissions or expanded evidence, they frequently do so under the guise of due process and "fundamental fairness". Unfortunately, in the experience of the participants, arbitral tribunals frequently accede to such requests and tolerate procedural conduct that violates the inherent duty[84]) to arbitrate in good faith. The participants identified the following as the main reasons for arbitrators adopting such an attitude: (i) the concern that relevant facts or arguments might be omitted from their analyses, and (ii) the phenomenon of due process paranoia, which still "*paralyzes tribunals*"[85]), undermining their willingness to exercise the very powers conferred by procedural rules and inherent authority.

## 5. How Proactive are External and In-House Counsel?

When asked how they promote efficiency in arbitral proceedings in their roles as external or in-house counsel, the participants highlighted disciplined advocacy and a familiar set of good practices: adhering to procedural timetables, avoiding unnecessary extensions or unsolicited submissions[86]) and preparing evidence well in advance. Participants from the Nordic jurisdictions added that arbitral proceedings in their region are typically front-loaded, with very concise submissions considered normal, even in high-value disputes.

The discussion revealed, however, that parties and their counsel rarely take a proactive role in proposing specific case-management measures to enhance efficiency, such as tighter procedural calenders, page limits,[87]) or midstream conferences.[88]) Three main reasons were identified for this lack of initiative:

---

[83]) Kirby, *supra*, at 689, 691.

[84]) *See* Sabrina Pearson-Wenger, *Good Faith in International Commercial Arbitration: Its Application by Arbitral Tribunals to the Parties' Contract and the Arbitration Agreement*, International Arbitration Law Library (2024), 493–558.

[85]) Toby Landau KC, Adjectives, Abuse and Bad Faith – Reconsidering Ethics and the Rule of Law, Gaillaird Lecture of 14 May 2025 (available online: https://youtu.be/-8pgR9FL0lA).

[86]) Which will prompt replies by the opposing side and can quickly evolve to "letter writing campaigns", unless stopped by the arbitral tribunal, *see* Ugo Draetta, *The Dark Side of Arbitration* (2018), 285.

[87]) In the 2021 Queen Mary Survey, the majority of the respondents (61 %) considered limiting the length of written submissions as the best procedural option to save time and costs in arbitration, see 2021 Queen Mary University/W&C International Arbitration Survey: Adapting arbitration to a changing world, p. 13.

[88]) Jörg Risse, *The Fishbone Paradox: About Efficiency in Arbitration,* SchiedsVZ 2025, 61, argues that parties and in-house counsel are complicit in the inefficiency they

*First*, discussants broadly agreed that tight procedural calenders are oftentimes not feasible, even in less complex disputes. Those acting as counsel pointed out that accelerated proceedings require additional resources (larger teams, more coordination, and higher fees) that are not always available. In-house counsel, for their part, observed that they are generally reluctant to press for shorter timeframes than their external counsel can accommodate, emphasizing that communication with external counsel regarding availability and time management in the proceedings is sometimes insufficient. They added, however, that more generous time limits for written submissions are often preferred, as they create opportunities for settlement between pleading rounds.

*Second*, lawyers' billing structures significantly impact the conduct of proceedings. Hourly rates, by their nature, reward time spent rather than time saved.[89]) Although drafting concise and persuasive submissions often requires more – and not less – time and skill, discussants observed that there is, in practice, little financial incentive to shorten or simplify proceedings.[90])

*Third*, beyond general reluctance to appear as "policing" the arbitral tribunal in procedural matters, counsel often fear that if they narrow their submissions or support shorter filing deadlines or hearings, the tribunal may fail to fully grasp their client's case. Counsel do not wish to be accused of not having done everything possible to win the case.[91]) Some participants recognized that this concern often leads to overly lengthy or unfocused submissions and unnecessary evidence, which, instead of assisting, confuse arbitral tribunals,[92]) prolong the process and generate more costs. In this context, in-house counsel added that they should have a filtering function when it comes to document management and that they should not overwhelm external counsel with documents, creating the impression that every document is relevant and should be submitted as evidence.

---

complain about: they seldom propose tighter procedural calendars or early case assessments, and never offer incentives for arbitrators to decide more swiftly.

[89]) Legal costs usually represent the largest share of the overall costs of arbitration. According to the ICC Commission Report, Decisions on Costs in International Arbitration, ICC Dispute Resolution Bulletin 3 (2015), party costs (including lawyers' fees and expenses and other costs incurred by the parties for the arbitration) make up on average 83 % of the overall costs of the proceedings.

[90]) *See* Hans Mikael (Mika) Savola, *Ten Fail-Safe Ways to Irritate, Alienate and Antagonize Your Arbitral Tribunal*, in Scherer (ed), ASA Bulletin (2025, Issue 1), 46–57, at point 4: "*Drawn-out proceedings also create more opportunities to bill the client even for unnecessary services. To the Bad Advocate, arbitration is strictly business, not some high-minded pursuit of justice.*"

[91]) Bodenheimer, *supra*, at 470.

[92]) Landau, *supra*; see also Bodenheimer, *supra*, at 477, 478.

## 6. Poor Advocacy and Sanctions for Procedural Misconduct

The discussion turned to examples of advocacy that not only undermine efficiency but also raise questions of professional ethics. Beyond frivolous procedural objections, arbitrator challenges and late introduction of evidence, participants noted a growing trend to employ accusatory or even aggressive advocacy as part of case strategy. Indeed, this behavior mirrors what Toby Landau described as the *"progressive degeneration of advocacy"* in the 2025 Gaillard lecture: a spectrum that begins with the use of empty intensifiers in pleadings ("clearly", "obviously", "undoubtedly") that do not add any substance, escalates into accusations of dishonesty ("deliberately", "knowingly", "intentionally"), and culminates in *ad hominem* attacks vis-à-vis the opposing side and their counsel.[93])

Poor advocacy not only irritates[94]) arbitrators, it also undermines the integrity of the arbitral process. It should therefore be prohibited and, where appropriate, sanctioned. However, the discussion revealed that this rarely occurs.

There was broad consensus among the participants that procedural conduct which wastes resources and violates the duty to arbitrate in good faith should be reflected in adverse cost awards.[95]) Most institutional rules already grant arbitral tribunals discretion to take party conduct into account when allocating costs.[96]) In practice, however, arbitral tribunals often hesitate to exercise these powers and penalize misconduct, largely because of persistent due process paranoia (see section 4. above). As a result, one of the most effective tools for deterring obstructive conduct remains underutilized.

## 7. Conclusion

The discussion underscored that it is the parties and their counsel who use their autonomy to shape the arbitral process. When both sides agree on multiple rounds of submissions and generous timetables – and they often do – arbitral tribunals will rarely have a legitimate basis for imposing stricter schedules that contradict the parties' own procedural choices. Likewise, initiatives to limit the length of pleadings or streamline evidentiary phases will only succeed if they align with the parties' perception of due process and their procedural strategy in light of the specific circumstances of each case.

---

93) Landau, *supra*.

94) Draetta, *supra*, at 282; Savola, *supra*, at 46–57.

95) *See* Robin Moser, *Effects of Procedural Misconduct on the Allocation of Costs in International Arbitration*, in Scherer, ASA BULLETIN, (2022, Issue 4), 822–843.

96) *See, e.g.*, Art. 38(2) of the Swiss Rules, Art. 38(5) of the ICC Rules, Art. 28.4 of the LCIA Rules, Art. 42 of the UNCITRAL, and Art. 40 of the Swiss Rules.

Hence, while procedural efficiency is a shared responsibility among all stakeholders, it is the parties and their counsel who most directly shape the process. Therefore, all participants agreed that they (should) remain the principal drivers of efficiency in arbitration.

# I. Greater Efficiency in International Arbitration Proceedings – Impulses from Young Arbitration Voices

*Antonia Cermak-Kietaibl/Ondrej Cech*

## 1. Introduction

Efficiency (and inefficiency) in ADR proceedings can take many forms and reasonable lawyers can easily disagree on what brings efficiency into the proceedings and what does not. At the Vienna Arbitration Days 2025 World Café, our table gathered an interesting selection of young practitioners and law students with whom we explored what efficiency means for them and what efficiency-enhancing techniques could be overlooked by their more senior colleagues.

The topics discussed may be divided into two distinct fields, which warrant further exploration. The first field concerns efficiency within the proceedings, encompassing all the usual suspects ranging from cumbersome document production to the use of new technologies in the preparation of submissions. The second field addresses the preparation of students and young practitioners for entering the field of arbitration and the barriers they face. In the following report we summarize some of the views expressed at the World Café event and follow up with some further comments on the topics discussed.

## 2. Efficiency within the proceedings

Although arbitration is intended to be the more efficient alternative to litigation, reliance on arbitration as a dispute resolution method is not a universal cure for all procedural inefficiencies. International arbitration may be able to eliminate some sources of inefficiencies that are present in litigation (e.g., full appeals or random selection of judges who may lack the required specialization to address specific disputes) but in turn produces some new ones.

### a) Meaning of Efficiency

For young practitioners, efficiency has many forms. Time, costs, procedural clarity, and accessibility were among the issues discussed. Some viewed efficiency primarily as speed, while others stressed predictability and accuracy of outcomes. Participants agreed that efficiency is a shared responsibility.

While arbitrators can play their role by setting effective timelines, reasonable page limits and maintaining communication, counsels contribute by keeping submissions concise and well-structured, avoiding unnecessary arguments or last-minute submissions of new evidence.

At the same time, too strict page limits or very short deadlines can backfire. When lawyers are forced to rush their work or cut essential content, quality suffers, and time may be lost later when issues need to be clarified. Striking the right balance between speed and quality is therefore crucial.

### b) Document Production and Procedural Challenges

The production of documents was the area that received the most criticism, as it often represents a compromise between different legal traditions but fails to fully satisfy either. Some felt that trying to find a middle ground between broad common-law discovery and narrow civil-law disclosure only adds complexity and costs without proportional benefit. According to discussion participants, a clearer approach, either limiting production to specific requests or allowing full discovery where appropriate, could make the process more transparent, predictable, and therefore more efficient.

Questions were also raised about whether existing procedural rules, such as the IBA Rules on the Taking of Evidence or major institutional frameworks, are flexible enough to meet the needs of modern disputes. Some of the ideas discussed included more tribunal initiative in tailoring procedures, for example by setting reasonable limits on witness statements and submissions early on.

### c) Technology as a Tool

Technology continues to change arbitration practice. Electronic filing, virtual hearings, and online document platforms are now common, simplifying long-distance collaboration, cutting down on paper use, and saving travel time. Furthermore, artificial intelligence, a promising but still evolving tool, is increasingly transforming how arbitration practitioners work. While AI may speed up tasks such as document review or research, its use still raises – amongst others -questions about accuracy, confidentiality and accountability. In addition to that participants expressed concern that AI might reduce opportunities for young lawyers to develop foundational research skills, as AI manages many of the entry-level research tasks traditionally given to them. The general view was that technology should support the work of a lawyer, not replace it.

### d) User-Centric Arbitration

Another theme was how arbitration should primarily serve the needs of its end users, i.e. the clients who rely on it to solve their disputes. Some noted that arbitration can feel designed for lawyers and arbitrators rather than for clients. Clients often expect quick, cost-effective solutions but instead encounter lengthy procedures and high fees. Making arbitration more client-focused could involve shorter, more streamlined submissions, clearer cost estimates, and more effective procedural planning. Younger professionals, typically more adaptable and comfortable with technology, could help bridge this gap between clients, practitioners and institutions.

## 3. Preparing the Next Generation for Arbitration Practice

The second major theme discussed was how young lawyers and students are trained and educated and how easily they can enter the field of Arbitration after completing their studies.

### a) Real-life Skills and Education

A debate took place about whether universities adequately prepare students for practical work. Many young practitioners felt that law schools remain too focused on theory, with limited attention to real-life skills like drafting, advocacy, or case management. Others argued that theory still has value as it gives a solid foundation of knowledge that can later be developed into practical skills once students enter the legal profession.

In the end, the best approach might be to combine the best of both. Internships, moot competitions, and ADR-focused clinics were discussed as effective ways to bridge the gap between academia and practice. Such options, moot competitions in particular, allow students to experience the day-to-day work, pressure, and team cooperation in a much more realistic setting.

The group also discussed whether arbitration should be given a bigger role in standard legal education, at least as an elective subject. While universities might not be able to teach practice in depth, exposing students early to arbitration as a dispute resolution method would enhance its visibility and accessibility. Access and Early Opportunities

Entering the field of arbitration remains difficult for many young lawyers. It is often perceived as a small and close-knit community, that is difficult to penetrate. Few students are aware of arbitration before graduation, and those who are, may find it hard to find their first role in this field. Discussion participants felt that law firms, arbitral institutions, and established practitioners could play a more active role in reaching out to young lawyers and students. Open days, guest lectures, mentorship programs, and junior counsel appointments can make a significant difference. Tribunal secretary roles were also seen as a valuable way for young professionals to gain hands-on experience. Some suggested that institutions or professional bodies could develop centralized databases or "marketplaces" to match young professionals with such roles and increase accessibility.

### b) Diversity and Arbitrator Selection

The group agreed that diversity in arbitrator appointments can contribute not only to fairness but also to efficiency. A broader mix of professional, cultural, and generational backgrounds can lead to better solutions overall. Greater transparency and objective, merit-based appointment criteria in the appointment process were considered essential to opening opportunities for younger professionals to join the arbitrator pool.

## 4. Conclusion

In conclusion, the group shared a range of practical ideas to make arbitration work more effectively. Rather than advocating radical reform, the suggestions focused on better cooperation, openness, inclusion, and slight intentional modifications. Specific ideas included promoting diversity, setting reasonable page limits for submissions, trying new fee models, building stronger mentoring relationships between senior and junior practitioners, opening up job and internship opportunities, and taking ideas from other fields such as technology.

# Chapter III

# The Award and the Courts

# Surprise, Surprise – One Aspect for the Setting Aside of Awards

*Antje Baumann/Amaryllis Germanidis/Vivian Elvers*

## I. Introduction

The setting aside of arbitral awards is an evergreen in international commercial arbitration. One reason for the setting aside are so-called surprise decisions (*Überraschungsentscheidungen*). The losing party alleges that the arbitral tribunal based its decision on a fact or a legal argument that was neither previously addressed by one of the parties nor discussed by the arbitrators.

This article provides an overview of the relevant case law, primarily from the German perspective, setting out the hurdles that must be overcome to annul an award based on the legal argument of a surprise decision. Its aim is to provide clear guidance on how to recognize, avoid, and minimize the risk of surprise decisions in arbitral proceedings. It concludes with some practical tips for counsels involved in arbitrations on how to preserve and assert rights on which a later challenge might be based.

## II. Overview Over Relevant Case Law

Before addressing surprise decisions in detail, this chapter will first provide a brief overview of the general requirements for setting aside arbitral awards. The discussion then turns to the notion of a surprise decision and the key standards developed by German case law that may provide grounds for setting aside an award.

### A. What are the General Prerequisites for Setting Aside an Award?

The German procedure for setting aside an arbitral award under Section 1059 of the German Code of Civil Procedure ("ZPO") is not a second instance for reviewing facts or law.[1]) As repeatedly emphasized by the German Federal Court of Justice (*Bundesgerichtshof*) and the German Higher Regional

[1]) Federal Court of Justice, decision of 28 January 2014 – III ZB 40/13, NJW 2014, 1597, 1598; Higher Regional Court of Jena, decision of 8 August 2007 – 4 Sch 3/06, BeckRS 2008, 2869; *Münch*, Münchner Kommentar zur ZPO, 6th ed. 2022, Section 1059

Courts (*Oberlandesgerichte*), the procedure for setting aside an arbitral award serves only as a narrow corrective mechanism to safeguard the fundamental minimum standards of arbitral proceedings.[2]) The statutory framework aims at protecting the finality and the binding nature of properly rendered arbitral awards. State interference is limited to exceptional circumstances.[3]) This aim is safeguarded by prohibiting the so-called révision au fond – that is, a substantive re-examination of the case's merits.[4])

Section 1059 ZPO contains an exhaustive enumeration of the grounds on which an arbitral award may be set aside. The state court can only review and potentially set aside an award on the following grounds:[5])

- The arbitration agreement was invalid.
- A party was not given proper notice of the appointment of an arbitrator or of the arbitral proceedings, **or was otherwise unable to assert the means of its attack or defense.**
- The award deals with a dispute not contemplated by, or not falling within, the terms of the arbitration agreement.
- The composition of the arbitral tribunal or the arbitral procedure was not in accordance with the parties' agreement or, failing such agreement, **with the applicable statutory provisions.**[6])

In addition, an arbitral award may be set aside if:

- The subject matter of the dispute is not capable of settlement by arbitration under German law.
- **The recognition or enforcement of the award would lead to a result contrary to the German or international *ordre public*.**[7])

---

para. 5 and 7; *Althammer*, Zöller, ZPO, 36th ed. 10/2025; Section 1059; para. 74 et seqq., in particular para. 86.

[2]) Federal Court of Justice, decision of 28 January 2014 – III ZB 40/13, NJW 2014, 1597, 1598; Higher Regional Court of Jena, decision of 8 August 2007 – 4 Sch 3/06, BeckRS 2008, 2869; *Münch*, Münchner Kommentar zur ZPO, 6th ed. 2022, Section 1059 para. 5 and 7; *Althammer*, Zöller, ZPO, 36th ed. 10/2025, Section 1059; para. 74 et seqq., in particular para. 86.

[3]) *Wilske/Markert*, BeckOK ZPO, as of 1 July 2025, Section 1059, para. 1; *Münch*, Münchner Kommentar zur ZPO, 6th ed. 2022, Section 1059, para. 5; *Voit*, Musielak/Voit, ZPO, 22nd ed. 2025, Section 1059 para. 1 et seq.; *Buchwitz*, Schiedsverfahrensrecht, 1st ed. 2019, p. 274.

[4]) Federal Court of Justice, decision of 28 January 2014 – III ZB 40/13, NJW 2014, 1597, 1598; Higher Regional Court of Bavaria, decision of 15 January 2025 – 102 Sch 250/23, para. 40,70 and 88; *Münch*, Münchner Kommentar zur ZPO, 6th ed. 2022, Section 1059, para. 5 and 8.

[5]) Federal Court of Justice, decision of 28 January 2014 – III ZB 40/13, NJW 2014, 1597, 1598.

[6]) Section 1059 (2) No 1 ZPO.

[7]) Section 1059 (2) No 2 ZPO.

A mere error of law by the arbitral tribunal does not justify an annulment.[8]) German courts consistently reaffirm that material correctness of the award is not subject to review. Errors in legal reasoning, statutory interpretation, or evaluation of evidence are therefore irrelevant unless they reach the threshold of an *ordre public* violation.[9]) This threshold is, however, very high.

The first four paragraphs of Section 1059 ZPO correspond to Article 34 of the UNCITRAL Model Law on International Commercial Arbitration, as of 1985, with amendments as adopted in 2006 ("UNICITRAL Model Law").[10]) The grounds for setting aside an award set out in Article 34 (2) of the UNCITRAL Model Law, in turn, were taken verbatim from Article V of the United Nations Convention on the Recognition and Enforcement of Foreign Arbitral, as of 10 June 1958 ("New York Convention").[11]) Given that Section 1059 ZPO is modelled on Article 34 of the UNCITRAL Model Law, which in turn mirrors Article V of the New York Convention, it is hardly surprising that the grounds for setting aside an arbitral award, and the standards developed by German courts when applying these grounds, largely correspond to international practice.[12])

This international alignment partly extends to how surprise decisions are treated by courts.[13])

## B. What is a 'Surprise Decision'

In short, a surprise decision is a decision based on facts or legal arguments not discussed by either party during the arbitral proceedings.[14]) In other words, a decision is surprising when the arbitral tribunal bases its decision on a **legal** or **factual** aspect that

---

[8]) Federal Court of Justice, decision of 28 January 2014 – III ZB 40/13, NJW 2014, 1597, 1598; Federal Court of Justice, decision of 24 July 2014 – III ZB 83/13, NJW 2014, 3652, 3653, para. 12; Federal Court of Justice, decision of 21 December 2023 – I ZB 37/23 SchiedsVZ 2024, 115; Higher Regional Court of Bavaria, decision of 26 June 2024, 101 Sch 116/23, para. 79.

[9]) Higher Regional Court of Frankfurt am Main, decision of 11 April 2014 – 26 Sch 13/13, SchiedsVZ 2014, 154, 160; *Althammer*, Zöller, ZPO; 36th ed. 10/2025; Section 1059; para. 86; Higher Regional Court of Frankfurt am Main, decision of 26 November 2020 – 26 Sch 14/20; *Anders*, Anders/Gehle, ZPO, 83rd ed. 2025, Section 1059 para. 3.

[10]) *Wilske/Markert*, BeckOK ZPO, 1 July 2025, Section 1059, para. 2.

[11]) *Wilske/Markert*, BeckOK ZPO, 1 July 2025, Section 1059, para. 2.1.

[12]) *Adolphsen*, Münchner Kommentar zur ZPO, 6th ed. (2022), Article 6 UNÜ. para. 5; Balthasar, Int. Commercial Arbitration, 2nd ed. 2021, A. para. 1 and 113 et seqq.

[13]) Balthasar, Int. Commercial Arbitration, 2nd ed. 2021, A. para. 129.

[14]) *E.g.*, Chapter 25: Annulment of International Arbitral Awards (December 2023), Gary B. Born, International Commercial Arbitration (Third ed.) 2023.

- neither party raised in the previous course of the proceedings,
- and on which, therefore, they had no opportunity to comment.

Parties may be surprised to either find new facts in the award or to find that the arbitral tribunal based its decision on a legal basis that was not discussed during the arbitration. In the latter case the decision may also have factual implications, particularly if the arbitral tribunal bases its decision on a legal basis that the parties did not anticipate, and which would have required different factual submissions.[15]) Likewise, an arbitral tribunal may depart from a previously expressed legal view without further notice, but where the parties have justifiably relied on the earlier view.[16])

In annulment proceedings, however, it must be examined on a case-by-case basis whether the decision was actually surprising, meaning it was unforeseeable for the parties.

## C. Requirements for Annulment due to Surprise

A surprise decision may lead to the annulment of the award.

German courts, like Austrian courts,[17]) considered surprise decisions under various grounds for annulment under Section 1059 (2) ZPO: a violation of the right to assert the means of attack or defense,[18]) a procedural violation with regard to notice requirements of the tribunal,[19]) or a violation of the *ordre public*.[20]) All these reasons for annulment are an embodiment of the right to be heard pursuant to Article 103 (1) of the Basic Law for the Federal Republic of Germany ("GG").[21]) Based on Article V of the New York Convention, *e.g.*, Austrian procedural law contains similar grounds for annulment under Section 611 (2) of the Code of Civil Procedure. A differentiation between the grounds is often difficult, and a clear boundary is hard to discern.[22])

---

[15]) *E.g.*, Higher Regional Court of Cologne, decision of 28 June 2011 – 19 Sch 11/10, SchiedsVZ 2012, 161, 166.

[16]) Higher Regional Court of Frankfurt am Main, decision of 28 May 2020 – 26 Sch 7/19, para. 113; Higher Regional Court of Frankfurt am Main, decision of 17 October 2019 – 26 Sch 2/19, para. 48; Higher Regional Court of Stuttgart, decision of 30 July 2010 – 1 Sch 3/10, SchiedsVZ 2011, 49, 53.

[17]) *See, e.g., Schifferl* and *Wong*, Chapter III: The Award and the Courts, Decisions of the Austrian Supreme Court on Arbitration in 2015 and 2016, in: Christian Klausegger, Peter Klein, et al. (eds), Austrian Yearbook on International Arbitration 2017, Volume 2017, p. 225.

[18]) Section 1059 (2) No. 1 b) ZPO).

[19]) Section 1059 (2) No. 1 d) ZPO).

[20]) Section 1059 (2) No. 2 b) ZPO).

[21]) *Münch*, Münchner Kommentar zur ZPO, 6th ed. 2022, Section 1059, para. 27.

[22]) *Münch*, Münchner Kommentar zur ZPO, 6th ed. 2022, Section 1059, para. 27; *Wilske/Markert*, BeckOK ZPO, 58th ed. 1 September 2025, ZPO Section 1059, para. 65;

### 1. Violation of the Right to Present all Means of Attack or Defense

First, in some cases the surprise decision is considered a procedural error, violating Section 1059 (2) No. 1 b) ZPO in conjunction with Section 1042 (1) ZPO.[23])

Section 1042 of the ZPO ensures the parties' right to present their case and to assert the available means of attack or defense.[24]) The parties must be given the opportunity to submit all arguments and facts they consider necessary in support of their position.[25]) This right may be violated if, due to a surprise decision, the parties were not enabled to make the relevant submissions in advance.[26])

However, there is no general obligation for the arbitral tribunal to disclose its legal views, or to conduct a legal dialogue with the parties.[27]) Duties of clarification or guidance,[28]) apply only where the parties have expressly agreed thereto.[29]) Accordingly, the parties have no right to be informed in advance of the arbitral tribunal's intended legal assessment.[30])

Only if the arbitral tribunal **has expressed a specific legal opinion and later departs therefrom without prior notice,** a violation of the right to be heard may be assumed if this prevents a party from making further necessary factual or legal submissions.[31]) If a party is taken by surprise by the decision that differs from the previously expressed position of the arbitral tribunal,

---

Higher Regional Court of Frankfurt am Main, decision of 17 October 2019 – 26 Sch 2/19, para. 45 et seq.

[23]) Higher Regional Court of Frankfurt am Main, decision of 10 September 2015 – 26 Sch 1/15, 2014, SchiedsVZ, 154, 160; Higher Regional Court of Munich, decision of 14 March 2011 – 34 Sch 08/10, SchiedsVZ, 2011, 159, 165; *Wilske/Markert,* BeckOK ZPO, as of July 1, 2025, Section 1059, para. 42.1; *Münch*, Münchner Kommentar zur ZPO, 6th ed. 2022, ZPO Section 1059 para. 52–55.

[24]) *Münch*, Münchner Kommentar zur ZPO, 6th ed. 2022, Section 1042, para. 32.

[25]) *Münch*, Münchner Kommentar zur ZPO, 6th ed. 2022, Section 1042, para. 32.

[26]) *Münch*, Münchner Kommentar zur ZPO, 6th ed. 2022, Section 1042, para. 30 et seqq.

[27]) Federal Court of Justice, decision of 12 May 2020 – VIII ZR 171/19, NJW 2020, 2730, 2731, para. 12 et seq.

[28]) *E.g.* 139 (1), (3) ZPO.

[29]) Federal Court of Justice, decision of 12 May 2020 – VIII ZR 171/19, NJW 2020, 2730, 2731, para. 12 et seq.

[30]) *Risse*, Salger/Trittmann, IntSchiedsVerf-HdB, 1st ed. 2019, § 12. para. 36; Higher Regional Court of Frankfurt am Main, decision of 28 May 2020 – 26 Sch 7/19, para. 113.

[31]) *Münch*, Münchner Kommentar zur ZPO, 6th ed. 2022, Section 1042, para. 32; Higher Regional Court of Munich, decision of 14 March 2011 – 34 Sch 08/10, SchiedsVZ, 2011, 159, 165.

it may invoke a violation of the right to present all means of attack or defense.[32])

In other jurisdictions, a violation of the right to be heard is more readily recognized.[33]) Any decision based on a statutory or contractual provisions or arguments raised *sua sponte* by the arbitrators – without giving the parties the opportunity to be heard – constitutes a surprise decision and ground for annulment.[34])

For example, the French perspective appears to be much stricter than the German standard in that regard. In this context, the *Paris Cour d'Appel* ruled that arbitral tribunals are prohibited from raising new factual or legal arguments ex officio without first giving the parties an opportunity to comment.[35]) As set out above, this "absolute right" to comment on the arbitral tribunal's findings does not exist under German law as a means of attack or defense.

A violation of the right to present all means of attack or defense[36]) must be specifically invoked and substantiated by the applicant.[37]) In order to successfully challenge an award on this basis, the party must demonstrate that the arbitral tribunal provided an indication or notice during the proceedings and that the subsequent award contradicts this indication in legal or factual terms. Furthermore, the party must demonstrate that, had it been aware of the arbitral tribunal's deviation, it would have presented different legal or factual submissions or offered additional evidence.[38])

---

[32]) Section 1059 (2) No. 1 (b) ZPO in conjunction with Section 1042 (1) ZPO; *Münch*, Münchner Kommentar zur ZPO, 6th ed. 2022, Section 1042, para. 32; Higher Regional Court of Munich, decision of 14 March 2011 – 34 Sch 08/10, SchiedsVZ, 2011, 159, 165.

[33]) Chapter 25: Annulment of International Arbitral Awards (December 2023), in: Gary B. Born, International Commercial Arbitration (Third Edition) 2023, with further references.

[34]) Chapter 25: Annulment of International Arbitral Awards (December 2023), in: Gary B. Born, International Commercial Arbitration (Third Edition) 2023, with further references.

[35]) Paris *Cour d'Appel*, Thyssen Stahlunion GmbH v. Maaden General Foreign Trade Organisation Bulding Materials, decision of 6 April 1995, 1995 Rev. Arb. 448 (annulling award where tribunal selected interest rate without given the parties the opportunity to be heard "*Considering that the arbitrator's task is to settle the dispute within the limits set by the parties both in the terms of reference and in their briefs; that the principle of adversarial proceedings requires that no factual or legal argument be raised ex officio by the arbitral tribunal without the parties having been invited to comment on it [...].*"); *see also* French *Cour de Cassation* (Civ. 1), decision of 18 March 2015, Case No. 13-22.391.

[36]) Section 1059 (2) No. 1 b) ZPO in conjunction with Section 1042 (1) ZPO.

[37]) *Münch*, Münchner Kommentar zur ZPO, 6th ed. 2022, Section 1059, para. 59 et seqq.; *Wilske/Markert*, BeckOK ZPO, 1 July 2025, Section 1059, para. 68 et seqq.

[38]) OLG Frankfurt am Main, decision of 29 Oktober 2009 – 26 Sch 12/09, SchiedsVZ 2010, 52, 55.

## 2. Procedural Error Resulting from a Breach of the Arbitral Tribunal's Notice Obligation

Second, a surprise decision can also be challenged as a procedural error pursuant to Section 1059 Abs. 2 No. 1 d) ZPO.[39])

Section 1059 (2) No. 1 d) ZPO aims to safeguard procedural fairness by addressing violations of the procedural rules governing an arbitration, including, in particular, infringements of the right to be heard.[40])

Pursuant to Section 1059 (2) No. 2 d) ZPO in conjunction with Section 139 ZPO, an arbitral award can be set aside if the arbitral tribunal, contrary to the impression previously conveyed during the proceedings, ultimately adopts a different assessment in its award.[41]) In such a case, the arbitral tribunal breaches its obligation to give notice.[42]) While a mere failure to provide such an indication does not, as a rule, amount to a violation of the right to be heard in arbitration, the situation is different where the tribunal silently departs from a previously communicated legal view and thereby prevents the parties from presenting or adapting their arguments and evidence accordingly.[43]) Therefore, the exceptional duty to provide notice, can also serve as grounds for an annulment of the award.[44])

Likewise, the Swiss *Tribunal Fédéral* has indicated that there may be exceptional cases in which also the reliance on different legal facts may lead to an annulment of the award.[45]) In particular in cases where the arbitral tribunal adopts a legal position different from what it previously communicated to the parties, the arbitral tribunal is required to inform the parties and provide them with an opportunity to be heard on the issue.

---

[39]) Higher Regional Court of Frankfurt am Main, decision of 30 March 2006 – 26 Sch 12/05.

[40]) *Wilske/Markert*, BeckOK ZPO, 1 July 2025, Section 1059, para. 53 et seqq.

[41]) Higher Regional Court of Frankfurt am Main, decision of 30 March 2006 – 26 Sch 12/05.

[42]) Section 139 ZPO; Higher Regional Court of Frankfurt am Main, decision of 30 March 2006 – 26 Sch 12/05.

[43]) Higher Regional Court of Frankfurt am Main, decision of 30 March 2006 – 26 Sch 12/05; Federal Court of Justice, decision of 11 November 1982 – III ZR 77/81, NJW 1983, 867, 868.

[44]) Section 1059 (2) No. 1 b) ZPO and Section 1059 (2) No. 1 d) ZPO.

[45]) Swiss *Tribunal Fédéral*, decision of 27 June 2016, DFT 4A_322/2015, para. 4.1 ("*Exceptionally, the parties should be consulted when the judge or arbitral tribunal intends to base its decision on a legal norm or consideration that was not raised during the proceedings and whose relevance could not reasonably have been anticipated by the parties (ATF 130 III 35 consid. 5 and references). Determining what is unforeseeable is, moreover, a matter of discretion. For this reason, the Federal Tribunal applies this rule restrictively, also taking into account the particularities of this type of proceeding and aiming to prevent the argument of surprise from being used to obtain a substantive review of the award by the appellate authority (judgment 4A_634/2014 of 21 May 2015 consid. 4.1 and cited cases).*", translated from the original.

The applicant must demonstrate that the arbitral tribunal initially provided notice on the matter, and that the subsequent award issued by the tribunal deviated from this initial notice, thereby violating the applicant's right to be properly notified and to make further necessary submission.[46])

### 3. Violation of the *Ordre Public*

Finally, in other cases surprise decisions were considered as a violation of the procedural *ordre public* pursuant to Section 1059(2) No. 2 b) ZPO, since the right to be heard is considered a fundamental principle of procedural fairness.[47])

According to the German Federal Court of Justice, an award violates the *ordre public* if it is clearly incompatible with the fundamental principles of German law.[48]) German law distinguishes between the substantive and the procedural *ordre public*. The substantive *ordre public* encompasses the fundamental principles of justice and morality underlying the German legal order. This includes breaches of rules governing the basis of state or economic life, or awards that clearly contradict German notions of justice.[49]) The procedural *ordre public*, on the other hand, safeguards core procedural guarantees for a fair hearing, such as equality of arms, impartiality of the tribunal and the right to be heard (Article 103 (1) GG).[50])

Therefore, to challenge an award pursuant due to a violation of the *ordre public*, a violation of the right to be heard must be alleged.

However, according to German case law, a surprise decision is only an impermissible violation of the right to be heard if the arbitral tribunal evaluates facts or arguments in a manner that a diligent and competent involved party (*gewissenhafter und kundiger Prozessbeteiligter*) could not reasonably have

---

[46]) *Anders*, Anders/Gehle, ZPO, 83rd ed.2025, Section 1059 para. 26.

[47]) Higher Regional Court of Frankfurt am Main, decision of 5 June 2014 – 26 Sch 1/14, para. 54; Higher Regional Court of Munich, decision of 23 January 2012 – 34 Sch 33/11 (2), SchiedsVZ 2012, 107, 110; Higher Regional Court of Cologne, decision of 28 June 2011 – 19 Sch 11/10, SchiedsVZ 2012, 161, 166; Higher Regional Court of Stuttgart, decision of 30 July 2010 – 1 Sch 3/10, SchiedsVZ 2011, 49, 53.

[48]) Federal Court of Justice, decision of 10 March 2016 – I ZB 99/14, NJW-RR 2016, 892, 895, para. 92.; Federal Court of Justice, decision of 28 January 2014 – III ZB 40/13, NJW 2014, 1597, 1598; Higher Regional Court of Cologne, decision of 9 March 2018 – 19 Sch 21/17 para. 21, 94 and 97; *Anders*, Anders/Gehle, ZPO, 83rd ed. 2025, Section 1059 para. 26; *Voit*, Musielak/Voit, ZPO, 22nd ed. 2025, Section 1059 para. 29.

[49]) Federal Court of Justice, decision of 10 March 2016 – I ZB 99/14, NJW-RR 2016, 892, 895, para. 92; Federal Court of Justice, decision of 28 January 2014 – III ZB 40/13, NJW 2014, 1597, 1598; Higher Regional Court of Cologne, decision of 9 March 2018 – 19 Sch 21/17 para. 21, 94 and 97; *Anders*, Anders/Gehle, ZPO, 83rd ed. 2025, Section 1059 para. 26; *Voit*, Musielak/Voit, ZPO, 22nd ed. 2025, Section 1059 para. 29.

[50]) *Münch*, Münchner Kommentar zur ZPO, 6th ed. 2022, ZPO Section 1059 para. 52–55.

anticipated based on the previous course of the proceedings.[51]) Similarly, if the arbitral tribunal imposes requirements on the parties' submissions in its award without prior notice that even a diligent party to the proceedings would not have been able to anticipate, the decision may be surprising.[52])

When anticipating all possible subsequent assessments of the arbitral tribunal, the diligent and competent party must consider every justifiable legal opinion *(Berücksichtigung der Vielfalt vertretbarer Rechtsauffassungen).*[53]) Therefore, a decision is not a surprise merely because the arbitral tribunal interprets facts or draws conclusions differently from what a party expected or considered correct.[54])

Other civil law jurisdictions,[55]) in line with this argumentation and the principle of *jura novit curia*, recognize that arbitral tribunals enjoy greater latitude to base their decision on legal grounds not raised by the parties than to rely on factual grounds that have not been addressed by them.[56]) For example, the Swiss *Tribunal Fédéral* established that in Swiss arbitration law, the right to be heard primarily concerns the establishment and discussion of facts.[57])

---

[51]) Federal Court of Justice, decision of 12 May 2020 – VIII ZR 171/19, NJW 2020, 2730, para. 13; Higher Regional Court of Frankfurt am Main, decision of 5 June 2014 – 26 Sch 1/14, para. 56.

[52]) Higher Regional Court of Cologne, decision of 28 June 2011 – 19 Sch 11/10, SchiedsVZ 2012, 161, 166.

[53]) Higher Administrative Court of Münster, decision of 7 January 2022 – 19 A 2358/22.A, para. 10, with further references; Federal Court of Justice, decision of 12 May 2020 – VIII ZR 171/19, NJW 2020, 2730, para. 14.

[54]) Higher Administrative Court of Münster, decision of 7 January 2022 – 19 A 2358/22.A, para. 10, with further references.

[55]) *Knuts*, Jura Novit Curia and the Right to Be Heard: An Analysis of Recent Case Law, 28 Arb. Int'l 669, 671 (2012) ("*The principle of jura novit curia is widely accepted in court litigation, in particular in civil law jurisdictions like Germany, Switzerland, Sweden and Finland*").

[56]) Chapter 25: Annulment of International Arbitral Awards (December 2023), in: Gary B. Born, International Commercial Arbitration (Third Edition) 2023.

[57]) Swiss *Tribunal Fédéral*, decision of 27 June 2016, DFT 4A_322/2015, para. 4.1 ("*In Switzerland, the right to be heard primarily relates to the determination of facts. The parties' right to be consulted on legal questions is recognized only to a limited extent. As a general rule, in accordance with the principle of jura novit curia, state or arbitral courts have discretion to assess the legal implications of the facts and may also decide on the basis of legal rules other than those invoked by the parties. Consequently, provided that the arbitration agreement does not limit the arbitral tribunal's mandate to the legal arguments raised by the parties, the parties do not need to be specifically consulted regarding the scope to be given to the legal rules. […] This case law does not concern the establishment of facts. In this domain, the right to be heard indeed allows each party to comment on the facts essential to the award, to propose evidence on the relevant facts, and to participate in the hearings of the arbitral tribunal. However, it does not require the arbitrators to seek the parties' views on the weight to be given to each piece of evidence, nor does it permit a party to limit the tribunal's autonomy in assessing a particular item of evidence based on the purpose assigned to it by that party. If, hypothetically, each party*

While parties are entitled to comment on the facts essential to the award and to present evidence, their right to be consulted on legal issues is limited.[58]) Under the principle of *jura novit curia*, arbitral tribunals may apply legal rules beyond those invoked by the parties.[59]) However, the right to be heard does not extend to influencing how arbitrators weigh individual pieces of evidence, as this would undermine the tribunal's autonomy and the principle of free evaluation of evidence.[60])

As set out above, in Swiss and in Germany, this principle does not apply without limits. In this regard, a violation of the right to be heard may also arise from a decision that deviates from an assessment made by the arbitral tribunal in a prior notice, as outlined above. In practice, the aforementioned grounds for annulment under Section 1059 (2) No. 1 b) and d) ZPO are often asserted under Section 1059 (2) No. 2 b) ZPO as well.[61])

The grounds under Section 1059 (2) No. 2 ZPO are examined *ex officio*.[62]) Nevertheless, the applicant needs to put forward the facts regarding the alleged surprise decision.[63])

## 4. Conclusion

In conclusion, German courts determine on a case-by-case basis whether:

- A diligent and competent party could, considering all reasonable legal positions and the previous course of the proceedings, have anticipated the arbitral tribunal's legal reasoning; and as a subset of this, whether:
- The arbitral tribunal imposed unexpected requirements on the parties' submissions, which a diligent party could not have deemed necessary

---

*could pre-determine, for every piece of evidence submitted, the evidentiary consequence the tribunal would be permitted to draw from it, the principle of free evaluation of evidence – which constitutes a cornerstone of international arbitration – would be rendered meaningless*"); *see also* Swiss Tribunal Fédéral, decision of 17 January 2013, 4A_538/2012, para. 5.1.

[58]) Swiss *Tribunal Fédéral*, decision of 27 June 2016, DFT 4A_322/2015, para. 4.1; *see also* Swiss *Tribunal Fédéral*, decision of 17 January 2013, 4A_538/2012, para. 5.1.

[59]) Swiss *Tribunal Fédéral*, decision of 27 June 2016, DFT 4A_322/2015, para. 4.1; *see also* Swiss *Tribunal Fédéral*, decision of 17 January 2013, 4A_538/2012, para. 5.1.

[60]) Swiss *Tribunal Fédéral*, decision of 27 June 2016, DFT 4A_322/2015, para. 4.1; *see also* Swiss *Tribunal Fédéral*, decision of 17 January 2013, 4A_538/2012, para. 5.1.

[61]) *Münch*, Münchner Kommentar zur ZPO, 6th ed. 2022, Section 1059, para. 27; *Wilske/Markert*, BeckOK ZPO, 58th ed. 1 September 2025, ZPO Section 1059, para. 65; Higher Regional Court of Frankfurt am Main, decision of October 17, 2019 – 26 Sch 2/19, para. 45 et seq.

[62]) *Münch*, Münchner Kommentar zur ZPO, 6th ed. 2022, Section 1059, para. 59 et seqq.; *Wilske/Markert*, BeckOK ZPO, 1 July 2025, Section 1059, para. 68 et seqq.

[63]) *Münch*, Münchner Kommentar zur ZPO, 6th ed. 2022, Section 1059, para. 59 et seqq.; *Wilske/Markert*, BeckOK ZPO, 1 July 2025, Section 1059, para. 68 et seqq.

based on the previous course of the proceedings, without providing appropriate prior notice; or

- The arbitral tribunal had previously rejected or excluded a relevant legal position and subsequently revised its stance without prior notice.

## D. Further Requirements to be Met in order to Set Aside an Award Due to a 'Surprise Decision': Causality

Under German law, the annulment of an arbitral award on the grounds of a surprise decision is subject to a causality requirement *(Entscheidungserheblichkeit).* The alleged grounds for annulment must thus be relevant to the arbitral tribunal's decision. This applies equally to the annulment following a surprise decision based on Section 1059(2) No. 2 b) ZPO or on Section 1059 (2) No 1. b) and d) ZPO.[64])

Therefore, to decide whether a party's right to be heard has been violated by a surprise decision, it must be examined whether the arbitral tribunal would have reached a different conclusion had this right not been violated.[65]) This is not the case if the disregarded submission is not relevant to the decision anyway, for example because the arbitral tribunal rejected or justified the case on other grounds.[66]) If an impact is deemed possible, the second step is to examine whether the disregarded submission would have been sufficient to cause the arbitral tribunal to decide differently.[67]) If the submission is clearly unsuitable, this is not the case.[68]) This must be assessed from the perspective of the arbitral tribunal that was seized with the matter.[69])

[64]) Bavarian Higher Regional Court, decision of 17 May 2023 – 102 Sch 44/22, para. 42; Higher Regional Court of Frankfurt am Main, decision of 17 October 2019 – 26 Sch 2/19, para. 50; Federal Court of Justice, decision of 15 January 2009 – III ZB 83/07, SchiedsVZ 2009, 126, 127; Saarland Higher Regional Court, decision of 29 October 2002 – 4 Sch 2/02 SchiedsVZ 2003, 92, 94; *Voit*, Musielak/Voit, ZPO, 22nd ed. 2025, Section 1059 para. 13, 22, 27.

[65]) *Voit*, Musielak/Voit, ZPO, 22nd ed. 2025, Section 1059 para. 13, 22, 27, Federal Court of Justice, decision of 18 July 2019 – I ZB 90/18, SchiedsVZ 2020, 46, para. 32.

[66]) *Voit*, Musielak/Voit, ZPO, 22nd ed. 2025, Section 1059 para. 27.

[67]) *Voit*, Musielak/Voit, ZPO, 22nd ed. 2025, Section 1059 para. 27.

[68]) *Voit*, Musielak/Voit, ZPO, 22nd ed. 2025, Section 1059 para. 27.

[69]) *Voit*, Musielak/Voit, ZPO, 22nd ed. 2025, Section 1059 para. 27; Munich Higher Regional Court, decision of 12 April 2011 – 34 Sch 28/10, SchiedsVZ 2011, 230, 232.

## III. Concluding Remarks and Practical Guidance for Counsel

Case law shows that surprise decisions are primarily case-by-case decisions. Even the grounds for setting aside an arbitral award under Section 1059 ZPO due to a surprise decision are not applied uniformly. This lack of coherence stems from the broad wording of Section 1059 ZPO and Articles V of the New York Convention and 34 of the UNCITRAL Model Law. Nevertheless, national courts have developed their own understandings of what constitutes an impermissible "surprise", ranging from procedural ambush to unanticipated legal reasoning.

Even though the treatment of surprise decision varies, some general guidance can be identified: To minimize the risk of a surprise decision, counsel must actively seek to ensure procedural fairness throughout the arbitration. Counsel should make comprehensive submissions that address not only the main legal theories, but also any alternative interpretations that the arbitral tribunal might consider. Counsel should pay close attention to procedural directions and indications from the arbitral tribunal during the proceedings. Whenever uncertainty arises regarding the arbitral tribunal's understanding of a factual or legal issue, it is helpful to seek clarification or request an opportunity to comment.

If a party seeks to set aside an award on the basis of a surprise decision, counsel must establish that the arbitral tribunal's reasoning was genuinely unforeseeable and that it significantly impacted the outcome. The challenge should focus on demonstrating that a diligent and competent party could not have anticipated the arbitral tribunal's approach, and that this lack of notice deprived the party of a meaningful opportunity to be heard. In this regard, practitioners can draw on a wide range of case law that illustrates different "surprising" scenarios. Given the close connection between Section 1059 ZPO, the UNCITRAL Model Law, and the New York Convention, it may also be persuasive to draw analogies from decisions rendered in other jurisdictions.

On the other hand, when defending against the allegation of a surprise decision, counsel should emphasize that the arbitral tribunal's reasoning fell within the range of reasonably predictable legal interpretations and that the party had sufficient opportunity to address the relevant issues during the proceedings. Establishing causality – showing whether the result would have been different absent the alleged violation – is decisive for both sides.

# Valuation on Trial: Rethinking How Tribunals Calculate Damages

*Arush Khanna/Rishika Jain*

## I. Introduction

Quantification of damages often remains the least developed part of an arbitral award. For all the intellectual energy poured into jurisdiction and liability, the quantification of damages often remains the least developed part of an award.[1])

A recent study on damages in international arbitration found that tribunals awarded, on average, only 40 per cent of the amounts claimed.[2]) These statistics are no longer exceptional; they represent the norm.

Despite its growing sophistication, arbitration as a field has not yet developed a consistent or disciplined approach to assessing damages. Tribunals still oscillate between divergent expert valuations, inconsistent methodologies, and, at times, minimal reasoning.[3]) The result is predictable: parties question not only the outcome but the intellectual integrity of the process itself.

As damages grow in scale and complexity, so does the pressure on tribunals to demonstrate analytical rigour.[4]) Most arbitrators are lawyers, not economists; most lawyers are advocates, not valuers.[5]) The result is a per-

---

[1]) Derek A. Soller, "What Would Have Happened If? The Role of Hypothesis, Assumptions, Good Faith Estimates and Speculation in Determining the Quantum of Damages", in Carlos González-Bueno (ed), *40 under 40 International Arbitration, 37* (Kluwer Law International, 2018); Mark W. Friedman, "Quantum Academy", 17 Disp Resol Int'l 69, 70–71 (2023).

[2]) PricewaterhouseCoopers (PwC), *International Arbitration Damages Study,* 9 (Mar 2024) https://www.pwccn.com/en/risk-assurance/publications/international-arbitration-damages-study-mar2024.pdf.

[3]) Mara Senn, Dawn Yamane Hewett and Stephanie I. Fine, "Damages in International Arbitration: Understanding the Theories and Methods of Damages Valuation and Compensation", in Laurence Shore, Tai-Heng Cheng and John Beechey (eds), *International Arbitration in the United States* 423 (Kluwer Law International 2017).

[4]) *Eaed.*

[5]) Adam Douglas, "Procedural Tools to Facilitate the Quantification of Damages in Investor-State Arbitration", in Christina L. Beharry (ed), *Contemporary and Emerging Issues on the Law of Damages and Valuation in International Investment Arbitration,* 3 (Brill Nijhoff 2018).

sistent gap between law's search for certainty and finance's tolerance for uncertainty.[6])

This article examines that gap. It looks at how arbitral tribunals have approached valuation, how damages reasoning of quantification has evolved, and why despite decades of jurisprudence, quantum remains an Achilles' heel in the arbitration eco-system. Drawing on recent studies, valuation standards, and cases, it argues for a more transparent, coherent, and economically grounded approach to damages.

## II. From Asset-Based Valuation to Forward-Looking Damages

For much of the twentieth century, arbitral practice was anchored in asset-based valuation, measuring loss by reference to what the investor had put in, not what might have been earned.[7]) This approach, focusing on tangible investment costs, physical assets, or balance-sheet figures, dominated both commercial and investment arbitration throughout the 1980s and 1990s.[8]) It reflected a cautious legal culture: tribunals were more comfortable compensating what could be counted than what could be forecast.[9]) Asset-based methods were straightforward and verifiable but limited. They could capture what had been spent yet failed to capture what had been lost in terms of future earning potential.[10])

However, by turn of the century, the paradigm shifted. As cross-border investment deepened and projects became more capital-intensive, tribunals began to recognize that focusing only on sunk costs could under-compensate investors whose ventures had genuine profit potential.[11]) This shift gave rise to forward-looking valuation methods, most notably the Discounted Cash Flow (DCF) model.

DCF treats an enterprise as a *going concern* – an operating, profit-generating business. Instead of valuing what is already there, it values what the business is expected to produce in the future. In practice, the method estimates projected cash flows over a defined period and discounts them back to their present value using a rate that reflects risk and time preference.[12]) In essence, it translates expected future income into today's dollars.

---

[6]) *Id.*

[7]) Irmgard Marboe, "International Standards, Bases of Value, and Valuation Approaches", in *Calculation of Compensation and Damages in International Investment Law* 201 (2nd ed., Oxford International Arbitration Series, OUP 2017).

[8]) *Ead.*

[9]) *Ead.*

[10]) *Ead.* at 202.

[11]) *Ead., supra* note 7, at 201–207.

[12]) Senn, Hewett & Fine, *supra* note 3, at 434.

To see how DCF works in practice, consider a simple illustration. Imagine a project expected to generate USD 1 million each year for the next three years. If the hypothetical discount rate is 10 %,[13]) those future profits, once discounted, translate to present values of roughly USD 0.91 million, USD 0.83 million, and USD 0.75 million, for each of the respective years. The total amount, about USD 2.49 million, represents what those three years of income are worth today.[14]) Even in this modest scenario, a slight change in the discount rate or projected cash flows can dramatically alter the result. It is this sensitivity magnified in multi-billion-dollar disputes that makes DCF both powerful and, at times, perilous in arbitration.

This approach marks more than just a methodological change; it reflects a conceptual shift in how international law understands economic loss. Traditionally, compensation in arbitration was backward-looking, *i.e.*, it measured what was spent or lost, not what might have been earned.[15]) But as tribunals began to focus on the value of future profits, the inquiry expanded from accounting for the past to forecasting the future.

Under international law, that broader inquiry is captured through two classic categories: *damnum emergens* and *lucrum cessans*.[16]) The first, *damnum emergens*, refers to the actual and immediate loss – the tangible harm or out-of-pocket expenditure caused by the breach. It includes invested capital, construction costs, fees, or expenses already incurred.[17]) In simple terms, it measures the financial hole created by the wrongful act.

The second, *lucrum cessans*, concerns lost profit – the income that would have been earned "but for" the breach.[18]) This structure mirrors the doctrine articulated in the *Chorzów Factory* case: a claimant must be placed, as far as possible, in the financial position it would have occupied but for the wrongful act.[19])

Together, these two heads of loss represent the principle of full reparation in international law: compensation must wipe out all the consequences of the

---

[13]) In practice, the selection of a discount rate is rarely so straightforward. It is typically derived from the project's weighted average cost of capital (WACC) and adjusted to reflect jurisdictional, industry, and project-specific risks. *See also:* James M. Hosking, "Important Components of DCF Valuations", in Mark A. Kantor (ed), *Valuation for Arbitration: Compensation Standards, Valuation Methods and Expert Evidence* 159–163 (Kluwer Law International 2008).

[14]) Lyn Alden, "Discounted Cash Flow Analysis: Complete Tutorial with Examples", *StockDelver* (2018), https://www.lynalden.com/discounted-cash-flow-analysis/.

[15]) Senn, Hewett & Fine, *supra* note 3, at 414–417.

[16]) *Eaed.*

[17]) *Eaed.*

[18]) Senn, Hewett & Fine, *supra* note 3, at 418–419.

[19]) Senn, Hewett & Fine, *supra* note 3, at 414–417; *Factory at Chorzów (Germany v. Poland) (Merits)*, Judgment, 1928 P.C.I.J. (ser. A) No. 17.

wrongful act, both past and future.[20] *Damnum emergens* repairs what has been destroyed; *lucrum cessans* restores what has been denied.

In practice, tribunals often need to balance both. An investor whose project was operational and profitable before expropriation may justifiably claim for *lucrum cessans*; one whose project never reached production may be limited to *damnum emergens*.[21] The line between the two is not rigid, but it anchors the logic of damages.

However, the transition from tangible loss to projected value has not been smooth. The DCF method, despite its mathematical sophistication, often conceals more uncertainty than precision.[22] Its output depends entirely on its inputs, being, assumptions about multiple variable factors like commodity prices, production volumes, regulatory stability, or geopolitical disruptions, all of which are susceptible to variation.[23] Even minor adjustments in these variables can change the valuation by hundreds of millions of dollars.[24]

The problem is not with DCF itself, but with how it is applied. In principle, it works well for established, profitable businesses with verifiable financial histories.[25] In practice, it is frequently used for projects that are speculative, incomplete, or still under construction, like ventures for which there is little or no operating data.[26] Tribunals, pressed by parties for a single number, often accept models built more on optimism than evidence.[27]

The World Bank Guidelines echo this warning, advising that DCF should be applied only where future profits are "reasonably predictable" and avoided for new or unproven projects.[28] The United Nations Compensation Com-

---

20) *Factory at Chorzów (Germany v. Poland)*, Judgment, 1928 P.C.I.J. (ser. A) No. 17, at 47.

21) Senn, Hewett & Fine, *supra* note 3, at 414–417.

22) *Eaed.*, *supra* note 3, at 427–429.

23) Gervase MacGregor & Michael Smith, "Best Practices and Issues That Arise in DCF Models", in *The Guide to Damages in International Arbitration* (6th ed., Law Business Research 2024), https://globalarbitrationreview.com/guide/the-guide-damages-in-international-arbitration/6th-edition/article/best-practices-and-issues-arise-in-dcf-models.

24) *Eid.*

25) *See* Meg Kinnear, "Damages in Investment Treaty Arbitration", in Katia Yannaca-Small (ed), *Arbitration Under International Investment Agreements: A Guide to the Key Issues* 551, 552 (Oxford University Press 2010); *Burlington Resources Inc. v. Republic of Ecuador*, ICSID Case No ARB/08/5, Decision on Reconsideration and Award, ¶ 160 (7 February 2017).

26) Kinnear, *supra* note 25, at 563.

27) *Ead.*

28) World Bank, *Guidelines on the Treatment of Foreign Direct Investment* § IV(5) (1992).

mission and the MIGA Operational Regulations similarly restrict its use to ongoing, profit-generating enterprises.[29])

Yet claimants routinely present DCF valuations grounded in best-case scenarios, assuming high growth, stable regulation, and perfect efficiency.[30]) Respondents counter with conservative or pessimistic models. Arbitrators, typically lawyers, are then left to choose between two competing fictions, often with little guidance on how to test the underlying economics.[31])

This explains why damages reasoning in arbitration has drawn increasing criticism. The more tribunals rely on DCF, the greater the gap between the *appearance* of precision and the *reality* of uncertainty.[32]) The method's elegance has become its trap: it creates the illusion of objectivity while quietly embedding layers of speculation.[33])

## III. The Fair Market Value Standard

The Fair Market Value ("FMV") standard is the prevailing benchmark for determining compensation in investment arbitration and is increasingly being adopted in commercial arbitrations.[34]) Defined as the price a willing and informed buyer would pay, today, for the future profits of an enterprise, FMV translates legal entitlement into an economic number.[35])

In principle, FMV should reflect a "meeting of minds" between buyer and seller, a balance of risk and reward determined by the market. However, in practice, valuations in arbitration rarely undergo this market test.[36]) FMV, in practice, thus, is not established through real transactions but through financial models built on expert assumptions.[37])

Building on the earlier illustration under DCF, if the same enterprise projected to earn USD 1 million annually were valued under the FMV standard, the DCF calculation would represent only one method for estimating that fair

29) United Nations Compensation Commission (UNCC), *Decision 1 – Principles Governing Claims* (1993); Multilateral Investment Guarantee Agency (MIGA), *Operational Regulations* art. 14 (2013); Marboe, *supra* note 7, at 169–170.

30) Marboe, *supra* note 7, at 209–211.

31) *Ead.*

32) *Ead.*

33) *Ead.*

34) Marboe, *supra* note 7, at 180; Juan Carlos Boué, "The Determination of Quantum and Claim Inflation", in *Rethinking Investment Law,* 205 (David Schneiderman & Gus Van Harten eds., Oxford University Press 2023).

35) United Nations Conference on Trade and Development (UNCTAD), *Fair Market Value in Investment Arbitration* (2020).

36) Boué, *supra* note 34, at 207.

37) International Valuation Standards Council (IVSC), *International Valuation Standards (IVS)* (effective January 31, 2024; published January 31, 2024) (London: IVSC 2024).

market value. The model would discount those anticipated cash flows – USD 909,000, USD 826,000, USD 751,000, USD 683,000, and USD 621,000 – to arrive at an aggregate present value of about USD 3.79 million.[38]) This figure, however, does not *prove* market value; it merely *infers* it, subject to the assumptions underlying each input.

In a real market transaction, price would also reflect comparable sales, asset condition, and investor sentiment – all variables that pure financial modelling cannot capture. This distinction between FMV as a legal standard and DCF as an economic tool underlies much of the tension in arbitral valuation.[39])

The growing reliance on the DCF model reflected a deeper conceptual shift toward FMV as the benchmark for compensation in investment arbitration.[40]) FMV represents not a method but a standard of value, the legal *goal* of compensation, while DCF is one of several valuation methods used to reach that goal.[41])

FMV expresses the amount a willing and informed buyer would pay to a willing and informed seller for an asset in an open market, without compulsion.[42]) DCF, by contrast, estimates the present value of expected future cash flows by discounting them at a rate that reflects both the risk of the investment and the time value of money.[43]) In short, FMV is the *destination*; DCF is one possible *path* toward it.

Tribunals apply FMV when the governing treaty or applicable law explicitly requires compensation at fair market value. This principle flows directly from investment treaties and customary international law, both of which recognize compensation at "the fair market value immediately before the expropriation".[44])

A leading example is *Compañía del Desarrollo de Santa Elena S.A. v. Costa Rica*, where the tribunal held that compensation for expropriation should be based on the FMV of the property "at the date of expropriation", not at the date

[38]) Investopedia, "Discounted Cash Flow (DCF) Explained with Formula and Examples" (17 Oct. 2025) https://www.investopedia.com/terms/d/dcf.asp.

[39]) Boué, *supra* note 34, at 208.

[40]) William C. Lieblich, "Determinations by International Tribunals of the Economic Value of Expropriated Enterprises", 7 *J. Int'l Arb.* 37 (1990).

[41]) Philip Haberman & Liz Perks, "Overview of Methodologies for Assessing Fair Market Value", in *The Guide to Damages in International Arbitration* (4th ed., Global Arbitration Review/Law Business Research 2021), https://globalarbitrationreview.com/guide/the-guide-damages-in-international-arbitration/4th-edition/article/overview-of-methodologies-assessing-fair-market-value.

[42]) *Eid.*

[43]) *Eid.*

[44]) United Nations Conference on Trade and Development (UNCTAD), *Fair Market Value in Investment Arbitration* 6 (2020).

of payment, affirming that the critical moment for valuation is the state's act of interference.[45])

Similarly, in *CME v. Czech Republic*, the tribunal preferred a market-comparables approach over DCF, citing the availability of reliable sale data that allowed for an objective market-based valuation.[46]) Tribunals consistently favour FMV when there is objective market evidence – such as share prices, merger-and-acquisition data, or comparable company transactions, that can anchor the valuation in actual market behaviour rather than hypothetical projections.

In *Yukos v. Russia*,[47]) the tribunal applied FMV standard under the treaty and used a mix of methods, *i.e.*, DCF, comparable company analysis, and market multiples, to estimate the value of Yukos shares before the expropriation.[48]) The approach reflected a pragmatic recognition that no single valuation model is definitive; triangulating several methods provides a more balanced and credible estimate of value.

When market data exists, FMV is straightforward. The challenge arises when it does not; when the expropriated enterprise is privately held, early-stage, or operating in a market without reliable comparable. In such cases, tribunals turn to DCF as a proxy for FMV. DCF is not, in itself, a standard of value; it is a tool for estimating what the market would have paid if one had existed.[49])

Tribunals ought to remain cautious since DCF relies on forecasts, and forecasts can be wrong. It demands a strong evidentiary foundation: historical performance, audited accounts, and demonstrable profitability.[50]) Where those conditions are absent, DCF ceases to be valuation and becomes speculation.

The contrast is clear in two oft-cited cases. In *Occidental Petroleum Corporation v. Ecuador*, the tribunal accepted DCF to assess FMV because Occidental had a long operational record, audited financial statements, and a proven production history.[51]) However, it reduced the damages by 25 per cent

---

45) *Compañía del Desarrollo de Santa Elena S.A. v. Republic of Costa Rica*, ICSID Case No. ARB/96/1, Award ¶¶ 72–78 (17 February, 2000).

46) *CME Czech Republic B.V. v. Czech Republic*, UNCITRAL, Final Award ¶ 595–604 (Mar. 14, 2003).

47) *Yukos Universal Ltd. (Isle of Man) v. Russian Federation*, PCA Case No. AA 227, Final Award ¶¶ 1785–1790 (July 18, 2014).

48) *Ibid.*, Final Award ¶¶ 1788–1793 (July 18, 2014).

49) Aswath Damodaran, "Ten Myths About Discounted Cash Flow" (NYU Stern School of Business 2022), https://pages.stern.nyu.edu/~adamodar/pdfiles/country/DCFmythsTemasek.pdf.

50) Greig Taylor & Alexander Lee, "Discounted Cash Flow" (Practice Note, Thomson Reuters/AlixPartners LLP 2019), https://www.alixpartners.com/media/13644/discounted-cash-flow-w-021-0210.pdf.

51) *Occidental Petroleum Corp. & Occidental Exploration & Production Co. v. Republic of Ecuador*, ICSID Case No. ARB/06/11, Award ¶¶ 708–710, 830 (October 5, 2012).

which reflected that even within DCF analysis, results can be adjusted for equity and risk.

By contrast, in *Siag and Vecchi v. Egypt*,[52]) the tribunal rejected DCF entirely, finding that the claimants' tourism project was still under development and lacked an operational record.[53]) The projected cash flows were "too speculative to serve as a reliable basis for valuation".[54])

These decisions capture the uneasy balance between law's demand for certainty and economics' acceptance of risk. As the master of the proceedings, the tribunal must decide not only which valuation method to use but also how and when to apply it. Valuation models often give the impression of precision, but that precision is largely dependent on the assumptions behind them. The real difficulty lies not in running the numbers, but in making sure those numbers rest on solid, verifiable evidence rather than optimistic projections or advocacy.

## IV. The Problem of Optimistic Forecasts

Optimism is built into both corporate life and legal pleadings. Business plans rarely model mediocrity. Strategic optimism is an institutional habit, boardrooms are wired to expect success, not failure. Yet when those same projections are later repurposed as evidence of loss, they may create a false sense of certainty.

Long-term business plans prepared before a dispute often overstate revenues and understate risks.[55]) Experts who rely on internal forecasts effectively "stack the deck" toward higher valuations by assuming that every variable capable of improvement will indeed improve, and every risk capable of occurring will conveniently not.[56])

This optimism bias becomes especially problematic in unrealised or aborted projects. Tribunals have, at times, awarded damages for ventures that never existed beyond feasibility studies. In *Metalclad v. Mexico*, for instance, the tribunal used DCF to calculate lost profits for a landfill that had never operated – a decision criticised by later tribunals and commentators as

---

[52]) *Siag & Vecchi v. Arab Republic of Egypt*, ICSID Case No. ARB/05/15, Award ¶¶ 575–582 (June 1, 2009).

[53]) *Ibid.* Award ¶¶ 543–545 (June 1, 2009).

[54]) David Caryl, James Nicholson & Lee Buchheit, "Early-Stage Investments and the 'Modern' DCF Method", in *The Guide to Damages in International Arbitration* (John A. Trenor ed., 4th ed., Global Arbitration Review 2021), https://globalarbitrationreview.com/guide/the-guide-damages-in-international-arbitration/4th-edition/article/early-stage-investments-and-the-modern-dcf-method.

[55]) Senn, Hewett & Fine, *supra* note 3, at 427–428.

[56]) *Eaed.*

untethered from economic reality.[57]) The World Bank Guidelines themselves warn that DCF should not be used to calculate lost profits for "a beginning industry and unperformed work".[58])

These distortions reveal a deeper discomfort: tribunals and advocates, trained in law not finance, are often forced to navigate evidence that feels scientific but is built on assumptions. This is where the real difficulty begins.

## V. When Arbitrators Play Economists

At the root of the problem lies a simple institutional fact: most arbitrators are trained in law, not finance. Their expertise lies in interpretation of contracts and evaluation of evidence, and not necessarily in determining quantum and valuing future income. This leaves them heavily reliant on party-appointed experts, professionals paid by each side, according to competing narratives.[59])

While expert evidence is indispensable, its adversarial nature can exacerbate divergence rather than resolve it.[60]) Experts may use the same data but reach radically different conclusions, often because they are instructed to start from different assumptions. Divergent models, discount rates, and forecasting horizons can turn the same facts into dramatically different valuations. When one expert says a project is worth USD 1 billion and other values it at USD 100 million, tribunals are left navigating a chasm disguised as science.[61])

Lacking financial training, many tribunals resolve this discomfort by seeking middle ground. The instinct is understandable: if two extremes seem equally credible, the "truth" must lie somewhere in between. But arithmetic balance is not analytical fairness. As several annulment decisions have shown, tribunals that simply average expert valuations without explaining why expose their awards to challenge for lack of reasoning.[62])

Some institutions have tried to bridge this gap. The ICC encourages concurrent expert testimony, colloquially known as "hot-tubbing", allowing experts to respond to each other in real time.[63]) The LCIA promotes joint expert statements to identify areas of agreement and isolate disputes.[64]) The

---

[57]) *Metalclad Corporation v United Mexican States*, ICSID Case No ARB(AF)/97/1, Award (August 30, 2000).

[58]) World Bank, *supra* note 28.

[59]) Douglas, *supra* note 5, at 6.

[60]) *Id.*

[61]) *Id.*, at 6–8.

[62]) *Occidental*, *supra* note 51; *see also Siag*, *supra* note 52.

[63]) International Chamber of Commerce (ICC), *Note to Parties and Arbitral Tribunals on the Conduct of Arbitration* (January 1, 2021), available at https://iccwbo.org/publication/note-to-parties-and-arbitral-tribunals-on-the-conduct-of-arbitration/.

[64]) London Court of International Arbitration (LCIA), *Guidance Note* (2020); *see also LCIA Arbitration Rules* art 14.5 (2020).

2022 ICSID Arbitration Rules explicitly empower tribunals to appoint independent experts.[65]) Yet these tools remain underused. Too often, experts still speak past each other, and tribunals remain spectators in their own evidentiary process.

This discomfort with numbers shapes how awards are written. Liability sections are meticulous, layered with authorities and precedent. Quantum sections, by contrast, are often thin – a few pages summarising expert opinions, followed by a conclusory figure. The imbalance is striking. Lawyers dissect liability with surgical precision but approach valuation as if it were an afterthought – a technical appendix rather than the heart of the dispute.

The problem is not just stylistic; it's structural. Quantum determines whether the judgment of law becomes a judgment of value; whether a legal victory translates into an economic one. Yet tribunals often devote ten pages to fault and ten lines to consequence. This intellectual asymmetry erodes confidence in the process and, at times, the enforceability of the award.

The answer lies not in adding more experts but in engaging more deeply with them. Lawyers who understand valuation models can frame better questions, challenge implausible assumptions, and guide the tribunal toward the core of the dispute. A tribunal that treats quantum as part of liability, the financial reflection of the wrong, is far less likely to deliver an incoherent result.

## VI. Liability vs. Quantum: The Uneven Attention Problem

The imbalance between liability and quantum runs deeper than drafting habits; it reflects the profession's comfort zone. Lawyers are fluent in causation and breach, not in discount rates or cash-flow models. Quantum requires a different form of reasoning, one that blends legal principle with economic probability.

Tribunals and counsel alike pour analytical energy into establishing fault but devote a fraction of that rigour to quantifying consequence.[66]) This imbalance has consequences of its own: parties may leave the hearing feeling that the law was debated, but the loss was guessed.

Moreover, the sequencing of proceedings often compounds this problem. Quantum is usually postponed until the final phase, long after the factual and legal foundation has been laid. Experts are brought in late, pleadings treat valuation mechanically, and tribunals, fatigued by months of argument,

[65]) International Centre for Settlement of Investment Disputes (ICSID), *Rules of Procedure for Arbitration Proceedings (Arbitration Rules)* r. 39 (effective July 1, 2022).

[66]) Boué, *supra* note 34, at 201.

summarise competing figures instead of analysing them.[67]) By that stage, the evidentiary base for a proper valuation may no longer exist.

This procedural reality exposes a deeper conceptual divide. Arbitration's fact-finding mission is retrospective it examines what happened. Damages analysis, by contrast, is hypothetical, assessing what would have happened but for the wrongful act. This "*but-for*" conundrum is not provable in the ordinary evidentiary sense; it is constructed through assumptions and models. This conceptual divide explains much of the discomfort tribunals experience when moving from liability to quantum.[68])

A well-reasoned liability section may satisfy the lawyer's mind, but quantum is where the award meets reality. It determines whether the victory has substance or only symbolism. An award that is doctrinally sound but economically incoherent is, in reality, half an award.

Closing this gap demands a cultural shift. Tribunals must treat damages not as an arithmetic epilogue but as part of liability itself. If liability answers *who* is responsible and *for what*, quantum answers *how much* that responsibility costs. Without the latter, the former is merely declaratory.

## VII. Legal Standards: Causation, Certainty, and the Limits of Speculation

Law and valuation meet uneasily. Law demands causation, foreseeability, and proof "with reasonable certainty". Valuation, by contrast, accepts probability, modelling, and assumption as unavoidable. The art of damages lies in reconciling those two instincts – turning the economist's prediction into a lawyer's proof.

As *Christoph Brunner* notes in his commentary on CISG Article 74, the principle of full compensation is bounded by two guardrails: foreseeability and reasonable certainty.[69]) Losses must be both causally linked to the breach and sufficiently ascertainable. This standard, though framed in contract law, resonates across international arbitration. It defines not just how much can be claimed, but how far a tribunal may travel into conjecture.

*Causation* sits at the core of this framework. It is not a procedural formality but the intellectual bridge between liability and quantum.[70]) The claimant must establish a direct and proximate link between the wrongful act and the

[67]) Douglas, *supra* note 5, at 8.

[68]) *Ibid.*

[69]) Christoph Brunner, Nils Schmidt-Ahrendts and Benjamin Gottlieb, "Article 74 [General Rule for Measuring Damages]", in Christoph Brunner and Benjamin Gottlieb (eds), *Commentary on the UN Convention on the International Sale of Goods (CISG)* 511–512 (Kluwer Law International 2019).

[70]) *Eid.* at 514–515.

economic loss alleged.[71]) Every model, every figure, every spreadsheet ultimately stands or falls on that link. Without it, valuation becomes narrative, untethered from the breach.

Tribunals, however, often conflate the existence of loss with its magnitude. They find causation once liability is established, assuming that damages naturally follow. But liability and quantum are not cause and effect; they are separate inquiries. The existence of a breach does not prove the existence of profit, only the potential for it.[72]) The fact that a contract was cancelled does not mean every future dollar imagined in a business plan was lost *because* of that cancellation. The question is not whether loss occurred, but how much of that loss is legally attributable to the wrongful act.

This distinction matters. In *CMS v. Argentina*, for example, the tribunal accepted that Argentina's economic crisis reduced the value of the claimant's investment but struggled to separate the effect of the state's measures from wider market collapse.[73]) That difficulty of causal apportionment between wrongful acts and external shocks, recurs in nearly every major arbitration.

The factual existence of loss must be proven; its quantification may rest on assumptions, provided those assumptions are reasonable and transparent.[74]) The danger lies in reversing that logic, *i.e.*, using assumption to prove loss, rather than to measure it. When tribunals treat speculation as evidence, they cross from inference into invention.

This is where legal and financial reasoning must align. A tribunal that makes its assumptions visible can be wrong in its numbers and still right in its reasoning. Ultimately, the legitimacy of the award depends less on *which* valuation model is chosen than on *how transparently* it is applied.[75])

## VIII. The "Split-the-Baby" Dilemma

The phrase "split the baby" traces back to the biblical *Judgment of Solomon* in the *Book of Kings*.[76]) Two women claim to be the mother of the same infant; Solomon, faced with no evidence, proposes to cut the child in half so that each receives an equal share. The true mother, horrified, begs to give the baby to the other woman rather than see it killed, revealing her identity. Over time, the image of "cutting the baby in two" became shorthand for a decision that divides

---

[71]) *Eid.*

[72]) *Eid.*

[73]) *CMS Gas Transmission Co. v. Argentine Republic*, ICSID Case No. ARB/01/8, Award (May 12, 2005).

[74]) Marboe, *supra* note 7, 207–209.

[75]) *Ead.*

[76]) Royal Collection Trust, *The Judgement of Solomon* (1519), https://www.rct.uk/collection/406032/the-judgement-of-solomon (last accessed October 10, 2023).

the disputed object in half, a resolution that seems fair in form but hollow in substance.

In legal and arbitral discourse, "splitting the baby" refers to the perception that tribunals tend to craft compromise awards, granting partial relief to each side rather than a decisive victory. It suggests an instinct toward arithmetic neutrality, an attempt to appear even-handed when evidence is inconclusive, even though they risk annulment for lack of reasoning.[77)]

Empirical studies show that outright compromise is rare. A review of more than 2,500 commercial arbitration awards found that over 90 % decisively favoured one party; only 5.5 % fell within the "split zone".[78)] Yet the myth persists because partial victories are remembered, and total defeats are not.

The "split the baby" trope persists largely because it *feels* true. Arbitration encourages fairness and flexibility; when a result gives neither side everything it sought, it is easy for both to assume the tribunal compromised.

Still, perception matters. The urge to compromise too early can distort deliberations and turn fairness into appeasement.[79)] In collegial tribunals, where consensus-building is prized, that instinct can suppress real debate and produce half-reasoned decisions.[80)]

Compromise itself is not illegitimate; unexplained compromise is. Arbitration promises fairness through reasoning, not through symmetry. Transparency, not precision, is what sustains legitimacy.

Ultimately, the "split the baby" debate is not about whether tribunals divide outcomes; it is about whether they explain them. Parties can live with losing, but not with *not knowing* why.

The more speculative the projection, and subsequent decision, the further arbitration drifts from the principle of full reparation, towards conjecture disguised as science. When hypothetical spreadsheets replace empirical evidence, it risks quantification of damages to becoming the most sophisticated form of guesswork.

## IX. The "Honest Guesswork" Principle

Not all loss can be proven to the decimal. The law recognizes this. Tribunals and courts alike have accepted that where exact quantification is impossible, a reasonable estimate "honest guesswork" is permissible.

The idea traces back to the early common-law treatment of damages, where courts distinguished between speculative claims and reasonable inferences. The classic view, expressed by Lord Shaw, was that the absence of

77) *Metalclad, supra* note 57.

78) Richard Naimark & Stephanie Keer, "Arbitrators Do Not 'Split the Baby': Empirical Evidence on the Accuracy of Arbitration Awards", 18(1) *J. Int'l Arb.* 1 (2002).

79) *Eid.*

80) *Eid.*

mathematical precision should not deprive a party of compensation if the fact of loss is certain.[81]) The court's duty, he said, is to do its best with the evidence available.[82])

This principle firmed its roots in Indian jurisprudence, reflecting a pragmatic compromise: if liability is established and evidence exists to support a loss, tribunals may make a reasoned approximation.[83]) The *ICSID* tribunal in *Vivendi v. Argentina*[84]) acknowledged that precise calculation is not always possible and that tribunals may reach their best estimate on the evidence available.

Honest guesswork has limits. Indian courts have, time and again, tested the limits of the applicability of this principle. Awards have been set aside where tribunals, lacking proof, invented their own formulae or applied abstract percentage reductions without a discernible rationale.[85]) Conversely, Indian courts have upheld estimates that rested on disclosed assumptions and logical analysis of imperfect data, recognizing that a fair approximation is often the best the facts allow.[86])

International tribunals have adopted a similar approach. Where the existence of loss is proven but its extent uncertain, arbitral panels have accepted reasonable estimation provided that the method and assumptions are made explicit.[87]) What matters is not numerical precision but the integrity of the reasoning process, *i.e.*, the transparency with which the tribunal explains how it arrived at its figure.

Ultimately, honest guesswork operates in the narrow space between inference and conjecture. It acknowledges the limits of proof without surrendering to speculation. Arbitral guesswork is legitimate only when it rests on disclosed assumptions and coherent reasoning. Anything beyond that ceases to be guesswork.

## X. The Way Forward: Building a Culture of Reasoned Damages

Arbitration rules already give tribunals broad procedural discretion, framed by the basic tenets of fairness, equality, and due process. Within that flexibility lies an underused set of tools that can dramatically improve the

[81]) *Watson, Laidlaw & Co. v. Pott, Cassels & Williamson*, [1914] A.C. 25 (H.L.).

[82]) *Ibid.*

[83]) *A.T. Brij Paul Singh v. State of Gujarat*, (1984) 4 SCC 59 (India).

[84]) *Compañía de Aguas del Aconquija S.A. & Vivendi Universal v. Argentine Republic*, ICSID Case No. ARB/97/3, Award (August 20, 2007).

[85]) *SMS Ltd. v. Konkan Railway Corp.*, OMP 279/2017, Judgment (Del. HC 2017).

[86]) *Bata India Ltd. v. Sagar Roy*, 2019 SCC OnLine Cal 1899 (Cal. HC).

[87]) *Lemire v. Ukraine*, ICSID Case No. ARB/06/18, Award (March 28, 2011); *Metalclad, supra* note 57; *Compañía de Aguas, supra* note 84.

quality and legitimacy of damages reasoning. The goal is not more complexity, but more clarity and discipline in how tribunals reach and explain quantum outcomes.

## A. Engage Early with Quantum

Quantification of damages should not be an afterthought. Early coordination between all stakeholders, including tribunal, counsel and experts, shape discovery, witness selection, and even liability arguments. Fact development and valuation must move together, not sequentially.

Tribunals can also take a proactive approach through early case management tools. The *Kaplan Opening*, pioneered by Neil Kaplan, invites early engagement between tribunal and counsel to identify the key legal and factual assumptions that underpin valuation.[88]) Such interventions help align the evidentiary record with the financial analysis and prevent damages from becoming a siloed, end-stage exercise.

## B. Use Expert Conferencing and Joint Reports

"Hot-tubbing" and joint expert statements can transform the way tribunals understand complex valuation evidence.[89]) Having both experts testify together and respond directly to each other's analysis allows the tribunal to distinguish genuine methodological disputes from advocacy-driven exaggerations.[90])

Concurrent expert testimony has, in practice, enabled tribunals to narrow complex quantum disputes by reconciling competing DCF models and identifying points of genuine divergence.[91]) Joint expert examination has also proved valuable in clarifying assumptions on key variables, such as pricing and capacity utilization, allowing tribunals to dismiss inflated projections and focus on the evidence that truly matters.[92]) These techniques promote analytical

---

[88]) Smitha Menon, "Inadequate Handling of Damages in International Arbitration", 17 *Dispute Resolution Int'l* 79, 84 (2023).

[89]) Douglas, *supra* note 5, at 21.

[90]) *Id.* at 22; Sophie Lamb, David Brown and Matthew Secomb, "Procedural Issues", in John A. Trenor (ed), *The Guide to Damages in International Arbitration* 107, 119 (Global Arbitration Review 2016); Klaus Sachs and Nils Schmidt-Ahrendts, "Protocol on Expert Teaming: A New Approach to Expert Evidence", in Albert Jan van den Berg (ed), *Arbitration Advocacy in Changing Times*, ICCA Congress Series, vol. 15, 135, 139 (Kluwer Law International 2011).

[91]) *Caratube International Oil Company LLP v. Republic of Kazakhstan*, ICSID Case No. ARB/08/12, Award (27 September 2017).

[92]) *Antaris Solar GmbH & Dr. Michael Göde v. Czech Republic*, PCA Case No. 2014-01, Award (May 2, 2018).

convergence: they reveal what is agreed, isolate what is not, and steer the debate toward substance rather than spectacle.

## C. Normalise Tribunal-Appointed Experts

Tribunal-appointed experts remain underused but can provide a neutral anchor in complex financial disputes. Their purpose is not to displace party experts but to offer an independent benchmark against which competing analyses can be tested.

The 2022 ICSID Arbitration Rules, for example, explicitly empower tribunals to appoint experts in technical or financial matters.[93]) Tribunal's use of a neutral financial expert, often helps bridge gaps between competing discount-rate models and enhanced the transparency of its reasoning.[94]) Neutral expertise strengthens legitimacy; independence reduces distortion.

## D. Strengthen Arbitrator Competence

Arbitrators do not need to be economists, but they must be economically literate. Arbitral institutions should integrate valuation principles and financial reasoning into their arbitrator training curriculum.[95]) An arbitrator who cannot read a DCF spreadsheet critically cannot meaningfully test the credibility of an expert's model.

As tribunals increasingly adjudicate cases worth hundreds of millions of dollars, economic literacy is not an advantage; it is a necessity. The credibility of arbitral reasoning now depends on an arbitrator's ability to engage meaningfully with quantitative evidence.

## E. Institutionalize Transparency in Damages Reasoning

Awards should explicitly explain the logic behind key valuation variables: the chosen methodology, discount rate, projection period, and interest rate.[96]) It is not mathematical precision that sustains legitimacy, but transparent reasoning. An award can survive a wrong number, but not a missing reason.[97])

---

93) International Centre for Settlement of Investment Disputes (ICSID), *Rules of Procedure for Arbitration Proceedings* (Arbitration Rules), Rule 39 (effective July 1, 2022).

94) *Giovanni Alemanni & Others v. Argentine Republic*, ICSID Case No. ARB/07/8, Decision on Jurisdiction & Admissibility (November 17, 2014).

95) Menon, *supra* note 88, at 83.

96) Douglas, *supra* 5, at 4.

97) *Id.*

This is particularly relevant under ICSID Convention Article 52(1)(e), where a "failure to state reasons" remains one of the most common grounds for annulment.[98]) Reasoned transparency not only strengthens enforceability but also enhances public confidence in arbitral decision-making.

### F. Close the Lawyer–Expert Gap

Finally, practitioners themselves must "level up". Counsels who understand the logic of valuation can craft sharper instructions, challenge weak assumptions, and align their case theory with financial reality.[99]) Bridging the communication gap between lawyers and quantum experts can eliminate much of the analytical drift that undermines damages submissions.[100]) Better lawyering means better expert evidence, and, in turn, better awards.

## XI. Conclusion: Credibility as the Real Currency

In the end, valuation in arbitration is not just about numbers, it is about credibility. The legitimacy of an award does not rise or fall with the size of the figure, but with the clarity of the reasoning that supports it.

Damages assessment sits at the intersection of law, economics, and judgment. To navigate it, tribunals must blend legal principle with economic realism; lawyers must learn to argue in numbers without losing the discipline of law. The bridge between advocacy and analysis is not technical; it is intellectual.

The future of international arbitration will not be measured by how much money it awards, but by how well it explains why. The field's endurance depends on tribunals showing how they reasoned, not just what they decided.

When numbers decide justice, the reasoning behind them must carry the same integrity as the law itself. Clarity, honesty, and coherence are no longer virtues; they are the currencies of trust on which the entire system now trades.

---

[98]) *See also:* Chapter 16, Christina L. Beharry, *Post-award Challenges of Damages Assessments*, at Section 2.5.3.

[99]) Menon, *supra* note 88, at 83.

[100]) *Id.*

# Corruption in Arbitration
## Limits of Arbitral Tribunals

*Sofia Elena Cozac**)

## I. Introduction

Arbitration has long been heralded as a cornerstone of international dispute resolution, valued for its efficiency, confidentiality, and neutrality. Yet, as the global fight against corruption intensifies, questions have emerged about the ability of arbitral tribunals to effectively address corruption-related issues. When allegations of bribery, fraud, or undue influence surface, arbitral tribunals often find themselves navigating a delicate balance between upholding party autonomy and safeguarding the integrity of the arbitral process.

The challenge lies in the inherent limits of arbitral authority. Unlike national courts, arbitral tribunals lack coercive powers of investigation, rely heavily on party cooperation, and operate within procedural frameworks that were not designed to uncover or sanction corruption. As a result, tribunals may be ill-equipped to deal with the evidentiary and jurisdictional complexities that corruption cases present.

This article examines the boundaries of arbitral competence in addressing corruption, exploring how existing procedural mechanisms, principles of international public policy, and judicial oversight interact to define these limits. It also considers recent jurisprudence and institutional developments that reflect a growing recognition of the need for arbitral systems to confront corruption without overstepping their mandate. Through this lens, the discussion seeks to illuminate the tension between the promise of arbitration as a neutral forum and its constraints in the face of one of the most persistent challenges in global commerce.

In close connection with this issue, the paper also looks at the issue of proving the existence of corruption in complex cases, as well as the sensitive topic of the adequate standard of proof. The article also briefly discusses the famous EDF v. Romania ICSID case and the law principles deriving from the tribunal's ruling in the case, pertaining to admissibility of evidence and state responsibility. As a natural continuation, the main possible consequences of finding corruption are also considered, alongside the general topic of restitution in case of nullity of the contract due to corruption issues.

---

*) Attorney-at-law, VIAC Ambassador for Romania.

## II. Approaches to Corruption in Arbitration

Concerning the impact that alleged instances of corruption may exert on the arbitrability of disputes and on arbitral tribunals' willingness to adjudicate them, the traditional approach of arbitration practice was one of avoidance. Historically, arbitral tribunals tended to refrain from engaging in cases that involved any suggestion of corruption. This approach was epitomized by a landmark decision rendered in 1963, widely recognized as the first international arbitral award to address issues of corruption.[1]) The case has since become emblematic of the arbitral practice of declining jurisdiction when even a suspicion of corruption arises.[2])

The decision in question was issued by sole arbitrator Gunnar Lagergren, who was tasked with determining a claim for the enforcement of alleged commission payments under a contract. The payments were, however, intended as bribes for Argentine officials, and the contract itself had been concluded between a British corporation and an Argentine engineer, engaged primarily for his political connections within the Argentine government.

A straightforward resolution would have been to declare the contract null and void on grounds of illegality, immorality, and violation of public policy, thereby rejecting the claim on the merits. Lagergren, however, adopted a more far-reaching position. He held that in cases involving such egregious and manifest corruption, the arbitral tribunal not only should not[3]) but also does not possess jurisdiction to hear the dispute.

This self-imposed denial of jurisdiction was grounded in a broader legal principle invoked by the arbitrator, namely, that contracts which seriously contravene *bonos mores* or international public policy are invalid or unenforceable and therefore cannot be sanctioned by courts or arbitral tribunals. In other words, certain agreements are deemed so reprehensible that they do not merit judicial consideration.

Beyond the substantive outcome, the award is also notable for the arbitrator's proactive conduct. Lagergren pursued evidence of the alleged corrupt payments *sua sponte*, even after both parties requested that these allegations be

---

[1]) E. Mujic, *Corruption in International Commercial Arbitration: The Right of the Arbitrator to Conduct Self-initiated Investigation of Corruption, Master's Thesis in International Process Law,* International Commercial Arbitration, Upsala University, 2013, p. 5, available at www.diva-portal.se.

[2]) ICC Award no. 1110, 1963 by G. Lagergren, YCA 1996, para. 47 *et seq.*, www.trans-lex.org.

[3]) The arbitrator concluded to this effect of arbitrability not only as a consequence of the law but also as a punishment for parties who try to use the law for illicit purposes: *"Parties who ally themselves in an enterprise of the present nature must realize that they have forfeited any right to ask for assistance of the machinery of justice (national courts or arbitral tribunals) in settling their disputes."* ICC Award no. 1110, *supra* note 2, para. 23.

disregarded. Due to the gravity of the issues involved, he determined that no specific legal basis was required for examining arbitrability on his own initiative and for declining jurisdiction, invoking instead "the interest of due administration of justice"[4]) and "general principles denying arbitrators to entertain disputes of this nature"[5]) rather than any national rules on arbitrability.

Although Lagergren maintained that a lack of arbitrability – and consequently, jurisdiction – was the proper response to cases of serious corruption, he nevertheless cautioned against allowing this approach to enable a party acting in bad faith to profit from its own misconduct by unjustly enriching itself at the expense of the other.

While unprecedented at the time, the decision initiated a broader discourse on the appropriate treatment of corruption in arbitration. It also attracted criticism from scholars who viewed it as inconsistent with the principle of separability,[6]) whereas others defended Lagergren's reasoning as an affirmation of *Kompetenz-Kompetenz* and as a catalyst for the development of civil-law instruments aimed at combating corruption.

Several courts have subsequently endorsed Lagergren's reasoning, even decades later. For instance, the Supreme Court of Pakistan ruled[7]) that although mere allegations of corruption or fraud do not render disputes non-arbitrable, cases supported by *prima facie* evidence of corruption fall outside the scope of arbitration due to public policy considerations, as such matters involve determinations of alleged criminality.

This conservative stance can be explained by the view that jurisdiction over corruption-related disputes should rest with state courts, which possess superior means of investigation and enforcement, including the ability to compel evidence and pursue criminal liability where appropriate.

More than sixty years after the seminal Lagergren decision, however, the international arbitration community has largely evolved in its approach. Contemporary doctrine overwhelmingly accepts that arbitral tribunals should not deny jurisdiction solely on the basis of suspected or even proven corruption, provided that they approach the matter with due diligence and care in establishing the underlying facts.

Accordingly, both arbitral tribunals and national courts have, in recent decades, departed from Lagergren's restrictive view, affirming the competence

---

[4]) ICC Award no. 1110, *supra* note 2, para. 2.

[5]) ICC Award no. 1110, *supra* note 2, para. 23.

[6]) K. Löf, *A Story of Corruption A Case Study of How Bribery Affects the Validity of Performed Commercial Contracts in Forward! Essays in Honour of Prof Dr Kaj Hobér*, Iustus, January 2019, p. 209, available at www.mannheimerswartling.se.

[7]) *The Hub Power Company Ltd (HUBCO) v Pakistan WAPDA and Federation of Pakistan*, Supreme Court of Pakistan, 14 June 2000, apud J. Lew, L. Mistelis, S. Kroll, *Comparative International Commercial Arbitration*, Kluwer Law International, 2003, p. 213.

of arbitrators to adjudicate disputes involving allegations of illegality, including bribery and corruption. For instance, an ICC tribunal[8]) rejected a jurisdictional objection of this nature, emphasizing that such objections are analogous to cases of unilateral withdrawal from an arbitration agreement. The tribunal upheld its jurisdiction notwithstanding the allegations of corruption and fraud, reasoning that denying jurisdiction would contravene the transnational public policy principle of good faith.

Although this modern approach may appear risky to those skeptical of arbitration's capacity to address such sensitive issues, it is important to recall that arbitral awards remain subject to judicial review at the enforcement stage. National courts retain the authority to refuse enforcement of awards that endorse contracts tainted by corruption, as such awards would contravene public policy and are therefore unenforceable in virtually all jurisdictions.[9])

## III. Investigating Corruption in Arbitration: Duties, Procedures, and Standards of Proof

### A. The Duty of Arbitrators to Investigate Corruption

Corruption represents a pervasive challenge in international arbitration, particularly in the context of complex commercial transactions that span multiple jurisdictions. The phenomenon of corruption in arbitration is not merely a matter of private dispute resolution; it engages public policy concerns, questions of enforceability, and the ethical integrity of the arbitral process. Contemporary practice recognizes that arbitral tribunals may and indeed should address allegations of corruption, yet the mechanisms for doing so are neither straightforward nor uniform. Tribunals must navigate a delicate balance between proactive investigation, party autonomy, procedural fairness, and enforceability requirements. Failure to appropriately address corruption may result in awards being annulled, unenforceable, or otherwise undermined, and can compromise the legitimacy of arbitration as a credible forum for resolving cross-border commercial disputes.

Within this context, one needs to make a comprehensive examination of the duties of arbitrators in investigating corruption, the procedural strategies and evidentiary tools available to them, and the standards of proof appropriate to such inquiries. The procedural and substantive considerations necessary for tribunals to discharge their obligations effectively become relevant. For this purpose, it is important to determine how tribunals may act proactively, inclusively by resorting to *sua sponte* investigations, while maintaining adherence

[8]) *ICC Partial Award No. 6474 of 1992*, YCA 2000, at 279 et seq., para. 38, available at www.trans-lex.org.

[9]) J. Lew, L. Mistelis, S. Kroll, *supra* note 7, p. 214.

to the parties' mandate and safeguarding procedural fairness. Ultimately, one should consider the broader consequences for the legitimacy, enforceability, and perception of international arbitration as a forum equipped to handle issues of both private and public significance.

## 1. Truth-Finding as a Core Obligation

Central to the role of any arbitral tribunal is the obligation to establish the factual matrix underpinning the dispute. Fact-finding is widely recognized[10]) as an intrinsic component of the tribunal's mandate, particularly in international commercial arbitration, where the parties often rely on the expertise and impartiality of the tribunal. This duty encompasses all matters of fact relevant to the dispute, including allegations of corruption, given their potential to invalidate the award or implicate public policy concerns. The tribunal's function as a fact-finder is heightened by the trust and confidence the parties place in it, often choosing arbitration over national courts precisely because arbitrators are perceived as more capable of addressing complex commercial arrangements efficiently and expertly.

The principle of truth-finding is explicitly codified in many civil law systems, including Romania, which requires judges to actively seek the truth in civil proceedings.[11]) This "*judicial activism*" principle, though originally applied to state courts, may be adapted to arbitration, obliging tribunals to undertake diligent inquiry into all matters potentially affecting the integrity of the award.[12]) In essence, tribunals are tasked not only with resolving the dispute according to the law and evidence presented by the parties but also with ensuring that their award is not tainted by unaddressed improprieties, such as corruption or bribery, which could undermine enforceability.

---

[10]) D. Malik, G. Kamat, *Corruption in International Commercial Arbitration: Arbitrability, Admissibility & Adjudication*, International Commercial Arbitration Brief, Volume 5, Issue 1, Washington College of Law, 2018, p. 13, available at digitalcommons.wcl.american.edu.

[11]) Romanian Civil Code of Civil Procedure art. 22:

"*Fundamental principles of civil procedure Art. 22 The role of the judge in ascertaining the truth*

*(1) The judge shall resolve the dispute in accordance with the applicable rules of law.*

*(2) The judge has the duty to use all legal means to prevent any error in finding the truth in the case, based on the establishment of the facts and the correct application of the law, in order to deliver a well-founded and lawful judgment. To this end, with regard to the facts and legal grounds invoked by the parties, the judge shall be entitled to ask them to provide explanations, orally or in writing, to bring any factual or legal circumstances into the debate, even if they are not mentioned in the application or in the response, to order the administration of the evidence he considers necessary, as well as other measures provided for by law, even if the parties object.*"

[12]) M. Storme, *A Single Civil Procedure for Europe: A Cathedral Builder's Dream*, Ritsumeikan Law Review no. 22/2005.

## 2. Justifications for Tribunal Proactivity

The rationale for proactive tribunal investigation of corruption is threefold. First, the enforceability of arbitral awards is at stake; corruption may invalidate an award either directly, if the conduct breaches mandatory law or public policy, or indirectly, if the award is rendered without addressing critical aspects of fact relevant to the allegations. Second, tribunals are expected to uphold the reasonable expectations of the parties, who rely on their expertise and impartiality to resolve complex disputes effectively. Ignoring red flags or indications of corruption risks undermining the legitimacy of the proceedings. Third, although arbitration is a private forum, corruption implicates the public interest, as it may involve unlawful conduct that contravenes fundamental legal norms. Tribunals, therefore, have an ethical and legal obligation to ensure that their awards do not facilitate or endorse illicit activity. Consequently, the duty to investigate corruption constitutes an extension of the tribunal's general responsibility to administer justice and render enforceable,[13]) equitable awards.

## 3. Sua Sponte Investigations: Powers and Limits

A critical question in the context of corruption investigations is whether tribunals may act *sua sponte*, initiating inquiries without prompting from the parties. *Sua sponte* investigations allow tribunals to address misconduct that may be concealed or deliberately omitted from party submissions. However, this approach entails risks, particularly the possibility of exceeding the scope of the arbitration agreement, which may result in awards being challenged for *ultra petita*.[14]) Consequently, tribunals must carefully balance the need for proactive investigation against their duty to respect the parties' consent and procedural boundaries.

English law, through the Arbitration Act 1996, explicitly empowers tribunals to determine the extent to which they may take the initiative in ascertaining facts and law.[15]) This statutory provision supports proactive investigations while emphasizing adherence to party autonomy and the scope of the arbitration agreement. Under this framework, tribunals are permitted to request clarifications, additional documentation, and expert opinions, provided such inquiries are proportional and aligned with the parties' submissions.

---

[13]) This principle is expressly included in the rules of several arbitral institutions. In this respect, art. 42 of the ICC 2021 Arbitration Rules: "*In all matters not expressly provided for in the Rules, the Court and the arbitral tribunal shall act in the spirit of the Rules and shall make every effort to make sure that the award is enforceable at law.*"

[14]) According to the provisions of Romanian law, this is a ground for annulment of the award, expressly provided for, alongside with *extra petita*: "*the arbitral tribunal has ruled on things that were not requested or has given more than was requested*", Romanian Code of Civil Procedure, art. 608 "Grounds for annulment of arbitral awards", paragraph 1, letter (f).

[15]) English Arbitration Act, 1996 c. 23, art. 34 (2) (g).

Romanian arbitration law similarly grants tribunals broad discretionary powers.[16]) Tribunals may request explanations, conduct evidentiary procedures, and examine facts beyond the parties' submissions. These powers, grounded in civil law principles of truth-finding, reinforce the tribunal's duty to ensure that the award is both fair and enforceable. The statutory framework acknowledges that tribunals may encounter situations in which allegations of corruption necessitate proactive investigation, including instances in which neither party explicitly raises the issue.

In exercising *sua sponte* powers, tribunals face competing risks. Acting beyond the parties' claims may render the award vulnerable to annulment for *ultra petita*. Conversely, failing to investigate credible indicators of corruption may compromise the enforceability of the award or contravene public policy. Tribunals must also avoid transforming arbitration into a criminal investigation, which could undermine procedural fairness. Striking the appropriate balance requires tribunals to carefully evaluate evidence, contextual indicators, and the proportionality of investigative measures.[17])

Proactive investigations are particularly justified in two scenarios. First, when a party raises corruption allegations, tribunals must investigate these claims thoroughly, while remaining alert to potential tactical misuse, such as attempts to delay proceedings or create procedural complications. Second, tribunals may observe indications of possible misconduct even in the absence of formal allegations, prompting a need to clarify facts and safeguard the integrity and enforceability of the award. In both cases, careful documentation of investigative steps is essential to demonstrate proportionality, transparency, and procedural fairness.

## B. Procedural Strategies for Investigating Corruption

Corruption is a factual matter that requires tribunals to adopt systematic evidence-gathering methods. Document analysis is fundamental, with contracts, invoices, correspondence, and financial records examined for irregularities or hidden arrangements. Witness testimony, whether oral or written, provides critical context and corroborates documentary evidence. Expert opinion is often indispensable, particularly in complex commercial cases involving intricate financial or technical matters. Experts may identify patterns or anomalies that are not apparent to lay arbitrators. Furthermore, external sources, including public registries or ongoing criminal investigations,

---

[16]) Romanian Code of Civil Procedure, art. 586 (2), art. 575 (2), art. 22 (2).

[17]) E. O. Igbokwe, *Dealing with Bribery and Corruption in International Commercial Arbitration: To Probe or Not to Probe*, Kluwer Law International, 2022, p. 250.

can supplement tribunal inquiries where permissible under applicable law and procedural rules.

The Basel Institute on Governance has developed a toolkit[18]) for arbitrators to aid in detecting and addressing corruption and money laundering. The toolkit identifies key indicators, or "red flags," including intermediaries with unclear qualifications or inappropriate political connections, unusual commissions or fees, discrepancies between contractual terms and performance, and patterns suggesting circumvention of regulatory requirements. While the presence of a single red flag does not establish misconduct, multiple converging indicators warrant more intensive investigation.

Tribunals may request additional evidence, convene hearings for witness examination, engage expert consultants, and, where appropriate, draw adverse inferences from a party's failure to provide requested information. These measures, although potentially encroaching on party autonomy, are justified where public policy or enforceability concerns are implicated. Institutional guidelines, such as the IBA Rules on the Taking of Evidence and the Basel Institute Toolkit, offer structured frameworks for balancing tribunal initiative with procedural fairness.

## C. Standards of Proof in Corruption Allegations

Proving corruption is inherently challenging due to its secretive nature. Direct evidence is rarely available, and parties may deliberately conceal or obscure improper conduct. Arbitration, as a private law forum, does not impose the criminal standard of *"beyond reasonable doubt"*. Instead, the *preponderance-of-evidence* standard is generally considered appropriate, reflecting the tribunal's need to balance fairness with the practical realities of evidence-gathering in complex commercial disputes.[19])

While the party alleging corruption carries the primary burden of proof, the respondent also bears an obligation to provide adequate explanations where allegations are plausible. Complete silence or refusal to engage may justify adverse inferences, ensuring that parties cannot exploit procedural gaps to conceal misconduct. Tribunals may rely on circumstantial evidence,[20]) such as anomalous financial patterns, repeated red flags, or unusual transactional behavior, to establish the likelihood of corruption indirectly. Evaluating such

[18]) M. Pieth, K. Betz, Competence Centre Arbitration and Crime, University of Basel and Basel Institute on Governance, *Corruption and Money Laundering in International Arbitration. A Toolkit for Arbitrators*, 2019, available at www.baselgovernance.org.

[19]) C. Partasides, *Proving Corruption in International Arbitration: A Balanced Standard for the Real World*, ICSID Review – Foreign Investment Law Journal, Volume 25, Issue 1, 2010, p. 48.

[20]) C. Partasides, *supra* note 19, p. 61.

evidence requires careful consideration of timing, source credibility, context, and potential impact on the enforceability of the award.

Given that arbitration is not a criminal trial, applying the *"beyond any reasonable doubt"* standard is evidently too stringent. Furthermore, in certain situations, even the *"clear and convincing evidence"* standard may lead to unfair results. Although the matter at hand – corruption – is of considerable gravity, it must be examined within the framework of private law. Accordingly, the standard of proof should be adapted as appropriate, assessing not only the evidence itself but also, among other factors, the timing and source of its submission.

Therefore, in striving to establish and articulate judicial truth as faithfully as possible to the actual truth, the tribunal should avoid being constrained by inflexible standards. Otherwise, it risks – albeit unintentionally and unknowingly – contributing to the concealment of corruption.

Proactive investigation of corruption strengthens the credibility and legitimacy of international arbitration. By employing structured evidence-gathering, expert consultation, and procedural safeguards, tribunals can ensure that awards are enforceable and ethically sound. Effective investigations also support global anti-corruption initiatives, discourage unethical conduct, and reinforce confidence in arbitration as a reliable mechanism for cross-border dispute resolution. The tribunal's ability to act proactively, within the limits of party autonomy and procedural fairness, demonstrates that arbitration is capable of addressing complex legal, ethical, and public policy concerns, thereby enhancing its role as a credible and legitimate forum.

Arbitrators should maintain vigilance for indications of corruption throughout the proceedings and exercise discretionary powers proportionately. Institutional guidelines, including the IBA Rules on Evidence and the Basel Toolkit, provide practical tools for identifying and addressing misconduct. Tribunals should document investigative measures meticulously, apply flexible standards of proof based on circumstantial evidence and adverse inferences, and consider comparative legal perspectives to guide proactive investigations effectively. Balancing diligence, fairness, and proportionality is critical in preserving both procedural integrity and award enforceability.

## IV. Conclusion

Arbitrators possess both the power and duty to investigate corruption in international arbitration. While respecting party autonomy and procedural fairness, tribunals must proactively identify and examine indications of misconduct to ensure that awards are fair, enforceable, and consistent with public policy. Through systematic evidence-gathering, expert consultation, and flexible standards of proof, tribunals can address corruption effectively without transforming arbitration into a criminal investigation. Such practices not only safeguard the immediate dispute but also enhance the credibility, integrity, and legitimacy of international arbitration as a mechanism for ethical and transparent dispute resolution.

In commercial arbitration, arbitral tribunals should retain their jurisdiction even when a party alleges that the tribunal is not competent to hear the dispute because it involves corruption issues. In investment arbitration, arbitrators should be very cautious when a host state argues the lack of jurisdiction of the tribunal because the investment does not comply with the host state law. Declaring that the tribunal is not competent on that basis can allow the host state to participate and benefit from corruption activities while, at the same time, not being subject to review by an arbitral tribunal. The investor would lose the protection of the bilateral investment treaty (BIT) in terms of fair and equitable treatment, expropriation, most-favored nation treatment and other typical standards of protection contained in BITs.

Moreover, it is now generally accepted that arbitrators have a duty to investigate corruption even when no party raises such matter. Arbitrators should use the powers granted by arbitration rules and laws to order the production of documents, to compel a witness to testify, or even to appoint an investigator or auditor to review documents and guide the tribunal in its assessment.

# Implementation of Article 16(3) of the UNCITRAL Model Law in the Balkan Region

## Balancing Efficiency and Judicial Control in Jurisdictional Challenges

*Milica Savić*

## I. Introduction

Article 16 of the UNCITRAL Model Law on International Commercial Arbitration embodies the principle of kompetenz-kompetenz, empowering arbitral tribunals to decide on their own jurisdiction. Paragraph (3) of this article, however, has generated extensive debate and inconsistent practice, especially in jurisdictions that adopted the Model Law without further procedural refinement that would be in line with the procedural tradition and legislation of each particular jurisdiction. Its primary aim was to ensure that jurisdictional challenges are resolved swiftly and efficiently, while allowing arbitration to proceed with the least interruption possible.

This paper explores the purpose of Article 16(3) and assesses whether this purpose was met and efficiently implemented in selected Balkan jurisdictions – namely Serbia, Montenegro, Croatia, and Slovenia. The analysis considers whether the regional approaches have fulfilled the intended goals of procedural efficiency and finality, or whether ambiguities have led to uncertainty and inconsistent judicial interpretation.

## II. The Purpose and Structure of Article 16(3)

Article 16(3) of the UNCITRAL Model Law on International Commercial Arbitration is intended as a procedural safeguard within the broader kompetenz-kompetenz framework established by Article 16. It provides that when an arbitral tribunal rules as a preliminary matter that it has jurisdiction, any party may, within thirty days of receiving notice of that ruling, request the local court to decide the issue. The court's decision is final and not subject to appeal, while the arbitral tribunal may continue the proceedings and render an award during the pendency of the judicial review.

The provision thus serves a dual purpose: it ensures judicial control over the tribunal's assumption of jurisdiction, while simultaneously protecting the efficiency and autonomy of the arbitral process by preventing dilatory tactics that could otherwise suspend proceedings. It tends to balance between limited court intervention and the uninterrupted progress of arbitration.

Importantly, Article 16(3) leaves procedural aspects such as the form of the tribunal's ruling, the scope of court review, and the interaction between concurrent arbitral and judicial processes to the discretion of national legislators. This deliberate openness has allowed flexible adaptation but has also led to interpretative divergences across Model Law jurisdictions, particularly where domestic laws have not clarified the procedural framework for judicial review of jurisdictional decisions.

## III. Regional Implementation and Legislative Nuances

Although most Balkan jurisdictions have adopted the Model Law, they differ in how they interpret and operationalize Article 16(3). These divergences primarily concern the form of the tribunal's decision on jurisdiction, the nature of the court's review, and the procedural effect of the 'no appeal' rule.

### A. Form and Terminology

The Model Law does not specify whether a decision on jurisdiction should be characterized as an award or a procedural order. This ambiguity has led to varying solutions in national jurisdictions as it was up to national legislators to decide on potential additional interpretations and specific wording that would avoid ambiguity in light of national procedural rules.

There are jurisdictions that decided to address this issue in a straightforward manner. For instance, Croatia's Arbitration Act defines an award strictly as a decision on the merits and treats jurisdictional determinations as separate procedural decisions reviewable through a non-contentious process. Slovenia follows a similar approach, clearly distinguishing between a tribunal's 'resolution on jurisdiction' and its award on the merits. In these jurisdictions there was also consistent court practice in understanding what the scope of judicial review in terms of arbitral tribunal's competence entails, and the intent behind Article 16(3) of the Model Law was followed (i) to preserve arbitral efficiency by preventing delays caused by jurisdictional challenges; (ii) to ensure a single, narrowly defined opportunity for judicial control; and (iii) to guarantee finality through a no-appeal rule. The Model Law thereby aims to maintain the momentum of arbitration while preventing fragmented multi-level judicial oversight.

In contrast, Serbia and Montenegro have largely replicated the Model Law verbatim. Their arbitration statutes refer simply to an 'odluka' (decision), without distinguishing its nature. This term in both Serbian and Montenegrin procedural rules is a generic term that may relate to any type of decision, either a judgment (decision on merits), which is by definition subject to several instances of judicial review or any type of procedural decisions which do not undergo judicial review, but can only be reviewed through an appeal on merits within the process they were rendered. This type of possible judicial review over any general decision is the distinction relevant for further considerations on whether Article 16(3) is implemented with its core purpose being achieved.

## B. The Nature and Scope of Judicial Review

Article 16(3) leaves open the extent of the court's review of a tribunal's jurisdictional finding. Linguistic and conceptual precision in national legislation determines the course of judicial review of the tribunal's ruling on its own jurisdiction.

As mentioned, Croatia and Slovenia have dealt with this issue in a straightforward manner, clearly distinguishing between procedural decision and decisions on merits, which has set the clear path on what type of review would the tribunal's decision on jurisdiction receive. It is a decision in a specific single-instance procedure that is not further reviewed.

On the other hand, lack of clarity of language and legal concept in Serbia and in Montenegro has allowed local courts to interpret tribunal's jurisdictional rulings inconsistently – sometimes as procedural decisions, sometimes as awards subject to annulment standards which has led to different procedural consequences in this judicial review.

## C. Procedural Nature of Review under Article 16(3)

The procedural nature of the court review under Article 16(3) raises complex questions. It can be argued that this review constitutes a distinct procedural mechanism, separate from the action to set aside an arbitral award, which is done in several-instance litigation proceedings. While both proceedings involve judicial oversight of arbitral decisions, the review contemplated in Article 16(3) does not entail annulment of an award; rather, it concerns a tribunal's preliminary determination of its own jurisdiction. Serbian and Montenegrin Laws on Arbitration copy the Model Law verbatim, so they also provide no detailed specification of this process, merely stating that a party may request the court to "decide the matter," with no appeal permitted. This textual simplicity has led some commentators to conclude that the review should be conducted as a single-instance, non-contentious proceeding.

In the absence of statutory guidance on the criteria and standards of review, national courts have tended to treat this review as analogous to the setting-aside procedure. Available case law demonstrates that judges often apply the same standards used for annulment proceedings when examining a tribunal's jurisdictional ruling. This approach, however, can be questioned both conceptually and functionally. Setting aside a final award has a definitive effect: it eliminates the award itself and terminates the tribunal's mandate. In contrast, judicial review of a tribunal's decision on jurisdiction occurs in a fundamentally different procedural environment. Article 16(3) expressly allows the tribunal to continue the proceedings and even render an award while the court review is pending. In practice, arbitral tribunals almost invariably exercise this discretion, seeking to preserve the efficiency and continuity of the arbitration.

Difficulties arise if courts apply annulment-type standards to jurisdictional rulings. For example, if a respondent claims a procedural violation – such as the inability to present its case – should the court's focus be on the procedural irregularity or on the substantive correctness of the jurisdictional determination? If the tribunal's reasoning on jurisdiction is sound, annulling it on purely procedural grounds would make little sense within the Model Law framework, which aims to limit judicial interference to essential matters of fairness and legality.

Ultimately, the open-textured drafting of Article 16(3) has left these interpretative questions to domestic courts. The experience in the Balkan region suggests that this has not always yielded optimal results. Owing to the relative scarcity of such cases and the limited familiarity of judges with arbitration-specific doctrines, national courts have sometimes struggled to apply the competence-competence principle consistently or to delineate the proper scope of review. The Serbian case law, in particular, provides examples where courts have misconstrued the purpose and procedural design of Article 16(3), leading to uncertainty and doctrinal inconsistency.

In a much-discussed case in Serbia, the Supreme Court reviewed a tribunal's jurisdictional decision by applying the same criteria as for setting aside a final award under Article 34 of the Model Law. This interpretation blurred the distinction between a preliminary review and annulment proceedings, undermining the intended procedural efficiency.

The court's willingness to admit the legal remedy and decide on it, despite the 'no appeal' rule, also contradicts the Model Law's structure. Such judicial expansion reveals a tension between domestic procedural instincts – favoring layered review – and the Model Law's philosophy of limited interference.

## D. Parallel Proceedings and Procedural Overlap

Another difficulty arises when arbitral proceedings continue while the court reviews the tribunal's jurisdictional decision. Although Article 16(3) allows the tribunal to proceed, in practice this can result in overlapping reviews. The same jurisdictional objections may appear both in the court review and later in a setting-aside action, leading to conflicting judicial outcomes. None of the Balkan arbitration laws explicitly regulate this procedural intersection, creating uncertainty for parties and tribunals alike.

### E. The "No Appeal" Rule

The "no appeal" rule was intended to ensure finality and expedite proceedings. In Croatia and Slovenia, courts have largely respected this rule, preserving the efficiency of the process. In Serbia and Montenegro, however, courts have sometimes reopened the question of jurisdiction through alternative procedural avenues, diluting the rule's finality. The absence of clear legislative guidance has thus produced divergent judicial practices and undermined the predictability that the Model Law strived to achieve.

## IV. Conclusion – Has the Purpose Been Achieved?

Article 16(3) of the UNCITRAL Model Law was drafted to reconcile efficiency with judicial oversight. Yet, its success depends on domestic adaptation. The Balkan experience reveals that formal adoption of the Model Law does not automatically ensure uniformity or efficiency. In theory, Article 16(3) was designed to promote autonomy, efficiency, and finality. In practice, however, the lack of procedural detail has encouraged judicial experimentation. Courts often apply domestic civil procedure analogies, extending review beyond the intended limits and thereby prolonging disputes.

Where legislatures intervened to clarify procedure – as in Croatia and Slovenia – the review process is more coherent and aligned with the Model Law's spirit. By contrast, jurisdictions that merely transposed the Model Law's text without elaboration, such as Serbia and Montenegro, face recurring interpretative dilemmas. The regional trend suggests that legislative precision, not mere adoption, determines successful implementation.

The absence of procedural clarity – particularly regarding the form of the tribunal's decision, the scope of judicial review, and the mechanics of the 'no appeal' rule – has resulted in uneven application and, at times, counterproductive judicial practice.

Nearly two decades after the enactment of Serbia's Law on Arbitration, experience suggests that legislative refinement is overdue. Clarifying the procedural framework for jurisdictional review would enhance both efficiency and predictability, ensuring that Article 16(3) fulfills its intended role: safeguarding arbitral autonomy while preserving essential judicial control. True alignment with the Model Law's objectives will require not just adoption, but careful, context-sensitive implementation.

# Conservatory Measures against States in Enforcement Proceedings

*Agis Georgiades/Chrystalla Christoforou**)

## I. Introduction

This article looks at the particularly thorny subject of conservatory measures against states, mainly from a common law perspective. The possibility of obtaining such measures is often of determinative importance in disputes. When the measures are obtained in time, they can provide sufficient security to the claimant and often give good reasons for settlement negotiations. On the contrary, when they are not obtained at all, or not obtained timely, this may render the whole claim nugatory, with no real prospect of actual enforcement. In arbitration proceedings, when the respondent is a state or state entity, a claimant who considers applying for such measures often faces the additional obstacle of state immunity. It may be the case that obtaining such measures is not a possibility in the premises. Even where such possibility exists, the claimant may find additional complications and impediments in enforcing such measures, especially where the state is reluctant to comply. It is shown that such conservatory measures are more effective when compliance with them depends on third parties against which, contrary to states, diplomats and state officials, contempt proceedings are generally available.

## II. Conservatory Measures

'Conservatory measures' or 'measures of constraint' in this context means the "full variety of pre- and post-judgment measures available in national legal systems, from injunctions preventing a respondent state, from disposing of certain assets pending resolution of a dispute, to attachment or seizure orders against a foreign state's property for enforcing a final judgment". Importantly, such measures cannot be taken *in personam* against officials of the foreign state.[1]) Instead, most attempts focus on the property of the foreign state.[2])

---

*) *CGA, Nicosia,* www.georgiades-law.com.

[1]) Jame Crawford, *Bronlie's Principles of Public International Law* (Oxford: 8th ed., 2012, OUP), p. 502.

[2]) Nelson Goh, "State immunity and court-ordered relief in support of arbitration" *Arbitration* (2018) 84(1), 89–95, p. 93.

Injunctions that are not intended to freeze, prevent or limit the exercise by states of rights to property or assets are beyond the scope of this article.

The applicable laws or rules may give power to state courts or arbitral tribunals to issue conservatory measures. However, the powers, the conditions for their exercise and the scope of such measures vary significantly between different jurisdictions. It is generally considered that common law jurisdictions afford state courts with wider powers in this matter.

## III. Immunity

### A. International Conventions

When looking at state immunity, the starting point is the principle that each state should respect the sovereignty of and should not take jurisdiction over another state, unless that other state has submitted to the jurisdiction.[3]) In the past, a person who traded or invested abroad faced a "serious and immediate barrier to judicial remedies", as state immunity was generally considered to be absolute.[4]) Over the years, the rigid rule of absolute immunity has given room to limited immunity.[5])

Immunity can be raised at different stages of the proceedings, with different scope. Therefore, the fact that a state agrees to refer disputes to arbitration does not amount to an automatic waiver of its right to raise state immunity in the arbitration proceedings.[6]) It may also invoke immunity at the stage of recognition of the arbitral award or its enforcement over state property, unless the state has waived such right expressly and particularly.[7])

In respect of conservatory measures during proceedings for the enforcement of arbitral awards, immunity rules of different states vary. But it can be said that the general rule under customary international law is that conser-

---

[3]) C. Dionysiou, *Recognition and Enforcement of Foreign Judgments in Cyprus* (Nicosia: Hippasus, 2025), pp. 435–438.

[4]) Sabahi, Rubins & Wallace, *Investor-State Arbitration* (Oxford: 2nd ed., 2019, OUP, pp. 2.07–2.10 & 2.18–2.20.

[5]) Jame Crawford, *Bronlie's Principles of Public International Law* (Oxford: 8th ed., 2012, OUP), p. 503; *Unitica Enterprises v Slovak Republic* [1999] 1 A.A.D. 284 (Cyprus), p. 293; and *Seckersavvas and another v Turkish Republic*, Civil Appeal No. 415/2019, Judgment dated 31 October 2024 (Cyprus), available at: https://www.cylaw.org/cgi-bin/open.pl?file=/courtOfAppeal/2024/202410-415-19PolEf.html (last accessed on November 3, 2025).

[6]) *Reliance Industries v Union of India* [2018] EWHC 822 (Comm), paras. 117, 125 & 126; and *Infrastructure Services Luxembourg S.À.R.L. v. Kingdom of Spain and Border Timbers Limited v. Republic of Zimbabwe* [2024] EWCA Civ 1257.

[7]) *Redfern and Hunter on International Arbitration* (Oxford: 7th ed., 2022, OUP), paras. 11.152–11.154 & 11.157–11.167; and *Russell on Arbitration* (London: 24th ed., 2015, Sweet & Maxwell), para. 3-021.

vatory measures against states are not available without that state giving its consent to such measures.[8])

In 1972, the Council of Europe introduced the European Convention on State Immunity ("**the European Convention**").[9]) Accordingly, a state may not raise immunity when sued in the courts of another member state, if the former state has undertaken to submit to the jurisdiction of that state (Article 2). The European Convention goes on to enumerate various other instances where state immunity cannot be invoked (Articles 2–14), and then states the general rules that immunity can be raised in all other instances (Article 15).

Where a judgment is issued against a state in relation to an industrial or commercial activity, it may be executed against property used exclusively in connection with such activity (Article 26). In respect of execution, the European Convention provides that "no measures of execution or preventive measures against the property […] may be taken […] except where and to the extent that the State has expressly consented thereto in writing in any particular case" (Article 23). A state that is party to proceedings may not be subjected to any measure of coercion (Article 18) or ordered to give security for costs (Article 17).

Another important instrument in the regulation of state immunity is the United Nations Convention on Jurisdictional Immunities and Their Property, of 2004 ("**the UN Convention**").[10]) The preamble of the Convention considers that the issue of state immunity is an established principle under rules of customary international law. It does not seek to supersede such rules, but rather to supplement them by regulating certain aspects of the principle. Accordingly, a state is generally immune from the jurisdiction of the courts of another state (Article 6), unless the first state expressly consents otherwise (Article 7). However, immunity cannot be invoked when a state engages in a commercial transaction with a foreign person (Article 10). For this purpose, the Convention identifies three categories of transactions which are within the definition of a 'commercial transaction' (Article 2).

In respect of pre-judgment measures of constraint, the UN Convention reiterates the general rule that they are not available against a foreign state unless that state expressly consented to the taking of such measures or allocated or earmarked property for the satisfaction of the claim (Article 18). The same exceptions apply for post-judgment measures of constraint, with an additional exception in the event that it is established that the property is specifically in use or intended for use by the state for other than government non-commercial

[8]) *Dicey, Morris & Collins on the Conflict of Laws* (London: 15th ed., 2012, Sweet & Maxwell), paras. 10-014–10-015.

[9]) Available at: https://rm.coe.int/16800730b1 (last accessed on November 3, 2025).

[10]) Available at: https://legal.un.org/ilc/texts/instruments/english/conventions/4_1_2004.pdf (last accessed on November 3, 2025).

purposes. (Article 19). The purpose test is a "means of balancing respect for state sovereignty and the judgment debtor's rights to be paid amounts judged due and owing".[11])

The UN Convention makes it clear that consent to jurisdiction does not imply consent to the taking of measures of constraint (Articles 20 & 21). A failure by the state to comply with such measures may only entail consequences in relation to the merits of the case, not including a fine or penalty to the state. It is not possible for such measures to obligate a state to provide any security, bond, deposit or security for costs (Article 24). However, a general consent to enforcement measures, unconnected to any specific category of property or enforcement measure, is insufficient to permit execution.[12])

The above show that, under international law, conservatory measures are generally not permitted against states. The common exception in the instruments mentioned above is where the state consents to such measures being issued or indicates specific property located in another state, against which a judgment or award can be enforced. The position is less clear in respect of property used exclusively for commercial purposes, where the state did not consent to conservatory measures being issued or indicate that property as available for enforcement purposes. It may be that the 'commercial purpose' criterion is seen as a condition to be met before property becomes subject to conservatory measures, that is additional to the condition of 'consent' or 'earmarking'. Such view is in line with the principle that conservatory measures should not be issued against state property if a judgment or award cannot be enforced against the same. By contrast, the 'commercial purpose' criterion may be seen as an independent condition which can allow the taking of such measures even where the other conditions are not present.

## B. English Law

In England and Wales, the matter is dealt with in the Sovereign Immunity Act 1978.[13]) In Singapore, the State Immunity Act 1979[14]) uses very similar wording.

S.13(2)(a) of the English act provides that "relief shall not be given against a State by way of injunction ...". However, s.13(3) goes on the state that s.13(2)

[11]) Jame Crawford, *Bronlie's Principles of Public International Law* (Oxford: 8th ed., 2012, OUP), p. 504.

[12]) Hazel Fox, "State Immunity (Jurisdictional Immunities of States and Their Property)", in *Max Planck Encyclopedia of Public International Law* (Oxford: Oxford University Press, 2008; updated 2021), para. 41.

[13]) Available at: https://www.legislation.gov.uk/ukpga/1978/33/2023-02-23 (last accessed on November 3, 2025).

[14]) Available at: https://sso.agc.gov.sg/Act/SIA1979 (last accessed on November 3, 2025).

does "not prevent the giving of any relief or the issue of any process with the written consent of the State concerned; and any such consent (which may be contained in a prior agreement) may be expressed so as to apply to a limited extent or generally; but a provision merely submitting to the jurisdiction of the courts is not to be regarded as a consent for the purposes of this subsection".

On the basis of s.13(3), a freezing injunction was granted in *A Company Ltd v. Republic of X*,[15]) where the state concerned had agreed to an express provision waiving "whatever defense it may have [had] of sovereign immunity for itself or its property".[16]) In order to obtain an injunction, the claimant must show that the wording of the waiver was sufficiently wide to include injunctive relief and that the intended use of the property that is the subject matter of the injunction is for commercial purposes.[17]) Also, the property must not be immune from execution. It must be property against which the claimant may satisfy a judgment or award.[18])

By implication, property that an award or judgment cannot be enforced against cannot be the subject of conservatory measures. S.13(4) provides that property is excluded from enforcement if, "it is for the time being in use or intended for use for commercial purposes". In *SerVaas Incorporated (Appellant) v Rafidain Bank and others (Respondents)*,[19]) when considering whether the property in question fell within this exception, the Supreme Court found that the nature of the underlying transaction was irrelevant. What mattered was the current use or intended use of that property (paras. 17, 22 & 32).

In *UK P&I Club N.V. and United Kingdom Mutual Steam Ship Assurance Association Ltd v República Bolivariana de Venezuela RCGS "Resolute"*,[20]) the Court proceeded with a thorough analysis of case law on immunity on conservatory measures. It confirmed the long-established position that states are immune from such measures. It seems that the same applies in respect of conservatory measures issued by arbitration tribunals, as waiver of immunity is a precondition to the exercise of such power.[21])

It would therefore appear that conservatory measures are not available against a foreign state without that state's consent or waiver. There has been case law suggesting that conservatory measures could be available even in the

[15]) [1990] 2 Lloyd's Rep. 520.

[16]) Steven Gee, *Commercial Injunctions* (London: 6th ed., 2016, Sweet & Maxwell), para. 3-037.

[17]) *Ibid.* para. 3-038. *See also:* Nelson Goh, "State immunity and court-ordered relief in support of arbitration" *Arbitration* (2018) 84(1), 89–95, p. 93; and *EIT Euro Telecom International NV v Republic of Bolivia* [2008] 2 Lloyd's Rep. 421; *c.f. Pearl Petroleum Co Ltd v Kurdistan Regional Government of Iraq* [2015] EWCH 3361.

[18]) *Ibid.*, para. 3-039.

[19]) [2012] UKSC 40.

[20]) [2022] EWHC 1655 (Comm), paras. 120–124, 128 & 129.

[21]) *The London Steam-Ship Owners' Mutual Insurance Association Limited v The Kingdom of Spain* [2020] EWHC 1582 (Comm).

absence or consent or waiver. In particular, it was found in *Benkharbouche v Embassy of the Republic of Sudan*[22]) that an immunity established by domestic law may result in a denial of access to justice, when it is not required by international law. However, in *UK P&I Club N.V. and United Kingdom Mutual Steam Ship Assurance Association Ltd v República Bolivariana de Venezuela RCGS "Resolute"*,[23]) the English High Court held that the provisions of s.13(2)(a) where consistent with current international standards (para. 116). It is therefore still the case that consent is a necessary condition under English for conservatory measures against states.

## IV. Practical Difficulties Resulting from Lack of Coercive Measures

When an injunction is issued against a state, it is reasonable to expect that the state will comply with it. If it does not, it is unlikely for a court to fine or sequestrate assets of the state or even enforce the injunction against individuals connected with the state. But it may deal with the matter with a declaration or an award of costs. Importantly, however, the injunction can have effects against third parties, such as banks or other asset holders.[24]) The problem becomes most acute when a state disregards interim or conservatory measures issued in arbitral proceedings. Even where such measures are properly granted, claimants have limited procedural avenues to compel compliance.[25]) Proceedings for contempt, which in ordinary litigation serve as a deterrent against non-compliance, are not realistically available against a sovereign. State immunity operates as a barrier to coercive enforcement, reflecting the broader principles of *comity* and *par in parem non habet imperium*.[26])

The approach of the European Convention, in theory, reflects a deliberate balance between the principle of sovereign equality and the need to ensure the effectiveness of adjudicatory processes, including arbitral proceedings. In practice, however, the said convention's strict consent requirement hinders enforcement mechanisms against non-complying sovereigns, as arbitral tribunals themselves lack coercive powers.[27]) Even where an arbitral award is

---

[22]) [2017] UKSC 62, para. 34.

[23]) [2022] EWHC 1655 (Comm).

[24]) Steven Gee, *Commercial Injunctions* (London: 6th ed., 2016, Sweet & Maxwell), para. 3-040.

[25]) Aman Prasad, *"Enforceability of Interim Measures Ordered by Arbitral Tribunals: The Issue and Possible Remedies in International Commercial Arbitration"* (2020) SSRN, p. 3.

[26]) J. Finke, "Sovereign Immunity: Rule, Comity or Something Else?", (2010) *European Journal of International Law* 21(4) 853, 856–860.

[27]) Y. Dautaj, *Enforcing Arbitral Awards Against States and the Defense of Sovereign Immunity from Execution: A U.S. Perspective*, 11 Penn St. J.L. & Int'l Aff. 97 (2023), pp. 116 & 140.

recognized, its execution often depends on the willingness of domestic courts to exercise their enforcement powers in the face of state immunity or restrictive national provisions (*e.g.*, the State Immunity Act 1978, ss. 13(2) & (4)).

In *UK P&I Club*,[28]) the English High Court explained that the reasoning behind s.13(2)(a) was that contempt proceedings are not available against states. The rule prohibiting interim measures against states emanated from international sensitivity relating to comity and procedural propriety (para. 122).

Diplomatic immunity further shields state officials from personal lability, while broader public policy considerations preclude the use of punitive or coercive measures against the state itself. As a result, both arbitral tribunals and national courts are left without any meaningful means of enforcement beyond declaratory or cost-based remedies. Interim measures, though binding in theory, therefore rely almost entirely on voluntary observance. Ultimately, the award creditor may possess a binding, internationally recognized award, yet no enforceable route to compel compliance or seize assets unless a clear and specific waiver of execution immunity exists.

## V. Indirect Coercion Through 3rd Parties

Although courts and arbitral tribunals lack direct coercive power over states, they may nevertheless exert indirect pressure through third parties that hold or manage state assets. This mechanism of indirect coercion operates by compelling third-parties, such as commercial banks, trustees, or state-owned enterprises, to comply with judicial or arbitral orders or risk contempt themselves. While such measures do not bind the state in a strict sense, they can significantly limit its ability to dispose of or access its assets and may therefore encourage compliance with the underlying award or injunction.

For instance, Mareva injunctions directed at financial institutions may freeze accounts or prevent the transfer of funds belonging to a state. Similarly, orders served on counterparties or contractual intermediaries can disrupt ongoing transactions or commercial arrangements involving the respondent state. These effects, though collateral, may create practical leverage, particularly where the state's commercial operations or credit reputation are affected. In *NML Capital Ltd v Republic of Argentina*,[29]) the US courts permitted discovery and restraint orders against third-party financial institutions in an effort to trace and limit Argentina's access to assets.

However, the scope of such indirect coercion remains limited. Third parties may resist compliance on the ground that any interference with state property constitutes a coercive measure against the sovereign itself. In *AIG*

[28]) [2022] EWHC 1655 (Comm).

[29]) F.3d 246 (2d Cir. 2012), pp.18-19; affirmed by the US Supreme Court, 573 U.S. 134 (2014), pp 4–5.

*Capital Partners Inc v Republic of Kazakhstan,*[30]) the English Commercial Court reaffirmed that orders directed at third parties must not in effect circumvent the immunity afforded to state property used for sovereign purposes.

Domestic courts tend to exercise considerable restraint when extending enforcement measures to third-parties, particularly where this would undermine the principles of comity or frustrate diplomatic relations. Ultimately, the permissibility and effectiveness of such indirect coercion depend upon the domestic legislation and judicial approach of the jurisdiction in which enforcement is sought.

## VI. Conclusion

'Consent' remains relevant and necessary for obtaining conservatory measures against states. But even where all the conditions are met and such measures are issued against a state, their effectiveness may be negated by the inability of the counterparty to coerce compliance. Nevertheless, as such measures often involve various intermediaries, who do not benefit from state immunity, the risk that such intermediaries may face contempt proceedings is often a decisive factor in relation to the effectiveness of the conservatory measures.

[30]) [2005] EWHC 2239 (Comm), paras. 91–94.

# Enforcement of Intra-EU Investment Awards
## Trends Within and Beyond the EU

*Eveli Lume/Matej Pustay**)

## I. Introduction

This article examines the evolving practice and jurisprudence of the enforcement of intra-EU investment awards – *i.e.*, awards rendered in disputes between a European Union ("**EU**") Member State and an investor from another Member State – across selected jurisdictions.

The enforcement of intra-EU investment arbitration awards has emerged as a particularly contentious and complex issue in contemporary international investment law. This development follows the decisions of the Court of Justice of the European Union ("**CJEU**") in *Achmea v. Slovakia*, *Komstroy v. Moldova*, and *PL Holdings v. Poland*, which found arbitration clauses providing for intra-EU investment arbitration to be incompatible with EU law.

These decisions had a significant impact on enforcement of intra-EU investment awards within the EU. At the same time, their impact outside of the EU has been limited. This divergence between EU and non-EU approaches has resulted in a fragmented enforcement landscape – one in which the fate of an intra-EU award often depends on the jurisdiction in which enforcement is sought.

According to the United Nations Conference on Trade and Development (UNCTAD) Investment Dispute Settlement Navigator, 81 intra-EU investment arbitration cases have been decided since 2018,[1]) and another eight cases are currently pending.[2])

---

*) The authors wish to thank *Ms. Helena Švandová* and *Ms. Oleksandra Hnatiuk* (both Squire Patton Boggs) for their valuable assistance with research for this article.

[1]) With the exclusion of the cases which were discontinued and decided in favor of neither party.

[2]) UNCTAD's Investment Dispute Settlement Navigator, available at https://investmentpolicy.unctad.org/investment-dispute-settlement (last accessed: 3 November 2025).

## II. The *Achmea, Komstroy* and *PL Holdings* Decisions

The CJEU has rendered three landmark decisions concerning the compatibility of intra-EU investment arbitration agreements with EU law. The first was the Grand Chamber's decision in *Achmea v. Slovakia* in which the CJEU held that arbitration clauses contained in intra-EU bilateral investment treaties ("**BITs**") are incompatible with EU law.[3]) The CJEU based its conclusion on Articles 267 and 344 of the Treaty on the Functioning of the European Union ("**TFEU**"), finding that these provisions confer exclusive authority to interpret EU law to the courts of the EU Member States and, ultimately, on the CJEU.

Accordingly, EU Member States are precluded from submitting disputes that could involve interpretation of EU law to investment tribunals, which remain outside of the EU judicial system.[4]) The CJEU also relied on the principle of mutual trust between the Member States, enshrined in Article 4(3) of the Treaty on European Union ("**TEU**"), which requires that EU law be respected and applied uniformly throughout the Union.[5])

Following the *Achmea* decision, on 15 January 2019, EU Member States signed a declaration on the legal consequences of the *Achmea* decision and on investment protection in which the Member States recognized the consequences of the *Achmea* decision and committed to terminate the intra-EU BITs (the "**2019 Declaration**").[6])

On 29 May 2020, all the Member States – except for Austria, Finland, Sweden, and Ireland – signed the Agreement for the termination of Bilateral Investment Treaties between the Member States of the European Union (the "**Termination Agreement**"). Member States agreed to terminate their intra-EU BITs along with their sunset clauses, designed to afford post-termination treaty protection to investments made prior to the termination.[7])

---

[3]) *Slovak Republic v Achmea BV*, Case C-284/16, ECLI:EU:C:2018:158 (CJEU 2018).

[4]) *Ibid.*, at 62.

[5]) *Ibid.*, at 34, 58.

[6]) Finland, Luxembourg, Malta, Slovenia, Sweden, and Hungary did not sign the declaration. *See* European Commission, *Declaration of the Member States of 15 January 2019 on the legal consequences of the Achmea judgment and on investment protection*, Directorate-General for Financial Stability, Financial Services and Capital Markets Union, 17 January 2019, available at https://finance.ec.europa.eu/publications/declaration-member-states-15-january-2019-legal-consequences-achmea-judgment-and-investment_en (last accessed: 1 November 2025).

[7]) Official Journal of the European Union, *Agreement for the termination of Bilateral Investment Treaties between the Member States of the European Union*, OJ L 169, 29 May 2020, pp. 1–41. ELI: 22020A0529(01) (last accessed: 1 November 2025).

The CJEU subsequently extended the *Achmea* reasoning in its Grand Chamber decision of 2 September 2021 in *Komstroy v Moldova*,[8]) holding that the arbitration clause in Article 26 of the Energy Charter Treaty ("**ECT**") is also incompatible with EU law insofar as it applies to intra-EU disputes.

Finally, in *PL Holdings v. Poland* (decision of 26 October 2021),[9]) the CJEU addressed the question whether an *ad hoc* arbitration agreement between an EU Member State and an investor from another EU Member State that is, in substance, identical to the arbitration clause in the intra-EU BIT between these EU Member States is compatible with EU law. Such an *ad hoc* agreement was considered to have been concluded tacitly under *lex arbitri* (Swedish law) based on Poland's conduct in the arbitration. The CJEU held that Articles 267 and 344 TFEU preclude national legislation allowing for the conclusion of such *ad hoc* agreements.[10])

Further to the *Komstroy* decision on the arbitration clause in the ECT, on 26 June 2024, all EU Member States except for Hungary issued a declaration, stating a common understanding that in light of the *Komstroy* decision, the investor-state arbitration clause in Article 26 of the ECT should be interpreted as not being applicable to intra-EU investment disputes.[11]) Following that declaration, on 10 September 2025, the European Parliament and Council approved the Agreement between the Member States on the interpretation and application of the Energy Charter Treaty, which mirrors the 26 June 2024 declaration. It provides that the ECT "*could not in the past and cannot now or in the future*" serve as the legal basis for an intra-EU arbitration.[12])

These developments have prompted objections to the jurisdiction of investment tribunals (a so-called intra-EU objection) in the ongoing intra-EU investment arbitrations as well as new investment arbitrations commenced ever since. Investment tribunals have not approached these objections consistently. Many investments tribunals have rejected the intra-EU objection

---

[8]) *Republic of Moldova v. Komstroy LLC*, Case C-741/19, ECLI:EU:C:2021:655 (CJEU 2021).

[9]) *Republic of Poland v. PL Holdings Sàrl*, Case C109/20, ECLI:EU:C:2021:875 (CJEU 2021).

[10]) *Ibid.*, at 70.

[11]) European Commission, *Declaration on the legal consequences of the judgment of the Court of Justice in Komstroy and common understanding on the nonapplicability of Article 26 of the Energy Charter Treaty as a basis for intraEU arbitration*, Directorate-General for Energy, 28 June 2024, available at https://energy.ec.europa.eu/publications/declaration-legal-consequences-judgment-court-justice-komstroy-and-common-under standing-non_en (last accessed: 1 November 2025).

[12]) Hungary is not a party to the agreement. European Parliament and Council of the European Union, *Decision (EU) 2025/1904 of the European Parliament and of the Council of 10 September 2025 on the approval by the Union of the Agreement on the interpretation and application of the Energy Charter Treaty*, OJ L, 19 September 2025, available at https://eur-lex.europa.eu/eli/dec/2025/1904/oj (last accessed: 3 November 2025).

and upheld their jurisdiction in intra-EU investment arbitrations.[13]) However, there are also investments tribunals that upheld the intra-EU objection.[14])

# III. Enforcement of Intra-EU Awards

## A. General Comments

Enforcement of investment awards is primarily governed by two international conventions: the 1958 Convention on the Recognition and Enforcement of Foreign Arbitral Awards (the "**NYC**"), to the extent the award qualifies under that Convention, and the 1966 Convention on the Settlement of Investment Disputes between States and Nationals of Other States (the "**ICSID Convention**"). The latter establishes a self-contained regime for enforcement of investment awards rendered under the ICSID framework.

Article V of the NYC sets forth specific grounds for rejection of recognition and enforcement of arbitral awards.[15]) As explained in Section B below,

[13]) *E.g., NextEra Energy Global Holdings B.V. and NextEra Energy Spain Holdings B.V. v. Kingdom of Spain*, ICSID Case No. ARB/14/11, Decision on Jurisdiction, Liability and Principles of Quantum, 12 March 2019, para. 357; *B3 Croatian Courier Coöperatief U.A. v. Republic of Croatia*, ICSID Case No. ARB/15/5, Award (Excerpts), 5 April 2019, para. 567; *VM Solar Jerez GmbH, M Solar Verwaltungs GmbH, Solarizz Holding Verwaltungs-GmbH, M Solar GmbH & Co. KG, Solarizz Holding GmbH & Co. KG and Helmut Vorndran v. Kingdom of Spain*, ICSID Case No. ARB/19/30, Decision on Jurisdiction, Liability and Principles of Quantum, 14 May 2025, paras. 326–328; *United Utilities (Tallinn) B.V. and Aktsiaselts Tallinna Vesi v. Republic of Estonia*, ICSID Case No. ARB/14/24, Award, 21 June 2019, paras. 531–560.

[14]) *E.g., Green Power K/S and Obton A/S v. Spain*, SCC Case No. V 2016/135, 16 June 2022.

[15]) Article V (1) of the NYC provides that recognition and enforcement of the award may be refused if "*(a) [t]he parties to the agreement referred to in article II were, under the law applicable to them, under some incapacity, or the said agreement is not valid under the law to which the parties have subjected it or, failing any indication thereon, under the law of the country where the award was made; or (b) [t]he party against whom the award is invoked was not given proper notice of the appointment of the arbitrator or of the arbitration proceedings or was otherwise unable to present his case; or (c) [t]he award deals with a difference not contemplated by or not falling within the terms of the submission to arbitration, or it contains decisions on matters beyond the scope of the submission to arbitration, provided that, if the decisions on matters submitted to arbitration can be separated from those not so submitted, that part of the award which contains decisions on matters submitted to arbitration may be recognized and enforced; or (d) [t]he composition of the arbitral authority or the arbitral procedure was not in accordance with the agreement of the parties, or, failing such agreement, was not in accordance with the law of the country where the arbitration took place; or (e) [t]he award has not yet become binding on the parties, or has been set aside or suspended by a competent authority of the country in which, or under the law of which, that award was made.*" Additionally, recognition and enforcement of an arbitral award may also be

respondent States have invoked several of these grounds to oppose recognition and enforcement of intra-EU investment awards, in particular the invalidity of the underlying arbitration agreement, the annulment of the award at the seat of arbitration, or the contention that recognition or enforcement of the intra-EU investment award would contradict the enforcing State's public policy.[16])

In contrast, the ICSID Convention requires each contracting State to *"recognize [awards] rendered pursuant to [the ICSID Convention] as binding and enforce the pecuniary obligations imposed by [those awards] within [their] territories as if [they] were a final judgment of a court in [those States]"*.[17]) Consequently, respondent States opposing the enforcement of ICSID intra-EU awards have also relied on more general defenses – most notably, sovereign immunity.

In addition to the above defenses, a further issue arises uniquely in the context of enforcement of intra-EU awards: the question of unlawful state aid under EU law. The EU Commission, the CJEU and certain courts of the Member States have repeatedly found that intra-EU investment awards may represent unlawful stated aid under EU law and, thus, cannot be enforced by the Member States' courts with the consequence that any amounts already paid should be recovered by the EU Member States.

This issue was first addressed with respect to an intra-EU ICSID case *Ioan Micula, Viorel Micula and others v. Romania (1)*. In that case, claimants prevailed and obtained an ICSID award upholding their claim for damages.[18]) The EU Commission, however, subsequently issued a decision stating that the tribunal's award represents unlawful state aid ("**Decision 2015/1470**").[19]) As a result, the EU Commission ordered that Romania shall not pay the damages

---

refused under Article V (2) of the NYC in the instances when *"(a) [t]he subject matter of the difference is not capable of settlement by arbitration under the law of that country; or (b) [t]he recognition or enforcement of the award would be contrary to the public policy of that country." See Convention on the Recognition and Enforcement of Foreign Arbitral Awards*, 10 June 1958, 21 U.S.T. 2543, 330 U.N.T.S. 38, Art. V.

[16]) *Convention on the Recognition and Enforcement of Foreign Arbitral Awards*, 10 June 1958, 21 U.S.T. 2543, 330 U.N.T.S. 38, Arts. V(1)(a), V(1)(e) and V(2)(b).

[17]) *Convention on the Settlement of Investment Disputes between States and Nationals of Other States*, 18 March 1965, 575 U.N.T.S. 159, Art. 54(1).

[18]) *Ioan Micula, Viorel Micula, S.C. European Food S.A, S.C. Starmill S.R.L. and S.C. Multipack S.R.L. v. Romania [I]*, ICSID Case No. ARB/05/20, Final Award, 11 December 2013, para. 1329.

[19]) *Micula v. Romania*, 2015/1470, 30 March 2015, (EU) 2015/1470 OJ L 232, pp. 43–70. European Commission, *Commission Decision (EU) 2015/1470 of 30 March 2015 on State aid SA.38517 (2014/C) (ex 2014/NN) implemented by Romania — Arbitral award Micula v Romania of 11 December 2013, Official Journal of the European Union* L 232/43, 4 September 2015, Article 1. This decision was subject to further proceedings but was eventually upheld by the General Court of the EU in October 2024.

awarded in the award and shall recover any payments that had already been made under the award.[20])

Decision 2015/1470 was, subsequently, challenged by claimants, who prevailed in the first instance. The General Court concluded that the EU Commission did not have competence to order Romania to refrain from paying the damages and that the legal classification of the arbitral award as an *"advantage"* and *"aid"* for the purposes of Article 107 of the TFEU was incorrect. As a result, the General Court annulled the Decision 2015/1470.[21])

The General Court's decision was, however, annulled by the CJEU on 25 January 2022 and the case was remanded back to the General Court.[22]) The CJEU noted, *inter alia*, that *"with effect from Romania's accession to the European Union, the system of judicial remedies provided for by the EU and TFEU Treaties replaced that arbitration procedure"* and, as a result, *"the consent given to that effect by Romania, from that time onwards, lacked any force"*.[23])

In its subsequent decision, the General Court upheld the Decision 2015/1470.[24]) The court found that the award issued by the *Micula* tribunal was *"adopted by the arbitral tribunal on 11 December 2013, that is to say, after Romania's accession to the European Union"* and, as a result, the award *"cannot [...] produce any effects and cannot thus be executed with a view to paying the compensation granted by that award"*.[25]) The General Court held that, as a consequence, *"a court or tribunal of a Member State ruling on the enforcement of an arbitral award is required to set aside that award and, therefore, may not*

[20]) European Commission, *Commission Decision (EU) 2015/1470 of 30 March 2015 on State aid SA.38517 (2014/C) (ex 2014/NN) implemented by Romania — Arbitral award Micula v Romania of 11 December 2013, Official Journal of the European Union* L 232/43, 4 September 2015, Article 2. In a more recent case, the EU Commission issued essentially the same decision with respect to the investment award issued in *Infrastructure Services (Antin) v. Spain. See* European Commission, *Commission Decision (EU) 2025/1235 of 24 March 2025 on the measure State aid SA.54155 (2021/NN) implemented by Spain – Arbitration award to Antin (notified under document C(2025) 1781)*, OJ L, 25 June 2025.

[21]) *European Food SA and Others v European Commission*, Joined Cases T-624/15 RENV, T-694/15 RENV & T-704/15 RENV, Judgment of 2 October 2024, ECLI:EU:T:2024:659 (GC 2024), para. 28.

[22]) *Commission v European Food SA and Others* (Case C-638/19 P), ECLI:EU:C:2022:50 (CJEU 2022) para. 156.

[23]) *Ibid.*, at 145.

[24]) Judgment of the General Court in Case T-624/15 RENV, 2 October 2024, para. 431.

[25]) *European Food SA and Others v European Commission*, Joined Cases T-624/15 RENV, T-694/15 RENV & T-704/15 RENV, Judgment of 2 October 2024, ECLI:EU:T:2024:659 (GC 2024), para. 101.

*in any case proceed with its enforcement in order to enable its beneficiaries to obtain payment of damages which it awarded them".*[26])

The prohibition of enforcing intra-EU awards by the Member States' courts was also confirmed by the CJEU in its decision on a request for a preliminary ruling filed by the Brussels Court of Appeal, which was seized to enforce the *Micula* award.[27]) In that decision, the CJEU concluded that *"Articles 267 and 344 TFEU, must be interpreted as meaning that a court of a Member State seised of the enforcement of the arbitral award which was the subject of Commission Decision (EU) 2015/1470 of 30 March 2015 concerning State aid SA.38517 (2014/C) (ex 2014/NN) implemented by Romania – Arbitral award in the Micula v Romania case of 11 December 2013, is required to disregard that award and, consequently, may not in any case proceed with its enforcement in order to enable its beneficiaries to obtain payment of the damages awarded to them".*[28])

This shows that, in the view of the EU Commission and the CJEU, intra-EU investment awards and their enforcement qualify as unlawful state aid, requiring the Member States' courts to deny their enforcement and to recover any amounts already paid under such awards.

---

[26]) *European Food SA and Others v European Commission*, Joined Cases T-624/15 RENV, T-694/15 RENV & T-704/15 RENV, Judgment of 2 October 2024, ECLI:EU:T:2024:659 (GC 2024), para. 102.

[27]) The Brussels Court of Appeal referred the following preliminary questions to the CJEU: *"1) Should Decision 2015/1470 be understood as referring to payments due from Romania even in the event that the payments are recovered [from it] following enforcement proceedings for the arbitral award [...] of 11 December 2013, initiated before the courts of a Member State other than Romania?; 2) Does Union law require, in itself and ex officio, that a court of a Member State (other than Romania), seised of an action [against] enforcement proceedings of an arbitral award [...] which has the force of res judicata under the national procedural rules of that Member State, set aside that award, solely on the ground that a non-final decision of the Commission adopted after the award considers that enforcement of the award is contrary to the [Union] State aid regime?; 3) Does EU law, in particular the principle of sincere cooperation or the principle of res judicata, allow a national court of a Member State (other than Romania) to fail to comply with its international obligations under the ICSID Convention if the Commission has adopted a decision subsequent to the award, which considers that the enforcement of the award would be contrary to the EU State aid regime, even if the Commission participated in the arbitration proceedings (including the application to set aside the award) and raised its arguments relating to the EU State aid regime?" DA and Others v Romanian Air Traffic Services Administration (Romatsa) and Others*, Case C-333/19, Order of 21 September 2022 (CJEU Tenth Chamber 2022), para. 22.

[28]) *DA and Others v Romanian Air Traffic Services Administration (Romatsa) and Others*, Case C-333/19, Order of 21 September 2022 (CJEU Tenth Chamber 2022), para. 46.

## B. Comparative Overview of the Practice of Recognition and Enforcement of Intra-EU Awards

This section examines approaches taken by certain national courts, both within and outside the EU, regarding intra-EU investment awards.[29]) The section primarily focuses on decisions issued in the context of recognition and enforcement proceedings but discusses also certain decisions in set-aside proceedings.

This is because the arguments raised by respondent States in set-aside proceedings often mirror those raised in enforcement proceedings, typically relying on the CJEU's reasoning in the *Achmea*, *Komstroy* and *PL Holdings* decisions. Accordingly, to fully understand how national courts approach the CJEU's reasoning – and how they may respond to efforts to enforce intra-EU investment awards – it is helpful to consider decisions from both recognition and enforcement and set-aside contexts.

### 1. Recognition and Enforcement Within the EU

#### a) Germany

German courts have played a notable role in applying the CJEU's case law on the compatibility of investor-state arbitration clauses with EU law. The German Federal Court of Justice (*Bundesgerichtshof*, "**BGH**") was the referring court in the *Achmea v. Slovakia* proceedings that led to the CJEU's *Achmea* decision. Following that decision, on 31 October 2018, the *Achmea* award was set aside.[30])

Thereafter, German courts have continued to apply *Achmea*'s reasoning, consistently finding intra-EU investment arbitration clauses to be incompatible with EU law. A notable example is the BGH decision of 27 March 2025 concerning the recognition and enforcement of the UNCITRAL intra-EU investment award in *Antaris and Michael Gode v. Czech Republic*.[31]) In that case, the BGH refused recognition and enforcement of a cost award rendered in favor of the Czech Republic against German investors. The investors had initiated investment arbitration under arbitration clauses in Article 10(2) of the Czechia-Germany BIT and Article 26(2) of the ECT.

---

[29]) This section provides certain examples of national court decisions that are considered as representative of how the intra-EU awards are treated in various jurisdictions. Given the limited scope of this article, this section does not aim to provide the full list and overview of all national courts' decision addressing enforcement or setting aside of the intra-EU awards.

[30]) German Federal Court of Justice (BGH), Decision dated 31 October 2018, I ZB 2/15.

[31]) German Federal Court of Justice (BGH), Decision dated 27 March 2025, I ZB 2/15.

The tribunal upheld its jurisdiction but dismissed the investors' claim and awarded costs to the Czech Republic. Referring to the *Achmea* and *Komstroy* decisions, the BGH found both arbitration clauses incompatible with Articles 267 and 344 of the TFEU and therefore invalid under the law governing these arbitration clauses within the meaning of Article V(1)(a) of the NYC. The court interpreted that law to be public international law, including EU law.[32])

The BGH further concluded that in terms of enforceability, a cost award in favor of a Member State should not be treated differently from an award granting damages to an investor, where both are based on an invalid arbitration clause.[33]) It remains to be seen how German courts would address a cost award arising from a tribunal's declining jurisdiction in intra-EU investment arbitration.

Noteworthy are also the BGH's rulings extending the *Achmea* and *Komstroy* reasoning to ICSID arbitrations. On 27 July 2023, the BGH issued a trio of rulings concerning three separate intra-EU ICSID arbitrations under the ECT.[34]) One proceeding was brought against Germany (*Mainstream Renewable Power Ltd and others v. Federal Republic of Germany*),[35]) while two others involved German investors bringing claims against the Netherlands (*RWE AG and RWE Eemshaven Holding II BV v. Kingdom of the Netherlands, Uniper SE, Uniper Benelux Holding B.V. and Uniper Benelux N.V. v. Kingdom of the Netherlands*).[36]) In all three cases, the respondent States requested German courts to declare the inadmissibility of the respective ICSID proceedings. Section 1032(2) of the German Civil Procedure Code ("**ZPO**") allows such a determination before the tribunal is formed. The BGH found that German courts had jurisdiction to decide over Germany's and the Netherland's requests by applying Section 1032(2) of the ZPO by analogy to delocalized proceedings, such as ICSID arbitrations.[37])

---

[32]) German Federal Court of Justice (BGH), Decision dated 27 March 2025, I ZB 2/15, para 35 *et seq.*

[33]) German Federal Court of Justice (BGH), Decision dated 27 March 2025, I ZB 2/15, para 40 *et seq.*

[34]) German Federal Court of Justice (BGH), Decision dated 27 July 2023, I ZB 43/22; German Federal Court of Justice (BGH), Decision dated 27 July 2023, I ZB 74/22; German Federal Court of Justice (BGH), Decision dated 27 July 2023, I ZB 75/22.

[35]) *Mainstream Renewable Power, Ltd., International Mainstream Renewable Power, Ltd., Mainstream Renewable Power Group Finance, Ltd., Horizont I Development, GmbH, Horizont II Renewable, GmbH and Horizont III Power GmbH v. Federal Republic of Germany*, ICSID Case No. ARB/21/26.

[36]) *RWE AG and RWE Eemshaven Holding II BV v. Kingdom of the Netherlands*, ICSID Case No. ARB/21/4; *Uniper SE, Uniper Benelux Holding B.V. and Uniper Benelux N.V. v. Kingdom of the Netherlands*, ICSID Case No. ARB/21/22.

[37]) German Federal Court of Justice (BGH), Decision dated 27 July 2023, I ZB 75/22, paras. 33–48; German Federal Court of Justice (BGH), Decision dated 27 July 2023, I ZB 43/22, paras. 33–49; German Federal Court of Justice (BGH), Decision dated 27 July 2023, I ZB 74/22, paras. 18–44.

The court further held that a review under Section 1032(2) of the ZPO was not precluded by the *Kompetenz-Kompetenz* principle enshrined in Article 41(1) of the ICSID Convention, even if – unlike under German law – that principle applied from the commencement of the ICSID proceedings, rather than from the constitution of the arbitral tribunal. In the BGH's view, the specific circumstances arising from the obligation to safeguard the primacy of EU law justified such a review. Here, the court relied on the principle of effectiveness of EU law (*effet utile*). Referring to the CJEU's decisions issued with respect to the *Micula* award, the BGH found that if a post-award review of ICSID awards by the Member States' courts is mandatory, a pre-award (upstream) review must likewise be permissible. The court found this to be even more the case, because a finding of inadmissibility under Section 1032(2) of the ZPO would preclude any later declaration of enforceability in Germany.[38])

Relying on *Komstroy*, the BGH concluded that the arbitration clause in Article 26 of the ECT was incompatible with EU law and accordingly held the arbitral proceedings inadmissible.[39])

German courts have also entertained Section 1032(2) requests regarding localized intra-EU arbitrations seated in Germany. A well-known example is the 11 February 2021 decision of the Higher Regional Court of Frankfurt, which concerned a UNCITRAL arbitration under the Austria-Netherlands BIT. The court held the arbitration to be inadmissible due to the BIT's arbitration clause's incompatibility with EU law,[40]) and the BGH subsequently dismissed the investors' appeal.[41])

---

[38]) German Federal Court of Justice (BGH), Decision dated 27 July 2023, I ZB 75/22, para. 52; German Federal Court of Justice (BGH), Decision dated 27 July 2023, I ZB 43/22, para. 52; German Federal Court of Justice (BGH), Decision dated 27 July 2023, I ZB 74/22, para. 47.

[39]) German Federal Court of Justice (BGH), Decision dated 27 July 2023, I ZB 75/22, paras. 126–127; German Federal Court of Justice (BGH), Decision dated 27 July 2023, I ZB 43/22, paras. 117–120. In the proceedings concerning the cases *RWE AG and RWE Eemshaven Holding II BV v. Kingdom of the Netherlands* and *Uniper SE, Uniper Benelux Holding B.V. and Uniper Benelux N.V. v. Kingdom of the Netherlands*, the Cologne Higher Regional Court had also found the arbitral proceedings to be incompatible with EU law. In the first case, this finding was appealed by investors and in the second case, such an appeal was later withdrawn. The BGH thus only had to confirm the finding of the Cologne Higher Regional Court in the first case. In addition, in both cases, the Netherlands had also requested an abstract declaration of inadmissibility of any arbitration proceedings between the parties based on the arbitration clause in the ECT. The BGH rejected this application by finding that such an abstract request was not covered by Section 1032(2) of the ZPO (German Federal Court of Justice (BGH), Decision dated 27 July 2023, I ZB 74/22, paras. 45 *et seq.*; German Federal Court of Justice (BGH), Decision dated 27 July 2023, I ZB 75/22, paras. 140 *et seq.*).

[40]) Higher Regional Court of Frankfurt (OLG Frankfurt), Decision dated 11 February 2021, 26 SchH 2/20.

[41]) German Federal Court of Justice (BGH), Decision dated 17 November 2021, I ZB 16/21.

### b) Sweden

Swedish courts have likewise followed the CJEU's rulings. Unlike German courts – which have primarily relied on the invalidity of the underlying arbitration clause – Swedish courts have based their reasoning on public policy (*ordre public*) considerations, finding that the enforcement of intra-EU awards would be manifestly incompatible with Swedish public policy.

One example is the 27 May 2024 decision of the Svea Court of Appeal in *CEF Energia v. Italy*, which concerned Italy's request to have an investment award rendered in an ECT arbitration pursuant to the SCC Arbitration Rules and seated in Stockholm declared invalid and set aside. Relying on *Achmea* and *Komstroy* decisions, the court upheld this request on the ground that the arbitration clause in Article 26 of the ECT was incompatible with EU law, rendering any award based on it unlawful. The court held that as the enforcement of such an award would manifestly contradict Swedish public policy, it must be declared invalid.[42])

In another case concerning a cost award in favor of Poland, Swedish courts distinguished the effects of such an award based on the investors' nationality. The case, *Festorino Invest Limited and others v. Poland,* concerned an ECT arbitration under the SCC Arbitration Rules seated in Stockholm and involved four investors from EU Member States and one Swiss citizen domiciled in Switzerland.[43]) On 20 December 2023, the Svea Court of Appeal found the that the entire arbitral award must be declared invalid on the ground that it contradicted Swedish public policy.[44])

However, Poland requested that the award be upheld to the extent it dismissed the Swiss investor's claims and awarded Poland its costs. On 26 May 2025, the Swedish Supreme Court partially reinstated the award on that basis, holding that the incompatibility of Article 26 of the ECT with EU law – and therefore with Swedish public policy – applied only to the part of the award concerning EU investors.[45]) The Supreme Court, however, upheld the Svea Court of Appeal's decision to invalidate the award to the extent it concerned EU investors.[46])

---

[42]) *CEF Energia BV v. Italian Republic*, SCC Case No. 2015/158, Judgment of the Svea Court of Appeal, 27 May 2024, paras. 53–54.

[43]) *Festorino Invest Limited, Fosontal Limited, Petry Salesny, Peter Derendinger and Petra Roijcka v. The Republic of Poland*, SCC Case No. 2018/098, Award, 30 June 2021.

[44]) *Festorino Invest Limited, Fosontal Limited, Petry Salesny, Peter Derendinger and Petra Roijcka v. The Republic of Poland*, SCC Case No. 2018/098, Judgment of the Svea Court of Appeal, 20 December 2023.

[45]) *Festorino Invest Limited, Fosontal Limited, Petry Salesny, Peter Derendinger and Petra Roijcka v. The Republic of Poland*, SCC Case No. 2018/098, Judgment of the Supreme Court of Sweden, 26 May 2025.

[46]) *Ibid.*, at 26.

### c) France

French courts addressed the effects of the intra-EU investment awards in the context of two annulment proceedings brought by the Republic of Poland against two investment awards rendered in *Strabag et al. v. Poland*, an intra-EU arbitration under the Austria-Poland BIT,[47]) and *Slot Group v. Poland*, an intra-EU arbitration under the Czechia-Poland BIT, both seated in Paris.[48]) In both cases, the Paris Court of Appeal, referring to the CJEU's reasoning in *Achmea* and *PL Holdings*, held that investment tribunals had wrongly asserted jurisdiction based on dispute resolution clauses in the respective intra-EU BITs, as those clauses were incompatible with EU law.[49])

The court further found that, since Poland's consent expressed in the arbitration clauses of the relevant BITs was contrary to EU law, which is binding on all Member States, it was unnecessary to assess the validity of the arbitration agreement under the Vienna Convention on the Law of Treaties ("**VCLT**") or the parties' common intention, both of which it deemed irrelevant for the outcome.[50])

Consequently, the Court of Appeal annulled the awards issued in both cases.[51])

### d) The Netherlands

Dutch courts addressed issues concerning enforceability of intra-EU investment awards when Spain applied for a declaratory judgment[52]) confirming that the investment award issued in *AES and others v. Spain*, an ECT

[47]) *Strabag SE, Raiffeisen Centrobank AG and Syrena Immobilien Holding AG v. Republic of Poland*, ICSID Case No. ADHOC/15/1, Judgment of the Paris Court of Appeal 19 April 2022.

[48]) *Slot Group a.s. v. Republic of Poland*, PCA Case No. 2017-10, Judgment of the Paris Court of Appeal (Department 5 – Chamber 16) 20/14581, 19 April 2022.

[49]) *Slot Group a.s. v. Republic of Poland*, PCA Case No. 2017-10, Judgment of the Paris Court of Appeal (Department 5 – Chamber 16) 20/14581, 19 April 2022, paras. 68–69; *Strabag SE, Raiffeisen Centrobank AG and Syrena Immobilien Holding AG v. Republic of Poland*, ICSID Case No. ADHOC/15/1, Judgment of the Paris Court of Appeal 19 April 2022, paras. 85–91.

[50]) *Slot Group a.s. v. Republic of Poland*, PCA Case No. 2017-10, Judgment of the Paris Court of Appeal (Department 5 – Chamber 16) 20/14581, 19 April 2022, para. 70; *Strabag SE, Raiffeisen Centrobank AG and Syrena Immobilien Holding AG v. Republic of Poland*, ICSID Case No. ADHOC/15/1, Judgment of the Paris Court of Appeal 19 April 2022, para. 90.

[51]) *Slot Group a.s. v. Republic of Poland*, PCA Case No. 2017-10, Judgment of Paris Court of Appeal on Set-Aside Application, 19 April 2022; *Strabag SE, Raiffeisen Centrobank AG and Syrena Immobilien Holding AG v. Republic of Poland*, ICSID Case No. ADHOC/15/1, Judgment of the Paris Court of Appeal 19 April 2022.

[52]) Spain applied for the declaratory judgment in the context of proceedings that it initiated against the beneficiaries of the award and in which it sought an order preventing the beneficiaries from enforcing the award. *See AES Solar and others (PV*

arbitration under the UNCITRAL Arbitration Rules seated in Switzerland, represented an unlawful state aid. On 5 February 2025, the Amsterdam District Court granted Spain's request, finding that the compensation awarded to the claimants by the investment tribunal constituted unlawful state aid unless the EU Commission declares the award compatible with the internal market. The court also ordered the investors to repay the amount already recovered under the award.[53])

#### e) Lithuania

The Supreme Court of Lithuania addressed the issue of enforcement of intra-EU investment awards in the context of domestic litigation initiated by Lithuania against the investors during the pendency of a related ICSID arbitration, *Veolia et al. v. Lithuania*, initiated under the France-Lithuania BIT.[54]) Lithuania initiated the domestic proceedings following the *Achmea* decision, after withdrawing its counterclaim in the ICSID arbitration and opting to pursue the matter before its national courts instead.

Referring to the *Achmea*, *Komstroy*, and *PL Holdings* rulings, on 18 January 2022, the Lithuanian Supreme Court held in proceedings related to Lithuania's counterclaim that the arbitration clause in the France-Lithuania BIT was incompatible with EU law. Consequently, it found that when the investors initiated ICSID arbitration, no valid offer to arbitrate existed, and thus no valid arbitration agreement could have been formed.[55])

In a separate decision on the investors' request to stay the domestic proceedings over Lithuania's counterclaim pending the outcome of the ICSID arbitration, the Supreme Court found no sufficient grounds for suspension. Referring to its 18 January 2022 decision, the CJEU's jurisprudence, and the Termination Agreement, the court concluded that *"EU Member States cannot recognize and enforce arbitral awards made under intra-EU bilateral investment*

---

*Investors) v. The Kingdom of Spain*, PCA Case No. 2012-14, Judgment of the Amsterdam District Court, 5 February 2025, sections I–IV.

[53]) *AES Solar and others (PV Investors) v. The Kingdom of Spain*, PCA Case No. 2012-14, Judgment of the Amsterdam District Court, 5 February 2025, para. 7.59

[54]) Hristina Todorovic, *Lithuanian Supreme Court declines to stay domestic court proceedings pending outcome of parallel intra-EU ICSID arbitration, signaling state's intention to deny recognition and enforcement of ICSID award*, 7 March 2025, available at https://www.iareporter.com/articles/lithuanian-supreme-court-declines-to-stay-domestic-court-proceedings-pending-outcome-of-parallel-intra-eu-icsid-arbitration-signaling-states-intention-to-deny-recognition-and-enforcement-of/ (last accessed: 3 November 2025); *Veolia Environnement S.A., Veolia Energie International S.A., UAB Vilniaus Energija and UAB Litesko v. Republic of Lithuania*, ICSID Case No. ARB/16/3, Judgment of the Supreme Court of Lithuania, 18 November 2024.

[55]) *Veolia Environnement S.A., Veolia Energie International S.A., UAB Vilniaus Energija and UAB Litesko v. Republic of Lithuania*, ICSID Case No. ARB/16/3, Decision of the Supreme Court of Lithuania, 18 January 2022.

*treaties, as this would be contrary to the principle of supremacy of EU law".*[56]) The court held that there was no need to stay the domestic proceedings because any future ICSID award *"under EU law will not be able to produce legal effects and be enforced in the territory of the Republic of Lithuania".*[57])

## 2. Recognition and Enforcement Outside the EU

### a) United Kingdom

The United Kingdom ("**UK**") occupies a rather distinct position in relation to intra-EU investment arbitrations. When the CJEU rendered its *Achmea* judgment, the UK was still an EU Member State. However, it did not sign the Termination Agreement in 2020.[58])

Shortly after its withdrawal from the EU but before the end of the transition period, the UK Supreme Court addressed the enforcement of the intra-EU ICSID award in *Ioan Micula, Viorel Micula and others v. Romania (1).* On 19 February 2020, the court lifted the stay of enforcement that had been stayed pending the outcome of EU proceedings concerning the EU Commission's decision prohibiting Romania from paying the award on the grounds that it constituted illegal state aid.[59]) The Supreme Court held that *"the duty of sincere co-operation* [between EU and Member States] *is not applicable in this case and there is no impediment to the lifting of the stay, which is an unlawful measure in international law and unjustified and unlawful in domestic law".*[60]) It further concluded that maintaining the stay would be incompatible with the UK's obligations to enforce ICSID awards under Article 54(1) of the ICSID Convention.[61])

---

[56]) *Veolia Environnement S.A., Veolia Energie International S.A., UAB Vilniaus Energija and UAB Litesko v. Republic of Lithuania*, ICSID Case No. ARB/16/3, Judgment of the Supreme Court of Lithuania, 18 November 2024, para. 55.

[57]) Hristina Todorovic, *Lithuanian Supreme Court declines to stay domestic court proceedings pending outcome of parallel intra-EU ICSID arbitration, signaling state's intention to deny recognition and enforcement of ICSID award,* 7 March 2025, available at https://www.iareporter.com/articles/lithuanian-supreme-court-declines-to-stay-domestic-court-proceedings-pending-outcome-of-parallel-intra-eu-icsid-arbitration-signaling-states-intention-to-deny-recognition-and-enforcement-of/ (last accessed: 3 November 2025); *Veolia Environnement S.A., Veolia Energie International S.A., UAB Vilniaus Energija and UAB Litesko v. Republic of Lithuania*, ICSID Case No. ARB/16/3, Judgment of the Supreme Court of Lithuania, 18 November 2024, para. 56.

[58]) The UK was, however, a signatory to the 2019 Declaration preceding the Termination Agreement. *See supra*, Section I; *Agreement for the termination of Bilateral Investment Treaties between the Member States of the European Union*, 2020 O.J. (L 169), 1.

[59]) *Micula and others v. Romania*, [2020] UKSC 5, paras. 29–36.

[60]) *Ibid.*, para. 118.

[61]) *Ibid.*, para. 86.

The UK courts subsequently addressed the enforcement of intra-EU investment awards also with respect to *Infrastructure Services (Antin) v. Spain*, an ICSID arbitration under the ECT. Spain resisted enforcement of the award issued in that case, invoking state immunity from the UK domestic proceedings under the UK State Immunity Act 1978.[62]) Spain argued that the exception from state immunity based on Section 9(1)[63]) of the UK State Immunity Act 1978, on which investors relied in their submissions, did not apply.[64])

While Spain did not dispute that the UK State Immunity Act 1978 removed state immunity where a state had agreed in writing to submit a dispute to arbitration, it challenged the effect of the arbitration clause in Article 26 of the ECT on the grounds that the *Achmea* and *Komstroy* decisions confirmed that this provision did not apply between EU Member States and investors from EU Member States.[65])

The High Court dismissed Spain's reliance on the *Achmea* and *Komstroy* decisions, finding no basis to conclude that Article 26 of the ECT did not extend to the investors.[66]) The High Court further held that Spain could not rely on immunity because, by acceding to the ICSID Convention, it had consented in writing to submit investment disputes to arbitration, thereby satisfying the exception from immunity under Article 9(1) of the UK State Immunity Act 1978.[67])

Finally, referring to the UK's obligations under the ICSID Convention, the High Court held that it would be *"wrong in law to allow [...] argument by Spain based on EU law, as explained in Achmea and Komstroy by the CJEU, to trump the existing treaty obligations of the ICSID Convention, as enacted into domestic law here by the 1966 Act".*[68])

**b) Switzerland**

In the reported cases, Swiss courts have rejected the respondent State's challenges based on the intra-EU objection. For example, on 3 April 2024, the Swiss Supreme Court dismissed Spain's application to set aside an intra-EU

---

[62]) *Infrastructure Services Luxembourg S.à r.l. v. Spain*, [2023] EWHC 1226 (Comm), paras. 4, 40, 53.

[63]) Under this exception, a state's adjudicative immunity is removed with respect to proceedings related to an arbitration in which it has agreed to arbitrate, including proceedings for the recognition of any resulting award.

[64]) *Infrastructure Services Luxembourg S.à r.l. v. Spain*, [2023] EWHC 1226 (Comm), paras. 91–92.

[65]) *Infrastructure Services Luxembourg S.à r.l. v. Spain*, [2023] EWHC 1226 (Comm), paras. 44–45, 101, 104; *Infrastructure Services Luxembourg S.à r.l. v. Spain*, [2024] EWCA Civ 1257, para. 8(i).

[66]) *Infrastructure Services Luxembourg S.à r.l. v. Spain*, [2023] EWHC 1226 (Comm), paras. 87–88, 101.

[67]) *Ibid.*, paras. 95, 114.

[68]) *Ibid.*, para. 125.

award in *EDF Energies Nouvelles v. Spain*, an UNCITRAL Arbitration initiated under the ECT and seated in Geneva.[69]) Spain had argued, relying on the reasoning of the *Komstroy* decision, that its consent to arbitrate in Article 26 of the ECT did not extend to intra-EU disputes.[70])

Interpreting Article 26 of the ECT pursuant to the principles in Article 31 of the VCLT, the Supreme Court found no indication that Article 26 of the ECT excluded disputes with investors from EU Member States.[71]) The court further rejected Spain's reliance on the 2019 Declaration, finding that it did not constitute a subsequent agreement on interpretation of the ECT or a subsequent practice within the meaning of Articles 31(3)(a) and (b) of the VCLT. The court reasoned that the 2019 Declaration had not been signed by all Member States, referred only to the *Achmea* judgment – which it considered irrelevant for ECT arbitrations – and could not have retroactive effect on arbitral proceedings that had already been initiated against Spain.[72]) As for the *Komstroy* judgment, the Supreme Court found that it was not binding on it, as Switzerland is not an EU Member State.[73])

In a disagreement with the CJEU, the Swiss Supreme Court held that no conflict existed between Article 26 of the ECT on the one hand and Articles 267 and 344 of the TFEU on other hand.[74]) It also ruled out the application of Article 30(3) of the VCLT, which governs the relationship between successive treaties relating to the same subject matter, finding that the ECT and the TFEU concern different subject matters.[75])

Finally, the Supreme Court held that Article 16 of the ECT confirms that Article 26 of the ECT should take precedence over any less favorable dispute resolution method in the TFEU. This provisions states that "[w]*here two or more Contracting Parties [...] enter into a subsequent international agreement, whose terms in either case concern the subject matter of Part III or V of this Treaty [...] nothing in such terms of the other agreement shall be construed to derogate from any provision of Part III or V of this Treaty or from any right to dispute resolution with respect thereto under this Treaty, where any such provision is more favourable to the Investor or Investment*".[76]) The court found this to be a specific conflict rule adopted by the parties to the ECT, confirming

[69]) *EDF Energies Nouvelles S.A. v. Kingdom of Spain*, PCA Case No. AA613, Final Award, 11 April 2023.

[70]) *EDF Energies Nouvelles S.A. v. Kingdom of Spain*, Case No. 4A_244/2023 (Swiss Fed. Trib. 3 April 2024), para. 7.2.1.

[71]) *Ibid.*, para. 7.7.6.

[72]) *Ibid.*, para. 7.7.5.

[73]) *Ibid.*, para. 7.8.2.

[74]) *Ibid.*, para. 7.8.2.

[75]) *Ibid.*, para. 7.8.3.2.

[76]) *Energy Charter Treaty*, Dec. 17 1994, 2080 U.N.T.S. 95, art. 16.

that the investor's right to submit a dispute to arbitration in accordance with Article 26 of the ECT must be guaranteed.[77])

Swiss courts have also dismissed challenges to other intra-EU awards such as the ECT awards in *AES and others v. Spain* discussed above[78]) and in *Natland Investment Group et al. v. Czech Republic.*[79])

#### c) United States

The United States ("**U.S.**") have become a significant forum for the recognition and enforcement of intra-EU investment awards. A large bulk of the available case law concerns intra-EU investment awards issued against Spain. Early case law on such awards produced divergent outcomes, leading Spain to file a petition for certiorari to the U.S. Supreme Court,[80]) which remains pending.

The initial cases concerned the recognition petitions relating to three intra-EU renewable energy awards rendered under the ECT against Spain, all brought before the U.S. District Court for the District of Columbia ("**D.C. District Court**"). Similarly to the *Infrastructure Services (Antin)* case before UK courts, in reliance on the *Komstroy* decision, Spain argued that it was immune from enforcement under the U.S. Foreign Sovereign Immunities Act ("**FSIA**") because there was no valid arbitration agreement.

The judges within the D.C. District Court reached differing results. With respect to the ICSID awards in the ECT arbitrations *NextEra*[81]) and *9Ren*,[82]) on 15 February 2023, one judge held that the FSIA arbitration exception applied because the relevant consideration under that exception is whether there exists an arbitration agreement or not. That judge found that Spain's challenge based on the CJEU's rulings did not affect the agreement's existence but the question of the agreement's arbitrability.[83]) The judge also issued an anti-anti-suit

[77]) *EDF Energies Nouvelles S.A. v. Kingdom of Spain*, Case No. 4A_244/2023 (Swiss Fed. Trib. 3 April 2024), para. 7.8.3.2.

[78]) *AES and others ("The PV Investors") v. Spain*, Case No. 4A_187/2020 (Swiss Fed. Trib. 23 February 2021).

[79]) *Natland Investment Group v. Czech Republic*, Case No. 4A_66/2024 (Swiss Fed. Trib. 13 June 2024).

[80]) *Kingdom of Spain v. Blasket Renewable Investments, LLC, et al.*, Petition for Writ of Certiorari to the U.S. Court of Appeals for the D.C. Circuit, No. 23-7031 (U.S. filed 1 May 2025).

[81]) *NextEra Energy Global Holdings B.V. and NextEra Energy Spain Holdings B.V. v. Kingdom of Spain*, ICSID Case No. ARB/14/11, Award, 31 May 2019.

[82]) *9REN Holding S.a.r.l v. Kingdom of Spain, ICSID Case No. ARB/15/15*, Award, 31 May 2019.

[83]) *NextEra Energy Global Holdings B.V., et al. v. Kingdom of Spain*, No. 1:2019 cv 01618 (D.D.C. 15 February 2023), Memorandum Opinion, p. 14; *NextEra Energy Global Holdings B.V., et al. v. Kingdom of Spain*, No. 1:2019-cv-01618 (D.D.C. 15 February 2023), Order; *9Ren Holding S.a.r.l. v. Kingdom of Spain*, No. 1:19-cv-01871 (D.D.C.

injunction against Spain who had sought injunctions before EU domestic courts to restrain the US enforcement.[84])

In contrast, concerning an UNCITRAL award in *AES and Others v. Spain*, on 29 March 2023, a different judge of the D.C. District Court dismissed the enforcement petition. The judge disagreed with *NextEra* and *9Ren*, holding that the intra-EU objection concerned the validity of the arbitration agreement itself. On that basis, the court found no valid agreement to arbitrate and dismissed the case for lack of jurisdiction under the FSIA.[85])

The issue then proceeded to the Circuit Court of Appeals for the District of Columbia, which held on 16 August 2024 that U.S. courts could accept jurisdiction under the FSIA arbitration exception, but that they lack authority to issue anti-anti-suit injunctions.[86]) It also found that the doctrine of *forum non conveniens*, which allows courts to decline jurisdiction in favor of a more appropriate forum, does not apply to international arbitral awards sought to be enforced under the ICSID or the NYC.[87]) The court added, however, that it does not *"address the merits question whether [ECT's] arbitration provision extends to EU nationals and thus whether Spain ultimately entered into legally valid agreements with the companies"*,[88]) leaving that issue open.

In May 2025, Spain filed a petition for a writ of certiorari with the U.S. Supreme Court, challenging the appellate court's conclusions.[89]) In October 2025, the Supreme Court invited the U.S. Solicitor General to submit briefs presenting the views of the United States.[90])

While the Supreme Court proceedings are pending, the D.C. District Court has, in 2025 alone, issued several decisions against Spain concerning other intra-EU investment awards in support of their recognition, including in

---

15 February 2023), Memorandum Opinion, p. 13; *9Ren Holding S.a.r.l. v. Kingdom of Spain*, No. 1:19-cv-01871 (D.D.C. 15 February 2023), Order.

[84]) *NextEra Energy Global Holdings B.V., et al. v. Kingdom of Spain*, No. 1:2019-cv-01618 (D.D.C. 15 February 2023), Order; *9Ren Holding S.a.r.l. v. Kingdom of Spain*, No. 1:19-cv-01871 (D.D.C. 15 February 2023), Order.

[85]) *Blasket Renewable Investments LLC v. Kingdom of Spain*, No. 21-3249 (D.D.C. 29 March 2023), Memorandum Opinion, pp. 17–20; *Blasket Renewable Investments LLC v. Kingdom of Spain*, No. 21-3249 (D.D.C. 29 March 2023), Order.

[86]) *NextEra Energy Global Holdings B.V., et al. v. Kingdom of Spain*, No. 23-7031, (D.C. Cir. 16 August 2024), Opinion of the D.C. Cir., p. 41.

[87]) *Ibid.*, at 29.

[88]) *Ibid.*, at 28.

[89]) *Kingdom of Spain v. Blasket Renewable Investments, LLC, et al.*, Petition for Writ of Certiorari to the U.S. Court of Appeals for the D.C. Circuit, No. 23-7031 (U.S. filed 1 May 2025).

[90]) The Supreme Court of the United States, *Orders in Pending Cases*, Order List: 607 U.S., 6 October 2025, p. 3, ref. 24-1130.

*RREEF v. Spain*,[91]) *InfraRed v. Spain* on the next day,[92]) *Watkins v. Spain*,[93]) *Antin v. Spain*,[94]) and *Cube v. Spain*[95]). All of these cases involved ICSID awards. In addition to the arguments considered in *NextEra*, *9Ren*, and *AES*, the court has also rejected Spain's reliance on the foreign sovereign compulsion doctrine, with Spain arguing that it should allow the court to defer to foreign laws or courts to avoid Spain paying unlawful state aid if the awards were enforced. The court held that this does not override the concrete comity obligations imposed on the U.S. by international treaties, including the ICSID Convention, which requires U.S. courts to enforce ICSID awards.[96])

A different approach has been recently taken in cases involving investment awards that have been set aside in the EU. On 8 September 2025, the D.C. District Court rejected the enforcement of an SCC award in an ECT arbitration in *Mercuria Energy Group v. Poland (2)* on the grounds that it had been set aside in Sweden based on the CJEU's jurisprudence on the incompatibility of the underlying arbitration clause with EU law. While the court stated that foreign judgments annulling arbitral awards may be disregarded if they were

[91]) *Blasket Renewable Investments LLC v. Kingdom of Spain*, No. 1:19-cv-3783 (D.D.C. 12 August 2025), Memorandum Opinion; *Blasket Renewable Investments LLC v. Kingdom of Spain*, No. 1:2019-cv-01618 (D.D.C. 12 August 2025), Order.

[92]) *Blasket Renewable Investments LLC v. Kingdom of Spain*, Civil Action No. 20-817 (JDB) (D.D.C. 13 August 2025), Memorandum Opinion; *Blasket Renewable Investments LLC v. Kingdom of Spain*, Civil Action No. 20-817 (JDB) (D.D.C. 13 August 2025), Order.

[93]) *Blasket Renewable Investments LLC v. Kingdom of Spain*, Civil Action No. 20-1081 (BAH) (D.D.C. 11 September 2025), Memorandum Opinion; *Blasket Renewable Investments LLC v. Kingdom of Spain*, Civil Action No. 20-1081 (BAH) (D.D.C. 11 September 2025), Order.

[94]) *Infrastructure Services Luxembourg s.a.r.l., et al. v. Kingdom of Spain*, Civil Action No. 18-1753 (LLA) (D.D.C. 12 August 2025), Memorandum Opinion & Order.

[95]) *Cube Infrastructure Fund SICAV v. Kingdom of Spain*, Civil Action No. 20-1708 (LLA) (D.D.C. 14 August 2025), Memorandum Opinion; *Cube Infrastructure Fund SICAV v. Kingdom of Spain*, Civil Action No. 20-1708 (LLA) (D.D.C. 14 August 2025), Order.

[96]) *Blasket Renewable Investments LLC v. Kingdom of Spain*, No. 1:19-cv-3783 (D.D.C. 12 August 2025), Memorandum Opinion, pp. 10–12; *Blasket Renewable Investments LLC v. Kingdom of Spain*, Civil Action No. 20-817 (JDB) (D.D.C. 13 August 2025), Memorandum Opinion, pp. 15–20; *Blasket Renewable Investments LLC v. Kingdom of Spain*, Civil Action No. 20-1081 (BAH) (D.D.C. 11 September 2025), Memorandum Opinion, pp. 17–18; *Infrastructure Services Luxembourg s.a.r.l., et al. v. Kingdom of Spain*, Civil Action No. 18 1753 (LLA) (D.D.C. 12 August 2025), Memorandum Opinion, pp. 11–14; *Cube Infrastructure Fund SICAV v. Kingdom of Spain*, Civil Action No. 20-1708 (LLA) (D.D.C. 14 August 2025), Memorandum Opinion, pp. 7–8.

*"'repugnant to fundamental notions of what is decent and just in the' United States,"* the court found this standard not to be met in the *Mercuria*'s case.[97])

Finally, the interaction between enforcement of intra-EU investment awards and EU state aid rules was addressed in the enforcement proceedings of the ICSID award in *Ioan Micula, Viorel Micula and others v. Romania (1)*, initiated in 2014. After the EU Commission found that payment of the award would constitute unlawful state aid, the D.C. District Court stayed enforcement proceedings. In 2019, it lifted the stay and confirmed the *Micula* award, holding that EU state aid rules could not serve as a defense against the award's enforcement and that the U.S. was obliged to enforce the award under the ICSID Convention.[98]) The D.C. Circuit Court of Appeals upheld this ruling in 2022, reaffirming that in U.S. courts, the enforcement obligations of the U.S. under the ICSID Convention prevail over EU law considerations.[99])

#### d) Australia

Like U.S. courts, the Federal Court of Australia addressed enforcement of intra-EU ICSID awards in the cases *RREEF*, *Watkins*, *NextEra*, and *9REN* against Spain.[100]) Spain opposed the enforcement of these awards by arguing that they were not binding under Article 53 of the ICSID Convention due to the conflict of the dispute resolution systems under the ECT and the ICSID Convention with *"the principle of autonomy"* of the EU judicial system. Spain argued that such conflict had to be resolved in favor of EU law.[101])

The Australian court rejected this argument, finding that it *"made good only within the EU system"* and that such conflict can be *"resolved in favour of the EU foundational treaties, but only within the EU system"*.[102]) The court thus rejected the notion that such conflict would relieve Spain from obligations under the ICSID Convention.[103])

The Federal Court found that the *Achmea* and *Komstroy* rulings addressed only EU law and did not assert that it had primacy over international law outside the EU legal system.[104]) The court also rejected the relevance of the

---

[97]) *Mercuria Energy Group Limited v. Republic of Poland*, Case No. 1:23-cv-03572 (D.D.C. 8 September 2025), Memorandum Opinion, p. 9.

[98]) *Ioan Micula, et al. v. Government of Romania,* Case No. 17-cv-02332 (APM) (D.D.C. 11 September 2019), Memorandum Opinion; *Ioan Micula, et al. v. Government of Romania,* Case No. 17-cv-02332-APM (D.D.C. 20 September 2019), Order and Final Judgment.

[99]) *Ioan Micula, et al. v. Government of Romania,* No. 20-7116 (D.C. Cir. 24 June 2022), Judgment.

[100]) *Blasket Renewable Investments LLC v Kingdom of Spain* [2025] FCA 1028, 29 August 2025, paras. 1, 7.

[101]) *Ibid.*, para. 78.

[102]) *Ibid.*, para. 205.

[103]) *Ibid.*, para. 205.

[104]) *Ibid.*, para. 206.

26 June 2024 declaration on the basis that it was issued long after the awards had been rendered, not all Member States had signed the declaration, and that it did not purport to modify the ICSID Convention.[105]) It concluded that *"as a matter of public international law, Spain is obliged to the other Contracting States to the ICSID Convention to comply with the ICSID awards against it; it is no answer, on the international plane, for Spain to say that to do so would be in conflict with its EU obligations (including as to State aid)"*.[106])

## IV. Conclusion

Since the CJEU's *Achmea*, *Komstroy*, and *PL Holdings* decisions, a growing body of case law from national courts both within and outside the EU has emerged concerning intra-EU investment awards. This case law provides valuable insight into how courts interpret the CJEU's reasoning and how they may approach enforcement of such awards.

Within the EU, national courts have thus far aligned with the CJEU's position, finding intra-EU investment arbitration clauses incompatible with EU law. While much of the case law concerns set-aside proceedings, it strongly indicates that enforcement would be likewise denied. Notably, in the rulings of the BGH in *Antaris and Michael Gode v. Czech Republic* and of the Swedish Supreme Court in *Festorino Invest Limited and others v. Poland*, this approach was extended to cost awards in favor of respondent States, with courts drawing no distinction between investor- and State-favorable awards where the underlying arbitration clause is incompatible with EU law. Although relatively few ICSID intra-EU awards have been tested in EU courts, the decisions of the BGH and the Lithuanian Supreme Court suggest that such awards would face similarly significant obstacles.

Outside the EU, on the other hand, most reported enforcement actions have involved ICSID awards, which have proven more resilient to EU law objections. Courts in jurisdictions such as the United Kingdom, Switzerland, the United States, and Australia have largely rejected defenses based on the intra-EU objection or EU state aid rules, relying instead on their international obligations under the ICSID Convention. These courts have upheld the validity of intra-EU arbitration agreements and permitted enforcement. However, a recent decision of the D.C. District Court in *Mercuria Energy Group v. Poland (2)* indicates that enforcement of non-ICSID awards annulled in the EU on *Achmea*-related grounds may still be refused.

Enforcement within the EU presents further challenges due to the potential application of EU state aid rules. The EU Commission, the CJEU, and certain courts of the Member States have held that intra-EU investment awards qualify

---

[105]) *Ibid.*, paras. 217 *et seq.*

[106]) *Ibid.*, para. 212.

as unlawful stated aid under EU law, thereby precluding the payment of the awarded sums by the respondent State – either voluntarily or involuntarily through enforcement proceedings. From the perspective of the Member States, this position appears to apply irrespective of the jurisdiction in which enforcement is sought. According to the EU Commission and the CJEU, Member States are also under obligation to recover any awarded amounts already paid – either voluntarily or involuntarily through enforcement proceedings – to investors under such awards. Relying on this reasoning, such a recovery was ordered by the Amsterdam District Court *AES and others v. Spain* where investors currently seek enforcement before U.S. courts.

Taken together, these developments reveal a fragmented enforcement landscape. Within the EU, enforcement of intra-EU awards – including ICSID and non-ICSID awards – is effectively precluded, whereas outside the EU, enforcement continues, albeit with varying degrees of scrutiny depending on the award's status and the jurisdiction in question.

# Enforcing Foreign Arbitral Awards Through the AIFC Court: Constitutionally Reconciled, Yet Untested

*Dina Berkaliyeva/Arman Shaikenov/Valikhan Shaikenov**)

## I. As Kazakhstan's National Gateway: Open the Door or Call It Unconstitutional[1])

Here is a blunt thesis: the Court of the Astana International Financial Centre (AIFC Court) can and – on first principles – should be used as a national gateway to recognize foreign arbitral awards for enforcement across Kazakhstan, even where the award debtor has no assets and no presence in the AIFC. That follows from the Constitution of the Republic of Kazakhstan (the Constitution)'s supreme force, the AIFC Court's general (not "special") civil jurisdiction properly understood, and the Convention on the Recognition and Enforcement of Foreign Arbitral Awards (New York Convention)'s twin duties of recognition and enforcement.

But here is the paradox that makes this controversial: the very constitutional logic that unlocks this gateway also threatens the Court's own existential footing. Read strictly, Kazakhstan's Constitution forbids special courts – and the AIFC Court has sometimes been treated as exactly that. Press the

*) Acknowledgment: The authors gratefully acknowledge the assistance provided by Madiyar Akhmetov and Damira Zhumanova in the preparation of this article.

[1]) While this Article's manuscript was still with the publishing house and had not yet been published, the AIFC Court, on October 30, 2025, issued two judgments addressing the questions raised in the Article. The two judgments are:

*Road Department of the Ministry of Infrastructure of Georgia v Todini Costruzioni Generali S.p.A.* [AIFC-C/CFI/2025/0025]; and

*Pacific Trade House Limited v (1) Altay Polymetals LLP (2) Terekty Ken Bayytu LLP* [AIFC-C/CFI/2025/0034].

The first judgment recognized and enforced an arbitral award rendered in an ICC arbitration seated in France. The second judgment recognized and enforced an arbitral award rendered in a SIAC arbitration seated in Singapore. In both cases, the Court based its reasoning on the Russian (original) version of the Constitutional Statute, finding that Article 14(1) established the grounds for its jurisdiction. However, both judgments were made without notice and remain subject to appeal. Moreover, the Court did not, on its own initiative, consider whether the award debtor possessed any assets or other connections to the AIFC, leaving room for further argument on that point.

Constitution too hard and the Court risks declaring itself unconstitutional; avoid the Constitution and it risks shrinking into a walled garden with little utility beyond the AIFC's borders.

This article cuts through the polite ambiguity. We show why the AIFC Court, acting "after the Constitution of the Republic of Kazakhstan", can issue stand-alone recognition orders for foreign awards and why those orders should carry nationwide effect on a parity footing with judgments of the ordinary courts. And we explain, candidly, why the Court has so far dodged constitutional engagement, why politics – not doctrine – may keep the gate half-closed, and what that means for award creditors deciding whether to try this "AIFC route".

In short: the law points to a door that is constitutionally reconciled yet untested. This piece maps the hinges, the locks, and the likely hands that will try to keep it shut.

## II. AIFC As a Parallel Jurisdiction: Constitutional Dilemma

The AIFC constitutes a separate onshore common law jurisdiction within the territory of the Republic of Kazakhstan:

1. The AIFC has its own judiciary composed entirely of foreign judges – primarily retired English judges. For example, Lord Burnett of Maldon, the former Lord Chief Justice of England and Wales, currently serves as the Chief Justice of the AIFC Court.
2. The AIFC Courts are not subject to supervision by the Supreme Court of Kazakhstan.
3. The AIFC operates under its own regulatory framework, distinct from that of the rest of Kazakhstan: acts of the AIFC are not subordinate to the laws of Parliament, nor are they adopted by Parliament.

Nevertheless, the AIFC and the AIFC Court were established as a political decision of the former President of Kazakhstan Nursultan Nazarbayev, despite strong objections from the legal community.[2]

---

[2]) *See* Farkhad Karagusov (Фархад Карагусов), O popytke sozdat' pravovuyu osnovu dlya funktsionirovaniya dvukh yurisdiktsiy na territorii Respubliki Kazakhstan [On the Attempt to Create a Legal Basis for the Functioning of Two Jurisdictions on the Territory of the Republic of Kazakhstan], Online Zakon (February 15, 2016), https://online.zakon.kz/Document/?doc_id=39979088; *see also* Arman Shaikenov (Арман Шайкенов) & Valikhan Shaikenov (Валихан Шайкенов), Konstitutsionen li MFTSA i pomogut li popravki v Konstitutsiyu? [Is the AIFC Constitutional and Will Constitutional Amendments Help?], Forbes Kazakhstan (March 7, 2017), https://forbes.kz/process/expertise/konstitutsionen_li_mftsa_i_pomogut_li_popravki_v_konstitutsiyu/; *see also* Maidan Suleimenov (Майдан Сулейменов), Sistema prava i sistema zakonodatel'stva Kazakhstana: vybor puti [Kazakhstan's Legal and Legislative System:

This point is important to bear in mind, as it directly informs the subsequent analysis. A number of propositions on which our analysis rests are grounded in the Constitution, require its *direct* application, and presuppose recognition that the AIFC Courts should be understood as part of the judicial system of the Republic of Kazakhstan and therefore possessing general jurisdiction (rather than *special jurisdiction*, as may be suggested by certain acts regulating the status of the AIFC).

The general nature of the AIFC Courts' jurisdiction, coupled with their fundamental authority to recognize foreign arbitral awards, could *theoretically* support the conclusion that the AIFC Court is empowered to recognize a foreign arbitral award even in circumstances where the debtor has no assets or organizational presence within the AIFC, with the possibility of subsequent enforcement elsewhere in Kazakhstan, outside the AIFC.

At the same time, however, direct application of the Constitution creates an existential risk for the AIFC. The Constitution expressly prohibits the creation of special courts, which the AIFC Court essentially represents. Accordingly, if the Constitution were to be applied strictly and directly, the AIFC Court would be compelled to conclude that it is itself unconstitutional. For existential reasons, therefore, we consider it likely that the AIFC Court may deliberately avoid *a strict application of the Constitution.*

## III. Summary

In theory, the AIFC Court could, and arguably should, recognize a foreign arbitral award even absent any territorial connection to the AIFC, with such recognition being enforceable throughout Kazakhstan. This view is grounded in the Court's *general jurisdiction* (which, we submit, it does possess), the supremacy of the Constitution, and the Court's statutory parity with the national courts (which the AIFC Court itself frequently refers to as the "ordinary courts"). Moreover, there are no formal indications that the AIFC was intended as a parallel jurisdiction.

In practice, however, Kazakhstan's judiciary (outside the AIFC) remains subject to political influence, and the AIFC Court has so far interpreted its jurisdiction restrictively without addressing constitutional arguments. Recognition of awards unconnected to the AIFC would risk shifting control away from the Kazakh executive, making it politically sensitive.

Accordingly, while the legal grounds are persuasive, the practical prospects of success cannot be regarded as high.

---

Choosing a Path], Online Zakon (April 15, 2011), https://online.zakon.kz/Document/?doc_id=31102841; *see also* Farkhad Karagusov (Фархад Карагусов), Snova o Mezhdunarodnom finansovom tsentre "Astana" [Once Again on the Astana International Financial Centre], Online Zakon (March 9, 2022), https://online.zakon.kz/Document/?doc_id=39068058.

# IV. Legal Analysis

## A. Does the AIFC Court Have General or Special Jurisdiction?

### 1. Mislabelled and Unfounded: The "Special Jurisdiction" Myth about the AIFC Court

There are no formal indications in Kazakh legislation or in any official statements that the AIFC was designed as either an off- or onshore parallel jurisdiction. On the contrary, public officials, including the President of Kazakhstan, have consistently emphasized that the AIFC does not infringe the constitutional principle of the unitary character of the Republic of Kazakhstan.

Nevertheless, there persists a perception that the AIFC and its Courts exercise a special jurisdiction limited to matters connected with the AIFC itself. This perception has even been reflected in AIFC Court practice. In *Michael Wilson & Partners, Limited v. CJSC Kazsubton and others* (AIFC-C/CFI/2023/0002, judgment dated September 26, 2023), Lord Mance observed:

> *"The drafters were therefore careful in these provisions to distinguish between judgments and awards emanating within and outside Kazakhstan. AIFC Court judgments are enforceable without more in both the AIFC and the Republic, just as judgments of the ordinary Kazakh court are enforceable in Kazakhstan and the AIFC. Arbitration awards are enforceable in the AIFC and the Republic if the arbitration was seated in the AIFC and the award has been ratified by the AIFC Court. But in other cases arbitration awards are only enforceable 'within the AIFC'. It is also very noticeable here that there are no provisions relating to the enforcement, either in the AIFC Court and still less in the Republic, of judgments from outside Kazakhstan."* (para 39)

This conclusion was premised on the presupposition that *"the jurisdiction of the AIFC Court is a special, and carefully delimited jurisdiction. The AIFC Court is not a court of general, let alone inherent, jurisdiction" (para 47).*

Yet such a position directly contradicts Article 75(4) of the Constitution, which prohibits the creation of "special" and "extraordinary" courts. Importantly, Lord Mance did not address this constitutional prohibition in reaching his conclusion, nor any party invoked this argument; had he done so, his reasoning might have been different.

One of the objectives in any possible enforcement attempt will therefore be to overcome Lord Mance's conclusion. At the same time, it must be acknowledged that the perception of the AIFC Court as a body of *special jurisdiction* exists and has already found expression in its case law.

## 2. Possible Consequences of the Perception of the AIFC Court's Special Jurisdiction

The perception of the AIFC Court as a body of special and *limited jurisdiction* may lead to the conclusion that its authority to recognize and enforce foreign arbitral awards is confined to situations where there is a demonstrable connection to the AIFC territory. Such a connection could be established, for example, through the debtor's presence within the AIFC or the location of the debtor's assets there.

If this view were to prevail, it would substantially narrow the role of the AIFC Court in recognition and enforcement matters, effectively excluding cases in which the debtor has no territorial nexus to the AIFC. In turn, this would undermine the potential of the AIFC Court to act as a broader forum for recognition of foreign arbitral awards in Kazakhstan, reducing it instead to a jurisdiction of limited reach.

This restrictive interpretation, in our view, conflicts with the Constitution's prohibition on *special courts*. Nevertheless, while we do not agree with such an interpretation and would regard it as unconstitutional, we must recognize that it may well, and, in our view, is likely to be adopted by the AIFC Court in practice.

## 3. Distinction Between "Special" and "Specialized" Courts from the Constitutional Perspective

The Constitutional Council of Kazakhstan, in its Normative Resolution No. 1 of April 14, 2006 (Normative Resolution No. 1), provided an authoritative interpretation of Article 75(4) of the Constitution, which prohibits the establishment of *special and extraordinary courts*. The Council clarified that the purpose of this prohibition is to safeguard the unity of the judicial system and to prevent the creation of parallel or exceptional tribunals that might infringe fundamental rights.

The Council defined *special courts* as judicial bodies that possess at least one of the following *unconstitutional* features:

1. Their organization, competence and creation are regulated by special normative acts outside the Constitution and the Constitutional Law *"On the Judicial System and Status of Judges"*.
2. They administer justice with derogations from the procedural rules binding on other courts.
3. Their formation and functioning are subject to organizational dependence on the executive, contrary to the principle of separation of powers.
4. In contrast, the Council drew a sharp line between "special courts" (*spetsialnye sudy*), which are constitutionally prohibited, and "specialized courts" (*spetsializirovannye sudy*), which are constitutionally permissible.

Specialized courts – such as economic, administrative, military, or juvenile courts – are allowed provided that they:

- form an integral part of the *unified judicial system of Kazakhstan* as local courts;
- are established by a constitutional law, not by special *ad hoc* normative acts;
- conduct proceedings exclusively in the general forms of civil, criminal, or other procedural law applicable to all courts;
- are subject to full appellate and supervisory review, including by the Supreme Court; and
- respect equality before the law and ensure full protection of constitutional rights.
- Thus, the Constitution does not prohibit functional specialization of courts. What it forbids is the establishment of judicial bodies with parallel or exceptional jurisdiction outside the unified judicial system.

## 4. Implications of Article 75(4) of the Constitution for the AIFC Court

This distinction is of decisive importance for assessing the status of the AIFC Court. By describing the AIFC Court as a *"special, carefully delimited jurisdiction"* and *"not a court of general, let alone inherent jurisdiction"*, Lord Mance effectively positioned the AIFC Court outside the unified judicial system of Kazakhstan. Such a reading is difficult to reconcile with the Constitutional Council's binding interpretation: if the AIFC Court is indeed separate from the ordinary and specialized courts, then it risks falling within the definition of a "special court" prohibited by Article 75(4).

In other words, Lord Mance's conclusion rests on a presupposition that the Constitutional Council has expressly rejected. The Council's jurisprudence shows that the AIFC Court must either be understood as part of Kazakhstan's unified judicial system (as a form of specialized court, albeit with focus on certain types of mattes) or else it cannot be reconciled with the Constitution. By failing to address this constitutional prohibition and its authoritative interpretation, Lord Mance overlooked a decisive issue – one that might have led him to a different conclusion.

## 5. Does the AIFC Constitutional Statute Establish the AIFC Court's Special Jurisdiction?

If read through the lens of Article 75(4) of the Constitution and in the context of the AIFC Court Regulations dated December 5, 2017 (AIFC Court Regulations), Article 13 of the Constitutional Law of the Republic of Kazakhstan on the Astana International Financial Centre dated December 7, 2015 (AIFC

Constitutional Statute) should be understood as granting the AIFC Court "exclusive jurisdiction" over certain categories of commercial disputes specifically connected to the AIFC, while at the same time preserving its *general jurisdiction over all other civil and commercial disputes* within the scope of AIFC law. This means that the Court's jurisdiction is exclusive only *vis-à-vis* other courts of Kazakhstan, not "special" in the constitutionally prohibited sense.

#### a) Text of the AIFC Constitutional Statute

Article 13 of the AIFC Constitutional Statute defines the AIFC Court. It provides, *inter alia*, that:

- disputes listed in paragraph 4 of Article 13 are to be heard only by the AIFC Court (Article 13(1));
- the Court has "exclusive jurisdiction" in relation to three categories of disputes:
  - disputes between AIFC participants, bodies of the AIFC and/or their foreign employees;
  - disputes concerning operations conducted in the AIFC and subject to AIFC law;
  - disputes referred to the Court by agreement of the parties (Article 13(4)).

The AIFC Constitutional Statute also makes clear that the AIFC Court does not exercise criminal or administrative jurisdiction.

#### b) AIFC Court Regulations

The AIFC Court Regulations reinforce these provisions. Article 26.1 repeats the categories of disputes listed in Article 13 of the Constitutional Statute. Article 26.4 expressly excludes criminal and administrative matters, and Article 26.8 confirms that the Court has jurisdiction in respect of any matters conferred on it by the AIFC Constitutional Statute or the AIFC Court Regulations, including authority to support arbitration.

The AIFC Court Regulations thus, in our view, confirm that the AIFC Court's civil and commercial jurisdiction is exclusive within the AIFC framework, but also general in scope as regards civil and commercial disputes unless expressly carved out.

#### c) Analysis: Exclusive but Not "Special"

The critical interpretive issue is whether the AIFC Court's "exclusive jurisdiction" under Article 13 amounts to the kind of *special jurisdiction* that is constitutionally prohibited under Article 75(4) of the Constitution.

- A *special jurisdiction* in the constitutional sense functions on an *enumerated powers model:* it may adjudicate only the specific categories of disputes exhaustively listed in its constitutive act. Under this model, it would be unnecessary to expressly exclude criminal or administrative matters, as they would already fall outside the Court's competence by default.

- By contrast, a *general jurisdiction* court operates under a *residual powers model*: it may hear all disputes within a certain legal sphere (here, civil and commercial matters under AIFC law), except for those expressly excluded. In this context, the carve-out of criminal and administrative cases in Article 26.4 serves a meaningful purpose – it removes these matters from what would otherwise be a comprehensive civil and commercial jurisdiction.

The presence of such a carve-out strongly suggests that the AIFC Court's jurisdiction is not narrowly "special" in the constitutional sense. Instead, it is an *exclusive civil and commercial jurisdiction vis-à-vis other courts.* It displaces the jurisdiction of national courts over disputes within the AIFC's sphere but does so on a general model applicable to all civil and commercial matters falling under AIFC law, rather than on an enumerated special-purpose basis.

#### d) Implications

This interpretation is consistent with the Normative Resolution No. 1, which prohibited the creation of *special courts* outside the unified judicial system but permitted *specialised courts* as long as they did not derogate from general forms of justice or operate under exceptional procedures. The AIFC Court's jurisdictional design – exclusive yet general within its sphere, with criminal and administrative matters expressly excluded – aligns it more closely with the model of a specialized court than with a prohibited special court.

Thus, while Article 13 of the Constitutional Statute describes the AIFC Court as having "exclusive jurisdiction", this exclusivity should be understood as exclusivity *vis-à-vis other courts* in Kazakhstan, not as a constitutionally impermissible *special jurisdiction*.

## B. On the AIFC Court's Independence from the National Judiciary

The AIFC Constitutional Statute establishes the AIFC Court as an independent judicial body and expressly defines its relationship with the national judiciary. Article 13.2 of the AIFC Constitutional Statute provides:

*"The [AIFC Court] is independent in its activities and is not part of the judicial system of the Republic of Kazakhstan."*

At first sight, this provision appears to distance the AIFC Court from the broader judicial system of Kazakhstan. One might argue – correctly – that such language weakens the prospects for enforcement of foreign arbitral awards outside the AIFC through the AIFC Court. Specifically, the AIFC Court itself could (and likely would) invoke Article 13.2 to assert that it is not a court of general jurisdiction, but rather a special court whose authority is confined to the AIFC, and which therefore does not form part of the unified judicial system of Kazakhstan.

In theory, however, Article 13.2 of the AIFC Constitutional Statute should not be read in isolation. In our view, the provision declaring that the AIFC Court *"is not part of the judicial system of the Republic of Kazakhstan"* directly contradicts Article 75(4) of the Constitution, which prohibits the creation of special and extraordinary courts. To the extent of such conflict, the Constitution must prevail, given its supreme legal force and direct effect throughout Kazakhstan.

Accordingly, we take the position that the relevant wording of Article 13.2 of the AIFC Constitutional Statute should (again, in theory) be treated as inoperative. On this basis, the AIFC Court should be regarded as forming an integral part of the unified judicial system of Kazakhstan, notwithstanding its functional and institutional independence. This understanding is consistent with the constitutional principle of the unitary character of the Republic and avoids treating the AIFC Court as a special jurisdiction in violation of the Constitution.

## C. Engagement of the AIFC Court with Constitutional Law

Further below we conclude that the Constitution of Kazakhstan, by virtue of its supreme legal force and direct effect under Article 4.2, forms part of the applicable law of the AIFC alongside the AIFC Constitutional Statute, regulations, and international treaties. This conclusion is reinforced by the Message of the Constitutional Council of the Republic of Kazakhstan dated June 16, 2016, No. 09-2/1, *"On the State of Constitutional Legality in the Republic of Kazakhstan" (Constitutional Council's Message)* and the AIFC's Practice Direction No. 2: AIFC Court Guide to Judicial Conduct dated October 18, 2023 (Practice Direction), which requires judges to act "after the Constitution of the Republic of Kazakhstan".

In practice, however, the AIFC Court has so far avoided engaging with constitutional arguments, confining its reasoning to the Constitutional Statute and relying on expert opinions. While the framework supports reliance on the Constitution – an important element of our further analysis – there has not yet been any AIFC Court practice addressing the issue from this perspective.

## 1. Constitution's Supreme Legal Force and Direct Effect

Our legal analysis is based on the following legal sources:

1. the Constitution;
2. the AIFC Constitutional Statute;
3. the Law of the Republic of Kazakhstan on Enforcement Procedures and Enforcement Officers dated April 2, 2010, as amended (the Enforcement Law); the AIFC Court Regulations; the AIFC Arbitration Regulations;
4. other rules and regulations of the AIFC;
5. applicable international treaties; and
6. the existing judicial practice of the AIFC Court.

Under Article 4.2 of the Constitution, *"[t]he Constitution has supreme legal force and direct effect throughout the territory of the Republic"*. Although Kazakhstan has a Constitutional Court (formerly the Constitutional Council) vested with authority to declare legislative acts unconstitutional where they infringe upon the constitutional rights and freedoms of individuals and citizens, the rule on the direct effect of the Constitution is not merely declaratory but carries binding legal meaning and effect.

In particular, the Constitutional Council's Message expressly stated that

*"[t]he recommendations of the Constitutional Council to state bodies, including judicial bodies, on their obligation to refer in their decisions to the relevant provisions of the Constitution remain valid, as follows from Article 4(2) of the Constitution on the supreme legal force and direct effect of the norms of the Basic Law. ... Direct effect of the Constitution of the country may thus be exercised."*

## 2. AIFC Constitutional Statute's Hierarchy of Normative Sources

It also follows from the AIFC Constitutional Statute that the Constitution forms part of the applicable law of the AIFC:

*"Article 4. Applicable Law of the Centre*

1. The applicable law of the Centre is based on the Constitution of the Republic of Kazakhstan and consists of:
   *1) this Constitutional Law;*
   *2) acts of the Centre not contradicting this Constitutional Law, which may be based on the principles, rules and precedents of the law of England and Wales and/or standards of the world's leading financial centres, adopted by the Centre's bodies within the powers conferred by this Constitutional Law;*

> *3) the applicable law of the Republic of Kazakhstan, which applies insofar as it is not regulated by this Constitutional Law and acts of the Centre."*

Accordingly, it should be recognized that the AIFC Court is bound not only by the AIFC Constitutional Statute and subordinate acts of the AIFC, but also by the Constitution, and that in the event of any conflict between them, priority must always be given to the Constitution as an instrument of supreme legal force and direct effect throughout the Republic.

## 3. AIFC Court's Practice Direction on the Effect of Constitution

Furthermore, this understanding is expressly reflected in Practice Direction adopted by The Rt. Hon. The Lord Mance, Chief Justice of the AIFC Court, *"for and on behalf of all the Judges of the AIFC Court"*. The Practice Direction provides that:

> *"The Judges of the Astana International Financial Centre Court ('the Court') have decided to adopt this Guide to Judicial Conduct with regard to their individual and collective conduct as Judges of the Court. The Guide relates to principles which are fundamental to the rule of law and to a fair trial, and is observed by all Judges of the Court in their decisions and the processes by which their decisions are reached. The Guide draws significantly on the United Nations-endorsed Bangalore Principles of Judicial Conduct."*
>
> *The Judicial Affirmation required of each Judge expressly states:*
>
> *"I, [name], do solemnly, sincerely, and truly declare and affirm that I will well and truly serve the Republic of Kazakhstan as a Judge of the Astana International Financial Centre Court and I will do right to all manner of people after the Constitution of the Republic of Kazakhstan and acting law of the AIFC, without fear or favour, affection or ill will."*

This underscores that, at least at the level of judicial affirmation and professional guidance, AIFC Court judges expressly acknowledge their duty to act *"after the Constitution of the Republic of Kazakhstan,"* thereby reaffirming the Constitution's role as part of the applicable law governing the Court's work.

The Practice Direction further notes that it *draws significantly on the United Nations-endorsed Bangalore Principles of Judicial Conduct (Bangalore Principles), which state in their preamble:*

> *"WHEREAS a competent, independent and impartial judiciary is likewise essential if the courts are to fulfil their role in upholding constitutionalism and the rule of law ..."*

One may therefore argue that it is the constitutional duty of the AIFC Court judges to uphold the constitutionalism of the Republic of Kazakhstan by giving effect to the Constitution's *"supreme legal force and direct effect throughout the territory of the Republic"*, as explicitly required by Article 4.2 of the Constitution.

The Practice Direction also sets out duties of competence and diligence. Among other things, it requires that:

> *"6.2. To that end, the Judges shall keep themselves informed about the constitution, laws, procedures and jurisprudence of the Court, as these exist and develop from time to time, as well as of any relevant international law."*

This provision may support the view that constitutional norms, at least in the Practice Direction's interpretation, form part of the applicable law of the AIFC and must guide the Court's decision-making.

At the same time, it must be acknowledged that, in practice, the judges of the AIFC Court so far have not engaged with the Constitution in their decisions and, at best, have confined their reasoning to the level of the AIFC Constitutional Statute. Several factors may explain this. Chief among them is that the English judges serving on the Court are not specialists in Kazakh law and, even when resolving issues of Kazakh civil law, tend in most cases to rely on expert opinions. It is also possible that arguments expressly invoking the Constitution have simply not yet been presented to the AIFC Court, and therefore the AIFC Court has not faced the necessity of undertaking such analysis.

There is also a possibility that the judges may take the view that questions of constitutional conflict fall within the exclusive competence of the Constitutional Court. While we do not share this position (and will elaborate on this further below), such a development cannot be ruled out.

In any event, since the argumentation in our case rests to a significant extent on a deep understanding of constitutional law, it will require the AIFC Court to undertake a constitutional law analysis. This is likely to be the first case of its kind in the AIFC Court's practice.

## D. Does the AIFC Law Provide for the Recognition of Foreign Arbitral Awards?

### 1. Distinction Between Recognition and Enforcement under the AIFC Arbitration Regulations

The AIFC Arbitration Regulations expressly distinguish between *recognition* and *enforcement* of arbitral awards, establishing them as related but distinct legal processes.

Article 45(1) sets the overall framework:

*"An arbitral award, irrespective of the State or jurisdiction in which it was made, shall be recognised as binding within the AIFC and, upon application*

*in writing to the AIFC Court, shall be enforced within the AIFC subject to the provisions of this Article and of Articles 46 and 47 ...*"

This provision clearly separates two legal effects.

First, arbitral awards "*shall be recognised as binding within the AIFC*" – an acknowledgment of their validity within the AIFC legal order that does not require further action. Recognition ensures that awards have binding legal status, such as *res judicata* effect, and may be relied upon in subsequent proceedings.

Second, enforcement is conditional: it requires "*application in writing to the AIFC Court*" and compliance with further provisions, enabling the award to be executed against assets.

Article 45(2) addresses the procedural requirements for both recognition and enforcement:

"*The party relying on an award or applying for its enforcement shall supply the original award or duly certified copy and the original arbitration agreement referred to in Article 15 or a duly certified copy. If the award or the agreement is not made in English, the AIFC Court may request the party to supply a duly certified translation.*"

The phrase "*relying on an award*" may reasonably be understood as covering situations where a party seeks the award's recognition, in contrast to "*applying for its enforcement*". In either case, however, the Regulations impose the same documentary requirements: production of the award, the arbitration agreement, and – where necessary – a certified translation. This drafting, in our view, confirms that recognition and enforcement are treated as distinct processes, yet both are subject to parallel procedural safeguards.

Article 46(1) provides expressly for recognition as a self-standing judicial determination:

"*Where, upon the application of a party for recognition of an arbitral award, the AIFC Court decides that the award shall be recognised, it shall issue an order to that effect.*"

Such an order has independent legal effect, irrespective of enforcement, and is itself sufficient proof of recognition. Article 46(2) further requires that the recognition order be issued in English and Russian or Kazakh, highlighting its formal and binding nature.

Finally, Article 47(1) sets out the grounds upon which "*recognition or enforcement*" may be refused, including invalid arbitration agreements, lack of notice, excess of jurisdiction, improper tribunal composition, or conflict with public policy. The fact that these grounds apply equally to both recognition and enforcement confirms that the Regulations treat them as separate, though subject to the same substantive limitations.

Taken together, Articles 45–47 demonstrate that recognition and enforcement under the AIFC Arbitration Regulations are distinct legal mechanisms:

- *Recognition* is the acknowledgment of an arbitral award as binding within the AIFC, with independent legal significance even without enforcement.
- *Enforcement* requires a written application and compliance with documentary requirements, enabling the award to be executed against assets.

As it will be demonstrated below, this dual framework mirrors the structure of the New York Convention, which likewise separates recognition as binding from enforcement through local procedure.

## 2. Do the AIFC Arbitration Regulations Limit the Recognition and Enforcement of Foreign Arbitral Awards to the AIFC Territory?

At first glance, the wording of Article 45(1) of the AIFC Arbitration Regulations might create some confusion. It provides:

> *"An arbitral award, irrespective of the State or jurisdiction in which it was made, shall be recognised as binding within the AIFC and, upon application in writing to the AIFC Court, shall be enforced within the AIFC subject to the provisions of this Article and of Articles 46 and 47 …"*

Read literally, the reference to recognition and enforcement "within the AIFC" may suggest that the legal effect of such acts is territorially confined. This interpretation, however, overlooks the nature of the AIFC legislation. By design, the legal effect of the AIFC Regulations is territorially limited to the AIFC, and it is therefore unsurprising that the Regulations employ such wording. Even where certain AIFC provisions appear to extend beyond the AIFC territory (as has occasionally occurred), their effect cannot in practice exceed the AIFC's territorial boundaries.

The decisive question, then, is not what the AIFC Arbitration Regulations say, but rather which legislative instruments govern the status and external effect of judicial acts rendered by the AIFC Court. That competence lies exclusively with constitutional laws of the Republic of Kazakhstan, which determine both the powers of the "ordinary courts" and those of the AIFC Court.

Accordingly, it is for the AIFC Constitutional Statute to regulate the effect of AIFC Court decisions – including those concerning recognition and enforcement of foreign arbitral awards – beyond the AIFC territory.

## E. Enforcement Parity of AIFC Court and 'Ordinary' Courts' Judicial Acts

One of the key provisions for the present analysis is Article 13.8 of the AIFC Constitutional Statute, which establishes the principle of parity of enforcement between the acts of the AIFC Court and those of the national ('ordinary') courts:

> *"The enforcement of decisions of the Court of the Centre in the Republic of Kazakhstan shall be carried out in the same manner and on the same conditions as the enforcement of judicial acts of the courts of the Republic of Kazakhstan. At the same time, a translation of decisions of the Court of the Centre into the Kazakh or Russian language must be ensured in the manner determined by the acts of the Centre."*

The provision refers to "decisions" (*resheniya*) of the AIFC Court, but does not expressly confine enforcement to judgments on the merits. The distinction in terminology – "decisions" for the AIFC Court and "judicial acts" for national courts – does not reflect a substantive limitation on enforceability. The legislative history confirms that the intent was not to narrow the scope of enforceable AIFC Court instruments.

In its prior version, Article 13.8 provided that

> *"the enforcement of decisions of the Court of the Centre in the Republic of Kazakhstan shall be carried out in the same manner and on the same conditions as the enforcement of decisions of the courts of the Republic of Kazakhstan,"*

with no qualification as to the type of decision.

The legislative dossier to the May 2019 draft law amending the AIFC Constitutional Law further clarified the intention, noting that under Article 21 of the Kazakhstan Civil Procedure Code adopted December 27, 1994 (CPC), a court of first instance issues judicial acts in the form of judicial orders, decisions, rulings, and resolutions. To ensure uniform application of AIFC Court acts, the amendment proposed equating the "decisions" of the AIFC Court with *all* types of judicial acts of national courts.

Such an interpretation is supported by functional necessity. Effective judicial protection cannot be guaranteed if only one category of AIFC Court instruments were subject to enforcement across Kazakhstan. For instance, interim measures – which are indispensable for preserving rights pending final resolution – are not issued in the form of "decisions" (*resheniya*) but must nonetheless be enforceable nationwide for proceedings before the AIFC Court to be meaningful.

Accordingly, a proper construction of Article 13.8 supports the conclusion that all binding judicial instruments of the AIFC Court – whether decisions on the merits, orders recognizing foreign arbitral awards, interim measures, or other binding rulings – are enforceable throughout Kazakhstan on equal footing with the judicial acts of national courts.

## F. Does the New York Convention Bind the AIFC Court to Recognize a Foreign Arbitral Award?

There is an ongoing scholarly debate among lawyers regarding the status of the New York Convention in Kazakhstan, in particular whether Kazakhstan has in fact ratified it. However, since the ratification status has never been challenged in court practice to date, we do not dwell on this issue.[3] For the purposes of this article, we proceed on the assumption that the Republic of Kazakhstan has ratified the Convention and is duly bound by its obligations.

### 1. AIFC Court Bound by Kazakhstan's International Treaty Obligations

As our further analysis will, *inter alia*, rely on the provisions of the New York Convention, it is first necessary to determine whether the AIFC Court is bound by it.

Article 45.1 of the AIFC Arbitration Regulations reads as follows:

*"(1) ... For the avoidance of doubt, where the Republic of Kazakhstan has entered into an applicable treaty for the mutual enforcement of judgments, orders or awards, the AIFC Court shall comply with the terms of such treaty."*

Thus, we conclude that the AIFC Court must be regarded as bound by the Convention.

### 2. AIFC Court Standing in the Position of the Contracting State under the New York Convention

In this context, it is important to note that, while the AIFC is not itself a sovereign State and therefore cannot technically qualify as a "Contracting

---

[3]) A detailed analysis of this debate can be found in: Valikhan Shaikenov, *A Call to Ratify the New York and European Conventions: Silence That Upsets the Investors and the Law*, Arbitration.ru, 2019, No. 6 (10), available at https://www.aequitas.kz/en/press-center/publications/v-shaikenov-a-call-to-ratify-the-new-york-and-european-conventions-silence-that-upsets-the-investors-and-the-law-arbitration-ru-2019-6-10. *See also* Valikhan Shaikenov & Ardak Idayatova, *4.6 Kazakhstan: Recognition and Enforcement of Foreign Arbitral Awards*, in Roman Zykov (ed.), *Recognition and Enforcement of Foreign Arbitral Awards in Russia and Former USSR States* (Kluwer Law International, 2021), pp. 379–416.

State" under the Convention, Article 45.1 of the AIFC Arbitration Regulations makes clear that the AIFC Court is required to *"comply with the terms"* of treaties to which the Republic of Kazakhstan is a party. Since Kazakhstan has ratified the New York Convention, its obligations under that treaty necessarily extend to all judicial bodies within its territory, including the AIFC Court.

Accordingly, in our view, the correct interpretative approach is that when the Convention refers to a "Contracting State", the AIFC Court should understand this term to apply *mutatis mutandis* to the AIFC as a judicial jurisdiction within Kazakhstan. In other words, for the purpose of recognition and enforcement under the Convention, the AIFC Court should treat the AIFC as standing in the position of the Contracting State and apply the Convention as if references to "the courts of a Contracting State" encompassed the AIFC Court.

This ensures both fidelity to Kazakhstan's treaty obligations and uniformity with the Convention's object and purpose, namely the facilitation of recognition and enforcement of foreign arbitral awards.

## 3. Does the New York Convention Distinguish Between Recognition and Enforcement of Foreign Arbitral Awards

The New York Convention makes a clear distinction between the obligations to recognize and to enforce foreign arbitral awards. Contracting States are bound both (1) to recognize awards as binding and (2) to enforce them in accordance with local procedural rules – two related but independent duties. This distinction is evident not only from the very title of the New York Convention – *Convention on the Recognition and Enforcement of Foreign Arbitral Awards* – but also from Articles I and III. Article III provides:

> *"Each Contracting State shall recognize arbitral awards as binding and enforce them in accordance with the rules of procedure of the territory where the award is relied upon, under the conditions laid down in the following articles. There shall not be imposed substantially more onerous conditions or higher fees or charges on the recognition* ***or*** *enforcement of arbitral awards to which this Convention applies than are imposed on the recognition or enforcement of domestic arbitral awards."* (emphasis added)

The UNCITRAL Secretariat Guide on the Convention on the Recognition and Enforcement of Foreign Arbitral Awards (2016) (Guide) confirms that the Convention deliberately treats recognition and enforcement as distinct concepts. It notes that the Convention does not itself define the two terms and that case law remains relatively scarce. However, it records that courts and commentators generally accept the following distinction:

- *Recognition* concerns the legal acknowledgment of an award's binding effect. For example, a Colombian court held that recognition establishes the legal force of an award, while *enforcement* concerns the compelled execution of that award once recognized (Guide, Article I, para. 7).
- Commentators broadly agree that recognition means treating the arbitral award as binding but not necessarily enforceable, while enforcement is the process of giving effect to the award through the mechanisms of the enforcing State (Guide, Article I, para. 8).

The Guide also highlights that national courts have diverged on whether recognition and enforcement must be sought together. In a 1981 decision, the German Supreme Court construed them as interrelated and not separable (Guide, Article I, para. 10). By contrast, other courts have accepted recognition on its own. The Indian Supreme Court held that recognition may be requested *"as a shield against re-agitation of issues with which the award deals"*, allowing an award creditor to rely on the award defensively without seeking coercive execution (Guide, Article I, para. 11). Similarly, courts in Portugal and the United States have confirmed that recognition can be sought independently of enforcement (Guide, Article I, para. 12).

This understanding is reinforced by the *travaux préparatoires* and by scholarly commentary, which both support the view that recognition can be sought separately (Guide, Article I, para. 13).

In sum, the New York Convention expressly distinguishes between recognition and enforcement. Recognition establishes the binding character of the award, enabling reliance upon it (for instance, to bar re-litigation of the same issues), while enforcement involves the use of judicial machinery to compel compliance. Both obligations are distinct but complementary and must be upheld by Contracting States under Articles I and III of the Convention.

## 4. Does the New York Convention Require the Debtor to Have Assets in the Jurisdiction for Recognition of a Foreign Arbitral Award?

The text of the New York Convention contains no requirement that the award debtor possess assets in the jurisdiction where recognition and enforcement is sought. Article III obliges Contracting States both to recognize foreign arbitral awards as binding and to enforce them in accordance with local procedural rules, but neither this provision nor any other article of the Convention conditions recognition or enforcement on the presence of assets.

As noted in the Guide, while in practice creditors often choose to apply for recognition or enforcement in jurisdictions where the debtor's assets are located or expected to be located, this is a matter of strategy rather than a legal requirement. With the exception of an isolated German decision (*Kammergericht*, Berlin, August 10, 2006, 20 Sch 07/04), the courts of Contracting States have not treated the absence of assets as a bar to recognition or enforcement. On the contrary, judicial practice across multiple jurisdictions confirms that recognition may be sought even where no assets are currently located in the forum state.

Leading commentators further support this interpretation, noting that recognition may serve purposes independent of immediate enforcement – such as establishing the binding force of an award, providing *res judicata* effect, or creating a basis for interim measures and asset tracing.[4]

Accordingly, recognition under the New York Convention should not be understood as contingent upon the existence of debtor assets in the jurisdiction.

## 5. Does the New York Convention Require the Debtor to Have Legal Presence in the Jurisdiction for Recognition of a Foreign Arbitral Award?

The New York Convention does not require the award debtor to have legal presence in the jurisdiction where recognition of the award is sought.

Article I of the Convention was deliberately drafted to avoid any limitation based on the parties' nationality, residence, or legal presence. During the *travaux préparatoires*, the earlier requirement under the 1927 Geneva Convention – restricting enforcement to parties *"subject to the jurisdiction"* of a Contracting State – was considered *"vague and ambiguous"* and was deliberately removed. A proposal to reinstate such a condition was expressly rejected, confirming that *"the scope of application of the New York Convention does not depend on the nationality or residence of the parties to the arbitration proceedings"* (Guide, Article I, Analysis, paras. 4–5).

The Guide also emphasizes that the "conditions" for recognition and enforcement are exhaustively set out in Articles IV and V of the Convention. National courts have confirmed that no additional conditions may be imposed. As the Guide states, *"the 'conditions' referred to in article III are those exclusively listed in the Convention and no other condition contained in the Contracting States' national laws shall apply at the recognition and enforcement stage"* (Guide, Article III, Analysis, para. 16).

---

[4]) Emilia Onyema, 'Formalities of the Enforcement Procedure (Articles III and IV)' in Emmanuel Gaillard and Domenico Di Pietro (eds), *Enforcement of Arbitration Agreements and International Arbitral Awards: The New York Convention in Practice* (Cameron May 2008), p. 603: "In certain arbitral proceedings where declaratory awards are sought, either party or both parties may apply for recognition of the award. In other cases, recognition of an award may be sought to preclude a re-litigation of the dispute or to, 'acknowledg[e] a *status quo* as ruled in an award rendered by an arbitral tribunal'." *See also*: Albert Jan van den Berg, *Consolidated Commentary* (1996), p. 301, 'Procedure for Enforcement, in General', stating that the presence of assets in the jurisdiction is not a precondition to the enforcement of the award.

This approach has been upheld in practice by national courts. For example, in *Nigi Agricoltura srl v. Inter Eltra Kommerz und Produktion GmbH*, the Italian Supreme Court (July 23, 2009, No. 17312) confirmed that recognition under the Convention cannot be conditioned on requirements not expressly set out in the treaty. Similarly, in *Privilegiata Fabbrica Maraschino Excelsior Girolamo Luxardo SpA v. Agrarcommerz AG*, the Italian Court of Cassation (January 15, 1992, XVIII Y.B. Com. Arb. 427 (1993)) stressed that the Convention's framework excludes the imposition of supplementary requirements by domestic law.

Accordingly, one may argue that the absence of a debtor's legal presence in the enforcing jurisdiction (in our case the AIFC) cannot serve as a bar to recognition of a foreign arbitral award under the New York Convention.

## G. Does the New York Convention Supersede the AIFC Constitutional Statute and AIFC Arbitration Regulations?

Under Kazakh constitutional law, the hierarchy of norms is clear: the Constitution has supreme legal force, followed by ratified international treaties, and only thereafter by national laws and subordinate legislation. Article 4(3) of the Constitution of the Republic of Kazakhstan expressly provides that international treaties ratified by Kazakhstan "*have priority over its laws*". This principle has been repeatedly confirmed by the Constitutional Council, which has stated that ratified international treaties and laws on accession are equal in legal force and consequences, and that such treaties prevail over ordinary legislation in case of conflict (Constitutional Council's Normative Resolution No. 2 of May 18, 2006).

Accordingly, the New York Convention, assuming it is considered by the AIFC Court as a ratified international treaty, enjoys priority over both the AIFC Constitutional Statute and the AIFC Arbitration Regulations. These AIFC instruments are national legislation (the former being a constitutional law, the latter subordinate acts) and cannot derogate from Kazakhstan's treaty obligations. The AIFC Court, as a judicial body established within Kazakhstan's legal order, is bound by Article 45.1 of the AIFC Arbitration Regulations, which expressly mandates compliance with Kazakhstan's treaty obligations on mutual enforcement of awards and judgments.

The Guide also underscores that Contracting States may not impose additional requirements beyond those contained in the New York Convention. Article III, for instance, prohibits Contracting States from subjecting recognition and enforcement of foreign arbitral awards to "substantially more onerous conditions or higher fees or charges" than those applied to domestic awards. This principle ensures the supremacy of the Convention over conflicting national provisions that might restrict enforcement.

## V. Conclusion: What Kazakhstan's Constitution Actually Demands

If the Constitution is taken seriously – not selectively invoked but fully respected – the path is clear. The AIFC Court is a court "after the Constitution", not a forbidden "special court". Its civil jurisdiction exists because the Constitution and the AIFC's Constitutional Statute say it may exist. On that footing, a foreign-award creditor should be able to obtain a stand-alone recognition order from the AIFC Court and carry that order to nationwide enforcement – without inventing extra hurdles that the New York Convention does not recognize.

What follows from that constitutional settlement is simple:

1. *One country, one supremacy clause.* The Constitution binds all state organs equally. If the AIFC Court issues a recognition order within its conferred jurisdiction, national enforcement bodies must act on it – across Kazakhstan, not just within the AIFC.
2. *Convention compliance without embellishment*. The New York Convention requires recognition and enforcement; it does not require a duplicate trip through ordinary courts. The debtor's objections are the Convention's objections – no broader.
3. *Comity, not competition.* Ordinary courts and the AIFC Court are partners in a single constitutional order. They should give each other *res judicata* effect, respect *lis pendens*, and avoid parallel, duplicative review. The right comparison is horizontal harmony, not jurisdictional turf.
4. *Equal dignity of judgments.* An AIFC recognition order should circulate with the same executory force as a judgment of the ordinary courts. Anything less resurrects the very "special court" suspicion the Constitution rejects.

The payoff is not academic. For award creditors, it means a predictable, single-door route to recognition; for state institutions, it means fewer conflicts and cleaner case management; for Kazakhstan, it means a credible message to investors: the country keeps its constitutional promises and its treaty promises – without pitting one against the other.

This is neither AIFC exceptionalism nor constitutional purism. Properly read, the Constitution authorizes the AIFC Court and disciplines it. Honor both halves, and the "AIFC route" becomes what the law already points to: a national gateway to recognition that strengthens, rather than strains, the unity of Kazakhstan's legal order. Open the gate.

# Chapter IV

# Investment Arbitration

*Markus Petsche*
Reflections on the Nature of Investment
in International Investment Law

*Duarte G. Henriques/Rita de Carvalho*
Funding Counterclaims of Host States in ISDS
New Balances or New Risks?

*Johannes Tropper*
The Exclusion of Protection for Fossil Fuel Investments
under the Modernized ECT and in the Event of Withdrawal
from the ECT
Should EU States Remain Parties to the ECT or Withdraw?

*Sára Darnót*
Hungary's 'Solo Run' in Investor-State Arbitration:
Safeguarding Arbitral Integrity –
or Something Else?

# Reflections on the Nature of Investment in International Investment Law

*Markus Petsche*

## I. Introduction

One of the most controversial questions in international investment law (and arbitration) pertains to the meaning of the central concept of investment.[1]) This is an issue of considerable practical relevance given that the existence of an investment constitutes a jurisdictional requirement in all

[1]) For scholarly writings on this topic, see, for example, Noah Rubins, *The Notion of "Investment" in International Investment Arbitration* in Norbert Horn and Stefan Kröll (eds), *Arbitrating Foreign Investment Disputes: Procedural and Substantive Legal Aspects* (2004 Kluwer Law International) 283; Farouk Yala, *The Notion of "Investment" in ICSID Case Law: A Drifting Jurisdictional Requirement?* 22 J Int'l Arb 105 (2004); Michael Waibel, *Opening Pandora's Box: Sovereign Bonds in International Arbitration* 101 AJIL 711 (2007); Sébastien Manciaux, *The Notion of Investment: New Controversies* 9 JWIT 443 (2008); Emmanuel Gaillard, *Identify or Define? Reflections on the Evolution of the Concept of Investment in ICSID Practice* in Christina Binder, Ursula Kriebaum, August Reinisch and Stephan Wittich (eds), *International Investment Law for the 21st Century: Essays in Honour of Christoph Schreuer* (2009 Oxford University Press) 403; Michael Hwang and Jennifer Lee Cheng Fong, *Definition of "Investment" – A Voice from the Eye of the Storm* (2011) 1 Asian J Int Law 99 (2011); Helena Jung Engfeldt, *Should ICSID Go Gangnam Style in Light of Non-Traditional Foreign Investments Including Those Spurred on by Social Media – Applying an Industry-Specific Lens to the Salini Test to Determine Article 25 Jurisdiction* 32 Berkeley J Int'l L 44 (2014); Michael Waibel, *Investment Arbitration: Jurisdiction and Admissibility* Legal Studies Research Paper Series, University of Cambridge Faculty of Law, Paper No 9/2014 (2014); Alex Grabowski, *The Definition of Investment under the ICSID Convention: A Defense of Salini* 15 Chi J Int'l L 287 (2014); Jeremy Marc Exelbert, *Consistently Inconsistent: What Is a Qualifying Investment Under Article 25 of the ICSID Convention and Why the Debate Must End* 85 Fordham L Rev 1243 (2016); Stratos Pahis, *Investment Misconceived: The Investment-Commerce Distinction in International Investment Law* 45 Yale J Int'l L 69 (2020); Michael Waibel, *Subject Matter Jurisdiction: The Notion of Investment* 19 ICSID Reports 25 (2021); Darius Chan and Justin Lai, *Two decades after Salini v Morocco: the case for retaining the Salini test with modifications* 39 Arb Int'l 63 (2023); Okechukwu Emmanuel Wali, *A Contemporary Evaluation of Decisions and Approaches Shaping the Conceptualization of an "ICSID Investment"* 90 Arbitration: The International Journal of Arbitration, Mediation and Dispute Management 224 (2024); Markus Petsche, *The Concept of Investment in ICSID Arbitration* (2024 Oxford University Press).

forms of investor-state arbitration. The matter is far from being purely theoretical. In fact, there are numerous decisions in which tribunals have held that the claimant had not made, or did not own, an investment in the sense of the applicable legal instrument(s), thus declining jurisdiction to hear the cases referred to them (either in whole or in part).[2])

The primary issue, both in arbitral case law and the scholarly discussion, is the meaning of "investment" under Article 25 ICSID Convention. This is because, unlike most international investment agreements (IIAs) (or investment treaties) and investment laws, the ICSID Convention lacks a definition of the notion of investment. This has given rise to two controversial questions: (1) whether the concept of investment under the ICSID Convention has any independent meaning at all (a question that has arisen because some tribunals have taken the view that the definition contained in the applicable instrument of consent – investment treaty or law – is solely relevant[3])) and (2), in the affirmative, what that meaning is.

Today, there is widespread consensus that the notion of investment under Article 25 ICSID Convention does indeed have an independent meaning and that the so-called *Salini* test, established by the Tribunal in *Salini v. Morocco*,[4]) adequately encapsulates the relevant legal requirements. While most com-

---

[2]) For recent rulings, see, for example, *Nova Scotia Power Incorporated (Canada) v. The Bolivarian Republic of Venezuela*, ICSID Case No. ARB(AF)/11/1, Award (30 April 2014) para 113 (deciding that a contract under which a company controlled by Venezuelan state-owned entities agreed to supply certain quantities of coal to the Claimant (or the rights arising under such contract) did not qualify as an investment under the BIT between Canada and Venezuela); *Poštová banka A.S. and others v. The Hellenic Republic*, ICSID Case No. ARB/13/8, Award (9 April 2015) para 359 (holding that "the definition of investment in the BIT at issue does not extend to Poštová banka's GGBs [Greek Government Bonds]"); *Raymond Charles Eyre and others v. Democratic Socialist Republic of Sri Lanka*, ICSID Case No. ARB/16/25, Award (5 March 2020) para 303 (holding that a plot of land owned by the Claimants did not constitute an investment under either the ICSID Convention or the BIT between the United Kingdom and Sri Lanka); *Rand Investments Ltd., William Archibald Rand, Kathleen Elizabeth Rand, Allison Ruth Rand, Robert Harry Leander Rand and Sembi Investment Limited v. Republic of Serbia*, ICSID Case No. ARB/18/8, Award (29 June 2023) para 277 (holding, *inter alia*, that Mr. William Archibald Rand's beneficial ownership of BD Agro shares constituted an investment under the ICSID Convention, while certain payments made to this company, as well as his indirect shareholding, did not); *Kaloti Metals & Logistics, LLC v. Republic of Peru*, ICSID Case No. ARB/21/29, Award (14 May 2024) paras 383–87 (ruling that the Claimant's gold export business in Peru did not constitute an investment under the applicable treaty).

[3]) See, for example, *Waguih Elie George Siag and Clorinda Vecchi v. The Arab Republic of Egypt*, ICSID Case No. ARB/05/15, Decision on Jurisdiction (11 April 2007) para 207; *ATA Construction, Industrial and Trading Company v. The Hashemite Kingdom of Jordan*, ICSID Case No. ARB/08/2, Award (18 May 2010) para 111.

[4]) *Salini Costruttori S.P.A. and Italstrade S.P.A. v. Kingdom of Morocco*, ICSID Case No. ARB/00/4, Decision on Jurisdiction (23 July 2001).

mentators and tribunals agree that the existence of a contribution, a minimum duration, and risk are core elements of the *Salini* test, there is significant controversy regarding the applicability of additional requirements, most importantly of a requirement that the investment contribute to the host State's economic development.[5]) In addition, there is also major disagreement with regard to the precise meaning of the core *Salini* criteria, including the relevant thresholds.[6])

These controversies have received so much attention from both scholars and tribunals that another, arguably more crucial, issue has gone almost entirely unnoticed. This is the question of the "nature" of investment. This "nature" does not refer to the various criteria that are relevant to determine the existence of an investment in individual cases, but to the more fundamental question of what "type of thing" an investment is. As will be shown in this article, there is no unanimous answer to this question, with two main competing views co-existing: (1) the view that an investment consists of an asset (something that an investor *has*) and (2) the view that an investment consists of an activity or operation (something that an investor *does*).

The question of the nature of investment has not only gone under the radar, but it is also poorly understood. This has caused a number of logical inconsistencies and contrasting approaches in arbitral and treaty practice, generating a high level of legal uncertainty. Against this background, the purpose of the present contribution is to create increased awareness of the question of the nature of investment and the related problems. This article is organized as follows. Section 2 explores the nature of investment under investment treaties (the most common legal basis of investor-state claims), showing that these instruments typically contain asset-based definitions of investment, *i.e.*, view investments as assets. Section 3 examines the nature of investment under the *Salini* test and explains that the implicit assumption of this test is that investments are operations or activities. Section 4 analyzes the different problems that arise in arbitral and treaty practice as a result of the co-existence of these conflicting approaches. Section 5 offers concluding remarks.

---

[5]) For decisions upholding the relevance of this requirement, see, for example, *Phoenix Action, Ltd. v. The Czech Republic*, ICSID Case No. ARB/06/5, Award (15 April 2009) paras 83–85; *Cortec Mining Kenya Limited and others v. Republic of Kenya*, ICSID Case No. ARB/15/29, Award (22 October 2018) para 291. For contrary decisions, see *Quiborax S.A. v. Plurinational State of Bolivia*, ICSID Case No. ARB/06/2, Decision on Jurisdiction (27 September 2012) para 225; *Deutsche Bank AG v. Democratic Socialist Republic of Sri Lanka*, ICSID Case No. 09/02, Award (31 October 2012) para 306; *Rand Investments Ltd., William Archibald Rand, Kathleen Elizabeth Rand, Allison Ruth Rand, Robert Harry Leander Rand and Sembi Investment Limited v. Republic of Serbia*, ICSID Case No. ARB/18/8, Award (29 June 2023) para 228.

[6]) See Petsche, *supra* note 1, paras 4.14–4.38.

# II. The Nature of Investment in Investment Treaties

## A. The Prevailing Approach: Investments as Assets

A typical asset-based definition of investment contains a general definition followed by a (usually non-exhaustive) list of assets that qualify as investments. Article 1(a) of the Bilateral Investment Treaty (BIT) between Japan and Georgia, for example, defines "investment" as "every kind of asset owned or controlled, directly or indirectly, by an investor of a Contracting Party, that is made in the territory of the other Contracting Party".[7]) This provision then goes on to list various categories of assets that are considered investments under the treaty. These include, for example, "shares, stocks, or other forms of equity participation in an enterprise", "rights under contracts …", "claims to money …", "intellectual property rights …", and a catch-all category covering "any other tangible and intangible, movable and immovable property …".[8])

Asset-based definitions are vastly predominant in investment treaty practice. According to UNCTAD's investment treaty database, which maps investment treaties signed between 1959 and 2019, 2518 out of 2598 IIAs (roughly 97 %) contain such definitions.[9]) The percentage of treaties featuring asset-based definitions has dropped slightly in recent years, with "only" 49 out of 55 investment treaties signed between 2015 and 2019 (roughly 89 %) adopting such definitions.[10]) However, as this data suggests, asset-based definitions remain clearly prevalent.

## B. Alternative Approaches: Investments as Enterprises or Activities

There are two alternative, much less common, approaches to asset-based definitions of "investment". The first such approach consists of so-called "enterprise-based" definitions under which, as the concept suggests, investments are viewed as enterprises. An example of a treaty containing such a definition is the BIT between Morocco and Nigeria, which defines "investment" as "an enterprise within the territory of one State established, acquired, expanded or operated … by an investor of the other State … taken together

[7]) Agreement between Japan and Georgia for the Liberalisation, Promotion and Protection of Investment (adopted 29 January 2021, entered into force 23 July 2021) Art. 1(a).

[8]) *Ibid.*

[9]) UNCTAD, *International Investment Agreements Navigator* <https://investmentpolicy.unctad.org/international-investment-agreements/iia-mapping> accessed 9 November 2025.

[10]) *Ibid.*

with the asset (sic!) of the enterprise".[11]) This definition also lists a number of assets that enterprises typically own, and which also qualify as investments.[12])

Treaties adopting enterprise-based definitions typically explain what is meant by "enterprise". The BIT between Austria and Kyrgyzstan, for example, defines "enterprise" as "any legal entity or other organisation constituted or organised under the national law of a Contracting Party", specifying that an enterprise may notably take the form of "a corporation, partnership, joint venture or any other association, as well as a trust, a sole proprietorship, or a branch".[13]) A similar definition of "enterprise" can be found in the BIT between Canada and Mongolia.[14])

It should be observed that while enterprise-based definitions of the term "investment" are indeed distinguishable from asset-based definitions, they are not fundamentally opposed to the latter. An enterprise – at least to the extent that it is defined as a legal entity such as a corporation – is, in fact, a particular type of asset. In that sense, it could be said that enterprise-based definitions are simply narrower asset-based definitions that cover only a particular category of assets.

Under the second alternative approach, investments are viewed as projects or activities. Definitions following such an approach often have the appearance of asset-based definitions (and are frequently characterized as such). However, they contain a requirement that qualifying assets must be associated with specific investment activities or projects, thus making the existence of such activities or projects a basic, and arguably the most central, requirement for the existence of an investment. An illustrative example is the BIT between Hungary and Oman, which provides that an investment comprises "every kind of asset owned or controlled by an Investor of one Contracting Party in the Territory of the other Contracting Party in connection with *economic activities* pursuant to the laws and regulations of the latter …".[15])

---

[11]) Reciprocal Investment Promotion and Protection Agreement between the Government of the Kingdom of Morocco and the Government of the Federal Republic of Nigeria (adopted 3 December 2016, not in force) Art. 1 (hereafter Morocco–Nigeria BIT).

[12]) *Ibid.*

[13]) Agreement for the Promotion and Protection of Investment between the Government of the Republic of Austria and the Government of the Kyrgyz Republic (adopted 22 April 2016, entered into force 1 October 2017) Art. 1(2).

[14]) Agreement between Canada and Mongolia for the Promotion and Protection of Investments (adopted 8 September 2016, entered into force 24 February 2017) Art. 1.

[15]) Agreement between the Government of the Sultanate of Oman and the Government of Hungary for the Promotion and Reciprocal Protection of Investments (adopted 2 February 2022, entered into force 24 October 2022) Art .1(1) (emphasis added).

# III. The Nature of Investment under the *Salini* Test

## A. The *Salini* Decision

*Salini* involved a contract for the construction of a highway concluded between two Italian companies, Salini Costruttori and Italstrade, and the competent Moroccan state entity, the *Société Nationale des Autoroutes du Maroc*. A dispute arose between the parties concerning the level of remuneration due for the work, with Salini and Italstrade ultimately filing an ICSID arbitration claim. Before the Tribunal, Morocco raised various jurisdictional objections, including an allegation that the Claimants had not made any investment in Morocco.

Addressing this objection, the Tribunal first found that the Claimants had made an investment within the meaning of the asset-based definition contained in the applicable treaty, the BIT between Italy and Morocco.[16]) It further held that, under the ICSID Convention, an investment required "contributions", "a certain duration of performance of the contract", "a participation in the risks of the transaction", as well as a "contribution to the economic development of the host State".[17]) The Tribunal noted that the first three criteria were generally recognized in legal scholarship, and that the fourth one could be derived from the ICSID Convention's Preamble, which refers to the objective of "international cooperation for economic development" and mentions the "role" that "private international investment" plays in that context.[18])

On the facts, the Tribunal found that all four requirements were met. It ruled that the investors had made various contributions (mentioning, for example, know-how, equipment, and personnel), that the 36-month performance of the contract satisfied the applicable duration requirement, that the claimants had faced multiple risks (risks flowing from the contractual prerogatives granted to the state party, as well as various economic and regulatory risks), and that it could not be doubted that the works performed by the claimants, which took the form of a "construction of infrastructure", contributed to Morrocco's economic development.[19])

## B. The *Salini* Test

As has been explained above, the *Salini* tribunal considered that the existence of an investment required the presence of contributions, a minimum

[16]) *Salini*, *supra* note 4, para 49.

[17]) *Ibid.* para 52.

[18]) *Ibid.*

[19]) *Ibid.*, paras 53–57.

duration, risk, and a contribution to the host State's economic development. In the majority of recent decisions, however, tribunals have taken the view that the contribution-to-the-economic-development criterion was not part of the *Salini* test, chiefly because they regarded the reference to the goal of economic development contained in the ICSID Convention's Preamble as too far removed from the definition of the term "investment".[20])

In addition to the three core criteria of contributions, duration, and risk, several tribunals have held that "regularity of profits and returns" was a further requirement. This criterion, which originated from the decision of the Tribunal in *Fedax v. Venezuela*,[21]) has notably been referred to in *Joy Mining v. Egypt*[22]) and *Malaysian Historical Salvors v. Malaysia*.[23]) Moreover, at least one tribunal has considered that legality and good faith were also relevant factors under Article 25 ICSID Convention.[24])

## C. The *Salini* Test's Implied View that Investments are Operations or Activities

The *Salini* case law is almost entirely silent on the issue of the "nature" of investment. In fact, most tribunals state that the existence of an investment "infers", "requires", or "supposes" that certain requirements are met; they do not generally attempt to provide actual definitions of this term, *i.e.*, they do not hold that an investment "is", or "consists of" something. Despite this omission in the relevant case law, the nature of the *Salini* criteria unambiguously suggests that the *Salini* test does *not* view investments as assets, but rather as "operations" or "activities."

This conclusion derives, first of all, from the three core *Salini* criteria. In fact, none of these criteria can sensibly apply to assets. For instance, an asset such as a piece of land or shares in a company does not have any duration. Also, an asset as such does not involve any risks. Nor is it particularly meaningful to speak of the contribution made to (or by?) an asset. On the contrary, when

[20]) See the cases referred to *supra*, note 5. For additional rulings denying the applicability of this criterion, see *L.E.S.I.-DIPENTA v. Democratic and Popular Republic of Algeria*, ICSID Case No. ARB/03/08, Award (10 January 2005) para 13; *Victor Pey Casado and Foundation 'Presidente Allende' v. Republic of Chile*, ICSID Case No. ARB/98/2, Award (8 May 2008) para 232; *Mr. Saba Fakes v. Republic of Turkey*, ICSID Case No. ARB/07/20, Award (14 July 2010) para 111.

[21]) *Fedax N.V. v. The Republic of Venezuela*, ICSID Case No. ARB/96/3, Decision of the Tribunal on Objections to Jurisdiction (11 July 1997) para 43.

[22]) *Joy Mining Machinery Limited v. The Arab Republic of Egypt*, ICSID Case No. ARB/03/11, Award on Jurisdiction (6 August 2004) para 53.

[23]) *Malaysian Historical Salvors Sdn, Bhd v. Malaysia*, ICSID Case No. ARB/05/10, Award on Jurisdiction (17 May 2007) para 108.

[24]) *Phoenix Action, Ltd. v. The Czech Republic*, ICSID Case No. ARB/06/5, Award (15 April 2009) para 114.

applied to an investor's operations or activities in the host State, these criteria make sense. In fact, such activities necessarily have a certain duration, and they are also likely to involve various risks (such as, for example, the occurrence of events that will undermine the profitability of those activities). Finally, investment operations will typically require certain contributions on the part of the investor (most importantly, the use or commitment of capital).

The same inference can be drawn from the additional *Salini* criteria that are occasionally referred to. "Regularity of profits and returns", for instance, may be a characteristic of certain operations, but it does not reasonably describe assets *per se*. Similarly, to speak of the legality and good faith of an asset does not have any logical meaning; again, these features are only useful when applied to the activities carried out by an investor.

Additional support for the proposition that investments are perceived as activities under the *Salini* test is provided by the context and language of the *Salini* decision itself, as well as subsequent developments in arbitral case law. In fact, as has been explained, the *Salini* decision was rendered in connection with a contract for the construction of a highway, *i.e.*, a transaction under which the investors were to carry out specific activities. The very formulation of the duration requirement in *Salini* (there has to be a "certain duration of performance of the *contract*") (emphasis added) also suggests that the *Salini* test focuses on investment contracts and related activities.

Recent refinements of the "contributions" and "risk" requirements are similarly telling. Indeed, a number of tribunals have taken the view that the relevant contributions should consist of contributions "to an economic *venture*",[25]) thus implicitly endorsing the view that an investment consists of investment operations. As far as the risk criterion is concerned, several tribunals have held that only certain types of risks qualify under the *Salini* test and that those risks are "investment" or "operational" risks,[26]) again highlighting the central role of investment activities for the existence of an investment under the *Salini* test.

[25]) See, for example, *Poštová banka, a.s. v. The Hellenic Republic*, ICSID Case No. ARB/13/8, Award (9 April 2015) para 360; *MNSS B.V. and Recupero Credito Acciaio N.V. v. Montenegro*, ICSID Case No. ARB(AF)/12/8, Award (4 May 2016) para 189; *Raymond Charles Eyre and others v. Democratic Socialist Republic of Sri Lanka*, ICSID Case No. ARB/16/25, Award (5 March 2020) para 294.

[26]) See, for example, *Poštová banka*, *supra* note 25, para 369; *Eyre*, *supra* note 25, para 293.

# IV. Problems

## A. Overview

Under the current legal framework, arbitral tribunals deciding on the existence of an investment will frequently have to apply two separate tests, and those tests are likely to be based on opposing views regarding the nature of investment. Firstly, they will apply the definition contained in the applicable instrument of consent (typically an investment treaty), which, in most cases, will be asset-based. Secondly, they will apply the *Salini* test under the ICSID Convention, which, as has been shown, implicitly views investments as activities or operations.

As practice has shown, this state of affairs has been a source of difficulties for arbitral tribunals, leading not only to conflicting approaches but also to inadequate reasoning. Several specific problems that have arisen in arbitral (and treaty) practice are examined in this Section. Those include (1) the inadequate application of the *Salini* test to assets, (2) the potentially confusing incorporation of the *Salini* criteria into asset-based treaty definitions of "investment", (3) rejection of asset-based definitions by arbitral tribunals, and (4) conflicting decisions.

## B. Application of the *Salini* Test to Assets

The *Salini* test's silence on the nature of investment, coupled with the overwhelming predominance of asset-based definitions of "investment" in IIAs, creates an obvious risk that arbitral tribunals will apply the *Salini* criteria to the investor's asset(s), rather than the relevant investment operations (if any). As has been explained above, such an approach is conceptually flawed and leads to inadequate rulings, further enhancing the uncertainty surrounding the question of the nature of investment and the meaning of "investment" more generally.

The problem is particularly acute in cases where an investor does not actually engage in specific operations, but merely makes a portfolio investment, for example by purchasing corporate shares without exercising any control over, or participating in the management of, the relevant company. In such a scenario, given the breadth and vagueness of the *Salini* criteria, a tribunal may be able to identify a contribution (the funds used to purchase the shares) and a risk (the risk of a drop in the value of those shares). Still, it may – rightly so – find it inappropriate to apply the *Salini* test's duration requirement. In fact, the application of this requirement would mean that the shares purchased by the investor are not investments from the time of the purchase, but only acquire such status once a certain period of time has passed. For obvious reasons, this is not a satisfactory solution, and arbitral tribunals are therefore likely to adopt very flexible interpretations of the duration requirement, largely depriving this criterion of any substance.

The decision of the Tribunal in *Phoenix v. Czech Republic* is illustrative of this problem. In this case, the Tribunal held that the two companies purchased by the Claimant qualified as investments under the ICSID Convention because the Claimant had purchased them in 2002 and only sold them in 2008, several years after initiating ICSID proceedings.[27]) The implication of this decision is that, if the Claimant's ownership had been more limited in time, it may not have been sufficient to meet the *Salini* test's duration requirement. As this example shows, the application of a duration requirement (and of the *Salini* criteria more generally) to individual assets is conceptually flawed and thus inappropriate.

## C. Incorporation of the *Salini* Criteria into Asset-Based Investment Treaty Definitions

A related problem is that an increasing number of investment treaties contain asset-based definitions of investment that incorporate the *Salini* criteria. It is not entirely clear what has motivated this trend, but two factors are likely to have played a role: (1) the widespread recognition that the *Salini* test enjoys, and (2) the desire to have the *Salini* criteria apply in non-ICSID investment arbitrations, either to ensure uniformity across all forms of investor-state arbitration or to limit the scope of asset-based definitions, which are sometimes considered as excessively broad.

This incorporation of the *Salini* test has been achieved by introducing the requirement that an investment must present certain characteristics that largely overlap with the *Salini* criteria. An example of such a provision can be found in the BIT between Japan and Georgia, which defines "investment" as "every kind of asset … that has the characteristics of an investment, including such characteristics as the commitment of capital or other resources, the expectation of gain or profit, or the assumption of risk".[28]) While the mentioned characteristics do not fully coincide with the three core *Salini* criteria, the two tests can be regarded as largely identical, notably because of the non-exhaustive nature of the features listed in treaty-based "characteristics" requirements.

Whatever the reason behind this innovation may be, it is likely to create further confusion as far as the nature of investment is concerned. In fact, if one transplants a test that has been elaborated on the assumption that investments consist of operations to definitions that expressly endorse the conflicting asset-based approach, this inevitably leads to tensions and contradictions,

[27]) *Phoenix*, *supra* note 3, para 124.

[28]) Japan-Georgia BIT, *supra* note 7, Art. 1(a).

detrimentally affecting the coherence of the legal framework and, by way of consequence, arbitral rulings.

## D. Growing Rejection of Asset-Based Definitions

Another problematic development is that several tribunals have rejected asset-based definitions, holding that they do not constitute definitions properly speaking, and that they must be amended to take into account the "objective" meaning of the term "investment".[29]) According to the relevant tribunals, this objective meaning consists of the three core *Salini* criteria of contribution, duration, and risk. By supplementing asset-based treaty definitions with the *Salini* test, these tribunals have indirectly rejected the notion that, for the purposes of the relevant treaties, an investment must be regarded as an asset.

The Tribunal in *Nova Scotia*, for example, expressed doubts as to whether the asset-based definition of "investment" in the BIT between Canada and Venezuela could "be properly described as a definition",[30]) holding that it lacked a reference to the term's objective meaning, *i.e.*, the *Salini* criteria.[31]) Taking this analysis one step further, the Tribunal in *Doutremepuich v. Mauritius* expressly denied that the definition contained in the BIT between France and Mauritius constituted an actual definition, holding that it merely provided examples of possible forms of investment, without specifying the relevant characteristics or criteria.[32]) These and other similar decisions have created further confusion regarding the question of the nature of investment.

## E. Conflicting Decisions

Unsurprisingly, the uncertainty surrounding the nature of investment has generated contradictory rulings. A particularly striking example is *Mitchell v. Congo*. The Claimant, Mr. Mitchell, operated a legal consultancy firm in the Republic of the Congo. In the ICSID proceedings brought against the Republic, he argued that various measures taken by the Congolese government amounted to an unlawful expropriation in violation of the BIT between Zaïre and the United States of America. The Respondent challenged the jurisdiction of the

[29]) For a discussion of the relevant cases, see Petsche, *supra* note 1, paras 6.44–6.65.

[30]) *Nova Scotia Power Incorporated (Canada) v. Bolivarian Republic of Venezuela*, ICSID Case No. ARB(AF)/11/1, Award (30 April 2014) para 77.

[31]) *Id.* para 84.

[32]) *Professor Christian Doutremepuich and Antoine Doutremepuich v. The Republic of Mauritius*, PCA Case No. 2018-37, Award on Jurisdiction (23 August 2019) para 117.

Tribunal, contending that Mr. Mitchell's consultancy firm did not constitute a qualifying investment.

In its award, the Tribunal held that the Claimant owned various types of assets within the meaning of the treaty's asset-based definition (notably movable property, know-how and goodwill, as well as the legal right to provide consultancy services), thus affirming the existence of an investment under the treaty.[1]) As far as the ICSID Convention was concerned, the Tribunal took the view that the *Salini* criteria did not constitute formal requirements, but merely elements that are "frequently present in investment projects".[2]) It thus concluded that Mr. Mitchell owned (or had owned) an investment in the Congo.

The *ad hoc* Committee hearing the Congo's annulment claim found the reasoning of the Tribunal to be inadequate, holding that it was constitutive of both a manifest excess of powers and a failure to state reasons.[3]) Of particular interest in this context was the *ad hoc* Committee's disagreement with what the Tribunal had identified as being Mr. Mitchell's investment. Indeed, the Committee noted that the Tribunal had confused "the economic operation or project – which, if it fulfills certain characteristics, becomes the investment within the meaning of the Convention and the Treaty" with "the rights and assets protected by the Treaty because they are part of the operation or project".[4]) As this statement suggests, the Tribunal and the *ad hoc* Committee took different positions as to the nature of Mr. Mitchell's investment. Relying on the applicable BIT, the Tribunal considered that the investment consisted of the various assets owned by the Claimant, while the *ad hoc* Committee held that an investment consisted not of assets, but of an operation or project. The annulment was, therefore, (at least in part) due to these divergent approaches.

## V. Conclusion

This article has shown that, beyond the controversy surrounding the *Salini* test and its criteria, there is a more fundamental unresolved question concerning the concept of investment: the issue of its "nature". The ICSID Convention's silence on the meaning of "investment" and the *Salini* test's failure to specify what it perceives to be the nature of investments have created regrettable legal uncertainty. This has been enhanced by the conflation, in both arbitral and treaty practice, of conflicting approaches, respectively viewing

[1]) *Patrick H. Mitchell v. The Democratic Republic of the Congo*, ICSID Case No. ARB/99/7, Award (9 February 2004) para 55.

[2]) *Ibid.* para 56.

[3]) *Mr Patrick Mitchell v. the Democratic Republic of the Congo*, ICSID Case No. ARB/99/7, Decision on the Application for Annulment of the Award (1 November 2006) para 67.

[4]) *Ibid.* para 38.

investments as assets and operations. This has led to contradictory rulings (as the *Mitchell* case shows) and conceptually flawed analysis and rulemaking (the application of the *Salini* criteria to assets and their incorporation into asset-based definitions of "investment").

The purpose of this contribution has been to raise greater awareness of these issues. More reflection will be needed to design solutions to remedy the current problems. Such solutions will not be easy to put forward, given that the current legal framework is both fragmented (*i.e.*, mostly comprised of bilateral treaties) and largely based on case law. Also, it is not obvious what a potential reform should look like. Should one recognize the asset nature of investments or, on the contrary, espouse the idea that investments consist of activities or operations? Or both/neither?

For the time being, however, it would already be an improvement if the various stakeholders (arbitrators, party representatives, and States) were able to develop a better understanding of the question of the nature of investment, gaining awareness of the co-existence of the conflicting viewpoints examined in this study. While this may not suffice to create a fully coherent and uniform legal framework, such awareness may usefully inform debates amongst scholars and practitioners, preventing at least some of the contradictions and misunderstandings described in this article.

# Funding Counterclaims of Host States in ISDS

## New Balances or New Risks?

*Duarte G. Henriques/Rita de Carvalho*

## I. Introduction

The last decade has witnessed an extraordinary transformation in the practice of third-party funding ("TPF") in international arbitration. What began as an experimental mechanism to enable impecunious claimants to pursue meritorious cases has evolved into a sophisticated, global industry.[1])

Today, commercial funders, ranging from specialized finance boutiques to institutional investors, play an increasingly visible role in the resolution of cross-border disputes, including those arising under investment treaties. Their growing involvement in investor–State dispute settlement ("ISDS") has generated both enthusiasm and anxiety: enthusiasm because TPF promises to democratize access to arbitration by leveling the playing field between capital-constrained investors and sovereign respondents; anxiety because it also introduces new layers of commercial interest, potential conflicts of interest, and systemic risk.[2])

Despite its rapid expansion, reliable empirical data on the prevalence of funding in ISDS remains scarce. Under the 2022 ICSID Arbitration Rules,[3]) parties must now disclose the existence and identity of any funder, a reform intended to improve transparency and address conflicts of interest. Since these rules entered into force, ICSID has reported that approximately sixteen percent of newly registered cases disclosed third-party funding arrangements, offering

---

[1]) Stavros Brekoulakis & Catherine A. Rogers, "Third-Party Funding in Investment Arbitration", in Chaisse, J., Choukroune, L., Jusoh, S. (eds.), *Handbook of International Investment Law and Policy* (Springer, 2021), pp. 1397–1422, p. 1398.

[2]) Frank J. Garcia, *The Case Against Third-Party Funding in Investment Arbitration*, (Investment Treaty News, 30 Jul. 2018), online: International Institute for Sustainable Development (IISD) https://www.iisd.org/itn/en/2018/07/30/the-case-against-third-party-funding-in-investment-arbitration-frank-garcia/ (all web pages last accessed on November 3, 2025).

[3]) International Centre for Settlement of Investment Disputes (ICSID), *ICSID Arbitration Rules* (as amended, effective), art. 14.

the first systematic indication of the practice's diffusion within treaty arbitration.[4])

Even so, the true extent of TPF is almost certainly higher, as many arrangements remain confidential, particularly in non-institutional or *ad hoc* proceedings. The growing visibility of funding, combined with the opacity of its operation, has consequently drawn the attention of regulators and reform bodies. UNCITRAL's Working Group III on ISDS Reform has placed TPF squarely on its agenda, with States deeply divided between those calling for strict regulation or outright prohibition and those favoring a more flexible, disclosure-based approach.[5])

In parallel, national and regional initiatives have begun to scrutinize the financing of international disputes.[6]) The European Parliamentary Research Service, for instance, has urged the adoption of safeguards to ensure that litigation and arbitration funding does not undermine fairness or public accountability.[7])

At the same time, investigative reporting has revealed how hedge funds and private-equity investors are profiting from environmentally and politically sensitive treaty claims, fueling renewed concern that TPF may amplify speculative or high-stakes litigation.[8])

Against this backdrop, the debate surrounding the legitimacy and regulation of TPF has become one of the most contentious aspects of the ongoing reform of investor–State dispute settlement ("ISDS").

Within this broader debate, one issue has received little systematic attention: the potential role of TPF in supporting counterclaims by respondent States. While funding has traditionally been associated with claimants seeking

[4]) Toby McIntosh, *New Information Disclosed on Level of Third-Party Funding of Investor Disputes, Eye on Global Transparency* (May 1, 2025), online: Eye on Global Transparency https://eyeonglobaltransparency.net/2025/05/01/new-information-disclosed-on-level-of-third-party-funding-of-investor-disputes/.

[5]) UNCITRAL, Working Group III, *Draft Provisions on Procedural Reform (A/CN.9/WG.III/WP.219)* (July 11, 2022), online: UN https://docs.un.org/en/A/CN.9/WG.III/WP.219.

[6]) European Commission, *Study on Mapping Third-Party Litigation Funding in the European Union*, DG Justice and Consumers (March 21, 2025), online: European Commission, https://commission.europa.eu/document/download/65adb710-1a36-4550-a4c6-a606adbff061_en?filename=Final%20Report%20EC%20Mapping%20TPLF%20 in%20the%20EU.pdf.

[7]) Jérôme Saulnier with Ivona Koronthalyova & Klaus Müller, *Responsible Private Funding of Litigation: European Added Value Assessment*, PE 662.612 (March 2021), online: EPRS https://www.europarl.europa.eu/RegData/etudes/STUD/2021/662612/EPRS_STU(2021)662612_EN.pdf, pp. 15–23.

[8]) Patrick Greenfield & Phoebe Weston, *Revealed: How Wall Street Is Making Millions Betting Against Green Laws*, The Guardian (March 5, 2025), online: The Guardian https://www.theguardian.com/environment/2025/mar/05/revealed-how-wall-street-is-making-millions-betting-against-green-laws-isds-aoe.

damages from governments, the growing normalization of counterclaims, particularly in cases involving environmental or human-rights obligations, raises the question of whether funders might also enable States to pursue their own claims for relief.

In principle, such financing could serve to equalize access to justice within ISDS, allowing resource-constrained governments to advance legitimate counterclaims rather than merely defend against investor actions.

In practice, however, extending funding to sovereign respondents introduces a new set of legal, ethical, and political complexities. Would such arrangements compromise the independence of the State? Could they expose public interests to commercial capture, or conversely, strengthen accountability by ensuring that violations of domestic or international law are not left unremedied?

## II. Counterclaims by State Respondents

A counterclaim can be defined as an autonomous, reactive and incidental claim of a respondent party against a claimant, aimed at obtaining more than mere dismissal of the principal claim. This right to counterclaim is a fundamental element of the respondent's right to present its case on an equal footing with the original claimant.[9])

Although counterclaims by State respondents are in principle possible in ISDS, their legal regime is far from straightforward. Under the major procedural frameworks, including the ICSID and UNCITRAL Arbitration Rules, counterclaims are not excluded, as tribunals may hear them provided certain conditions are met.

For example, Article 46 of ICSID's Arbitration Rules States that:

> *Except as the parties otherwise agree, the Tribunal shall, if requested by a party, determine any incidental or additional claims or counterclaims arising directly out of the subject-matter of the dispute provided that they are within the scope of the consent of the parties and are otherwise within the jurisdiction of the Centre.*

Those conditions of consent, connection and jurisdiction have, however, proved to be significant hurdles to State respondents who, in practice, wish to submit their counterclaims regarding the violation of international or national

---

[9]) Anna De Luca & Crina Baltag, *Counterclaims in Investment Arbitration: Reflections on UNCITRAL WG III Reform*, *Kluwer Arbitration Blog* (November 5, 2021), online: Kluwer https://legalblogs.wolterskluwer.com/arbitration-blog/counterclaims-in- investment-arbitration-reflections-on-uncitral-wg-iii-reform/.

law by investor claimants, considering that tribunals have often interpreted both the consent and the "the same dispute" requirements narrowly.[10])

Additionally, traditional bilateral investment treaties (BITs) routinely impose obligations on host States but rarely impose corresponding obligations on investors.[11]) As a result, most counterclaims grounded in treaty law have been rejected.[12])

However, recent treaty practice is beginning to shift. "New-generation" agreements, such as the EU–Vietnam Free Trade Agreement (2020), and provisions in the Comprehensive and Progressive Agreement for Trans-Pacific Partnership (CPTPP) (2018),[13]) expressly reference investor obligations on issues such as environmental protection, corporate social responsibility, or anti-corruption.[14]) These provisions provide a clearer jurisdictional basis for counterclaims, though they remain relatively rare.

Case Law has also begun to open the door for counterclaims, though cautiously. In *Saluka v. Czech Republic* (2006), the tribunal confirmed that counterclaims are theoretically possible but insisted they must be directly connected to the investor's claims.[15]) In *Paushok v. Mongolia* (2011), the tribunal dismissed counterclaims because the BIT contained no investor obligations.[16]) More significantly, in *Urbaser v. Argentina* (2016), the tribunal accepted jurisdiction over Argentina's counterclaim that the investor had violated the human right to water. Although Argentina's claim ultimately failed on the merits, the award was groundbreaking in recognizing that investors may, at least in principle, bear obligations under international law

---

[10]) Anna De Luca & Crina Baltag, *Counterclaims in Investment Arbitration: Reflections on UNCITRAL WG III Reform, Kluwer Arbitration Blog* (November 5, 2021), online: Kluwer https://legalblogs.wolterskluwer.com/arbitration-blog/counterclaims-in-investment-arbitration-reflections-on-uncitral-wg-iii-reform/.

[11]) Mees Brenninkmeijer & Fabien Gélinas, *Counterclaims in Investment Arbitration: Towards an Integrated Approach* (July 18, 2023), online: ICSID https://icsid.world bank.org/news-and-events/speeches-articles/counterclaims-investment-arbitration-towards-integrated-approach.

[12]) Ishikawa T., *Corporate Environmental Responsibility in Investor-State Dispute Settlement: The Unexhausted Potential of Current Mechanisms* (Cambridge University Press, 2023), pp. 87–116.

[13]) Chapter 13 of the EU-Vietnam Free Trade Agreement is entirely dedicated to trade and sustainable development, whereas Chapters 19, 20, 23 and 26 of the CPTPP are dedicated to issues such as labor, environment, development, and transparency and anti-corruption.

[14]) On this topic, Ishikawa T., *Corporate Environmental Responsibility in Investor-State Dispute Settlement: The Unexhausted Potential of Current Mechanisms* (Cambridge University Press, 2023), pp. 23–55.

[15]) *Saluka Investments BV v. Czech Republic*, UNCITRAL, Partial Award (March 17, 2006), online: https://www.italaw.com/cases/961.

[16]) *Sergey Paushok, CJSC Golden East Company and CJSC Vostokneftegaz Company v. Government of Mongolia*, UNCITRAL, Award on Jurisdiction and Liability (April 28, 2011), online: https://www.italaw.com/cases/816.

that could ground counterclaims.[17] In *Burlington v. Ecuador* (2017)[18] and *Perenco v. Ecuador* (2019),[19] ICSID tribunals went further, granting Ecuador substantial damages for environmental harm caused by oil companies.

Although these cases demonstrate that counterclaims based on domestic law obligations incorporated into the arbitration agreement can succeed, obstacles remain, such as the structural imbalance between capital-exporting investors and capital-importing host States has long been at the center of debates on investment treaty arbitration.

Arbitration proceedings under the ICSID or UNCITRAL frameworks are notoriously expensive. Average costs for States defending claims often exceed USD 6 million, while the median cost is approximately USD 4.7 million, excluding enforcement or annulment proceedings. Claimants typically incur slightly higher costs, and total tribunal and institutional expenses can add another USD 1 million or more to each case.[20]

For developing and least-developed countries, these sums represent a significant diversion of scarce public resources away from pressing social and developmental needs. This financial burden does not end with legal fees. If an arbitral award is rendered against the State, damages can amount to hundreds of millions (or even billions) of dollars, far exceeding the national budgets of many small economies.

Procedural disadvantages compound these substantive challenges. Well-resourced investors can retain leading international law firms and engage expert witnesses, while impoverished States may struggle to secure comparable representation.[21] In practice, States often rely on a small pool of international firms willing to accept reduced fees or success-based arrangements (typically under public procurement procedures), which can create dependency and limit strategic flexibility.

These dynamics have fed into the broader legitimacy crisis of ISDS. Critics argue that the system entrenches a structural asymmetry between

---

17) *Urbaser S.A. and Consorcio de Aguas Bilbao Bizkaia, Bilbao Biskaia Ur Partzuergoa v. The Argentine Republic*, ICSID Case No. ARB/07/26, Award (December 6, 2016), online: https://www.italaw.com/cases/1144.

18) *Burlington Resources Inc. v. Republic of Ecuador*, ICSID Case No. ARB/08/5, Decision on Counterclaims (February 7, 2017), online: https://www.italaw.com/cases/181.

19) *Perenco Ecuador Ltd. v. Republic of Ecuador and Empresa Estatal Petróleos del Ecuador (PetroEcuador)*, ICSID Case No. ARB/08/6, Award (September 27, 2019), online: https://www.italaw.com/cases/819.

20) British Institute of International and Comparative Law (BIICL), *Costs, Damages and Duration in Investor-State Arbitration* (June 2021), pp. 21–23, online: BIICL https://www.biicl.org/documents/136_isds-costs-damages-duration_june_2021.pdf.

21) On this topic, GAR – Know-How Investment Treaty Arbitration, on several jurisdictions, online: GAR https://globalarbitrationreview.com/insight/know-how/investment-treaty-arbitration.

global investors and States, effectively allowing capital to discipline sovereign decision-making.[22]) For less developed States, the challenge is not only financial but systemic: investment arbitration often reinforces patterns of dependency and disempowerment, limiting policy space[23]) at precisely the moment when it is most needed for development.

## III. Rebalancing Through Counterclaims and the Role of Third-Party Funding

The precarious position of less-developed host States in the investment arbitration system underscores the urgency of exploring mechanisms that can restore a measure of balance. One such mechanism is the counterclaim.

Allowing States to assert claims against investors (*e.g.*, environmental concerns, corruption, or breaches of domestic law) provides a potential means of shifting arbitration away from a purely defensive posture. In principle, counterclaims can help States recover damages for harms caused by investors, while also reinforcing the notion that investment protection must be accompanied by investor responsibility.[24])

This is where the debate over TPF takes on renewed significance. This mechanism operates on a simple but powerful premise: an external financier provides the resources necessary to pursue or defend a legal claim in exchange for a share of the eventual recovery. In investment arbitration, where proceedings are notoriously expensive and often extend over many years, the involvement of funders can be decisive in determining whether a claim or counterclaim is financially viable.

To date, TPF has largely been associated with claimants, particularly investors pursuing costly arbitration against States. For respondents, however, funding could in theory offer a lifeline. If adapted to support State counterclaims, TPF could enable impoverished governments to pursue affirmative relief against investors whose conduct has caused measurable harm.

---

[22]) Cruz Trabanino, P., "State Counterclaims and the 'Legitimacy Crisis' in Investment Treaty Arbitration", in: Bäumler, J., et al. *European Yearbook of International Economic Law 2021*, European Yearbook of International Economic Law, vol 12 (2022), pp. 203–228.

[23]) Columbia Center on Sustainable Investment, *ISDS Reform Without Remedy: A Report from the 51st Session of UNCITRAL Working Group III* (2024), online: CCSI https://ccsi.columbia.edu/sites/ccsi.columbia.edu/files/content/pics/CCSI-ISDS-Reform-Without-Remedy.pdf, pp. 9–11.

[24]) Ishikawa T., *Corporate Environmental Responsibility in Investor-State Dispute Settlement: The Unexhausted Potential of Current Mechanisms* (Cambridge University Press, 2022), pp. 148–156.

The cases of *Burlington v. Ecuador*[25]) and *Perenco v. Ecuador*[26]) illustrate the financial stakes of such counterclaims: environmental damage awards against investors exceeded hundreds of millions of dollars. For a resource-constrained State, securing funding to pursue similar claims could mean the difference between recovering vital resources and abandoning claims for lack of capacity.

At the same time, the prospect of TPF in support of State counterclaims introduces new complexities. Funders are traditionally reluctant to finance respondents, given the asymmetrical risk profile[27]) and the difficulty of enforcing awards against private investors. Moreover, the involvement of commercial funders in counterclaims might invite skepticism: are they enabling host States to defend their sovereignty, or are they merely monetizing State claims in ways that replicate existing power imbalances? For impoverished States, the danger is that reliance on funders could replace one form of dependency with another.

Thus, counterclaims and TPF sit at the heart of a broader paradox. On the one hand, they represent potential equalizers in a system long criticized for privileging investors. On the other, they risk entrenching new vulnerabilities, whether through funders' control over litigation strategy, the heightened exposure of investors to speculative counterclaims, or the political consequences of outsourcing sovereign disputes to private financiers.

The challenge, then, is to assess whether these evolving tools can genuinely rebalance the ISDS system in favor of host States, or whether they simply reshape the asymmetry in new and more complex forms.

## IV. Challenges to Third-Party Funding of Host States

For private investors, entering into a funding agreement is a commercial transaction. By contrast, when the respondent is a sovereign State, the arrangement can fall within the scope of domestic rules governing public finances, procurement, and the management of State assets.

Many legal systems impose strict requirements on how States may contract private parties, especially where contingency fees or success-based payments

---

25) *Burlington Resources Inc. v. Republic of Ecuador*, ICSID Case No. ARB/08/5, Decision on Counterclaims (February 7, 2017), online: https://www.italaw.com/cases/181.

26) *Perenco Ecuador Ltd. v. Republic of Ecuador and Empresa Estatal Petróleos del Ecuador (PetroEcuador)*, ICSID Case No. ARB/08/6, Award (27 Sept. 2019), online: https://www.italaw.com/cases/819.

27) Victoria Sahani, *Rethinking the Impact of Third-Party Funding on Access to Civil Justice*, (69 DePaul Law Review, 2020), pp. 611–632, online: https://scholarship.law.bu.edu/faculty_scholarship/3473.

are involved. A funding agreement in which a State promises a share of a potential arbitral award could be construed as alienating sovereign resources or pledging future revenues, raising constitutional or statutory obstacles. In some jurisdictions, procurement rules mandate competitive tendering for financial services, which is difficult to reconcile with the confidentiality and bespoke nature of TPF agreements.

Even where no explicit prohibition exists, the absence of a clear legal framework can create political and reputational risks. A government that turns to TPF to pursue a counterclaim against an investor may face domestic criticism for "selling off" sovereign claims to foreign financiers. This risk is particularly acute in developing States where the legitimacy of public spending is closely scrutinized and where opposition groups may weaponize perceptions of external interference in sovereign disputes.

Beyond procurement law, other structural challenges complicate TPF intervention on the respondent side. Enforcement is a key concern. Whereas investors typically enforce awards against States through international enforcement regimes such as the ICSID Convention or the New York Convention 1958,[28]) States seeking to collect on counterclaims must often pursue private investors through domestic courts, where assets may be shielded or dissipated. This enforcement asymmetry makes counterclaims less attractive to funders, as the risks of non-recovery are high.

A related difficulty concerns the financing of legal costs, especially when the State's defense is led by public servants. In many States, international arbitration is handled primarily by government ministries or in-house legal departments.

This raises the question: what exactly is the funder financing if attorneys' salaries are already covered by the public purse? While funders can cover tribunal fees, expert costs, and adverse cost risks, their ability to fund the core legal team is limited if that team consists of salaried civil servants. If the State decides to retain external international counsel, which is often necessary in high-stakes disputes, this will almost always require adherence to procurement rules, adding another layer of complexity.

Another challenge lies in regulatory uncertainty. In some jurisdictions, litigation funding has been treated with suspicion by courts or regulators, and in others it has been restricted or declared unenforceable. The UK's *PACCAR* decision in 2023,[29]) which briefly rendered many funding agreements unenforceable before reform proposals emerged, highlights the fragility of

[28]) Andrew Battisson & Tamlyn Mills, *Enforcement and Recovery: Theory, GAR: The Guide to Investment Treaty Protection and Enforcement* (2nd ed., 26 Feb. 2024), online: GAR https://globalarbitrationreview.com/guide/the-guide-investment-treaty-protection-and-enforcement/second-edition/article/enforcement-and-recovery-theory.

[29]) *R (on the application of PACCAR Inc & Others) v. Competition Appeal Tribunal & Others*, [2023] UKSC 28 (U.K. Sup. Ct. July 26, 2023), https://www.supreme court.uk/cases/uksc-2021-0078.html.

funding arrangements even in advanced legal systems. For developing host States, the uncertainty is compounded: even if a funding agreement is permissible under international arbitration rules, it may later be challenged under domestic law.

Further, if one accepts the legitimacy of TPF to support host States in investment arbitration, a delicate paradox emerges. Allowing States to secure external financing for their defense or counterclaims would make it difficult, if not impossible, to continue condemning investors for relying on the same mechanism.

The very arguments often levelled against claimant-side funding (*e.g.*, that it commercializes justice, distorts incentives, and invites speculative claims) would apply with equal force to respondent-side arrangements. If TPF is accepted as a means of empowering under-resourced States, then it must also be recognized as a legitimate tool for investors seeking access to justice against powerful sovereigns.

This symmetry risks diluting the moral and political critique of TPF, shifting the debate from one about legitimacy to one about regulation. The challenge, therefore, lies in distinguishing between funding as a vehicle of access and funding as a vehicle of speculation. Without a coherent framework to make that distinction, the normalization of TPF for State respondents could inadvertently legitimize the very dynamics that have drawn criticism — transforming what was once viewed as an instrument of imbalance into a universally sanctioned market for sovereign disputes.

And indeed, funders face reputational challenges of their own. While claimant-side funding is increasingly normalized, funders who back sovereign respondents risk being portrayed as politicizing disputes or profiting from State sovereignty. This is especially sensitive in the context of investment arbitration's ongoing legitimacy crisis.

In addition, one can raise concerns about the terms of funding agreements themselves. Critics argue that some arrangements verge on usury, with funders demanding returns of 30 to 50 percent of any award or multiples of three to four times the capital invested.[30]) For a State respondent that wins a counterclaim, the optics of handing over a large share of recovered damages to a private financier can be politically explosive. This raises the broader ethical concern of whether access to justice is being provided on fair terms, or whether funders are exploiting vulnerable States in desperate financial straits.

More broadly still, the rise of TPF in ISDS feeds into anxieties about the commoditization of justice. By turning disputes into financial assets, subject to investment analysis and portfolio diversification, there is a risk that justice

[30]) David Gaukrodger, *Third-Party Funding in International Investor-State Arbitration* (ASIL Insights Vol. 22, Issue 16, 2022), online: American Society of International Law https://www.asil.org/insights/volume/22/issue/16/third-party-funding-international-investor-state-arbitration.

itself is reframed as a tradable commodity. For claimants, this has already sparked debate about whether funders encourage speculative litigation.[31]) For States, the danger is that sovereignty disputes – questions of public interest regulation, human rights, and environmental stewardship – may be reduced to profit opportunities for external financiers. This commodification risks undermining the legitimacy of ISDS even further, reinforcing perceptions that the system serves private capital rather than balancing the interests of States and investors.

Taken together, these challenges explain why, despite the theoretical appeal of TPF as a tool for empowering host States, actual practice has remained heavily skewed toward claimant-side financing. Overcoming these obstacles would likely require legal reforms in both international and domestic frameworks, including clearer treaty provisions on funding, explicit carve-outs from procurement rules, and enhanced transparency measures to mitigate political concerns. Even if such reforms were enacted, the deeper question would persist: can justice in sovereign disputes ever be reconciled with a model that treats litigation as a financial asset to be traded and leveraged?

## V. Creating New Balances or New Risks?

The emergence of third-party funding (TPF) in investment arbitration has sparked a fundamental debate about whether it can serve as a corrective to the systemic asymmetries of ISDS or whether it merely multiplies the risks facing already vulnerable actors. At the heart of this tension lies the question of counterclaims. For States, particularly impoverished host States, counterclaims represent one of the few mechanisms by which they can move beyond a defensive posture and hold investors accountable for misconduct. If TPF could make such counterclaims financially viable, it would constitute a powerful rebalancing tool in a system long criticized for privileging investors.

On one level, the enabling potential of TPF is evident. By underwriting the high costs of arbitral proceedings – expert witnesses, tribunal fees, enforcement actions – funders could make it possible for resource-constrained States to pursue environmental, human rights, or anti-corruption counterclaims that would otherwise remain dormant. The jurisprudence of cases such as *Burlington v. Ecuador* and *Perenco v. Ecuador*, where counterclaims yielded substantial damages for environmental harm, shows that the financial stakes of such actions can be considerable. If external financing were available, impoverished States might be empowered to transform counterclaims from a theoretical possibility into a practical tool of accountability. In this sense, TPF holds out

[31]) Patrick Greenfield & Phoebe Weston, *Revealed: How Wall Street Is Making Millions Betting Against Green Laws* (The Guardian, March 5, 2025), online: The Guardian https://www.theguardian.com/environment/2025/mar/05/revealed-how-wall-street-is-making-millions-betting-against-green-laws-isds-aoe.

the promise of leveling the playing field: just as it has allowed claimants with limited means to challenge powerful States, it could enable weak States to confront powerful investors.

Yet, the risks are equally compelling. The involvement of funders in sovereign disputes raises thorny questions of legitimacy and control. Funding agreements are often permissible to grant financiers significant influence over litigation strategy, including decisions on settlement or withdrawal. If a funder, motivated by return on investment, pushes a State to litigate aggressively or to reject reasonable settlement offers, the result may be an erosion of sovereign autonomy. Far from rebalancing the system, TPF could entrench new dependencies, replacing financial vulnerability to investors with vulnerability to financiers.

The political optics are especially troubling. An impoverished State that secures a major award through a counterclaim but is then compelled to transfer a large portion of that recovery to a private funder risk appearing to have "sold off" its sovereignty. Domestic constituencies may view this as exploitative or illegitimate, particularly where funding agreements are opaque, and the returns resemble usurious profit margins. In this respect, TPF risks worsening the legitimacy crisis of ISDS by reinforcing the perception that disputes are no longer about justice or regulation but about monetizing sovereign conflict.

Beyond optics, structural risks abound. The commoditization of justice is perhaps the deepest concern: when litigation is treated as a financial asset, the substantive public interests at stake in ISDS, such as health, environment, human rights, economic development, risk being subordinated to the logic of profit. Moreover, enforcement asymmetries make funders cautious about backing counterclaims. Unlike investors, States cannot easily enforce awards across borders; investors may have fewer attachable assets or may restructure holdings to evade liability. This asymmetry means that funders may only support counterclaims in rare cases with exceptionally strong prospects of recovery, leaving the broader promise of funding as an equalizer unfulfilled.

The dilemma, then, is stark. On the one hand, TPF offers a pathway to empowerment, giving impoverished host States the resources to assert counterclaims that would otherwise be unattainable. On the other, it risks introducing new vulnerabilities, exposing States to accusations of commodifying justice, undermining political legitimacy, and surrendering strategic control to private financiers.

Whether TPF ultimately functions as an enabler or a destabilizer will depend heavily on how the legal and institutional frameworks evolve. Robust disclosure requirements, procurement law adaptations, safeguards against exploitative terms, and clearer treaty bases for counterclaims could tilt the balance toward empowerment. Absent such reforms, however, TPF may simply deepen the contradictions of a system already struggling with questions of fairness and legitimacy.

# VI. Conclusion

The evolution of third-party funding (TPF) in investment arbitration illustrates both the resilience and fragility of the ISDS system.

On the one hand, TPF has become a normalized tool to expand access to justice, enabling parties who could not otherwise bear the heavy costs of arbitration to bring their claims. On the other, its application to state counterclaims remains deeply uncertain.

The caselaw has demonstrated that counterclaims are possible in principle, and new-generation treaties increasingly create legal space for them, but the practical obstacles, from treaty asymmetry to enforcement challenges, remain formidable.

For less developed host States, these dynamics cut both ways. TPF could represent a new avenue for accountability, allowing States to pursue damages against investors for environmental degradation, corruption, or violations of domestic law. At the same time, reliance on external financiers' risks creating new dependencies, exposing States to exploitative terms, political backlash, and the perception that sovereignty has been commodified. The very features that make TPF attractive, such as its ability to underwrite expensive proceedings and assume litigation risk, are the same features that raise concerns about control, legitimacy, and the subordination of justice to profit.

The future trajectory of TPF in ISDS will depend on whether institutional and treaty reforms can channel its use toward genuine rebalancing rather than exploitation. Stronger disclosure obligations, adaptations of public procurement rules, safeguards against usurious terms, and clearer treaty provisions imposing investor obligations could tilt the balance toward enabling States to use counterclaims effectively. Without such reforms, however, the involvement of commercial funders may exacerbate rather than alleviate the asymmetries of ISDS, deepening the system's legitimacy crisis.

In this light, the question posed at the outset – whether third-party funding enables counterclaims or creates new risks – admits of no simple answer. It is both. TPF holds out the promise of empowering host States, particularly those with limited resources, to move beyond a purely defensive role. Yet, it also threatens to entrench new forms of dependency and commodification.

The challenge for policymakers, arbitrators, and treaty drafters is to ensure that TPF evolves not as another instrument of imbalance, but as a mechanism that contributes to a fairer and more sustainable framework for resolving disputes between investors and States.

# The Exclusion of Protection for Fossil Fuel Investments under the Modernized ECT and in the Event of Withdrawal from the ECT

## Should EU States Remain Parties to the ECT or Withdraw?

*Johannes Tropper*

## I. Introduction

In December 2024, the Energy Charter Conference adopted amendments[1]) to modernize the Energy Charter Treaty (ECT),[2]) following a process initiated in 2017 that culminated in an agreement in principle in June 2022.[3]) The ECT is a sectoral trade and investment agreement which was concluded in 1994 and entered into force in 1998. It includes investment protection standards for foreign investors from other contracting parties of the ECT and access to international arbitration. Critics have argued that investment agreements in general, and the ECT in particular, hinder regulatory action against fossil fuel-based energy producers, as investment arbitration may lead to damages awards for alleged breaches of treaty protections.[4]) Thus, the modernization of the ECT aimed, *inter alia,* to align the ECT's investment protection regime with the Paris Agreement[5]) and to support the clean energy

---

[1]) Energy Charter Conference, *Decision on Amendments to the Energy Charter Treaty*, CCDEC 2024 12 GEN (3 December 2024): https://www.energycharter.org/fileadmin/DocumentsMedia/CCDECS/2024/CCDEC202412_EN.pdf.

[2]) Energy Charter Treaty (Annex I of the Final Act of the European Energy Charter Conference), 17 December 1994, 2080 U.N.T.S. 95 [hereinafter: ECT].

[3]) Agreement in Principle on the Modernisation of the Energy Charter Treaty, CC 750 Rev (24 June 2022): https://www.bilaterals.org/IMG/pdf/reformed_ect_text.pdf [hereinafter: Amended ECT].

[4]) *See, e.g.,* Kyla Tienhaara & Lorenzo Cotula, *Raising the Cost of Climate action? Investor-State Dispute Settlement and Compensation for Stranded Fossil Fuel Assets*, IIED (September 2020), https://pubs.iied.org/sites/default/files/pdfs/migrate/17660IIED.pdf (last visited 24 October 2025). *See also* Clémentine Baldon & Rosanne Craveia, *Overview of Recent Fossil Fuel Arbitration Cases Under the Energy Charter Treaty*, IISD (27 January 2025), https://www.iisd.org/itn/2025/01/27/overview-recent-fossil-fuel-arbitration-cases-under-energy-charter-treaty-clementine-baldon-rosanne-craveia/ (last visited 24 October 2025).

[5]) Paris Agreement, 12 December 2015, 3156 U.N.T.S. 79.

transition. The European Union (EU) was the main driver of the modernization[6]) of the ECT and also proposed a (gradual) exclusion of investment protection for fossil fuel-based investments, including energy production.[7]) A carve-out for fossil fuel-based investments for all contracting parties was not supported by the other contracting parties to the ECT. Instead, the modernized ECT introduces what the ECT Secretariat and the contracting parties call a "flexibility mechanism"[8]) in Annex NI ("Non-Applicable Energy Materials and Products for Definitions of 'Economic Activity in the Energy Sector'") to the ECT.[9]) This allows states to phase out protection for fossil fuel investments on the basis of a decision of the Energy Charter Conference, *i.e.*, meeting of all contracting parties to the ECT.[10])

Nonetheless, dissatisfaction with the modernization process after the conclusion of the agreement in principle led many EU member states to withdraw from the ECT, arguing that the envisaged reforms fell short of expectations.[11]) These states also blocked the EU from voting in favor of modernization in the Energy Charter Conference scheduled to take place in November 2022,[12]) delaying its adoption until December 2024 after a compromise had been

[6]) *See, e.g.*, Johannes Tropper & Kilian Wagner, *The European Union Proposal for the Modernisation of the Energy Charter Treaty – A Model for Climate-Friendly Investment Treaties?*, 23(4-6) J. World Invest. & Trade 813 (2022).

[7]) European Union Text Proposal for the Modernisation of the Energy Charter Treaty, Additional Submission (2021), https://energy.ec.europa.eu/system/files/2021-02/eu_submission_-_revised_definition_of_economic_activity_in_the_energy_sector_0.pdf (last visited 24 October 2025).

[8]) Energy Charter Conference, *Public Communication explaining the main changes contained in the agreement in principle*, CCDEC 2022 10 GEN (24 June 2022): https://www.energycharter.org/fileadmin/DocumentsMedia/CCDECS/2022/CCDEC202210.pdf.

[9]) Energy Charter Conference, *Decision on Modifications and Changes to Annexes to the Energy Charter Treaty*, CCDEC 2024 13 GEN (3 December 2024): https://www.energycharter.org/fileadmin/DocumentsMedia/CCDECS/2024/CCDEC202413_EN.pdf.

[10]) ECT Art. 34.

[11]) *See, e.g.*, Arthur Neslen, *France becomes latest country to leave controversial energy charter treaty*, The Guardian (21 October 2022), https://www.theguardian.com/world/2022/oct/21/france-becomes-latest-country-to-leave-controversial-energy-charter-treaty (last visited 24 October 2025); Frédéric Simon, *Netherlands follows Spain in quitting Energy Charter Treaty*, Euractiv (19 October 2022), https://www.euractiv.com/section/eet/news/netherlands-follows-spain-in-quitting-energy-charter-treaty/ (last visited 24 October 2025).

[12]) Frédéric Simon, *Brussels calls for pause in ECT reform talks after losing key EU vote*, Euractiv (21 November 2022), https://www.euractiv.com/section/energy/news/brussels-calls-for-pause-in-ect-reform-talks-after-losing-key-eu-vote/ (last visited 24 October 2025).

reached in May 2024.[13]) The compromise among EU member states was that the EU, as a contracting party to the ECT in its own right, would withdraw,[14]) as would the European Atomic Energy Community (Euratom),[15]) while those member states wishing to remain parties would retain the right to vote in favor of the modernization.[16])

Continued membership in the ECT implies that EU member states will benefit from the phase-out mechanism for fossil fuel investments but remain otherwise bound by the ECT. By contrast, withdrawal from the ECT eliminates protection for all investments once it takes effect, although the so-called sunset clause of the treaty extends protections for existing investments – including fossil fuels – for 20 years under the unreformed ECT. To mitigate this, the EU has adopted what can be characterized as an *inter se* agreement among its member states to exclude the application of the sunset clause in intra-EU disputes.[17]) This agreement still needs to be ratified by the member states and enter into force, but it could arguably eliminate access to investment arbitration in intra-EU relations (for investors operating in fossil fuel-based energy production).

Against this backdrop, this paper compares continued membership under the modernized ECT (II.) with the applicable rules on withdrawal and the EU's *inter se* agreement (III.) to assess which approach more effectively excludes fossil fuel investments from protection under the ECT. The paper concludes with a brief comparative assessment of the risks associated with both amending the ECT and withdrawing from the ECT (IV.). The conclusion also argues that, in some respects, the broader debate on modernization or withdrawal is incomplete if the objective is to remove protection for fossil fuel investors, as

---

[13]) Council of the EU, *Press release: Energy Charter Treaty: EU notifies its withdrawal* (27 June 2024), https://www.consilium.europa.eu/en/press/press-releases/2024/06/27/energy-charter-treaty-eu-notifies-its-withdrawal/#:~:text=With%20the%20two%20decisions%20adopted,over%20continued%20fossil%20fuel%20investments (last visited 24 October 2025).

[14]) Council Decision (EU) 2024/1638 of 30 May 2024 on the withdrawal of the Union from the Energy Charter Treaty, 2024 O.J. (L 1638), 5 June 2024.

[15]) Council Decision (EU) 2024/1677 of 30 May 2024 on the approval of the withdrawal of the European Atomic Energy Community from the Energy Charter Treaty, 2024 O.J. (L 1677), 13 June 2024.

[16]) Council Decision (EU) 2024/1644 of 30 May 2024 on the position to be taken on behalf of the European Union in the Energy Charter Conference, 2024 O.J. (L 1644), 6 June 2024; Council Decision (Euratom) 2024/1645 of 30 May 2024 on the position to be taken on behalf of Euratom in the Energy Charter Conference, 2024 O.J. (L 1645), 6 June 2024.

[17]) Decision (EU) 2025/1904 of the European Parliament and of the Council of 10 September 2025 on the approval by the Union of the Agreement on the interpretation and application of the Energy Charter Treaty, 2025 O.J. L, 2025/1904, 19 September 2025 [hereinafter: *Inter se* agreement].

numerous bilateral investment treaties continue to coexist with the ECT in extra-EU relations.

## II. Excluding Protection of Fossil Fuel Investments by Changing an Annex

This section outlines how the modernized ECT gradually removes protection for certain fossil fuel-based investments with respect to specific contracting parties. It begins with a general overview of how amendments to Annex NI of the ECT are connected to the protective scope of the investment provisions (A.). Subsequently, it addresses the exclusion of protection for new fossil fuel-based investments set out in Section B of Annex NI (B.) and the phase-out for existing fossil fuel-based investments set out in Section C of Annex NI (C.).

### A. Annex NI and the Link to "Investments" in the ECT

The modernized ECT only partially eliminates investment protection for fossil fuel-based investments. Contrary to the original proposal by the EU, fossil fuel investments are not excluded from the ECT for all contracting parties. Instead, certain contracting parties can remove the protection of fossil fuel-based investments within their territories through Annex NI[18]) of the ECT. The EU, the UK and Switzerland have done so. The latter opted for the narrowest exclusion, essentially limited to the making of new investments in the hydrocarbon sector after 5 September 2025. The UK's exclusion was wider but since the UK withdrew from the ECT the changes to the Annex concerning the UK's fossil fuel investments are without effect. In contrast, for EU member states which still remain party to the ECT, the changes in the Annex take effect.

Changes to the annexes of the ECT must be made by the Energy Charter Conference which includes all contracting parties to the ECT (currently 40 states).[19]) Its decisions are taken by unanimity,[20]) thus all Contracting Parties had to approve the elimination of protection of fossil fuel investments for those states wanting to remove such protection within their territories. However, in contrast to amending the treaty provisions, changes to the annexes do not normally have to follow the ratification procedure foreseen for amend-

[18]) *Decision on Modifications and Changes to Annexes, supra* note 9.

[19]) Of these 40 states, one (Lithuania) already notified its withdrawal and Romania and Ireland expressed an intention to notify a withdrawal from the ECT as well.

[20]) ECT Art. 36(1).

ments of the treaty.[21]) Accordingly, changes to an annex can generally be made more swiftly than changes to the text of the ECT. This is particularly relevant because the contracting parties have committed to reviewing Annex NI in the future and making further changes if necessary.[22])

Annex NI excludes investment protection for fossil fuel-based investments, as it is indirectly connected to the definition of "investment", which constitutes the object of protection under various standards of treatment in the ECT, such as the expropriation clause. Generally, both the old ECT[23]) and the modernized ECT[24]) provide for a relatively broad definition of "investment". However, only those investments are protected that are "associated with an Economic Activity in the Energy Sector".[25]) The term "Economic Activity in the Energy Sector" is linked – both under the old ECT[26]) as well as under the modernized ECT[27]) – to the term "Energy Materials and Products except those included in Annex NI". Thus, the ECT provides that certain activities related to energy materials and products, such as their extraction and distribution, qualify as economic activities, unless these energy materials and products are explicitly excluded in the Annex NI. In addition, "Energy Materials and Products" are defined as "items included in Annexes EM I or EM II". Thus, Annex EM I and Annex NI must be read together in order to determine which specific materials are indeed

[21]) Compare ECT Art. 34(3)(m) and Art. 36(1)(d) with Art. 34(3)(l), Art. 42(2), 36(1)(a) and Art. 42(2).

[22]) *Public Communication*, *supra* note 8.

[23]) ECT Art. 1(6) ("'Investment' means every kind of asset, owned or controlled directly or indirectly by an Investor and includes: a. tangible and intangible, and movable and immovable, property, and any property rights such as leases, mortgages, liens, and pledges; b. a company or business enterprise, or shares, stock, or other forms of equity participation in a company or business enterprise, and bonds and other debt of a company or business enterprise; c. claims to money and claims to performance pursuant to contract having an economic value and associated with an Investment; d. Intellectual Property; e. Returns; f. any right conferred by law or contract or by virtue of any licences and permits granted pursuant to law to undertake any Economic Activity in the Energy Sector. […]").

[24]) The amendment to ECT Art. 1(6) primarily clarifies that the investment is protected if it "is made or acquired in accordance with the applicable law in the Host Contracting Party and that has the characteristics of an investment, such as the commitment of capital or other resources, the expectation of gain or profit, certain duration or the assumption of risk".

[25]) ECT Art. 1(6), *see also* amendment to ECT Art. 1(6) ("'Investment' refers to assets associated with an Economic Activity in the Energy Sector").

[26]) ECT Art. 1(5) ("'Economic Activity in the Energy Sector' means an economic activity concerning the exploration, extraction, refining, production, storage, land transport, transmission, distribution, trade, marketing, or sale of Energy Materials and Products except those included in Annex NI, or concerning the distribution of heat to multiple premises.").

[27]) Amended ECT Art. 1(5).

excluded in Annex NI because the Annex NI refers to the subheadings in Annex EM I.

## B. The Exclusion of Protection for New Fossil Fuel-Based Investments

Specifically, Section A of Annex NI excludes energy materials, such as fuel wood and wood charcoal, from the scope of the ECT for all contracting parties. Apart from the addition of the new heading (Section A), there is nothing new about the exclusion of these materials from the scope of the ECT.

In contrast, Section B introduces the exclusion of certain energy materials for the EU, Switzerland, and the United Kingdom as of 3 September 2025. Any investments made on or after that date in relation to these materials will only be protected to the extent provided in the Annex. Türkiye, Switzerland, and Japan have introduced a reciprocal carve-out for investors from the EU, Switzerland, and the United Kingdom. This measure denies access to arbitration or protection to investments in energy materials that the latter three parties have excluded from ECT protection (see Section B(4) of Annex NI and Annex NPT and IA-NI).

Importantly, the modernized ECT, *i.e.*, the amendments to old ECT, only enter into force upon ratification by three-fourths of the contracting parties.[28]) In order to facilitate a more rapid implementation, the parties agreed to provisionally apply the treaty amendments as of 3 September 2025.[29]) As of that date, the amendments to the text of the ECT are being provisionally applied by all contracting parties,[30]) except those which have opted out from provisional application.[31]) Initially, ten states opted out from provisional application of the amendments,[32]) namely the Netherlands,[33]) the Czech Republic, Latvia, Finland, Liechtenstein, Switzerland, Belgium, Lithuania,

[28]) ECT Art. 42(4).

[29]) Energy Charter Conference, *Decision on Entry into Force and Provisional Application of Amendments to the Energy Charter Treaty and Changes and Modifications to its Annexes*, CCDEC 2024 15 GEN (3 December 2024): https://www.energycharter.org/fileadmin/DocumentsMedia/CCDECS/2024/CCDEC202415_EN.pdf.

[30]) Sec 2, *ibid.*

[31]) Sec 3, *ibid.*

[32]) *See* Lisa Bohmer, *[Updated] Netherlands, Czech Republic, Latvia, Finland, Liechtenstein, Switzerland, Belgium, Lithuania, Japan and Estonia decline provisional application of modernized ECT*, IAReporter (28 February 2025), https://www.iareporter.com/articles/finland-declines-provisional-application-of-modernized-ect/ (last visited 24 October 2025).

[33]) The notification by the Netherlands was in fact not necessary as its withdrawal from the ECT became effective in June 2025.

Japan and Estonia. In August 2025, two more states, Austria[34]) and Romania,[35]) notified the ECT Secretariat that they could not provisionally apply the amendments.

In contrast to the treaty amendments, the changes to Section B of Annex NI automatically entered into force on 3 September 2025.[36]) Thus, irrespective of whether and when the "modernization"-amendments enter into force or are provisionally applied, certain newly made fossil fuel-based investments will no longer be protected in EU states that remain party to the ECT.

In the territory of an EU member state party to the ECT, any newly made investment in connection with coal, natural gas, petroleum and petroleum products, as well as electrical energy produced from them no longer qualifies as a protected investment.[37]) In addition, hydrogen, with the exception of low carbon hydrogen and renewable hydrogen, will no longer be protected in the EU under the ECT.[38]) The EU also excludes synthetic fuels except low carbon fuels.[39]) Finally, all "[e]conomic activities concerning the capture, utilisation and storage of carbon dioxide",[40]) in other words carbon capture and storage, are excluded from the protective scope of the ECT in the EU.

However, the Annex provides for additional exceptions in Section B(1)(b), which essentially allow for maintaining protection for investments in the production of electrical energy from petroleum gases and hydrocarbons through power plants and infrastructure that can also be used for renewable or low-carbon gases, provided that the electricity generated from fossil fuel gases has a carbon intensity below 380 grams of $CO_2$ per kilowatt-hour (kWh). If

---

[34]) Energy Charter Secretariat, *Communication from the Republic of Austria in relation to Paragraph 2 of the Energy Charter Conference Decision CCDEC 2024 15 GEN* (1 September 2025), https://www.energycharter.org/media/news/article/communication-from-the-republic-of-austria-in-relation-to-paragraph-2-of-the-energy-charter-conferen/?tx_news_pi1%5Bcontroller%5D=News&tx_news_pi1%5Baction%5D=detail&cHash=2fc1ab15477440f6b2500ea9f85f605e.

[35]) Energy Charter Secretariat, *Communication from Romania in relation to Paragraph 2 of the Energy Charter Conference Decision CCDEC 2024 15 GEN* (26 September 2025), https://www.energycharter.org/media/news/article/communication-from-romania-in-relation-to-paragraph-2-of-the-energy-charter-conference-decision-ccde/?tx_news_pi1%5Bcontroller%5D=News&tx_news_pi1%5Baction%5D=detail&cHash=44a0e1ff92132f713dc671ec1acd4ce0.

[36]) Sec 1(b)(i), *Decision on Entry into Force and Provisional Application of Amendments to the Energy Charter Treaty and Changes and Modifications to its Annexes*, *supra* note 29.

[37]) Sec B(1)(a)(i) *Decision on Modifications and Changes to Annexes*, *supra* note 9.

[38]) Sec B(1)(a)(ii), *ibid.* Low carbon hydrogen is defined as "hydrogen produced from non-renewable sources, with significantly reduced full life-cycle emissions resulting in less than 3tCO2eq/tH2". Renewable hydrogen is "hydrogen produced from renewable sources, with the exception of biomass, resulting in full life-cycle emissions of less than 3tCO2eq/tH2".

[39]) Sec B(1)(a)(iii), *ibid.*

[40]) Sec B(1)(a)(iv), *ibid.*

these requirements are fulfilled, the cut-off date for protection of investments in production of electricity in such manner will be 31 December 2030.[41]) A slightly longer transition period (September 2035) applies if these investments replace electrical energy production based on coal and petroleum oil.[42]) In addition, investments in the transport of "petroleum gases and other gaseous hydrocarbons [...] through pipelines, provided that the pipelines are able to transport safe and sustainable renewable and low carbon gases, including hydrogen"[43]) will only lose protection after September 2035. In comparison to the EU, Switzerland only excludes protection for new investments in relation to hydrogen or synthetic fuels.[44])

The various transitional periods for newly made investments in the fossil fuel energy sector render the phase-out mechanism relatively complex, leaving certain gaps to a quick exit from protection for fossil fuel investments. Nonetheless, they eliminate the protection of most newly made investments in the fossil fuel energy sector as of 3 September 2025 and this covers those forms of energy production that emit the most carbon dioxide. Importantly, the exclusion in Section B of Annex NI has full effect rather than being applied on a provisional basis. It takes effect irrespective of whether the amendments to the ECT are provisionally applied or ever enter into force.

## C. The Exclusion of Protection for Existing Fossil Fuel-Based Investments

The EU has also made use of the possibility to phase out protection for existing fossil fuel-based investments under the ECT, *i.e.*, investments made before 3 September 2025. The UK would have made use of a similar mechanism,

---

[41]) Sec B(1)(b)(i), *ibid.* ("Electrical energy (subheading 27.16) produced from petroleum gases and other gaseous hydrocarbons (subheading 27.11) through power plants and infrastructures enabling the use of renewable and low carbon gases, and emitting less than 380 g of CO2 of fossil fuel origin per kWh of electricity, shall be excluded from the definition of Economic Activity in the Energy Sector only in respect of Part III of this Treaty after 31 December 2030.")

[42]) Sec B(1)(b)(ii), *ibid.* ("Electrical energy (subheading 27.16) produced from petroleum gases and other gaseous hydrocarbons (subheading 27.11) through power plants and infrastructures enabling the use of renewable and low carbon gases, and emitting less than 380 g of CO2 of fossil fuel origin per kWh of electricity, related to investments that replace existing investments producing electrical energy (subheading 27.16) from Energy Materials and Products under the subheadings 27.01 to 27.10, shall be excluded from the definition of Economic Activity in the Energy Sector only in respect of Part III of this Treaty ten years after the date of entry into force of the modifications in Section B of this Annex approved on 3 December 2024."). As Section B enters into force on 3 September 2025, ten years means 4 September 2035.

[43]) Sec B(1)(b)(iii), *ibid.*

[44]) Sec B(2), *ibid.*

while Switzerland opted against it. Under Section C of the Annex, investments made before 3 September 2025 in relation to the energy materials listed in Section B(1)(a) will lose protection under the ECT "ten years after the date of entry into force of the modifications in Section C of this Annex approved on 3 December 2024 but no later than 31 December 2040".[45])

Notably, the phase-out mechanism of Section C only applies to those energy materials listed in Section B(1)(a), *i.e.*, coal, natural gas, petroleum, etc. The additional exceptions for the production of electrical energy from petroleum gases and hydrocarbons using certain power plants, for which specific timelines are listed in Section B(1)(b), are not covered. The wording in section B(1)(b) seems to suggest that any newly made investments as well as existing investments with respect to such energy production would lose protection at the same time, namely 2030[46]) and 2035[47]) respectively. Provided that this reading of Section B(1)(b) is correct, a more radical phase-out mechanism appears to exist for some of the already existing investments in the production of electrical energy based on petroleum gases and hydrocarbons than for those based on petroleum and coal. The only other plausible interpretation of Section B(1)(b) – which, however, does not seem to be supported by the text of the Annex – would imply that no phase-out applies at all to the production of electrical energy from petroleum gases and hydrocarbons under certain circumstances.

In any event, the ten-year phase-out period under Section C starts to run when Section C enters into force and its entry into force is tied to the entry into force of the amendments of the ECT. Thus, unlike the changes to Section A and B, the phase-out period under Section C does not start to run automatically on 3 September 2025. Provisional application seems to be a substitute for full entry into force.[48]) However, for the states that have opted out from provisional application, the modifications in Section C will also not apply on a provisional basis. Thus, different cut-off dates for the protection of existing investments may apply, depending on when provisional application or entry into force has commenced between the contracting parties. For instance, Hungary and Jordan have not opted out from provisional application. Thus, the ten-year period for Jordanian investors having hypothetically made investments in the Hungarian petroleum sector would normally have started to run on 3 September 2025. In comparison, Japan has notified that it would not provisionally apply the changes. Thus, the ten-year period would only start in relation to Hungary as soon as Japan notifies its provisional application or if the amend-

[45]) Sec C(1), *ibid.*

[46]) *See supra* note 41.

[47]) *See supra* note 42.

[48]) Sec 2, *Decision on Entry into Force and Provisional Application of Amendments to the Energy Charter Treaty and Changes and Modifications to its Annexes, supra* note 29.

ments entered into force and Japan also ratified the amendments so that they entered into force for Japan as well. As this may take some years, the explicitly mentioned cut-off date of "no later than 31 December 2040" might be triggered in relation to investors from such states that do not provisionally apply or ratify the modernized ECT or do so relatively late.

## III. The EU's *inter se* Agreement to Exclude Access to Investment Arbitration Under the ECT

Despite the fact that modernized ECT adopted many aspects of the EU proposal,[49]) EU member states were dissatisfied with the modernized ECT and started withdrawing from the ECT.[50]) Apart from Italy, which had already notified its withdrawal on 31 December 2014, no other contracting party to the ECT had withdrawn before. The first EU member to start the wave of withdrawals was France, which notified its withdrawal on 7 December 2022 and whose withdrawal became effective on 8 December 2023. This was followed by Germany (effective on 20 December 2023), Poland (effective on 29 December 2023), Luxembourg (effective on 17 June 2024), Slovenia (effective on 14 October 2024), Portugal (effective on 2 February 2025), Spain (effective on 17 April 2025), the Netherlands (effective on 28 June 2025) and Denmark (effective on 4 September 2025). In addition, the EU and Euratom notified their withdrawals on 27 June 2024, and the withdrawals became effective on 28 June 2025. In August 2025, Lithuania notified its withdrawal, which becomes effective on 8 August 2026. Romania is also preparing to start the withdrawal process.[51]) In addition, the United Kingdom decided to withdraw as well, and its withdrawal became effective on 27 April 2025. It is fairly likely that other EU member states will also decide to withdraw from the ECT, in particular those that have opted out from provisional application of the amendments.

Withdrawal ensures that the withdrawing state is taken out of the investment protection system and thus enhances the regulatory space compared to participation in the modernized ECT. However, while withdrawal from the ECT ends investment protection and access to investment arbitration, including for "fossil fuel investors", withdrawal does not automatically become effective. Instead, there is a one year notice period before withdrawal becomes effective

---

[49]) *See, e.g.*, Johannes Tropper & Kilian Wagner, *Modernisation*, *supra* note 6.

[50]) The notifications of withdrawal, including the dates on which they become effective, are available on the website of the Energy Charter Treaty Secretariat, *see* https://www.energycharter.org/media/all-news/ (last visited 24 October 2025).

[51]) *See* Lisa Bohmer, *Romanian Government decides to withdraw from Energy Charter Treaty*, IAReporter (23 October 2024), https://www.iareporter.com/articles/romanian-government-decides-to-withdraw-from-energy-charter-treaty/ (last visited 24 October 2025).

(Article 47(2) ECT[52])) and like other investment treaties, the ECT contains a so-called sunset clause providing that any investments made prior to withdrawal continue to remain protected under the ECT for another 20 years (Article 47(3) ECT).[53]) Accordingly, any existing fossil fuel investments continue to be protected for 20 years after the withdrawal. For instance, hypothetical investors from Switzerland which have made investments in Germany before 20 December 2023 can continue to institute arbitral proceedings against Germany for alleged breaches of the ECT until 20 December 2043. This poses a risk to regulatory action taken against fossil fuel investments as evinced by pending proceedings against Germany.[54])

In order to militate this problem and due to CJEU's finding that intra-EU investment arbitration under the ECT is incompatible with EU law,[55]) the EU prepared a so-called *inter se* agreement to remove the applicability of investor-state dispute settlement (ISDS) in intra-EU relations, including the applicability of the sunset clause of the ECT. This would incidentally also eliminate access to ISDS for fossil fuel investors from one EU member state intending to bring claims under the ECT against another EU member state.

Generally, a modification of a multilateral treaty between a subset of contracting parties to the treaty is permissible, as laid out in Article 41 of the Vienna Convention on the Law of Treaties (VCLT),[56]) which reflects customary international law.[57]) This implies that the content of a multilateral treaty may

[52]) ECT Art. 47(2) ("Any such withdrawal shall take effect upon the expiry of one year after the date of the receipt of the notification by the Depositary, or on such later date as may be specified in the notification of withdrawal.").

[53]) ECT Art. 47(3) ("The provisions of this Treaty shall continue to apply to Investments made in the Area of a Contracting Party by Investors of other Contracting Parties or in the Area of other Contracting Parties by Investors of that Contracting Party as of the date when that Contracting Party's withdrawal from the Treaty takes effect for a period of 20 years from such date.").

[54]) *See, e.g., Azienda Elettrica Ticinese v. Federal Republic of Germany*, ICSID Case No. ARB/23/47. The investment dispute concerns the Swiss claimant's investment in a coal-fired power plant located in Lünen, which is affected by the German Government's 2020 decision to phase out coal-based energy production, requiring the plant's closure by 2031.

[55]) C-741/19, *République de Moldavie v. Komstroy LLC*, ECLI:EU:C:2021:655, paras. 41–64 (2 September 2021).

[56]) Vienna Convention on the Law of Treaties, 23 May 1969, 1155 U.N.T.S. 331 [hereinafter: VCLT].

[57]) Strictly speaking, the VCLT itself is not applicable, but rather the customary norms reflected in the VCLT because France and Romania have never ratified the VCLT. More precisely, it is the customary norm reflected in Article 41 of the Vienna Convention on the Law of Treaties between States and International Organizations or Between International Organizations (VCLT-IO) which applies because the EU, which is also supposed to be a party to the *inter se* treaty, is not a State. However, this paper simply refers to the VCLT because the customary norms and the provision of the VCLT-IO are identical to Article 41 of the VCLT.

differ between these states which have joined the *inter se* agreement and states that have not. However, there are certain limitations under Article 41 VCLT and further limitations may arise from the ECT itself, as interpreted by arbitral tribunals established under the ECT.

This section briefly discusses the content of the *inter se* agreement of the EU and its qualification as an *inter se* modification under Article 41 VCLT (A.). It subsequently addresses the question of whether Article 16 ECT can be read as an explicit prohibition of an *inter se* modification which excludes investment arbitration and the applicability of the sunset clause in intra-EU relations (B.). Subsequently, it discusses whether the EU's *inter se* agreement can be described as being incompatible with the effective execution of the object and purpose of the treaty as a whole under Article 41(1)(b)(ii) VCLT (C.). Finally, it argues that, provided such *inter se* agreements are lawful, they do not bind other contracting parties to the ECT. Thus, to fully remove the possibility of ISDS claims after withdrawal, the EU would need to negotiate *inter se* agreements with other contracting parties to the ECT (D.).

## A. The EU's *inter se* Agreement

In September 2025, the EU adopted the decision approving the "Agreement on the Interpretation and Application of the Energy Charter Treaty", the *inter se* agreement.[58]) It was signed by the EU and all EU member states, except Hungary. The agreement formalizes the declaration on the legal consequences following from the CJEU's *Komstroy* judgment[59]) on intra-EU arbitration and that declaration was agreed upon between the EU and all EU member states (except Hungary[60])) in June 2024.[61]) The *inter se* agreement is subject to ratification[62]) and enters into force 30 days after the second instrument of ratification is submitted.[63])

[58]) *See supra* note 17.

[59]) C-741/19, *République de Moldavie v. Komstroy LLC*, ECLI:EU:C:2021:655, paras. 41–66 (2 September 2021).

[60]) Hungary issued a separate declaration, *see Declaration of the Representative of the Government of Hungary of 26 June 2024 on the Legal Consequences of the Judgment of the Court of Justice in* Komstroy *and Common Understanding on the Non-Applicability of Article 26 of the Energy Charter Treaty as Basis for Intra-EU Arbitration Proceedings* (26 June 2024), https://perma.cc/NTR9-RLY3.

[61]) *Declaration on the Legal Consequences of the Judgment of the Court of Justice in* Komstroy *and Common Understanding on the Non-Applicability of Article 26 of the Energy Charter Treaty as Basis for Intra-EU Arbitration Proceedings* (26 June 2024), OJ L 2121, https://perma.cc/MN5K-5C5L.

[62]) *Inter se* agreement Art. 5.

[63]) *Inter se* agreement Art. 6(1).

The *inter se* agreement stipulates that

[t]he Contracting Parties hereby reaffirm, for greater certainty, that they share a common understanding on the interpretation and application of the Energy Charter Treaty, according to which Article 26 of that Treaty cannot and never could serve as a legal basis for intra-EU arbitration proceedings.[64])

It also provides that

[t]he Contracting Parties reaffirm, for greater certainty, that they share the common understanding that, as a result of the absence of legal basis for intra-EU arbitration proceedings pursuant to Article 26 of the Energy Charter Treaty, Article 47, paragraph 3, of the Energy Charter Treaty cannot extend, and could not have been extended, to such proceedings. Accordingly, in that respect, Article 47, paragraph 3, of the Energy Charter Treaty cannot have produced any legal effects in intra-EU relations when a Member State withdrew from the Energy Charter Treaty prior to this agreement, nor will it produce any legal effects in intra-EU relations if a Contracting Party withdraws from the Energy Charter Treaty subsequently.[65])

Finally, it clarifies in Article 2(3) that

[f]or greater certainty, the Contracting Parties are in agreement that in accordance with the common understanding expressed in paragraphs 1 and 2, and without prejudice thereto, *Article 26 of the Energy Charter Treaty does not apply as a basis for intra-EU arbitration proceedings and that, in that respect, Article 47, paragraph 3, of the Energy Charter Treaty will not produce legal effects in intra-EU relations.*[66])

The EU and its member states are reluctant to explicitly state that the agreement constitutes an *inter se* modification of the ECT pursuant to Article 41 VCLT, given that such modifications can only operate prospectively. Instead, the *inter se* treaty uses language suggesting that these provisions are clarifications and have a retroactive element ("cannot and never could", "cannot extend, and could not have been extended", "cannot have produced"). This arguably follows from the requirements of EU law and the interpretations of the CJEU, which has taken the view that there was no consent to intra-EU investment arbitration at the time when both the home State of the investor and host state of the investment became parties to the respective intra-EU investment treaty.[67]) As there was never valid consent to intra-EU investment

[64]) *Inter se* agreement Art. 2(1).

[65]) *Inter se* agreement Art. 2(2).

[66]) *Inter se* agreement Art. 2(3) (emphasis added).

[67]) C-638/19 P, *European Commission v. European Food SA and Others*, ECLI:EU:C:2022:50, paras. 144-145 (25 January 2022); *see also* C-284/16, *Slowakische Republik*

arbitration, a prospective removal of consent under international law would be incompatible with these holdings of the CJEU.[68])

However, the italicized part of Article 2(3) quoted above can reasonably be understood as prospective in nature and as amounting to a modification of the ECT from the perspective of international law, since it states that Article 26 ECT "does not apply" and the sunset clause "will not produce legal effects". Thus, the *inter se* agreement at least also includes provisions which are modifications in addition to provisions which are mere clarifications.[69]) Accordingly, the *inter se* agreement should also be qualified as an *inter se* modification pursuant to Article 41 VCLT. The question is whether the envisaged *inter se* modification is permissible or prohibited under Article 41 VCLT, which will be addressed in the next two sections.

## B. The (Im)Permissibility of the *inter se* Modification Pursuant to Article 16 ECT

Article 41(1)(b) VCLT provides that an *inter se* modification is only permissible if "the modification in question is not prohibited by the treaty". The ECT does not contain an explicit prohibition of *inter se* modifications, but it may be questioned whether Article 16 ECT also precludes the type of *inter se* modification proposed by the EU and its member states.

Article 16 ECT provides that:

> [w]here two or more Contracting Parties have entered into a prior international agreement, or enter into a subsequent international agreement, whose terms in either case concern the subject matter of Part III (*i.e.*, Investment Promotion and Protection) or V of this Treaty (*i.e.*, Dispute Settlement),
>
> (1) nothing in Part III or V of this Treaty shall be construed to derogate from any provision of such terms of the other agreement or from any right to dispute resolution with respect thereto under that agreement; and

---

*(Slovak Republic) v. Achmea BV*, ECLI:EU:C:2018:158 (6 March 2018); C-741/19, *République de Moldavie v. Komstroy LLC*, ECLI:EU:C:2021:655, paras. 41–66 (2 September 2021).

68) From the perspective of international law, the retroactive removal of consent is problematic, at least as far as already pending proceedings are concerned, *see VM Solar Jerez GmbH and others v. Kingdom of Spain*, ICSID Case No. ARB/19/30, Decision on Jurisdiction, Liability and Principles of Quantum, paras. 322–323 (14 May 2025).

69) Johannes Tropper, *The* Komstroy *Declarations and the* Inter Se *Treaty on intra-EU Investment Arbitration under the ECT: Entering Unchartered Legal Territory*, 10(1) Eur. Invest. L. & Arb. Rev. 13, 26–27 (2025). *See also* Luca Pantaleo, *The EU's Withdrawal from the Energy Charter Treaty between Treaty Law and International Responsibility Issues*, 26(5) J. World Invest. & Trade 981, 986 (2025).

(2) nothing in such terms of the other agreement shall be construed to derogate from any provision of Part III or V of this Treaty or from any right to dispute resolution with respect thereto under this Treaty,

where any such provision is more favourable to the Investor or Investment.

This section outlines both the arguments in favor (1.) and against the permissibility of an *inter se* modification under Article 16(2) ECT (2.). It ends with an interim conclusion (3.)

### 1. Arguments in favor of the Permissibility of the *inter se* Modification

A reasonable argument can be made that the envisaged *inter se* modification is not affected by Article 16(2) ECT. With respect to Article 16(2) ECT, arbitral tribunals have noted that it is a conflict clause[70]) in case of competing regimes, which provides priority of the investment protection regime under the ECT. It is doubtful that Article 16 ECT, as a conflict clause, would apply to an agreement explicitly modifying the ECT *inter se.*[71]) Arguably, treaties not containing investment standards or investment arbitration, such as the *inter se* treaty, do not have the same subject matter as the ECT. Article 16 ECT applies only in case of conflicts between treaties containing some form of investment provisions or access to arbitration that is either better or worse than the one provided for in the ECT. The EU's modification agreement, however, provides neither worse investment protection standards nor worse alternative access to arbitration, but completely removes access to arbitration and thus does not result in the kind of conflict that Article 16 ECT intends to settle in favor of the ECT.[72]) It might also be argued that the starting point for treaty conflicts is Article 30 VCLT (to which Article 16 ECT is *lex specialis*) and the provision of the VCLT clearly acknowledges that *inter se* agreements are possible.[73]) Finally, to the extent that Article 16 ECT applies, it can be argued that Article 16 ECT only preserves access to arbitration and investment protection standards, not the sunset clause which falls outside of the protective scope of Article 16.[74]) The sunset clause is not found in Part III or Part V of the ECT, but Article 16 ECT only addresses agreements concerning Part III or V of the ECT ("whose terms in either case concern the subject matter of Part III or V of this Treaty"). Thus, even if an *inter se* agreement does not remove consent in intra-EU relations, it could remove the applicability of the ECT and consent to arbitration that

---

[70]) *See, e.g., Vattenfall AB and* Others *v. Federal Republic of Germany (II)*, ICSID Case No. ARB/12/12, Decision on the *Achmea* Issue, paras. 227, 229 (31 August 2018).

[71]) *See, e.g.,* Nikos Braoudakis, Rosanne Craveia & Clémentine Baldon, *Neutralising the ECT Sunset Clause* Inter Se, 39(2) ICSID Rev. 347, 361–362 (2024).

[72]) Tropper, *Inter Se Treaty, supra* note 69, at 33.

[73]) VCLT Art. 30(5) ("without prejudice to article 41").

[74]) Tropper, *Inter Se Treaty, supra* note 69, at 33.

would otherwise remain applicable in the survival period under the sunset clause. This could effectively eliminate the applicability of the ECT in cases where a withdrawal takes place.

## 2. Arguments against the Permissibility of the *inter se* Modification

A counterargument can be made that Article 16 ECT requires the setting aside of any modification agreement that eliminates access to arbitration because "Article 16(2) ECT [...] accords priority to the ECT over less favourable agreements".[75]) For instance, the tribunal in *Landesbank v. Spain* insinuated as much when it held that

> the recent Declaration of Twenty-Two Member States regarding the effects of the *Achmea* Judgment cannot by itself alter the obligations of those States under the ECT even *inter se*. To hold otherwise would be to ignore the effects of Article 16 of the ECT and the clear intention of the Contracting Parties to the ECT that the same text should apply to all Contracting Parties – an intention manifested in their agreement not to permit reservations to the ECT.[76])

Treating Article 16(2) ECT as an obstacle to *inter se* agreements removing access to investment arbitration and the sunset clause may follow from a literal interpretation of Article 16(2) ECT. Article 16 ECT applies to any subsequent agreement which *concerns* the subject matter of investment protection or arbitration. The term "concerns" means "relates to" or "refers to".[77]) A modification agreement that removes access to arbitration necessarily concerns investment arbitration insofar, as it tries to regulate that mechanism by eliminating it.[78]) Such an interpretation does not require strict identity between subject matters and thus extends the scope of application from investment treaties to any treaties that touch upon the investment standards or arbitration. This reading would imply that an *inter se* agreement removing access to intra-EU arbitration is not permissible as it affects Part V of the ECT.

[75]) Pantaleo, *Withdrawal*, *supra* note 69, at 987. *See also* Tibisay Morgandi & Lorand Bartels, *Exiting the Energy Charter Treaty under the Law of Treaties*, 34(1) King's L. J. 145, 158 (2023).

[76]) *Landesbank Baden-Württemberg and others v. Kingdom of Spain*, ICSID Case No. ARB/15/45, Decision on the Intra-EU Jurisdictional Objection, para. 192 (25 February 2019).

[77]) "Concern", Oxford English Dictionary, https://www.oed.com/dictionary/concern_v?tab=meaning_and_use#8642731 (last visited 24 October 2025).

[78]) Stefan Mayr, *How to Put an End to intra-EU investment Arbitration under the Energy Charter Treaty (Fast): Amendment, Withdrawal Modification?*, 30(2) Eur. Foreign Aff. Rev. 223, 242 (2025).

In addition, it might also be argued that an *inter se* removal of the sunset clause is impermissible under Article 16 ECT because it indirectly touches upon the applicability of investment protection and investment arbitration. Article 16 ECT provides that "nothing in such terms of the other agreement shall be construed to derogate from any provision of Part III or V of this Treaty or from any right to dispute resolution with respect thereto under this Treaty". It may be argued that removing the applicability of the sunset clause, which itself is not found in Part III or V, affects "any right to dispute resolution with respect [to Part III or V] under this Treaty". Therefore the sunset clause, which provides that "[t]he provisions of this Treaty shall continue to apply [...] for a period of 20 years [...]", arguably concerns "any right to dispute resolution" under the ECT and thus an *inter se* modification affecting the sunset clause would be contrary to Article 16 ECT.

### 3. Interim Conclusion

In conclusion, reasonable arguments can be made in favor of and against the permissibility of an *inter se* modification in light of Article 16(2) ECT. In the present author's opinion, Article 16(2) ECT was not intended to apply to such an *inter se* modification. Doubts may arise whether this intention can clearly be deduced from the text of Article 16 ECT.[79]) The view that this intention does not follow Article 16 ECT is certainly not unreasonable. Accordingly, it would have been advisable to remove Article 16 ECT in intra-EU relations through the EU *inter se* agreement as well, or at least to clarify that the provision does not apply between EU member states. An explicit *inter se* removal of Article 16 would not have been precluded by Article 16 ECT.[80]) Some arbitral tribunals seem to have suggested this in *obiter dicta*.[81])

[79]) On the irrelevance of presumed intention not reflected in the text, *see, e.g.*, *Wintershall Aktiengesellschaft v. Argentine Republic*, ICSID Case No. ARB/04/14, Award, paras. 78, 87–88 (8 December 2008).

[80]) *See* Braoudakis, Craveia & Baldon, *Neutralising the Sunet Clause*, *supra* note 71, at 363 ("States could therefore expressly override the conflict clause in Article 16 in accordance with the general rule that 'a later expression of intention is to be presumed to prevail over an earlier one'".); Pantaleo, *Withdrawal*, *supra* note 69, at 987. *See*, however, Mayr, *End*, supra note 78, at 243–244. Out of an abundance of caution, the prohibition of reservations in Article 46 ECT, which does not regulate *inter se* agreements, should have also been removed *inter se*, *see* Tropper, *Inter Se Treaty*, *supra* note 69, at 33–35 and 38.

[81]) *See, e.g.*, *RWE Innogy GmbH and RWE Innogy Aersa S.A.U. v. Kingdom of Spain*, ICSID Case No. ARB/14/34, Decision on Jurisdiction, Liability, and Certain Issues of Quantum, para. 341 (30 December 2019).

## C. The (Im)Permissibility of the *inter se* Modification pursuant to Article 41 VCLT

Even if no explicit prohibition can be deduced from the ECT, scholarship and arbitral tribunals have suggested that the envisaged *inter se* modification might be implicitly prohibited as it may "relate to a provision, derogation from which is incompatible with the effective execution of the object and purpose of the treaty as a whole" (Article 41(1)(b)(ii) VCLT). Generally, the threshold for such an implicit prohibition is very high, as it requires not merely incompatibility with the object and purpose of the treaty, but incompatibility with the effective execution of the treaty as a whole.

This section outlines both the arguments in favor (1.) and against the permissibility of an *inter se* modification under Article 41(1)(b)(ii) VCLT (2.). It ends with an interim conclusion (3.)

### 1. Arguments in favor of the Permissibility of the *inter se* Modification

The International Law Commission (ILC) and scholars have generally suggested that absolute, integral treaties and treaties containing rights *erga omnes partes* cannot (easily) be modified *inter se*.[82]) For instance, the prohibition of torture in the Convention Against Torture (CAT)[83]) enshrines an absolute, *ius cogens* right and qualifies as an obligation *erga omnes* and *erga omnes partes*. An *inter se* modification to the CAT allowing some states to torture people of their nationality or other states' nationality would clearly not be a permissible *inter se* modification. In contrast, treaties containing bilateral, reciprocal rights should be capable of modification *inter se*. This includes, for instance, the Vienna Convention on Diplomatic Relations and the Vienna Convention on Consular Relations as the obligations contained in this multilateral treaty are typically owed vis-à-vis individual states that have established diplomatic missions in the territory of the other state. It would generally be possible to alter the specific rules in their mutual relations. The ECT has been described as a treaty containing bilateral rights or constituting

---

[82]) *See, e.g.,* Kerstin von der Decken, *Article 41*, in *Vienna Convention on the Law of Treaties: A Commentary* 777, 783 (Oliver Dörr & Kirsten Schmalenbach eds, 2nd ed. Springer 2018); Anne Rigaux, et al., *1969 Vienna Convention: Article 41 Agreements to modify multilateral treaties between certain of the parties only*, in *The Vienna Conventions on the Law of Treaties: A Commentary* 986, 1003–1004 (Olivier Corten & Pierre Klein eds, Oxford University Press 2011); *see further* ILC, *Fragmentation of International Law: Difficulties Arising from the Diversification and Expansion of International Law*, UN Doc. A/CN.4/L.682 (13 April 2006), para. 312.

[83]) Convention against Torture and Other Cruel, Inhuman or Degrading Treatment or Punishment, 10 December 1984, 1465 U.N.T.S. 85.

a web of bilateral investment treaties,[84]) which would seem to suggest that a modification of rights under the ECT between some states is not incompatible with the effective execution of the object and purpose as a whole.

Even if the ECT were deemed to contain rights of an *erga omnes partes* nature,[85]) it could still be argued that an *inter se* modification is permissible, as the International Court of Justice (ICJ) has accepted the validity of reservations to the dispute settlement clause of the Genocide Convention. The Genocide Convention contains *erga omnes partes* obligations and grants every contracting party the right to invoke breaches of the Convention by another contracting party before the ICJ.[86]) Nonetheless, a reservation to the dispute settlement clause of the Convention was not treated as incompatible with its object and purpose. According to the ICJ, reservations to the dispute settlement clause do not affect substantive obligations but merely exclude a specific form of dispute settlement.[87]) Thus, one might argue that if a reservation to the dispute settlement clause of the Genocide Convention is deemed compatible with the Convention's object and purpose, then an *inter se* modification of the ECT should, *a fortiori*, not be regarded as affecting the effective execution of its object and purpose as a whole.

### 2. Arguments against the Permissibility of the *inter se* Modification

Nevertheless, one may question whether the argument made in the previous subsection truly does justice to the investor-state dispute settlement mechanism and the rights of investors. While investors' rights do not qualify

---

[84]) *See, e.g.*, C-741/19, *République de Moldavie v. Komstroy LLC*, ECLI:EU:C:2021:655, para. 64 (2 September 2021); Michael De Boeck, *EU Law and International Investment Arbitration: The compatibility of ISDS in Bilateral Investment Treaties (BITs) and the Energy Charter Treaty (ECT) with the autonomy of EU law* 93 (Brill Nijhoff 2022).

[85]) *See, e.g.*, *Landesbank Baden-Württemberg and others v. Kingdom of Spain*, ICSID Case No. ARB/15/45, Decision on the Intra-EU Jurisdictional Objection, para. 148 (25 February 2019) ("the ECT, as a multilateral treaty, involves obligations by each Contracting Party towards all other Contracting Parties; it is more than just a network of bilateral relationships and is therefore quite different from a BIT. The nature of the ECT as a single legal instrument in force in the same terms and to the same effect between all its Contracting Parties is reinforced by the fact that reservations to the ECT are expressly prohibited by Article 46 of the ECT").

[86]) *Application of the Convention on the Prevention and Punishment of the Crime of Genocide* (*The Gambia v. Myanmar*), Preliminary Objections, Judgment, I.C.J. Reports 2022, p. 477, para. 108.

[87]) *Armed Activities on the Territory of the Congo (New Application: 2002)* (*Democratic Republic of the Congo v. Rwanda*), Jurisdiction and Admissibility, Judgment, I.C.J. Reports 2006, p. 6, paras. 64–67. *See also Application of the Convention on the Prevention and Punishment of the Crime of Genocide in Sudan* (*Sudan v. United Arab Emirates*) Order, 5 May 2025, paras. 28–33.

as human rights as they are not universal rights and only granted to nationals of one state with respect to another state,[88]) access to arbitration is nonetheless an essential feature. The substantive obligations of the ECT will become practically unenforceable and lose their purpose if investors cannot have access to arbitration. The private party enforcement mechanism distinguishes the ECT from treaties such as the Genocide Convention, which, despite providing protection to individuals, only foresees a state-to-state dispute settlement mechanism. A further distinguishing factor is the explicit prohibition of reservations in the ECT,[89]) which is absent from the Genocide Convention. While the prohibition of reservations under the ECT does not apply to *inter se* modifications,[90]) it may indicate that the ECT should be a unified whole, and not be characterized by different obligations applying between states.[91]) This would suggest that an *inter se* modification removing arbitration and the sunset clause would also be more likely to be contrary to the effective execution of the object and purpose of the treaty as a whole.[92])

Arbitral tribunals have stressed the importance of access to arbitration as a key feature of the ECT which cannot be removed through an *inter se* modification. This view was held in connection with the argument that EU law implicitly results in an *inter se* modification of the ECT. Notably, the tribunal in *Baywa v. Spain* found that

> it is very doubtful whether the abrogation *inter se* of the ECT as between EU Member States is compatible "with the effective execution of the object and purpose of the [ECT] as a whole". Article 16 of the ECT suggests that it is not, since it evinces an intent, even as between treaties on the same subject matter, to preserve the rights of investors and investments, which constitute a major plank of that multilateral treaty.[93])

[88]) *See, e.g.,* De Boeck, *EU Law and International Investment Arbitration*, supra note 84, at 94.

[89]) ECT Art. 46 ("No reservations may be made to this Treaty.").

[90]) Tropper, *Inter Se Treaty, supra* note 69, at 33–35.

[91]) *See also Landesbank Baden-Württemberg and others v. Kingdom of Spain*, ICSID Case No. ARB/15/45, Decision on the Intra-EU Jurisdictional Objection, para. 192 (25 February 2019).

[92]) *See also* the conclusion reached in Philipp Kehl & Sebastian Wuschka, *The Energy Charter Treaty at a Tipping Point – Modernization Efforts, Withdrawal Plans and their Legal Consequences*, 1 ZEuS 59, 73 (2024) ("A removal of the sunset clause among certain states would also remove dispute settlement between them and investors from other EU member states altogether. This cannot be compatible with the effective execution of the ECT's object and purpose").

[93]) *BayWa r.e. renewable energy GmbH and BayWa r.e. Asset Holding GmbH v. Kingdom of Spain*, ICSID Case No. ARB/15/16, Decision on Jurisdiction, Liability and Directions on Quantum para. 276 (2 December 2019).

### 3. Interim Conclusion

There are good arguments that the ECT, containing a bilateral web of investment treaties, can be modified as no implicit prohibition can be deduced from Article 41 VCLT. Also, if it contained *erga omnes partes* obligations, a removal of access to arbitration could still be permissible. However, it appears that arbitral practice is skeptical about *inter se* modifications removing access to arbitration under the ECT, based on an interplay between Article 16 ECT and Article 41 VCLT. Nonetheless, arbitral practice has not addressed an explicit modification agreement of the ECT yet.[94]) Thus, no definitive conclusion can be reached on whether a tribunal would consider the *inter se* modification of the ECT to be incompatible with Article 41 of the VCLT.

## D. The Need for Additional *inter se* Agreements

If *inter se* agreements removing the applicability of the sunset clause are compatible with international law, they can only eliminate the applicability of the sunset clause between those contracting parties to the ECT that have signed up for the respective *inter se* agreements. As follows from Article 34 VCLT,[95]) third states are not bound by a treaty or any other kind of agreement, unless they consent to it. Also, Article 41(1)(b)(i) VCLT provides that an *inter se* modification is only permissible if it "does not affect the enjoyment by the other parties of their rights under the treaty or the performance of their obligations".[96])

This illustrates one of the limitations associated with the withdrawal route. For withdrawal to be fully effective, negotiations are required not only with EU member states, but also with other parties to the ECT. This is because investors from non-EU states could still initiate arbitral proceedings under the treaty's sunset clause. In the absence of *inter se* agreements with non-EU states eliminating the application of the sunset clause, withdrawal still leaves states exposed to claims by fossil fuel investors. These agreements with non-EU states which are contracting parties to the ECT are arguably even more important than the EU *inter se* agreement given the limited possibilities of enforcing intra-EU investment awards and the applicability of state aid law to such

[94]) Apart from *Landesbank v. Spain*, which seemed to reject the *Achmea* Declarations as possible *inter se* agreements, *see supra* note 76. The tribunal in *VM Solar Jerez v. Spain* briefly discussed the draft *inter se* agreement, but with respect to VCLT Art. 31(3)(a), *see VM Solar Jerez GmbH and others v. Kingdom of Spain*, ICSID Case No. ARB/19/30, Decision on Jurisdiction, Liability and Principles of Quantum, paras. 321–323 (14 May 2025).

[95]) VCLT Art. 34 ("A treaty does not create either obligations or rights for a third State without its consent".).

[96]) VCLT Art. 41(1)(b)(i).

investment awards.[97]) Moreover, regulatory measures targeting fossil fuel investments would primarily affect existing investments of companies from other contracting parties, rather than investments made after withdrawal which would not be protected by the ECT any longer.

There is also a risk that investors have restructured their investments in such a manner as to continue to have access to arbitration under the ECT. Corporate restructuring to be subject to an investment treaty (so-called nationality planning) is generally permissible as long as a dispute is not foreseeable.[98]) In contrast to the modernized ECT, the definition of investor in the old ECT does not, in principle, pose a significant obstacle for restructuring to remain protected under the ECT. The old ECT[99]) does not require "substantial business activities"[100]) in the home State for a corporation to qualify as an "investor". Thus, an EU energy company that has restructured its investments in an EU state through the establishment of a letterbox company in another non-EU ECT contracting party prior to withdrawal and the foreseeability of a dispute (*e.g.*, Switzerland, Iceland or Liechtenstein which are in the EEA) could continue to be protected under the sunset clause for 20 years as long as no *inter se* agreement is concluded with these states to eliminate the applicability of the sunset clause.

## IV. Concluding Remarks: To Stay in the Modernized ECT or to Withdraw?

Whether a contracting party opts for withdrawal from the ECT or stays on board with the modernized ECT depends on policy preferences and legal

[97]) *See, e.g., Commission Decision (EU) 2025/1235 of 24 March 2025 on the measure State aid SA.54155 (2021/NN) implemented by Spain – Arbitration award to Antin (notified under document C(2025) 1781)*, 2025 O.J. (L 1235) 25 June 2025.

[98]) *See, e.g., Philip Morris Asia Limited v. The Commonwealth of Australia*, UNCITRAL, PCA Case No. 2012-12, Award on Jurisdiction and Admissibility, para. 554 (17 December 2015) ("the initiation of a treaty-based investor-State arbitration constitutes an abuse of rights (or an abuse of process, the rights abused being procedural in nature) when an investor has changed its corporate structure to gain the protection of an investment treaty at a point in time when a specific dispute was foreseeable. The Tribunal is of the opinion that a dispute is foreseeable when there is a reasonable prospect [...] that a measure which may give rise to a treaty claim will materialise.").

[99]) ECT Art. 1(7).

[100]) Amended ECT Art. 1(7)(i) ("investor means [...] a company or other organisation constituted in accordance with the law applicable in a Contracting Party and with substantial business activities in the Area of that Contracting Party. The existence of substantial business activities should be established by an overall examination, on a case-by-case basis, of the relevant circumstances, which may include whether the enterprise (a) has a physical presence in the Area of that Contracting Party; (b) employs staff in the Area of that Contracting Party; (c) generates turnover in the Area of that Contracting Party; or (d) pays taxes in the Area of that Contracting Party.").

considerations. From the legal point of view there are advantages and disadvantages for both the continued membership and withdrawal.

The advantage of remaining party to the ECT for EU member states is the removal of intra-EU[101]) arbitration in the modernized ECT which will become effective as soon as the amendments of the ECT are being provisionally applied. However, most EU member states have opted out from provisional application. In addition, under the modernized ECT, most fossil fuel investors making investments in the territory of EU member states on or after 3 September 2025 will no longer be protected under the treaty. In this respect, the outcome within the territory of EU member states is effectively the same as if a withdrawal had taken place. A further advantage is a potentially earlier phase-out for most existing fossil fuel investments within ten years after entry into force of modernized ECT. The ten-year phase-out period is notably shorter than the 20-year survival clause provided under the ECT. However, much depends on when the modernized ECT enters into force or when it begins to apply provisionally with respect to a given contracting party. There is a risk that the final cut-off date of 31 December 2040 may apply to certain states that either do not opt for provisional application or fail to ratify the modernized ECT in time. In such cases, the phase-out for existing fossil fuel investments could nearly match the duration envisaged under the ECT's sunset clause.

In contrast, withdrawal leads to a clean slate with respect to the ECT. New fossil fuel investors lose protection one year after the notification of withdrawal, but already existing investments continue to be protected under the sunset clause for another 20 years. However, to the extent that the *inter se* agreement among EU member states, which is intended to eliminate the sunset clause, is effective, its application is limited to intra-EU relations. For extra-EU relations, the sunset clause and the associated full protection for existing fossil fuel investors remain in effect for the entire 20-year period following withdrawal from the treaty. Accordingly, the phase-out for existing fossil fuel investments through withdrawal from the ECT will be slower than under the modernized ECT, unless the EU member states manage to negotiate *inter se* agreements with these non-EU contracting parties to the ECT.

Both modernization and withdrawal in conjunction with the *inter se* agreement result in the non-application of the ECT in intra-EU proceedings. The real issue of modernization, therefore, concerns only extra-EU relations raising the question whether withdrawal is indeed more effective from a climate policy perspective. The assertion that withdrawal should facilitate the clean energy transition is certainly at odds with the reality that fossil fuel investors with existing investments could be protected for a longer period under the withdrawal framework than under the phase-out mechanism in Section C of Annex NI. The worst case scenario under the modernized ECT, the final cut-off date of 2040 in the ECT, would still end protection three years

[101]) Amended ECT Art. 24(3).

earlier than the survival period applicable to France, which initiated the current wave of withdrawals by submitting its notification of withdrawal on 7 December 2022.

Nonetheless, it should be noted that irrespective of whether an EU state remains party to the modernized ECT or withdraws, many extra-EU BITs remain in force with non-EU contracting parties to the ECT. Claims may be brought by fossil fuel investors under these BITs irrespective of what happens with respect to the ECT and EU investors may continue to start proceedings against non-EU contracting parties to the ECT. Such claims may also be initiated with respect to new fossil fuel investments made after withdrawal from the ECT. For instance, Austria has BITs with 18 of the 23 non-EU contracting parties to the ECT[102]) and Germany has BITs with 19 non-EU contracting parties.[103]) Evidently, these BITs neither contain phase-out mechanisms nor are there any publicly discussed plans to modify or terminate them. This implies that the plan to withdraw from the ECT and conclude *inter se* agreements, much like the plan to modernize the ECT, is a half-baked effort if the objective is to eliminate protection for fossil fuel investments, as long as extra-EU BITs continue to exist in their unreformed form.

[102]) The five states with which Austria does not maintain a BIT are Afghanistan, Iceland, Japan, Liechtenstein and Switzerland.

[103]) The four states with which Germany does not maintain a BIT are Iceland, Japan, Liechtenstein and Switzerland.

# Hungary's 'Solo Run' in Investor-State Arbitration: Safeguarding Arbitral Integrity – or Something Else?

*Sára Darnót**)

## I. Introduction

In July 2024, the European Commission initiated an infringement procedure (case INFR (2024) 2206) against Hungary, challenging the latter's unilateral declaration regarding the application of the Court of Justice of the European Union's (CJEU) judgment in *République de Moldavie v Komstroy LLC* (C-741/19) under the Energy Charter Treaty (ECT).[1]) The procedure followed the usual two-stage Commission framework: first, a letter of formal notice was issued on 25 July 2024, inviting Hungary to comply within two months.[2]) As the Hungarian Government did not amend its position, the Commission delivered a reasoned opinion in March 2025, concluding that the Hungarian declaration violated the duty of sincere cooperation under Article 4(3) TEU and the principles of primacy and uniformity of EU law. Finally, on 17 July 2025, the Commission decided to refer the matter to the Court of Justice under Article 258 TFEU.[3]) As of the time of writing, no final judgment has been rendered, and the case remains pending before the Court.

The controversy stems from Hungary's distinct position within the EU's collective reaction to *Komstroy*. While twenty-six Member States joined the Inter-se Declaration of 26 June 2024 – stating that Article 26 ECT has "never applied" to intra-EU disputes – Hungary simultaneously issued a separate unilateral declaration to "ensure consistency with international law", narrowing the applicability of *Komstroy* to future disputes only, and only after a formal

---

*) Attorney-at-law, Lakatos Köves and Partners

[1]) Judgment of the Court (Grand Chamber) of 2 September 2021. République de Moldavie v Komstroy LLC. Request for a preliminary ruling from the Cour d'appel de Paris.

[2]) Investment Treaty News, 9 October 2024 (https://www.iisd.org/itn/2024/10/09/european-commission-challenges-hungary-regarding-its-approach-to-intra-eu-arbitrations-under-the-energy-charter-treaty).

[3]) Commission refers HUNGARY to the Court of Justice of the European Union for contradicting the Union's position on intra-EU arbitrations under the Energy Charter Treaty.

amendment of the ECT.[4]) This "solo run", as several commentators have called it, sparked debate: is Hungary protecting arbitral autonomy and legal certainty, or pursuing other strategic objectives, notably its energy-policy relationship with Russia?

The question is not merely theoretical. Hungary has positioned itself at odds with the EU's progressive dismantling of intra-EU investor-state arbitration since *Achmea BV v Slovak Republic* (C-284/16), while at the same time adopting domestic decrees that restrict the enforcement of arbitral awards adverse to Hungarian energy interests. This juxtaposition of "arbitration-friendly" rhetoric and state-protective practice raises doubts about the government's underlying motivations.

The purpose of this article is therefore twofold:

1. to reconstruct the legal background of *Achmea* and *Komstroy* and the subsequent EU and Hungarian policy reactions; and
2. to assess whether Hungary's stance represents a genuine defence of arbitral integrity and legal certainty or, instead, a manifestation of geopolitical and economic pragmatism.

To that end, the article proceeds as follows. Section II contrasts *Achmea* and *Komstroy* and situates Hungary's energy context within the ECT framework. Section III analyses the EU's collective reaction, including the Inter-se Declaration and Hungary's divergent statement. Section IV evaluates Hungary's reasoning in light of international-law principles and state interests. Section V presents academic critiques of the CJEU's jurisdiction and reasoning in *Komstroy*. Section VI examines the "Lex Orlen" decree and its implications for award enforcement. Section VII discusses the broader consequences for investment arbitration and energy governance in the EU. Finally, Section VIII concludes by reflecting on the tensions between EU legal integration, arbitral autonomy, and national strategic interests.

## II. Background: *Achmea* and *Komstroy*

### A. The *Achmea* Judgment (C-284/16)

As we all recall, the *Achmea* decision of 6 March 2018 marked the turning point in the EU's attitude toward intra-EU investment arbitration. The dispute arose from a bilateral investment treaty (BIT) between the Netherlands and the Slovak Republic. The CJEU held that Article 8 of that BIT, allowing investors of one Member State to initiate arbitration against another Member State, was

---

[4]) Statement by Hungary on its implementation of the Komstroy judgment (https://kormany.hu/hirek/magyarorszag-nyilatkozata-a-komstroy-iteletnek-valo-tagal lami-megfelelesrol).

incompatible with the autonomy of the EU legal order.[5]) According to the Court, such a clause deprived domestic courts – and ultimately the CJEU – of their exclusive competence to interpret EU law under Article 267 TFEU, thereby violating the principle of mutual trust and the requirement of uniform application of Union law.[6])

The ruling rested on three pillars:

(a) the autonomy of EU law, guaranteeing that interpretation remains within the Union's judicial system;

(b) the principle of mutual trust, ensuring that Member States regard each other's courts as capable of safeguarding EU law; and

(c) the exclusivity of Article 267 TFEU preliminary references, which arbitral tribunals could not make. The Court thus concluded that the investor-state arbitration mechanism in intra-EU BITs "has an adverse effect on the autonomy of EU law".[7])

This reasoning had immediate systemic impact. Member States, including Hungary, signed the Agreement for the Termination of Intra-EU BITs in 2020,[8]) which annulled approximately 190 bilateral treaties within the EU. However, the *Achmea* judgment formally concerned only intra-EU BITs – treaties between Member States – and not multilateral frameworks such as the Energy Charter Treaty.

## B. The Komstroy Judgment (C-741/19)

Three years later, the CJEU extended *Achmea*'s rationale in *République de Moldavie v Komstroy LLC*, decided on 2 September 2021.[9]) The underlying facts concerned an energy-supply contract between a Ukrainian investor and Moldova. The dispute was brought under Article 26 ECT, which provides that disputes between a "Contracting Party" and an investor of another Contracting Party "shall, if possible, be settled amicably", and if not, may be submitted to arbitration under the ICSID, UNCITRAL or Stockholm Chamber of Commerce rules.[10]) While neither party to the dispute was an EU Member State, the place of arbitration – Paris – was within the EU, enabling the Court to exercise jurisdiction through a preliminary-ruling request by the Paris Court of Appeal (during the annulment procedure against the award).[11])

---

[5]) C-284/16 *Achmea BV* v *Slovak Republic*, ECLI:EU:C:2018:158, para. 60.

[6]) *Ibid.*, paras 33–37.

[7]) *Ibid.*, para. 58.

[8]) Agreement for the Termination of Intra-EU BITs, OJ L 169/1 (29 May 2020).

[9]) C-741/19 *Komstroy*, ECLI:EU:C:2021:655.

[10]) Energy Charter Treaty, Art. 26(1)–(2).

[11]) C-741/19 *Komstroy*, para. 21.

The CJEU held that Article 26 ECT "must be interpreted as not applicable to disputes between a Member State and an investor of another Member State".[12]) It reasoned that allowing intra-EU arbitration under the ECT would undermine the autonomy and primacy of EU law for the same reasons identified in *Achmea*. The Court's reasoning relied on Articles 267 and 344 TFEU and stressed that arbitral tribunals under the ECT "cannot be regarded as courts or tribunals of a Member State within the meaning of Article 267 TFEU".[13]) Consequently, such tribunals lack competence to request preliminary rulings or ensure uniform application of EU law.

This extension was controversial. Unlike *Achmea*, the ECT is a multilateral treaty involving both EU and non-EU Contracting Parties (including Russia, Kazakhstan, and Azerbaijan). The EU and its Member States are themselves ECT parties, and the Treaty's preamble emphasises the promotion of long-term energy cooperation "on the basis of complementarities and mutual benefits".[14]) The Court's assumption that intra-EU relationships can be severed from the multilateral context has been criticised as lacking treaty-text support.[15]) Furthermore, Russia – while having signed but not ratified the ECT – remains bound provisionally under Article 45 ECT, reflecting its central role in the European energy network.[16]) Given Hungary's heavy dependence on Russian gas and nuclear-fuel imports, the ruling inevitably intersected with Hungary's strategic interests.

## C. Comparative Analysis

Although *Achmea* and *Komstroy* share the same doctrinal core – protection of EU-law autonomy – they differ materially in scope and implications. In *Achmea*, the arbitral clause was embedded in a bilateral treaty entirely within the EU legal space; in *Komstroy*, the dispute concerned a multilateral treaty whose reach extended beyond the EU. Thus, *Komstroy* raised two novel questions:

(1) Can the CJEU legitimately interpret provisions of a treaty that also binds non-EU states? and

(2) Can the Union unilaterally alter the operation of such a treaty among its own members without the consent of other Contracting Parties?

---

12) *Ibid.*, para. 66.

13) *Ibid.*, para. 49.

14) ECT Preamble.

15) Odermatt, J., Is EU Law International? (European Papers 2021) (https://www.europeanpapers.eu/europeanforum/is-eu-law-international-case-moldova-v-komstroy-and-autonomy-of-eu-legal-order).

16) Energy Charter Secretariat, "List of Signatories and Contracting Parties" (2024).

The Court answered both implicitly in the affirmative, grounding its competence on the EU's status as an ECT party and on the necessity to preserve the coherence of Union law. Critics argue, however, that such reasoning blurs the distinction between EU internal constitutional autonomy and international treaty interpretation.[17]) From a pragmatic standpoint, the judgment extended the *Achmea* logic to the energy sector, effectively nullifying intra-EU arbitration under the ECT and compelling Member States to handle investor disputes exclusively before domestic or EU courts.

### D. Energy Context and Hungarian Implications

For Hungary, the significance of *Komstroy* cannot be overstated. The country relies on Russian gas for roughly 80 percent of its consumption and has long-term contracts through Gazprom Export. Hungary's approach to investor-state arbitration therefore intertwines with energy security: maintaining flexibility in arbitration may shield its state-owned energy enterprises (notably MVM Group and Paks II Nuclear Plant) from EU-law-based challenges. By resisting a blanket intra-EU exclusion, Hungary could preserve the possibility of invoking arbitration in disputes where Russian or other non-EU entities are involved.

In this light, Hungary's subsequent unilateral declaration – limiting *Komstroy*'s application to future disputes only – fits a broader pattern of aligning legal positions with energy-policy priorities. Sections III and IV explore these declarations and their political-legal motivations in more depth.

## III. EU Reaction

### A. The Inter-se Declaration of 26 June 2024

Following the *Komstroy* judgment, the European Commission coordinated the adoption of a collective position among Member States to ensure consistency within the Union's external energy-investment framework. On 26 June 2024, twenty-six EU Member States and the Union itself issued the *Declaration on the legal consequences of the judgment of the Court of Justice in Komstroy and common understanding on the non-applicability of Article 26 of the Energy*

[17]) Mayr, Stefan, 'How to Put an End to intra-EU Investment Arbitration under the Energy Charter Treaty (Fast): Amendment, Withdrawal, Modification?'. European Foreign Affairs Review 30, no. 2 (2025): 223–248. © 2025 Kluwer Law International BV, The Netherlands

*Charter Treaty as a basis for intra-EU arbitration proceedings* (the "Inter-se Declaration").[18])

The Declaration stated that, "pursuant to Articles 267 and 344 TFEU, as interpreted by the Court of Justice, Article 26 ECT cannot serve, and has never served, as a legal basis for investor-state arbitration proceedings between investors of one Member State and another Member State".[19]) It added that any pending or future arbitral proceedings relying on Article 26 ECT in intra-EU contexts were "incompatible with the EU Treaties and must therefore be discontinued or not initiated".[20])

This collective act went beyond the binding effect of a CJEU preliminary ruling. Under Article 267 TFEU, a preliminary judgment is formally binding only on the referring national court and subsequently on other courts applying the same provision.[21]) Yet the Union's political-legal reaction effectively "constitutionalised" the *Komstroy* interpretation across Member States, treating it as *erga omnes* within the EU. In doing so, the Declaration converted a judicial interpretation into a quasi-legislative commitment.[22])

For the Commission, the Declaration was necessary to pre-empt arbitral tribunals seated within the EU from asserting jurisdiction in pending Energy Charter Treaty (ECT) cases. It also reflected the Commission's broader campaign – launched after *Achmea* – to eradicate intra-EU investor-state dispute settlement (ISDS) mechanisms deemed inconsistent with the Union's legal order.[23]) The Inter-se Declaration thus represented the culmination of a policy line dating back to 2018, transforming *Komstroy* from a doctrinal ruling into an administrative enforcement instrument.

## B. Hungary's Separate Unilateral Declaration

On the same day – 26 June 2024 – the Government of Hungary did not sign the Inter-se Declaration but simultaneously issued an independent unilateral declaration titled "Statement by Hungary on its implementation of the *Komstroy* judgment".[24]) The preamble explains that the declaration was

[18]) European Commission, Declaration on the legal consequences of *Komstroy*, 26 June 2024.

[19]) *Ibid.*, para. 1.

[20]) *Ibid.*, para. 3.

[21]) TFEU Art. 267.

[22]) Odermatt, J., Is EU Law International?, European Papers 2021 (https://www.europeanpapers.eu/europeanforum/is-eu-law-international-case-moldova-v-komstroy-and-autonomy-of-eu-legal-order).

[23]) European Commission, Infringement Package – Key Decisions Energy, 25 July 2024.

[24]) Government of Hungary, Statement by Hungary on its implementation of *Komstroy*, 26 June 2024.

adopted *"in order to ensure consistency with international law"* and by *"considering the judicial practice of international arbitration"*.[25])

The operative part of the Hungarian declaration provides that:

> *"THE GOVERNMENT OF HUNGARY DECLARES THAT HUNGARY SHARES THE FOLLOWING UNDERSTANDING ON THE NON-APPLICABILITY OF ARTICLE 26(2)(c) OF THE ENERGY CHARTER TREATY AS A BASIS FOR INTRA-EU ARBITRATION PROCEEDINGS:*
>
> 1. *For the sake of clarity, Hungary confirms that Article 26(2)(c) of the Energy Charter Treaty shall be interpreted and applied in such a way that it shall no longer serve as a legal basis for disputes between an investor of one Member State and another Member State in connection with an investment in the territory of that other Member State.*
>
> *The understanding is based on the following elements of Union law:*
>
> i. *the interpretation of the Court of Justice of the European Union pursuant to which Article 26(2)(c) of the Energy Charter Treaty does not apply as a basis for intra-EU arbitration proceedings; and*
>
> ii. *the primacy of European Union law, recalled in Declaration No 17, annexed to the Final Act of the Intergovernmental Conference which adopted the Treaty of Lisbon, as a rule of international law governing conflict of norms in their mutual relations with the result that in any event Article 26(2)(c) of the Energy Charter Treaty does not apply as a basis for intra-EU arbitration proceedings.*
>
> *The understanding is based on the following elements of international law:*
>
> 1. *The withdrawal of the applicability of Article 26(2)(c) of the Energy Charter Treaty in intra-EU arbitration proceedings may be ensured in accordance with international law by a future amendment of the Energy Charter Treaty through bilateral or multilateral treaty between all or certain parties to the treaty, in accordance with Article 40 or 41 of the Vienna Convention on the Law of Treaties.*
> 2. *Paragraph 1 is without prejudice to the interpretation and application of other provisions of the Energy Charter Treaty to the extent they concern intra-EU relations."*[26])

This formulation materially diverged from the Inter-se Declaration in two respects. First, Hungary limited the temporal scope of *Komstroy* to future disputes, whereas the Inter-se Declaration treated it as declaratory of existing law, applying retrospectively to all pending cases. Second, Hungary conditioned

[25]) Government of Hungary, Statement on Implementation of *Komstroy*, 26 June 2024 (https://kormany.hu/hirek/magyarorszag-nyilatkozata-a-komstroy-iteletnek-valo-tagallami-megfelelesrol).

[26]) Hungary's statement, operative part.

the judgment's full implementation on a formal amendment of the ECT, invoking public-international-law doctrines on treaty modification. This condition implies that *Komstroy* – in Hungary's view – does not by itself alter the ECT's text or the consent to arbitration already given under Article 26.[27])

By coupling these two limitations, Hungary implicitly asserted that EU law cannot unilaterally modify international obligations toward non-EU parties, echoing Article 39 of the Vienna Convention on the Law of Treaties (VCLT), which requires the consent of all contracting parties for treaty amendment. The declaration thus framed Hungary's position as one of treaty-law orthodoxy rather than defiance, portraying it as a defence of legal certainty and pacta sunt servanda.[28])

## C. The Commission's Response

The Commission immediately regarded Hungary's unilateral declaration as an infringement of Union law. In its press release of 25 July 2024, the Commission warned that "Hungary's interpretation undermines the uniform application of EU law and contradicts the Union's position that intra-EU arbitration under the ECT is incompatible with the Treaties".[29]) A *letter of formal notice* followed the same day, requiring compliance within two months. Hungary's reply reiterated that its declaration merely "clarified" international-law obligations, not EU law ones. After concluding that Hungary failed to align its position, the Commission issued a *reasoned opinion* in March 2025 and, on 17 July 2025, referred the matter to the CJEU under Article 258 TFEU.[30])

In its referral, the Commission alleged breaches of Articles 4(3) and 19 TEU, 267 and 344 TFEU, and of the general principles of autonomy, primacy and effectiveness of Union law. The Commission emphasised that Member States may not issue unilateral declarations that "restrict or condition the application of judgments of the Court of Justice".[31])

Hungary, by contrast, defended its position as a safeguard of legal certainty, arguing that applying *Komstroy* retroactively would disrupt existing arbitration proceedings and violate investors' legitimate expectations under the ECT. In public statements, the Hungarian Government described its

---

[27]) Vienna Convention on the Law of Treaties, Art. 39.

[28]) Mayr, Stefan, 'How to Put an End to intra-EU Investment Arbitration under the Energy Charter Treaty (Fast): Amendment, Withdrawal, Modification?'. European Foreign Affairs Review 30, no. 2 (2025): 223–248. © 2025 Kluwer Law International BV, The Netherlands

[29]) European Commission Press Release IP-24-3228, 25 July 2024.

[30]) European Commission, IP/25/1799, 17 July 2025.

[31]) *Ibid.*

declaration as "a balanced legal clarification ensuring consistency with international law".[32])

The resulting standoff laid bare a structural tension between EU constitutional autonomy and Member-State sovereignty under international law. While the Commission interpreted *Komstroy* as definitive for all intra-EU contexts, Hungary invoked international-law orthodoxy to defend its own declaration. This confrontation – unique among Member States – set the stage for the 2025 infringement case now pending before the CJEU.

## IV. Doctrinal Legality or political Strategy? Assessing Hungary's *Komstroy* Declaration

### A. Hungary's Framing: Legal Certainty and Arbitral Autonomy

In its exchanges with the European Commission and in public communications, the Hungarian Government has consistently portrayed its unilateral declaration not as defiance but as "a clarification ensuring the harmonious application of international and Union law".[33]) The official narrative emphasises legal certainty and the continuity of consent under the Energy Charter Treaty (ECT). According to this view, the *Komstroy* judgment – binding within the EU legal order – cannot of itself rewrite a multilateral treaty that also binds non-EU Contracting Parties.

This reasoning rests on two well-established doctrines of public international law:

- Pacta sunt servanda (VCLT Article 26), requiring treaties to be performed in good faith; unilateral reinterpretation of the ECT through EU law, Hungary argues, would breach this duty toward non-EU partners.[34])
- VCLT Article 27, prohibiting states from invoking internal law – including EU law – to justify non-performance of international obligations.[35])

By conditioning the effect of *Komstroy* on a formal amendment of the ECT, Hungary positioned itself as defending the orthodox understanding of treaty stability rather than opposing the EU per se. From a doctrinal perspective, the argument is not without merit: in a consent-based system of dispute

---

[32]) Government of Hungary, Statement on Implementation of Komstroy, 26 June 2024

[33]) *Ibid.*

[34]) Vienna Convention on the Law of Treaties, Art. 26.

[35]) *Ibid.*, Art. 27.

settlement, an arbitral clause remains binding until lawfully withdrawn or amended. The Commission's contrary stance – treating *Komstroy* as having *erga omnes* effect within the Union – was therefore criticised in Hungary as retroactive and ultra vires.[36])

Nevertheless, the timing and political context of the declaration suggest that the appeal to legal orthodoxy also serves instrumental purposes. The insistence on international-law integrity conveniently aligns with Hungary's effort to shield its energy policy from supranational constraints, a point examined below.

## B. Jurisdictional Overreach and the Nature of a Preliminary Ruling

A principal academic criticism of *Komstroy* is that the CJEU stretched the preliminary-ruling mechanism of Article 267 TFEU beyond its legitimate boundaries. The reference originated from the Paris Court of Appeal, seized with an action to annul an arbitral award rendered under the ECT between Moldovan and Ukrainian parties.[37]) Neither party was an EU Member State; only the *seat* of arbitration (Paris) linked the dispute to EU territory.

Traditionally, Article 267 allows national courts to seek clarification of *EU law* – not public international law – relevant to a case before them.[38]) The ECT, however, is a mixed agreement: it binds the EU, its Member States, and third countries, and its interpretation normally falls under public-international-law methods, not EU constitutional review. By entertaining the reference, the Court effectively converted the ECT's dispute-settlement clause into an issue of EU constitutional autonomy. Critics describe this as a "jurisdictional leap" that conflates the EU's internal judicial hierarchy with its external treaty obligations.

Odermatt observes that *Komstroy* "extends EU constitutional reasoning into a sphere where the EU is only one of many contracting parties", thereby risking fragmentation between EU and non-EU interpretations of the ECT.[39]) Similarly, Mayr questions whether the Court's ruling has *erga omnes* effect,

[36]) https://www.portfolio.hu/gazdasag/20240725/nekiment-brusszel-a-kulonutas-magyar-kormanyzati-nyilatkozatnak-az-orosz-gazbeszerzest-vedo-lepest-is-erintheti-700581# .

[37]) C-741/19 *Komstroy*, para. 21.

[38]) TFEU Art. 267.

[39]) Odermatt J., Is EU Law International? (European Papers 2021) p. 9. (https://www.europeanpapers.eu/europeanforum/is-eu-law-international-case-moldova-v-komstroy-and-autonomy-of-eu-legal-order).

noting that "the CJEU cannot bind non-EU Contracting Parties, yet its interpretation unavoidably reshapes their treaty rights".[40])

From a doctrinal standpoint, the preliminary-ruling procedure does not authorise the Court to pronounce on the objective validity of an international treaty clause, only on the compatibility of its application within EU law. In *Komstroy*, the Court arguably moved from interpretation to *re-legislation* – a step that explains why Hungary later insisted that the decision required a formal ECT amendment before taking effect.[41])

## C. Substantive Critiques: Autonomy Versus Legal Certainty

The *Komstroy* reasoning also drew criticism for its substantive premises. The Court held that intra-EU investor-state arbitration "may adversely affect the autonomy and effectiveness of EU law" because arbitral tribunals are not "courts or tribunals of a Member State"[42]) and judicial review of their awards is not guaranteed in every case. On that basis, the Court concluded that only a complete exclusion of intra-EU investor-state arbitration could preserve the uniform interpretation of EU law – particularly since the Energy Charter Treaty, as far as it applies to Member States, must itself be treated as part of the Union's legal order. This reasoning, however, extends well beyond the ECT context: the absence of full judicial review is characteristic of nearly all international arbitrations, meaning that the Court's logic would effectively render EU law and arbitration mutually incompatible wherever EU law is incidentally applied. Critics therefore view *Komstroy* as codifying the CJEU's growing scepticism toward arbitration as an autonomous system of adjudication rather than a cooperative mechanism within the Union's legal framework.

Moreover, the judgment arguably undermines legal certainty for investors who relied on the ECT's explicit consent to arbitration. Retroactively invalidating that consent jeopardises legitimate expectations – a value enshrined in EU law itself.[43]) Hungary's declaration capitalised on this tension, arguing that applying *Komstroy* to pending proceedings would breach investors' expectations and violate Article 26 ECT's good-faith principle.

A further inconsistency lies in the Court's reliance on Article 344 TFEU (obligation of Member States not to submit disputes concerning EU law to

---

[40]) Mayr, Stefan, 'How to Put an End to intra-EU Investment Arbitration under the Energy Charter Treaty (Fast): Amendment, Withdrawal, Modification?'. European Foreign Affairs Review 30, no. 2 (2025): 223–248. © 2025 Kluwer Law International BV, The Netherlands.

[41]) Government of Hungary, Statement on Implementation of Komstroy (26 June 2024).

[42]) C-741/19 *Komstroy*, para. 49.

[43]) European Commission, Infringement Package – Energy (25 July 2024).

any method of settlement other than those provided by the Treaties). While Article 344 applies to inter-State disputes, the Court extended it to private investor claims, a category not covered by the provision's wording.[44]) Commentators describe this as a "category mistake" that converts a clause of interstate discipline into a universal bar on arbitration.

Ironically, while the EU rejects intra-EU ISDS on autonomy grounds, it continues to promote arbitration and investment protection in its external trade agreements – for example, under CETA or the EU–Singapore Investment Protection Agreement. These treaties incorporate appellate and review mechanisms designed precisely to ensure consistency with EU law.[45]),[46]) This duality reinforces Hungary's complaint that the Commission's position is politically selective: arbitration is condemned when it limits Brussels' control but celebrated when it extends EU regulatory reach abroad.

## D. Connecting the Critique to Hungary's Position

The academic objections above intersect directly with Hungary's defence strategy in the infringement case. By grounding its unilateral declaration in international-law orthodoxy – pacta sunt servanda and Article 27 VCLT – Hungary effectively aligns itself with those who see *Komstroy* as judicial overreach. Its insistence that the ruling should apply only prospectively mirrors the argument that a CJEU preliminary judgment cannot amend an international treaty *inter se* without explicit consent. In this sense, Hungary functions as a *proxy litigant* for a wider scholarly dissent within the EU legal community.

Nonetheless, Hungary's motives are not purely doctrinal. As Section VI will demonstrate, its domestic conduct – particularly the "Lex Orlen" decree restricting enforcement of certain arbitral awards – reveals how legal critique and economic self-interest converge. The overlap between principle and pragmatism remains the hallmark of Hungary's "arbitration-friendly" exceptionalism.

# V. Two Aspects of Energy Related Arbitration Protectiveness

Hungary's approach to arbitration in the energy sector reflects a complex duality: outwardly, the government defends the integrity of investor-state dispute settlement as a safeguard for Hungarian capital abroad; inwardly, it selectively limits enforcement of foreign awards to preserve its autonomy over

[44]) TFEU Art. 344.

[45]) EU–Canada (CETA) Investment Tribunal Rules, Art. 8.27.

[46]) EU-Singapore Free Trade Agreement, Investment Protection Agreement and Digital Trade Agreement, Chapter 14

strategic energy relations. These two trajectories – protection of outsourced investments and restriction of enforcement in energy-sensitive contexts – form the two sides of Hungary's arbitration policy.

The following subsections examine these dimensions in detail. Section A. analyses Hungary's external investment-protection logic through the lens of the *MOL v Croatia* case and the Energy Charter Treaty (ECT). Section B. explores the domestic counterpart, epitomised by the 2024 "Lex Orlen" decree, which curtails the enforcement of foreign arbitral awards in the name of energy security.

## A. The Other Side of the Story: Hungary's Protection of Outsourced Investments in the Energy Field – The *MOL v Croatia* Saga and Its Effect

Hungary's insistence on defending investor-state arbitration under the Energy Charter Treaty (ECT) cannot be fully understood without considering the strategic economic interests behind its position. While the official rhetoric often frames the issue as one of "arbitration integrity" or legal sovereignty, a closer look reveals a deeper logic: the protection of Hungary's largest multinational, MOL Group, whose extensive foreign energy investments rely heavily on international arbitration mechanisms. The MOL v Croatia case and its broader implications illustrate how national and corporate interests converge in shaping Hungary's policy stance.

### 1. The MOL v Croatia ICSID Case

The dispute between MOL Hungarian Oil and Gas Company Plc. and the Republic of Croatia (ICSID Case No. ARB/13/32) represents one of the most consequential intra-EU investment arbitrations of the past decade. Initiated in 2013 under the Energy Charter Treaty (ECT), MOL claimed that Croatia had breached its obligations by unlawfully interfering with MOL's shareholder rights and contractual control over the Croatian energy company INA d.d.

After nearly a decade of proceedings, the ICSID tribunal ruled in July 2022 that Croatia had violated the fair and equitable treatment (FET) standard, awarding USD 184 million plus interest to MOL.[47]) Croatia's defence, centred on allegations of corruption and EU law supremacy, was rejected. The tribunal confirmed that the ECT's protections applied and that the arbitration was valid despite the EU's evolving stance against intra-EU investor-state dispute settlement (ISDS).

---

[47]) *MOL Group Press Release*, "Decision by the ICSID Court of Arbitration", 22 July 2022, available at: https://molgroup.info/en/investor-relations/investor-news/decision-by-the-icsid-court-of-arbitration.

The case is emblematic for Hungary not only because the investor was a Hungarian national champion but also because the ruling tested the practical limits of EU law's primacy over international arbitration. Croatia's subsequent efforts to annul or resist enforcement of the award – citing the CJEU's *Achmea* and *Komstroy* judgments – highlighted precisely the legal uncertainty Hungary has sought to counter through its political and legal declarations.

## 2. The ECT and Its Role in Hungary's External Energy Interests

The Energy Charter Treaty provides a multilateral framework for protecting and promoting energy investments across borders, including guarantees of non-discrimination, fair and equitable treatment, and access to investor-state arbitration (Article 26 ECT). For MOL – and by extension Hungary – the ECT has long served as a pillar of investment security in volatile or politically sensitive jurisdictions.

Hungary's legal and diplomatic defence of the ECT must thus be seen in this context. The CJEU's restrictive interpretation in *Komstroy*, which effectively nullifies the possibility of intra-EU arbitration under the ECT, poses not only a doctrinal challenge but also an economic one: it threatens to dismantle a treaty network that Hungarian investors have historically depended on. As the EU moves toward a coordinated withdrawal from the ECT, Hungary's opposition to such withdrawal is aligned with the interests of its most globally exposed company.

## 3. The Prospect of Further Disputes: MOL's Expanding Investment Footprint

Beyond its operations in Croatia, MOL maintains an extensive portfolio of upstream, midstream, and downstream energy projects throughout Central Asia, the Middle East, and the Balkans, including significant exploration and production assets in Kazakhstan, Azerbaijan, and Iraq.[48]) These ventures operate in legal environments where domestic courts often lack the independence, procedural guarantees, or technical expertise required to adjudicate complex energy disputes.

In the absence of robust treaty protections like those under the ECT or ICSID Convention, MOL would face considerable political risk and would likely be compelled to seek remedies in local courts – a scenario that offers neither neutrality nor enforceability. The MOL v Croatia case, therefore, serves

[48]) https://molgroup.info/storage/documents/publikaciok/befektetoi_prezentaciok/2025/investor-presentation-202502.pdf; *IA Reporter*, "Hungarian MOL lodges second ECT/ICSID arbitration against Croatia, prolonging the parties' decades-old legal battles", 2024, available at: https://www.iareporter.com/articles/hungarian-mol-lodges-second-ect-icsid-arbitration-against-croatia-prolonging-the-parties-decades-old-legal-battles.

as a cautionary precedent for what could occur in other jurisdictions if the ECT's investor-state arbitration mechanism is dismantled.

### 4. The Necessity of Maintaining ECT Applicability and Arbitrability

For Hungary, the continued applicability and arbitrability of the ECT is not a matter of abstract legal theory but of concrete national interest. The treaty ensures that MOL and similar companies can operate abroad under a predictable regime of legal protection, backed by the enforceability of arbitral awards under the ICSID Convention and the New York Convention.

If the ECT were rendered inapplicable or non-arbitrable within the EU framework, Hungary's outward investments would lose a crucial layer of protection. This would not only expose MOL to geopolitical risk but could also weaken Hungary's regional energy influence, reducing its role from that of a net exporter and regional leader to a market dependent on domestic resources. The preservation of arbitration, in this light, serves as a strategic shield for Hungary's economic sovereignty abroad.

### 5. The Political Economy of Hungary's Separate Declaration

It is within this intersection of legal doctrine and economic pragmatism that Hungary's separate declaration before the CJEU must be understood. While officially presented as a defence of international law principles – particularly pacta sunt servanda and state consent under the Vienna Convention on the Law of Treaties – the declaration also reflects domestic lobbying pressures.

MOL, as Hungary's most globalised enterprise, has a vested interest in ensuring that international arbitration remains available and enforceable. Its success in the MOL v Croatia arbitration, coupled with ongoing exposure in high-risk jurisdictions, likely creates implicit pressure on the government to maintain a pro-arbitration stance within EU fora. In this sense, Hungary's position embodies a form of corporate–state symbiosis, where national policy functions as a defensive mechanism for key private-sector actors operating in geopolitically sensitive environments.

## B. Parallel Case: Enforcement & Energy Dependencies

If Section A. illuminated Hungary's external defence of arbitration, Section B. explores the domestic mirror image – the selective restriction of arbitration enforcement where it conflicts with national energy-security priorities.

## 1. Background: The "Lex Orlen" Decree

In late May 2024 the Hungarian government adopted Government Decree 117/2024 (V. 30.) – widely referred to as the "Lex Orlen" – as an emergency measure to prevent the enforcement in Hungary of certain foreign arbitral or judicial decisions that could interfere with the country's energy-supply payments.[49])

The immediate trigger was a warning letter from Poland's PKN Orlen SA to Hungary's state-owned gas wholesaler MVM CEEnergy, received roughly a month earlier.[50]) The letter stated that, following a Warsaw court's confirmation of an arbitration award rendered by the Stockholm Chamber of Commerce in favour of Orlen and against Gazprom Export, the Polish company intended to seize more than €350 million from MVM's forthcoming transfers to Gazprom to satisfy its claim (as an interim measure issued by regular courts of Poland).[51]) Similar notices were reportedly sent to companies in Austria and Slovakia. The underlying dispute stemmed from Orlen's refusal in 2022 to comply with Russia's new rouble-payment requirement for gas deliveries under the Yamal-Europe pipeline contract, which led Gazprom to halt supplies and prompted Orlen's USD 1.45 billion arbitration claim.[52])

According to contemporaneous reporting by Reuters and Portfolio.hu, this threat of third-party attachment prompted the Hungarian government to act "within days", issuing the decree on 30 May 2024 to block bailiffs or foreign creditors from intercepting Hungarian payments to Gazprom.[53]) The decree justified the prohibition as necessary "to ensure the uninterrupted operation of Hungary's strategic energy supply and to prevent enforcement actions contrary to public security".[54]) In practice, however, it barred enforcement authorities from recognising or executing foreign interim measures that might restrain transfers between MVM and Gazprom, explicitly invoking "public order" and "security of supply" as grounds.

## 2. Domestic Effects and International/ EU Law Implications

From an international-law standpoint, the decree overrode Hungary's obligations under both the New York Convention on the Recognition and Enforcement of Foreign Arbitral Awards and Article III ECT, which guarantee fair and equitable treatment and enforcement of investment-related awards

[49]) Government Decree 117/2024 (V. 30.), Magyar Közlöny No. 83/2024.

[50]) Portfolio.hu, "Orlen would seize MVM's money transfer to Gazprom", 27 June 2024.

[51]) *Ibid.*

[52]) Reuters dispatch cited in Portfolio.hu, 27 June 2024.

[53]) *Ibid.*

[54]) Explanatory Memorandum to Gov. Decree 117/2024.

(noting that the decision in question was issued by the regular court of Poland as interim measure supporting the pending SCC case).[55]) Domestic legal analysts noted that the "Lex Orlen" effectively created a sovereign-immunity-style shield for Hungarian energy assets under the banner of national security, casting doubt on whether such a measure would withstand judicial scrutiny abroad or protect Hungarian transfers routed through correspondent banks.[56])

The decree also revealed the geopolitical subtext of the *Komstroy* controversy: by invoking ordre public to pre-empt enforcement actions related to Russian gas payments, Hungary demonstrated that its invocation of international-law principles – whether in defending treaty stability or arbitral integrity – was inseparable from its priority of preserving energy relations with Russia. The "Lex Orlen" thus functions as the domestic mirror of Hungary's unilateral declaration under the ECT: both deploy the language of legality and sovereignty to secure room for manoeuvre in an increasingly politicised energy environment.

## 3. Geopolitical and Doctrinal Dimensions

Hungary was not alone in facing arbitration linked to energy-security measures. Slovakia, which relies on similar gas-supply arrangements through Gazprom, adopted a ministerial resolution in June 2024 temporarily staying enforcement of the same Polish interim measure order, though without enacting a general ban.[57]) Poland, by contrast, pursued enforcement proceedings in its national courts, invoking EU internal-market rules and alleging that Hungary's refusal breached mutual-recognition obligations under the Brussels I Regulation.[58])

This regional divergence is instructive. Whereas Poland framed the dispute as a test of EU legal solidarity, Hungary and, to a lesser extent, Slovakia treated it as a matter of energy sovereignty. Yet only Hungary combined this stance with a formal legislative barrier to enforcement, thereby placing itself at the outer edge of compliance with both EU and international arbitration norms.

The "Lex Orlen" episode crystallises the pattern already visible in Hungary's handling of the *Komstroy* fallout. In both cases, the government positioned itself as defending national autonomy against perceived EU overreach while simultaneously curtailing the practical operation of arbitration. This duality illustrates how energy dependency transforms legal doctrine into geopolitical instrument. Hungary's state-centric energy model, built on long-term Russian contracts and domestic price controls, makes external dispute-

---

[55]) Energy Charter Treaty Art. III; New York Convention Art. III.

[56]) External commentary in *Portfolio.hu*, 31 May 2024; Queritius Blog, June 2024.

[57]) Slovak Ministry of Economy Press Release, 14 June 2024.

[58]) Polish Ministry of Justice Report on Intra-EU Arbitration Cases, Nov 2024.

settlement mechanisms structurally inconvenient. The *Lex Orlen* thus functions not merely as an emergency decree but as the domestic counterpart to Hungary's international "clarification" of *Komstroy*: both shield the state's discretion in energy matters under the banner of arbitration integrity.

# VI. Implications, Outlook and Conclusions

## A. Reconfiguration of the EU Investment-Arbitration Landscape

The Hungarian infringement procedure epitomises the post-*Achmea* crisis of investor-state arbitration within the European Union. Since 2018, the European Commission has pursued a systematic policy to eradicate intra-EU investor-state dispute settlement (ISDS), culminating in the coordinated termination of bilateral investment treaties and, more recently, in the de facto neutralisation of the Energy Charter Treaty's arbitration clause.

The pending CJEU proceedings against Hungary now represent a constitutional-international crossroads. As the Global Arbitration Review reported, Hungary's unilateral declaration has placed it "at odds with the EU majority" for insisting that *Komstroy* must be implemented "only prospectively and consistently with international law", rather than retroactively and automatically across the Union.[59]) In effect, the Court must determine whether a Member State may interpret a CJEU judgment through the lens of pacta sunt servanda and the Vienna Convention on the Law of Treaties – or whether EU constitutional autonomy overrides those doctrines entirely.

A nuanced academic debate surrounds this issue. The Kluwer Arbitration Blog analysis by Veronika Korom and Szabolcs Nagy concludes that the Inter-Se Declaration adopted by twenty-six Member States is not binding on arbitral tribunals constituted under the ECT; tribunals remain free to accept jurisdiction and proceed with arbitration as a matter of international law.[60]) Yet, as this article emphasises, such reasoning overlooks the practical barrier of enforceability: awards rendered under the ECT in intra-EU contexts may indeed be issued – but without viable enforcement avenues within the EU, their legal victory risks becoming illusory. This tension between theoretical jurisdiction and effective recognition forms the core of the current arbitration-law impasse.

Hence, the pending Hungary v Commission case is not merely an infringement action; it is a litmus test for the CJEU's willingness to engage with

[59]) https://globalarbitrationreview.com/article/hungary-odds-eu-over-declaration-komstroy.

[60]) https://legalblogs.wolterskluwer.com/arbitration-blog/eu-member-states-diverging-declarations-on-the-intra-eu-applicability-of-the-ect-can-the-ect-be-disapplied-intra-eu-as-a-matter-of-international-law-without-modernization/.

international-law orthodoxy. A ruling that dismisses Hungary's invocation of treaty-consent principles would cement the internal closure of the EU to investor arbitration. Conversely, partial acceptance could open a limited corridor for reconciling EU constitutional supremacy with treaty-based consent to arbitrate – a reconciliation long urged by practitioners and scholars concerned with the stability of the international investment system.

## B. Hungary's Position and Its Dualities

Hungary's behaviour illustrates a dual strategy of arbitration protectiveness. Externally, through the MOL v Croatia arbitration, the government defends international-law-based investor protection to secure national capital abroad. Internally, through the Lex Orlen decree, it restricts enforcement of foreign awards to preserve discretion over domestic energy flows. Together, these policies reveal a calculated pragmatism: arbitration integrity when it safeguards outward investments; arbitration constraint when it endangers domestic energy stability.

From an international-law standpoint, Hungary's unilateral declaration invokes legitimate doctrines – pacta sunt servanda, Article 27 VCLT, and state consent to arbitration. It thus presents a rare test of how far the CJEU will engage with treaty-law reasoning. Should the Court consider these arguments substantively, Hungary could achieve a limited vindication of its legal orthodoxy even while losing procedurally on compliance grounds. Yet the Lex Orlen decree simultaneously undermines this narrative by revealing the domestic limits of Hungary's proclaimed arbitration integrity.

The outcome will thus determine whether the EU legal order recognises any residual space for international-law reasoning within its constitutional framework – or whether even treaty-consent doctrines must yield entirely to the logic of uniform interpretation.

## C. Broader Policy Outlook and Structural Implications

The MOL v Croatia – Lex Orlen dualities expose the deeper structural collision between EU legal integration and national energy sovereignty. The Commission's push to render intra-EU arbitration "non-existent" prioritises uniformity over adaptability, while Hungary's stance substitutes coherence with opportunism – defending arbitration abroad but curtailing it at home. Still, this contradiction serves a strategic function: it keeps both legal avenues – international arbitration and sovereign discretion – open as instruments of energy governance.

If the CJEU reaffirms the Commission's view, European investors may increasingly rely on external frameworks – Energy Community, EAEU or ad hoc BITs – for arbitration security. If, conversely, the Court acknowledges the treaty-law concerns raised by Hungary and noted in the Kluwer analysis, it could inaugurate a more pluralistic model of conditional autonomy, where EU law and international arbitration coexist within delineated spheres.

## D. Conclusions

- The EU's strategic direction remains toward full internalisation of investment protection and the eradication of intra-EU ISDS. The *Komstroy* doctrine, reinforced through the Inter-Se Declaration, effectively seals the Union's arbitral space.
- Hungary's dualism – MOL v Croatia externally and Lex Orlen domestically – demonstrates that "arbitration-friendliness" is functional, not principled. It serves as an outward shield for Hungarian investors and an inward barrier against external claims.
- The conclusion that tribunals may still form and proceed under the ECT (maybe even with a seat outside of the EU) is formally correct but incomplete: while jurisdiction may subsist, enforceability within the EU does not. Arbitration without enforcement remains, in practice, a hollow remedy.
- Doctrinally, the CJEU case offers an opportunity – perhaps the last – to re-engage with international-law consent theory and reconsider the compatibility of multilateral treaty obligations with the EU's constitutional order.

## E. Closing Reflection

Hungary's "solo run" thus mirrors the broader European struggle to balance constitutional autonomy with international legality. The dual narratives of MOL v Croatia and Lex Orlen show arbitration evolving from a neutral adjudicative tool into a strategic instrument of statecraft. Whether the CJEU's forthcoming judgment condemns or accommodates Hungary, it will define not only the future of intra-EU arbitration but also the credibility of Europe's commitment to the rule of law beyond its borders.